Codification of Statements on Standards for Attestation Engagements

(Including Statements on Standards for Attestation Engagements [Clarified])

Attestation Standards [AT]

Attestation Standards (Clarified) [AT-C]

Numbers 1 to 18

AS OF APRIL 2016

16893-349

AICPA®

Reprinted from
AICPA *Professional Standards*
Attestation Engagements Parts
(as of April 2016)

1 2 3 4 5 6 7 8 9 0 PrP 1 9 8 7 6

ISBN 978-1-94354-651-0

Printed in Canada

PREFACE

This publication, issued by the Accounting and Review Services Committee and the Auditing Standards Board (ASB), is a codification of Statements on Standards for Attestation Engagements (SSAEs) and the related attestation interpretations applicable to the preparation and issuance of attestation reports for all nonissuers. A *nonissuer* is any entity not subject to the Sarbanes-Oxley Act of 2002 or the rules of the SEC.

This publication contains the codified attestation standards and related attestation interpretations that are in effect through April 2017 (identified as "AT" sections) as well as the codified clarified attestation standards resulting from the issuance of SSAE No. 18, *Attestation Standards: Clarification and Recodification* (identified as "AT-C" sections). SSAE No. 18 is effective for reports dated on or after May 1, 2017.

SSAEs are issued by senior committees of the AICPA designated to issue pronouncements on attestation matters applicable to the preparation and issuance of attestation reports for entities that are nonissuers. The "Compliance With Standards Rule" (AICPA, *Professional Standards*, ET sec. 1.310.001) of the AICPA Code of Professional Conduct requires an AICPA member performing an attestation engagement for a nonissuer (a practitioner) to comply with standards promulgated by such senior committees. A practitioner must comply with an unconditional requirement in all cases in which such requirement is relevant. A practitioner also should comply with a presumptively mandatory requirement in all cases in which such requirement is relevant; however, in rare circumstances, the practitioner may depart from a presumptively mandatory requirement provided that the practitioner documents the justification for the departure and how the alternative procedures performed in the circumstances were sufficient to achieve the intent of that requirement.

Exhibits and interpretations to SSAEs are interpretive publications, as defined in AT-C section 105, *Concepts Common to All Attestation Engagements*. AT-C section 105 requires the practitioner to consider applicable interpretive publications in planning and performing an attestation engagement. Interpretive publications are not attestation standards. Interpretive publications are recommendations on the application of the SSAEs in specific circumstances, including engagements for entities in specialized industries. An interpretive publication is issued under the authority of the relevant senior technical committee after all members of the committee have been provided an opportunity to consider and comment on whether the proposed interpretive publication is consistent with the SSAEs. Attestation interpretations are included in the AT-C sections of AICPA *Professional Standards*. AICPA Guides and Attestation Statements of Position are listed in AT-C appendix A, "AICPA Guides and Statements of Position," of AICPA *Professional Standards*.

ACCOUNTING AND REVIEW
SERVICES COMMITTEE
Mike Fleming, Chair
Michael P. Glynn, Senior Technical Manager—
Audit and Attest Standards

AUDITING STANDARDS BOARD
Michael J. Santay, Chair
Charles E. Landes, Vice President—
Professional Standards and Services

WHAT'S NEW IN THIS EDITION

STANDARDS RECENTLY ISSUED

Statement	Title	Issue Date	Section
Statements on Standards for Attestation Engagements (SSAE) No. 18	*Statements on Standards for Attestation Engagements: Clarification and Recodification*	April 2016	AT-C 105 AT-C 205 AT-C 210 AT-C 215 AT-C 305 AT-C 310 AT-C 315 AT-C 320 AT-C 395

ADDITIONAL CHANGES

Section	Addition
AT 9201.01.19	Addition of section as a result of the issuance of Interpretation No. 1, "Third-Party Due Diligence Services Related to Asset-Backed Securitizations: SEC Release No. 34-72936," of AT section 201, *Agreed-Upon Procedures Engagements*.
U.S. Attestation Standards—AICPA (Clarified) [AT-C]	Addition of section as a result of the issuance of SSAE No. 18.

TABLE OF CONTENTS

HOW THIS PUBLICATION IS ORGANIZED

This publication is organized into two main sections.

The first section, "Attestation Standards [AT]," contains the codified attestation standards that will be applicable through April 2017, by which time substantially all engagements for which the AT sections were still effective are expected to be completed, and the related attestation interpretations.

The next section, "U.S. Attestation Standards—AICPA (Clarified) [AT-C]," contains the clarified codified attestation standards.

These sections are described in more detail in the following sections.

Attestation Standards [AT]

The AT sections include attestation standards issued through Statement on Standards for Attestation Engagements (SSAE) No. 17, *Reporting on Compiled Prospective Financial Statements When the Practitioner's Independence Is Impaired*. Superseded portions have been deleted, and all applicable amendments have been included. These sections are arranged as follows:

AT Cross-References to SSAEs

Defining Professional Requirements in Statements on Standards for Attestation Engagements

SSAE Hierarchy

Attest Engagements

Agreed-Upon Procedures Engagements

Financial Forecasts and Projections

Reporting on Pro Forma Financial Information

An Examination of an Entity's Internal Control Over Financial Reporting That Is Integrated With an Audit of Its Financial Statements

Compliance Attestation

Management's Discussion and Analysis

Reporting on Controls at a Service Organization

Appendixes

Topical Index

The AT Cross-References to SSAEs is a list of all issued SSAEs and a list of sources of sections in the current text.

The standards are divided into sections, each with its own section number. Each paragraph within a section is decimally numbered.

Attestation interpretations are numbered in the 9000 series with the last three digits indicating the section to which the interpretation relates. Interpretations immediately follow their corresponding section. For example, interpretations related to section 101 are numbered 9101, which directly follows section 101.

There are two appendixes relating to attestation standards as follows:

Appendix A provides a list of AICPA attestation guides and Statements of Position.

Appendix B identifies other attestation publications published by the AICPA that have been reviewed by the AICPA Audit and Attest Standards staff.

The AT topical index uses the key word method to facilitate reference to the statements and interpretations. The index is arranged alphabetically by topic with references to section and paragraph numbers.

U.S. Attestation Standards—AICPA (Clarified) [AT-C]

The AT-C sections include clarified accounting and review services standards issued by SSAE No. 18, *Attestation Standards: Clarification and Recodification*. These sections are arranged as follows:

AT-C Cross-References to SSAEs

AT-C Introduction

Common Concepts

Level of Service

Subject Matter

Exhibits

Appendixes

AT-C Topical Index

The AT-C Cross-References to SSAEs to SSAEs lists all issued SSAEs and the sources of sections created by SSAE No. 18 in the current text.

The AT-C Introduction describes the Auditing Standards Board project to revise and clarify all existing attestation standards in the Codification of Statements on Standards for Attestation Engagements.

The standards are divided into sections, each with its own section number. Each paragraph within a section is decimally numbered.

There is one exhibit relating to attestation standards as follows:

The exhibit provides a list of AT-C sections designated by SSAE No. 18 cross referenced to a list of AT sections.

There are two appendixes relating to attestation standards as follows:

Appendix A provides a list of AICPA attestation guides and Statements of Position.

Appendix B identifies other attestation publications published by the AICPA that have been reviewed by the AICPA Audit and Attest Standards staff.

The AT-C topical index uses the keyword method to facilitate reference to the pronouncements. The index is arranged alphabetically by topic and refers to major divisions, sections, and paragraph numbers.

AT Section

STATEMENTS ON STANDARDS FOR ATTESTATION ENGAGEMENTS

CONTENTS

AT CROSS-REFERENCES TO SSAEs

Statements on Standards for Attestation Engagements*

No.	Date Issued	Title	Section
1	Mar. 1986	Attestation Standards [Revised and recodified by SSAE No. 10; see AT sections 101, 301, and 401]	
1	Dec. 1987	Attest Services Related to MAS Engagements [Revised and recodified by SSAE No. 10; see AT sections 101, 301, and 401]	
1	Oct. 1985	Financial Forecasts and Projections [Revised and recodified by SSAE No. 10; see AT sections 101, 301, and 401]	
1	Sept. 1988	Reporting on Pro Forma Financial Information [Revised and recodified by SSAE No. 10; see AT sections 101, 301, and 401]	
2	May 1993	Reporting on an Entity's Internal Control Over Financial Reporting [Revised and recodified by SSAE No. 10; subsequently superseded by SSAE No. 15, see AT section 501]	
3	Dec. 1993	Compliance Attestation [Revised and recodified by SSAE No. 10; see AT section 601]	
4	Sept. 1995	Agreed-Upon Procedures Engagements [Revised and recodified by SSAE No. 10; see AT section 201]	
5	Nov. 1995	Amendment to Statement on Standards for Attestation Engagements No. 1, *Attestation Standards* [Revised and recodified by SSAE No. 10; see AT section 101]	
6	Dec. 1995	Reporting on an Entity's Internal Control Over Financial Reporting: An Amendment to Statement on Standards for Attestation Engagements No. 2 [Revised and recodified by SSAE No. 10]	
7	Oct. 1997	Establishing an Understanding With the Client [Revised and recodified by SSAE No. 10; see AT section 101]	

(continued)

* Pronouncements in effect are indicated in **boldface** type.

No.	Date Issued	Title	Section
8	Mar. 1998	Management's Discussion and Analysis [Revised and recodified by SSAE No. 10; see AT section 701]	
9	Jan. 1999	Amendments to Statement on Standards for Attestation Engagements Nos. 1, 2, and 3 [Revised and recodified by SSAE No. 10; see AT sections 101 and 601]	
10	**Jan. 2001**	**Attestation Standards: Revision and Recodification**[1]	
11	**Jan. 2002**	**Attest Documentation**[2]	
12	**Sept. 2002**	**Amendment to Statement on Standards for Attestation Engagements No. 10, *Attestation Standards: Revision and Recodification***[3]	
13	**Dec. 2005**	**Defining Professional Requirements in Statements on Standards for Attestation Engagements**	20
14	**Nov. 2006**	**SSAE Hierarchy**	50
15	**Sept. 2008**	**An Examination of an Entity's Internal Control Over Financial Reporting That Is Integrated With an Audit of Its Financial Statements**	501
16	**April 2010**	**Reporting on Controls at a Service Organization**	801
17	**Dec. 2010**	**Reporting on Compiled Prospective Financial Statements When the Practitioner's Independence Is Impaired**[4]	

[1] SSAE No. 10 has been integrated within AT sections 101, 201, 301, 401, 601, and 701.

[2] SSAE No. 11 has been integrated within AT sections 101.100–[.108], 201[.27–.30], 301[.17], and 301[.32].

[3] SSAE No. 12 has been integrated within AT sections 101.17–.18.

[4] SSAE No. 17 has been integrated within AT section 301.23.

Sources of Sections in Current Text

AT Section	*Contents*	*Source*
20	Defining Professional Requirements in Statements on Standards for Attestation Engagements	SSAE No. 13
50	SSAE Hierarchy	SSAE No. 14
101	Attest Engagements	SSAE No. 10
201	Agreed-Upon Procedures Engagements	SSAE No. 10
301	Financial Forecasts and Projections	SSAE No. 10
401	Reporting on Pro Forma Financial Information	SSAE No. 10
501	An Examination of an Entity's Internal Control Over Financial Reporting That Is Integrated With an Audit of Its Financial Statements	SSAE No. 15
601	Compliance Attestation	SSAE No. 10
701	Management's Discussion and Analysis	SSAE No. 10
801	Reporting on Controls at a Service Organization	SSAE No. 16

ATTESTATION STANDARDS

Introduction

The accompanying "attestation standards" provide guidance and establish a broad framework for a variety of attest services increasingly demanded of the accounting profession. The standards and related interpretive commentary are designed to provide professional guidelines that will enhance both consistency and quality in the performance of such services.

For years, attest services generally were limited to expressing a positive opinion on historical financial statements on the basis of an audit in accordance with generally accepted auditing standards (GAAS). However, certified public accountants increasingly have been requested to provide, and have been providing, assurance on representations other than historical financial statements and in forms other than the positive opinion. In responding to these needs, certified public accountants have been able to generally apply the basic concepts underlying GAAS to these attest services. As the range of attest services has grown, however, it has become increasingly difficult to do so.

Consequently, the main objective of adopting these attestation standards and the related interpretive commentary is to provide a general framework for and set reasonable boundaries around the attest function. As such, the standards and commentary (*a*) provide useful and necessary guidance to certified public accountants engaged to perform new and evolving attest services and (*b*) guide AICPA standard-setting bodies in establishing, if deemed necessary, interpretive standards for such services.

The attestation standards are a natural extension of the ten generally accepted auditing standards. Like the auditing standards, the attestation standards deal with the need for technical competence, independence in mental attitude, due professional care, adequate planning and supervision, sufficient evidence, and appropriate reporting; however, they are much broader in scope. (The eleven attestation standards are listed below.) Such standards apply to a growing array of attest services. These services include, for example, reports on descriptions of systems of internal control; on descriptions of computer software; on compliance with statutory, regulatory, and contractual requirements; on investment performance statistics; and on information supplementary to financial statements. Thus, the standards have been developed to be responsive to a changing environment and the demands of society.

These attestation standards apply only to attest services rendered by a certified public accountant in public practice—that is, a practitioner as defined in footnote 1 of paragraph .01.

The attestation standards do not supersede any of the existing standards in Statements on Auditing Standards (SASs) and Statements on Standards for Accounting and Review Services (SSARSs). Therefore, the practitioner who is engaged to perform an engagement subject to these existing standards should follow such standards.

Attestation Standards

General Standards

1. The practitioner must have adequate technical training and proficiency to perform in the attestation engagement.
2. The practitioner must have adequate knowledge of the subject matter.
3. The practitioner must have reason to believe that the subject matter is capable of evaluation against criteria that are suitable and available to users.
4. The practitioner must maintain independence in mental attitude in all matters relating to the engagement.
5. The practitioner must exercise due professional care in the planning and performance of the engagement and the preparation of the report.

Standards of Fieldwork

1. The practitioner must adequately plan the work and must properly supervise any assistants.
2. The practitioner must obtain sufficient evidence to provide a reasonable basis for the conclusion that is expressed in the report.

Standards of Reporting

1. The practitioner must identify the subject matter or the assertion being reported on and state the character of the engagement in the report.
2. The practitioner must state the practitioner's conclusion about the subject matter or the assertion in relation to the criteria against which the subject matter was evaluated.
3. The practitioner must state all of the practitioner's significant reservations about the engagement, the subject matter, and, if applicable, the assertion related thereto in the report.
4. The practitioner must state in the report that the report is intended solely for the information and use of the specified parties under the following circumstances:
   - When the criteria used to evaluate the subject matter are determined by the practitioner to be appropriate only for a limited number of parties who either participated in their establishment or can be presumed to have an adequate understanding of the criteria
   - When the criteria used to evaluate the subject matter are available only to specified parties
   - When reporting on subject matter and a written assertion has not been provided by the responsible party
   - When the report is on an attestation engagement to apply agreed-upon procedures to the subject matter

[As amended, effective for attest reports issued on or after June 30, 1999, by SSAE No. 9. As amended, effective when the subject matter or assertion is as of or for a period ending on or after June 1, 2001, by SSAE No. 10. Revised, December 2006, to reflect conforming changes necessary due to the issuance of SSAE No. 14. Revised, January 2015, to reflect conforming changes necessary due to the issuance of the revised AICPA Code of Professional Conduct, effective December 15, 2014]

AT Section

STATEMENTS ON STANDARDS FOR ATTESTATION ENGAGEMENTS

The following is a Codification of currently effective Statements on Standards for Attestation Engagements ("SSAEs") and related Attestation Interpretations. Statements on Standards for Attestation Engagements are issued by senior committees of the AICPA designated to issue pronouncements on attestation matters. The "Compliance With Standards Rule" of the AICPA Code of Professional Conduct (ET sec. 1.310.001) requires an AICPA member who performs an attest engagement (a practitioner) to comply with such pronouncements. A practitioner is required to comply with an unconditional requirement in all cases in which the circumstances exist to which the unconditional requirement applies. A practitioner is also required to comply with a presumptively mandatory requirement in all cases in which the circumstances exist to which the presumptively mandatory requirement applies; however, in rare circumstances, the practitioner may depart from a presumptively mandatory requirement provided the practitioner documents his or her justification for the departure and how the alternative procedures performed in the circumstances were sufficient to achieve the objectives of the presumptively mandatory requirement.

Attestation Interpretations are recommendations on the application of SSAEs in specific circumstances, including engagements for entities in specialized industries, issued under the authority of AICPA senior committees. An interpretation is not as authoritative as a pronouncement; however, if a practitioner does not apply an attestation interpretation, the practitioner should be prepared to explain how he or she complied with the SSAE provisions addressed by such attestation interpretation. The specific terms used to define professional requirements in the SSAEs are not intended to apply to interpretations because interpretations are not attestation standards. It is the Auditing Standards Board's intention to make conforming changes to the interpretations over the next several years to remove any language that would imply a professional requirement where none exists.

TABLE OF CONTENTS

AT Section 20

Defining Professional Requirements in Statements on Standards for Attestation Engagements

Source: SSAE No. 13.

Effective December 2005.

Introduction

.01 This section sets forth the meaning of certain terms used in Statements on Standards for Attestation Engagements (SSAEs) issued by the Auditing Standards Board in describing the professional requirements imposed on practitioners.

Professional Requirements

.02 SSAEs contain professional requirements together with related guidance in the form of explanatory material. Practitioners have a responsibility to consider the entire text of an SSAE in carrying out their work on an engagement and in understanding and applying the professional requirements of the relevant SSAEs.

.03 Not every paragraph of an SSAE carries a professional requirement that the practitioner is expected to fulfill. Rather, the professional requirements are communicated by the language and the meaning of the words used in the SSAEs.

.04 SSAEs use two categories of professional requirements, identified by specific terms, to describe the degree of responsibility they impose on practitioners, as follows:

- *Unconditional requirements.* The practitioner is required to comply with an unconditional requirement in all cases in which the circumstances exist to which the unconditional requirement applies. SSAEs use the words *must* or *is required* to indicate an unconditional requirement.
- *Presumptively mandatory requirements.* The practitioner is also required to comply with a presumptively mandatory requirement in all cases in which the circumstances exist to which the presumptively mandatory requirement applies; however, in rare circumstances, the practitioner may depart from a presumptively mandatory requirement provided the practitioner documents his or her justification for the departure and how the alternative procedures performed in the circumstances were sufficient to achieve the objectives of the presumptively mandatory requirement. SSAEs use the word *should* to indicate a presumptively mandatory requirement.

If an SSAE provides that a procedure or action is one that the practitioner "should consider," the consideration of the procedure or action is presumptively required, whereas carrying out the procedure or action is not. The professional requirements of an SSAE are to be understood and applied in the context of the explanatory material that provides guidance for their application.

Explanatory Material

.05 Explanatory material is defined as the text within an SSAE (excluding any related appendixes or interpretations[1]) that may:

- Provide further explanation and guidance on the professional requirements; or
- Identify and describe other procedures or actions relating to the activities of the practitioner.

.06 Explanatory material that provides further explanation and guidance on the professional requirements is intended to be descriptive rather than imperative. That is, it explains the objective of the professional requirements (where not otherwise self-evident); it explains why the practitioner might consider or employ particular procedures, depending on the circumstances; and it provides additional information for the practitioner to consider in exercising professional judgment in performing the engagement.

.07 Explanatory material that identifies and describes other procedures or actions relating to the activities of the practitioner is not intended to impose a professional requirement for the practitioner to perform the suggested procedures or actions. Rather, these procedures or actions require the practitioner's attention and understanding; how and whether the practitioner carries out such procedures or actions in the engagement depends on the exercise of professional judgment in the circumstances consistent with the objective of the standard. The words *may*, *might*, and *could* are used to describe these actions and procedures.

Application

.08 The provisions of this section are effective upon issuance.[2]

---

[1] Interpretive publications differ from explanatory material. Interpretive publications, for example, interpretations of the Statements on Standards for Attestation Engagements (SSAEs), appendixes to the SSAEs and AICPA auditing Statements of Position, are issued under the authority of the Auditing Standards Board (ASB). In contrast, explanatory material is always contained within the standards sections of the SSAE and is meant to be more descriptive in nature.

[2] The specific terms used to define professional requirements in this attestation standard are not intended to apply to any interpretive publications issued under the authority of the ASB, for example, interpretations of the SSAEs, or appendixes to the SSAEs, since interpretive publications are not attestation standards. (See footnote 1.) It is the ASB's intention to make conforming changes to the interpretive publications over the next several years to remove any language that would imply a professional requirement where none exists. It is the ASB's intention that such language would only be used in the standards sections of the SSAEs.

AT Section 50

SSAE Hierarchy

Source: SSAE No. 14.

Effective when the subject matter or assertion is as of or for a period ending on or after December 15, 2006.

.01 A practitioner plans, conducts, and reports the results of an attestation engagement in accordance with attestation standards. Attestation standards provide a measure of quality and the objectives to be achieved in the attestation engagement. Attestation procedures differ from attestation standards. Attestation procedures are acts that the practitioner performs during the course of the attestation engagement to comply with the attestation standards.

Attestation Standards

.02 The general, fieldwork, and reporting standards (the 11 attestation standards) approved and adopted by the membership of the AICPA, as amended by the AICPA Auditing Standards Board (ASB), are as follows:

General Standards

1. The practitioner must have adequate technical training and proficiency to perform the attestation engagement.
2. The practitioner must have adequate knowledge of the subject matter.
3. The practitioner must have reason to believe that the subject matter is capable of evaluation against criteria that are suitable and available to users.
4. The practitioner must maintain independence in mental attitude in all matters relating to the engagement.
5. The practitioner must exercise due professional care in the planning and performance of the engagement and the preparation of the report.

Standards of Fieldwork

1. The practitioner must adequately plan the work and must properly supervise any assistants.
2. The practitioner must obtain sufficient evidence to provide a reasonable basis for the conclusion that is expressed in the report.

Standards of Reporting[1]

1. The practitioner must identify the subject matter or the assertion being reported on and state the character of the engagement in the report.
2. The practitioner must state the practitioner's conclusion about the subject matter or the assertion in relation to the criteria against which the subject matter was evaluated in the report.
3. The practitioner must state all of the practitioner's significant reservations about the engagement, the subject matter, and, if applicable, the assertion related thereto in the report.

---

[1] The reporting standards apply only when the practitioner issues a report.

4. The practitioner must state in the report that the report is intended solely for the information and use of the specified parties under the following circumstances:
   - When the criteria used to evaluate the subject matter are determined by the practitioner to be appropriate only for a limited number of parties who either participated in their establishment or can be presumed to have an adequate understanding of the criteria.
   - When the criteria used to evaluate the subject matter are available only to specified parties.
   - When reporting on subject matter and a written assertion has not been provided by the responsible party.
   - When the report is on an attestation engagement to apply agreed-upon procedures to the subject matter.

Footnote 1 is also to be added to the heading *Standards of Reporting* preceding paragraph .63 of section 101, *Attest Engagements*.

.03 Statements on Standards for Attestation Engagements (SSAEs) are issued by senior committees of the AICPA designated to issue pronouncements on attestation matters. The "Compliance With Standards Rule" (ET sec. 1.310.001) of the AICPA Code of Professional Conduct requires an AICPA member who performs an attestation engagement (the practitioner) to comply with such pronouncements.[2] SSAEs are developed and issued through a due process that includes deliberation in meetings open to the public, public exposure of proposed SSAEs, and a formal vote. The SSAEs are codified within the framework of the 11 attestation standards. [Revised, January 2015, to reflect conforming changes necessary due to the issuance of the revised AICPA Code of Professional Conduct, effective December 15, 2014.]

.04 The nature of the 11 attestation standards and the SSAEs requires the practitioner to exercise professional judgment in applying them. When, in rare circumstances, the practitioner departs from a presumptively mandatory requirement, the practitioner must document in the working papers his or her justification for the departure and how the alternative procedures performed in the circumstances were sufficient to achieve the objectives of the presumptively mandatory requirement.[3]

Attestation Interpretations[4]

.05 Attestation interpretations consist of Interpretations of the SSAEs, appendixes to the SSAEs, attestation guidance included in AICPA Audit and Accounting Guides, and AICPA attestation Statements of Position. Attestation interpretations are recommendations on the application of SSAEs in specific circumstances, including engagements for entities in specialized industries, issued under the authority of the AICPA senior committees.

.06 The practitioner should be aware of and consider attestation interpretations applicable to the attestation engagement. If the practitioner does not

---

[2] In certain engagements, the practitioner also may be subject to other attestation requirements, such as *Government Auditing Standards* issued by the comptroller general of the United States.

[3] The term *presumptively mandatory requirement* is defined in section 20, *Defining Professional Requirements in Statements on Standards for Attestation Engagements*.

[4] Appendixes to Statements on Standards for Attestation Engagements (SSAEs) referred to in paragraph .05 of this section do not include previously issued appendixes to original pronouncements that, when adopted, modified other SSAEs.

apply the attestation guidance included in an applicable attestation interpretation, the practitioner should be prepared to explain how he or she complied with the SSAE provisions addressed by such attestation guidance.

Other Attestation Publications

.07 Other attestation publications include AICPA attestation publications not referred to above; attestation articles in the *Journal of Accountancy* and other professional journals; attestation articles in the AICPA *CPA Letter*; continuing professional education programs and other instruction materials, textbooks, guide books, attest programs, and checklists; and other attestation publications from state CPA societies, other organizations, and individuals.[5] Other attestation publications have no authoritative status; however, they may help the practitioner understand and apply the SSAEs.

.08 A practitioner may apply the attestation guidance included in an other attestation publication if he or she is satisfied that, in his or her judgment, it is both relevant to the circumstances of the attestation engagement, and appropriate. In determining whether an other attestation publication is appropriate, the practitioner may wish to consider the degree to which the publication is recognized as being helpful in understanding and applying SSAEs and the degree to which the issuer or author is recognized as an authority in attestation matters. Other attestation publications published by the AICPA that have been reviewed by the AICPA Audit and Attest Standards Staff are presumed to be appropriate.

.09 This section is effective when the subject matter or assertion is as of or for a period ending on or after December 15, 2006.

---

[5] The practitioner is not expected to be aware of the full body of other attestation publications.

AT Section 101

Attest Engagements

Source: SSAE No. 10; SSAE No. 11; SSAE No. 12; SSAE No. 14.

See section 9101 for interpretations of this section.

Effective when the subject matter or assertion is as of or for a period ending on or after June 1, 2001, unless otherwise indicated.

Applicability

.01 This section applies to engagements, except for those services discussed in paragraph .04, in which a certified public accountant in public practice[1] (hereinafter referred to as a *practitioner*) is engaged to issue or does issue an examination, a review, or an agreed-upon procedures report on subject matter, or an assertion about the subject matter (hereafter referred to as *the assertion*), that is the responsibility of another party.[2] [Revised, January 2015, to reflect conforming changes necessary due to the issuance of the revised AICPA Code of Professional Conduct, effective December 15, 2014.]

.02 This section establishes a framework for attest[3] engagements performed by practitioners and for the ongoing development of related standards. For certain subject matter, specific attestation standards have been developed to provide additional requirements for engagement performance and reporting.

.03 When a practitioner undertakes an attest engagement for the benefit of a government body or agency and agrees to follow specified government standards, guides, procedures, statutes, rules, and regulations, the practitioner is obliged to follow those governmental requirements as well as the applicable attestation standards.

.04 Professional services provided by practitioners that are not covered by this SSAE include the following:

a. Services performed in accordance with Statements on Auditing Standards (SASs)

b. Services performed in accordance with Statements on Standards for Accounting and Review Services (SSARSs)

c. Services performed in accordance with the Statement on Standards for Consulting Services (SSCS), such as engagements in which the practitioner's role is solely to assist the client (for example, acting as the company accountant in preparing information other than financial

---

[1] For a definition of the term *public practice*, see ET section 0.400, *Definitions*. [Footnote revised, January 2015, to reflect conforming changes necessary due to the issuance of the revised AICPA Code of Professional Conduct, effective December 15, 2014.]

[2] See paragraph .02 of section 301, *Financial Forecasts and Projections*, for additional guidance on applicability when engaged to provide an attest service on a financial forecast or projection.

[3] The term *attest* and its variants, such as *attesting* and *attestation,* are used in a number of state accountancy laws, and in regulations issued by state boards of accountancy under such laws, for different purposes and with different meanings from those intended by this section. Consequently, the definition of *attest engagements* set out in paragraph .01, and the attendant meaning of *attest* and *attestation* as used throughout the section, should not be understood as defining these terms and similar terms, as they are used in any law or regulation, nor as embodying a common understanding of the terms which may also be reflected in such laws or regulations.

statements), or engagements in which a practitioner is engaged to testify as an expert witness in accounting, auditing, taxation, or other matters, given certain stipulated facts

d. Engagements in which the practitioner is engaged to advocate a client's position—for example, tax matters being reviewed by the Internal Revenue Service

e. Tax engagements in which a practitioner is engaged to prepare tax returns or provide tax advice

.05 An attest engagement may be part of a larger engagement, for example, a feasibility study or business acquisition study may also include an examination of prospective financial information. In such circumstances, these standards apply only to the attest portion of the engagement.

.06 Any professional service resulting in the expression of assurance must be performed under AICPA professional standards that provide for the expression of such assurance. Reports issued by a practitioner in connection with other professional standards should be written to be clearly distinguishable from and not to be confused with attest reports. For example, a practitioner performing an engagement which is intended solely to assist an organization in improving its controls over the privacy of client data should not issue a report as a result of that engagement expressing assurance as to the effectiveness of such controls. Additionally, a report that merely excludes the words, " ...was conducted in accordance with attestation standards established by the American Institute of Certified Public Accountants..." but is otherwise similar to an examination, a review or an agreed-upon procedures attest report may be inferred to be an attest report.

Definitions and Underlying Concepts

Subject Matter

.07 The subject matter of an attest engagement may take many forms, including the following:

a. Historical or prospective performance or condition (for example, historical or prospective financial information, performance measurements, and backlog data)

b. Physical characteristics (for example, narrative descriptions, square footage of facilities)

c. Historical events (for example, the price of a market basket of goods on a certain date)

d. Analyses (for example, break-even analyses)

e. Systems and processes (for example, internal control)

f. Behavior (for example, corporate governance, compliance with laws and regulations, and human resource practices)

The subject matter may be as of a point in time or for a period of time.

Assertion

.08 An assertion is any declaration or set of declarations about whether the subject matter is based on or in conformity with the criteria selected.

.09 A practitioner may report on a written assertion or may report directly on the subject matter. In either case, the practitioner should ordinarily obtain a written assertion in an examination or a review engagement. A written assertion may be presented to a practitioner in a number of ways, such as in a narrative description, within a schedule, or as part of a representation letter appropriately identifying what is being presented and the point in time or period of time covered.

.10 When a written assertion has not been obtained, a practitioner may still report on the subject matter; however, the form of the report will vary depending on the circumstances and its use should be restricted.[4] In this section, see paragraphs .58 and .60 on gathering sufficient evidence and paragraphs .73–.75 and .78–.80 for reporting guidance.

Responsible Party

.11 The *responsible party* is defined as the person or persons, either as individuals or representatives of the entity, responsible for the subject matter. If the nature of the subject matter is such that no such party exists, a party who has a reasonable basis for making a written assertion about the subject matter may provide such an assertion (hereinafter referred to as the *responsible party*).

.12 The practitioner may be engaged to gather information to enable the responsible party to evaluate the subject matter in connection with providing a written assertion. Regardless of the procedures performed by the practitioner, the responsible party must accept responsibility for its assertion and the subject matter and must not base its assertion solely on the practitioner's procedures.[5]

.13 Because the practitioner's role in an attest engagement is that of an *attester*, the practitioner should not take on the role of the responsible party in an attest engagement. Therefore, the need to clearly identify a responsible party is a prerequisite for an attest engagement. A practitioner may accept an engagement to perform an examination, a review or an agreed-upon procedures engagement on subject matter or an assertion related thereto provided that one of the following conditions is met.

a. The party wishing to engage the practitioner is responsible for the subject matter, or has a reasonable basis for providing a written assertion about the subject matter if the nature of the subject matter is such that a responsible party does not otherwise exist.

b. The party wishing to engage the practitioner is not responsible for the subject matter but is able to provide the practitioner, or have a third party who is responsible for the subject matter provide the practitioner, with evidence of the third party's responsibility for the subject matter.

.14 The practitioner should obtain written acknowledgment or other evidence of the responsible party's responsibility for the subject matter, or the written assertion, as it relates to the objective of the engagement. The responsible party can acknowledge that responsibility in a number of ways, for example, in an engagement letter, a representation letter, or the presentation of the subject matter, including the notes thereto, or the written assertion. If the practitioner is not able to directly obtain written acknowledgment, the practitioner should obtain other evidence of the responsible party's responsibility for the subject matter (for example, by reference to legislation, a regulation, or a contract).

---

[4] When the practitioner is unable to perform the inquiry and analytical or other procedures that he or she considers necessary to achieve the limited assurance contemplated by a review, or when the client is the responsible party and does not provide the practitioner with a written assertion, the review will be incomplete. A review that is incomplete is not an adequate basis for issuing a review report and, accordingly, the practitioner should withdraw from the engagement.

[5] See paragraph .112 regarding the practitioner's assistance in developing subject matter or criteria.

Applicability to Agreed-Upon Procedures Engagements

.15 An agreed-upon procedures attest engagement is one in which a practitioner is engaged to issue a report of findings based on specific procedures performed on subject matter. The general, fieldwork, and reporting standards for attest engagements set forth in this section are applicable to agreed-upon procedures engagements. Because the application of these standards to agreed-upon procedures engagements is discussed in section 201, *Agreed-Upon Procedures Engagements*, such engagements are not discussed further in this section.

The Relationship of Attestation Standards to Quality Control Standards

.16 The practitioner is responsible for compliance with the American Institute of Certified Public Accountants' (AICPA's) Statements on Standards for Attestation Engagements (SSAEs) in an attest engagement. The "Compliance With Standards Rule" (ET sec. 1.310.001) of the AICPA Code of Professional Conduct requires members to comply with such standards when conducting professional services. [Revised, January 2015, to reflect conforming changes necessary due to the issuance of the revised AICPA Code of Professional Conduct, effective December 15, 2014.]

.17 A firm of practitioners has a responsibility to adopt a system of quality control in the conduct of a firm's attest practice.[6] Thus, a firm should establish quality control policies and procedures to provide it with reasonable assurance that its personnel comply with the attestation standards in its attest engagements. The nature and extent of a firm's quality control policies and procedures depend on factors such as its size, the degree of operating autonomy allowed its personnel and its practice offices, the nature of its practice, its organization, and appropriate cost-benefit considerations. [As amended, effective September 2002, by SSAE No. 12.]

.18 Attestation standards relate to the conduct of individual attest engagements; quality control standards relate to the conduct of a firm's attest practice as a whole. Thus, attestation standards and quality control standards are related and the quality control policies and procedures that a firm adopts may affect both the conduct of individual attest engagements and the conduct of a firm's attest practice as a whole. However, deficiencies in or instances of noncompliance with a firm's quality control policies and procedures do not, in and of themselves, indicate that a particular engagement was not performed in accordance with attestation standards. [As amended, effective September 2002, by SSAE No. 12.]

General Standards

Training and Proficiency

.19 The first general standard is—*The practitioner must have adequate technical training and proficiency to perform the attestation engagement.* [As

---

[6] The elements of a system of quality control are identified in Statement on Quality Control Standards (SQCS) No. 8, *A Firm's System of Quality Control* (QC sec. 10). A system of quality control consists of policies designed to provide the firm with reasonable assurance that the firm and its personnel comply with professional standards and applicable legal and regulatory requirements and that reports issued by the firm are appropriate in the circumstances, and the procedures necessary to implement and monitor compliance with those policies. [As amended, effective September 2002, by SSAE No. 12. Footnote amended due to the issuance of SQCS No. 7, December 2008.]

amended, effective when the subject matter or assertion is as of or for a period ending on or after December 15, 2006, by SSAE No. 14.]

.20 Performing attest services is different from preparing and presenting subject matter or an assertion. The latter involves collecting, classifying, summarizing, and communicating information; this usually entails reducing a mass of detailed data to a manageable and understandable form. On the other hand, performing attest services involves gathering evidence to support the subject matter or the assertion and objectively assessing the measurements and communications of the responsible party. Thus, attest services are analytical, critical, investigative, and are concerned with the basis and support for the subject matter or the assertion.

Adequate Knowledge of Subject Matter

.21 The second general standard is—*The practitioner must have adequate knowledge of the subject matter.* [As amended, effective when the subject matter or assertion is as of or for a period ending on or after December 15, 2006, by SSAE No. 14.]

.22 A practitioner may obtain adequate knowledge of the subject matter through formal or continuing education, including self-study, or through practical experience. However, this standard does not necessarily require a practitioner to personally acquire all of the necessary knowledge in the subject matter to be qualified to express a conclusion. This knowledge requirement may be met, in part, through the use of one or more specialists on a particular attest engagement if the practitioner has sufficient knowledge of the subject matter (*a*) to communicate to the specialist the objectives of the work and (*b*) to evaluate the specialist's work to determine if the objectives were achieved.

Suitability and Availability of Criteria

.23 The third general standard is—*The practitioner must have reason to believe that the subject matter is capable of evaluation against criteria that are suitable and available to users.* [As amended, effective when the subject matter or assertion is as of or for a period ending on or after December 15, 2006, by SSAE No. 14.]

Suitability of Criteria

.24 Criteria are the standards or benchmarks used to measure and present the subject matter and against which the practitioner evaluates the subject matter.[*] Suitable criteria must have each of the following attributes:

- *Objectivity*—Criteria should be free from bias.
- *Measurability*—Criteria should permit reasonably consistent measurements, qualitative or quantitative, of subject matter.
- *Completeness*—Criteria should be sufficiently complete so that those relevant factors that would alter a conclusion about subject matter are not omitted.
- *Relevance*—Criteria should be relevant to the subject matter.

---

[*] An example of suitable criteria are the Trust Services criteria developed by the AICPA's Assurance Services Executive Committee. These criteria may be used when the subject matter of the engagement is the security, availability, or processing integrity of a system, or the confidentiality or privacy of the information processed or stored by that system. The Trust Services criteria are presented in TSP sections 100 and 200 of the AICPA's *Trust Services Principles and Criteria*. [Footnote added by the Assurance Services Executive Committee, January 2003. Footnote revised, May 2006, to reflect conforming changes necessary due to the issuance of Generally Accepted Privacy Principles.]

.25 Criteria that are established or developed by groups composed of experts that follow due process procedures, including exposure of the proposed criteria for public comment, ordinarily should be considered suitable. Criteria promulgated by a body designated by the AICPA Governing Council under the AICPA Code of Professional Conduct are, by definition, considered to be suitable.

.26 Criteria may be established or developed by the client, the responsible party, industry associations, or other groups that do not follow due process procedures or do not as clearly represent. the public interest. To determine whether these criteria are suitable, the practitioner should evaluate them based on the attributes described in paragraph .24.

.27 Regardless of who establishes or develops the criteria, the responsible party or the client is responsible for selecting the criteria and the client is responsible for determining that such criteria are appropriate for its purposes.

.28 The use of suitable criteria does not presume that all persons or groups would be expected to select the same criteria in evaluating the same subject matter. There may be more than one set of suitable criteria for a given subject matter. For example, in an engagement to express assurance about customer satisfaction, a responsible party may select as a criterion for customer satisfaction that all customer complaints are resolved to the satisfaction of the customer. In other cases, another responsible party may select a different criterion, such as the number of repeat purchases in the three months following the initial purchase.

.29 In evaluating the measurability attribute as described in paragraph .24, the practitioner should consider whether the criteria are sufficiently precise to permit people having competence in and using the same measurement criterion to be able to ordinarily obtain materially similar measurements. Consequently, practitioners should not perform an engagement when the criteria are so subjective or vague that reasonably consistent measurements, qualitative or quantitative, of subject matter cannot ordinarily be obtained. However, practitioners will not always reach the same conclusion because such evaluations often require the exercise of considerable professional judgment.

.30 For the purpose of assessing whether the use of particular criteria can be expected to yield reasonably consistent measurement and evaluation, consideration should be given to the nature of the subject matter. For example, *soft information*, such as forecasts or projections, would be expected to have a wider range of reasonable estimates than *hard* data, such as the calculated investment performance of a defined portfolio of managed investment products.

.31 Some criteria may be appropriate for only a limited number of parties who either participated in their establishment or can be presumed to have an adequate understanding of the criteria. For instance, criteria set forth in a lease agreement for override payments may be appropriate only for reporting to the parties to the agreement because of the likelihood that such criteria would be misunderstood or misinterpreted by parties other than those who have specifically agreed to the criteria. Such criteria can be agreed upon directly by the parties or through a designated representative. If a practitioner determines that such criteria are appropriate only for a limited number of parties, the use of the report should be restricted to those specified parties who either participated in their establishment or can be presumed to have an adequate understanding of the criteria.

.32 The third general standard in paragraph .23 applies equally regardless of the level of the attest service to be provided. Consequently, it is inappropriate to perform a review engagement if the practitioner concludes that an examination cannot be performed because competent persons using the same criteria would not be able to obtain materially similar evaluations.

Availability of Criteria

.33 The criteria should be available to users in one or more of the following ways:

a. Available publicly

b. Available to all users through inclusion in a clear manner in the presentation of the subject matter or in the assertion

c. Available to all users through inclusion in a clear manner in the practitioner's report

d. Well understood by most users, although not formally available (for example, "The distance between points A and B is twenty feet;" the criterion of distance measured in feet is considered to be well understood)

e. Available only to specified parties; for example, terms of a contract or criteria issued by an industry association that are available only to those in the industry

.34 If criteria are only available to specified parties, the practitioner's report should be restricted to those parties who have access to the criteria as described in paragraphs .78 and .80.

Independence

.35 The fourth general standard is—*The practitioner must maintain independence in mental attitude in all matters relating to the engagement.*[7] [As amended, effective when the subject matter or assertion is as of or for a period ending on or after December 15, 2006, by SSAE No. 14.]

.36 The practitioner should maintain the intellectual honesty and impartiality necessary to reach an unbiased conclusion about the subject matter or the assertion. This is a cornerstone of the attest function.

.37 In the final analysis, independence in mental attitude means objective consideration of facts, unbiased judgments, and honest neutrality on the part of the practitioner in forming and expressing conclusions. It implies not the attitude of an advocate or an adversary but an impartiality that recognizes an obligation for fairness. Independence in mental attitude presumes an undeviating concern for an unbiased conclusion about the subject matter or an assertion no matter what the subject matter or the assertion may be.

.38 The profession has established, through the AICPA's Code of Professional Conduct, precepts to guard against the *presumption* of loss of independence. Presumption is stressed because the possession of intrinsic independence is a matter of personal quality rather than of rules that formulate certain objective tests. Insofar as these precepts have been incorporated in the

---

[7] The practitioner performing an attest engagement should be independent pursuant to "Independence Rule" (ET sec. 1.200.001) of the AICPA Code of Professional Conduct. The "Independence Standards for Engagements Performed in Accordance With Statements on Standards for Attestation Engagements" subtopic (ET sec. 1.297) provides guidance about its application to certain attest engagements. [Footnote revised, December 2012, to reflect conforming changes necessary due to the revision of Ethics Interpretation 101-11. Footnote revised, January 2015, to reflect conforming changes necessary due to the issuance of the revised AICPA Code of Professional Conduct, effective December 15, 2014.]

profession's code, they have the force of professional law for the independent practitioner.

Due Professional Care

.39 The fifth general standard is—*The practitioner must exercise due professional care in the planning and performance of the engagement and the preparation of the report.* [As amended, effective when the subject matter or assertion is as of or for a period ending on or after December 15, 2006, by SSAE No. 14.]

.40 Due professional care imposes a responsibility on each practitioner involved with the engagement to observe each of the attestation standards. Exercise of due professional care requires critical review at every level of supervision of the work done and the judgment exercised by those assisting in the engagement, including the preparation of the report.

.41 *Cooley on Torts*, a legal treatise, describes the obligation for due care as follows:

> Every man who offers his services to another and is employed assumes the duty to exercise in the employment such skill as he possesses with reasonable care and diligence. In all these employments where peculiar skill is requisite, if one offers his services, he is understood as holding himself out to the public as possessing the degree of skill commonly possessed by others in the same employment, and if his pretentions are unfounded, he commits a species of fraud upon every man who employs him in reliance on his public profession. But no man, whether skilled or unskilled, undertakes that the task he assumes shall be performed successfully, and without fault or error; he undertakes for good faith and integrity, but not for infallibility, and he is liable to his employer for negligence, bad faith, or dishonesty, but not for losses consequent upon mere errors of judgment.[8]

Standards of Fieldwork

Planning and Supervision

.42 The first standard of fieldwork is—*The practitioner must adequately plan the work and must properly supervise any assistants.* [As amended, effective when the subject matter or assertion is as of or for a period ending on or after December 15, 2006, by SSAE No. 14.]

.43 Proper planning and supervision contribute to the effectiveness of attest procedures. Proper planning directly influences the selection of appropriate procedures and the timeliness of their application, and proper supervision helps ensure that planned procedures are appropriately applied.

.44 Planning an attest engagement involves developing an overall strategy for the expected conduct and scope of the engagement. To develop such a strategy, practitioners need to have sufficient knowledge to enable them to understand adequately the events, transactions, and practices that, in their judgment, have a significant effect on the subject matter or the assertion.

.45 Factors to be considered by the practitioner in planning an attest engagement include the following:

a. The criteria to be used

[8] D. Haggard, *Cooley on Torts*, 472 (4th ed., 1932).

b. Preliminary judgments about attestation risk[9] and materiality for attest purposes

c. The nature of the subject matter or the items within the assertion that are likely to require revision or adjustment

d. Conditions that may require extension or modification of attest procedures

e. The nature of the report expected to be issued

.46 The practitioner should establish an understanding with the client regarding the services to be performed for each engagement.[10] Such an understanding reduces the risk that either the practitioner or the client may misinterpret the needs or expectations of the other party. For example, it reduces the risk that the client may inappropriately rely on the practitioner to protect the entity against certain risks or to perform certain functions that are the client's responsibility. The understanding should include the objectives of the engagement, management's responsibilities, the practitioner's responsibilities, and limitations of the engagement. The practitioner should document the understanding in the working papers, preferably through a written communication with the client. If the practitioner believes an understanding with the client has not been established, he or she should decline to accept or perform the engagement.

.47 The nature, extent, and timing of planning will vary with the nature and complexity of the subject matter or the assertion and the practitioner's prior experience with management. As part of the planning process, the practitioner should consider the nature, extent, and timing of the work to be performed to accomplish the objectives of the attest engagement. Nevertheless, as the attest engagement progresses, changed conditions may make it necessary to modify planned procedures.

.48 Supervision involves directing the efforts of assistants who participate in accomplishing the objectives of the attest engagement and determining whether those objectives were accomplished. Elements of supervision include instructing assistants, staying informed of significant problems encountered, reviewing the work performed, and dealing with differences of opinion among personnel. The extent of supervision appropriate in a given instance depends on many factors, including the nature and complexity of the subject matter and the qualifications of the persons performing the work.

.49 Assistants should be informed of their responsibilities, including the objectives of the procedures that they are to perform and matters that may affect the nature, extent, and timing of such procedures. The practitioner with final responsibility for the engagement should direct assistants to bring to his or her attention significant questions raised during the attest engagement so that their significance may be assessed.

.50 The work performed by each assistant should be reviewed to determine whether it was adequately performed and to evaluate whether the results are consistent with the conclusion to be presented in the practitioner's report.

---

[9] *Attestation risk* is the risk that the practitioner may unknowingly fail to appropriately modify his or her attest report on the subject matter or an assertion that is materially misstated. It consists of (*a*) the risk (consisting of *inherent risk* and *control risk*) that the subject matter or assertion contains deviations or misstatements that could be material and (*b*) the risk that the practitioner will not detect such deviations or misstatements (*detection risk*).

[10] See paragraph 29 of SQCS No. 8. [Footnote amended due to the issuance of SQCS No. 7, December 2008. Footnote revised, December 2012, due to the issuance of SQCS No. 8.]

Obtaining Sufficient Evidence

.51 The second standard of fieldwork is—*The practitioner must obtain sufficient evidence to provide a reasonable basis for the conclusion that is expressed in the report.* [As amended, effective when the subject matter or assertion is as of or for a period ending on or after December 15, 2006, by SSAE No. 14.]

.52 Selecting and applying procedures that will accumulate evidence that is sufficient in the circumstances to provide a reasonable basis for the level of assurance to be expressed in the attest report requires the careful exercise of professional judgment. A broad array of available procedures may be applied in an attest engagement. In establishing a proper combination of procedures to appropriately restrict attestation risk, the practitioner should consider the following presumptions, bearing in mind that they are not mutually exclusive and may be subject to important exceptions.

a. Evidence obtained from independent sources outside an entity provides greater assurance about the subject matter or the assertion than evidence secured solely from within the entity.

b. Information obtained from the independent attester's direct personal knowledge (such as through physical examination, observation, computation, operating tests, or inspection) is more persuasive than information obtained indirectly.

c. The more effective the controls over the subject matter, the more assurance they provide about the subject matter or the assertion.

.53 Thus, in the hierarchy of available attest procedures, those that involve search and verification (for example, inspection, confirmation, or observation), particularly when using independent sources outside the entity, are generally more effective in restricting attestation risk than those involving internal inquiries and comparisons of internal information (for example, analytical procedures and discussions with individuals responsible for the subject matter or the assertion). On the other hand, the latter are generally less costly to apply.

.54 In an attest engagement designed to provide a high level of assurance (referred to as an *examination*), the practitioner's objective is to accumulate sufficient evidence to restrict attestation risk to a level that is, in the practitioner's professional judgment, appropriately low for the high level of assurance that may be imparted by his or her report. In such an engagement, a practitioner should select from all available procedures—that is, procedures that assess inherent and control risk and restrict detection risk—any combination that can restrict attestation risk to such an appropriately low level.

.55 In an attest engagement designed to provide a moderate level of assurance (referred to as a *review*), the objective is to accumulate sufficient evidence to restrict attestation risk to a moderate level. To accomplish this, the types of procedures performed generally are limited to inquiries and analytical procedures (rather than also including search and verification procedures).

.56 Nevertheless, there will be circumstances in which inquiry and analytical procedures (*a*) cannot be performed, (*b*) are deemed less efficient than other procedures, or (*c*) yield evidence indicating that the subject matter or the assertion may be incomplete or inaccurate. In the first circumstance, the practitioner should perform other procedures that he or she believes can provide him or her with a level of assurance equivalent to that which inquiries and analytical procedures would have provided. In the second circumstance, the practitioner may perform other procedures that he or she believes would be more efficient to provide him or her with a level of assurance equivalent to that which inquiries and analytical procedures would provide. In the third circumstance, the practitioner should perform additional procedures.

.57 The extent to which attestation procedures will be performed should be based on the level of assurance to be provided and the practitioner's consideration of (*a*) the nature and materiality of the information to be tested to the subject matter or the assertion taken as a whole, (*b*) the likelihood of misstatements, (*c*) knowledge obtained during current and previous engagements, (*d*) the responsible party's competence in the subject matter, (*e*) the extent to which the information is affected by the asserter's judgment, and (*f*) inadequacies in the responsible party's underlying data.

.58 As part of the attestation procedures, the practitioner considers the written assertion ordinarily provided by the responsible party. If a written assertion cannot be obtained from the responsible party, the practitioner should consider the effects on his or her ability to obtain sufficient evidence to form a conclusion about the subject matter. When the practitioner's client is the responsible party, a failure to obtain a written assertion should result in the practitioner concluding that a scope limitation exists.[11] When the practitioner's client is not the responsible party and a written assertion is not provided, the practitioner may be able to conclude that he or she has sufficient evidence to form a conclusion about the subject matter.

Representation Letter

.59 During an attest engagement, the responsible party makes many representations to the practitioner, both oral and written, in response to specific inquiries or through the presentation of subject matter or an assertion. Such representations from the responsible party are part of the evidential matter the practitioner obtains.

.60 Written representations from the responsible party ordinarily confirm representations explicitly or implicitly given to the practitioner, indicate and document the continuing appropriateness of such representations, and reduce the possibility of misunderstanding concerning the matters that are the subject of the representations. Accordingly, in an examination or a review engagement, a practitioner should consider obtaining a representation letter from the responsible party. Examples of matters that might appear in such a representation letter include the following:[12]

a. A statement acknowledging responsibility for the subject matter and, when applicable, the assertion

b. A statement acknowledging responsibility for selecting the criteria, where applicable

---

[11] When the client is the responsible party, it is presumed that the client will be capable of providing the practitioner with a written assertion regarding the subject matter. Failure to provide the written assertion in this circumstance is a client-imposed limitation on the practitioner's evidence-gathering efforts. In an examination, the practitioner should modify the report for the scope limitation. In a review engagement, such a scope limitation results in an incomplete review and the practitioner should withdraw from the engagement.

[12] Specific written representations will depend on the circumstances of the engagement (for example, whether the client is the responsible party) and the nature of the subject matter and the criteria. For example, when the client is not the responsible party but has selected the criteria, the practitioner might obtain the representation regarding responsibility for selection of the criteria from the client rather than the responsible party (see paragraph .61).

c. A statement acknowledging responsibility for determining that such criteria are appropriate for its purposes, where the responsible party is the client

d. The assertion about the subject matter based on the criteria selected

e. A statement that all known matters contradicting the assertion and any communication from regulatory agencies affecting the subject matter or the assertion have been disclosed to the practitioner

f. Availability of all records relevant to the subject matter

g. A statement that any known events subsequent to the period (or point in time) of the subject matter being reported on that would have a material effect on the subject matter (or, if applicable, the assertion) have been disclosed to the practitioner

h. Other matters as the practitioner deems appropriate

.61 When the client is not the responsible party, the practitioner should consider obtaining a letter of written representations from the client as part of the attest engagement. Examples of matters that might appear in such a representation letter include the following:

a. A statement that any known events subsequent to the period (or point in time) of the subject matter being reported on that would have a material effect on the subject matter (or, if applicable, the assertion) have been disclosed to the practitioner

b. A statement acknowledging the client's responsibility for selecting the criteria, where applicable

c. A statement acknowledging the client's responsibility for determining that such criteria are appropriate for its purposes

d. Other matters as the practitioner deems appropriate

.62 If the responsible party or the client refuses to furnish all written representations that the practitioner deems necessary, the practitioner should consider the effects of such a refusal on his or her ability to issue a conclusion about the subject matter. If the practitioner believes that the representation letter is necessary to obtain sufficient evidence to issue a report, the responsible party's or the client's refusal to furnish such evidence in the form of written representations constitutes a limitation on the scope of an examination sufficient to preclude an unqualified opinion and is ordinarily sufficient to cause the practitioner to disclaim an opinion or withdraw from an examination engagement. However, based on the nature of the representations not obtained or the circumstances of the refusal, the practitioner may conclude, in an examination engagement, that a qualified opinion is appropriate. Further, the practitioner should consider the effects of the refusal on his or her ability to rely on other representations. When a scope limitation exists in a review engagement, the practitioner should withdraw from the engagement. (See paragraph .75.)

Standards of Reporting[13]

.63 The first standard of reporting is—*The practitioner must identify the subject matter or the assertion being reported on and state the character of the engagement in the report.* [As amended, effective when the subject matter or assertion is as of or for a period ending on or after December 15, 2006, by SSAE No. 14.]

---

[13] The reporting standards apply only when the practitioner issues a report. [Footnote added, effective when the subject matter or assertion is as of or for a period ending on or after December 15, 2006, by SSAE No. 14.]

.64 The practitioner who accepts an attest engagement should issue a report on the subject matter or the assertion or withdraw from the attest engagement. If the practitioner is reporting on the assertion, the assertion should be bound with or accompany the practitioner's report or the assertion should be clearly stated in the practitioner's report.[14]

.65 The statement of the character of an attest engagement includes the following two elements: (*a*) a description of the nature and scope of the work performed and (*b*) a reference to the professional standards governing the engagement. The terms *examination* and *review* should be used to describe engagements to provide, respectively, a high level and a moderate level of assurance. The reference to professional standards should be accomplished by referring to "attestation standards established by the American Institute of Certified Public Accountants."

.66 The second standard of reporting is—*The practitioner must state the practitioner's conclusion about the subject matter or the assertion in relation to the criteria against which the subject matter was evaluated in the report.* However, if conditions exist that, individually or in combination, result in one or more material misstatements or deviations from the criteria, the practitioner should modify the report and, to most effectively communicate with the reader of the report, should ordinarily express his or her conclusion directly on the subject matter,[15] not on the assertion. [As amended, effective when the subject matter or assertion is as of or for a period ending on or after December 15, 2006, by SSAE No. 14.]

.67 The practitioner should consider the concept of materiality in applying this standard. In expressing a conclusion, the practitioner should consider an omission or a misstatement to be material if the omission or misstatement—individually or when aggregated with others—is such that a reasonable person would be influenced by the omission or misstatement. The practitioner should consider both qualitative and quantitative aspects of omissions and misstatements.

.68 The term *general use* applies to attest reports that are not restricted to specified parties. General-use attest reports should be limited to two levels of assurance: one based on a restriction of attestation risk to an appropriately low level (an *examination*) and the other based on a restriction of attestation risk to a moderate level (a *review*). In an engagement to achieve a high level of assurance (an *examination*), the practitioner's conclusion should be expressed in the form of an opinion. When attestation risk has been restricted only to a moderate level (a *review*), the conclusion should be expressed in the form of negative assurance.

.69 A practitioner may report on subject matter or an assertion at multiple dates or covering multiple periods during which criteria have changed (for example, a report on comparative information). In those circumstances, the practitioner should determine whether the criteria are clearly stated or described for each of the dates or periods, and whether the changes have been adequately disclosed.

---

[14] The use of a "hot link" within the practitioner's report to management's assertion, such as might be used in a WebTrust^{SM} report, would meet this requirement. [Footnote renumbered by the issuance of SSAE No. 14, November 2006.]

[15] Specific standards may require that the practitioner express his or her conclusion directly on the subject matter. For example, if management states in its assertion that a material weakness exists in the entity's internal control over financial reporting, the practitioner should state his or her opinion directly on the effectiveness of internal control, not on management's assertion related thereto. [Footnote renumbered by the issuance of SSAE No. 14, November 2006.]

.70 If the criteria used for the subject matter for the current date or period differ from those criteria used for the subject matter for a preceding date or period and the subject matter for the prior date or period is not presented, the practitioner should consider whether the changes in criteria are likely to be significant to users of the report. If so, the practitioner should determine whether the criteria are clearly stated or described and the fact that the criteria have changed is disclosed. (See paragraphs .76–.77.)

.71 The third standard of reporting is—*The practitioner must state all of the practitioner's significant reservations about the engagement, the subject matter, and, if applicable, the assertion related thereto in the report.* [As amended, effective when the subject matter or assertion is as of or for a period ending on or after December 15, 2006, by SSAE No. 14.]

.72 *Reservations about the engagement* refers to any unresolved problem that the practitioner had in complying with these attestation standards, interpretive standards, or the specific procedures agreed to by the specified parties. The practitioner should not express an unqualified conclusion unless the engagement has been conducted in accordance with the attestation standards. Such standards will not have been complied with if the practitioner has been unable to apply all the procedures that he or she considers necessary in the circumstances.

.73 Restrictions on the scope of an engagement, whether imposed by the client or by such other circumstances as the timing of the work or the inability to obtain sufficient evidence, may require the practitioner to qualify the assurance provided, to disclaim any assurance, or to withdraw from the engagement. For example, if the practitioner's client is the responsible party, a failure to obtain a written assertion should result in the practitioner concluding that a scope limitation exists. (See paragraph .58.)

.74 The practitioner's decision to provide a qualified opinion, to disclaim an opinion, or to withdraw because of a scope limitation in an examination engagement depends on an assessment of the effect of the omitted procedure(s) on his or her ability to express assurance. This assessment will be affected by the nature and magnitude of the potential effects of the matters in question, and by their significance to the subject matter or the assertion. If the potential effects are pervasive to the subject matter or the assertion, a disclaimer or withdrawal is more likely to be appropriate. When restrictions that significantly limit the scope of the engagement are imposed by the client or the responsible party, the practitioner generally should disclaim an opinion or withdraw from the engagement. The reasons for a qualification or disclaimer should be described in the practitioner's report.

.75 In a review engagement, when the practitioner is unable to perform the inquiry and analytical or other procedures he or she considers necessary to achieve the limited assurance contemplated by a review, or when the client is the responsible party and does not provide the practitioner with a written assertion, the review will be incomplete. A review that is incomplete is not an adequate basis for issuing a review report and, accordingly, the practitioner should withdraw from the engagement.

.76 *Reservations about the subject matter or the assertion* refers to any unresolved reservation about the assertion or about the conformity of the subject matter with the criteria, including the adequacy of the disclosure of material matters. They can result in either a qualified or an adverse opinion, depending on the materiality of the departure from the criteria against which the subject matter or the assertion was evaluated, or a modified conclusion in a review engagement.

.77 Reservations about the subject matter or the assertion may relate to the measurement, form, arrangement, content, or underlying judgments and assumptions applicable to the subject matter or the assertion and its appended notes, including, for example, the terminology used, the amount of detail given, the classification of items, and the bases of amounts set forth. The practitioner considers whether a particular reservation should affect the report given the circumstances and facts of which he or she is aware at the time.

.78 The fourth standard of reporting is—*The practitioner must state in the report that the report is intended solely for the information and use of the specified parties under the following circumstances:*

- *When the criteria used to evaluate the subject matter are determined by the practitioner to be appropriate only for a limited number of parties who either participated in their establishment or can be presumed to have an adequate understanding of the criteria*
- *When the criteria used to evaluate the subject matter are available only to specified parties*
- *When reporting on subject matter and a written assertion has not been provided by the responsible party*
- *When the report is on an attestation engagement to apply agreed-upon procedures to the subject matter*

[As amended, effective when the subject matter or assertion is as of or for a period ending on or after December 15, 2006, by SSAE No. 14.]

.79 The need for restriction on the use of a report may result from a number of circumstances, including the purpose of the report, the criteria used in preparation of the subject matter, the extent to which the procedures performed are known or understood, and the potential for the report to be misunderstood when taken out of the context in which it was intended to be used. A practitioner should consider informing his or her client that restricted-use reports are not intended for distribution to nonspecified parties, regardless of whether they are included in a document containing a separate general-use report.[16, 17] However, a practitioner is not responsible for controlling a client's distribution of restricted-use reports. Accordingly, a restricted-use report should alert readers to the restriction on the use of the report by indicating that the report is not intended to be and should not be used by anyone other than the specified parties.

.80 An attest report that is restricted as to use should contain a separate paragraph at the end of the report that includes the following elements:

a. A statement indicating that the report is intended solely for the information and use of the specified parties

---

[16] In some cases, restricted-use reports filed with regulatory agencies are required by law or regulation to be made available to the public as a matter of public record. Also, a regulatory agency as part of its oversight responsibility for an entity may require access to restricted-use reports in which they are not named as a specified party. [Footnote renumbered by the issuance of SSAE No. 14, November 2006.]

[17] This section does not preclude the practitioner, in connection with establishing the terms of the engagement, from reaching an understanding with the client that the intended use of the report will be restricted, and from obtaining the client's agreement that the client and the specified parties will not distribute the report to parties other than those identified in the report. [Footnote renumbered by the issuance of SSAE No. 14, November 2006.]

b. An identification of the specified parties to whom use is restricted

c. A statement that the report is not intended to be and should not be used by anyone other than the specified parties

An example of such a paragraph is the following.

> This report is intended solely for the information and use of [*the specified parties*] and is not intended to be and should not be used by anyone other than these specified parties.

.81 Other attestation standards may specify situations that require restricted reports such as the following:

a. A review report on management's discussion and analysis

b. A report on prospective financial information when the report is intended for use by the responsible party alone, or by the responsible party and third parties with whom the responsible party is negotiating directly, as described in paragraph .10 of section 301, *Financial Forecasts and Projections*.

Furthermore, nothing in this section precludes a practitioner from restricting the use of any report.

.82 If a practitioner issues a single combined report covering both (*a*) subject matter or presentations that require a restriction on use to specified parties and (*b*) subject matter or presentations that ordinarily do not require such a restriction, the use of such a single combined report should be restricted to the specified parties.

.83 In some instances, a separate restricted-use report may be included in a document that also contains a general-use report. The inclusion of a separate restricted-use report in a document that contains a general-use report does not affect the intended use of either report. The restricted-use report remains restricted as to use, and the general-use report continues to be for general use.

Examination Reports

.84 When expressing an opinion, the practitioner should clearly state whether, in his or her opinion, (*a*) the subject matter is based on (or in conformity with) the criteria in all material respects or (*b*) the assertion is presented (or fairly stated), in all material respects, based on the criteria. Reports expressing an opinion may be qualified or modified for some aspect of the subject matter, the assertion or the engagement (see the third reporting standard). However, as stated in paragraph .66, if conditions exist that, individually or in combination, result in one or more material misstatements or deviations from the criteria, the practitioner should modify the report and, to most effectively communicate with the reader of the report, should ordinarily express his or her conclusion directly on the subject matter, not on the assertion. In addition, such reports may emphasize certain matters relating to the attest engagement, the subject matter, or the assertion. The form of the practitioner's report will depend on whether the practitioner opines on the subject matter or the assertion.

.85 The practitioner's examination report on subject matter should include the following:

a. A title that includes the word *independent*

b. An identification of the subject matter and the responsible party

c. A statement that the subject matter is the responsibility of the responsible party

d. A statement that the practitioner's responsibility is to express an opinion on the subject matter based on his or her examination

e. A statement that the examination was conducted in accordance with attestation standards established by the American Institute of Certified Public Accountants, and, accordingly, included procedures that the practitioner considered necessary in the circumstances

f. A statement that the practitioner believes the examination provides a reasonable basis for his or her opinion

g. The practitioner's opinion on whether the subject matter is based on (or in conformity with) the criteria in all material respects

h. A statement restricting the use of the report to specified parties under the following circumstances (see paragraphs .78–.83):

(1) When the criteria used to evaluate the subject matter are determined by the practitioner to be appropriate only for a limited number of parties who either participated in their establishment or can be presumed to have an adequate understanding of the criteria

(2) When the criteria used to evaluate the subject matter are available only to the specified parties

(3) When a written assertion has not been provided by the responsible party (The practitioner should also include a statement to that effect in the introductory paragraph of the report.)

i. The manual or printed signature of the practitioner's firm

j. The date of the examination report

Appendix A [paragraph .114], *Examination Reports*, includes a standard examination report on subject matter. (See example 1.)

.86 The practitioner's examination report on an assertion should include the following:

a. A title that includes the word *independent*

b. An identification of the assertion and the responsible party (When the assertion does not accompany the practitioner's report, the first paragraph of the report should also contain a statement of the assertion.)

c. A statement that the assertion is the responsibility of the responsible party

d. A statement that the practitioner's responsibility is to express an opinion on the assertion based on his or her examination

e. A statement that the examination was conducted in accordance with attestation standards established by the American Institute of Certified Public Accountants, and, accordingly, included procedures that the practitioner considered necessary in the circumstances

f. A statement that the practitioner believes the examination provides a reasonable basis for his or her opinion

g. The practitioner's opinion on whether the assertion is presented (or fairly stated), in all material respects, based on the criteria (However, see paragraph .66.)

h. A statement restricting the use of the report to specified parties under the following circumstances (see paragraphs .78–.83):

(1) When the criteria used to evaluate the subject matter are determined by the practitioner to be appropriate only for a limited number of parties who either participated in their establishment

or can be presumed to have an adequate understanding of the criteria

(2) When the criteria used to evaluate the subject matter are available only to the specified parties

i. The manual or printed signature of the practitioner's firm

j. The date of the examination report

Appendix A [paragraph .114] includes a standard examination report on an assertion. (See example 2.)

.87 Nothing precludes the practitioner from examining an assertion but opining directly on the subject matter. (See Appendix A [paragraph .114], example 3.)

Review Reports

.88 In a review report, the practitioner's conclusion should state whether any information came to the practitioner's attention on the basis of the work performed that indicates that (*a*) the subject matter is not based on (or in conformity with) the criteria or (*b*) the assertion is not presented (or fairly stated) in all material respects based on the criteria. (As discussed more fully in the commentary to the third reporting standard, if the subject matter or the assertion is not modified to correct for any such information that comes to the practitioner's attention, such information should be described in the practitioner's report.)

.89 The practitioner's review report on subject matter should include the following:

a. A title that includes the word *independent*

b. An identification of the subject matter and the responsible party

c. A statement that the subject matter is the responsibility of the responsible party

d. A statement that the review was conducted in accordance with attestation standards established by the American Institute of Certified Public Accountants

e. A statement that a review is substantially less in scope than an examination, the objective of which is an expression of opinion on the subject matter, and accordingly, no such opinion is expressed

f. A statement about whether the practitioner is aware of any material modifications that should be made to the subject matter in order for it to be based on (or in conformity with), in all material respects, the criteria, other than those modifications, if any, indicated in his or her report

g. A statement restricting the use of the report to specified parties under the following circumstances (see paragraphs .78–.83):

(1) When the criteria used to evaluate the subject matter are determined by the practitioner to be appropriate only for a limited number of parties who either participated in their establishment or can be presumed to have an adequate understanding of the criteria

(2) When the criteria used to evaluate the subject matter are available only to the specified parties

(3) When a written assertion has not been provided by the responsible party and the responsible party is not the client (The practitioner should also include a statement to that effect in the introductory paragraph of the report.)

h. The manual or printed signature of the practitioner's firm

i. The date of the review report

Appendix B [paragraph .115] *Review Reports*, includes a standard review report on subject matter. (See example 1.) Appendix B [paragraph .115] also includes a review report on subject matter that is the responsibility of a party other than client; the report is restricted as to use because a written assertion has not been provided by the responsible party. (See example 2.)

.90 The practitioner's review report on an assertion should include the following:

a. A title that includes the word *independent*

b. An identification of the assertion and the responsible party (When the assertion does not accompany the practitioner's report, the first paragraph of the report should also contain a statement of the assertion.)

c. A statement that the assertion is the responsibility of the responsible party

d. A statement that the review was conducted in accordance with attestation standards established by the American Institute of Certified Public Accountants

e. A statement that a review is substantially less in scope than an examination, the objective of which is an expression of opinion on the assertion, and accordingly, no such opinion is expressed

f. A statement about whether the practitioner is aware of any material modifications that should be made to the assertion in order for it to be presented (or fairly stated), in all material respects, based on (or in conformity with) the criteria, other than those modifications, if any, indicated in his or her report (However, see paragraph .66.)

g. A statement restricting the use of the report to specified parties under the following circumstances (see paragraphs .78–.83):

(1) When the criteria used to evaluate the subject matter are determined by the practitioner to be appropriate only for a limited number of parties who either participated in their establishment or can be presumed to have an adequate understanding of the criteria

(2) When the criteria used to evaluate the subject matter are available only to the specified parties

h. The manual or printed signature of the practitioner's firm

i. The date of the review report

Appendix B [paragraph .115] includes a review report on an assertion that is restricted as to use because the criteria are available only to the specified parties. (See example 3.)

Other Information in a Client-Prepared Document Containing the Practitioner's Attest Report[18]

.91 A client may publish various documents that contain information (hereinafter referred to as *other information*) in addition to the practitioner's attest report on subject matter (or on an assertion related thereto). Paragraphs .92–.94 provide guidance to the practitioner when the other information is contained in (*a*) annual reports to holders of securities or beneficial interests, annual reports of organizations for charitable or philanthropic purposes distributed to the public, and annual reports filed with regulatory authorities under the Securities Exchange Act of 1934 or (*b*) other documents to which the practitioner, at the client's request, devotes attention. These paragraphs are not applicable when an attest report appears in a registration statement filed under the Securities Act of 1933. (See AU-C section 920, *Letters for Underwriters and Certain Other Requesting Parties*, and AU-C section 925, *Filings With the U.S. Securities and Exchange Commission Under the Securities Act of 1933*.) Also, these paragraphs are not applicable to other information on which the practitioner or another practitioner is engaged to issue an opinion. [Revised, December 2012, to reflect conforming changes necessary due to the issuance of SAS Nos. 122–126.]

.92 The practitioner's responsibility with respect to other information in such a document does not extend beyond the information identified in his or her report, and the practitioner has no obligation to perform any procedures to corroborate any other information contained in the document. However, the practitioner should read the other information not covered by the practitioner's report or by the report of the other practitioner and consider whether it, or the manner of its presentation, is materially inconsistent with the information appearing in the practitioner's report. If the practitioner believes that the other information is inconsistent with the information appearing in the practitioner's report, he or she should consider whether the practitioner's report requires revision. If the practitioner concludes that the report does not require revision, he or she should request the client to revise the other information. If the other information is not revised to eliminate the material inconsistency, the practitioner should consider other actions, such as revising his or her report to include an explanatory paragraph describing the material inconsistency, withholding the use of his or her report in the document, or withdrawing from the engagement.

.93 If, while reading the other information for the reasons set forth in paragraph .92, the practitioner becomes aware of information that he or she believes is a material misstatement of fact that is not a material inconsistency as described in paragraph .92, he or she should discuss the matter with the client. In connection with this discussion, the practitioner should consider that he or she may not have the expertise to assess the validity of the statement, that there may be no standards by which to assess its presentation, and that there may be valid differences of judgment or opinion. If the practitioner concludes he or she has a valid basis for concern, the practitioner should propose that the client consult with some other party whose advice may be useful, such as the entity's legal counsel.

---

[18] Such guidance pertains only to other information in a client-prepared document. The practitioner has no responsibility to read information contained in documents of nonclients. Further, the practitioner is not required to read information contained in electronic sites, or to consider the consistency of other information in electronic sites with the original documents since electronic sites are a means of distributing information and are not "documents" as that term is used in this section. Practitioners may be asked by their clients to render attest services with respect to information in electronic sites, in which case, other attest standards may apply to those services. [Footnote renumbered by the issuance of SSAE No. 14, November 2006.]

.94 If, after discussing the matter, the practitioner concludes that a material misstatement of fact remains, the action taken will depend on his or her judgment in the circumstances. The practitioner should consider steps such as notifying the client's management and audit committee in writing of his or her views concerning the information and consulting his or her legal counsel about further action appropriate in the circumstances.[19]

Consideration of Subsequent Events in an Attest Engagement

.95 Events or transactions sometimes occur subsequent to the point in time or period of time of the subject matter being tested but prior to the date of the practitioner's report that have a material effect on the subject matter and therefore require adjustment or disclosure in the presentation of the subject matter or assertion. These occurrences are referred to as *subsequent events*. In performing an attest engagement, a practitioner should consider information about subsequent events that comes to his or her attention. Two types of subsequent events require consideration by the practitioner.

.96 The first type consists of events that provide additional information with respect to conditions that existed at the point in time or during the period of time of the subject matter being tested. This information should be used by the practitioner in considering whether the subject matter is presented in conformity with the criteria and may affect the presentation of the subject matter, the assertion, or the practitioner's report.

.97 The second type consists of those events that provide information with respect to conditions that arose subsequent to the point in time or period of time of the subject matter being tested that are of such a nature and significance that their disclosure is necessary to keep the subject matter from being misleading. This type of information will not normally affect the practitioner's report if the information is appropriately disclosed.

.98 While the practitioner has no responsibility to detect subsequent events, the practitioner should inquire of the responsible party (and his or her client if the client is not the responsible party) as to whether they are aware of any subsequent events, through the date of the practitioner's report, that would have a material effect on the subject matter or assertion.[20] If the practitioner has decided to obtain a representation letter, the letter ordinarily would include a representation concerning subsequent events. (See paragraphs .60–.61.)

.99 The practitioner has no responsibility to keep informed of events subsequent to the date of his or her report; however, the practitioner may later become aware of conditions that existed at that date that might have affected the practitioner's report had he or she been aware of them. In such circumstances, the practitioner may wish to consider the guidance in AU-C section

---

[19] If the client does not have an audit committee, the practitioner should communicate with individuals whose authority and responsibility are equivalent to those of an audit committee, such as the board of directors, the board of trustees, an owner in a owner-managed entity, or those who engaged the practitioner. [Footnote renumbered by the issuance of Statement on SSAE No. 14, November 2006.]

[20] For certain subject matter, specific subsequent event standards have been developed to provide additional requirements for engagement performance and reporting. Additionally, a practitioner engaged to examine the design or effectiveness of internal control over items not covered by section 501, *An Examination of an Entity's Internal Control Over Financial Reporting That Is Integrated With an Audit of Its Financial Statements*, or section 601, *Compliance Attestation*, should consider the subsequent events guidance set forth in paragraphs .129–.134 of section 501 and paragraphs .50–.52 of section 601. [Footnote renumbered by the issuance of SSAE No. 14, November 2006.]

560, *Subsequent Events and Subsequently Discovered Facts*. [Revised, December 2012, to reflect conforming changes necessary due to the issuance of SAS Nos. 122–126.]

Attest Documentation[21]

.100 The practitioner should prepare and maintain attest documentation, the form and content of which should be designed to meet the circumstances of the particular attest engagement.[22] Attest documentation is the principal record of attest procedures applied, information obtained, and conclusions or findings reached by the practitioner in the engagement. The quantity, type, and content of attest documentation are matters of the practitioner's professional judgment. [As amended, effective for attest engagements when the subject matter or assertion is as of or for a period ending on or after December 15, 2002, by SSAE No. 11.]

.101 Attest documentation serves mainly to:

a. Provide the principal support for the practitioner's report, including the representation regarding observance of the standards of fieldwork, which is implicit in the reference in the report to attestation standards.[23]

b. Aid the practitioner in the conduct and supervision of the attest engagement.

For examinations of prospective financial statements, attest documentation ordinarily should indicate that the process by which the entity develops its prospective financial statements was considered in determining the scope of the examination. [Paragraph added, effective for attest engagements when the subject matter or assertion is as of or for a period ending on or after December 15, 2002, by SSAE No. 11.]

.102 Examples of attest documentation are work programs, analyses, memoranda, letters of confirmation and representation, abstracts or copies of entity documents, and schedules or commentaries prepared or obtained by the practitioner. Attest documentation may be in paper form, electronic form, or other media. [Paragraph renumbered and amended, effective for attest engagements when the subject matter or assertion is as of or for a period ending on or after December 15, 2002, by SSAE No. 11.]

.103 Attest documentation should be sufficient to (*a*) enable members of the engagement team with supervision and review responsibilities to understand the nature, timing, extent, and results of attest procedures performed,

---

[21] *Attest documentation* also may be referred to as *working papers*. [Footnote added, effective for attest engagements when the subject matter or assertion is as of or for a period ending on or after December 15, 2002, by SSAE No. 11. Footnote renumbered by the issuance of SSAE No. 14, November 2006.]

[22] [Footnote renumbered and deleted by the issuance of SSAE No. 11, January 2002. Footnote subsequently renumbered by the issuance of SSAE No. 14, November 2006.]

[23] However, there is no intention to imply that the practitioner would be precluded from supporting his or her report by other means in addition to attest documentation. [Footnote added, effective for attest engagements when the subject matter or assertion is as of or for a period ending on or after December 15, 2002, by SSAE No. 11. Footnote renumbered by the issuance of SSAE No. 14, November 2006.]

and the information obtained[24] and (*b*) indicate the engagement team member(s) who performed and reviewed the work. [Paragraph added, effective for attest engagements when the subject matter or assertion is as of or for a period ending on or after December 15, 2002, by SSAE No. 11.]

.104 Attest documentation is the property of the practitioner, and some states recognize this right of ownership in their statutes. The practitioner should adopt reasonable procedures to retain attest documentation for a period of time sufficient to meet the needs of his or her practice and to satisfy any applicable legal or regulatory requirements for records retention.[25, [26]] [Paragraph renumbered and amended, effective for attest engagements when the subject matter or assertion is as of or for a period ending on or after December 15, 2002, by SSAE No. 11.]

.105 The practitioner has an ethical, and in some situations a legal, obligation to maintain the confidentiality of client information or information of the responsible party.[27] Because attest documentation often contains confidential information, the practitioner should adopt reasonable procedures to maintain the confidentiality of that information.[†] [Paragraph added, effective for attest engagements when the subject matter or assertion is as of or for a period ending on or after December 15, 2002, by SSAE No. 11.]

.106 The practitioner also should adopt reasonable procedures to prevent unauthorized access to attest documentation. [Paragraph added, effective for attest engagements when the subject matter or assertion is as of or for a period ending on or after December 15, 2002, by SSAE No. 11.]

.107 Certain attest documentation may sometimes serve as a useful reference source for the client, but it should not be regarded as a part of, or a substitute for, the client's records. [Paragraph renumbered and amended, effective for attest engagements when the subject matter or assertion is as of or for a period ending on or after December 15, 2002, by SSAE No. 11.]

[.108] [Paragraph renumbered and deleted by the issuance of SSAE No. 11, January 2002.]

---

[24] A firm of practitioners has a responsibility to adopt a system of quality control policies and procedures to provide the firm with reasonable assurance that its personnel comply with applicable professional standards, including attestation standards, and the firm's standards of quality in conducting individual attest engagements. Review of attest documentation and discussions with engagement team members are among the procedures a firm performs when monitoring compliance with the quality control policies and procedures that it has established. (Also, see paragraphs .17–.18.) [Footnote added, effective for attest engagements when the subject matter or assertion is as of or for a period ending on or after December 15, 2002, by SSAE No. 11. Footnote renumbered by the issuance of SSAE No. 14, November 2006.]

[25] The procedures should enable the practitioner to access electronic attest documentation throughout the retention period. [Footnote added, effective for attest engagements when the subject matter or assertion is as of or for a period ending on or after December 15, 2002, by SSAE No. 11. Footnote renumbered by the issuance of SSAE No. 14, November 2006.]

[[26]] [Footnote renumbered and deleted by the issuance of SSAE No. 11, January 2002. Footnote subsequently renumbered by the issuance of SSAE No. 14, November 2006.]

[27] Also, see the "Confidential Client Information Rule" (ET sec. 1.700.001) of the AICPA Code of Professional Conduct. [Footnote added, effective for attest engagements when the subject matter or assertion is as of or for a period ending on or after December 15, 2002, by SSAE No. 11. Footnote renumbered by the issuance of SSAE No. 14, November 2006. Footnote revised, January 2015, to reflect conforming changes necessary due to the issuance of the revised AICPA Code of Professional Conduct, effective December 15, 2014.]

[†] ***Note:*** See Interpretation No. 4, "Providing Access to or Copies of Attest Documentation to a Regulator," of section 101 (sec. 9101 par. .43–.46).

Attest Services Related to Consulting Service Engagements

Attest Services as Part of a Consulting Service Engagement

.109 When a practitioner provides an attest service (as defined in this section) as part of a consulting service engagement, this SSAE applies only to the attest service. The SSCS applies to the balance of the consulting service engagement. [Paragraph renumbered by the issuance of SSAE No. 11, January 2002.]

.110 When the practitioner determines that an attest service is to be provided as part of a consulting service engagement, the practitioner should inform the client of the relevant differences between the two types of services and obtain concurrence that the attest service is to be performed in accordance with the appropriate professional requirements. The practitioner should take such actions because the professional requirements for an attest service differ from those for a consulting service engagement. [Paragraph renumbered by the issuance of SSAE No. 11, January 2002.]

.111 The practitioner should issue separate reports on the attest engagement and the consulting service engagement and, if presented in a common binder, the report on the attest engagement or service should be clearly identified and segregated from the report on the consulting service engagement. [Paragraph renumbered by the issuance of SSAE No. 11, January 2002.]

Subject Matter, Assertions, Criteria, and Evidence

.112 An attest service may involve subject matter, an assertion, criteria, or evidential matter developed during a concurrent or prior consulting service engagement. Subject matter or an assertion developed with the practitioner's advice and assistance as the result of such consulting services engagement may be the subject of an attest engagement, provided the responsible party accepts and acknowledges responsibility for the subject matter or assertion. (See paragraph .12.) Criteria developed with the practitioner's assistance may be used to evaluate subject matter in an attest engagement, provided such criteria meet the requirements of this section. Relevant information obtained in the course of a concurrent or prior consulting service engagement may be used as evidential matter in an attest engagement, provided the information satisfies the requirements of this section. [Paragraph renumbered by the issuance of SSAE No. 11, January 2002.]

Effective Date

.113 This section is effective when the subject matter or assertion is as of or for a period ending on or after June 1, 2001. Early application is permitted. [Paragraph renumbered by the issuance of SSAE No. 11, January 2002.]

.114

Appendix A

Examination Reports

Example 1

This is a standard examination report on subject matter for general use. This report pertains to subject matter for which suitable criteria exist and are available to all users through inclusion in a clear manner in the presentation of the subject matter. (See paragraphs .78–.83 for guidance on restricting the use of the report when criteria are available only to specified parties; see Example 4 for an illustration of such a report.) A written assertion has been obtained from the responsible party.

Independent Accountant's Report

We have examined the [*identify the subject matter—for example, the accompanying schedule of investment returns of XYZ Company for the year ended December 31, 20XX*]. XYZ Company's management is responsible for the schedule of investment returns. Our responsibility is to express an opinion based on our examination.

Our examination was conducted in accordance with attestation standards established by the American Institute of Certified Public Accountants and, accordingly, included examining, on a test basis, evidence supporting [*identify the subject matter—for example, XYZ Company's schedule of investment returns*] and performing such other procedures as we considered necessary in the circumstances. We believe that our examination provides a reasonable basis for our opinion.

[*Additional paragraph(s) may be added to emphasize certain matters relating to the attest engagement or the subject matter.*]

In our opinion, the schedule referred to above presents, in all material respects, [*identify the subject matter—for example, the investment returns of XYZ Company for the year ended December 31, 20XX*] based on [*identify criteria—for example, the ABC criteria set forth in Note 1*].

[*Signature*]

[*Date*]

Example 2

This report is a standard examination report on an assertion for general use. The report pertains to subject matter for which suitable criteria exist and are available to all users through inclusion in a clear manner in the presentation of the subject matter. (See paragraphs .78–.83 for guidance on restricting the use of the report when criteria are available only to specified parties.) A written assertion has been obtained from the responsible party.

Independent Accountant's Report

We have examined management's assertion that [*identify the assertion—for example, the accompanying schedule of investment returns of XYZ Company for the year ended December 31, 20XX is presented in accordance with ABC criteria set forth in Note 1*]. XYZ Company's management is responsible for the assertion. Our responsibility is to express an opinion on the assertion based on our examination.

Our examination was conducted in accordance with attestation standards established by the American Institute of Certified Public Accountants and, accordingly, included examining, on a test basis, evidence supporting management's assertion and performing such other procedures as we considered necessary in the circumstances. We believe that our examination provides a reasonable basis for our opinion.

[*Additional paragraph(s) may be added to emphasize certain matters relating to the attest engagement or the assertion.*]

In our opinion, management's assertion referred to above is fairly stated, in all material respects, based on [*identify established or stated criteria—for example, the ABC criteria set forth in Note 1*].

[*Signature*]

[*Date*]

Example 3

This is an examination report for general use; the introductory paragraph states the practitioner has examined management's assertion but the practitioner opines directly on the subject matter (see paragraph .87). The report pertains to subject matter for which suitable criteria exist and are available to all users through inclusion in a clear manner in the presentation of the subject matter. (See paragraphs .78–.83 for guidance on restricting the use of the report when criteria are available only to specified parties.) A written assertion has been obtained from the responsible party.

Independent Accountant's Report

We have examined management's assertion that [*identify the assertion—for example, the accompanying schedule of investment returns of XYZ Company for the year ended December 31, 20XX is presented in accordance with the ABC criteria set forth in Note 1*]. XYZ Company's management is responsible for the assertion. Our responsibility is to express an opinion based on our examination.

Our examination was conducted in accordance with attestation standards established by the American Institute of Certified Public Accountants and, accordingly, included examining, on a test basis, evidence supporting [*identify the subject matter—for example, XYZ Company's schedule of investment returns*] and performing such other procedures as we considered necessary in the circumstances. We believe that our examination provides a reasonable basis for our opinion.

[*Additional paragraph(s) may be added to emphasize certain matters relating to the attest engagement or the assertion.*]

In our opinion, the schedule referred to above, presents, in all material respects, [*identify the subject matter—for example, the investment returns of XYZ Company for the year ended December 31, 20XX*] based on [*identify criteria—for example, the ABC criteria set forth in Note 1*].

[*Signature*]

[*Date*]

Example 4

This is an examination report on subject matter. Although suitable criteria exist, use of the report is restricted because the criteria are available only to specified parties. (See paragraph .34.) A written assertion has been obtained from the responsible party.

Independent Accountant's Report

We have examined the accompanying schedule of investment returns of XYZ Company for the year ended December 31, 20XX. XYZ Company's management is responsible for the schedule of investment returns. Our responsibility is to express an opinion based on our examination.

Our examination was conducted in accordance with attestation standards established by the American Institute of Certified Public Accountants and, accordingly, included examining, on a test basis, evidence supporting [*identify the subject matter—for example, XYZ Company's schedule of investment returns*] and performing such other procedures as we considered necessary in the circumstances. We believe that our examination provides a reasonable basis for our opinion.

[*Additional paragraph(s) may be added to emphasize certain matters relating to the attest engagement or the assertion.*]

In our opinion, the schedule referred to above, presents, in all material respects, [*identify the subject matter—for example, the investment returns of XYZ Company for the year ended December 31, 20XX*] based on the ABC criteria referred to in the investment management agreement between XYZ Company and DEF Investment Managers, Ltd., dated November 15, 20X1.

This report is intended solely for the information and use of XYZ Company and [*identify other specified parties—for example, DEF Investment Managers, Ltd.*] and is not intended to be and should not be used by anyone other than these specified parties.

[*Signature*]

[*Date*]

Example 5

This is an examination report with a qualified opinion because conditions exist that, individually or in combination, result in one or more material misstatements or deviations from the criteria; the report is for general use. The report pertains to subject matter for which suitable criteria exist and are available to all users through inclusion in a clear manner in the presentation of the subject matter. (See paragraphs .78–.83 for guidance on restricting the use of the report when criteria are available only to specified parties.) A written assertion has been obtained from the responsible party.

Independent Accountant's Report

We have examined the accompanying schedule of investment returns of XYZ Company for the year ended December 31, 20XX. XYZ Company's management is responsible for the schedule of investment returns. Our responsibility is to express an opinion based on our examination.

Our examination was conducted in accordance with attestation standards established by the American Institute of Certified Public Accountants and, accordingly, included examining, on a test basis, evidence supporting [*identify the subject matter—for example, XYZ Company's schedule of investment returns*] and performing such other procedures as we considered necessary in the circumstances. We believe that our examination provides a reasonable basis for our opinion.

Our examination disclosed the following [*describe condition(s) that, individually or in the aggregate, resulted in a material misstatement or deviation from the criteria*].

In our opinion, except for the material misstatement [*or deviation from the criteria*] described in the preceding paragraph, the schedule referred to above, presents, in all material respects, [*identify the subject matter—for example, the investment returns of XYZ Company for the year ended December 31, 20XX*] based on [*identify criteria—for example, the ABC criteria set forth in Note 1*].

[*Signature*]

[*Date*]

Example 6

This is an examination report that contains a disclaimer of opinion because of a scope restriction. (See paragraph .74 for reporting guidance when there is a scope restriction.) The report pertains to subject matter for which suitable criteria exist and are available to all users through inclusion in a clear manner in the presentation of the subject matter.

Independent Accountant's Report

We were engaged to examine the accompanying schedule of investment returns of XYZ Company for the year ended December 31, 20XX. XYZ Company's management is responsible for the schedule of investment returns.

[*Scope paragraph should be omitted.*]

[*Include paragraph to describe scope restrictions.*]

Because of the restriction on the scope of our examination discussed in the preceding paragraph, the scope of our work was not sufficient to enable us to express, and we do not express, an opinion on whether the schedule referred to above presents, in all material respects, [*identify the subject matter—for example, the investment returns of XYZ Company for the year ended December 31, 20XX*] based on [*identify criteria—for example, the ABC criteria set forth in Note 1*].

[*Signature*]

[*Date*]

Example 7

This is an examination report on subject matter that is the responsibility of a party other than the client. The report is restricted as to use since a written assertion has not been provided by the responsible party. (See paragraph .78.) The subject matter pertains to criteria that are suitable and are available to the client.

Independent Accountant's Report

To the Board of Directors

DEF Company:

We have examined the [*identify the subject matter—for example, the accompanying schedule of investment returns of XYZ Company for the year ended December 31, 20XX*]. XYZ Company's management is responsible for the schedule of investment returns. XYZ management did not provide us a written assertion about their schedule of investment returns for the year ended December 31, 20XX. Our responsibility is to express an opinion based on our examination.

Our examination was conducted in accordance with attestation standards established by the American Institute of Certified Public Accountants and, accordingly, included examining, on a test basis, evidence supporting [*identify the subject matter—for example, XYZ Company's schedule of investment returns*] and performing such other procedures as we considered necessary in the circumstances. We believe that our examination provides a reasonable basis for our opinion.

[*Additional paragraph(s) may be added to emphasize certain matters relating to the attest engagement or the subject matter.*]

In our opinion, the schedule referred to above presents, in all material respects, [*identify the subject matter—for example, the investment returns of XYZ Company for the year ended December 31, 20XX*] based on [*identify criteria—for example, the ABC criteria set forth in Note 1*].

This report is intended solely for the information and use of the management and board of directors of DEF Company and is not intended to be and should not be used by anyone other than these specified parties.

[*Signature*]

[*Date*]

[Paragraph renumbered by the issuance of SSAE No. 11, January 2002.]

.115

Appendix B

Review Reports

Example 1

This is a standard review report on subject matter for general use. The report pertains to subject matter for which suitable criteria exist and are available to all users through inclusion in a clear manner in the presentation of the subject matter. (See paragraphs .78–.83 for guidance on restricting the use of the report when criteria are available only to specified parties.) A written assertion has been obtained from the responsible party.

Independent Accountant's Report

We have reviewed the [*identify the subject matter—for example, the accompanying schedule of investment returns of XYZ Company for the year ended December 31, 20XX*]. XYZ Company's management is responsible for the schedule of investment returns.

Our review was conducted in accordance with attestation standards established by the American Institute of Certified Public Accountants. A review is substantially less in scope than an examination, the objective of which is the expression of an opinion on [*identify the subject matter—for example, XYZ Company's schedule of investment returns*]. Accordingly, we do not express such an opinion.

[*Additional paragraph(s) may be added to emphasize certain matters relating to the attest engagement or the subject matter.*]

Based on our review, nothing came to our attention that caused us to believe that the [*identify the subject matter—for example, schedule of investment returns of XYZ Company for the year ended December 31, 20XX*] is not presented, in all material respects, in conformity with [*identify the criteria—for example, the ABC criteria set forth in Note 1*].

[*Signature*]

[*Date*]

Example 2

This is a review report on subject matter that is the responsibility of a party other than the client. This review report is restricted as to use since a written assertion has not been provided by the responsible party. (See paragraph .78.) The subject matter pertains to criteria that are suitable and are available to the client.

Independent Accountant's Report

To the Board of Directors

DEF Company:

We have reviewed [*identify the subject matter—for example, the accompanying schedule of investment returns of XYZ Company for the year ended December 31, 20XX*]. XYZ Company's management is responsible for the schedule of investment returns. XYZ Company's management did not provide us a written assertion about their schedule of investment returns for the year ended December 31, 20XX.

Our review was conducted in accordance with attestation standards established by the American Institute of Certified Public Accountants. A review is substantially less in scope than an examination, the objective of which is the expression of an opinion on [*identify the subject matter—for example, XYZ Company's schedule of investment returns*]. Accordingly, we do not express such an opinion.

[*Additional paragraph(s) may be added to emphasize certain matters relating to the attest engagement or the subject matter.*]

Based on our review, nothing came to our attention that caused us to believe that [*identify the subject matter—for example, the schedule of investment returns of XYZ Company for the year ended December 31, 20XX*] is not presented, in all material respects, in conformity with [*identify the criteria—for example, the ABC criteria set forth in Note 1*].

This report is intended solely for the information and use of the management and board of directors of DEF Company and is not intended to be and should not be used by anyone other than these specified parties.

[*Signature*]

[*Date*]

Example 3

This is a review report on an assertion. Although suitable criteria exist for the subject matter, the report is restricted as to use since the criteria are available only to specified parties; if the criteria are available as described in paragraph .33(*a*)–(*d*), the paragraph restricting the use of the report would be omitted. A written assertion has been obtained from the responsible party.

Independent Accountant's Report

We have reviewed management's assertion that [*identify the assertion—for example, the accompanying schedule of investment returns of XYZ Company for the year ended December 31, 20XX is presented in accordance with the ABC criteria referred to in Note 1*]. XYZ Company's management is responsible for the assertion.

Our review was conducted in accordance with attestation standards established by the American Institute of Certified Public Accountants. A review is substantially less in scope than an examination, the objective of which is the expression of an opinion on management's assertion. Accordingly, we do not express such an opinion.

[*Additional paragraph(s) may be added to emphasize certain matters relating to the attest engagement or the assertion.*]

Based on our review, nothing came to our attention that caused us to believe that management's assertion referred to above is not fairly stated, in all material respects, based on [*identify the criteria—for example, the ABC criteria referred to in the investment management agreement between XYZ Company and DEF Investment Managers, Ltd., dated November 15, 20X1*].

This report is intended solely for the information and use of XYZ Company and [*identify other specified parties—for example, DEF Investment Managers, Ltd.*] and is not intended to be and should not be used by anyone other than these specified parties.

[*Signature*]

[*Date*]

[Paragraph renumbered by the issuance of SSAE No. 11, January 2002.]

AT Section 9101

Attest Engagements: Attest Engagements Interpretations of Section 101

1. Defense Industry Questionnaire on Business Ethics and Conduct[1]

.01 *Question*—Certain defense contractors have made a commitment to adopt and implement six principles of business ethics and conduct contained in the *Defense Industry Initiatives on Business Ethics and Conduct* (initiatives). One of those principles concerns defense contractors' public accountability for their commitment to the initiatives. That public accountability begins by the contractor completing an annual *Public Accountability Questionnaire* (questionnaire).

.02 Each of the participating signatory companies (signatories) completes a questionnaire concerning certain policies, procedures, and programs that were to have been in place during the reporting period. The public accountability process requires signatories to perform internal audits and to provide officer certifications as to whether the responses to the questionnaire are current and accurate.

.03 Alternatively, a defense contractor may request its independent public accountant (practitioner) to examine or review its responses to the questionnaire for the purpose of expressing a conclusion about the appropriateness of those responses in a report. Would such an engagement be an attest engagement under section 101, *Attest Engagements*?

.04 *Interpretation*—Section 101 states that the attestation standards apply when a CPA in public practice is engaged to issue or does issue an examination, a review, or an agreed-upon procedures report on subject matter, or an assertion about the subject matter that is the responsibility of another party. When a practitioner is engaged by a defense contractor to provide an examination or a review report on the contractor's written responses to the questionnaire, such an engagement involves subject matter that is the responsibility of the defense contractor. Consequently, section 101 applies to such engagements.

.05 *Question*—Paragraph .23 of section 101 specifies that "the practitioner must have reason to believe that the subject matter is capable of evaluation against criteria that are suitable and available to users." What are the criteria against which such subject matter is to be evaluated and are such criteria suitable and available?

.06 *Interpretation*—The criteria for evaluating the defense contractor's responses are set forth primarily in the questionnaire and the instructions thereto. The suitability of those criteria should be evaluated by assessing whether the criteria meet the characteristics discussed in paragraph .24 of section 101.

.07 The criteria set forth in the questionnaire and its instructions will, when properly followed, be suitable. Although these should provide suitable

---

[1] Information regarding the Defense Industry Initiative on Business Ethics and Conduct (DII) is available at DII's website www.dii.org.

criteria, the questionnaire and its instructions are not generally available. Therefore, the practitioner's report should normally be restricted. The availability requirement can be met if the defense contractor attaches the criteria to the presentation.

.08 *Question*—What is the nature of the procedures that should be applied to the questionnaire responses?

.09 *Interpretation*—The objective of the procedures performed in either an examination or a review engagement is to obtain evidential matter that the defense contractor has designed and placed in operation policies and programs in a manner that supports the signatory's responses to each of the questions on the questionnaire and that the policies and programs operated during the period covered by the questionnaire. The objective does not include providing assurance about whether the defense contractor's policies and programs operated effectively to ensure compliance with the defense contractor's code of business ethics and conduct on the part of individual employees or about whether the defense contractor and its employees have complied with federal procurement laws. In an examination, the evidential matter should be sufficient to limit attestation risk to a level that is appropriately low for the high degree of assurance imparted by an examination report. In a review, this evidential matter should be sufficient to limit attestation risk to a moderate level.

.10 Examination procedures include obtaining evidential matter by reading relevant policies and programs, making inquiries of appropriate defense contractor personnel, inspecting documents and records, confirming defense contractor assertions with its employees or others, and observing activities. In an examination it will be necessary for a practitioner's procedures to go beyond simply reading relevant policies and programs and making inquiries of appropriate defense contractor personnel. Alternatively, review procedures are generally limited to reading relevant policies and procedures and making inquiries of appropriate defense contractor personnel. When applying examination or review procedures, the practitioner should assess the appropriateness (including the comprehensiveness) of the policies and programs supporting the signatory's responses to each of the questions on the questionnaire.

.11 A particular defense contractor's policies and programs may vary from those of other defense contractors. As a result, evidential matter obtained from the procedures performed cannot be evaluated solely on a quantitative basis. Consequently, it is not practicable to establish only quantitative guidelines for determining the nature or extent of the evidential matter that is necessary to provide the assurance required in either an examination or a review. The qualitative aspects should also be considered.

.12 In determining the nature, timing, and extent of examination or review procedures, the practitioner should consider information obtained in the performance of other services for the defense contractor, for example, the audit of the defense contractor's financial statements. For multi-location defense contractors, whether policies and programs operated during the period should be evaluated for both the defense contractor's headquarters and for selected defense contracting locations. The practitioner may consider using the work of the defense contractor's internal auditors. AU-C section 610, *The Auditor's Consideration of the Internal Audit Function in an Audit of Financial Statements*, may be useful in that consideration.

.13 Examination procedures, and in some instances review procedures, may require access to information involving specific instances of actual or alleged noncompliance with laws. An inability to obtain access to such information because of restrictions imposed by a defense contractor (for example, to protect attorney-client privilege) may constitute a scope limitation. Paragraphs .73–.75 of section 101 provide guidance in such situations. The practitioner should assess the effect of the inability to obtain access to such information on his or her ability to form a conclusion about whether the related policy or program operated during the period. If the defense contractor's reasons for not permitting access to the information are reasonable (for example, the information is the subject of litigation or a governmental investigation) and have been approved by an executive officer of the defense contractor, the occurrences of restricted access to information are few in number, and the practitioner has access to other information about that specific instance or about other instances that is sufficient to permit a conclusion to be formed about whether the related policy or program operated during the period, the practitioner ordinarily would conclude that it is not necessary to disclaim assurance.

.14 If the practitioner's scope of work has been restricted with respect to one or more questions, the practitioner should consider the implications of that restriction on the practitioner's ability to form a conclusion about other questions. In addition, as the nature or number of questions on which the defense contractor has imposed scope limitations increases in significance, the practitioner should consider whether to withdraw from the engagement.

.15 *Question*—What is the form of report that should be issued to meet the requirements of section 101?

.16 *Interpretation*—The standards of reporting in section 101 provide guidance about report content and wording and the circumstances that may require report modification. Appendix A and appendix B provide illustrative reports appropriate for various circumstances. Paragraph .66 of section 101 permits the practitioner to report directly on the subject matter or on management's assertion. In either case, the practitioner should ordinarily obtain a written assertion. An illustrative defense contractor assertion is also presented in appendix A and appendix B.

.17 The engagements addressed in this interpretation do not include providing assurance about whether the defense contractor's policies and programs operated effectively to ensure compliance with the defense contractor's code of business ethics and conduct on the part of individual employees or about whether the defense contractor and its employees have complied with federal procurement laws. The practitioner's report should explicitly disclaim an opinion on the extent of such compliance.

.18 Because variations in individual performance and interpretation will affect the operation of the defense contractor's policies and programs during the period, adherence to all such policies and programs in every case may not be possible. In determining whether a reservation about a response in the questionnaire is sufficiently significant to result in an opinion modified for an exception to that response, the practitioner should consider the nature, causes, patterns, and pervasiveness of the instances in which the policies and programs did not operate as designed and their implications for that response in the questionnaire.

.19 When scope limitations have precluded the practitioner from forming an opinion on the responses to one or more questions, the practitioner's report should describe all such scope restrictions. If the defense contractor imposed such a scope limitation after the practitioner had begun performing procedures, that fact should be stated in the report.

.20 A defense contractor may request the practitioner to communicate to management, the board of directors, or one of its committees, either orally or in writing, conditions noted that do not constitute significant reservations about the answers to the questionnaire but that might nevertheless be of value to management. Agreed-upon arrangements between the practitioner and the defense contractor to communicate conditions noted may include, for example, the reporting of matters of less significance than those contemplated by the criteria, the existence of conditions specified by the defense contractor, the results of further investigation of matters noted to identify underlying causes, or suggestions for improvements in various policies or programs. Under these arrangements, the practitioner may be requested to visit specific locations, assess the effectiveness of specific policies or programs, or undertake specific procedures not otherwise planned. In addition, the practitioner is not precluded from communicating matters believed to be of value, even if no specific request has been made.

.21

Appendix A

Illustrative Defense Contractor Assertions and Examination Reports

Defense Industry Questionnaire on Business Ethics and Conduct

Illustration 1: Unqualified Opinion; General-Use Report; Criteria Attached to the Presentation

Defense Contractor Assertion

Statement of Responses to the Defense Industry Questionnaire on *Business Ethics and Conduct for the period from __________ to __________.*

The affirmative responses in the accompanying *Questionnaire on Business Ethics and Conduct with Responses by the XYZ Company for the period from __________ to __________* are based on policies and programs in operation for that period and are appropriately presented in conformity with the criteria set forth in the *Defense Industry Initiatives on Business Ethics and Conduct,* including the Questionnaire.

Attachments:

Defense Industry Initiatives on Business Ethics and Conduct

Instructions and Questionnaire on Business Ethics and Conduct with Responses by the XYZ Company for the period from __________ to __________.

Examination Report

Independent Accountant's Report

To the Board of Directors of the XYZ Company

We have examined the XYZ Company's *Statement of Responses to the Defense Industry Questionnaire on Business Ethics and Conduct for the period from __________ to __________*, and the Questionnaire and responses attached thereto. XYZ Company's management is responsible for its responses to the Questionnaire. Our responsibility is to express an opinion based on our examination.

Our examination was conducted in accordance with attestation standards established by the American Institute of Certified Public Accountants and, accordingly, included examining, on a test basis, evidence as to whether XYZ Company had policies and programs in operation during that period that support the affirmative responses to the *Questionnaire* and performing such other procedures as we considered necessary in the circumstances. We believe that our examination provides a reasonable basis for our opinion. Our examination procedures were not designed, however, to evaluate whether the aforementioned policies and programs operated effectively to ensure compliance with the Company's *Code of Business Ethics and Conduct* on the part of individual employees or to evaluate the extent to which the Company or its employees have complied with federal procurement laws, and we do not express an opinion or any other form of assurance thereon.

In our opinion, the affirmative responses in the Questionnaire accompanying the *Statement of Responses to the Defense Industry Questionnaire on Business Ethics and Conduct for the period from ________ to ________* referred to above are appropriately presented in conformity with the criteria set forth in the *Defense Industry Initiatives on Business Ethics and Conduct*, including the Questionnaire.

Illustration 2: Unqualified Opinion; Report Modified for Negative Responses to Defense Contractor Assertion; Use of the Report is Restricted Because Criteria are Available Only to Specified Parties

Defense Contractor Assertion

Statement of Responses to the Defense Industry Questionnaire on *Business Ethics and Conduct for the period from ________ to ________.*

The affirmative responses in the accompanying *Questionnaire on Business Ethics and Conduct with Responses by the XYZ Company for the period from ________ to ________* are based on policies and programs in operation for that period and are appropriately presented in conformity with the criteria set forth in the *Defense Industry Initiatives on Business Ethics and Conduct*, including the Questionnaire. Negative responses indicate that the Company did not have policies and programs in operation during that period with respect to those areas.

Attachments: None

(The responses could include an explanation of negative responses if the defense contractor so desired.)

Examination Report

Independent Accountant's Report

To the Board of Directors of the XYZ Company

We have examined the XYZ Company's *Statement of Responses to the Defense Industry Questionnaire on Business Ethics and Conduct for the period from ________ to ________*. XYZ Company's management is responsible for its responses to the Questionnaire. Our responsibility is to express an opinion based on our examination.

[*Standard Scope Paragraph*]

In our opinion, the affirmative responses in the Questionnaire referred to above are appropriately presented in conformity with the criteria set forth in the *Defense Industry Initiatives on Business Ethics and Conduct*, including the Questionnaire. The negative responses to Questions ________ and ________ in the Questionnaire indicate that the Company did not have policies and programs in operation during the period with respect to those areas.

This report is intended solely for the information and use of the XYZ Company and [*identify other specified parties—for example,* the Defense Industry Initiative] and is not intended to be and should not be used by anyone other than these specified parties.

Illustration 3: Opinion Modified for Exception on Certain Response

Defense Contractor Assertion

Statement of Responses to the Defense Industry Questionnaire on *Business Ethics and Conduct for the period from* __________ *to* __________ .

The affirmative responses in the accompanying *Questionnaire on Business Ethics and Conduct with Responses by the XYZ Company for the period from* __________ *to* __________ , are based on policies and programs in operation for that period and are appropriately presented in conformity with the criteria set forth in the *Defense Industry Initiatives on Business Ethics and Conduct*, including the Questionnaire.

Attachments:

Defense Industry Initiatives on Business Ethics and Conduct

Questionnaire on Business Ethics and Conduct with Responses by the XYZ Company for the period from __________ to __________ .

Examination Report

Independent Accountant's Report

To the Board of Directors of the XYZ Company

[*Standard Introductory and Scope Paragraphs*]

Management believes that an appropriate mechanism exists for informing employees of the results of any follow-up into their charges of violations of the Company's Code of Business Ethics and Conduct, and has accordingly answered Question 12 in the affirmative. That mechanism consists principally of distributing newspaper articles and press releases of violations of federal procurement laws that have been voluntarily reported to the appropriate governmental agencies. We do not believe that such a mechanism is sufficient, inasmuch as it does not provide follow-up information on violations reported by employees that are not deemed reportable to a governmental agency. Consequently, in our opinion, the affirmative response to Question 12 in the Questionnaire is not appropriately presented in conformity with the criteria set forth in the *Defense Industry Initiatives on Business Ethics and Conduct*, including the Questionnaire.

In our opinion, except for the response to Question 12 as discussed in the preceding paragraph, the affirmative responses in the Questionnaire accompanying the *Statement of Responses to the Defense Industry Questionnaire on Business Ethics and Conduct for the period from* __________ *to* __________ referred to above are appropriately presented in conformity with the criteria set forth in the Defense Industry Initiatives on Business Ethics and Conduct, including the Questionnaire.

Illustration 4: Opinion Modified for Exception on a Certain Response; Report also Modified for Negative Responses

Defense Contractor Assertion

Statement of Responses to the *Defense Industry Questionnaire on Business Ethics and Conduct for the period from* __________ *to* __________.

The affirmative responses in the accompanying *Questionnaire on Business Ethics and Conduct with Responses by the XYZ Company for the period from* __________ *to* __________ are based on policies and programs in operation for that period and are appropriately presented in conformity with the criteria set forth in the *Defense Industry Initiatives on Business Ethics and Conduct*, including the Questionnaire. Negative responses indicate that the Company did not have policies and programs in operation during that period with respect to those areas.

Attachments:

Defense Industry Initiatives on Business Ethics and Conduct

Questionnaire on Business Ethics and Conduct with Responses by the XYZ Company for the period from __________ to __________.

(The responses could include an explanation of negative responses if the defense contractor so desired.)

Examination Report

Independent Accountant's Report

To the Board of Directors of the XYZ Company

[*Standard Introductory and Scope Paragraphs*]

Management believes that an appropriate mechanism exists for letting employees know of the results of any follow-up into their charges of violations of the Company's Code of Business Ethics and Conduct, and has accordingly answered Question 12 in the affirmative. That mechanism consists principally of distributing newspaper articles and press releases of violations of federal procurement laws that have been voluntarily reported to the appropriate governmental agencies. We do not believe that such a mechanism is sufficient, inasmuch as it does not provide follow-up information on violations reported by employees that are not deemed reportable to a governmental agency. Consequently, in our opinion, the affirmative response to Question 12 in the Questionnaire is not appropriately presented in conformity with the criteria set forth in the Defense Industry Initiatives on Business Ethics and Conduct, including the Questionnaire.

In our opinion, except for the response to Question 12 as discussed in the preceding paragraph, the affirmative responses in the Questionnaire accompanying the *Statement of Responses to the Defense Industry Questionnaire on Business Ethics and Conduct for the period from* __________ *to* __________ referred to above are appropriately presented in conformity with the criteria set forth in the *Defense Industry Initiatives on Business Ethics and Conduct*, including the Questionnaire. The negative responses to Questions __________ and __________ in the Questionnaire indicate that the Company did not have policies and programs in operation during the period with respect to those areas.

Illustration 5: Opinion Disclaimed on Certain Responses Because of Scope Restrictions Imposed by Client

Defense Contractor Assertion

Statement of Responses to the Defense Industry Questionnaire on *Business Ethics and Conduct for the period from* __________ *to* __________.

The affirmative responses in the accompanying *Questionnaire on Business Ethics and Conduct with Responses by the XYZ Company for the period from ________ to ________* are based on policies and programs in operation for that period and are appropriately presented in conformity with the criteria set forth in the *Defense Industry Initiatives on Business Ethics and Conduct*, including the Questionnaire.

Attachments:

Defense Industry Initiatives on Business Ethics and Conduct

Questionnaire on Business Ethics and Conduct with Responses by the XYZ Company for the period from ________ to ________ .

Examination Report

Independent Accountant's Report

To the Board of Directors of the XYZ Company

[*Standard Introductory Paragraph*]

Except as described below, our examination was conducted in accordance with attestation standards established by the American Institute of Certified Public Accountants and, accordingly, included examining, on a test basis, evidence as to whether XYZ Company had policies and programs in operation during that period that support the affirmative responses to the *Questionnaire*. We believe that our examination provides a reasonable basis for our opinion. Our examination procedures were not designed, however, to evaluate whether the aforementioned policies and programs operated effectively to ensure compliance with the Company's *Code of Business Ethics and Conduct* on the part of individual employees or to evaluate the extent to which the Company or its employees have complied with federal procurement laws, and we do not express an opinion or any other form of assurance thereon.

We were not permitted to read relevant documents and files or interview appropriate employees to determine that the affirmative answers to Questions 6, 7, and 8 are appropriate. The nature of those questions precluded us from satisfying ourselves as to the appropriateness of those answers by means of other examination procedures.

In our opinion, the affirmative responses to Questions 1 through 5 and 9 through 17 in the Questionnaire accompanying the *Statement of Responses to the Defense Industry Questionnaire on Business Ethics and Conduct for the period from ________ to ________* referred to above are appropriately presented in conformity with the criteria set forth in the *Defense Industry Initiatives on Business Ethics and Conduct*, including the Questionnaire. Because of the matters discussed in the preceding paragraph, the scope of our work was not sufficient to express, and we do not express, an opinion on the appropriateness of the affirmative responses to Questions 6, 7, and 8 in the Questionnaire.

.22

Appendix B

Illustrative Defense Contractor Assertion and Review Report; Use of Report Is Restricted Because Criteria Are Available Only To Specified Parties

Defense Industry Questionnaire on Business Ethics and Conduct

Defense Contractor Assertion

Statement of Responses to the Defense Industry Questionnaire on *Business Ethics and Conduct for the period from* ________ *to* ________.

The affirmative responses in the accompanying *Questionnaire on Business Ethics and Conduct with Responses by the XYZ Company for the period from* ________ *to* ________ are based on policies and programs in operation during that period and are appropriately presented in conformity with the criteria set forth in the *Defense Industry Initiatives on Business Ethics and Conduct*, including the Questionnaire.

Attachments: None

Review Report

Independent Accountant's Report

To the Board of Directors of the XYZ Company

We have reviewed the XYZ Company's *Statement of Responses to the Defense Industry Questionnaire on Business Ethics and Conduct for the period from* ________ *to* ________. XYZ Company's management is responsible for the Statement of Responses to the Defense Industry Questionnaire on Business Ethics.

Our review was conducted in accordance with attestation standards established by the American Institute of Certified Public Accountants. A review is substantially less in scope than an examination, the objective of which is the expression of an opinion on the affirmative responses in the Questionnaire. Accordingly, we do not express such an opinion. Additionally, our review was not designed to evaluate whether the aforementioned policies and programs operated effectively to ensure compliance with the Company's *Code of Business Ethics and Conduct* on the part of individual employees or to evaluate the extent to which the Company or its employees have complied with federal procurement laws and we do not express an opinion or any other form of assurance thereon.

Based on our review, nothing came to our attention that caused us to believe that the affirmative responses in the Questionnaire referred to above are not appropriately presented in conformity with the criteria set forth in the *Defense Industry Initiatives on Business Ethics and Conduct*, including the Questionnaire.

This report is intended solely for the information and use of the XYZ Company and [*identify other specified parties—for example,* the Defense Industry Initiative] and is not intended to be and should not be used by anyone other than these specified parties.

[Issue Date: August 1987; Amended: February 1989;
Modified: May 1989; Revised: January 2001; November 2006; Revised:
December 2012; Revised: January 2015.]

2. Responding to Requests for Reports on Matters Relating to Solvency

.23 *Question*—Lenders, as a requisite to the closing of certain secured financings in connection with leveraged buyouts, recapitalizations and certain other financial transactions, have sometimes requested written assurance from an accountant regarding the prospective borrower's solvency and related matters.[2] The lender is concerned that such financings not be considered to include a fraudulent conveyance or transfer under the Federal Bankruptcy Code[3] or the relevant state fraudulent conveyance or transfer statute.[4] If the financing is subsequently determined to have included a fraudulent conveyance or transfer, repayment obligations and security interests may be set aside or subordinated to the claims of other creditors.

.24 May a practitioner provide assurance concerning *matters relating to solvency* as hereinafter defined?

.25 *Interpretation*—No. For reasons set forth subsequently, a practitioner should not provide any form of assurance, through examination, review, or agreed-upon procedures engagements, that an entity

- is not insolvent at the time the debt is incurred or would not be rendered insolvent thereby.
- does not have unreasonably small capital.
- has the ability to pay its debts as they mature.

---

[2] Although this interpretation describes requests from secured lenders and summarizes the potential effects of fraudulent conveyance or transfer laws upon such lenders, the interpretation is not limited to requests from lenders. All requests for assurance on matters relating to solvency are governed by this interpretation.

[3] Section 548 of the Federal Bankruptcy Code defines *fraudulent transfers and obligations* as follows:

> The trustee may avoid any transfer of an interest of the debtor in property or any obligation incurred by the debtor, that was made or incurred on or within one year before the date of the filing of the petition, if the debtor voluntarily or involuntarily—
>
> (1) made such transfer or incurred such obligation with actual intent to hinder, delay, or defraud any entity to which the debtor was or became, on or after the date that such transfer occurred or such obligation was incurred, indebted; or
>
> (2)(A) received less than a reasonably equivalent value in exchange for such transfer or obligation; and
>
> (2)(B)(i) was insolvent on the date that such transfer was made or such obligation was incurred, or became insolvent as a result of such transfer or obligation;
>
> (2)(B)(ii) was engaged in business or a transaction, or was about to engage in business or a transaction, for which any property remaining with the debtor was an unreasonably small capital; or
>
> (2)(B)(iii) intended to incur, or believed that the debtor would incur, debts that would be beyond the debtor's ability to pay as such debts matured. (Bankruptcy Law Reporter, 3 vols. [Chicago: Commerce Clearing House, 1986], vol. 1, 1339).

[4] State fraudulent conveyance or transfer statutes such as the Uniform Fraudulent Conveyance Act and the Uniform Fraudulent Transfer Act reflect substantially similar provisions. These state laws may be employed absent a declaration of bankruptcy or by a bankruptcy trustee under Section 544(1) of the Federal Bankruptcy Code. Although the statute of limitations varies from state to state, in some states financing transactions may be vulnerable to challenge for up to six years from closing.

In the context of particular transactions other terms are sometimes used or defined by the parties as equivalents of or substitutes for the terms listed above (for example, *fair salable value of assets exceeds liabilities*). These terms, and those matters listed previously, are hereinafter referred to as *matters relating to solvency*. The prohibition extends to providing assurance concerning all such terms.

.26 The third general attestation standard states that the practitioner must have reason to believe that the subject matter is capable of evaluation against criteria that are suitable and available to users. Suitable criteria must have each of the following attributes:

- *Objectivity*—Criteria should be free from bias.
- *Measurability*—Criteria should permit reasonably consistent measurements, qualitative or quantitative, of subject matter.
- *Completeness*—Criteria should be sufficiently complete so those relevant factors that would alter a conclusion about subject matter are not omitted.
- *Relevance*—Criteria should be relevant to the subject matter.

In addition, the second general attestation standard states that the practitioner must have adequate knowledge of the subject matter.

.27 The matters relating to solvency mentioned in paragraph .23 are subject to legal interpretation under, and varying legal definition in, the Federal Bankruptcy Code and various state fraudulent conveyance and transfer statutes. Because these matters are not clearly defined in an accounting sense, and are therefore subject to varying interpretations, they do not provide the practitioner with suitable criteria required to evaluate the subject matter or an assertion under the third general attestation standard. In addition, lenders are concerned with legal issues on matters relating to solvency and the practitioner is generally unable to evaluate or provide assurance on these matters of legal interpretation. Therefore, practitioners are precluded from giving any form of assurance on matters relating to solvency or any financial presentation of matters relating to solvency.

.28 Under existing AICPA standards, the practitioner may provide a client with various professional services that may be useful to the client in connection with a financing. These services include the following:

- Audit of historical financial statements
- Review of historical financial information (a review in accordance with AU-C section 930, *Interim Financial Information*, of interim financial information, or in accordance with AR section 90, *Review of Financial Statements*)
- Examination or review of pro forma financial information (section 401, *Reporting on Pro Forma Financial Information*)
- Examination or compilation of prospective financial information (section 301, *Financial Forecasts and Projections*)

.29 In addition, under existing AICPA attestation standards (section 201, *Agreed-Upon Procedures Engagements*), the practitioner can provide the client and lender with an agreed-upon procedures report. In such an engagement, a client and lender may request that specified procedures be applied to various financial presentations, such as historical financial information, pro forma financial information, and prospective financial information, which can be useful to a client or lender in connection with a financing.

.30 The practitioner should be aware that certain of the services described in paragraph .28 require that the practitioner have an appropriate level of knowledge of the entity's accounting and financial reporting practices and its internal control. This has ordinarily been obtained by the practitioner auditing historical financial statements of the entity for the most recent annual period or by otherwise obtaining an equivalent knowledge base. When considering acceptance of an engagement relating to a financing, the practitioner should consider whether he or she can perform these services without an equivalent knowledge base.

.31 A report on agreed-upon procedures should not provide any assurances on matters relating to solvency or any financial presentation of matters relating to solvency (for example, fair salable value of assets less liabilities or fair salable value of assets less liabilities, contingent liabilities, and other commitments). A practitioner's report on the results of applying agreed-upon procedures should contain the report elements set forth in paragraph .31 of section 201 (or paragraph .55 of section 301 if applying agreed upon procedures to prospective financial information). The practitioner's report on the results of applying agreed-upon procedures should state that

- the service has been requested in connection with a financing (no reference should be made to any solvency provisions in the financing agreement).
- no representations are provided regarding questions of legal interpretation.
- no assurance is provided concerning the borrower's (*a*) solvency, (*b*) adequacy of capital, or (*c*) ability to pay its debts.
- the procedures should not be taken to supplant any additional inquiries and procedures that the lender should undertake in its consideration of the proposed financing.
- where applicable, an audit of recent historical financial statements has previously been performed and that no audit of any historical financial statements for a subsequent period has been performed. In addition, if any services have been performed pursuant to paragraph .28, they may be referred to.

.32 The report ordinarily is dated at or shortly before the closing date. The financing agreement ordinarily specifies the date, often referred to as the cutoff date, to which the report is to relate (for example, a date three business days before the date of the report). The report should state that the inquiries and other procedures carried out in connection with the report did not cover the period from the cutoff date to the date of the report.

.33 The practitioner might consider furnishing the client with a draft of the agreed-upon procedures report. The draft report should deal with all matters expected to be covered in the terms expected to be used in the final report. The draft report should be identified as a draft in order to avoid giving the impression that the procedures described therein have been performed. This practice of furnishing a draft report at an early point permits the practitioner to make clear to the client and lender what they may expect the accountant to furnish and gives them an opportunity to change the financing agreement or the agreed-upon procedures if they so desire.

[Issue Date: May 1988; Amended: February 1993;
Revised: January 2001; November 2006; Revised: December 2012.]

3. Applicability of Attestation Standards to Litigation Services

.34 *Question*—Paragraph .04 of section 101 provides an example of a litigation service provided by practitioners that would not be considered an attest engagement as defined by section 101. When does section 101 not apply to litigation service engagements?

.35 *Interpretation*—Section 101 does not apply to litigation services that involve pending or potential formal legal or regulatory proceedings before a *trier of fact*[5] in connection with the resolution of a dispute between two or more parties in any of the following circumstances when the

a. practitioner has not been engaged to issue and does not issue an examination, a review, or an agreed-upon procedures report on subject matter, or an assertion about the subject matter that is the responsibility of another party.

b. service comprises being an expert witness.

c. service comprises being a trier of fact or acting on behalf of one.

d. practitioner's work under the rules of the proceedings is subject to detailed analysis and challenge by each party to the dispute.

e. practitioner is engaged by an attorney to do work that will be protected by the attorney's work product privilege and such work is not intended to be used for other purposes.

When performing such litigation services, the practitioner should comply with the "General Standards Rule" (ET sec. 1.300.001) of the AICPA Code of Professional Conduct. [Revised, January 2015, to reflect conforming changes necessary due to the issuance of the revised AICPA Code of Professional Conduct, effective December 15, 2014.]

.36 *Question*—When does section 101 apply to litigation service engagements?

.37 *Interpretation*—Section 101 applies to litigation service engagements only when the practitioner is engaged to issue or does issue an examination, a review, or an agreed-upon procedures report on subject matter, or an assertion about the subject matter, that is the responsibility of another party.

.38 *Question*—Paragraph .04(*c*) of section 101 provides the following example of litigation service engagements that are not considered attest engagements: "Services performed in accordance with the Statement on Standards for Consulting Services, such as.... engagements in which a practitioner is engaged to testify as an expert witness in accounting, auditing, taxation, or other matters, given certain stipulated facts."

What does the term *stipulated facts* as used in paragraph .04(*c*) of section 101 mean?

.39 *Interpretation*—The term *stipulated facts* as used in paragraph .04(*c*) of section 101 means facts or assumptions that are specified by one or more parties to a dispute to serve as the basis for the development of an expert opinion. It is not used in its typical legal sense of facts agreed to by all parties involved in a dispute.

.40 *Question*—Does Interpretation No. 2, "Responding to Requests for Reports on Matters Relating to Solvency," of section 101 (par. .23–.33), prohibit

---

[5] A *trier of fact* in this section means a court, regulatory body, or government authority; their agents; a grand jury; or an arbitrator or mediator of the dispute.

a practitioner from providing expert testimony, as described in paragraph .04(*c*) of section 101 before a trier of fact on matters relating to solvency?

.41 *Interpretation*—No. Matters relating to solvency mentioned in paragraph .25 are subject to legal interpretation under, and varying legal definition in, the Federal Bankruptcy Code and various state fraudulent conveyance and transfer statutes. Because these matters are not clearly defined in an accounting sense, and therefore subject to varying interpretations, they do not provide the practitioner with the suitable criteria required to evaluate the assertion. Thus, Interpretation No. 2 (par. .23–.33) prohibits a practitioner from providing any form of assurance in reporting upon examination, review, or agreed-upon procedures engagements about matters relating to solvency (as defined in paragraph .25).

.42 However, a practitioner who is involved with pending or potential formal legal or regulatory proceedings before a trier of fact in connection with the resolution of a dispute between two or more parties may provide an expert opinion or consulting advice about matters relating to solvency. The prohibition in paragraphs .23–.33 does not apply in such engagements because as part of the legal or regulatory proceedings, each party to the dispute has the opportunity to analyze and challenge the legal definition and interpretation of the matters relating to solvency and the criteria the practitioner uses to evaluate matters related to solvency. Such services are not intended to be used by others who do not have the opportunity to analyze and challenge such definitions and interpretations.

[Issue Date: July 1990; Revised: January 2001.]

4. Providing Access to or Copies of Attest Documentation to a Regulator

.43 *Question*—Interpretation No. 1, "Providing Access to or Copies of Audit Documentation to a Regulator," of AU-C section 230, *Audit Documentation* (AU-C sec. 9230 par .01–.15), contains guidance relating to providing access to or copies of audit documentation to a regulator. Is this guidance applicable to an attest engagement when a regulator requests access to or copies of the attest documentation?

.44 *Interpretation*—Yes. The guidance in Interpretation No. 1 (AU sec. 9230 par .01–.15) is applicable in these circumstances; however, the letter to a regulator should be tailored to meet the individual engagement characteristics or the purpose of the regulatory request, for example, a quality control review. Illustrative letters for an examination engagement performed in accordance with section 601, *Compliance Attestation*, and an agreed-upon procedures engagement performed in accordance with section 201, follow.

.45 Illustrative letter for examination engagement:

Illustrative Letter to Regulator [6]

[Date]

[Name and Address of Regulatory Agency]

Your representatives have requested access to our attest documentation in connection with our engagement to examine (*identify the subject matter examined*

[6] The practitioner should appropriately modify this letter when the engagement has been conducted in accordance with Statements on Standards for Attestation Engagements (SSAE) and also in accordance with additional attest requirements specified by a regulatory agency (for example, the requirements specified in *Government Auditing Standards* issued by the Comptroller General of the United States).

or restate management's assertion). It is our understanding that the purpose of your request is (*state purpose*: for example, "to facilitate your regulatory examination").[7]

Our examination was conducted in accordance with attestation standards[8] established by the American Institute of Certified Public Accountants, the objective of which is to form an opinion as to whether the subject matter (or management's assertion) is fairly stated, in all material respects, based on (*identify criteria*). Under these standards, we have the responsibility to plan and perform our examination to provide a reasonable basis for our opinion and to exercise due professional care in the performance of our examination. Our examination is subject to the inherent risk that material noncompliance, if it exists, would not be detected. In addition, our examination does not address the possibility that material noncompliance may occur in the future. Also, our use of professional judgment and the assessments of attestation risk and materiality for the purpose of our examination means that matters may have existed that would have been assessed differently by you. Our examination does not provide a legal determination on (*name of entity*)'s compliance with specified requirements.

The attest documentation was prepared for the purpose of providing the principal support for our opinion on (*name of entity*)'s compliance and to aid in the performance and supervision of our examination. The attest documentation is the principal record of attest procedures performed, information obtained, and conclusions reached in the examination. The procedures that we performed were limited to those we considered necessary under attestation standards[9] established by the American Institute of Certified Public Accountants to provide us with reasonable basis for our opinion. Accordingly, we make no representation as to the sufficiency or appropriateness, for your purposes, of either the procedures or information in our attest documentation. In addition, any notations, comments, and individual conclusions appearing on any of the attest documentation do not stand alone and should not be read as an opinion on any part of management's assertion or the related subject matter.

Our examination was conducted for the purpose stated above and was not planned or performed in contemplation of your (*state purpose*: for example, "regulatory examination"). Therefore, items of possible interest to you may not have been specifically addressed. Accordingly, our examination, and the attest documentation prepared in connection therewith, should not supplant other inquiries and procedures that should be undertaken by the (*name of regulatory agency*) for the purpose of monitoring and regulating (*name of entity*). In addition, we have not performed any procedures since the date of our report with respect to the subject matter (*or management's assertion related thereto*), and significant events or circumstances may have occurred since that date.

The attest documentation constitutes and reflects work performed or information obtained by us in the course of our examination. The documents contain trade secrets and confidential commercial and financial information of our firm and (*name of entity*) that is privileged and confidential, and we expressly reserve all rights with respect to disclosures to third parties. Accordingly, we request confidential treatment under the Freedom of Information Act or similar laws and regulations when requests are made for the attest documentation or

---

[7] If the practitioner is not required by law, regulation, or engagement contract to provide a regulator access to the attest documentation but otherwise intends to provide such access (see Interpretation No. 1, "Providing Access to or Copies of Audit Documentation to a Regulator," of AU-C section 230, *Audit Documentation* [AU-C sec. 9230 par. .11–.15]), the letter should include a statement that: "Management of (*name of entity*) has authorized us to provide you access to our attest documentation for (*state purpose*)." [Footnote revised, December 2012, to reflect conforming changes necessary due to the issuance of SAS Nos. 122–126.]

[8] Refer to footnote 6.

[9] Refer to footnote 6.

information contained therein or any documents created by the (*name of regulatory agency*) containing information derived there from. We further request that written notice be given to our firm before distribution of the information in the attest documentation (or copies thereof) to others, including other governmental agencies, except when such distribution is required by law or regulation.[10]

[*If it is expected that copies will be requested, add the following*:

Any copies of our attest documentation we agree to provide you will contain a legend "Confidential Treatment Requested by (*name of practitioner, address, telephone number*)."]

[*Firm signature*]

.46 Example letter for agreed-upon procedures engagements:

Illustrative Letter to Regulator[11]

[*Date*]

[*Name and Address of Regulatory Agency*]

Your representatives have requested access to our attest documentation in connection with our engagement to perform agreed-upon procedures on (*identify the subject matter or management's assertion*). It is our understanding that the purpose of your request is (*state purpose:* for example, "to facilitate your regulatory examinations").[12]

Our agreed-upon procedures engagement was conducted in accordance with attestation standards[13] established by the American Institute of Certified Public Accountants. Under these standards, we have the responsibility to perform the agreed-upon procedures to provide a reasonable basis for the findings expressed in our report. We were not engaged to, and did not, perform an examination, the objective of which would be to form an opinion on (*identify the subject matter or management's assertion*). Our engagement is subject to the inherent risk that material misstatement of (*identify the subject matter or management's assertion*), if it exists, would not be detected. (*The practitioner may add the following:* "In addition, our engagement does not address the possibility that material misstatement of (*identify the subject matter or management's assertion*) may occur in the future.") The procedures that we performed were limited to those agreed to by the specified users, and the sufficiency of these procedures is solely the responsibility of the specified users of the report. Further, our engagement does not provide a legal determination on (*name of entity*)'s compliance with specified requirements.

The attest documentation was prepared to document agreed-upon procedures applied, information obtained, and findings reached in the engagement. Accordingly, we make no representation, for your purposes, as to the sufficiency

---

[10] This illustrative paragraph may not in and of itself be sufficient to gain confidential treatment under the rules and regulations of certain regulatory agencies. The practitioner should consider tailoring this paragraph to the circumstances after consulting the regulations of each applicable regulatory agency and, if necessary, consult with legal counsel regarding the specific procedures and requirements necessary to gain confidential treatment.

[11] The practitioner should appropriately modify this letter when the engagement has been conducted in accordance with the SSAEs and also in accordance with additional attest requirements specified by a regulatory agency (for example, the requirements specified in *Government Auditing Standards* issued by the Comptroller General of the United States).

[12] If the practitioner is not required by law, regulation or engagement contract to provide a regulator access to the attest documentation but otherwise intends to provide such access (see Interpretation No. 1 of AU-C section 230) the letter should include a statement that: "Management of (*name of entity*) has authorized us to provide you access to our attest documentation for (*state purpose*)." [Footnote revised, December 2012, to reflect conforming changes necessary due to the issuance of SAS Nos. 122–126.]

[13] Refer to footnote 6.

or appropriateness of the information in our attest documentation. In addition, any notations, comments, and individual findings appearing on any of the attest documentation should not be read as an opinion on management's assertion or the related subject matter, or any part thereof.

Our engagement was performed for the purpose stated above and was not performed in contemplation of your (*state purpose*: for example, "regulatory examination"). Therefore, items of possible interest to you may not have been specifically addressed. Accordingly, our engagement, and the attest documentation prepared in connection therewith, should not supplant other inquiries and procedures that should be undertaken by the (*name of regulatory agency*) for the purpose of monitoring and regulating (*name of client*). In addition, we have not performed any procedures since the date of our report with respect to the subject matter or management's assertion related thereto, and significant events or circumstances may have occurred since that date.

The attest documentation constitutes and reflects procedures performed or information obtained by us in the course of our engagement. The documents contain trade secrets and confidential commercial and financial information of our firm and (*name of client*) that is privileged and confidential, and we expressly reserve all rights with respect to disclosures to third parties. Accordingly, we request confidential treatment under the Freedom of Information Act or similar laws and regulations when requests are made for the attest documentation or information contained therein or any documents created by the (*name of regulatory agency*) containing information derived therefrom. We further request that written notice be given to our firm before distribution of the information in the attest documentation (or copies thereof) to others, including other governmental agencies, except when such distribution is required by law or regulation.[14]

[*If it is expected that copies will be requested, add the following:*

Any copies of our attest documentation we agree to provide you will contain a legend "Confidential Treatment Requested by (*name of practitioner, address, telephone number*)."]

[*Firm signature*]

[Issue Date: May 1996; Revised: January 2001; January 2002; Revised: December 2012.]

5. Attest Engagements on Financial Information[15] Included in eXtensible Business Reporting Language Instance Documents

.47 *Question*—What is eXtensible Business Reporting Language (XBRL) and an XBRL Instance Document?

.48 *Interpretation*—XBRL, the business reporting aspect of the Extensible Markup Language (XML), is a freely licensable open technology standard, which makes it possible to store and transfer data along with the complex hierarchies, data processing rules, and descriptions that enable analysis and

---

[14] This illustrative paragraph may not in and of itself be sufficient to gain confidential treatment under the rules and regulations of certain regulatory agencies. The practitioner should consider tailoring this paragraph to the circumstances after consulting the regulations of each applicable regulatory agency and, if necessary, consult with legal counsel regarding the specific procedures and requirements necessary to gain confidential treatment.

[15] Financial information includes data presented in audited or reviewed financial statements or other financial information (for example, management discussion and analysis).

distribution.[16] An entity may make its financial information available in the form of an XBRL Instance Document (instance document). An *instance document* is essentially a machine-readable format of financial information (that is, a computer can read the data, search for information, or perform calculations). Through the XBRL tagging process, a mapping of the financial information is created that enables a user to extract specific information, facilitating analysis. For example, XBRL would enable a user to use a software tool to automatically extract certain financial line items and automatically import those amounts into a worksheet calculating financial ratios.

.49 The instance document consists of various data points and their corresponding XBRL tags (that describe the financial information) and may include references to other items such as a PDF (Adobe Acrobat) version of financial information. Hence, an instance document is a stand-alone document that may be published using a website, e-mail, and other electronic distribution means.

.50 *Question*—What are the practitioner's considerations when the practitioner has been engaged to examine and report on whether the instance document accurately reflects the financial information?

.51 *Interpretation*—The third general attestation standard states that the practitioner shall perform the engagement only if he or she has reason to believe that the subject matter is capable of evaluation against criteria that are suitable and available to users. Two related criteria, XBRL taxonomies and XBRL International Technical Specifications, meet the available and suitable attributes under the attestation standards because a panel of experts developed the criteria and followed due process procedures that included exposure of the proposed criteria for public comment. The entity has the ability to extend the XBRL taxonomy by creating its own entity extension taxonomy. The entity may also create one or more custom entity taxonomies (for example, for a unique industry that is not yet represented by an XBRL taxonomy). Because neither the XBRL entity extension nor the custom taxonomy typically undergoes due process procedures when developed, the practitioner should evaluate whether the XBRL entity extension or custom taxonomy represents suitable and available criteria as described in paragraphs .24–.34 of section 101.

.52 The practitioner should perform procedures he or she believes are necessary to obtain sufficient evidential matter to form an opinion. Example procedures the practitioner should consider performing include the following:

- Compare the rendered[17] instance document to the financial information.
- Trace and agree the instance document's tagged information to the financial information.
- Test that the financial information is appropriately tagged and included in the instance document.
- Test for consistency of tagging (for example, an entity may use one taxonomy tag for one year and then switch to a different tag for the same financial information the following year. In this case, the financial information for both years should use the same tag).

---

[16] The eXtensible Business Reporting Language (XBRL) tags and their relationship to other XBRL tags are represented in a taxonomy. The XBRL taxonomy is needed for a full rendering of the XBRL Instance Document.

[17] A rendered instance document converts the machine-readable format to a human readable version through a software tool.

- Test that the entity extension or custom taxonomy meets the XBRL International Technical Specification (for example, through the use of a validation tool).

.53 When the client is the responsible party, the client will provide the practitioner with a written assertion regarding the subject matter. An example of a written assertion follows:

> We assert that the accompanying XBRL Instance Document accurately reflects the data presented in the financial statements of XYZ Company as of December 31, 20XX, and for the year then ended in conformity with [*identify the criteria—for example, specify XBRL taxonomy, such as "XBRL U.S. Consumer and Industrial Taxonomy," and where applicable, the company extension taxonomy, such as "XYZ Company's extension taxonomy" and the XBRL International Technical Specifications (specify version)*].

.54 The practitioner should identify in his or her report whether the underlying financial information has been audited or reviewed, and should refer to the report of such audit or review.[18] If the underlying information has not been audited or reviewed, the practitioner should disclaim an opinion on the underlying information. Any information in the Instance Document that is not covered by the practitioner's report should clearly be identified as such.

.55 Report Examples

Example 1: Reporting on the Subject Matter

Independent Accountant's Report

> We have examined the accompanying XBRL Instance Document of XYZ Company, which reflects the data presented in the financial statements of XYZ Company as of December 31, 20XX, and for the year then ended [*optional to include the location of the financial statements, such as "included in the Company's Form 10-K for the year ended December 31, 20XX"*]. XYZ Company's management is responsible for the XBRL Instance Document. Our responsibility is to express an opinion based on our examination.
>
> Our examination was conducted in accordance with attestation standards established by the American Institute of Certified Public Accountants and, accordingly, included examining, on a test basis, evidence supporting the XBRL Instance Document and performing such other procedures as we considered necessary in the circumstances. We believe that our examination provides a reasonable basis for our opinion.
>
> In our opinion, the XBRL Instance Document of XYZ Company referred to above accurately reflects, in all material respects, the data presented in the financial statements in conformity with [*identify the criteria—for example, specific XBRL taxonomy, such as the "XBRL U.S. Consumer and Industrial Taxonomy," and where applicable, the company extension taxonomy, such as "XYZ Company's extension taxonomy," and the XBRL International Technical Specifications 2.0*].
>
> We have also audited, in accordance with auditing standards generally accepted in the United States of America, the financial statements of XYZ Company as of December 31, 20XX, and for the year then ended, and in our report dated

[18] When no audit or review report has been issued, no reference to a report is required.

[*Month*] XX, 20XX, we expressed an unqualified opinion on those financial statements.[19, 20]

[*Signature*]

[*Date*]

Example 2: Reporting on Management's Assertions

<u>Independent Accountant's Report</u>

We have examined management's assertion that [*identify the assertion—for example, the accompanying XBRL Instance Document accurately reflects the data presented in the financial statements of XYZ Company as of December 31, 20XX, and for the year then ended in conformity with (identify the criteria—for example, specific XBRL taxonomy, such as the "XBRL U.S. Consumer and Industrial Taxonomy," and where applicable, the company extension taxonomy, such as "XYZ Company's extension taxonomy," and the XBRL International Technical Specifications 2.0)*]. XYZ Company's management is responsible for the assertion. Our responsibility is to express an opinion on the assertion based on our examination.

We have also audited, in accordance with auditing standards generally accepted in the United States of America, the financial statements of XYZ Company, which comprise the balance sheet as of December 31, 20XX, and the related statements of income, changes in stockholders' equity, and cash flows, for the year then ended, and the related notes to the financial statements. In our report dated [*Month*] XX, 20XX, we expressed an unmodified opinion on those financial statements.

Our examination was conducted in accordance with attestation standards established by the American Institute of Certified Public Accountants and, accordingly, included examining, on a test basis, evidence supporting the XBRL Instance Document and performing such other procedures as we considered necessary in the circumstances. We believe that our examination provides a reasonable basis for our opinion.

In our opinion, management's assertion referred to above is fairly stated, in all material respects, in conformity with [*identify the criteria—for example, specific XBRL taxonomy, such as the "XBRL U.S. Consumer and Industrial Taxonomy," and where applicable, the company extension taxonomy, such as "XYZ Company's extension taxonomy," and the XBRL International Technical Specifications 2.0*].

[*Signature*]

[*Date*]

[Issue Date: September 2003; Revised: December 2012.]

---

[19] If the financial statements have been reviewed, the sentence would read: "We have also reviewed, in accordance with [*standards established by the American Institute of Certified Public Accountants*] [*Statements on Standards for Accounting and Review Services issued by the American Institute of Certified Public Accountants*], the financial statements of XYZ Company as of March 31, 20XX, and for the three months then ended, the objective of which was the expression of limited assurance on such financial statements, and issued our report thereon dated [*Month*] XX, 20XX, [*describe any modifications of such report*]."

If the financial information has not been audited or reviewed, no reference to a report is required. The sentence would read: "We were not engaged to and did not conduct an audit or review of the [*identify information*], the objectives of which would have been the expression of an opinion or limited assurance on such [*identify information*]. Accordingly, we do not express an opinion or any other assurance on [*it*] [*them*]."

[20] If the audit opinion on the related financial statements is other than unqualified, the practitioner should disclose that fact, and any substantive reasons therefore.

6. Reporting on Attestation Engagements Performed in Accordance With *Government Auditing Standards*[21]

.56 *Question*—Chapter 5, "Standards for Attestation Engagements," of the 2011 revision of *Government Auditing Standards* (commonly referred to as the Yellow Book) sets forth additional fieldwork and reporting standards for attestation engagements performed pursuant to generally accepted government auditing standards (GAGAS). Practitioners performing attestation engagements under GAGAS are also required to follow the general standards set forth in chapter 3, "General Standards," of the Yellow Book, as well as the guidance and requirements in chapters 1, "Government Auditing: Foundation and Ethical Principles," and 2, "Standards for Use and Application of GAGAS." For examination attestation engagements performed pursuant to GAGAS, paragraph 5.18 of the Yellow Book prescribes additional reporting standards[22] that go beyond the standards of reporting set forth in paragraphs .63–.90 of section 101. When a practitioner performs an attestation examination in accordance with GAGAS, how should the report be modified?

.57 *Interpretation*—The practitioner should modify the scope paragraph of the attestation report to indicate that the examination or review was "conducted in accordance with attestation standards established by the American Institute of Certified Public Accountants and the standards applicable to attestation engagements contained in *Government Auditing Standards* issued by the Comptroller General of the United States."

.58 Additionally, GAGAS require the practitioner's attestation report to disclose any matters (often referred to as findings) that are set forth in paragraphs 5.20–.26 of the revised Yellow Book. Paragraphs 5.27–.28 of the revised Yellow Book set forth the presentation requirements that the practitioner should use, to the extent possible, in reporting a finding. The following illustration is a standard examination report modified to make reference to a schedule of findings when any of the matters set forth in paragraphs 5.20–.26 have been identified. This report pertains to subject matter for which suitable criteria exist and are available to all users through inclusion in a clear manner in the presentation of the subject matter. A written assertion has been obtained from the responsible party. Although the following illustrative report modifications would comply with the Yellow Book requirement, this illustration is not intended to preclude a practitioner from complying with these additional Yellow Book reporting requirements in other ways. In this illustrative report, the practitioner is reporting on the subject matter.

Independent Accountant's Report

We have examined [*identify the subject matter—for example, the accompanying schedule of performance measures of XYZ Agency for the year ended December*

---

[21] Although separate interpretations for other AT sections have not been issued to deal with attestation engagements performed in accordance with *Government Auditing Standards*, a practitioner may use this guidance to help him or her appropriately modify an attest report pursuant to other AT sections.

[22] Paragraph 5.18 of the Yellow Book sets forth the additional reporting requirements: (*a*) reporting auditors' compliance with generally accepted government auditing standards, (*b*) reporting deficiencies in internal control, fraud, noncompliance with provisions of laws, regulations, contracts, and grant agreements, and abuse, (*c*) reporting views of responsible officials, (*d*) reporting confidential or sensitive information, and (*e*) distributing reports. [Footnote revised, January 2008, to reflect conforming changes necessary due to the issuance of the 2007 revised *Government Auditing Standards*. Footnote revised, December 2012, to reflect conforming changes necessary due to the issuance of the 2011 revision of *Government Auditing Standards*.]

31, 20XX].[23] XYZ Agency's management is responsible for the [*identify the subject matter—for example, schedule of performance measures*]. Our responsibility is to express an opinion based on our examination.

Our examination was conducted in accordance with attestation standards established by the American Institute of Certified Public Accountants and the standards applicable to attestation engagements contained in *Government Auditing Standards* issued by the Comptroller General of the United States and, accordingly, included examining, on a test basis, evidence supporting [*identify the subject matter—for example, XYZ Agency's schedule of performance measures*] and performing such other procedures as we considered necessary in the circumstances. We believe that our examination provides a reasonable basis for our opinion.

[*Additional paragraph(s) may be added to emphasize certain matters relating to the attest engagement or the subject matter.*]

In our opinion, the schedule referred to above presents, in all material respects, [*identify the subject matter—for example, the performance measures of XYZ Agency for the year ended December 31, 20XX*], in conformity with [*identify criteria—for example, the criteria set forth in Note 1*].

[*When any of the matters set forth in paragraphs 5.20–.26 of the Yellow Book have been identified the following paragraph would be added.*]

In accordance with *Government Auditing Standards*, we are required to report all deficiencies that are considered to be significant deficiencies or material weaknesses in internal control; fraud and noncompliance with provisions of laws or regulations that have a material effect on [*identify the subject matter—for example, XYZ Agency's schedule of performance measures*]; and any other instances that warrant the attention of those charged with governance; noncompliance with provisions of contracts or grant agreements, and abuse that has a material effect on the subject matter.[24] We are also required to obtain and report the views of responsible officials concerning the findings, conclusions, and recommendations, as well as any planned corrective actions. We performed our examination to express an opinion on whether [*identify the subject matter—for example, XYZ Agency's schedule of performance measures*] is presented in accordance with the criteria described above and not for the purpose of expressing an opinion on the internal control over [*identify the subject matter—for example, reporting of performance measures*] or on compliance and other matters; accordingly, we express no such opinions. Our examination disclosed certain findings that are required to be reported under *Government Auditing Standards* and

---

[23] If the practitioner is reporting on an assertion about the subject matter, the practitioner would identify the assertion rather than the subject matter, for example, "management's assertion that the accompanying schedule presents the performance measures of XYZ Agency for the year ended December 31, 20XX in conformity with the criteria in Note 1." [Footnote added, December 2012, to reflect conforming changes necessary due to the issuance of the 2011 revision of *Government Auditing Standards*.]

[24] Note that paragraph 5.25 of *Government Auditing Standards* states that when auditors detect instances of noncompliance with provisions of contracts or grant agreements, or abuse that have an effect on the subject matter or an assertion about the subject matter that is less than material but warrant the attention of those charged with governance, they should communicate those findings in writing to entity officials. When auditors detect any instances of fraud, noncompliance with provisions of laws, regulations, contracts, or grant agreements, or abuse that do not warrant the attention of those charged with governance, the auditors' determination of whether and how to communicate such instances to audited entity officials is a matter of professional judgment. [Footnote added, January 2008, to reflect conforming changes necessary due to the issuance of the 2007 revised *Government Auditing Standards*. Footnote renumbered and revised, December 2012, to reflect conforming changes necessary due to the issuance of the 2011 revision of *Government Auditing Standards*.]

those findings, along with the views of responsible officials, are described in the attached Schedule of Findings.[25]

[*Signature*]

[*Date*]

[25] [Footnote renumbered and deleted to reflect conforming changes necessary due to the issuance of the 2007 revised *Government Auditing Standards*. Footnote renumbered, December 2012, to reflect conforming changes necessary due to the issuance of the 2011 revision of *Government Auditing Standards*.]

Illustrative Schedule of Findings

XYZ Agency
Schedule of Findings[26]
Year Ended December 31, 20XX

Finding No. 1

Criteria

Condition

Cause

Effect or Potential Effect

Management's Response

Finding No. 2

Criteria

Condition

Cause

Effect or Potential Effect

Management's Response

[Issue Date: December 2004; Revised: January 2008; Revised: December 2012.]

[26] Refer to paragraphs 5.11–.15 of the Yellow Book regarding the content of the schedule of findings. [Footnote renumbered and revised: January 2008, to reflect conforming changes necessary due to the issuance of the 2007 revised *Government Auditing Standards*. Footnote renumbered and revised, December 2012, to reflect conforming changes necessary due to the issuance of the 2011 revision of *Government Auditing Standards*.]

7. Reporting on the Design of Internal Control

.59 *Question*—A practitioner may be asked to report on the suitability[27] of the design of an entity's internal control over financial reporting (internal control) for preventing or detecting and correcting material misstatements of the entity's financial statements on a timely basis. Such requests may be made by, for example,

- an entity applying for a government grant or contract that is required to submit a written preaward survey by management about the suitability of the design of the entity's internal control or a portion of the entity's internal control, together with a practitioner's report thereon.
- a new casino applying for a license to operate that is required by a regulatory agency to submit a practitioner's report on whether the entity's internal control *that it plans to implement* is suitably designed to provide reasonable assurance that the control objectives specified in the regulatory agency's regulations would be achieved. (In this situation the casino would not yet have begun operations, and audited financial statements or financial data relevant to the period covered by the engagement may not exist.)

May a practitioner report on the suitability of the design of an entity's internal control based on the risk assessment procedures the auditor performs to obtain a sufficient understanding of the entity and its environment, including its internal control, in an audit of the entity's financial statements?

.60 *Interpretation*—No. In a financial statement audit, the purpose of the auditor's understanding of the entity and its environment, including its internal control, is to enable the auditor to assess the risk of material misstatement of the financial statements whether due to error or fraud, and to design the nature, timing, and extent of further audit procedures. The understanding obtained in a financial statement audit does not provide the practitioner with a sufficient basis to report on the suitability of the design of an entity's internal control or any portion thereof.

.61 *Question*—How may a practitioner report on the suitability of the design of an entity's internal control or a portion thereof?

.62 *Interpretation*—The practitioner may perform an examination under section 101, or apply agreed-upon procedures under section 201, to management's written assertion about the suitability of the design of the entity's internal control. Footnote 4 of section 501, *An Examination of an Entity's Internal Control Over Financial Reporting That is Integrated With an Audit of Its Financial Statements*, states that although section 501 does not directly apply when an auditor is engaged to examine the suitability of design of an entity's internal control, it may be useful in planning and performing such engagements. Paragraphs .57–.59 of section 501 discuss how the auditor evaluates the design effectiveness of controls.

.63 When the engagement involves the application of agreed-upon procedures to a written assertion about the suitability of the design of an entity's internal control over compliance with specified requirements, the practitioner should also follow the provisions of paragraphs .09 and .11–.29 of section 601.

---

[27] In this interpretation, the *suitability of the design of internal control* means the same thing as the *design effectiveness of an entity's internal control.* [Footnote renumbered, December 2012, to reflect conforming changes necessary due to the issuance of the 2011 revision of *Government Auditing Standards*.]

.64 The following is an illustrative report a practitioner may issue when reporting on the suitability of the design of an entity's internal control that has been implemented. The report may be modified, as appropriate, to fit the particular circumstances.

Independent Accountant's Report

[*Introductory paragraph*]

We have examined the suitability of the design of W Company's internal control over financial reporting to prevent or detect and correct material misstatements in its financial statements on a timely basis as of December 31, 20XX, based on [*identify criteria*].[28] W Company's management is responsible for the suitable design of internal control over financial reporting. Our responsibility is to express an opinion on the design of internal control based on our examination.

[*Scope paragraph*]

Our examination was conducted in accordance with attestation standards established by the American Institute of Certified Public Accountants and, accordingly, included obtaining an understanding of internal control over financial reporting, evaluating the design of internal control, and performing such other procedures as we considered necessary in the circumstances. We believe that our examination provides a reasonable basis for our opinion. We were not engaged to examine and report on the operating effectiveness of W Company's internal control over financial reporting as of December 31, 20XX, and, accordingly, we express no opinion on operating effectiveness.

[*Inherent limitations paragraph*]

Because of its inherent limitations, internal control over financial reporting may not prevent or detect and correct misstatements. Also, projections of any evaluation of effectiveness to future periods are subject to the risk that controls may become inadequate because of changes in conditions, or that the degree of compliance with the policies or procedures may deteriorate.

[*Opinion paragraph*]

In our opinion, W Company's internal control over financial reporting was suitably designed, in all material respects, to prevent or detect and correct material misstatements in the financial statements on a timely basis as of December 31, 20XX, based on [*identify criteria*].

[*Signature*]

[*Date*]

.65 When reporting on the suitability of the design of an entity's internal control that has not yet been implemented, the practitioner would be unable to confirm that the controls have been implemented and should disclose that information in the practitioner's report. In those circumstances, the practitioner should modify (1) the scope paragraph of the illustrative report in paragraph .64 to inform readers that the controls identified in the report have not yet been implemented and (2) the inherent limitations paragraph to reflect the related risk. Following are modified illustrative report paragraphs for use when controls have not yet been implemented. (New language is shown in boldface italics. Deleted language is shown in strikethrough.)

---

[28] This report assumes that the control criteria are both suitable and available to users as discussed in paragraphs .23–.33 of section 101. Therefore, the use of this report is not restricted. [Footnote renumbered, December 2012, to reflect conforming changes necessary due to the issuance of the 2011 revision of *Government Auditing Standards*.]

Our examination was conducted in accordance with attestation standards established by the American Institute of Certified Public Accountants and, accordingly, included obtaining an understanding of internal control over financial reporting, evaluating the design of internal control, and performing such other procedures as we considered necessary in the circumstances. We believe that our examination provides a reasonable basis for our opinion. ***Because operations had not begun as of December 31, 20XX, we could not confirm that the specified controls were implemented. Accordingly, our report solely addresses the suitability of the design of the Company's internal control and does not address whether the controls were implemented. Furthermore, because the specified controls have not yet been implemented, we were unable to test, and did not test,*** the operating effectiveness of W Company's internal control over financial reporting as of December 31, 20XX, and, accordingly, we express no opinion on operating effectiveness.

[*Inherent limitations paragraph*]

Because of its inherent limitations, internal control over financial reporting may not prevent or detect and correct misstatements. Also, projections of any evaluation of effectiveness to future periods are subject to the risk that controls ***may not be implemented as intended when operations begin or*** may become inadequate because of changes in conditions~~, or that the degree of compliance with the policies or procedures may deteriorate~~.

.66 *Question*—A practitioner may be asked to sign a prescribed form developed by the party to whom the form is to be submitted regarding the design of an entity's internal control. What are the practitioner's responsibilities when requested to sign such a form if it includes language that is not consistent with the practitioner's function or responsibility or with the reporting requirements of professional standards?

.67 *Interpretation*—Paragraphs .22–.23 of AU-C section 800, *Special Considerations—Audits of Financial Statements Prepared in Accordance With Special Purpose Frameworks*, address such situations in the context of an audit of financial statements and indicate that the auditor should either reword the prescribed form of report or attach an appropriately worded separate report that conforms with the auditor's function or responsibility and professional standards. When reporting on the suitability of the design of an entity's internal control under section 101, the practitioner's report should contain all of the elements in either paragraphs .85 or .86, as applicable, which can be accomplished by either rewording the prescribed form of report or attaching an appropriately worded separate report in place of the prescribed form.

.68 *Question*—An entity may be required to submit a practitioner's report about an entity's *ability* to establish suitably designed internal control (or its assertion thereon). May a practitioner issue such a report based on (*a*) the risk assessment procedures related to existing internal control that the auditor performs in an audit of an entity's financial statements or (*b*) the performance of an attest engagement?

.69 *Interpretation*—No. Neither the risk assessment procedures the auditor performs in an audit of an entity's financial statements nor the performance of an attest engagement provide the practitioner with a basis for issuing a report on the *ability* of an entity to establish suitably designed internal control. There are no suitable criteria for evaluating an entity's ability to establish suitably designed internal control. The requesting party may be willing to accept a report of the practitioner on a consulting service. The practitioner may include in the consulting service report *a.* a statement that the practitioner is unable to perform an attest engagement that addresses the entity's ability to establish suitably designed internal control because there are no suitable criteria for evaluating the entity's ability to do so;

b. a description of the nature and scope of the practitioner's services; and

c. the practitioner's findings.

The practitioner may refer to the guidance in CS section 100, *Consulting Services: Definitions and Standards*.

[Issue Date: December 2008; Revised: December 2012.]

8. Including a Description of Tests of Controls or Other Procedures, and the Results Thereof, in an Examination Report

.70 *Question*—Section 801, *Reporting on Controls at a Service Organization*, addresses examination engagements undertaken by a service auditor to report on controls at organizations that provide services to user entities when those controls are likely to be relevant to user entities' internal control over financial reporting (ICFR). For a type 2 report resulting from such an examination engagement, section 801 provides for a separate section of the report that includes a description of the service auditor's tests of controls likely to be relevant to user entities' ICFR and the results of those tests. This information is intended for user auditors who may need detailed information about the results of such tests of controls to determine how the results affect a particular user entity's financial statements.

.71 Paragraph .02 of section 801 refers the practitioner to section 101, when a practitioner is engaged to examine and report on controls at a service organization other than those likely to be relevant to user entities' ICFR (for example, controls at a service provider that are relevant to user entities' compliance with laws or regulations or controls at a service provider that are relevant to the privacy of user entities' information).[29] If a practitioner performs an examination engagement under section 101, may the practitioner's examination report include, in a separate section, a description of tests of controls or other procedures performed in support of the practitioner's opinion resulting from such an engagement?

.72 *Interpretation*—Nothing in section 101 precludes a practitioner from including in a separate section of his or her examination report a description of tests of controls or other procedures performed and the results thereof. However, in some cases, such a description may overshadow the practitioner's overall opinion or may cause report users to misunderstand the opinion. Therefore, the circumstances of the particular engagement are relevant to the practitioner's consideration regarding whether to include a description of tests of controls or other procedures performed, and the results thereof, in a separate section of the practitioner's examination report. In determining whether to include such a description in the practitioner's examination report, the following considerations are relevant:

---

[29] As indicated in paragraph A2 of section 801, *Reporting on Controls at a Service Organization*, paragraph .02 of section 801 is not intended to permit a report that combines reporting on a service organization's controls likely to be relevant to user entities' internal control over financial reporting (ICFR) with reporting on controls that are not likely to be relevant to user entities' ICFR. [Footnote renumbered, December 2012, to reflect conforming changes necessary due to the issuance of the 2011 revision of *Government Auditing Standards*.]

- Whether there has been a request for such information and whether the specified parties making the request have an appropriate business need or reasonable basis for requesting the information (for example, the specified parties are required to maintain and monitor controls that either encompass or are dependent on controls that are the subject of the examination and, therefore, need information about the tests of controls to enable them to have a basis for concluding that they have met the requirements applicable to them)
- Whether the specified parties have an understanding of the nature and subject matter of the engagement and experience in using the information in such reports
- Whether including such a description in the examination report is likely to cause report users to misunderstand the opinion
- Whether the practitioner's tests of controls or other procedures performed directly relate to the subject matter of the engagement

Paragraph .79 of section 101 states, "The need for restriction on the use of a report may result from a number of circumstances, including the purpose of the report, the criteria used in preparation of the subject matter, the extent to which the procedures performed are known or understood, and the potential for the report to be misunderstood when taken out of the context in which it was intended to be used." The addition of a description of tests of controls or other procedures performed, and the results thereof, in a separate section of an examination report may increase the need for use of the report to be restricted to specified parties.

[Issue Date: July 2010.]

AT Section 201

Agreed-Upon Procedures Engagements

Source: SSAE No. 10; SSAE No. 11.

Effective when the subject matter or assertion is as of or for a period ending on or after June 1, 2001, unless otherwise indicated.

Introduction and Applicability

.01 This section sets forth attestation standards and provides guidance to a practitioner concerning performance and reporting in all agreed-upon procedures engagements, except as noted in paragraph .02. A practitioner also should refer to the following sections of this Statement on Standards for Attestation Engagements (SSAE), which provide additional guidance for certain types of agreed-upon procedures engagements:

a. Section 301, *Financial Forecasts and Projections*

b. Section 601, *Compliance Attestation*

.02 This section does not apply to the following:[1]

a. Situations in which an auditor reports on specified compliance requirements based solely on an audit of financial statements, as addressed in AU-C section 806, *Reporting on Compliance With Aspects of Contractual Agreements or Regulatory Requirements in Connection With Audited Financial Statements*

b. Engagements for which the objective is to report in accordance with AU-C section 935, *Compliance Audits*, unless the terms of the engagement specify that the engagement be performed pursuant to SSAEs

c. Engagements covered by AU-C section 920, *Letters for Underwriters and Certain Other Requesting Parties*

d. Certain professional services that would not be considered as falling under this section as described in paragraph .04 of section 101, *Attest Engagements*

[Revised, December 2010, to reflect conforming changes necessary due to the issuance of SAS No. 117. Revised, August 2011, to reflect conforming changes necessary due to the issuance of SSAE No. 16. Revised, December 2012, to reflect conforming changes necessary due to the issuance of SAS Nos. 122–126.]

Agreed-Upon Procedures Engagements

.03 An agreed-upon procedures engagement is one in which a practitioner is engaged by a client to issue a report of findings based on specific procedures performed on subject matter. The client engages the practitioner to assist specified parties in evaluating subject matter or an assertion as a result of a need

---

[1] Interpretation No. 2, "Responding to Requests for Reports on Matters Relating to Solvency," of section 101, *Attest Engagements* (sec. 9101 par. .23–.33), prohibits the performance of any attest engagements concerning matters of solvency or insolvency.

or needs of the specified parties.[2] Because the specified parties require that findings be independently derived, the services of a practitioner are obtained to perform procedures and report his or her findings. The specified parties and the practitioner agree upon the procedures to be performed by the practitioner that the specified parties believe are appropriate. Because the needs of the specified parties may vary widely, the nature, timing, and extent of the agreed-upon procedures may vary as well; consequently, the specified parties assume responsibility for the sufficiency of the procedures since they best understand their own needs. In an engagement performed under this section, the practitioner does not perform an examination or a review, as discussed in section 101, and does not provide an opinion or negative assurance.[3] (See paragraph .24.) Instead, the practitioner's report on agreed-upon procedures should be in the form of procedures and findings. (See paragraph .31.)

.04 As a consequence of the role of the specified parties in agreeing upon the procedures performed or to be performed, a practitioner's report on such engagements should clearly indicate that its use is restricted to those specified parties.[4] Those specified parties, including the client, are hereinafter referred to as *specified parties*.

Standards

.05 The general, fieldwork, and reporting standards for attestation engagements as established in section 50, *SSAE Hierarchy*, together with interpretive guidance regarding their application as addressed throughout this section, should be followed by the practitioner in performing and reporting on agreed-upon procedures engagements. [Revised, November 2006, to reflect conforming changes necessary due to the issuance of SSAE No. 14.]

Conditions for Engagement Performance

.06 The practitioner may perform an agreed-upon procedures attest engagement provided that—

a. The practitioner is independent.

b. One of the following conditions is met.

  (1) The party wishing to engage the practitioner is responsible for the subject matter, or has a reasonable basis for providing a written assertion about the subject matter when the nature of the subject matter is such that a responsible party does not otherwise exist.

  (2) The party wishing to engage the practitioner is not responsible for the subject matter but is able to provide the practitioner, or have a third party who is responsible for the subject matter provide the practitioner with evidence of the third party's responsibility for the subject matter.

c. The practitioner and the specified parties agree upon the procedures performed or to be performed by the practitioner.

---

[2] See paragraphs .08–.09 for a discussion of subject matter and assertion.

[3] For guidance on expressing an opinion on specified elements, accounts, or items of a financial statement based on an audit, see AU-C section 805, *Special Considerations—Audits of Single Financial Statements and Specific Elements, Accounts, or Items of a Financial Statement*. [Footnote revised, December 2012, to reflect conforming changes necessary due to the issuance of SAS Nos. 122–126.]

[4] See paragraphs .78–.83 of section 101 for additional guidance regarding restricted-use reports.

d. The specified parties take responsibility for the sufficiency of the agreed-upon procedures for their purposes.

e. The specific subject matter to which the procedures are to be applied is subject to reasonably consistent measurement.

f. Criteria to be used in the determination of findings are agreed upon between the practitioner and the specified parties.

g. The procedures to be applied to the specific subject matter are expected to result in reasonably consistent findings using the criteria.

h. Evidential matter related to the specific subject matter to which the procedures are applied is expected to exist to provide a reasonable basis for expressing the findings in the practitioner's report.

i. Where applicable, the practitioner and the specified parties agree on any materiality limits for reporting purposes. (See paragraph .25.)

j. Use of the report is restricted to the specified parties.

k. For agreed-upon procedures engagements on prospective financial information, the prospective financial statements include a summary of significant assumptions. (See paragraph .52 of section 301.)

Agreement on and Sufficiency of Procedures

.07 To satisfy the requirements that the practitioner and the specified parties agree upon the procedures performed or to be performed and that the specified parties take responsibility for the sufficiency of the agreed-upon procedures for their purposes, ordinarily the practitioner should communicate directly with and obtain affirmative acknowledgment from each of the specified parties. For example, this may be accomplished by meeting with the specified parties or by distributing a draft of the anticipated report or a copy of an engagement letter to the specified parties and obtaining their agreement. If the practitioner is not able to communicate directly with all of the specified parties, the practitioner may satisfy these requirements by applying any one or more of the following or similar procedures.

- Compare the procedures to be applied to written requirements of the specified parties.
- Discuss the procedures to be applied with appropriate representatives of the specified parties involved.
- Review relevant contracts with or correspondence from the specified parties.

The practitioner should not report on an engagement when specified parties do not agree upon the procedures performed or to be performed and do not take responsibility for the sufficiency of the procedures for their purposes. (See paragraph .36 for guidance on satisfying these requirements when the practitioner is requested to add other parties as specified parties after the date of completion of the agreed-upon procedures.)

Subject Matter and Related Assertions

.08 The subject matter of an agreed-upon procedures engagement may take many different forms and may be at a point in time or covering a period of time. In an agreed-upon procedures engagement, it is the specific subject matter to which the agreed-upon procedures are to be applied using the criteria selected. Even though the procedures are agreed upon between the practitioner and the specified parties, the subject matter and the criteria must meet the conditions set forth in the third general standard. (See paragraphs .23–.24 of section 101.) The criteria against which the specific subject matter needs to be measured may be recited within the procedures enumerated or referred to in the practitioner's report.

.09 An assertion is any declaration or set of declarations about whether the subject matter is based on or in conformity with the criteria selected. A written assertion is generally not required in an agreed-upon procedures engagement unless specifically required by another attest standard (for example, see paragraph .11 of section 601). If, however, the practitioner requests the responsible party to provide an assertion, the assertion may be presented in a representation letter or another written communication from the responsible party, such as in a statement, narrative description, or schedule appropriately identifying what is being presented and the point in time or the period of time covered.

Establishing an Understanding With the Client

.10 The practitioner should establish an understanding with the client regarding the services to be performed. When the practitioner documents the understanding through a written communication with the client (an *engagement letter*), such communication should be addressed to the client, and in some circumstances also to all specified parties. Matters that might be included in such an understanding include the following:

- The nature of the engagement
- Identification of the subject matter (or the assertion related thereto), the responsible party, and the criteria to be used
- Identification of specified parties (See paragraph .36.)
- Specified parties' acknowledgment of their responsibility for the sufficiency of the procedures
- Responsibilities of the practitioner (See paragraphs .12–.14 and .40.)
- Reference to attestation standards established by the American Institute of Certified Public Accountants (AICPA)
- Agreement on procedures by enumerating (or referring to) the procedures (See paragraphs .15–.18.)
- Disclaimers expected to be included in the practitioner's report
- Use restrictions
- Assistance to be provided to the practitioner (See paragraphs .22–.23.)
- Involvement of a specialist (See paragraphs .19–.21.)
- Agreed-upon materiality limits (See paragraph .25.)

Nature, Timing, and Extent of Procedures

Responsibility of the Specified Parties

.11 Specified parties are responsible for the sufficiency (nature, timing, and extent) of the agreed-upon procedures because they best understand their own needs. The specified parties assume the risk that such procedures might be insufficient for their purposes. In addition, the specified parties assume the risk that they might misunderstand or otherwise inappropriately use findings properly reported by the practitioner.

Practitioner's Responsibility

.12 The responsibility of the practitioner is to carry out the procedures and report the findings in accordance with the general, fieldwork, and reporting standards as discussed and interpreted in this section. The practitioner assumes the risk that misapplication of the procedures may result in inappropriate findings being reported. Furthermore, the practitioner assumes the risk that appropriate findings may not be reported or may be reported inaccurately. The practitioner's risks can be reduced through adequate planning and supervision and due professional care in performing the procedures, determining the findings, and preparing the report.

.13 The practitioner should have adequate knowledge in the specific subject matter to which the agreed-upon procedures are to be applied. He or she may obtain such knowledge through formal or continuing education, practical experience, or consultation with others.[5]

.14 The practitioner has no responsibility to determine the differences between the agreed-upon procedures to be performed and the procedures that the practitioner would have determined to be necessary had he or she been engaged to perform another form of attest engagement. The procedures that the practitioner agrees to perform pursuant to an agreed-upon procedures engagement may be more or less extensive than the procedures that the practitioner would determine to be necessary had he or she been engaged to perform another form of engagement.

Procedures to Be Performed

.15 The procedures that the practitioner and specified parties agree upon may be as limited or as extensive as the specified parties desire. However, mere reading of an assertion or specified information about the subject matter does not constitute a procedure sufficient to permit a practitioner to report on the results of applying agreed-upon procedures. In some circumstances, the procedures agreed upon evolve or are modified over the course of the engagement. In general, there is flexibility in determining the procedures as long as the specified parties acknowledge responsibility for the sufficiency of such procedures for their purposes. Matters that should be agreed upon include the nature, timing, and extent of the procedures.

---

[5] Paragraphs .19–.20 of section 601 provide guidance about obtaining an understanding of certain requirements in an agreed-upon procedures engagement on compliance.

.16 The practitioner should not agree to perform procedures that are overly subjective and thus possibly open to varying interpretations. Terms of uncertain meaning (such as general review, limited review, check, or test) should not be used in describing the procedures unless such terms are defined within the agreed-upon procedures. The practitioner should obtain evidential matter from applying the agreed-upon procedures to provide a reasonable basis for the finding or findings expressed in his or her report, but need not perform additional procedures outside the scope of the engagement to gather additional evidential matter.

.17 Examples of appropriate procedures include the following:

- Execution of a sampling application after agreeing on relevant parameters
- Inspection of specified documents evidencing certain types of transactions or detailed attributes thereof
- Confirmation of specific information with third parties
- Comparison of documents, schedules, or analyses with certain specified attributes
- Performance of specific procedures on work performed by others (including the work of internal auditors—see paragraphs .22–.23)
- Performance of mathematical computations

.18 Examples of inappropriate procedures include the following:

- Mere reading of the work performed by others solely to describe their findings
- Evaluating the competency or objectivity of another party
- Obtaining an understanding about a particular subject
- Interpreting documents outside the scope of the practitioner's professional expertise

Involvement of a Specialist[6]

.19 The practitioner's education and experience enable him or her to be knowledgeable about business matters in general, but he or she is not expected to have the expertise of a person trained for or qualified to engage in the practice of another profession or occupation. In certain circumstances, it may be appropriate to involve a specialist to assist the practitioner in the performance of one or more procedures. The following are examples.

- An attorney might provide assistance concerning the interpretation of legal terminology involving laws, regulations, rules, contracts, or grants.
- A medical specialist might provide assistance in understanding the characteristics of diagnosis codes documented in patient medical records.
- An environmental engineer might provide assistance in interpreting environmental remedial action regulatory directives that may affect

[6] A *specialist* is a person (or firm) possessing skill or knowledge in a particular field other than the attest function. As used herein, a specialist does not include a person employed by the practitioner's firm who participates in the attest engagement.

the agreed-upon procedures applied to an environmental liabilities account in a financial statement.

- A geologist might provide assistance in distinguishing between varying physical characteristics of a generic minerals group related to information to which the agreed-upon procedures are applied.

.20 The practitioner and the specified parties should explicitly agree to the involvement of the specialist in assisting a practitioner in the performance of an agreed-upon procedures engagement. This agreement may be reached when obtaining agreement on the procedures performed or to be performed and acknowledgment of responsibility for the sufficiency of the procedures, as discussed in paragraph .07. The practitioner's report should describe the nature of the assistance provided by the specialist.

.21 A practitioner may agree to apply procedures to the report or work product of a specialist that does not constitute assistance by the specialist to the practitioner in an agreed-upon procedures engagement. For example, the practitioner may make reference to information contained in a report of a specialist in describing an agreed-upon procedure. However, it is inappropriate for the practitioner to agree to merely read the specialist's report solely to describe or repeat the findings, or to take responsibility for all or a portion of any procedures performed by a specialist or the specialist's work product.

Internal Auditors and Other Personnel

.22 The agreed-upon procedures to be enumerated or referred to in the practitioner's report are to be performed entirely by the practitioner except as discussed in paragraphs .19–.21.[7] However, internal auditors or other personnel may prepare schedules and accumulate data or provide other information for the practitioner's use in performing the agreed-upon procedures. Also, internal auditors may perform and report separately on procedures that they have carried out. Such procedures may be similar to those that a practitioner may perform under this section.

.23 A practitioner may agree to perform procedures on information documented in the working papers of internal auditors. For example, the practitioner may agree to—

- Repeat all or some of the procedures.
- Determine whether the internal auditors' working papers contain documentation of procedures performed and whether the findings documented in the working papers are presented in a report by the internal auditors.

However, it is inappropriate for the practitioner to—

- Agree to merely read the internal auditors' report solely to describe or repeat their findings.
- Take responsibility for all or a portion of any procedures performed by internal auditors by reporting those findings as the practitioner's own.
- Report in any manner that implies shared responsibility for the procedures with the internal auditors.

---

[7] AU-C section 610, *The Auditor's Consideration of the Internal Audit Function in an Audit of Financial Statements*, does not apply to agreed-upon procedures engagements. [Footnote revised, December 2012, to reflect conforming changes necessary due to the issuance of SAS Nos. 122–126.]

Findings

.24 A practitioner should present the results of applying agreed-upon procedures to specific subject matter in the form of findings. The practitioner should not provide negative assurance about whether the subject matter or the assertion is fairly stated based on the criteria. For example, the practitioner should not include a statement in his or her report that "nothing came to my attention that caused me to believe that the [*identify subject matter*] is not presented based on [or the assertion is not fairly stated based on] [*identify criteria*]."

.25 The practitioner should report all findings from application of the agreed-upon procedures. The concept of materiality does not apply to findings to be reported in an agreed-upon procedures engagement unless the definition of materiality is agreed to by the specified parties. Any agreed-upon materiality limits should be described in the practitioner's report.

.26 The practitioner should avoid vague or ambiguous language in reporting findings. Examples of appropriate and inappropriate descriptions of findings resulting from the application of certain agreed-upon procedures follow.

Procedures Agreed Upon	*Appropriate Description of Findings*	*Inappropriate Description of Findings*
Inspect the shipment dates for a sample (agreed-upon) of specified shipping documents, and determine whether any such dates were subsequent to December 31, 20XX.	No shipment dates shown on the sample of shipping documents were subsequent to December 31, 20XX.	Nothing came to my attention as a result of applying that procedure.
Calculate the number of blocks of streets paved during the year ended September 30, 20XX, shown on contractors' certificates of project completion; compare the resultant number to the number in an identified chart of performance statistics.	The number of blocks of streets paved in the chart of performance statistics was Y blocks more than the number calculated from the contractors' certificates of project completion.	The number of blocks of streets paved approximated the number of blocks included in the chart of performance statistics.
Calculate the rate of return on a specified investment (according to an agreed-upon formula) and verify that the resultant percentage agrees to the percentage in an identified schedule.	No exceptions were found as a result of applying the procedure.	The resultant percentage approximated the predetermined percentage in the identified schedule.

Procedures Agreed Upon	*Appropriate Description of Findings*	*Inappropriate Description of Findings*
Inspect the quality standards classification codes in identified performance test documents for products produced during a specified period; compare such codes to those shown in an identified computer printout.	All classification codes inspected in the identified documents were the same as those shown in the computer printout except for the following: [*List all exceptions.*]	All classification codes appeared to comply with such performance documents.
Trace all outstanding checks appearing on a bank reconciliation as of a certain date to checks cleared in the bank statement of the subsequent month.	All outstanding checks appearing on the bank reconciliation were cleared in the subsequent month's bank statement except for the following: [*List all exceptions.*]	Nothing came to my attention as a result of applying the procedure.
Compare the amounts of the invoices included in the "over ninety days" column shown in an identified schedule of aged accounts receivable of a specific customer as of a certain date to the amount and invoice date shown on the outstanding invoice and determine whether or not the invoice dates precede the date indicated on the schedule by more than ninety days.	All outstanding invoice amounts agreed with the amounts shown on the schedule in the "over ninety days" column, and the dates shown on such invoices preceded the date indicated on the schedule by more than ninety days.	The outstanding invoice amounts agreed within approximation of the amounts shown on the schedule in the "over ninety days" column, and nothing came to our attention that the dates shown on such invoices preceded the date indicated on the schedule by more than ninety days.

Working Papers

[.27–.30] [Paragraphs deleted by the issuance of SSAE No. 11, January 2002.][8–9]

[8–9] [Footnotes deleted by the issuance of SSAE No. 11, January 2002.]

Reporting

Required Elements

.31 The practitioner's report on agreed-upon procedures should be in the form of procedures and findings. The practitioner's report should contain the following elements:

a. A title that includes the word *independent*

b. Identification of the specified parties (See paragraph .36.)

c. Identification of the subject matter[10] (or the written assertion related thereto) and the character of the engagement

d. Identification of the responsible party

e. A statement that the subject matter is the responsibility of the responsible party

f. A statement that the procedures performed were those agreed to by the specified parties identified in the report

g. A statement that the agreed-upon procedures engagement was conducted in accordance with attestation standards established by the AICPA

h. A statement that the sufficiency of the procedures is solely the responsibility of the specified parties and a disclaimer of responsibility for the sufficiency of those procedures

i. A list of the procedures performed (or reference thereto) and related findings (The practitioner should not provide negative assurance—see paragraph .24.)

j. Where applicable, a description of any agreed-upon materiality limits (See paragraph .25.)

k. A statement that the practitioner was not engaged to and did not conduct an examination[11,12] of the subject matter, the objective of which would be the expression of an opinion, a disclaimer of opinion on the subject matter, and a statement that if the practitioner had performed

---

[10] In some agreed-upon procedures engagements, the practitioner may be asked to apply agreed-upon procedures to more than one subject matter or assertion. In these engagements, the practitioner may issue one report that refers to all subject matter covered or assertions presented. (For example, see paragraph .28 of section 601.)

[11] If the practitioner also wishes to refer to a review, alternate wording would be as follows.

> A statement that the practitioner was not engaged to and did not conduct an examination or a review of the subject matter, the objectives of which would be the expression of an opinion or limited assurance, a disclaimer of opinion on the subject matter, and a statement that if the practitioner had performed additional procedures, other matters might have come to his or her attention that would have been reported.

[12] If the subject matter consists of elements, accounts, or items of a financial statement, this statement may be worded as follows.

> We were not engaged to and did not conduct an audit [*or a review*], the objective of which would be the expression of an opinion [*or limited assurance*] on the [*identify elements, accounts, or items of a financial statement*]. Accordingly, we do not express such an opinion [*or limited assurance*].

Alternatively, the wording may be the following.

> These agreed-upon procedures do not constitute an audit [*or a review*] of financial statements or any part thereof, the objective of which is the expression of opinion [or limited assurance] on the financial statements or a part thereof.

additional procedures, other matters might have come to his or her attention that would have been reported[13]

l. A statement of restrictions on the use of the report because it is intended to be used solely by the specified parties[14]

m. Where applicable, reservations or restrictions concerning procedures or findings as discussed in paragraphs .33, .35, and .39–.40

n. For an agreed-upon procedures engagement on prospective financial information, all items included in paragraph .55 of section 301

o. Where applicable, a description of the nature of the assistance provided by a specialist as discussed in paragraphs .19–.21

p. The manual or printed signature of the practitioner's firm

q. The date of the report

Illustrative Report

.32 The following is an illustration of an agreed-upon procedures report.

Independent Accountant's Report
<u>on Applying Agreed-Upon Procedures</u>

To the Audit Committees and Managements of ABC Inc. and XYZ Fund:

We have performed the procedures enumerated below, which were agreed to by the audit committees and managements of ABC Inc. and XYZ Fund, solely to assist you in evaluating the accompanying Statement of Investment Performance Statistics of XYZ Fund (prepared in accordance with the criteria specified therein) for the year ended December 31, 20X1. XYZ Fund's management is responsible for the statement of investment performance statistics. This agreed-upon procedures engagement was conducted in accordance with attestation standards established by the American Institute of Certified Public Accountants. The sufficiency of these procedures is solely the responsibility of those parties specified in this report. Consequently, we make no representation regarding the sufficiency of the procedures described below either for the purpose for which this report has been requested or for any other purpose.

[*Include paragraphs to enumerate procedures and findings.*]

We were not engaged to and did not conduct an examination, the objective of which would be the expression of an opinion on the accompanying Statement of Investment Performance Statistics of XYZ Fund. Accordingly, we do not express such an opinion. Had we performed additional procedures, other matters might have come to our attention that would have been reported to you.

This report is intended solely for the information and use of the audit committees and managements of ABC Inc. and XYZ Fund,[15] and is not intended to be and should not be used by anyone other than these specified parties.

[*Signature*]

[*Date*]

---

[13] [Footnote deleted, December 2012, to reflect conforming changes necessary due to the issuance of SSARS No. 19 and SAS Nos. 122–126.]

[14] The purpose of the restriction on the use of the practitioner's report on applying agreed-upon procedures is to restrict its use to only those parties that have agreed upon the procedures performed and taken responsibility for the sufficiency of the procedures. Paragraph .36 describes the process for adding parties who were not originally contemplated in the agreed-upon procedures engagement.

[15] The report may list the specified parties or refer the reader to the specified parties listed elsewhere in the report.

Explanatory Language

.33 The practitioner also may include explanatory language about matters such as the following:

- Disclosure of stipulated facts, assumptions, or interpretations (including the source thereof) used in the application of agreed-upon procedures (For example, see paragraph .26 of section 601.)
- Description of the condition of records, controls, or data to which the procedures were applied
- Explanation that the practitioner has no responsibility to update his or her report
- Explanation of sampling risk

Dating of Report

.34 The date of completion of the agreed-upon procedures should be used as the date of the practitioner's report.

Restrictions on the Performance of Procedures

.35 When circumstances impose restrictions on the performance of the agreed-upon procedures, the practitioner should attempt to obtain agreement from the specified parties for modification of the agreed-upon procedures. When such agreement cannot be obtained (for example, when the agreed-upon procedures are published by a regulatory agency that will not modify the procedures), the practitioner should describe any restrictions on the performance of procedures in his or her report or withdraw from the engagement.

Adding Specified Parties (Nonparticipant Parties)

.36 Subsequent to the completion of the agreed-upon procedures engagement, a practitioner may be requested to consider the addition of another party as a specified party (*a nonparticipant party*). The practitioner may agree to add a nonparticipant party as a specified party, based on consideration of such factors as the identity of the nonparticipant party and the intended use of the report.[16] If the practitioner does agree to add the nonparticipant party, he or she should obtain affirmative acknowledgment, normally in writing, from the nonparticipant party agreeing to the procedures performed and of its taking responsibility for the sufficiency of the procedures. If the nonparticipant party is added after the practitioner has issued his or her report, the report may be reissued or the practitioner may provide other written acknowledgment that the nonparticipant party has been added as a specified party. If the report is reissued, the report date should not be changed. If the practitioner provides written acknowledgment that the nonparticipant party has been added as a specified party, such written acknowledgment ordinarily should state that no procedures have been performed subsequent to the date of the report.

---

[16] When considering whether to add a nonparticipant party, the guidance in paragraphs .A27–.A28 of AU-C section 560, *Subsequent Events and Subsequently Discovered Facts*, may be helpful. [Footnote revised, December 2012, to reflect conforming changes necessary due to the issuance of SAS Nos. 122–126.]

Written Representations

.37 A practitioner may find a representation letter to be a useful and practical means of obtaining representations from the responsible party. The need for such a letter may depend on the nature of the engagement and the specified parties. For example, paragraph .68 of section 601 requires a practitioner to obtain written representations from the responsible party in an agreed-upon procedures engagement related to compliance with specified requirements.

.38 Examples of matters that might appear in a representation letter from the responsible party include the following:

a. A statement acknowledging responsibility for the subject matter and, when applicable, the assertion

b. A statement acknowledging responsibility for selecting the criteria and for determining that such criteria are appropriate for their purposes

c. The assertion about the subject matter based on the criteria selected

d. A statement that all known matters contradicting the subject matter or the assertion and any communication from regulatory agencies affecting the subject matter or the assertion has been disclosed to the practitioner

e. Availability of all records relevant to the subject matter and the agreed-upon procedures

f. Other matters as the practitioner deems appropriate

.39 The responsible party's refusal to furnish written representations determined by the practitioner to be appropriate for the engagement constitutes a limitation on the performance of the engagement. In such circumstances, the practitioner should do one of the following.

a. Disclose in his or her report the inability to obtain representations from the responsible party.

b. Withdraw from the engagement.[17]

c. Change the engagement to another form of engagement.

Knowledge of Matters Outside Agreed-Upon Procedures

.40 The practitioner need not perform procedures beyond the agreed-upon procedures. However, in connection with the application of agreed-upon procedures, if matters come to the practitioner's attention by other means that significantly contradict the subject matter (or written assertion related thereto) referred to in the practitioner's report, the practitioner should include this matter in his or her report.[18] For example, if, during the course of applying

---

[17] For an agreed-upon procedures engagement performed pursuant to section 601, management's refusal to furnish all required representations also constitutes a limitation on the scope of the engagement that requires the practitioner to withdraw from the engagement.

[18] If the practitioner has performed (or has been engaged to perform) an audit of the entity's financial statements to which an element, account, or item of a financial statement relates and the auditor's report on such financial statements includes a departure from a standard report (see AU-C section 805, *Special Considerations—Audits of Single Financial Statements and Specific Elements, Accounts, or Items of a Financial Statement*), he or she should consider including a reference to the auditor's report and the departure from the standard report in his or her agreed-upon procedures report. [Footnote revised, December 2012, to reflect conforming changes necessary due to the issuance of SAS Nos. 122–126.]

agreed-upon procedures regarding an entity's internal control, the practitioner becomes aware of a material weakness by means other than performance of the agreed-upon procedure, the practitioner should include this matter in his or her report.

Change to an Agreed-Upon Procedures Engagement From Another Form of Engagement

.41 A practitioner who has been engaged to perform another form of attest engagement or a nonattest service engagement may, before the engagement's completion, be requested to change the engagement to an agreed-upon procedures engagement under this section. A request to change the engagement may result from a change in circumstances affecting the client's requirements, a misunderstanding about the nature of the original services or the alternative services originally available, or a restriction on the performance of the original engagement, whether imposed by the client or caused by circumstances.

.42 Before a practitioner who was engaged to perform another form of engagement agrees to change the engagement to an agreed-upon procedures engagement, he or she should consider the following:

a. The possibility that certain procedures performed as part of another type of engagement are not appropriate for inclusion in an agreed-upon procedures engagement

b. The reason given for the request, particularly the implications of a restriction on the scope of the original engagement or the matters to be reported

c. The additional effort required to complete the original engagement

d. If applicable, the reasons for changing from a general-use report to a restricted-use report

.43 If the specified parties acknowledge agreement to the procedures performed or to be performed and assume responsibility for the sufficiency of the procedures to be included in the agreed-upon procedures engagement, either of the following would be considered a reasonable basis for requesting a change in the engagement—

a. A change in circumstances that requires another form of engagement

b. A misunderstanding concerning the nature of the original engagement or the available alternatives

.44 In all circumstances, if the original engagement procedures are substantially complete or the effort to complete such procedures is relatively insignificant, the practitioner should consider the propriety of accepting a change in the engagement.

.45 If the practitioner concludes, based on his or her professional judgment, that there is reasonable justification to change the engagement, and provided he or she complies with the standards applicable to agreed-upon procedures engagements, the practitioner should issue an appropriate agreed-upon procedures report. The report should not include reference to either the original engagement or performance limitations that resulted in the changed engagement. (See paragraph .40.)

Combined Reports Covering Both Restricted-Use and General-Use Subject Matter or Presentations

.46 When a practitioner performs services pursuant to an engagement to apply agreed-upon procedures to specific subject matter as part of or in addition to another form of service, this section applies only to those services described herein; other Standards would apply to the other services. Other services may include an audit, review, or compilation of a financial statement, another attest service performed pursuant to the SSAEs, or a nonattest service.[19] Reports on applying agreed-upon procedures to specific subject matter may be combined with reports on such other services, provided the types of services can be clearly distinguished and the applicable Standards for each service are followed. See paragraphs .82–.83 of section 101 regarding restricting the use of the combined report.

Effective Date

.47 This section is effective when the subject matter or assertion is as of or for a period ending on or after June 1, 2001. Early application is permitted.

---

[19] See paragraphs .105–.107 of section 101 for requirements relating to attest services provided as part of a consulting service engagement.

Appendix

Additional Illustrative Reports

The following are additional illustrations of reporting on applying agreed-upon procedures to elements, accounts, or items of a financial statement.

1. Report in Connection With a Proposed Acquisition

Independent Accountant's Report
on Applying Agreed-Upon Procedures

To the Board of Directors and Management of X Company:

We have performed the procedures enumerated below, which were agreed to by the Board of Directors and Management of X Company, solely to assist you in connection with the proposed acquisition of Y Company as of December 31, 20XX. Y Company is responsible for its cash and accounts receivable records. This agreed-upon procedures engagement was conducted in accordance with attestation standards established by the American Institute of Certified Public Accountants. The sufficiency of these procedures is solely the responsibility of the parties specified in this report. Consequently, we make no representation regarding the sufficiency of the procedures described below either for the purpose for which this report has been requested or for any other purpose.

The procedures and the associated findings are as follows:

Cash

1. We obtained confirmation of the cash on deposit from the following banks, and we agreed the confirmed balance to the amount shown on the bank reconciliations maintained by Y Company. We mathematically checked the bank reconciliations and compared the resultant cash balances per book to the respective general ledger account balances.

Bank	*General Ledger Account Balances as of December 31, 20XX*
ABC National Bank	$ 5,000
DEF State Bank	3,776
XYZ Trust Company regular account	86,912
XYZ Trust Company payroll account	5,000
	$110,688

We found no exceptions as a result of the procedures.

Accounts Receivable

2. We added the individual customer account balances shown in an aged trial balance of accounts receivable (identified as Exhibit A) and compared the resultant total with the balance in the general ledger account.

   We found no difference.

3. We compared the individual customer account balances shown in the aged trial balance of accounts receivable (Exhibit A) as of December 31, 19XX, to the balances shown in the accounts receivable subsidiary ledger.

   We found no exceptions as a result of the comparisons.

4. We traced the aging (according to invoice dates) for 50 customer account balances shown in Exhibit A to the details of outstanding invoices in the accounts receivable subsidiary ledger. The balances selected for tracing were determined by starting at the eighth item and selecting every fifteenth item thereafter.

   We found no exceptions in the aging of the amounts of the 50 customer account balances selected. The sample size traced was 9.8 percent of the aggregate amount of the customer account balances.

5. We mailed confirmations directly to the customers representing the 150 largest customer account balances selected from the accounts receivable trial balance, and we received responses as indicated below. We also traced the items constituting the outstanding customer account balance to invoices and supporting shipping documents for customers from which there was no reply. As agreed, any individual differences in a customer account balance of less than $300 were to be considered minor, and no further procedures were performed.

   Of the 150 customer balances confirmed, we received responses from 140 customers; 10 customers did not reply. No exceptions were identified in 120 of the confirmations received. The differences disclosed in the remaining 20 confirmation replies were either minor in amount (as defined above) or were reconciled to the customer account balance without proposed adjustment thereto. A summary of the confirmation results according to the respective aging categories is as follows.

		Accounts Receivable December 31, 20XX	
Aging Categories	*Customer Account Balances*	*Confirmations Requested*	*Confirmations Received*
Current	$156,000	$ 76,000	$ 65,000
Past due:			
Less than one month:	60,000	30,000	19,000
One to three months	36,000	18,000	10,000
Over three months	48,000	48,000	8,000
	$300,000	$172,000	$102,000

We were not engaged to and did not conduct an audit, the objective of which would be the expression of an opinion on cash and accounts receivable. Accordingly, we do not express such an opinion. Had we performed additional procedures, other matters might have come to our attention that would have been reported to you.

This report is intended solely for the information and use of the board of directors and management of X Company and is not intended to be and should not be used by anyone other than these specified parties.

[*Signature*]

[*Date*]

2. Report in Connection With Claims of Creditors

Independent Accountant's Report
on Applying Agreed-Upon Procedures

To the Trustee of XYZ Company:

We have performed the procedures described below, which were agreed to by the Trustee of XYZ Company, with respect to the claims of creditors solely to assist you in determining the validity of claims of XYZ Company as of May 31, 20XX, as set forth in the accompanying Schedule A. XYZ Company is responsible for maintaining records of claims submitted by creditors of XYZ Company. This agreed-upon procedures engagement was conducted in accordance with attestation standards established by the American Institute of Certified Public Accountants. The sufficiency of these procedures is solely the responsibility of the party specified in this report. Consequently, we make no representation regarding the sufficiency of the procedures described below either for the purpose for which this report has been requested or for any other purpose.

The procedures and associated findings are as follows:

1. Compare the total of the trial balance of accounts payable at May 31, 20XX, prepared by XYZ Company, to the balance in the related general ledger account.

   The total of the accounts payable trial balance agreed with the balance in the related general ledger account.

2. Compare the amounts for claims received from creditors (as shown in claim documents provided by XYZ Company) to the respective amounts shown in the trial balance of accounts payable. Using the data included in the claims documents and in XYZ Company's accounts payable detail records, reconcile any differences found to the accounts payable trial balance.

   All differences noted are presented in column 3 of Schedule A. Except for those amounts shown in column 4 of Schedule A, all such differences were reconciled.

3. Obtain the documentation submitted by creditors in support of the amounts claimed and compare it to the following documentation in XYZ Company's files: invoices, receiving reports, and other evidence of receipt of goods or services.

   No exceptions were found as a result of these comparisons.

We were not engaged to and did not conduct an audit, the objective of which would be the expression of an opinion on the claims of creditors set forth in the accompanying Schedule A. Accordingly, we do not express such an opinion. Had we performed additional procedures, other matters might have come to our attention that would have been reported to you.

This report is intended solely for the information and use of the Trustee of XYZ Company and is not intended to be and should not be used by anyone other than this specified party.

[*Signature*]

[*Date*]

AT Section 9201

Agreed-Upon Procedures Engagements: Attest Engagements Interpretation of Section 201

1. Third-Party Due Diligence Services Related to Asset-Backed Securitizations: SEC Release No. 34-72936

.01 SEC Release No. 34-72936, *Nationally Recognized Statistical Rating Organizations* (the release [1]), acknowledges that certain procedures often performed by practitioners as agreed-upon procedures (AUP) engagements related to asset-backed securitizations (ABS) are considered third-party *due diligence services* (as defined in the release). These include due diligence services that relate to checking the accuracy of the information or data about the assets provided by the securitizer or originator of the assets. For example, comparing the information on a loan tape with the information contained on the hard-copy documents in a loan file is an activity that falls within the definition of due diligence services.

.02 For an AUP engagement performed that is considered due diligence services, as defined in the release, the specified parties are typically only the issuer or the underwriter(s), or both.

.03 The release requires the following:

- The issuer or underwriter of any ABS to make publicly available the findings and conclusions of any third-party due diligence report obtained by the issuer or underwriter. The release further describes that the disclosure of the findings and conclusions includes disclosure of the criteria against which the loans were evaluated, and how the evaluated loans compared to those criteria, along with the basis for including any loans not meeting those criteria. This is accomplished by including such information in Form ABS-15G, "Asset-Backed Securitizer Report Pursuant to Section 15G of the Securities Exchange Act of 1934," which is required to be furnished by the issuer or underwriter to the SEC through the Electronic Data Gathering, Analysis, and Retrieval (EDGAR) system.
- Any third-party due diligence service provider to complete Form ABS Due Diligence-15E, "Certification of Provider of Third-Party Due Diligence Services for Asset-Backed Securities" (the prescribed form). The prescribed form elicits information about the due diligence performed, including a description of the work performed (Item 4 of the prescribed form) and a summary of findings and conclusions of the third party (Item 5 of the prescribed form).

---

[1] For purposes of this interpretation, the term *release* refers to the SEC rules amended by SEC Release No. 34-72936, *Nationally Recognized Statistical Rating Organizations*, and the accompanying release text.

.04 The release states the following:

> The Commission understands there may be particular considerations that would need to be taken into account under applicable professional standards that govern certain services provided by the accounting profession. The requirements and limitations resulting from relevant professional standards generally are described within the reports issued and, to the extent such requirements or limitations are based upon professional standards, the Commission would not object to the inclusion of the same description in the written certifications on [the prescribed form].

.05 The prescribed form is required to be signed by the due diligence provider. The prescribed form is also required to be provided to any nationally recognized statistical rating organization (NRSRO) that produces a credit rating for an ABS to which such due diligence services relate. The release describes that the due diligence provider will be deemed to have met this obligation by providing the prescribed form to the issuer, sponsor, or underwriter of the securitization that maintains the Rule 17g-5 website. The purpose of the Rule 17g-5 website is to make information related to ABS transactions accessible to all NRSROs. Additionally, the release requires the prescribed form to be provided to any NRSRO that specifically requests it.

.06 When the NRSRO produces a credit rating, the release requires that it publicly disclose each prescribed form that was posted to the Rule 17g-5 website. Such information is expected to be posted on the website of the specific NRSRO, not on the EDGAR system. The release indicates that the decision to allow the NRSRO to disclose the prescribed form in the manner previously described, instead of through the EDGAR system, was to limit additional cost that would be incurred from having the NRSRO submit the prescribed forms through the EDGAR system.

.07 In most instances, Form ABS-15G will be furnished through the EDGAR system either prior to or at the same time as the prescribed form is posted to the Rule 17g-5 website.

.08 Therefore, the procedures or findings, or both, of due diligence services (as defined in the release) conducted as AUP engagements are made public via Form ABS-15G through the EDGAR system or via the prescribed form through the process by which the NRSRO publishes its credit ratings, or both.

.09 *Question*—The release requires the public disclosure of the procedures or findings, or both, of the practitioner's due diligence services in the prescribed form and Form ABS-15G, as applicable. Is the distribution of such procedures or findings, or both, prohibited under section 201, *Agreed-Upon Procedures Engagements*, when such services are performed as an AUP engagement?

.10 *Interpretation*—No. The distribution of the procedures or findings, or both, of the practitioner's due diligence services in the prescribed form or Form ABS-15G is not prohibited. A practitioner is not required to prohibit the distribution of the procedures or findings, or both, contained in the AUP report that may be disclosed in the prescribed form or Form ABS-15G because the distribution of that information is required by regulation to be made available to the public, as described in paragraphs .01–.08 of this interpretation.

.11 Footnote 16 of section 101, *Attest Engagements*, states, "In some cases, restricted-use reports filed with regulatory agencies are required by law or regulation to be made available to the public as a matter of public record. Also, a regulatory agency as part of its oversight responsibility for an entity may require access to restricted-use reports in which they are not named as a specified party."

.12 *Question*—The prescribed form contains certain language that is inconsistent with language commonly used in AUP reports and could be misinterpreted by those who have access to the prescribed form (for example, the term *review* is included in the prescribed form). In addition, the prescribed form does not include all elements of an AUP report required by paragraph .31 of section 201.

.13 What are the practitioner's responsibilities when due diligence services (as defined in the release) have been performed as an AUP engagement and the practitioner is required to complete the prescribed form, which includes language that is inconsistent with the practitioner's function or responsibility, or is incomplete with respect to the reporting requirements of the professional standards?

.14 *Interpretation*—Paragraph .67 of section 9101, *Attest Engagements: Attest Engagements Interpretations of Section 101*, addresses such a situation in the context of reporting on the suitability of the design of an entity's internal control under section 101 and indicates that the practitioner should either reword the prescribed form of report or attach an appropriately worded separate report that conforms with the practitioner's function or responsibility and professional standards. Therefore, when completing the prescribed form for due diligence services that have been performed as an AUP engagement, the practitioner should include all of the elements in paragraph .31 of section 201 and any clarifying wording to avoid any misinterpretation. This may be accomplished by either adding wording to the prescribed form or attaching an appropriately worded separate report to the prescribed form, or both.

.15 *Question*—How might the practitioner modify the illustrative report wording in section 201 in order to clarify the requirements and limitations of AUP engagements and reports as it relates to due diligence services as defined in the release?

.16 *Interpretation*—Paragraph .79 of section 101 states the following:

> The need for restriction on the use of a report may result from a number of circumstances, including the purpose of the report, the criteria used in preparation of the subject matter, the extent to which the procedures performed are known or understood, and the potential for the report to be misunderstood when taken out of the context in which it was intended to be used. A practitioner should consider informing his or her client that restricted-use reports are not intended for distribution to non-specified parties, regardless of whether they are included in a document containing a separate general-use report.[16, 17] However, a practitioner is not responsible for controlling a client's distribution of restricted-use reports. Accordingly, a restricted-use report should alert readers to the restriction on the use of the report by indicating that the report is not intended to be and should not be used by anyone other than the specified parties.

[16, 17] Footnotes omitted for purposes of this interpretation.

.17 As noted in paragraph .31 of section 201 and paragraph .79 of section 101, a practitioner does have a responsibility to disclose certain limitations of AUP engagements in the AUP report. However, the modifications can be made only to meet the requirements of the professional standards.

.18 Because distribution of procedures or findings, or both, to non-specified parties may cause those non-specified parties to misunderstand the restricted use limitations of AUP reports, the practitioner may modify the illustrative language in paragraph .32 of section 201, consistent with the requirements in paragraph .31*l* of section 201, to clarify in the AUP report or prescribed form that the information with respect to the procedures or findings, or both, contained therein is not intended to be used by non-specified parties that may have access to the procedures or findings, or both, as required by the release (for example, NRSROs and investors).

.19 Because the prescribed form utilizes the term *review*, the practitioner may also add language in the prescribed form that the practitioner did not conduct a review in accordance with the AICPA attestation standards.

[Issue Date: February 2015.]

AT Section 301
Financial Forecasts and Projections

Source: SSAE No. 10; SSAE No. 11; SSAE No. 17.

Effective when the date of the practitioner's report is on or after June 1, 2001, unless otherwise indicated.

Introduction

.01 This section sets forth standards and provides guidance to practitioners who are engaged to issue or do issue examination (paragraphs .29–.50), compilation (paragraphs .12–.28), or agreed-upon procedures reports (paragraphs .51–.56) on prospective financial statements.

.02 Whenever a practitioner (*a*) submits, to his or her client or others, prospective financial statements that he or she has assembled, or assisted in assembling, that are or reasonably might be expected to be used by another (third) party[1] or (*b*) reports on prospective financial statements that are, or reasonably might be expected to be used by another (third) party, the practitioner should perform one of the engagements described in the preceding paragraph. In deciding whether the prospective financial statements are or reasonably might be expected to be used by a third party, the practitioner may rely on either the written or oral representation of the responsible party, unless information comes to his or her attention that contradicts the responsible party's representation. If such third-party use of the prospective financial statements is not reasonably expected, the provisions of this section are not applicable unless the practitioner has been engaged to examine, compile, or apply agreed-upon procedures to the prospective financial statements.

.03 This section also provides standards for a practitioner who is engaged to examine, compile, or apply agreed-upon procedures to partial presentations. A partial presentation is a presentation of prospective financial information that excludes one or more of the items required for prospective financial statements as described in appendix A [paragraph .68], "Minimum Presentation Guidelines."

.04 The practitioner who has been engaged to or does compile, examine, or apply agreed-upon procedures to a partial presentation should perform the engagement in accordance with the guidance in paragraphs .12–.28 for compilations, .29–.50 for examinations, and .51–.56 for agreed-upon procedures, respectively, modified to reflect the nature of the presentation as discussed in paragraphs .03 and .57–.58.

.05 This section does not provide standards or procedures for engagements involving prospective financial statements used solely in connection with litigation support services. A practitioner may, however, look to these standards because they provide helpful guidance for many aspects of such engagements and may be referred to as useful guidance in such engagements. Litigation support services are engagements involving pending or potential formal legal proceedings before a trier of fact in connection with the resolution

---

[1] However, paragraph .59 permits an exception to this for certain types of budgets.

of a dispute between two or more parties, for example, when a practitioner acts as an expert witness. This exception is provided because, among other things, the practitioner's work in such proceedings is ordinarily subject to detailed analysis and challenge by each party to the dispute. This exception does not apply, however, if either of the following occur.

a. The practitioner is specifically engaged to issue or does issue an examination, a compilation, or an agreed-upon procedures report on prospective financial statements.

b. The prospective financial statements are for use by third parties who, under the rules of the proceedings, do not have the opportunity for analysis and challenge by each party to a dispute in a legal proceeding.

For example, creditors may not have such opportunities when prospective financial statements are submitted to them to secure their agreement to a plan of reorganization.

.06 In reporting on prospective financial statements, the practitioner may be called on to assist the responsible party in identifying assumptions, gathering information, or assembling the statements.[2] The responsible party is nonetheless responsible for the preparation and presentation of the prospective financial statements because the prospective financial statements are dependent on the actions, plans, and assumptions of the responsible party, and only it can take responsibility for the assumptions. Accordingly, the practitioner's engagement should not be characterized in his or her report or in the document containing his or her report as including "preparation" of the prospective financial statements. A practitioner may be engaged to prepare a financial analysis of a potential project where the engagement includes obtaining the information, making appropriate assumptions, and assembling the presentation. Such an analysis is not and should not be characterized as a forecast or projection and would not be appropriate for general use. However, if the responsible party reviewed and adopted the assumptions and presentation, or based its assumptions and presentation on the analysis, the practitioner could perform one of the engagements described in this section and issue a report appropriate for general use.

.07 The concept of materiality affects the application of this section to prospective financial statements as materiality affects the application of generally accepted auditing standards (GAAS) to historical financial statements. Materiality is a concept that is judged in light of the expected range of reasonableness of the information; therefore, users should not expect prospective information (information about events that have not yet occurred) to be as precise as historical information.

Definitions

.08 For the purposes of this section the following definitions apply.

a. *Prospective financial statements*—Either financial forecasts or financial projections including the summaries of significant assumptions and accounting policies. Although prospective financial statements may cover a period that has partially expired, statements for periods that have completely expired are not considered to be prospective

[2] Some of these services may not be appropriate if the practitioner is to be named as the person reporting on an examination in a filing with the Securities and Exchange Commission (SEC). SEC Release Nos. 33-5992 and 34-15305, "Disclosure of Projections of Future Economic Performance," state that for prospective financial statements filed with the commission, "a person should not be named as an outside reviewer if he actively assisted in the preparation of the projection."

financial statements. Pro forma financial statements and partial presentations are not considered to be prospective financial statements.[3]

b. *Partial presentation*—A presentation of prospective financial information that excludes one or more of the items required for prospective financial statements as described in appendix A (paragraph .68), "Minimum Presentation Guidelines." Partial presentations are not ordinarily appropriate for general use; accordingly, partial presentations should be restricted for use by specified parties who will be negotiating directly with the responsible party.

c. *Financial forecast*—Prospective financial statements that present, to the best of the responsible party's knowledge and belief, an entity's expected financial position, results of operations, and cash flows. A financial forecast is based on the responsible party's assumptions reflecting the conditions it expects to exist and the course of action it expects to take. A financial forecast may be expressed in specific monetary amounts as a single point estimate of forecasted results or as a range, where the responsible party selects key assumptions to form a range within which it reasonably expects, to the best of its knowledge and belief, the item or items subject to the assumptions to actually fall. When a forecast contains a range, the range is not selected in a biased or misleading manner, for example, a range in which one end is significantly less expected than the other. Minimum presentation guidelines for prospective financial statements are set forth in appendix A (paragraph .68).

d. *Financial projection*—Prospective financial statements that present, to the best of the responsible party's knowledge and belief, given one or more hypothetical assumptions, an entity's expected financial position, results of operations, and cash flows. A financial projection is sometimes prepared to present one or more hypothetical courses of action for evaluation, as in response to a question such as, "What would happen if . . . ?" A financial projection is based on the responsible party's assumptions reflecting conditions it expects would exist and the course of action it expects would be taken, given one or more hypothetical assumptions. A projection, like a forecast, may contain a range. Minimum presentation guidelines for prospective financial statements are set forth in appendix A (paragraph .68).

e. *Entity*—Any unit, existing or to be formed, for which financial statements could be prepared in accordance with generally accepted accounting principles (GAAP) or a special purpose framework.[4] For example, an entity can be an individual, partnership, corporation, trust, estate, association, or governmental unit.

f. *Hypothetical assumption*—An assumption used in a financial projection to present a condition or course of action that is not necessarily expected to occur, but is consistent with the purpose of the projection.

---

3 The objective of pro forma financial information is to show what the significant effects on the historical financial information might have been had a consummated or proposed transaction (or event) occurred at an earlier date. Although the transaction in question may be prospective, this section does not apply to such presentations because they are essentially historical financial statements and do not purport to be prospective financial statements. See section 401, *Reporting on Pro Forma Financial Information*.

4 AU-C section 800, *Special Considerations—Audits of Financial Statements Prepared in Accordance With Special Purpose Frameworks*, defines a *special purpose framework* as a cash, tax, regulatory, or contractual basis of accounting (commonly referred to as *comprehensive bases of accounting other than GAAP*). [Footnote revised, December 2012, to reflect conforming changes necessary due to the issuance of SAS Nos. 122–126.]

g. *Responsible party*—The person or persons who are responsible for the assumptions underlying the prospective financial statements. The responsible party usually is management, but it can be persons outside of the entity who do not currently have the authority to direct operations (for example, a party considering acquiring the entity).

h. *Assembly*—The manual or computer processing of mathematical or other clerical functions related to the presentation of the prospective financial statements. Assembly does not refer to the mere reproduction and collation of such statements or to the responsible party's use of the practitioner's computer processing hardware or software.

i. *Key factors*—The significant matters on which an entity's future results are expected to depend. Such factors are basic to the entity's operations and thus encompass matters that affect, among other things, the entity's sales, production, service, and financing activities. Key factors serve as a foundation for prospective financial statements and are the bases for the assumptions.

[Revised, December 2012, to reflect conforming changes necessary due to the issuance of SAS Nos. 122–126.]

Uses of Prospective Financial Statements

.09 Prospective financial statements are for either *general use* or *limited use*. *General use* of prospective financial statements refers to the use of the statements by persons with whom the responsible party is not negotiating directly, for example, in an offering statement of an entity's debt or equity interests. Because recipients of prospective financial statements distributed for general use are unable to ask the responsible party directly about the presentation, the presentation most useful to them is one that portrays, to the best of the responsible party's knowledge and belief, the expected results. Thus, only a financial forecast is appropriate for general use.

.10 *Limited use* of prospective financial statements refers to the use of prospective financial statements by the responsible party alone or by the responsible party and third parties with whom the responsible party is negotiating directly. Examples include use in negotiations for a bank loan, submission to a regulatory agency, and use solely within the entity. Third-party recipients of prospective financial statements intended for limited use can ask questions of the responsible party and negotiate terms directly with it. Any type of prospective financial statements that would be useful in the circumstances would normally be appropriate for limited use. Thus, the presentation may be a financial forecast or a financial projection.

.11 Because a financial projection is not appropriate for general use, a practitioner should not consent to the use of his or her name in conjunction with a financial projection that he or she believes will be distributed to those who will not be negotiating directly with the responsible party, for example, in an offering statement of an entity's debt or equity interests, unless the projection is used to supplement a financial forecast.

Compilation of Prospective Financial Statements

.12 A compilation of prospective financial statements is a professional service that involves the following:

a. Assembling, to the extent necessary, the prospective financial statements based on the responsible party's assumptions

b. Performing the required compilation procedures,[5] including reading the prospective financial statements with their summaries of significant assumptions and accounting policies, and considering whether they appear to be presented in conformity with AICPA presentation guidelines[6] and not obviously inappropriate

c. Issuing a compilation report

.13 A compilation is not intended to provide assurance on the prospective financial statements or the assumptions underlying such statements. Because of the limited nature of the practitioner's procedures, a compilation does not provide assurance that the practitioner will become aware of significant matters that might be disclosed by more extensive procedures, for example, those performed in an examination of prospective financial statements.

.14 The summary of significant assumptions is essential to the reader's understanding of prospective financial statements. Accordingly, the practitioner should not compile prospective financial statements that exclude disclosure of the summary of significant assumptions. Also, the practitioner should not compile a financial projection that excludes either (*a*) an identification of the hypothetical assumptions or (*b*) a description of the limitations on the usefulness of the presentation.

.15 The following standards apply to a compilation of prospective financial statements and to the resulting report.

a. The compilation should be performed by a person or persons having adequate technical training and proficiency to compile prospective financial statements.

b. Due professional care should be exercised in the performance of the compilation and the preparation of the report.

c. The work should be adequately planned, and assistants, if any, should be properly supervised.

d. Applicable compilation procedures should be performed as a basis for reporting on the compiled prospective financial statements. (See appendix B [paragraph .69], "Training and Proficiency, Planning and Procedures Applicable to Compilations," for the procedures to be performed.)

e. The report based on the practitioner's compilation of prospective financial statements should conform to the applicable guidance in paragraphs .18–.28.

.16 The practitioner should consider, after applying the procedures specified in paragraph .69, whether representations or other information he or she has received appear to be obviously inappropriate, incomplete, or otherwise misleading, and if so, the practitioner should attempt to obtain additional or revised information. If he or she does not receive such information, the practitioner should ordinarily withdraw from the compilation engagement.[7] (Note that the

---

[5] See appendix B (paragraph .69), subparagraph 5, for the required procedures.

[6] AICPA presentation guidelines are detailed in AICPA Guide *Prospective Financial Information*.

[7] The practitioner need not withdraw from the engagement if the effect of such information on the prospective financial statement does not appear to be material.

omission of disclosures, other than those relating to significant assumptions, would not require the practitioner to withdraw. See paragraph .26.)

Working Papers

[.17] [Paragraph deleted by the issuance of SSAE No. 11, January 2002.]

Reports on Compiled Prospective Financial Statements

.18 The practitioner's standard report on a compilation of prospective financial statements should include the following:

a. An identification of the prospective financial statements presented by the responsible party

b. A statement that the practitioner has compiled the prospective financial statements in accordance with attestation standards established by the American Institute of Certified Public Accountants

c. A statement that a compilation is limited in scope and does not enable the practitioner to express an opinion or any other form of assurance on the prospective financial statements or the assumptions

d. A caveat that the prospective results may not be achieved

e. A statement that the practitioner assumes no responsibility to update the report for events and circumstances occurring after the date of the report

f. The manual or printed signature of the practitioner's firm

g. The date of the compilation report

.19 The following is the form of the practitioner's standard report on the compilation of a forecast that does not contain a range.[8]

> We have compiled the accompanying forecasted balance sheet, statements of income, retained earnings, and cash flows of XYZ Company as of December 31, 20XX, and for the year then ending, in accordance with attestation standards established by the American Institute of Certified Public Accountants.[9]
>
> A compilation is limited to presenting in the form of a forecast information that is the representation of management[10] and does not include evaluation of the support for the assumptions underlying the forecast. We have not examined the forecast and, accordingly, do not express an opinion or any other form of

---

[8] The forms of reports provided in this section are appropriate whether the presentation is based on GAAP or on a special purpose framework. [Footnote revised, December 2012, to reflect conforming changes necessary due to the issuance of SAS Nos. 122–126.]

[9] When the presentation is summarized as discussed in appendix A (paragraph .68), this sentence might read, "We have compiled the accompanying summarized forecast of XYZ Company as of December 31, 20XX, and for the year then ending in accordance with attestation standards established by the American Institute of Certified Public Accountants."

[10] If the responsible party is other than management, the references to management in the standard reports provided in this section should be changed to refer to the party who assumes responsibility for the assumptions.

assurance on the accompanying statements or assumptions. Furthermore, there will usually be differences between the forecasted and actual results, because events and circumstances frequently do not occur as expected, and those differences may be material. We have no responsibility to update this report for events and circumstances occurring after the date of this report.

[Signature]

[Date]

.20 When the presentation is a projection, the practitioner's compilation report should include the report elements set forth in paragraph .18. Additionally, the report should include a statement describing the special purpose for which the projection was prepared as well as a separate paragraph that restricts the use of the report because it is intended to be used solely by the specified parties. The following is the form of the practitioner's standard report on a compilation of a projection that does not contain a range.

> We have compiled the accompanying projected balance sheet, statements of income, retained earnings, and cash flows of XYZ Company as of December 31, 20XX, and for the year then ending, in accordance with attestation standards established by the American Institute of Certified Public Accountants.[11] The accompanying projection was prepared for [*state special purpose, for example, "the purpose of negotiating a loan to expand XYZ Company's plant"*].
>
> A compilation is limited to presenting in the form of a projection information that is the representation of management and does not include evaluation of the support for the assumptions underlying the projection. We have not examined the projection and, accordingly, do not express an opinion or any other form of assurance on the accompanying statements or assumptions. Furthermore, even if [*describe hypothetical assumption, for example, "the loan is granted and the plant is expanded,"*] there will usually be differences between the projected and actual results, because events and circumstances frequently do not occur as expected, and those differences may be material. We have no responsibility to update this report for events and circumstances occurring after the date of this report.
>
> The accompanying projection and this report are intended solely for the information and use of [*identify specified parties, for example, "XYZ Company and DEF Bank"*] and is not intended to be and should not be used by anyone other than these specified parties.
>
> *[Signature]*
>
> *[Date]*

.21 When the prospective financial statements contain a range, the practitioner's standard report should also include a separate paragraph that states that the responsible party has elected to portray the expected results of one or more assumptions as a range. The following is an example of the separate paragraph to be added to the practitioner's report when he or she compiles prospective financial statements, in this case a forecast, that contain a range.

> As described in the summary of significant assumptions, management of XYZ Company has elected to portray forecasted [*describe financial statement element*

---

[11] When the presentation is summarized as discussed in appendix A (paragraph .68), this sentence might read as follows.

> We have compiled the accompanying summarized projection of XYZ Company as of December 31, 20XX, and for the year then ending in accordance with attestation standards established by the American Institute of Certified Public Accountants.

or elements for which the expected results of one or more assumptions fall within a range, and identify the assumptions expected to fall within a range, for example, "revenue at the amounts of $X,XXX and $Y,YYY, which is predicated upon occupancy rates of XX percent and YY percent of available apartments,"] rather than as a single point estimate. Accordingly, the accompanying forecast presents forecasted financial position, results of operations, and cash flows [*describe one or more assumptions expected to fall within a range, for example, "at such occupancy rates."*] However, there is no assurance that the actual results will fall within the range of [*describe one or more assumptions expected to fall within a range, for example, "occupancy rates"*] presented.

.22 The date of completion of the practitioner's compilation procedures should be used as the date of the report.

.23 A practitioner may compile prospective financial statements for an entity with respect to which he or she is not independent.[12] In such circumstances, the practitioner's report should be modified to indicate his or her lack of independence in a separate paragraph of the practitioner's report. An example of such a disclosure would be

We are not independent with respect to XYZ Company.

The practitioner is not precluded from disclosing a description about the reason(s) that his or her independence is impaired. The following are examples of descriptions the practitioner may use:

a. We are not independent with respect to XYZ Company as of and for the year ended [*or ending, as applicable*] December 31, 20XX, because a member of the engagement team had a direct financial interest in XYZ Company.

b. We are not independent with respect to XYZ Company as of and for the year ended [*or ending, as applicable*] December 31, 20XX, because an immediate family member of one of the members of the engagement team was employed by XYZ Company.

c. We are not independent with respect to XYZ Company as of and for the year ended [*or ending, as applicable*] December 31, 20XX, because we performed certain accounting services (the practitioner may include a specific description of those services) that impaired our independence.

If the accountant elects to disclose a description about the reasons his or her independence is impaired, the accountant should ensure that all reasons are included in the description.

[As amended, effective for compilations of prospective financial statements for periods ending on or after December 15, 2010, by SSAE No. 17.]

.24 Prospective financial statements may be included in a document that also contains historical financial statements and the practitioner's report thereon.[13] In addition, the historical financial statements that appear in the document may be summarized and presented with the prospective financial statements for comparative purposes.[14] An example of the reference to the

---

[12] In making a judgment about whether he or she is independent, the practitioner should be guided by the AICPA Code of Professional Conduct. [Footnote amended, effective for compilations of prospective financial statements for periods ending on or after December 15, 2010, by SSAE No. 17.]

[13] Footnote revised, November 2002, to reflect conforming changes necessary due to the issuance of SSARS No. 9. Footnote deleted, December 2012, to reflect conforming changes necessary due to the issuance of SSARS No. 19 and SAS Nos. 122–126.]

[14] AU-C section 810, *Engagements to Report on Summary Financial Statements*, addresses the auditor's responsibilities relating to an engagement to report separately on summary financial

(continued)

practitioner's report on the historical financial statements when he or she audited, reviewed, or compiled those statements is presented below.

[*Concluding sentence of last paragraph*]

> The historical financial statements for the year ended December 31, 20XX, [*from which the historical data are derived*] and our report thereon are set forth on pages XX-XX of this document.

.25 In some circumstances, a practitioner may wish to expand his or her report to emphasize a matter regarding the prospective financial statements. Such information may be presented in a separate paragraph of the practitioner's report. However, the practitioner should exercise care that emphasizing such a matter does not give the impression that he or she is expressing assurance or expanding the degree of responsibility he or she is taking with respect to such information.[15] For example, the practitioner should not include statements in his or her compilation report about the mathematical accuracy of the statements or their conformity with presentation guidelines.

Modifications of the Standard Compilation Report

.26 An entity may request a practitioner to compile prospective financial statements that contain presentation deficiencies or omit disclosures other than those relating to significant assumptions. The practitioner may compile such prospective financial statements provided the deficiency or omission is clearly indicated in his or her report and is not, to his or her knowledge, undertaken with the intention of misleading those who might reasonably be expected to use such statements.

.27 Notwithstanding the preceding, if the compiled prospective financial statements are prepared in accordance with a special purpose financial reporting framework and do not include disclosure of the framework used, the framework should be disclosed in the practitioner's report. [Revised, December 2012, to reflect conforming changes necessary due to the issuance of SAS Nos. 122–126.]

.28 The following is an example of a paragraph that should be added to a report on compiled prospective financial statements, in this case a financial forecast, in which the summary of significant accounting policies has been omitted.

> Management has elected to omit the summary of significant accounting policies required by the guidelines for presentation of a forecast established by the American Institute of Certified Public Accountants. If the omitted disclosures were included in the forecast, they might influence the user's conclusions about the Company's financial position, results of operations, and cash flows for the forecast period. Accordingly, this forecast is not designed for those who are not informed about such matters.

Examination of Prospective Financial Statements

.29 An examination of prospective financial statements is a professional service that involves—

(footnote continued)

statements derived from financial statements audited in accordance with generally accepted auditing standards by the same auditor. [Footnote revised, December 2012, to reflect conforming changes necessary due to the issuance of SAS Nos. 122–126.]

[15] However, the practitioner may provide assurance on tax matters in order to comply with the requirements of regulations governing practice before the Internal Revenue Service (IRS) contained in 31 CFR pt. 10 (Treasury Department Circular No. 230).

a. Evaluating the preparation of the prospective financial statements.

b. Evaluating the support underlying the assumptions.

c. Evaluating the presentation of the prospective financial statements for conformity with AICPA presentation guidelines.[16]

d. Issuing an examination report.

.30 As a result of his or her examination, the practitioner has a basis for reporting on whether, in his or her opinion—

a. The prospective financial statements are presented in conformity with AICPA guidelines.

b. The assumptions provide a reasonable basis for the responsible party's forecast, or whether the assumptions provide a reasonable basis for the responsible party's projection given the hypothetical assumptions.

.31 The practitioner should follow the general, fieldwork, and reporting standards for attestation engagements established in section 50, *SSAE Hierarchy*, and further explained in section 101, *Attest Engagements*, in performing an examination of prospective financial statements and reporting thereon. (See paragraph .70 for standards concerning such technical training and proficiency, planning the examination engagement, and the types of procedures a practitioner should perform to obtain sufficient evidence for his or her examination report.) [Revised, November 2006, to reflect conforming changes necessary due to the issuance of SSAE No. 14.]

Working Papers

[.32] [Paragraph deleted by the issuance of SSAE No. 11, January 2002.]

Reports on Examined Prospective Financial Statements

.33 The practitioner's standard report on an examination of prospective financial statements should include the following:

a. A title that includes the word *independent*

b. An identification of the prospective financial statements presented

c. An identification of the responsible party and a statement that the prospective financial statements are the responsibility of the responsible party

d. A statement that the practitioner's responsibility is to express an opinion on the prospective financial statements based on his or her examination

e. A statement that the examination of the prospective financial statements was conducted in accordance with attestation standards established by the American Institute of Certified Public Accountants and, accordingly, included such procedures as the practitioner considered necessary in the circumstances

f. A statement that the practitioner believes that the examination provides a reasonable basis for his or her opinion

---

[16] AICPA presentation guidelines are detailed in AICPA Guide *Prospective Financial Information*.

g. The practitioner's opinion that the prospective financial statements are presented in conformity with AICPA presentation guidelines and that the underlying assumptions provide a reasonable basis for the forecast or a reasonable basis for the projection given the hypothetical assumptions[17]

h. A caveat that the prospective results may not be achieved

i. A statement that the practitioner assumes no responsibility to update the report for events and circumstances occurring after the date of the report

j. The manual or printed signature of the practitioner's firm

k. The date of the examination report

.34 The following is the form of the practitioner's standard report on an examination of a forecast that does not contain a range.

Independent Accountant's Report

We have examined the accompanying forecasted balance sheet, statements of income, retained earnings, and cash flows of XYZ Company as of December 31, 20XX, and for the year then ending.[18] XYZ Company's management is responsible for the forecast. Our responsibility is to express an opinion on the forecast based on our examination.

Our examination was conducted in accordance with attestation standards established by the American Institute of Certified Public Accountants and, accordingly, included such procedures as we considered necessary to evaluate both the assumptions used by management and the preparation and presentation of the forecast. We believe that our examination provides a reasonable basis for our opinion.

In our opinion, the accompanying forecast is presented in conformity with guidelines for presentation of a forecast established by the American Institute of Certified Public Accountants, and the underlying assumptions provide a reasonable basis for management's forecast. However, there will usually be differences between the forecasted and actual results, because events and circumstances frequently do not occur as expected, and those differences may be material. We have no responsibility to update this report for events and circumstances occurring after the date of this report.

[*Signature*]

[*Date*]

.35 When a practitioner examines a projection, his or her opinion regarding the assumptions should be conditioned on the hypothetical assumptions; that is, he or she should express an opinion on whether the assumptions provide a reasonable basis for the projection given the hypothetical assumptions. The practitioner's examination report on a projection should include the report elements set forth in paragraph .33. Additionally, the report should include a statement describing the special purpose for which the projection was prepared as well a separate paragraph that restricts the use of the report because it is

---

[17] The practitioner's report need not comment on the consistency of the application of accounting principles as long as the presentation of any change in accounting principles is in conformity with AICPA presentation guidelines as detailed in AICPA Guide *Prospective Financial Information*.

[18] When the presentation is summarized as discussed in appendix A (paragraph .68), this sentence might read, "We have examined the accompanying summarized forecast of XYZ Company as of December 31, 20XX, and for the year then ending."

intended to be used solely by specified parties. The following is the form of the practitioner's standard report on an examination of a projection that does not contain a range.

Independent Accountant's Report

We have examined the accompanying projected balance sheet, statements of income, retained earnings, and cash flows of XYZ Company as of December 31, 20XX, and for the year then ending.[19] XYZ Company's management is responsible for the projection, which was prepared for [*state special purpose, for example, "the purpose of negotiating a loan to expand XYZ Company's plant"*]. Our responsibility is to express an opinion on the projection based on our examination.

Our examination was conducted in accordance with attestation standards established by the American Institute of Certified Public Accountants and, accordingly, included such procedures as we considered necessary to evaluate both the assumptions used by management and the preparation and presentation of the projection. We believe that our examination provides a reasonable basis for our opinion.

In our opinion, the accompanying projection is presented in conformity with guidelines for presentation of a projection established by the American Institute of Certified Public Accountants, and the underlying assumptions provide a reasonable basis for management's projection [*describe the hypothetical assumption, for example, "assuming the granting of the requested loan for the purpose of expanding XYZ Company's plant as described in the summary of significant assumptions."*] However, even if [*describe hypothetical assumption, for example, "the loan is granted and the plant is expanded,"*], there will usually be differences between the projected and actual results, because events and circumstances frequently do not occur as expected, and those differences may be material. We have no responsibility to update this report for events and circumstances occurring after the date of this report.

The accompanying projection and this report are intended solely for the information and use of [*identify specified parties, for example, "XYZ Company and DEF National Bank"*] and is not intended to be and should not be used by anyone other than these specified parties.

[*Signature*]

[*Date*]

.36 When the prospective financial statements contain a range, the practitioner's standard report should also include a separate paragraph that states that the responsible party has elected to portray the expected results of one or more assumptions as a range. The following is an example of the separate paragraph to be added to the practitioner's report when he or she examines prospective financial statements, in this case a forecast, that contain a range.

As described in the summary of significant assumptions, management of XYZ Company has elected to portray forecasted [*describe financial statement element or elements for which the expected results of one or more assumptions fall within a range, and identify assumptions expected to fall within a range, for example, "revenue at the amounts of $X,XXX and $Y,YYY, which is predicated upon occupancy rates of XX percent and YY percent of available apartments,"*] rather than as a single point estimate. Accordingly, the accompanying forecast presents forecasted financial position, results of operations, and cash flows [*de-*

[19] When the presentation is summarized as discussed in appendix A (paragraph .68), this sentence might read, "We have examined the accompanying summarized projection of XYZ Company as of December 31, 20XX, and for the year then ending."

scribe one or more assumptions expected to fall within a range, for example, "at such occupancy rates."] However, there is no assurance that the actual results will fall within the range of [*describe one or more assumptions expected to fall within a range, for example, "occupancy rates"*] presented.

.37 The date of completion of the practitioner's examination procedures should be used as the date of the report.

Modifications to the Practitioner's Opinion[20]

.38 The following circumstances result in the following types of modified practitioner's report involving the practitioner's opinion.

a. If, in the practitioner's opinion, the prospective financial statements depart from AICPA presentation guidelines, he or she should express a qualified opinion (see paragraph .39) or an adverse opinion. (See paragraph .41.)[21] However, if the presentation departs from the presentation guidelines because it fails to disclose assumptions that appear to be significant, the practitioner should express an adverse opinion. (See paragraphs .41–.42.)

b. If the practitioner believes that one or more significant assumptions do not provide a reasonable basis for the forecast, or a reasonable basis for the projection given the hypothetical assumptions, he or she should express an adverse opinion. (See paragraph .41.)

c. If the practitioner's examination is affected by conditions that preclude application of one or more procedures he or she considers necessary in the circumstances, he or she should disclaim an opinion and describe the scope limitation in his or her report. (See paragraph .43.)

.39 *Qualified Opinion*. In a qualified opinion, the practitioner should state, in a separate paragraph, all substantive reasons for modifying his or her opinion and describe the departure from AICPA presentation guidelines. His or her opinion should include the words "except" or "exception" as the qualifying language and should refer to the separate explanatory paragraph. The following is an example of an examination report on a forecast that is at variance with AICPA guidelines for presentation of a financial forecast.

Independent Accountant's Report

We have examined the accompanying forecasted balance sheet, statements of income, retained earnings, and cash flows of XYZ Company as of December 31, 20XX, and for the year then ending. XYZ Company's management is responsible for the forecast. Our responsibility is to express an opinion on the forecast based on our examination.

Our examination was conducted in accordance with attestation standards established by the American Institute of Certified Public Accountants and, accordingly, included such procedures as we considered necessary to evaluate both the assumptions used by management and the preparation and presentation of the forecast. We believe that our examination provides a reasonable basis for our opinion.

---

[20] Paragraphs .38–.44 describe circumstances in which the practitioner's standard report on prospective financial statements may require modification. The guidance for modifying the practitioner's standard report is generally applicable to partial presentations. Also, depending on the nature of the presentation, the practitioner may decide to disclose that the partial presentation is not intended to be a presentation of financial position, results of operations, or cash flows. Illustrative reports on partial presentations may be found in AICPA Guide *Prospective Financial Information*.

[21] However, the practitioner may issue the standard examination report on a financial forecast filed with the SEC that meets the presentation requirements of article XI of Regulation S-X.

The forecast does not disclose significant accounting policies. Disclosure of such policies is required by guidelines for presentation of a forecast established by the American Institute of Certified Public Accountants.

In our opinion, except for the omission of the disclosure of the significant accounting policies as discussed in the preceding paragraph, the accompanying forecast is presented in conformity with guidelines for a presentation of a forecast established by the American Institute of Certified Public Accountants and the underlying assumptions provide a reasonable basis for management's forecast. However, there will usually be differences between the forecasted and actual results, because events and circumstances frequently do not occur as expected, and those differences may be material. We have no responsibility to update this report for events and circumstances occurring after the date of this report.

[*Signature*]

[*Date*]

.40 Because of the nature, sensitivity, and interrelationship of prospective information, a reader would find a practitioner's report qualified for a measurement departure,[22] the reasonableness of the underlying assumptions, or a scope limitation difficult to interpret. Accordingly, the practitioner should not express his or her opinion about these items with language such as "except for . . ." or "subject to the effects of. . . ." Rather, when a measurement departure, an unreasonable assumption, or a limitation on the scope of the practitioner's examination has led him or her to conclude that he or she cannot issue an unqualified opinion, he or she should issue the appropriate type of modified opinion described in paragraphs .41–.44.

.41 *Adverse Opinion.* In an adverse opinion the practitioner should state, in a separate paragraph, all of the substantive reasons for his or her adverse opinion. His or her opinion should state that the presentation is not in conformity with presentation guidelines and should refer to the explanatory paragraph. When applicable, his or her opinion paragraph should also state that, in the practitioner's opinion, the assumptions do not provide a reasonable basis for the prospective financial statements. An example of an adverse opinion on an examination of prospective financial statements is set forth below. In this case, a financial forecast was examined and the practitioner's opinion was that a significant assumption was unreasonable. The example should be revised as appropriate for a different type of presentation or if the adverse opinion is issued because the statements do not conform to the presentation guidelines.

Independent Accountant's Report

We have examined the accompanying forecasted balance sheet, statements of income, retained earnings, and cash flows of XYZ Company as of December 31, 20XX, and for the year then ending. XYZ Company's management is responsible for the forecast. Our responsibility is to express an opinion on the forecast based on our examination.

Our examination was conducted in accordance with attestation standards established by the American Institute of Certified Public Accountants and, accordingly, included such procedures as we considered necessary to evaluate

[22] An example of a measurement departure is the failure to capitalize a capital lease in a forecast where the historical financial statements for the prospective period are expected to be presented in accordance with GAAP.

both the assumptions used by management and the preparation and presentation of the forecast. We believe that our examination provides a reasonable basis for our opinion.

As discussed under the caption "Sales" in the summary of significant forecast assumptions, the forecasted sales include, among other things, revenue from the Company's federal defense contracts continuing at the current level. The Company's present federal defense contracts will expire in March 20XX. No new contracts have been signed and no negotiations are under way for new federal defense contracts. Furthermore, the federal government has entered into contracts with another company to supply the items being manufactured under the Company's present contracts.

In our opinion, the accompanying forecast is not presented in conformity with guidelines for presentation of a financial forecast established by the American Institute of Certified Public Accountants because management's assumptions, as discussed in the preceding paragraph, do not provide a reasonable basis for management's forecast. We have no responsibility to update this report for events or circumstances occurring after the date of this report.

[*Signature*]

[*Date*]

.42 If the presentation, including the summary of significant assumptions, fails to disclose assumptions that, at the time, appear to be significant, the practitioner should describe the assumptions in his or her report and express an adverse opinion. The practitioner should not examine a presentation that omits all disclosures of assumptions. Also, the practitioner should not examine a financial projection that omits (*a*) an identification of the hypothetical assumptions or (*b*) a description of the limitations on the usefulness of the presentation.

.43 *Disclaimer of Opinion.* In a disclaimer of opinion, the practitioner's report should indicate, in a separate paragraph, the respects in which the examination did not comply with standards for an examination. The practitioner should state that the scope of the examination was not sufficient to enable him or her to express an opinion with respect to the presentation or the underlying assumptions, and his or her disclaimer of opinion should include a direct reference to the explanatory paragraph. The following is an example of a report on an examination of prospective financial statements, in this case a financial forecast, for which a significant assumption could not be evaluated.

Independent Accountant's Report

We were engaged to examine the accompanying forecasted balance sheet, statements of income, retained earnings, and cash flows of XYZ Company as of December 31, 20XX, and for the year then ending. XYZ Company's management is responsible for the forecast.

As discussed under the caption "Income From Investee" in the summary of significant forecast assumptions, the forecast includes income from an equity investee constituting 23 percent of forecasted net income, which is management's estimate of the Company's share of the investee's income to be accrued for 20XX. The investee has not prepared a forecast for the year ending December 31, 20XX, and we were therefore unable to obtain suitable support for this assumption.

Because, as described in the preceding paragraph, we are unable to evaluate management's assumption regarding income from an equity investee and other assumptions that depend thereon, the scope of our work was not sufficient to express, and we do not express, an opinion with respect to the presentation of or the assumptions underlying the accompanying forecast. We have no responsibility to update this report for events and circumstances occurring after the date of this report.

[*Signature*]

[*Date*]

.44 When there is a scope limitation and the practitioner also believes there are material departures from the presentation guidelines, those departures should be described in the practitioner's report.

Other Modifications to the Standard Examination Report

.45 The circumstances described below, although not necessarily resulting in modifications to the practitioner's opinion, would result in the following types of modifications to the standard examination report.

.46 *Emphasis of a Matter.* In some circumstances, the practitioner may wish to emphasize a matter regarding the prospective financial statements but nevertheless intends to express an unqualified opinion. The practitioner may present other information and comments he or she wishes to include, such as explanatory comments or other informative material, in a separate paragraph of his or her report.

.47 *Evaluation Based in Part on a Report of Another Practitioner.* When more than one practitioner is involved in the examination, the guidance provided for that situation in connection with examinations of historical financial statements is generally applicable. When the principal practitioner decides to refer to the report of another practitioner as a basis, in part, for his or her own opinion, he or she should disclose that fact in stating the scope of the examination and should refer to the report of the other practitioner in expressing his or her opinion. Such a reference indicates the division of responsibility for the performance of the examination.

.48 *Comparative Historical Financial Information.* Prospective financial statements may be included in a document that also contains historical financial statements and a practitioner's report thereon.[23] In addition, the historical financial statements that appear in the document may be summarized and presented with the prospective financial statements for comparative purposes.[24] An example of the reference to the practitioner's report on the historical financial statements when he or she audited, reviewed, or compiled those statements is presented in paragraph .24.

.49 *Reporting When the Examination Is Part of a Larger Engagement.* When the practitioner's examination of prospective financial statements is part of a larger engagement, for example, a financial feasibility study or business acquisition study, it is appropriate to expand the report on the examination of the prospective financial statements to describe the entire engagement.

---

[23] [Footnote revised, November 2002, to reflect conforming changes necessary due to the issuance of SSARS No. 9. Footnote deleted, December 2012, to reflect conforming changes necessary due to the issuance of SAS Nos. 122–126.]

[24] AU-C section 810, *Engagements to Report on Summary Financial Statements*, addresses the auditor's responsibilities relating to an engagement to report separately on summary financial statements derived from financial statements audited in accordance with GAAS by the same auditor. [Footnote revised, December 2012, to reflect conforming changes necessary due to the issuance of SAS Nos. 122–126.]

.50 The following is a report that might be issued when a practitioner chooses to expand his or her report on a financial feasibility study.[25]

Independent Accountant's Report

a. The Board of Directors
Example Hospital
Example, Texas

b. We have prepared a financial feasibility study of Example Hospital's (the Hospital's) plans to expand and renovate its facilities. The study was undertaken to evaluate the ability of the Hospital to meet its operating expenses, working capital needs, and other financial requirements, including the debt service requirements associated with the proposed $25,000,000 [*legal title of bonds*] issue, at an assumed average annual interest rate of 10.0 percent during the five years ending December 31, 20X6.

c. The proposed capital improvements program (the Program) consists of a new two-level addition, which is to provide fifty additional medical-surgical beds, increasing the complement to 275 beds. In addition, various administrative and support service areas in the present facilities are to be remodeled. The Hospital administration anticipates that construction is to begin June 30, 20X2, and to be completed by December 31, 20X3.

d. The estimated total cost of the Program is approximately $30,000,000. It is assumed that the $25,000,000 of revenue bonds that the Example Hospital Finance Authority proposes to issue would be the primary source of funds for the Program. The responsibility for payment of debt service on the bonds is solely that of the Hospital. Other necessary funds to finance the Program are assumed to be provided from the Hospital's funds, from a local fund drive, and from interest earned on funds held by the bond trustee during the construction period.

e. Our procedures included analysis of the following:

- Program history, objectives, timing, and financing
- The future demand for the Hospital's services, including consideration of the following:
  - — Economic and demographic characteristics of the Hospital's defined service area
  - — Locations, capacities, and competitive information pertaining to other existing and planned area hospitals
  - — Physician support for the Hospital and its programs
  - — Historical utilization levels
- Planning agency applications and approvals
- Construction and equipment costs, debt service requirements, and estimated financing costs
- Staffing patterns and other operating considerations

[25] Although the entity referred to in the report is a hospital, the form of report is also applicable to other entities such as hotels or stadiums. Also, although the illustrated report format and language should not be departed from in any significant way, the language used should be tailored to fit the circumstances that are unique to a particular engagement (for example, the description of the proposed capital improvement program, paragraph *c*; the proposed financing of the program, paragraphs *b* and *d*; the specific procedures applied by the practitioner, paragraph *e*; and any explanatory comments included in emphasis-of-a-matter paragraphs, paragraph *i*, which deals with general matter; and paragraph *j*, which deals with specific matters).

- Third-party reimbursement policy and history
- Revenue/expense/volume relationships

f. We also participated in gathering other information, assisted management in identifying and formulating its assumptions, and assembled the accompanying financial forecast based on those assumptions.

g. The accompanying financial forecast for the annual periods ending December 31, 20X2, through 20X6, is based on assumptions that were provided by or reviewed with and approved by management. The financial forecast includes the following:

- Balance sheets
- Statements of operations
- Statements of cash flows
- Statements of changes in net assets

h. We have examined the financial forecast. Example Hospital's management is responsible for the forecast. Our responsibility is to express an opinion on the forecast based on our examination. Our examination was conducted in accordance with attestation standards established by the American Institute of Certified Public Accountants and, accordingly, included such procedures as we considered necessary to evaluate both the assumptions used by management and the preparation and presentation of the forecast. We believe that our examination provides a reasonable basis for our opinion.

i. Legislation and regulations at all levels of government have affected and may continue to affect revenues and expenses of hospitals. The financial forecast is based on legislation and regulations currently in effect. If future legislation or regulations related to hospital operations are enacted, such legislation or regulations could have a material effect on future operations.

j. The interest rate, principal payments, Program costs, and other financing assumptions are described in the section entitled "Summary of Significant Forecast Assumptions and Rationale." If actual interest rates, principal payments, and funding requirements are different from those assumed, the amount of the bond issue and debt service requirements would need to be adjusted accordingly from those indicated in the forecast. If such interest rates, principal payments, and funding requirements are lower than those assumed, such adjustments would not adversely affect the forecast.

k. Our conclusions are presented below.

- In our opinion, the accompanying financial forecast is presented in conformity with guidelines for presentation of a financial forecast established by the American Institute of Certified Public Accountants.
- In our opinion, the underlying assumptions provide a reasonable basis for management's forecast. However, there will usually be differences between the forecasted and actual results, because events and circumstances frequently do not occur as expected, and those differences may be material.

- The accompanying financial forecast indicates that sufficient funds could be generated to meet the Hospital's operating expenses, working capital needs, and other financial requirements, including the debt service requirements associated with the proposed $25,000,000 bond issue, during the forecast periods. However, the achievement of any financial forecast is dependent on future events, the occurrence of which cannot be assured.

l. We have no responsibility to update this report for events and circumstances occurring after the date of this report.

[*Signature*]

[*Date*]

Applying Agreed-Upon Procedures to Prospective Financial Statements

.51 The practitioner who accepts an engagement to apply agreed-upon procedures to prospective financial statements should follow the general, fieldwork, and reporting standards for attest engagements established in section 50, *SSAE Hierarchy*, and the guidance set forth herein and in section 201, *Agreed-Upon Procedures Engagements*. [Revised, November 2006, to reflect conforming changes necessary due to the issuance of SSAE No. 14.]

.52 A practitioner may perform an agreed-upon procedures attest engagement on prospective financial statements[26] provided the following conditions are met.

a. The practitioner is independent.

b. The practitioner and the specified parties agree upon the procedures performed or to be performed by the practitioner.

c. The specified parties take responsibility for the sufficiency of the agreed-upon procedures for their purposes.

d. The prospective financial statements include a summary of significant assumptions.

e. The prospective financial statements to which the procedures are to be applied are subject to reasonably consistent evaluation against criteria that are suitable and available to the specified parties.

f. Criteria to be used in the determination of findings are agreed upon between the practitioner and the specified parties.[27]

g. The procedures to be applied to the prospective financial statements are expected to result in reasonably consistent findings using the criteria.

h. Evidential matter related to the prospective financial statements to which the procedures are applied is expected to exist to provide a reasonable basis for expressing the findings in the practitioner's report.

---

[26] Practitioners should follow the guidance in AU-C section 920, *Letters for Underwriters and Certain Other Requesting Parties*, when requested to perform agreed-upon procedures on a forecast and report thereon in a letter for an underwriter. [Footnote revised, December 2012, to reflect conforming changes necessary due to the issuance of SAS Nos. 122–126.]

[27] For example, accounting principles and other presentation criteria as discussed in chapter 8, "Presentation Guidelines," of AICPA Guide *Prospective Financial Information*.

i. Where applicable, the practitioner and the specified users agree on any agreed-upon materiality limits for reporting purposes. (See paragraph .25 of section 201.)

j. Use of the report is to be restricted to the specified parties.[28]

.53 Generally, the practitioner's procedures may be as limited or as extensive as the specified parties desire, as long as the specified parties take responsibility for their sufficiency. However, mere reading of prospective financial statements does not constitute a procedure sufficient to permit a practitioner to report on the results of applying agreed-upon procedures to such statements. (See paragraph .15 of section 201.)

.54 To satisfy the requirements that the practitioner and the specified parties agree upon the procedures performed or to be performed and that the specified parties take responsibility for the sufficiency of the agreed-upon procedures for their purposes, ordinarily the practitioner should communicate directly with and obtain affirmative acknowledgment from each of the specified parties. For example, this may be accomplished by meeting with the specified parties or by distributing a draft of the anticipated report or a copy of an engagement letter to the specified parties and obtaining their agreement. If the practitioner is not able to communicate directly with all of the specified parties, the practitioner may satisfy these requirements by applying any one or more of the following or similar procedures:

- Compare the procedures to be applied to written requirements of the specified parties.
- Discuss the procedures to be applied with appropriate representatives of the specified parties involved.
- Review relevant contracts with or correspondence from the specified parties.

The practitioner should not report on an engagement when specified parties do not agree upon the procedures performed or to be performed and do not take responsibility for the sufficiency of the procedures for their purposes. (See paragraph .36 of section 201 for guidance on satisfying these requirements when the practitioner is requested to add other parties as specified parties after the date of completion of the agreed-upon procedures.)

Reports on the Results of Applying Agreed-Upon Procedures

.55 The practitioner's report on the results of applying agreed-upon procedures should be in the form of procedures and findings. The practitioner's report should contain the following elements:

a. A title that includes the word *independent*

b. Identification of the specified parties

c. Reference to the prospective financial statements covered by the practitioner's report and the character of the engagement

d. A statement that the procedures performed were those agreed to by the specified parties identified in the report

[28] In some cases, restricted-use reports filed with regulatory agencies are required by law or regulation to be made available to the public as a matter of public record. Also, a regulatory agency as part of its oversight responsibility for an entity may require access to restricted-use reports in which they are not named as a specified party. (See paragraph .79 of section 101.)

e. Identification of the responsible party and a statement that the prospective financial statements are the responsibility of the responsible party

f. A statement that the agreed-upon procedures engagement was conducted in accordance with attestation standards established by the American Institute of Certified Public Accountants

g. A statement that the sufficiency of the procedures is solely the responsibility of the specified parties and a disclaimer of responsibility for the sufficiency of those procedures

h. A list of the procedures performed (or reference thereto) and related findings (The practitioner should not provide negative assurance—see paragraph .24 of section 201.)

i. Where applicable, a description of any agreed-upon materiality limits (See paragraph .25 of section 201.)

j. A statement that the practitioner was not engaged to and did not conduct an examination of prospective financial statements; a disclaimer of opinion on whether the presentation of the prospective financial statements is in conformity with AICPA presentation guidelines and on whether the underlying assumptions provide a reasonable basis for the forecast, or a reasonable basis for the projection given the hypothetical assumptions; and a statement that if the practitioner had performed additional procedures, other matters might have come to his or her attention that would have been reported

k. A statement of restrictions on the use of the report because it is intended to be used solely by the specified parties

l. Where applicable, reservations or restrictions concerning procedures or findings as discussed in paragraphs .33, .35, and .39–.40 of section 201

m. A caveat that the prospective results may not be achieved

n. A statement that the practitioner assumes no responsibility to update the report for events and circumstances occurring after the date of the report

o. Where applicable, a description of the nature of the assistance provided by a specialist as discussed in paragraphs .19–.21 of section 201

p. The manual or printed signature of the practitioner's firm

q. The date of the report

.56 The following illustrates a report on applying agreed-upon procedures to the prospective financial statements. (See section 201.)

Independent Accountant's Report
<u>on Applying Agreed-Upon Procedures</u>

Board of Directors—XYZ Corporation

Board of Directors—ABC Company

At your request, we have performed certain agreed-upon procedures, as enumerated below, with respect to the forecasted balance sheet and the related forecasted statements of income, retained earnings, and cash flows of DEF Company, a subsidiary of ABC Company, as of December 31, 20XX, and for the year then ending. These procedures, which were agreed to by the Boards of

Directors of XYZ Corporation and ABC Company, were performed solely to assist you in evaluating the forecast in connection with the proposed sale of DEF Company to XYZ Corporation. DEF Company's management is responsible for the forecast.

This agreed-upon procedures engagement was conducted in accordance with attestation standards established by the American Institute of Certified Public Accountants. The sufficiency of these procedures is solely the responsibility of the specified parties. Consequently, we make no representation regarding the sufficiency of the procedures described below either for the purpose for which this report has been requested or for any other purpose.

[*Include paragraphs to enumerate procedures and findings.*]

We were not engaged to and did not conduct an examination, the objective of which would be the expression of an opinion on the accompanying prospective financial statements. Accordingly, we do not express an opinion on whether the prospective financial statements are presented in conformity with AICPA presentation guidelines or on whether the underlying assumptions provide a reasonable basis for the presentation. Had we performed additional procedures, other matters might have come to our attention that would have been reported to you. Furthermore, there will usually be differences between the forecasted and actual results, because events and circumstances frequently do not occur as expected, and those differences may be material. We have no responsibility to update this report for events and circumstances occurring after the date of this report.

This report is intended solely for the information and use of the Boards of Directors of ABC Company and XYZ Corporation and is not intended to be and should not be used by anyone other than these specified parties.

[*Signature*]

[*Date*]

Partial Presentations

.57 The practitioner's procedures on a partial presentation may be affected by the nature of the information presented. Many elements of prospective financial statements are interrelated. The practitioner should give appropriate consideration to whether key factors affecting elements, accounts, or items that are interrelated with those in the partial presentation he or she has been engaged to examine or compile have been considered, including key factors that may not necessarily be obvious to the partial presentation (for example, productive capacity relative to a sales forecast), and whether all significant assumptions have been disclosed. The practitioner may find it necessary for the scope of the examination or compilation of some partial presentations to be similar to that for the examination or compilation of a presentation of prospective financial statements. For example, the scope of a practitioner's procedures when he or she examines forecasted results of operations would likely be similar to that of procedures used for the examination of prospective financial statements since the practitioner would most likely need to consider the interrelationships of all accounts in the examination of results of operations.

.58 Because partial presentations are generally appropriate only for limited use, reports on partial presentations of both forecasted and projected information should include a description of any limitations on the usefulness of the presentation.

Other Information

.59 When a practitioner's compilation, review, or audit report on historical financial statements is included in a practitioner-submitted document containing prospective financial statements, the practitioner should either examine, compile, or apply agreed-upon procedures to the prospective financial statements and report accordingly, unless the following occur.

a. The prospective financial statements are labeled as a "budget."

b. The budget does not extend beyond the end of the current fiscal year.

c. The budget is presented with interim historical financial statements for the current year.

In such circumstances, the practitioner need not examine, compile, or apply agreed-upon procedures to the budget; however, he or she should report on it and—

a. Indicate that he or she did not examine or compile the budget.

b. Disclaim an opinion or any other form of assurance on the budget.

In addition, the budgeted information may omit the summaries of significant assumptions and accounting policies required by the guidelines for presentation of prospective financial statements established by the AICPA, provided such omission is not, to the practitioner's knowledge, undertaken with the intention of misleading those who might reasonably be expected to use such budgeted information, and is disclosed in the practitioner's report. The following is the form of the standard paragraphs to be added to the practitioner's report in this circumstance when the summaries of significant assumptions and accounting policies have been omitted.

> The accompanying budgeted balance sheet, statements of income, retained earnings, and cash flows of XYZ Company as of December 31, 20XX, and for the six months then ending, have not been compiled or examined by us, and, accordingly, we do not express an opinion or any other form of assurance on them.
>
> Management has elected to omit the summaries of significant assumptions and accounting policies required under established guidelines for presentation of prospective financial statements. If the omitted summaries were included in the budgeted information, they might influence the user's conclusions about the company's budgeted information. Accordingly, this budgeted information is not designed for those who are not informed about such matters.

.60 When the practitioner's compilation, review, or audit report on historical financial statements is included in a client-prepared document containing prospective financial statements, the practitioner should not consent to the use of his or her name in the document unless:

a. He or she has examined, compiled, or applied agreed-upon procedures to the prospective financial statements and his or her report accompanies them.

b. The prospective financial statements are accompanied by an indication by the responsible party or the practitioner that the practitioner has not performed such a service on the prospective financial statements and that the practitioner assumes no responsibility for them.

c. Another practitioner has examined, compiled, or applied agreed-upon procedures to the prospective financial statements and his or her report is included in the document.

In addition, if the practitioner has audited the historical financial statements and the prospective financial statements that he or she did not examine, compile, or apply agreed-upon procedures to are included in a document containing the audited historical financial statements and the auditor's report thereon,[29] he or she should refer to AU-C section 720, *Other Information in Documents Containing Audited Financial Statements*. [Revised, December 2010, to reflect conforming changes necessary due to the issuance of SAS Nos. 118–120. Revised, December 2012, to reflect conforming changes necessary due to the issuance of SAS Nos. 122–126.]

.61 The practitioner whose report on prospective financial statements is included in a client-prepared document containing historical financial statements should not consent to the use of his or her name in the document unless:

a. He or she has compiled, reviewed, or audited the historical financial statements and his or her report accompanies them.

b. The historical financial statements are accompanied by an indication by the responsible party or the practitioner that the practitioner has not performed such a service on the historical financial statements and that the practitioner assumes no responsibility for them.

c. Another practitioner has compiled, reviewed, or audited the historical financial statements and his or her report is included in the document.

.62 An entity may publish various documents that contain information other than historical financial statements in addition to the compiled or examined prospective financial statements and the practitioner's report thereon. The practitioner's responsibility with respect to information in such a document does not extend beyond the financial information identified in the report, and he or she has no obligation to perform any procedures to corroborate other information contained in the document. However, the practitioner should read the other information and consider whether such information, or the manner of its presentation, is materially inconsistent with the information, or manner of its presentation, appearing in the prospective financial statements.

.63 If the practitioner examines prospective financial statements included in a document containing inconsistent information, he or she might not be able to conclude that there is adequate support for each significant assumption. The practitioner should consider whether the prospective financial statements, his or her report, or both require revision. Depending on the conclusion he or she reaches, the practitioner should consider other actions that may be appropriate, such as issuing an adverse opinion, disclaiming an opinion because of a scope limitation, withholding the use of his or her report in the document, or withdrawing from the engagement.

.64 If the practitioner compiles the prospective financial statements included in the document containing inconsistent information, he or she should attempt to obtain additional or revised information. If he or she does not receive

---

[29] AU-C section 720 applies only to such prospective financial statements contained in annual reports (or similar documents) that are issued to owners (or similar stakeholders) and annual reports of governments and organizations for charitable or philanthropic purposes that are available to the public that contain audited financial statements and the auditor's report thereon. AU-C section 720 also may be applied, adapted as necessary in the circumstances, to other documents to which the auditor, at management's request, devotes attention. AU-C section 720 does not apply when the historical financial statements and report appear in a registration statement filed under the Securities Act of 1933 (in which case, see AU-C section 925, *Filings With the U.S. Securities and Exchange Commission Under the Securities Act of 1933*). [Footnote revised, December 2010, to reflect conforming changes necessary due to the issuance of SAS Nos. 118–120. Footnote revised, December 2012, to reflect conforming changes necessary due to the issuance of SAS Nos. 122–126.]

such information, the practitioner should withhold the use of his or her report or withdraw from the compilation engagement.

.65 If, while reading the other information appearing in the document containing the examined or compiled prospective financial statements, as described in the preceding paragraphs, the practitioner becomes aware of information that he or she believes is a material misstatement of fact that is not an inconsistent statement, he or she should discuss the matter with the responsible party. In connection with this discussion, the practitioner should consider that he or she may not have the expertise to assess the validity of the statement made, that there may be no standards by which to assess its presentation, and that there may be valid differences of judgment or opinion. If the practitioner concludes that he or she has a valid basis for concern, he or she should propose that the responsible party consult with some other party whose advice might be useful, such as the entity's legal counsel.

.66 If, after discussing the matter as described in paragraph .65, the practitioner concludes that a material misstatement of fact remains, the action he or she takes will depend on his or her judgment in the particular circumstances. The practitioner should consider steps such as notifying the responsible party in writing of his or her views concerning the information and consulting his or her legal counsel about further appropriate action in the circumstances.

Effective Date

.67 This section is effective when the date of the practitioner's report is on or after June 1, 2001. Early application is permitted.

.68

Appendix A

Minimum Presentation Guidelines*

1. Prospective information presented in the format of historical financial statements facilitates comparisons with financial position, results of operations, and cash flows of prior periods, as well as those actually achieved for the prospective period. Accordingly, prospective financial statements preferably should be in the format of the historical financial statements that would be issued for the period(s) covered unless there is an agreement between the responsible party and potential users specifying another format. Prospective financial statements may take the form of complete basic financial statements[1] or may be limited to the following minimum items (where such items would be presented for historical financial statements for the period).[2]

a. Sales or gross revenues

b. Gross profit or cost of sales

c. Unusual or infrequently occurring items

d. Provision for income taxes

e. Discontinued operations or extraordinary items

f. Income from continuing operations

g. Net income

h. Basic and diluted earnings per share

i. Significant changes in financial position[3]

j. A description of what the responsible party intends the prospective financial statements to present, a statement that the assumptions are based on the responsible party's judgment at the time the prospective information was prepared, and a caveat that the prospective results may not be achieved

---

* ***Note:*** This appendix describes the minimum items that constitute a presentation of a financial forecast or a financial projection, as specified in AICPA Guide *Prospective Financial Information*. Complete presentation guidelines for entities that choose to issue prospective financial statements, together with illustrative presentations, are included in the Guide. The guide also prescribes presentation guidelines for partial presentations.

[1] The details of each statement may be summarized or condensed so that only the major items in each are presented. The usual footnotes associated with historical financial statements need not be included as such. However, significant assumptions and accounting policies should be disclosed.

[2] Similar types of financial information should be presented for entities for which these terms do not describe operations. Further, similar items should be presented if a comprehensive basis of accounting other than GAAP is used to present the prospective financial statements. For example, if the cash basis were used, item a would be cash receipts.

[3] The responsible party should disclose significant cash flows and other significant changes in balance sheet accounts during the period. However, neither a balance sheet nor a statement of cash flows, as described in Financial Accounting Standards Board (FASB) *Accounting Standards Codification* (ASC) 230, *Statement of Cash Flows*, is required. Furthermore, none of the specific captions or disclosures required by FASB ASC 230 is required. Significant changes disclosed will depend on the circumstances; however, such disclosures will often include cash flows from operations. See AICPA Guide *Prospective Financial Information* exhibits 9-2 and 9-6 for illustrations of alternate methods of presenting significant cash flows. [Footnote revised, June 2009, to reflect conforming changes necessary due to the issuance of FASB ASC.]

k. Summary of significant assumptions

l. Summary of significant accounting policies

2. A presentation that omits one or more of the applicable minimum items *a–i* is a partial presentation, which would not ordinarily be appropriate for general use. If an omitted applicable minimum item is derivable from the information presented, the presentation would not be deemed to be a partial presentation. A presentation that contains the applicable minimum items *a–i*, but omits items *j–l*, is subject to all of the provisions of this section applicable to complete presentations.

.69

Appendix B

Training and Proficiency, Planning, and Procedures Applicable to Compilations

Training and Proficiency

1. The practitioner should be familiar with the guidelines for the preparation and presentation of prospective financial statements. The guidelines are contained in AICPA Guide *Prospective Financial Information*.

2. The practitioner should possess or obtain a level of knowledge of the industry and the accounting principles and practices of the industry in which the entity operates or will operate that will enable him or her to compile prospective financial statements that are in appropriate form for an entity operating in that industry.

Planning the Compilation Engagement

3. To compile the prospective financial statements of an existing entity, the practitioner should obtain a general knowledge of the nature of the entity's business transactions and the key factors upon which its future financial results appear to depend. He or she should also obtain an understanding of the accounting principles and practices of the entity to determine whether they are comparable to those used within the industry in which the entity operates.

4. To compile the prospective financial statements of a proposed entity, the practitioner should obtain knowledge of the proposed operations and the key factors upon which its future results appear to depend and that have affected the performance of entities in the same industry.

Compilation Procedures

5. In a compilation of prospective financial statements the practitioner should perform the following, where applicable.

a. Establish an understanding with the client regarding the services to be performed. The understanding should include the objectives of the engagement, the client's responsibilities, the practitioner's responsibilities, and limitations of the engagement. The practitioner should document the understanding in the working papers, preferably through a written communication with the client. If the practitioner believes an understanding with the client has not been established, he or she should decline to accept or perform the engagement.

b. Inquire about the accounting principles used in the preparation of the prospective financial statements.

(1) For existing entities, compare the accounting principles used to those used in the preparation of previous historical financial statements and inquire whether such principles are the same as those expected to be used in the historical financial statements covering the prospective period.

(2) For entities to be formed or entities formed that have not commenced operations, compare specialized industry accounting principles used, if any, to those typically used in the industry. Inquire whether the accounting principles used for the prospective financial statements are those that are expected to be used when or if the entity commences operations.

c. Ask how the responsible party identifies the key factors and develops its assumptions.

d. List, or obtain a list of the responsible party's significant assumptions providing the basis for the prospective financial statements and consider whether there are any obvious omissions in light of the key factors upon which the prospective results of the entity appear to depend.

e. Consider whether there appear to be any obvious internal inconsistencies in the assumptions.

f. Perform or test the mathematical accuracy of the computations that translate the assumptions into prospective financial statements.

g. Read the prospective financial statements, including the summary of significant assumptions, and consider whether—

(1) The statements, including the disclosures of assumptions and accounting policies, appear to be not presented in conformity with the AICPA presentation guidelines for prospective financial statements.[1]

(2) The statements, including the summary of significant assumptions, appear to be not obviously inappropriate in relation to the practitioner's knowledge of the entity and its industry and, for the following:

(a) Financial forecast, the expected conditions and course of action in the prospective period

(b) Financial projection, the purpose of the presentation

h. If a significant part of the prospective period has expired, inquire about the results of operations or significant portions of the operations (such as sales volume), and significant changes in financial position, and consider their effect in relation to the prospective financial statements. If historical financial statements have been prepared for the expired portion of the period, the practitioner should read such statements and consider those results in relation to the prospective financial statements.

i. Confirm his or her understanding of the statements (including assumptions) by obtaining written representations from the responsible party. Because the amounts reflected in the statements are not supported by historical books and records but rather by assumptions, the practitioner should obtain representations in which the responsible party indicates its responsibility for the assumptions. The representations should be signed by the responsible party at the highest

---

[1] Presentation guidelines for entities that issue prospective financial statements are set forth and illustrated in AICPA Guide *Prospective Financial Information*.

level of authority who the practitioner believes is responsible for and knowledgeable, directly or through others, about matters covered by the representations.

(1) For a *financial forecast*, the representations should include the responsible party's assertion that the financial forecast presents, to the best of its knowledge and belief, the expected financial position, results of operations, and cash flows for the forecast period and that the forecast reflects the responsible party's judgment, based on present circumstances, of the expected conditions and its expected course of action. The representations should also include a statement that the forecast is presented in conformity with guidelines for presentation of a forecast established by the American Institute of Certified Public Accountants. The representations should also include a statement that the assumptions on which the forecast is based are reasonable. If the forecast contains a range, the representation should also include a statement that, to the best of the responsible party's knowledge and belief, the item or items subject to the assumption are expected to actually fall within the range and that the range was not selected in a biased or misleading manner.

(2) For a *financial projection*, the representations should include the responsible party's assertion that the financial projection presents, to the best of its knowledge and belief, the expected financial position, results of operations, and cash flows for the projection period given the hypothetical assumptions, and that the projection reflects its judgment, based on present circumstances, of expected conditions and its expected course of action given the occurrence of the hypothetical events. The representations should also (*i*) identify the hypothetical assumptions and describe the limitations on the usefulness of the presentation, (*ii*) state that the assumptions are appropriate, (*iii*) indicate if the hypothetical assumptions are improbable, and (*iv*) if the projection contains a range, include a statement that, to the best of the responsible party's knowledge and belief, given the hypothetical assumptions, the item or items subject to the assumption are expected to actually fall within the range and that the range was not selected in a biased or misleading manner. The representations should also include a statement that the projection is presented in conformity with guidelines for presentation of a projection established by the American Institute of Certified Public Accountants.

j. Consider, after applying the preceding procedures, whether he or she has received representations or other information that appears to be obviously inappropriate, incomplete, or otherwise misleading and, if so, attempt to obtain additional or revised information. If he or she does not receive such information, the practitioner should ordinarily withdraw from the compilation engagement.[2] (Note that the omission of disclosures, other than those relating to significant assumptions, would not require the practitioner to withdraw; see paragraph .26.)

---

[2] The practitioner need not withdraw from the engagement if the effect of such information on the prospective financial statements does not appear to be material.

.70

Appendix C

Training and Proficiency, Planning, and Procedures Applicable to Examinations

Training and Proficiency

1. The practitioner should be familiar with the guidelines for the preparation and presentation of prospective financial statements. The guidelines are contained in AICPA Guide *Prospective Financial Information*.

2. The practitioner should possess or obtain a level of knowledge of the industry and the accounting principles and practices of the industry in which the entity operates or will operate that will enable him or her to examine prospective financial statements that are in appropriate form for an entity operating in that industry.

Planning an Examination Engagement

3. Planning the examination engagement involves developing an overall strategy for the expected scope and conduct of the engagement. To develop such a strategy, the practitioner needs to have sufficient knowledge to enable him or her to adequately understand the events, transactions, and practices that, in his or her judgment, may have a significant effect on the prospective financial statements.

4. Factors to be considered by the practitioner in planning the examination include the following:

a. The accounting principles to be used and the type of presentation

b. The anticipated level of attestation risk related to the prospective financial statements[1]

c. Preliminary judgments about materiality levels

d. Items within the prospective financial statements that are likely to require revision or adjustment

e. Conditions that may require extension or modification of the practitioner's examination procedures

f. Knowledge of the entity's business and its industry

g. The responsible party's experience in preparing prospective financial statements

h. The length of the period covered by the prospective financial statements

i. The process by which the responsible party develops its prospective financial statements

---

[1] *Attestation* risk is the risk that the practitioner may unknowingly fail to appropriately modify his or her examination report on prospective financial statements that are materially misstated, that is, that are not presented in conformity with AICPA presentation guidelines or have assumptions that do not provide a reasonable basis for management's forecast, or management's projection given the hypothetical assumptions. It consists of (*a*) the risk (consisting of *inherent risk* and *control risk*) that the prospective financial statements contain errors that could be material and (*b*) the risk (*detection risk*) that the practitioner will not detect such errors.

5. The practitioner should obtain knowledge of the entity's business, accounting principles, and the key factors upon which its future financial results appear to depend. The practitioner should focus on areas such as the following:

a. The availability and cost of resources needed to operate (Principal items usually include raw materials, labor, short-term and long-term financing, and plant and equipment.)

b. The nature and condition of markets in which the entity sells its goods or services, including final consumer markets if the entity sells to intermediate markets

c. Factors specific to the industry, including competitive conditions, sensitivity to economic conditions, accounting policies, specific regulatory requirements, and technology

d. Patterns of past performance for the entity or comparable entities, including trends in revenue and costs, turnover of assets, uses and capacities of physical facilities, and management policies

Examination Procedures

6. The practitioner should establish an understanding with the responsible party regarding the services to be performed. The understanding should include the objectives of the engagement, the responsible party's responsibilities, the practitioner's responsibilities, and limitations of the engagement. The practitioner should document the understanding in the working papers, preferably through a written communication with the responsible party. If the practitioner believes an understanding with the responsible party has not been established, he or she should decline to accept or perform the engagement. If the responsible party is different than the client, the practitioner should establish the understanding with both the client and the responsible party, and the understanding also should include the client's responsibilities.

7. The practitioner's objective in an examination of prospective financial statements is to accumulate sufficient evidence to restrict attestation risk to a level that is, in his or her professional judgment, appropriate for the level of assurance that may be imparted by his or her examination report. In a report on an examination of prospective financial statements, the practitioner provides assurance only about whether the prospective financial statements are presented in conformity with AICPA presentation guidelines and whether the assumptions provide a reasonable basis for management's forecast, or a reasonable basis for management's projection given the hypothetical assumptions. He or she does not provide assurance about the achievability of the prospective results because events and circumstances frequently do not occur as expected and achievement of the prospective results is dependent on the actions, plans, and assumptions of the responsible party.

8. In his or her examination of prospective financial statements, the practitioner should select from all available procedures—that is, procedures that assess inherent and control risk and restrict detection risk—any combination that can restrict attestation risk to such an appropriate level. The extent to which examination procedures will be performed should be based on the practitioner's consideration of the following:

a. The nature and materiality of the information to the prospective financial statements taken as a whole

b. The likelihood of misstatements

c. Knowledge obtained during current and previous engagements

d. The responsible party's competence with respect to prospective financial statements

e. The extent to which the prospective financial statements are affected by the responsible party's judgment, for example, its judgment in selecting the assumptions used to prepare the prospective financial statements

f. The adequacy of the responsible party's underlying data

9. The practitioner should perform those procedures he or she considers necessary in the circumstances to report on whether the assumptions provide a reasonable basis for the following.

a. *Financial forecast.* The practitioner can form an opinion that the assumptions provide a reasonable basis for the forecast if the responsible party represents that the presentation reflects, to the best of its knowledge and belief, its estimate of expected financial position, results of operations, and cash flows for the prospective period[2] and the practitioner concludes, based on his or her examination, (*i*) that the responsible party has explicitly identified all factors expected to materially affect the operations of the entity during the prospective period and has developed appropriate assumptions with respect to such factors[3] and (*ii*) that the assumptions are suitably supported.

b. *Financial projection given the hypothetical assumptions.* The practitioner can form an opinion that the assumptions provide a reasonable basis for the financial projection given the hypothetical assumptions if the responsible party represents that the presentation reflects, to the best of its knowledge and belief, expected financial position, results of operations, and cash flows for the prospective period given the hypothetical assumptions[4] and the practitioner concludes, based on his or her examination, that:

(1) The responsible party has explicitly identified all factors that would materially affect the operations of the entity during the prospective period if the hypothetical assumptions were to materialize and has developed appropriate assumptions with respect to such factors and

(2) The other assumptions are suitably supported given the hypothetical assumptions. However, as the number and significance of the hypothetical assumptions increase, the practitioner may not be able to satisfy himself or herself about the presentation as a whole by obtaining support for the remaining assumptions.

10. The practitioner should evaluate the support for the assumptions.

a. *Financial forecast*—The practitioner can conclude that assumptions are suitably supported if the preponderance of information supports each significant assumption.

---

[2] If the forecast contains a range, the representation should also include a statement that, to the best of the responsible party's knowledge and belief, the item or items subject to the assumption are expected to actually fall within the range and that the range was not selected in a biased or misleading manner.

[3] An attempt to list all assumptions is inherently not feasible. Frequently, basic assumptions that have enormous potential impact are considered to be implicit, such as conditions of peace and absence of natural disasters.

[4] If the projection contains a range, the representation should also include a statement that, to the best of the responsible party's knowledge and belief, given the hypothetical assumptions, the item or items subject to the assumption are expected to actually fall within the range and that the range was not selected in a biased or misleading manner.

b. *Financial projection*—In evaluating support for assumptions other than hypothetical assumptions, the practitioner can conclude that they are suitably supported if the preponderance of information supports each significant assumption given the hypothetical assumptions. The practitioner need not obtain support for the hypothetical assumptions, although he or she should consider whether they are consistent with the purpose of the presentation.

11. In evaluating the support for assumptions, the practitioner should consider—

a. Whether sufficient pertinent sources of information about the assumptions have been considered. Examples of external sources the practitioner might consider are government publications, industry publications, economic forecasts, existing or proposed legislation, and reports of changing technology. Examples of internal sources are budgets, labor agreements, patents, royalty agreements and records, sales backlog records, debt agreements, and actions of the board of directors involving entity plans.

b. Whether the assumptions are consistent with the sources from which they are derived.

c. Whether the assumptions are consistent with each other.

d. Whether the historical financial information and other data used in developing the assumptions are sufficiently reliable for that purpose. Reliability can be assessed by inquiry and analytical or other procedures, some of which may have been completed in past audits or reviews of the historical financial statements. If historical financial statements have been prepared for an expired part of the prospective period, the practitioner should consider the historical data in relation to the prospective results for the same period, where applicable. If the prospective financial statements incorporate such historical financial results and that period is significant to the presentation, the practitioner should make a review of the historical information in conformity with the applicable standards for a review.[5]

e. Whether the historical financial information and other data used in developing the assumptions are comparable over the periods specified or whether the effects of any lack of comparability were considered in developing the assumptions.

f. Whether the logical arguments or theory, considered with the data supporting the assumptions, are reasonable.

12. In evaluating the preparation and presentation of the prospective financial statements, the practitioner should perform procedures that will provide reasonable assurance as to the following.

---

[5] If the entity is an issuer, the practitioner should perform the procedures in paragraphs .13–.19 of AU section 722, *Interim Financial Information* (AICPA, *PCAOB Standards and Related Rules*, Interim Standards). If the entity is a nonissuer, the practitioner should perform the procedures in AR section 90, *Review of Financial Statements*, or in AU-C section 930, *Interim Financial Information*, when the review of interim financial information meets the provisions of that section. [Footnote revised, November 2002, to reflect conforming changes necessary due to the issuance of SAS No. 100 and SSARS No. 9. Footnote revised, May 2004, to reflect the conforming changes necessary due to the issuance of SSARS No. 10. Footnote revised, December 2012, to reflect conforming changes necessary due to the issuance of SAS Nos. 122–126 and SSARS No. 19.]

a. The presentation reflects the identified assumptions.

b. The computations made to translate the assumptions into prospective amounts are mathematically accurate.

c. The assumptions are internally consistent.

d. Accounting principles used in the—

(1) Financial forecast are consistent with the accounting principles expected to be used in the historical financial statements covering the prospective period and those used in the most recent historical financial statements, if any.

(2) Financial projection are consistent with the accounting principles expected to be used in the prospective period and those used in the most recent historical financial statements, if any, or that they are consistent with the purpose of the presentation.[6]

e. The presentation of the prospective financial statements follows the AICPA guidelines applicable for such statements.[7]

f. The assumptions have been adequately disclosed based on AICPA presentation guidelines for prospective financial statements.

13. The practitioner should consider whether the prospective financial statements, including related disclosures, should be revised because of any of the following:

a. Mathematical errors

b. Unreasonable or internally inconsistent assumptions

c. Inappropriate or incomplete presentation

d. Inadequate disclosure

14. The practitioner should obtain written representations from the responsible party acknowledging its responsibility for both the presentation and the underlying assumptions. The representations should be signed by the responsible party at the highest level of authority who the practitioner believes is responsible for and knowledgeable, directly or through others in the organization, about the matters covered by the representations. Paragraph .69, subparagraph 5*i* describes the specific representations to be obtained for a financial forecast and a financial projection. See paragraph .43 for guidance on the form of report to be rendered if the practitioner is not able to obtain the required representations.

---

[6] The accounting principles used in a financial projection need not be those expected to be used in the historical financial statements for the prospective period if use of different principles is consistent with the purpose of the presentation.

[7] Presentation guidelines for entities that issue prospective financial statements are set forth and illustrated in AICPA Guide *Prospective Financial Information*.

AT Section 401

Reporting on Pro Forma Financial Information

Source: SSAE No. 10.

Effective when the presentation of pro forma financial information is as of or for a period ending on or after June 1, 2001. Earlier application is permitted.

Introduction

.01 This section provides guidance to a practitioner who is engaged to issue or does issue an examination or a review report on pro forma financial information. Such an engagement should comply with the general and fieldwork standards established in section 50, *SSAE Hierarchy*, and the specific performance and reporting standards set forth in this section.[1] [Revised, November 2006, to reflect conforming changes necessary due to the issuance of SSAE No. 14.]

.02 When pro forma financial information is presented outside the basic financial statements but within the same document, and the practitioner is not engaged to report on the pro forma financial information, the practitioner's responsibilities are described in AU-C section 720, *Other Information in Documents Containing Audited Financial Statements*, and AU-C section 925, *Filings With the U.S. Securities and Exchange Commission Under the Securities Act of 1933*. [Revised, December 2012, to reflect conforming changes necessary due to the issuance of SAS Nos. 122–126.]

.03 This section does not apply in those circumstances when, for purposes of a more meaningful presentation, a transaction consummated after the balance-sheet date is reflected in the historical financial statements (such as a revision of debt maturities or a revision of earnings per share calculations for a stock split).[2]

Presentation of Pro Forma Financial Information

.04 The objective of pro forma financial information is to show what the significant effects on historical financial information might have been had a consummated or proposed transaction (or event) occurred at an earlier date. Pro forma financial information is commonly used to show the effects of transactions such as the following:

- Business combination
- Change in capitalization

---

[1] Paragraph .10 of AU-C section 920, *Letters for Underwriters and Certain Other Requesting Parties*, identifies certain parties who may request a letter. When one of those parties requests a letter or asks the practitioner to perform agreed-upon procedures on pro forma financial information in connection with an offering, the practitioner should follow the guidance in paragraphs .10, .13, .44, and .52–.53 of AU-C section 920. [Footnote revised, December 2012, to reflect conforming changes necessary due to the issuance of SAS Nos. 122–126.]

[2] In certain circumstances, generally accepted accounting principles may require the presentation of pro forma financial information in the financial statements or the accompanying notes. That information includes, for example, pro forma financial information required by Financial Accounting Standards Board (FASB) *Accounting Standards Codification* (ASC) 805, *Business Combinations*, or FASB ASC 250, *Accounting Changes and Error Corrections*. [Footnote revised, June 2009, to reflect conforming changes necessary due to the issuance of FASB ASC. Footnote revised, December 2012, to reflect conforming changes necessary due to the issuance of SAS Nos. 122–126.]

- Disposition of a significant portion of the business
- Change in the form of business organization or status as an autonomous entity
- Proposed sale of securities and the application of the proceeds

.05 This objective is achieved primarily by applying pro forma adjustments to historical financial information. Pro forma adjustments should be based on management's assumptions and give effect to all significant effects directly attributable to the transaction (or event).

.06 Pro forma financial information should be labeled as such to distinguish it from historical financial information. This presentation should describe the transaction (or event) that is reflected in the pro forma financial information, the source of the historical financial information on which it is based, the significant assumptions used in developing the pro forma adjustments, and any significant uncertainties about those assumptions. The presentation also should indicate that the pro forma financial information should be read in conjunction with related historical financial information and that the pro forma financial information is not necessarily indicative of the results (such as financial position and results of operations, as applicable) that would have been attained had the transaction (or event) actually taken place earlier.[3]

Conditions for Reporting

.07 The practitioner may agree to report on an examination or a review of pro forma financial information if the following conditions are met.

a. The document that contains the pro forma financial information includes (or incorporates by reference) complete historical financial statements of the entity for the most recent year (or for the preceding year if financial statements for the most recent year are not yet available) and, if pro forma financial information is presented for an interim period, the document also includes (or incorporates by reference) historical interim financial information for that period (which may be presented in condensed form).[4] In the case of a business combination, the document should include (or incorporate by reference) the appropriate historical financial information for the significant constituent parts of the combined entity.

b. The historical financial statements of the entity (or, in the case of a business combination, of each significant constituent part of the combined entity) on which the pro forma financial information is based have been audited or reviewed.[5] The practitioner's attestation risk

---

[3] For further guidance on the presentation of pro forma financial information included in filings with the Securities and Exchange Commission (SEC), see Article 11 of Regulation S-X.

[4] For pro forma financial information included in an SEC Form 8-K, historical financial information previously included in an SEC filing would meet this requirement. Interim historical financial information may be presented as a column in the pro forma financial information.

[5] The practitioner's audit or review report should be included (or incorporated by reference) in the document containing the pro forma financial information. For issuers, the review may be that as defined in AU section 722, *Interim Financial Information* (AICPA, *PCAOB Standards and Related Rules*, Interim Standards). For nonissuers, the review may be that as defined in AR section 90, *Review of Financial Statements*, or in AU-C section 930, *Interim Financial Information*, when the review of interim financial information meets the provisions of that section. [Footnote revised, November 2002, to reflect conforming changes necessary due to the issuance of SAS No. 100. Footnote revised, December 2012, to reflect conforming changes necessary due to the issuance of SAS Nos. 122–126 and SSARS No. 19.]

relating to the pro forma financial information is affected by the scope of the engagement providing the practitioner with assurance about the underlying historical financial information to which the pro forma adjustments are applied. Therefore, the level of assurance given by the practitioner on the pro forma financial information, as of a particular date or for a particular period, should be limited to the level of assurance provided on the historical financial statements (or, in the case of a business combination, the lowest level of assurance provided on the underlying historical financial statements of any significant constituent part of the combined entity). For example, if the underlying historical financial statements of each constituent part of the combined entity have been audited at year-end and reviewed at an interim date, the practitioner may perform an examination or a review of the pro forma financial information at year-end but is limited to performing a review of the pro forma financial information at the interim date.

c. The practitioner who is reporting on the pro forma financial information should have an appropriate level of knowledge of the accounting and financial reporting practices of each significant constituent part of the combined entity. This would ordinarily have been obtained by the practitioner auditing or reviewing historical financial statements of each entity for the most recent annual or interim period for which the pro forma financial information is presented. If another practitioner has performed such an audit or a review, the need, by a practitioner reporting on the pro forma financial information, for an understanding of the entity's accounting and financial reporting practices is not diminished, and that practitioner should consider whether, under the particular circumstances, he or she can acquire sufficient knowledge of these matters to perform the procedures necessary to report on the pro forma financial information.

Practitioner's Objective

.08 The objective of the practitioner's examination procedures applied to pro forma financial information is to provide reasonable assurance as to whether—

- Management's assumptions provide a reasonable basis for presenting the significant effects directly attributable to the underlying transaction (or event).
- The related pro forma adjustments give appropriate effect to those assumptions.
- The pro forma column reflects the proper application of those adjustments to the historical financial statements.

.09 The objective of the practitioner's review procedures applied to pro forma financial information is to provide negative assurance as to whether any information came to the practitioner's attention to cause him or her to believe that—

- Management's assumptions do not provide a reasonable basis for presenting the significant effects directly attributable to the underlying transaction (or event).
- The related pro forma adjustments do not give appropriate effect to those assumptions.

- The pro forma column does not reflect the proper application of those adjustments to the historical financial statements.

Procedures

.10 Other than the procedures applied to the historical financial statements,[6] the procedures the practitioner should apply to the assumptions and pro forma adjustments for either an examination or a review engagement are as follows.

a. Obtain an understanding of the underlying transaction (or event), for example, by reading relevant contracts and minutes of meetings of the board of directors and by making inquiries of appropriate officials of the entity, and, in cases, of the entity acquired or to be acquired.

b. Obtain a level of knowledge of each constituent part of the combined entity in a business combination that will enable the practitioner to perform the required procedures. Procedures to obtain this knowledge may include communicating with other practitioners who have audited or reviewed the historical financial information on which the pro forma financial information is based. Matters that may be considered include accounting principles and financial reporting practices followed, transactions between the entities, and material contingencies.

c. Discuss with management their assumptions regarding the effects of the transaction (or event).

d. Evaluate whether pro forma adjustments are included for all significant effects directly attributable to the transaction (or event).

e. Obtain sufficient evidence in support of such adjustments. The evidence required to support the level of assurance given is a matter of professional judgment. The practitioner typically would obtain more evidence in an examination engagement than in a review engagement. Examples of evidence that the practitioner might consider obtaining are purchase, merger or exchange agreements, appraisal reports, debt agreements, employment agreements, actions of the board of directors, and existing or proposed legislation or regulatory actions.

f. Evaluate whether management's assumptions that underlie the pro forma adjustments are presented in a sufficiently clear and comprehensive manner. Also, evaluate whether the pro forma adjustments are consistent with each other and with the data used to develop them.

g. Determine that computations of pro forma adjustments are mathematically correct and that the pro forma column reflects the proper application of those adjustments to the historical financial statements.

h. Obtain written representations from management concerning their—

  - Responsibility for the assumptions used in determining the pro forma adjustments

[6] See paragraph .07*b*.

- Assertion that the assumptions provide a reasonable basis for presenting all of the significant effects directly attributable to the transaction (or event), that the related pro forma adjustments give appropriate effect to those assumptions, and that the pro forma column reflects the proper application of those adjustments to the historical financial statements
- Assertion that the significant effects directly attributable to the transaction (or event) are appropriately disclosed in the pro forma financial information

i. Read the pro forma financial information and evaluate whether—

- The underlying transaction (or event), the pro forma adjustments, the significant assumptions and the significant uncertainties, if any, about those assumptions have been appropriately described.
- The source of the historical financial information on which the pro forma financial information is based has been appropriately identified.

Reporting on Pro Forma Financial Information

.11 The practitioner's report on pro forma financial information should be dated as of the completion of the appropriate procedures. The practitioner's report on pro forma financial information may be added to the practitioner's report on historical financial information, or it may appear separately. If the reports are combined and the date of completion of the procedures for the examination or review of the pro forma financial information is after the date of completion of the fieldwork for the audit or review of the historical financial information, the combined report should be dual-dated. (For example, "February 15, 20X2, except for the paragraphs regarding pro forma financial information as to which the date is March 20, 20X2.")

.12 A practitioner's examination report on pro forma financial information should include the following:

a. A title that includes the word *independent*

b. An identification of the pro forma financial information

c. A reference to the financial statements from which the historical financial information is derived and a statement that such financial statements were audited (The report on pro forma financial information should refer to any modification in the practitioner's report on the historical financial information.)

d. An identification of the responsible party and a statement that the responsible party is responsible for the pro forma financial information

e. A statement that the practitioner's responsibility is to express an opinion on the pro forma financial information based on his or her examination

f. A statement that the examination of the pro forma financial information was conducted in accordance with attestation standards established by the American Institute of Certified Public Accountants and, accordingly, included such procedures as the practitioner considered necessary in the circumstances

g. A statement that the practitioner believes that the examination provides a reasonable basis for his or her opinion

h. A separate paragraph explaining the objective of pro forma financial information and its limitations

i. The practitioner's opinion as to whether management's assumptions provide a reasonable basis for presenting the significant effects directly attributable to the transaction (or event), whether the related pro forma adjustments give appropriate effect to those assumptions, and whether the pro forma column reflects the proper application of those adjustments to the historical financial statements (see paragraphs .18 and .20)

j. The manual or printed signature of the practitioner's firm

k. The date of the examination report

.13 A practitioner's review report on pro forma financial information should include the following:

a. A title that includes the word *independent*

b. An identification of the pro forma financial information

c. A reference to the financial statements from which the historical financial information is derived and a statement as to whether such financial statements were audited or reviewed (The report on pro forma financial information should refer to any modification in the practitioner's report on the historical financial information.)

d. An identification of the responsible party and a statement that the responsible party is responsible for the pro forma financial information

e. A statement that the review of the pro forma financial information was conducted in accordance with attestation standards established by the American Institute of Certified Public Accountants

f. A statement that a review is substantially less in scope than an examination, the objective of which is the expression of an opinion on the pro forma financial information and, accordingly, the practitioner does not express such an opinion

g. A separate paragraph explaining the objective of pro forma financial information and its limitations

h. The practitioner's conclusion as to whether any information came to the practitioner's attention to cause him or her to believe that management's assumptions do not provide a reasonable basis for presenting the significant effects directly attributable to the transaction (or event), or that the related pro forma adjustments do not give appropriate effect to those assumptions, or that the pro forma column does not reflect the proper application of those adjustments to the historical financial statements (See paragraphs .19–.20.)

i. The manual or printed signature of the practitioner's firm

j. The date of the review report

.14 Nothing precludes the practitioner from restricting the use of the report (see paragraphs .78–.83 of section 101).

.15 Because a pooling-of-interests business combination is accounted for by combining historical amounts retroactively, pro forma adjustments for a proposed transaction generally affect only the equity section of the pro forma condensed balance sheet. Further, because of the requirements of Financial Accounting Standards Board *Accounting Standards Codification* 805, *Business Combinations*, a business combination effected as a pooling of interests would not ordinarily involve a choice of assumptions by management. Accordingly, a report on a proposed pooling transaction need not address management's assumptions unless the pro forma financial information includes adjustments to conform the accounting principles of the combining entities. (See paragraph .21.) [Revised, June 2009, to reflect conforming changes necessary due to the issuance of FASB ASC.]

.16 Restrictions on the scope of the engagement (see paragraphs .73–.75 of section 101), reservations about the propriety of the assumptions and the conformity of the presentation with those assumptions (including adequate disclosure of significant matters), or other reservations may require the practitioner to qualify the opinion, disclaim an opinion, or withdraw from the engagement.[7] The practitioner should disclose all substantive reasons for any report modifications. Uncertainty as to whether the transaction (or event) will be consummated would not ordinarily require a report modification. (See paragraph .22.)

Effective Date

.17 This section is effective when the presentation of pro forma financial information is as of or for a period ending on or after June 1, 2001. Early application is permitted.

[7] See paragraphs .76–.77 of section 101.

.18

Appendix A

Report on Examination of Pro Forma Financial Information

Independent Accountant's Report

We have examined the pro forma adjustments reflecting the transaction [*or event*] described in Note 1 and the application of those adjustments to the historical amounts in [*the assembly of*][8] the accompanying pro forma financial condensed balance sheet of X Company as of December 31, 20X1, and the pro forma condensed statement of income for the year then ended. The historical condensed financial statements are derived from the historical financial statements of X Company, which were audited by us, and of Y Company, which were audited by other accountants,[9] appearing elsewhere herein [*or incorporated by reference*].[10] Such pro forma adjustments are based upon management's assumptions described in Note 2. X Company's management is responsible for the pro forma financial information. Our responsibility is to express an opinion on the pro forma financial information based on our examination.

Our examination was conducted in accordance with attestation standards established by the American Institute of Certified Public Accountants and, accordingly, included such procedures as we considered necessary in the circumstances. We believe that our examination provides a reasonable basis for our opinion.

The objective of this pro forma financial information is to show what the significant effects on the historical financial information might have been had the transaction [*or event*] occurred at an earlier date. However, the pro forma condensed financial statements are not necessarily indicative of the results of operations or related effects on financial position that would have been attained had the above-mentioned transaction [*or event*] actually occurred earlier.

[*Additional paragraph(s) may be added to emphasize certain matters relating to the attest engagement or the subject matter.*]

In our opinion, management's assumptions provide a reasonable basis for presenting the significant effects directly attributable to the above-mentioned transaction [*or event*] described in Note 1, the related pro forma adjustments give appropriate effect to those assumptions, and the pro forma column reflects the proper application of those adjustments to the historical financial statement amounts in the pro forma condensed balance sheet as of December 31, 20X1, and the pro forma condensed statement of income for the year then ended.

[*Signature*]

[*Date*]

---

8 This wording is appropriate when one column of pro forma financial information is presented without separate columns of historical financial information and pro forma adjustments.

9 If either accountant's report includes an explanatory paragraph or is other than unqualified, that fact should be referred to within this report.

10 If the option in footnote 4 to paragraph .07*a* is followed, the report should be appropriately modified.

.19

Appendix B

Report on Review of Pro Forma Financial Information

Independent Accountant's Report

We have reviewed the pro forma adjustments reflecting the transaction [*or event*] described in Note 1 and the application of those adjustments to the historical amounts in [*the assembly of*][11] the accompanying pro forma condensed balance sheet of X Company as of March 31, 20X2, and the pro forma condensed statement of income for the three months then ended. These historical condensed financial statements are derived from the historical unaudited financial statements of X Company, which were reviewed by us, and of Y Company, which were reviewed by other accountants,[12, 13] appearing elsewhere herein [*or incorporated by reference*].[14] Such pro forma adjustments are based on management's assumptions as described in Note 2. X Company's management is responsible for the pro forma financial information.

Our review was conducted in accordance with attestation standards established by the American Institute of Certified Public Accountants. A review is substantially less in scope than an examination, the objective of which is the expression of an opinion on management's assumptions, the pro forma adjustments and the application of those adjustments to historical financial information. Accordingly, we do not express such an opinion.

The objective of this pro forma financial information is to show what the significant effects on the historical financial information might have been had the transaction [*or event*] occurred at an earlier date. However, the pro forma condensed financial statements are not necessarily indicative of the results of operations or related effects on financial position that would have been attained had the above-mentioned transaction [*or event*] actually occurred earlier.

[*Additional paragraph(s) may be added to emphasize certain matters relating to the attest engagement or the subject matter.*]

Based on our review, nothing came to our attention that caused us to believe that management's assumptions do not provide a reasonable basis for presenting the significant effects directly attributable to the above-mentioned transaction [*or event*] described in Note 1, that the related pro forma adjustments do

---

[11] This wording is appropriate when one column of pro forma financial information is presented without separate columns of historical financial information and pro forma adjustments.

[12] If either accountant's report includes an explanatory paragraph or is modified, that fact should be referred to within this report.

[13] Where one set of historical financial statements is audited and the other set is reviewed, wording similar to the following would be appropriate:

The historical condensed financial statements are derived from the historical financial statements of X Company, which were audited by us, and of Y Company, which were reviewed by other accountants, appearing elsewhere herein [*or incorporated by reference*].

[14] If the option in footnote 4 to paragraph .07*a* is followed, the report should be appropriately modified.

not give appropriate effect to those assumptions, or that the pro forma column does not reflect the proper application of those adjustments to the historical financial statement amounts in the pro forma condensed balance sheet as of March 31, 20X2, and the pro forma condensed statement of income for the three months then ended.

[*Signature*]

[*Date*]

.20

Appendix C

Report on Examination of Pro Forma Financial Information at Year-End With a Review of Pro Forma Financial Information for a Subsequent Interim Date

Independent Accountant's Report

We have examined the pro forma adjustments reflecting the transaction [*or event*] described in Note 1 and the application of those adjustments to the historical amounts in [*the assembly of*][15] the accompanying pro forma financial condensed balance sheet of X Company as of December 31, 20X1, and the pro forma condensed statement of income for the year then ended. The historical condensed financial statements are derived from the historical financial statements of X Company, which were audited by us, and of Y Company, which were audited by other accountants,[16] appearing elsewhere herein [*or incorporated by reference*].[17] Such pro forma adjustments are based upon management's assumptions described in Note 2. X Company's management is responsible for the pro forma financial information. Our responsibility is to express an opinion on the pro forma financial information based on our examination.

Our examination was conducted in accordance with attestation standards established by the American Institute of Certified Public Accountants and, accordingly, included such procedures as we considered necessary in the circumstances. We believe that our examination provides a reasonable basis for our opinion.

In addition, we have reviewed the pro forma adjustments and the application of those adjustments to the historical amounts in [*the assembly of*] the accompanying pro forma condensed balance sheet of X Company as of March 31, 20X2, and the pro forma condensed statement of income for the three months then ended. The historical condensed financial statements are derived from the historical financial statements of X Company, which were reviewed by us, and of Y Company, which were reviewed by other accountants,[18] appearing elsewhere herein [*or incorporated by reference*].[19] Such pro forma adjustments are based upon management's assumptions as described in Note 2. Our review

---

[15] This wording is appropriate when one column of pro forma financial information is presented without separate columns of historical financial information and pro forma adjustments.

[16] If either accountant's report includes an explanatory paragraph or is other than unqualified, that fact should be referred to within this report.

[17] If the option in footnote 4 to paragraph .07*a* is followed, the report should be appropriately modified.

[18] Where one set of historical financial statements is audited and the other set is reviewed, wording similar to the following would be appropriate:

The historical condensed financial statements are derived from the historical financial statements of X Company, which were audited by us, and of Y Company, which were reviewed by other accountants, appearing elsewhere herein [*or incorporated by reference*].

[19] If the option in footnote 4 to paragraph .07*a* is followed, the report should be appropriately modified.

was conducted in accordance with attestation standards established by the American Institute of Certified Public Accountants. A review is substantially less in scope than an examination, the objective of which is the expression of an opinion on management's assumptions, the pro forma adjustments, and the application of those adjustments to historical financial information. Accordingly, we do not express such an opinion on the pro forma adjustments or the application of such adjustments to the pro forma condensed balance sheet as of March 31, 20X2, and the pro forma condensed statement of income for the three months then ended.

The objective of this pro forma financial information is to show what the significant effects on the historical financial information might have been had the transactions [*or event*] occurred at an earlier date. However, the pro forma condensed financial statements are not necessarily indicative of the results of operations or related effects on financial position that would have been attained had the above-mentioned transaction [*or event*] actually occurred earlier.

[*Additional paragraph(s) may be added to emphasize certain matters relating to the attest engagements or the subject matter.*]

In our opinion, management's assumptions provide a reasonable basis for presenting the significant effects directly attributable to the above-mentioned transaction [*or event*] described in Note 1, the related pro forma adjustments give appropriate effect to those assumptions, and the pro forma column reflects the proper application of those adjustments to the historical financial statement amounts in the pro forma condensed balance sheet as of December 31, 20X1, and the pro forma condensed statement of income for the year then ended.

Based on our review, nothing came to our attention that caused us to believe that management's assumptions do not provide a reasonable basis for presenting the significant effects directly attributable to the above-mentioned transaction [*or event*] described in Note 1, that the related pro forma adjustments do not give appropriate effect to those assumptions, or that the pro forma column does not reflect the proper application of those adjustments to the historical financial statement amounts in the pro forma condensed balance sheet as of March 31, 20X2, and the pro forma condensed statement of income for the three months then ended.

[*Signature*]

[*Date*]

.21

Appendix D

Report on Examination of Pro Forma Financial Information Giving Effect to a Business Combination to Be Accounted for as a Pooling of Interests[20]

Independent Accountant's Report

We have examined the pro forma adjustments reflecting the proposed business combination to be accounted for as a pooling of interests described in Note 1 and the application of those adjustments to the historical amounts in the accompanying pro forma condensed balance sheet of X Company as of December 31, 20X1, and the pro forma condensed statements of income for each of three years in the period then ended. These historical condensed financial statements are derived from the historical financial statements of X Company, which were audited by us,[21] and of Y Company, which were audited by other accountants, appearing elsewhere herein [*or incorporated by reference*].[22] Such pro forma adjustments are based upon management's assumptions described in Note 2. X Company's management is responsible for the pro forma financial information. Our responsibility is to express an opinion on the pro forma financial information based on our examination.

Our examination was conducted in accordance with attestation standards established by the American Institute of Certified Public Accountants and, accordingly, included such procedures as we considered necessary in the circumstances. We believe that our examination provides a reasonable basis for our opinion.

The objective of this pro forma financial information is to show what the significant effects on the historical financial information might have been had the transactions [*or event*] occurred at an earlier date.

[*Additional paragraph(s) may be added to emphasize certain matters relating to the attest engagement or the subject matter.*]

In our opinion, the accompanying condensed pro forma financial statements of X Company as of December 31, 20X1, and for each of the three years in the period then ended give appropriate effect to the pro forma adjustments necessary to reflect the proposed business combination on a pooling of interests basis as described in Note 1 and the pro forma column reflects the proper application of those adjustments to the historical financial statements.

[*Signature*]

[*Date*]

---

[20] See paragraph .15 for a discussion of the form of the opinion on pro forma financial information in a pooling of interests business combination.

[21] If either accountant's report includes an explanatory paragraph or is other than unqualified, that fact should be referred to within this report.

[22] If the option in footnote 4 to paragraph .07*a* is followed, the report should be appropriately modified.

.22

Appendix E

Other Example Reports

An example of a report qualified because of a scope limitation follows.

Independent Accountant's Report

We have examined the pro forma adjustments reflecting the transaction [*or event*] described in Note 1 and the application of those adjustments to the historical amounts in [*the assembly of*][23] the accompanying pro forma condensed balance sheet of X Company as of December 31, 20X1, and the pro forma condensed statement of income for the year then ended. The historical condensed financial statements are derived from the historical financial statements of X Company, which were audited by us, and of Y Company, which were audited by other accountants,[24] appearing elsewhere herein [*or incorporated by reference*].[25] Such pro forma adjustments are based upon management's assumptions described in Note 2. X Company's management is responsible for the pro forma financial information. Our responsibility is to express an opinion on the pro forma financial information based on our examination.

Except as described below, our examination was conducted in accordance with attestation standards established by the American Institute of Certified Public Accountants and, accordingly, included such procedures as we considered necessary in the circumstances. We believe that our examination provides a reasonable basis for our opinion.

We are unable to perform the examination procedures we considered necessary with respect to assumptions relating to the proposed loan described in Adjustment E in Note 2.

[*Same paragraph as third paragraph in examination report in paragraph .18*]

In our opinion, except for the effects of such changes, if any, as might have been determined to be necessary had we been able to satisfy ourselves as to the assumptions relating to the proposed loan, management's assumptions provide a reasonable basis for presenting the significant effects directly attributable to the above-mentioned transaction [*or event*] described in Note 1, the related pro forma adjustments give appropriate effect to those assumptions, and the pro forma column reflects the proper application of those adjustments to the historical financial statement amounts in the pro forma condensed balance sheet as of December 31, 20X1, and the pro forma condensed statement of income for the year then ended.

[*Signature*]

[*Date*]

---

[23] This wording is appropriate when one column of pro forma financial information is presented without separate columns of historical financial information and pro forma adjustments.

[24] If either accountant's report includes an explanatory paragraph or is other than unqualified, that fact should be referred to within this report.

[25] If the option in footnote 4 to paragraph .07*a* is followed, the report should be appropriately modified.

An example of a report qualified for reservations about the propriety of assumptions on an acquisition transaction follows:

[*Same first three paragraphs as examination report in paragraph .18*]

As discussed in Note 2 to the pro forma financial statements, the pro forma adjustments reflect management's assumption that X Division of the acquired company will be sold. The net assets of this division are reflected at their historical carrying amount; generally accepted accounting principles require these net assets to be recorded at estimated net realizable value.

In our opinion, except for inappropriate valuation of the net assets of X Division, management's assumptions described in Note 2 provide a reasonable basis for presenting the significant effects directly attributable to the above-mentioned transaction [*or event*] described in Note 1, the related pro forma adjustments give appropriate effect to those assumptions, and the pro forma column reflects the proper application of those adjustments to the historical financial statement amounts in the pro forma condensed balance sheet as of December 31, 20X1, and the pro forma condensed statement of income for the year then ended.

[*Signature*]

[*Date*]

An example of a disclaimer of opinion because of a scope limitation follows:

<u>Independent Accountant's Report</u>

We were engaged to examine the pro forma adjustments reflecting the transaction [*or event*] described in Note 1 and the application of those adjustments to the historical amounts in [*the assembly of*][26] the accompanying pro forma financial condensed balance sheet of X Company as of December 31, 20X1, and the pro forma condensed statement of income for the year then ended. The historical condensed financial statements are derived from the historical financial statements of X Company, which were audited by us, and of Y Company, which were audited by other accountants,[27] appearing elsewhere herein [*or incorporated by reference*].[28] Such pro forma adjustments are based upon management's assumptions described in Note 2. X Company's management is responsible for the pro forma financial information.

As discussed in Note 2 to the pro forma financial statements, the pro forma adjustments reflect management's assumptions that the elimination of duplicate facilities would have resulted in a 30 percent reduction in operating costs. Management could not supply us with sufficient evidence to support this assertion.

[*Same paragraph as third paragraph in examination report in paragraph .18*]

Since we were unable to evaluate management's assumptions regarding the reduction in operating costs and other assumptions related thereto, the scope of our work was not sufficient to express and, therefore, we do not express an

---

[26] This wording is appropriate when one column of pro forma financial information is presented without separate columns of historical financial information and pro forma adjustments.

[27] If either accountant's report includes an explanatory paragraph or is other than unqualified, that fact should be referred to within this report.

[28] If the option in footnote 4 to paragraph .07*a* is followed, the report should be appropriately modified.

opinion on the pro forma adjustments, management's underlying assumptions regarding those adjustments and the application of those adjustments to the historical financial statement amounts in the pro forma condensed financial statement amounts in the pro forma condensed balance sheet as of December 31, 20X1, and the pro forma condensed statement of income for the year then ended.

[*Signature*]

[*Date*]

AT Section 501

An Examination of an Entity's Internal Control Over Financial Reporting That Is Integrated With an Audit of Its Financial Statements

Source: SSAE No. 15.

See section 9501 for interpretations of this section.

Effective when the subject matter or assertion is as of or for a period ending on or after December 15, 2008. Earlier application is permitted.

Notice of Pending Withdrawal of AT Section 501, *An Examination of an Entity's Internal Control Over Financial Reporting That Is Integrated With an Audit of Its Financial Statements*

In October 2015, the Auditing Standards Board (ASB) issued SAS No. 130, *An Audit of Internal Control Over Financial Reporting That Is Integrated With an Audit of Financial Statements* (sec. 940), which withdraws AT section 501. SAS No. 130 is effective for integrated audits for periods ending on or after December 15, 2016, at which time the content of this section will be removed. The ASB concluded that, because engagements performed under AT section 501 are required to be integrated with an audit of financial statements, it would be appropriate to move the content of this section from the attestation standards into generally accepted auditing standards.

Applicability

.01 This section establishes requirements and provides guidance that applies when a practitioner[1] is engaged to perform an examination of the design and operating effectiveness of an entity's internal control over financial reporting (*examination of internal control*)[2] that is integrated with an audit of financial statements (*integrated audit*).[3]

.02 Ordinarily, the auditor will be engaged to examine the effectiveness of the entity's internal control over financial reporting (hereinafter referred to as

---

[1] In this section, the *practitioner* is referred to as the *auditor* because the examination of internal control is integrated with an audit of financial statements, and an examination provides the same level of assurance as an audit.

[2] In this section, the phrase *examination of internal control* means an engagement to report directly on internal control or on management's assertion thereon. The performance guidance in this section applies equally to either reporting alternative.

[3] Certain regulatory bodies require the examination of internal control and the audit of the financial statements to be performed by the same auditor. There are difficulties inherent in integrating the examination of internal control and the audit of the financial statements to meet the requirements of this section when the audit of the financial statements is performed by a different auditor. In such circumstances, the requirements of this section, nevertheless, apply.

internal control) as of the end of the entity's fiscal year; however, management may select a different date. If the auditor is engaged to examine the effectiveness of an entity's internal control at a date different from the end of the entity's fiscal year, the examination should, nevertheless, be integrated with a financial statement audit (see paragraphs .18–.19).

.03 An auditor may be engaged to examine the effectiveness of an entity's internal control for a period of time. In that circumstance, the guidance in this section should be modified accordingly, and the examination of internal control should be integrated with an audit of financial statements that covers the same period of time.

.04 This section does not provide guidance for the following:

a. Engagements to examine the suitability of design of an entity's internal control. Such engagements may be developed and performed under section 101, *Attest Engagements* [4]

b. Engagements to examine controls over the effectiveness and efficiency of operations. Such engagements may be developed and performed under section 101.

c. Engagements to examine controls over compliance with laws and regulations. See section 601, *Compliance Attestation.*

d. Engagements to report on controls at a service organization. See section 801, *Reporting on Controls at a Service Organization.*

e. Engagements to perform agreed-upon procedures on controls. See section 201, *Agreed-Upon Procedures Engagements.*

[Revised, August 2011, to reflect conforming changes necessary due to the issuance of SSAE No. 16.]

.05 The auditor may be requested to perform certain nonattest services related to the entity's internal control in addition to the examination of internal control. The auditor should determine whether to perform such nonattest services after considering relevant ethical requirements.

.06 An auditor should not accept an engagement to review an entity's internal control or a written assertion thereon.

Definitions and Underlying Concepts

.07 For purposes of this section, the terms listed below are defined as follows:

Control objective. The aim or purpose of specified controls. Control objectives ordinarily address the risks that the controls are intended to mitigate. In the context of internal control, a control objective generally relates to a relevant assertion for a significant account or disclosure and addresses the risk that the controls in a specific area will not provide reasonable assurance that a misstatement or omission in that relevant assertion is prevented, or detected and corrected on a timely basis.

Deficiency. A deficiency in internal control exists when the design or operation of a control does not allow management or employees, in the normal course of performing their assigned functions, to prevent, or detect and correct misstatements on a timely basis. A deficiency in design exists when (*a*) a control necessary to meet the control objective is missing or (*b*) an existing

[4] Although this section does not apply when an auditor is engaged to examine the suitability of design of an entity's internal control, it may be useful in planning and performing such engagements.

control is not properly designed so that, even if the control operates as designed, the control objective would not be met. A deficiency in operation exists when a properly designed control does not operate as designed, or when the person performing the control does not possess the necessary authority or competence to perform the control effectively.

Detective control. A control that has the objective of detecting and correcting errors or fraud that has already occurred that could result in a misstatement of the financial statements.

Financial statements and related disclosures. An entity's financial statements and notes to the financial statements as presented in accordance with the applicable financial reporting framework.[5] References to financial statements and related disclosures do not extend to the preparation of other financial information presented outside an entity's basic financial statements and notes.

Internal control over financial reporting.[6] A process effected by those charged with governance,[7] management, and other personnel, designed to provide reasonable assurance regarding the preparation of reliable financial statements in accordance with the applicable financial reporting framework and includes those policies and procedures that[8]

i. pertain to the maintenance of records that, in reasonable detail, accurately and fairly reflect the transactions and dispositions of the assets of the entity;
ii. provide reasonable assurance that transactions are recorded as necessary to permit preparation of financial statements in accordance with the applicable financial reporting framework, and that receipts and

---

[5] The *applicable financial reporting framework* is defined in paragraph .14 of AU-C section 200, *Overall Objectives of the Independent Auditor and the Conduct of an Audit in Accordance With Generally Accepted Auditing Standards*, as "the financial reporting framework adopted by management and, when appropriate, those charged with governance in the preparation and fair presentation of the financial statements that is acceptable in view of the nature of the entity and the objective of the financial statements, or that is required by law or regulation." Paragraph .A31 of AU-C section 700, *Forming an Opinion and Reporting on Financial Statements*, provides the following examples of applicable financial reporting frameworks: accounting principles generally accepted in the United States of America (or U.S. generally accepted accounting principles), International Financial Reporting Standards promulgated by the International Accounting Standards Board (IASB), and *International Financial Reporting Standard for Small and Medium-Sized Entities* promulgated by the IASB. [Footnote revised, December 2012, to reflect conforming changes necessary due to the issuance of SAS Nos. 122–126.]

[6] For insured depository institutions (IDIs) subject to the internal control reporting requirements of Section 112 of the Federal Deposit Insurance Corporation Improvement Act (FDICIA), internal control includes controls over the preparation of the IDI's financial statements and related disclosures in accordance with GAAP and with the instructions to the *Consolidated Financial Statements for Bank Holding Companies*. Internal control also includes controls over the preparation of the IDI's financial statements and related disclosures in accordance with GAAP and controls over the preparation of schedules equivalent to the basic financial statements in accordance with the Federal Financial Institutions Examination Council Instructions for Consolidated Reports of Condition and Income (call report instructions) or with the Office of Thrift Supervision Instructions for Thrift Financial Reports (TFR instructions).

[7] The term *those charged with governance* is defined in paragraph .06 of AU-C section 260, *The Auditor's Communication With Those Charged With Governance*, as "the person(s) or organization(s) (for example, a corporate trustee) with responsibility for overseeing the strategic direction of the entity and the obligations related to the accountability of the entity. This includes overseeing the financial reporting process. Those charged with governance may include management personnel; for example, executive members of a governance board or an owner-manager." [Footnote revised, December 2012, to reflect conforming changes necessary due to the issuance of SAS Nos. 122–126.]

[8] The auditor's procedures performed as part of the integrated audit are not part of an entity's internal control.

expenditures of the entity are being made only in accordance with authorizations of management and those charged with governance; and

iii. provide reasonable assurance regarding prevention, or timely detection and correction of unauthorized acquisition, use, or disposition of the entity's assets that could have a material effect on the financial statements.

Internal control has inherent limitations. Internal control is a process that involves human diligence and compliance and is subject to lapses in judgment and breakdowns resulting from human failures. Internal control also can be circumvented by collusion or improper management override. Because of such limitations, there is a risk that material misstatements will not be prevented, or detected and corrected on a timely basis by internal control. However, these inherent limitations are known aspects of the financial reporting process.

Management's assertion. Management's conclusion about the effectiveness of the entity's internal control that is included in management's report on internal control.

Material weakness. A deficiency, or a combination of deficiencies, in internal control such that there is a reasonable possibility[9] that a material misstatement of the entity's financial statements will not be prevented, or detected and corrected on a timely basis.

Preventive control. A control that has the objective of preventing errors or fraud that could result in a misstatement of the financial statements.

Relevant assertion. A financial statement assertion[10] that has a reasonable possibility of containing a misstatement or misstatements that would cause the financial statements to be materially misstated. The determination of whether an assertion is a relevant assertion is made without regard to the effect of controls.

Significant account or disclosure. An account balance or disclosure that has a reasonable possibility that it could contain a misstatement that, individually or when aggregated with others, has a material effect on the financial statements, considering the risks of both overstatement and understatement. The determination of whether an account balance or disclosure is a significant account or disclosure is made without regard to the effect of controls.

Significant deficiency. A deficiency, or a combination of deficiencies, in internal control that is less severe than a material weakness, yet important enough to merit attention by those charged with governance.

.08 Effective internal control provides reasonable assurance regarding the reliability of financial reporting and the preparation of financial statements

[9] A reasonable possibility exists when the chance of the future event or events occurring is more than remote. [Footnote revised, June 2009, to reflect conforming changes necessary due to the issuance of FASB ASC. Footnote revised, December 2012, to reflect conforming changes necessary due to the issuance of SAS Nos. 122–126.]

[10] The financial statement assertions are described in paragraph .A114 of AU-C section 315, *Understanding the Entity and Its Environment and Assessing the Risks of Material Misstatement*. The auditor may use the financial statement assertions as they are described in AU-C section 315 or may express them differently, provided that all aspects described in AU-C section 315 have been covered. [Footnote revised, December 2012, to reflect conforming changes necessary due to the issuance of SAS Nos. 122–126.]

for external purposes. If one or more material weaknesses exist, the entity's internal control cannot be considered effective.

.09 The auditor's objective in an examination of internal control is to form an opinion on the effectiveness of the entity's internal control. Because an entity's internal control cannot be considered effective if one or more material weaknesses exist, to form a basis for expressing an opinion, the auditor should plan and perform the examination to obtain sufficient appropriate evidence to obtain reasonable assurance[11] about whether material weaknesses exist as of the date specified in management's assertion. A material weakness in internal control may exist even when financial statements are not materially misstated. The auditor is not required to search for deficiencies that, individually or in combination, are less severe than a material weakness.

.10 An auditor engaged to perform an examination of internal control should comply with the general, fieldwork, and reporting standards in section 101, and the specific performance and reporting requirements set forth in this section. In this section, the subject matter is the effectiveness of internal control, and the responsible party usually is management of the entity. Accordingly, the term *management* is used in this section to refer to the responsible party.

.11 The auditor should use the same suitable and available control criteria[12] to perform his or her examination of internal control as management uses for its evaluation of the effectiveness of the entity's internal control.

.12 An auditor may perform an examination of internal control only if the following conditions are met:

a. Management accepts responsibility for the effectiveness of the entity's internal control.

b. Management evaluates the effectiveness of the entity's internal control using suitable and available criteria.

c. Management supports its assertion about the effectiveness of the entity's internal control with sufficient appropriate evidence (see discussion beginning at paragraph .14).

d. Management provides its assertion about the effectiveness of the entity's internal control in a report that accompanies the auditor's report (see paragraph .95).

.13 Management's refusal to furnish a written assertion should cause the auditor to withdraw from the engagement. However, if law or regulation does

---

[11] The high, but not absolute, level of assurance that is intended to be obtained by the auditor is expressed in the auditor's report as obtaining reasonable assurance about whether effective internal control over financial reporting was maintained in all material respects as of the date specified in management's assertion. See paragraph .54 of section 101, *Attest Engagements*, and AU-C section 200. [Footnote revised, December 2012, to reflect conforming changes necessary due to the issuance of SAS Nos. 122–126.].

[12] According to paragraph .23 of section 101 "[t]he third general attestation standard is—*The auditor must have reason to believe that the subject matter is capable of evaluation against criteria that are suitable and available to users.*" The Committee of Sponsoring Organizations of the Treadway Commission's (COSO) report *Internal Control—Integrated Framework* provides suitable and available criteria against which management may evaluate and report on the effectiveness of the entity's internal control. *Internal Control—Integrated Framework* describes an entity's internal control as consisting of five components: control environment, risk assessment, information and communication, control activities, and monitoring. See AU-C section 315 for a discussion of these components. If management selects another framework, see paragraphs .23–.34 of section 101 for guidance on evaluating the suitability and availability of criteria. [Footnote revised, December 2012, to reflect conforming changes necessary due to the issuance of SAS Nos. 122–126.]

not allow the auditor to withdraw from the engagement and management refuses to furnish a written assertion, the auditor should disclaim an opinion on internal control.[13]

Evidence Supporting Management's Assertion

.14 Management is responsible for identifying and documenting the controls and the control objectives that they were designed to achieve. Such documentation serves as a basis for management's assertion. Documentation of the design of controls, including changes to those controls, is evidence that controls upon which management's assertion is based are

- identified.
- capable of being communicated to those responsible for their performance.
- capable of being monitored and evaluated by the entity.

.15 Management's documentation may take various forms, for example, entity policy manuals, accounting manuals, narrative memoranda, flowcharts, decision tables, procedural write-ups, or completed questionnaires. No one, particular form of documentation is prescribed, and the extent of documentation may vary depending upon the size and complexity of the entity and the entity's monitoring activities.

.16 Management's monitoring activities also may provide evidence of the design and operating effectiveness of internal control in support of management's assertion. Monitoring of controls is a process to assess the effectiveness of internal control performance over time. It involves assessing the effectiveness of controls on a timely basis, identifying and reporting deficiencies to appropriate individuals within the organization, and taking necessary corrective actions. Management accomplishes monitoring of controls through ongoing activities, separate evaluations, or a combination of the two.

.17 Ongoing monitoring activities are often built into the normal recurring activities of an entity and include regular management and supervisory activities. The greater the degree and effectiveness of ongoing monitoring, the less need for separate evaluations. Usually, some combination of ongoing monitoring and separate evaluations will ensure that internal control maintains its effectiveness over time.

Integrating the Examination With the Financial Statement Audit

.18 The examination of internal control should be integrated with an audit of financial statements. Although the objectives of the engagements are not the same, the auditor should plan and perform the integrated audit to achieve the objectives of both engagements simultaneously. The auditor should design tests of controls

- to obtain sufficient appropriate evidence to support the auditor's opinion on internal control as of the period-end; and

[13] See paragraphs .117–.121 when disclaiming an opinion, including the requirement for the auditor's report to include a description of any material weaknesses identified.

- to obtain sufficient appropriate evidence to support the auditor's control risk assessments for purposes of the audit of financial statements.

.19 The date specified in management's assertion (the as-of date of the examination) should correspond to the balance sheet date (or period ending date) of the period covered by the financial statements (see paragraph .02).

.20 Obtaining sufficient appropriate evidence to support the operating effectiveness of controls for purposes of the financial statement audit ordinarily allows the auditor to modify the substantive procedures that otherwise would have been necessary to opine on the financial statements. (Integration is described further beginning at paragraph .159.)

.21 In some circumstances, particularly in some audits of smaller, less complex entities, the auditor might choose not to test the operating effectiveness of controls for purposes of the audit of the financial statements. In such circumstances, the auditor's tests of the operating effectiveness of controls would be performed principally for the purpose of supporting his or her opinion on whether the entity's internal control is effective as of period-end. The auditor should consider the results of the financial statement auditing procedures in determining his or her risk assessments and the testing necessary to conclude on the operating effectiveness of a control.

Planning the Examination

.22 The auditor should plan the examination of internal control. Evaluating whether the following matters are important to the entity's financial statements and internal control and, if so, how they may affect the auditor's procedures, may assist the auditor in planning the examination:

- Knowledge of the entity's internal control obtained during other engagements performed by the auditor or, if applicable, during a review of a predecessor auditor's working papers
- Matters affecting the industry in which the entity operates, such as financial reporting practices, economic conditions, laws and regulations, and technological changes
- Matters relating to the entity's business, including its organization, operating characteristics, and capital structure
- The extent of recent changes, if any, in the entity, its operations, or its internal control
- The auditor's preliminary judgments about materiality, risk, and other factors relating to the determination of material weaknesses
- Deficiencies previously communicated to those charged with governance or management
- Legal or regulatory matters of which the entity is aware
- The type and extent of available evidence related to the effectiveness of the entity's internal control
- Preliminary judgments about the effectiveness of internal control
- Public information about the entity relevant to the evaluation of the likelihood of material financial statement misstatements and the effectiveness of the entity's internal control

- Knowledge about risks related to the entity evaluated as part of the auditor's client acceptance and retention evaluation
- The relative complexity of the entity's operations

Role of Risk Assessment

.23 Risk assessment underlies the entire examination process described by this section, including the determination of significant accounts and disclosures and relevant assertions, the selection of controls to test, and the determination of the evidence necessary to conclude on the effectiveness of a given control. When performing an examination of internal control that is integrated with an audit of financial statements, the same risk assessment process supports both engagements.[14]

.24 The auditor should focus more attention on the areas of highest risk. A direct relationship exists between the degree of risk that a material weakness could exist in a particular area of the entity's internal control and the amount of attention that would be devoted to that area. In addition, an entity's internal control is less likely to prevent, or detect and correct a misstatement caused by fraud than a misstatement caused by error. It is not necessary to test controls that, even if deficient, would not present a reasonable possibility of material misstatement to the financial statements.

Scaling the Examination

.25 The size and complexity of the entity, its business processes, and business units may affect the way in which the entity achieves many of its control objectives. Many smaller entities have less complex operations. Additionally, some larger, complex entities may have less complex units or processes. Factors that might indicate less complex operations include fewer business lines; less complex business processes and financial reporting systems; more centralized accounting functions; extensive involvement by senior management in the day-to-day activities of the business; and fewer levels of management, each with a wide span of control. Accordingly, a smaller, less complex entity, or even a larger, less complex entity might achieve its control objectives differently from a more complex entity.

.26 The size and complexity of the organization, its business processes, and business units also may affect the auditor's risk assessment and the determination of the necessary procedures and the controls necessary to address those risks. Scaling is most effective as a natural extension of the risk-based approach and applicable to examinations of all entities.

Addressing the Risk of Fraud

.27 When planning and performing the examination of internal control, the auditor should incorporate the results of the fraud risk assessment performed in the financial statement audit. As part of identifying and testing entity-level controls, as discussed beginning at paragraph .37, and selecting other controls to test, as discussed beginning at paragraph .54, the auditor should evaluate whether the entity's controls sufficiently address identified risks of material

---

[14] The risk assessment procedures performed in connection with a financial statement audit are described in AU-C section 315. [Footnote revised, December 2012, to reflect conforming changes necessary due to the issuance of SAS Nos. 122–126.]

misstatement due to fraud[15] and the risk of management override of other controls. Controls that might address these risks include

- controls over significant, unusual transactions, particularly those that result in late or unusual journal entries;
- controls over journal entries and adjustments made in the period-end financial reporting process;
- controls over related party transactions;
- controls related to significant management estimates; and
- controls that mitigate incentives for, and pressures on, management to falsify or inappropriately manage financial results.

.28 If the auditor identifies deficiencies in controls designed to prevent, or detect and correct misstatements caused by fraud during the examination of internal control, he or she should take into account those deficiencies when developing his or her response to risks of material misstatement during the financial statement audit, as provided in paragraphs .28–.33 of AU-C section 240, *Consideration of Fraud in a Financial Statement Audit.* [Revised, December 2012, to reflect conforming changes necessary due to the issuance of SAS Nos. 122–126.]

Using the Work of Others

.29 The auditor should evaluate the extent to which he or she will use the work of others to reduce the work the auditor might otherwise perform himself or herself.

.30 AU-C section 610, *The Auditor's Consideration of the Internal Audit Function in an Audit of Financial Statements*, applies in an integrated audit. For purposes of the examination of internal control, however, the auditor may use the work performed by, or receive direct assistance from, internal auditors, entity personnel (in addition to internal auditors), and third parties working under the direction of management or those charged with governance that provide evidence about the effectiveness of internal control. In an integrated audit, the auditor also may use this work to obtain evidence supporting the assessment of control risk for purposes of the financial statement audit. [Revised, December 2012, to reflect conforming changes necessary due to the issuance of SAS Nos. 122–126.]

.31 The auditor should obtain an understanding of the work of others sufficient to identify those activities related to the effectiveness of internal control that are relevant to planning the examination of internal control. The extent of the procedures necessary to obtain this understanding will vary, depending on the nature of those activities.

.32 The auditor should assess the competence and objectivity of the persons whose work the auditor plans to use to determine the extent to which the auditor may use their work. The higher the degree of competence and objectivity, the greater use the auditor may make of the work. The auditor should apply paragraphs .09–.11 of AU-C section 610 to assess the competence and objectivity of internal auditors. The auditor should apply the principles underlying those paragraphs to assess the competence and objectivity of persons

---

[15] See paragraphs .25–.27 of AU-C section 240, *Consideration of Fraud in a Financial Statement Audit*, regarding the auditor's identification and assessment of the risks of material misstatement due to fraud. [Footnote revised, December 2012, to reflect conforming changes necessary due to the issuance of SAS Nos. 122–126.]

other than internal auditors whose work the auditor plans to use. [Revised, December 2012, to reflect conforming changes necessary due to the issuance of SAS Nos. 122–126.]

.33 For purposes of using the work of others, competence means the attainment and maintenance of a level of understanding, knowledge, and skills that enables that person to perform ably the tasks assigned to them, and objectivity means the ability to perform those tasks impartially and with intellectual honesty. To assess competence, the auditor should evaluate factors about the person's qualifications and ability to perform the work that the auditor plans to use. To assess objectivity, the auditor should evaluate whether factors are present that either inhibit or promote a person's ability to perform with the necessary degree of objectivity the work that the auditor plans to use. The effect of the work of others on the auditor's work also depends on the relationship between the risk associated with a control and the competence and objectivity of those who performed the work. As the risk associated with a control decreases, the necessary level of competence and objectivity decreases as well. In higher risk areas (for example, controls that address specific fraud risks), use of the work of others would be limited, if it could be used at all.

.34 The extent to which the auditor may use the work of others also depends, in part, on the risk associated with the control being tested (see paragraph .62). As the risk associated with a control increases, the need for the auditor to perform his or her own work on the control increases.

Materiality

.35 In planning and performing the examination of internal control, the auditor should use the same materiality used in planning and performing the audit of the entity's financial statements.[16]

Using a Top-Down Approach

.36 The auditor should use a top-down approach[17] to the examination of internal control to select the controls to test. A top-down approach involves

- beginning at the financial statement level;
- using the auditor's understanding of the overall risks to internal control;
- focusing on entity-level controls;
- working down to significant accounts and disclosures and their relevant assertions;
- directing attention to accounts, disclosures, and assertions that present a reasonable possibility of material misstatement to the financial statements and related disclosures;
- verifying the auditor's understanding of the risks in the entity's processes; and
- selecting controls for testing that sufficiently address the assessed risk of material misstatement to each relevant assertion.

---

[16] See AU-C section 320, *Audit Risk and Materiality in Planning and Performing an Audit*, which provides additional explanation of materiality. [Footnote revised, December 2012, to reflect conforming changes necessary due to the issuance of SAS Nos. 122–126.]

[17] The top-down approach describes the auditor's sequential thought process in identifying risks and the controls to test, not necessarily the order in which the auditor will perform the examination procedures.

Identifying Entity-Level Controls

.37 The auditor should test those entity-level controls that are important to his or her conclusion about whether the entity has effective internal control. The auditor's evaluation of entity-level controls can result in increasing or decreasing the testing that he or she otherwise would have performed on other controls.

.38 Entity-level controls include

- controls related to the control environment;
- controls over management override;[18]
- the entity's risk assessment process;
- centralized processing and controls, including shared service environments;
- controls to monitor results of operations;
- controls to monitor other controls, including activities of the internal audit function, those charged with governance, and self-assessment programs;
- controls over the period-end financial reporting process; and
- programs and controls that address significant business control and risk management practices.

.39 Entity-level controls vary in nature and precision:

- Some entity-level controls, such as certain control environment controls, have an important but indirect effect on the likelihood that a misstatement will be prevented, or detected and corrected on a timely basis. These controls might affect the other controls that the auditor selects for testing and the nature, timing, and extent of procedures the auditor performs on other controls.
- Some entity-level controls monitor the effectiveness of other controls. Such controls might be designed to identify possible breakdowns in lower level controls, but not at a level of precision that would, by themselves, sufficiently address the assessed risk that material misstatements to a relevant assertion will be prevented, or detected and corrected on a timely basis. These controls, when operating effectively, might allow the auditor to reduce the testing of other controls.
- Some entity-level controls might be designed to operate at a level of precision that would adequately prevent, or detect and correct on a timely basis misstatements to one or more relevant assertions. If an entity-level control sufficiently addresses the assessed risk of material misstatement, the auditor need not test additional controls relating to that risk.

Control Environment

.40 Because of its importance to effective internal control, the auditor should evaluate the control environment at the entity. When evaluating the control environment, the auditor should apply paragraph .15 of AU-C section

---

[18] Controls over management override are important to effective internal control for all entities and may be particularly important at smaller, less complex entities because of the increased involvement of senior management in performing controls and in the period-end financial reporting process. For smaller, less complex entities, the controls that address the risk of management override might be different from those at a larger entity. For example, a smaller, less complex entity might rely on more detailed oversight by those charged with governance that focuses on the risk of management override.

315, *Understanding the Entity and Its Environment and Assessing the Risks of Material Misstatement*. As part of evaluating the control environment, the auditor should assess

- whether management's philosophy and operating style promote effective internal control;
- whether sound integrity and ethical values, particularly of top management, are developed and understood; and
- whether those charged with governance understand and exercise oversight responsibility over financial reporting and internal control.

[Revised, December 2012 and July 2013, to reflect conforming changes necessary due to the issuance of SAS Nos. 122–126.]

Period-End Financial Reporting Process

.41 Because of its importance to financial reporting and to the integrated audit, the auditor should evaluate the period-end financial reporting process.[19] The period-end financial reporting process includes the following:

- Procedures used to enter transaction totals into the general ledger
- Procedures related to the selection and application of accounting policies
- Procedures used to initiate, authorize, record, and process journal entries in the general ledger
- Procedures used to record recurring and nonrecurring adjustments to the financial statements
- Procedures for preparing financial statements and related disclosures

.42 As part of evaluating the period-end financial reporting process, the auditor should assess

- the inputs, procedures performed, and outputs of the processes the entity uses to produce its financial statements;
- the extent of IT involvement in the period-end financial reporting process;
- who participates from management;
- the locations involved in the period-end financial reporting process;
- the types of adjusting and consolidating entries; and
- the nature and extent of the oversight of the process by management and those charged with governance.

Identifying Significant Accounts and Disclosures and Their Relevant Assertions

.43 The auditor should identify significant accounts and disclosures and their relevant assertions. To identify significant accounts and disclosures and their relevant assertions, the auditor should evaluate the qualitative and quantitative risk factors related to the financial statement line items and disclosures. Risk factors relevant to the identification of significant accounts and disclosures and their relevant assertions include

- size and composition of the account;

[19] Because the annual period-end financial reporting process normally occurs after the as-of date of management's assertion, those controls usually cannot be tested until after the as-of date.

- susceptibility to misstatement due to errors or fraud;
- volume of activity, complexity, and homogeneity of the individual transactions processed through the account or reflected in the disclosure;
- nature of the account, class of transactions, or disclosure;
- accounting and reporting complexities associated with the account, class of transactions, or disclosure;
- exposure to losses in the account;
- possibility of significant contingent liabilities arising from the activities reflected in the account or disclosure;
- existence of related party transactions in the account; and
- changes from the prior period in the account, class of transactions, or disclosure characteristics.

.44 As part of identifying significant accounts and disclosures and their relevant assertions, the auditor also should determine the likely sources of potential misstatements that would cause the financial statements to be materially misstated. The auditor might determine the likely sources of potential misstatements by asking himself or herself "what could go wrong?" within a given significant account or disclosure.

.45 The risk factors that the auditor should evaluate in the identification of significant accounts and disclosures and their relevant assertions are the same in the examination of internal control as in the audit of the financial statements; accordingly, significant accounts and disclosures and their relevant assertions are the same in an integrated audit.[20]

.46 The components of a potential significant account or disclosure might be subject to significantly different risks. If so, different controls might be necessary to adequately address those risks.

.47 When an entity has multiple locations or business units, the auditor should identify significant accounts and disclosures and their relevant assertions based on the consolidated financial statements.

Understanding Likely Sources of Misstatement

.48 To further understand the likely sources of potential misstatements, and as a part of selecting the controls to test, the auditor should achieve the following objectives:

- Understand the flow of transactions related to the relevant assertions, including how these transactions are initiated, authorized, processed, and recorded
- Identify the points within the entity's processes at which a misstatement, including a misstatement due to fraud, could arise that, individually or in combination with other misstatements, would be material (for example, points at which information is initiated, transferred, or otherwise modified)
- Identify the controls that management has implemented to address these potential misstatements

---

[20] The risk assessment procedures performed in connection with a financial statement audit are described in AU-C section 315. [Footnote revised, December 2012, to reflect conforming changes necessary due to the issuance of SAS No. 122–126.]

- Identify the controls that management has implemented over the prevention, or timely detection and correction of unauthorized acquisition, use, or disposition of the entity's assets that could result in a material misstatement of the financial statements

.49 Because of the degree of judgment required, the auditor should either perform the procedures that achieve the objectives in paragraph .48 himself or herself or supervise the work of others who provide direct assistance to the auditor, as described in AU-C section 610. [Revised, December 2012, to reflect conforming changes necessary due to the issuance of SAS Nos. 122–126.]

.50 The auditor also should understand how IT affects the entity's flow of transactions and apply paragraph .22 of AU-C section 315. Paragraphs .A54–.A60 and .A98–.A101 of AU-C section 315 discuss the effect of IT on internal control and the risks to assess. [Revised, December 2012 and July 2013, to reflect conforming changes necessary due to the issuance of SAS Nos. 122–126.]

.51 The identification of risks and controls within IT is not a separate evaluation. Instead, it is an integral part of the top-down approach used to identify likely sources of misstatement and the controls to test, as well as to assess risk and allocate audit effort.

Performing Walkthroughs

.52 Performing walkthroughs will frequently be the most effective way of achieving the objectives in paragraph .48. A walkthrough involves following a transaction from origination through the entity's processes, including information systems, until it is reflected in the entity's financial records, using the same documents and IT that entity personnel use. Walkthrough procedures may include a combination of inquiry, observation, inspection of relevant documentation, recalculation, and control reperformance.

.53 A walkthrough includes questioning the entity's personnel about their understanding of what is required by the entity's prescribed procedures and controls at the points at which important processing procedures occur. These probing questions, combined with the other walkthrough procedures, allow the auditor to gain a sufficient understanding of the process and to be able to identify important points at which a necessary control is missing or not designed effectively. Additionally, probing questions that go beyond a narrow focus on the single transaction used as the basis for the walkthrough may provide an understanding of the different types of significant transactions handled by the process.

Selecting Controls to Test

.54 The auditor should test those controls that are important to the auditor's conclusion about whether the entity's controls sufficiently address the assessed risk of material misstatement to each relevant assertion.

.55 There might be more than one control that addresses the assessed risk of material misstatement to a particular relevant assertion; conversely, one control might address the assessed risk of material misstatement to more than one relevant assertion. It may not be necessary to test all controls related to a relevant assertion nor necessary to test redundant controls, unless redundancy is, itself, a control objective.

.56 The decision concerning whether a control would be selected for testing depends on which controls, individually or in combination, sufficiently address the assessed risk of material misstatement to a given relevant assertion rather than on how the control is labeled (for example, entity-level control, transaction-level control, control activity, monitoring control, preventive control, or detective control).

Testing Controls

Evaluating Design Effectiveness

.57 The auditor should evaluate the design effectiveness of controls by determining whether the entity's controls, if they are applied as prescribed by persons possessing the necessary authority and competence to perform the control effectively, satisfy the entity's control objectives, and can effectively prevent, or detect and correct misstatements caused by errors or fraud that could result in material misstatements in the financial statements.

.58 A smaller, less complex entity might achieve its control objectives in a different manner from a larger, more complex organization. For example, a smaller, less complex entity might have fewer employees in the accounting function, limiting opportunities to segregate duties and leading the entity to implement alternative controls to achieve its control objectives. In such circumstances, the auditor should evaluate whether those alternative controls are effective.

.59 Procedures performed to evaluate design effectiveness may include a mix of inquiry of appropriate personnel, observation of the entity's operations, and inspection of relevant documentation. Walkthroughs that include these procedures ordinarily are sufficient to evaluate design effectiveness.

Testing Operating Effectiveness

.60 The auditor should test the operating effectiveness of a control by determining whether the control is operating as designed and whether the person performing the control possesses the necessary authority and competence to perform the control effectively.[21]

.61 Procedures performed to test operating effectiveness may include a mix of inquiry of appropriate personnel, observation of the entity's operations, inspection of relevant documentation, recalculation, and reperformance of the control.

Relationship of Risk to the Evidence to Be Obtained

.62 For each control selected for testing, the evidence necessary to persuade the auditor that the control is effective depends upon the risk associated with the control. The risk associated with a control consists of the risk that the control might not be effective and, if not effective, the risk that a material weakness exists. As the risk associated with the control being tested increases, the evidence that the auditor should obtain also increases.

.63 Although the auditor should obtain evidence about the effectiveness of controls for each relevant assertion, he or she is not responsible for obtaining sufficient appropriate evidence to support an opinion about the effectiveness of

---

[21] In some situations, particularly in smaller, less complex entities, an entity might use a third party to provide assistance with certain financial reporting functions. When assessing the competence of personnel responsible for an entity's financial reporting and associated controls, the auditor may take into account the combined competence of entity personnel and other parties that assist with functions related to financial reporting.

each individual control. Rather, the auditor's objective is to express an opinion on the entity's internal control overall. This allows the auditor to vary the evidence obtained regarding the effectiveness of individual controls selected for testing based on the risk associated with the individual control.

.64 Factors that affect the risk associated with a control may include

- the nature and materiality of misstatements that the control is intended to prevent, or detect and correct;
- the inherent risk associated with the related account(s) and assertion(s);
- whether there have been changes in the volume or nature of transactions that might adversely affect control design or operating effectiveness;
- whether the account has a history of errors;
- the effectiveness of entity-level controls, especially controls that monitor other controls;
- the nature of the control and the frequency with which it operates;
- the degree to which the control relies on the effectiveness of other controls (for example, the control environment or IT general controls);
- the competence of the personnel who perform the control or monitor its performance and whether there have been changes in key personnel who perform the control or monitor its performance;
- whether the control relies on performance by an individual or is automated (that is, an automated control would generally be expected to be lower risk if relevant IT general controls are effective);[22] and
- the complexity of the control and the significance of the judgments that would be made in connection with its operation.[23]

.65 When the auditor identifies control deviations, he or she should determine the effect of the deviations on his or her assessment of the risk associated with the control being tested and the evidence to be obtained, as well as on the operating effectiveness of the control.

.66 Because effective internal control cannot and does not provide absolute assurance of achieving the entity's control objectives, an individual control does not necessarily have to operate without any deviation to be considered effective.

.67 The evidence provided by the auditor's tests of the effectiveness of controls depends upon the mix of the nature, timing, and extent of the auditor's procedures. Further, for an individual control, different combinations of the nature, timing, and extent of testing may provide sufficient appropriate evidence in relation to the risk associated with the control.

.68 Walkthroughs may include a combination of inquiry of appropriate personnel, observation of the entity's operations, inspection of relevant documentation, recalculation, and reperformance of the control and might provide sufficient appropriate evidence of operating effectiveness, depending on the risk

---

[22] A smaller, less complex entity or business unit with simple business processes and centralized accounting operations might have relatively simple information systems that make greater use of off-the-shelf packaged software without modification. In the areas in which off-the-shelf software is used, the auditor's testing of IT controls might focus on the application controls built into the prepackaged software that management relies on to achieve its control objectives and the IT general controls that are important to the effective operation of those application controls.

[23] Generally, a conclusion that a control is not operating effectively can be supported by less evidence than is necessary to support a conclusion that a control is operating effectively.

associated with the control being tested, the specific procedures performed as part of the walkthrough, and the results of those procedures.

Nature of Tests of Controls

.69 Some types of tests, by their nature, produce greater evidence of the effectiveness of controls than other tests. The following tests that the auditor might perform are presented in order of the evidence that they ordinarily would produce, from least to most: inquiry, observation, inspection of relevant documentation, recalculation, and reperformance of a control. Inquiry alone, however, does not provide sufficient appropriate evidence to support a conclusion about the effectiveness of a control.

.70 The nature of the tests of effectiveness that will provide sufficient appropriate evidence depends, to a large degree, on the nature of the control to be tested, including whether the operation of the control results in documentary evidence of its operation. Documentary evidence of the operation of some controls, such as management's philosophy and operating style, might not exist.

.71 A smaller, less complex entity or unit might have less formal documentation regarding the operation of its controls. In those situations, testing controls through inquiry combined with other procedures, such as observation of activities, inspection of less formal documentation, recalculation, or reperformance of certain controls, might provide sufficient appropriate evidence about whether the control is effective.

Timing and Extent of Tests of Controls

.72 Testing controls over a longer period of time provides more evidence of the effectiveness of controls than testing over a shorter period of time. Further, testing performed closer to the date of management's assertion provides more evidence than testing performed earlier in the year. The auditor should balance performing the tests of controls closer to the as-of date with the need to test controls over a sufficient period of time to obtain sufficient appropriate evidence of operating effectiveness.

.73 Prior to the date specified in management's assertion, management might implement changes to the entity's controls to make them more effective or efficient or to address deficiencies. If the auditor determines that the new controls achieve the related objectives of the control criteria and have been in effect for a sufficient period to permit the auditor to assess their design and operating effectiveness by performing tests of controls, he or she will not need to test the design and operating effectiveness of the superseded controls for purposes of expressing an opinion on internal control. If the operating effectiveness of the superseded controls is important to the auditor's control risk assessment in the financial statement audit, the auditor should test the design and operating effectiveness of those superseded controls, as appropriate. (Integration is discussed beginning at paragraph .159.)

.74 The more extensively a control is tested, the greater the evidence obtained from that test.

Rollforward Procedures

.75 When the auditor reports on the effectiveness of controls as of a specific date and obtains evidence about the operating effectiveness of controls at an interim date, he or she should determine what additional evidence concerning the operation of the controls for the remaining period is necessary.

.76 The additional evidence that is necessary to update the results of testing from an interim date to the entity's period-end depends on the following factors:[24]

- The specific control tested prior to the as-of date, including the risks associated with the control, the nature of the control, and the results of those tests
- The sufficiency of the evidence of operating effectiveness obtained at an interim date
- The length of the remaining period
- The possibility that there have been any significant changes in internal control subsequent to the interim date

Special Considerations for Subsequent Years' Examinations

.77 In subsequent years' examinations, the auditor should incorporate knowledge obtained during past examinations he or she performed of the entity's internal control into the decision making process for determining the nature, timing, and extent of testing necessary. This decision making process is described in paragraphs .62–.76.

.78 Factors that affect the risk associated with a control in subsequent years' examinations include those in paragraph .64 and the following:

- The nature, timing, and extent of procedures performed in previous examinations
- The results of the previous years' testing of the control
- Whether there have been changes in the control or the process in which it operates since the previous examination

.79 After taking into account the risk factors identified in paragraphs .64 and .78, the additional information available in subsequent years' examinations might permit the auditor to assess the risk as lower than in the initial year. This, in turn, might permit the auditor to reduce testing in subsequent years.

.80 The auditor also may use a benchmarking strategy for automated application controls in subsequent years' examinations. Benchmarking is described further beginning at paragraph .153.

.81 In addition, the auditor should vary the nature, timing, and extent of testing of controls from period to period to introduce unpredictability into the testing and respond to changes in circumstances. For this reason, the auditor might test controls at a different interim period, increase or reduce the number and types of tests performed, or change the combination of procedures used.

Evaluating Identified Deficiencies

.82 The auditor should evaluate the severity of each deficiency to determine whether the deficiency, individually or in combination, is a material weakness as of the date of management's assertion.

.83 The severity of a deficiency depends on

- the magnitude of the potential misstatement resulting from the deficiency or deficiencies; and

---

[24] In some circumstances, such as when evaluation of these factors indicates a low risk that the controls are no longer effective during the rollforward period, inquiry alone might be sufficient as a rollforward procedure.

- whether there is a reasonable possibility that the entity's controls will fail to prevent, or detect and correct a misstatement of an account balance or disclosure.

The severity of a deficiency does not depend on whether a misstatement actually occurred.

.84 Factors that affect the magnitude of the misstatement that might result from a deficiency or deficiencies include, but are not limited to, the following:

- The financial statement amounts or total of transactions exposed to the deficiency
- The volume of activity (in the current period or expected in future periods) in the account or class of transactions exposed to the deficiency

.85 In evaluating the magnitude of the potential misstatement, the maximum amount by which an account balance or total of transactions can be overstated is generally the recorded amount, whereas understatements could be larger.

.86 Risk factors affect whether there is a reasonable possibility that a deficiency, or a combination of deficiencies, will result in a misstatement of an account balance or disclosure. The factors include, but are not limited to, the following:

- The nature of the financial statement accounts, classes of transactions, disclosures, and assertions involved
- The susceptibility of the related asset or liability to loss or fraud
- The subjectivity, complexity, or extent of judgment required to determine the amount involved
- The interaction or relationship of the control with other controls
- The interaction among the deficiencies
- The possible future consequences of the deficiency

.87 The evaluation of whether a deficiency presents a reasonable possibility of misstatement may be made without quantifying the probability of occurrence as a specific percentage or range. Also, in many cases, the probability of a small misstatement will be greater than the probability of a large misstatement.

.88 Multiple deficiencies that affect the same significant account or disclosure, relevant assertion, or component of internal control increase the likelihood of material misstatement and may, in combination, constitute a material weakness, even though such deficiencies individually may be less severe. Therefore, the auditor should determine whether deficiencies that affect the same significant account or disclosure, relevant assertion, or component of internal control collectively result in a material weakness.

.89 Multiple deficiencies that affect the same significant account or disclosure, relevant assertion, or component of internal control also may collectively result in a significant deficiency.

.90 A compensating control can limit the severity of a deficiency and prevent it from being a material weakness. Although compensating controls can mitigate the effects of a deficiency, they do not eliminate the deficiency. The auditor should evaluate the effect of compensating controls when determining whether a deficiency or combination of deficiencies is a material weakness. To have a mitigating effect, the compensating control should operate at a level of precision that would prevent, or detect and correct a material misstatement. The auditor should test the operating effectiveness of compensating controls.

Indicators of Material Weaknesses

.91 Indicators of material weaknesses in internal control include

- identification of fraud, whether or not material, on the part of senior management;
- restatement of previously issued financial statements to reflect the correction of a material misstatement due to error or fraud;
- identification by the auditor of a material misstatement of financial statements under audit in circumstances that indicate that the misstatement would not have been detected and corrected by the entity's internal control; and
- ineffective oversight of the entity's financial reporting and internal control by those charged with governance.

.92 If the auditor determines that a deficiency, or a combination of deficiencies, is not a material weakness, he or she should consider whether prudent officials, having knowledge of the same facts and circumstances, would likely reach the same conclusion.

Concluding Procedures

Forming an Opinion

.93 The auditor should form an opinion on the effectiveness of internal control by evaluating evidence obtained from all sources, including the auditor's testing of controls, misstatements detected during the financial statement audit, and any identified deficiencies.

.94 As part of this evaluation, the auditor should review reports issued during the year by internal audit (or similar functions) that address controls related to internal control and evaluate deficiencies identified in those reports.

.95 After forming an opinion on the effectiveness of the entity's internal control, the auditor should evaluate management's report to determine whether it appropriately contains the following:

- A statement regarding management's responsibility for internal control
- A description of the subject matter of the examination (for example, controls over the preparation of the entity's financial statements in accordance with generally accepted accounting principles [GAAP])
- An identification of the criteria against which internal control is measured (for example, criteria established in the Committee of Sponsoring Organizations of the Treadway Commission's *Internal Control—Integrated Framework*)
- Management's assertion about the effectiveness of internal control
- A description of the material weaknesses, if any
- The date as of which management's assertion is made

.96 If the auditor determines that any required element of management's report is incomplete or improperly presented, the auditor should request management to revise its report. If management does not revise its report, the auditor should apply paragraph .116. If management refuses to furnish a report, the auditor should apply paragraph .13.

Obtaining Written Representations

.97 In an examination of internal control, the auditor should obtain written representations from management

a. acknowledging management's responsibility for establishing and maintaining effective internal control;

b. stating that management has performed an evaluation of the effectiveness of the entity's internal control and specifying the control criteria;

c. stating that management did not use the auditor's procedures performed during the integrated audit as part of the basis for management's assertion;

d. stating management's assertion about the effectiveness of the entity's internal control based on the control criteria as of a specified date;

e. stating that management has disclosed to the auditor all deficiencies in the design or operation of internal control, including separately disclosing to the auditor all such deficiencies that it believes to be significant deficiencies or material weaknesses in internal control;

f. describing any fraud resulting in a material misstatement to the entity's financial statements and any other fraud that does not result in a material misstatement to the entity's financial statements, but involves senior management or management or other employees who have a significant role in the entity's internal control;

g. stating whether the significant deficiencies and material weaknesses identified and communicated to management and those charged with governance during previous engagements pursuant to paragraph .100 have been resolved and specifically identifying any that have not; and

h. stating whether there were, subsequent to the date being reported on, any changes in internal control or other factors that might significantly affect internal control, including any corrective actions taken by management with regard to significant deficiencies and material weaknesses.

.98 The failure to obtain written representations from management, including management's refusal to furnish them, constitutes a limitation on the scope of the examination.[25] The auditor should evaluate the effects of management's refusal on his or her ability to rely on other representations, such as those obtained in the audit of the entity's financial statements.

.99 The auditor should apply AU-C section 580, *Written Representations*, as it relates to matters such as who should sign the letter, the period to be covered by the letter, and when to obtain an updated letter. [Revised, December 2012, to reflect conforming changes necessary due to the issuance of SAS Nos. 122–126.]

Communicating Certain Matters

.100 Deficiencies identified during the integrated audit that, upon evaluation, are considered significant deficiencies or material weaknesses should be communicated, in writing, to management and those charged with governance

---

[25] See paragraph .117 when the scope of the engagement has been restricted.

as a part of each integrated audit, including significant deficiencies and material weaknesses that were previously communicated to management and those charged with governance and have not yet been remediated. Significant deficiencies and material weaknesses that previously were communicated and have not yet been remediated may be communicated, in writing, by referring to the previously issued written communication and the date of that communication.

.101 If the auditor concludes that the oversight of the entity's financial reporting and internal control by the audit committee (or similar subgroups with different names) is ineffective, the auditor should communicate that conclusion, in writing, to the board of directors or other similar governing body if one exists.

.102 The written communications referred to in paragraphs .100–.101 should be made by the report release date,[26] which is the date the auditor grants the entity permission to use the auditor's report. For a governmental entity, the auditor is not required to make the written communications by the report release date, if such written communications would be publicly available prior to management's report on internal control, the entity's financial statements, and the auditor's report thereon. In that circumstance, the written communications should be made as soon as practicable, but no later than 60 days following the report release date.

.103 Because of the importance of timely communication, the auditor may choose to communicate significant matters during the course of the integrated audit. If the communication is made during the integrated audit, the form of interim communication would be affected by the relative significance of the identified deficiencies and the urgency for corrective follow-up action. Such early communication is not required to be in writing. However, regardless of how the early communication is delivered, the auditor should communicate all significant deficiencies and material weaknesses in writing to management and those charged with governance in accordance with paragraphs .100–.102, even if the significant deficiencies or material weaknesses were remediated during the examination.

.104 The auditor also should communicate to management, in writing, all deficiencies (those deficiencies that are not material weaknesses or significant deficiencies) identified during the integrated audit on a timely basis, but no later than 60 days following the report release date, and inform those charged with governance when such a communication was made. In making the written communication referred to in this paragraph, the auditor is not required to communicate those deficiencies that are not material weaknesses or significant deficiencies that were included in previous written communications, whether those communications were made by the auditor, internal auditors, or others within the organization.

.105 The auditor is not required to perform procedures that are sufficient to identify all deficiencies; rather, the auditor communicates deficiencies of which he or she is aware.

.106 Because the integrated audit does not provide the auditor with assurance that he or she has identified all deficiencies less severe than a material weakness, the auditor should not issue a report stating that no such deficiencies were identified during the integrated audit. Also, because the auditor's objective in an examination of internal control is to form an opinion on the effectiveness

---

[26] See paragraph .A2 of AU-C section 230, *Audit Documentation*, for additional guidance related to the report release date. [Footnote revised, December 2012, to reflect conforming changes necessary due to the issuance of SAS Nos. 122–126.]

of the entity's internal control, the auditor should not issue a report indicating that no material weaknesses were identified during the integrated audit.

Reporting on Internal Control

.107 The auditor's report on the examination of internal control should include the following elements:[27]

a. A title that includes the word *independent*

b. A statement that management is responsible for maintaining effective internal control and for evaluating the effectiveness of internal control

c. An identification of management's assertion on internal control that accompanies the auditor's report, including a reference to management's report

d. A statement that the auditor's responsibility is to express an opinion on the entity's internal control (or on management's assertion)[28] based on his or her examination[29]

e. A statement that the examination was conducted in accordance with attestation standards established by the American Institute of Certified Public Accountants

f. A statement that such standards require that the auditor plan and perform the examination to obtain reasonable assurance about whether effective internal control was maintained in all material respects

g. A statement that an examination includes obtaining an understanding of internal control, assessing the risk that a material weakness exists, testing and evaluating the design and operating effectiveness of internal control based on the assessed risk, and performing such other procedures as the auditor considers necessary in the circumstances

h. A statement that the auditor believes the examination provides a reasonable basis for his or her opinion

i. A definition of internal control (the auditor should use the same description of the entity's internal control as management uses in its report)

j. A paragraph stating that, because of inherent limitations, internal control may not prevent, or detect and correct misstatements and that projections of any evaluation of effectiveness to future periods are subject to the risk that controls may become inadequate because of changes in conditions, or that the degree of compliance with the policies or procedures may deteriorate

k. The auditor's opinion on whether the entity maintained, in all material respects, effective internal control as of the specified date, based on the control criteria; or, the auditor's opinion on whether management's assertion about the effectiveness of the entity's internal control as of the specified date is fairly stated, in all material respects, based on the control criteria

l. The manual or printed signature of the auditor's firm

m. The date of the report

---

[27] Report modifications are discussed further beginning at paragraph .115.

[28] The auditor may report directly on the entity's internal control or on management's written assertion, except as described in paragraph .112.

[29] Because the examination of internal control is integrated with the audit of the financial statements and an examination provides the same level of assurance as an audit, the auditor may refer to the examination of internal control as an audit in his or her report or other communications.

Separate or Combined Reports

.108 The auditor may choose to issue a combined report (that is, one report containing both an opinion on the financial statements and an opinion on internal control) or separate reports on the entity's financial statements and on internal control.

.109 If the auditor issues a separate report on internal control, he or she should add the following paragraph to the auditor's report on the financial statements:

> We also have examined [*or audited*][30] in accordance with attestation standards established by the American Institute of Certified Public Accountants, [*company name*]'s internal control over financial reporting as of December 31, 20X8, based on [*identify control criteria*] and our report dated [*date of report, which should be the same as the date of the report on the financial statements*] expressed [*include nature of opinion*].

The auditor also should add the following paragraph to the report on internal control:

> We also have audited, in accordance with auditing standards generally accepted in the United States of America, the [*identify financial statements*] of [*company name*] and our report dated [*date of report, which should be the same as the date of the report on internal control*] expressed [*include nature of opinion*].

Report Date

.110 The auditor should date the report no earlier than the date on which the auditor has obtained sufficient appropriate evidence to support the auditor's opinion. Because the examination of internal control is integrated with the audit of the financial statements, the dates of the reports should be the same.

Adverse Opinions

.111 Paragraphs .82–.92 describe the evaluation of deficiencies. If there are deficiencies that, individually or in combination, result in one or more material weaknesses as of the date specified in management's assertion, the auditor should express an adverse opinion on the entity's internal control, unless there is a restriction on the scope of the engagement.[31]

.112 When internal control is not effective because one or more material weaknesses exist, the auditor is prohibited from expressing an opinion on management's assertion and should report directly on the effectiveness of internal control. In addition, the auditor's report should include

- the definition of a material weakness.
- a statement that one or more material weaknesses have been identified and an identification of the material weaknesses described in management's assertion. The auditor's report need only refer to the material weaknesses described in management's report and need not include a description of each material weakness, provided each material weakness is included and fairly presented in all material respects in management's report, as described in the following paragraph.

---

[30] See footnote 29.

[31] See paragraph .117 when the scope of the engagement has been restricted.

.113 If one or more material weaknesses have not been included in management's report accompanying the auditor's report, the auditor's report should be modified to state that one or more material weaknesses have been identified but not included in management's report. Additionally, the auditor's report should include a description of each material weakness not included in management's report, which should provide the users of the report with specific information about the nature of each material weakness and its actual and potential effect on the presentation of the entity's financial statements issued during the existence of the weakness. In this case, the auditor also should communicate, in writing, to those charged with governance that one or more material weaknesses were not disclosed or identified as a material weakness in management's report. If one or more material weaknesses have been included in management's report but the auditor concludes that the disclosure of such material weaknesses is not fairly presented in all material respects, the auditor's report should describe this conclusion as well as the information necessary to fairly describe each material weakness.

.114 The auditor should determine the effect an adverse opinion on internal control has on his or her opinion on the financial statements. Additionally, the auditor should disclose whether his or her opinion on the financial statements was affected by the material weaknesses.[32]

Report Modifications

.115 The auditor should modify his or her report if any of the following conditions exist:

a. Elements of management's report are incomplete or improperly presented.

b. There is a restriction on the scope of the engagement.

c. The auditor decides to refer to the report of a component auditor as the basis, in part, for the auditor's own report.

d. There is other information contained in management's report.

[Revised, December 2012, to reflect conforming changes necessary due to the issuance of SAS Nos. 122–126.]

Elements of Management's Report Are Incomplete or Improperly Presented

.116 If the auditor determines that any required element of management's report (see paragraph .95) is incomplete or improperly presented and management does not revise its report, the auditor should modify his or her report to include an explanatory paragraph describing the reasons for this determination. If the auditor determines that the required disclosure about one or more material weaknesses is not fairly presented in all material respects, the auditor should apply paragraph .113.

Scope Limitations

.117 The auditor may express an opinion on the entity's internal control only if the auditor has been able to apply the procedures necessary in the

---

[32] If the auditor issues a separate report on internal control in this circumstance, the disclosure required by this paragraph may be combined with the report language described in paragraph .109. The auditor may present the combined language either as a separate paragraph or as part of the paragraph that identifies the material weakness.

circumstances. If there are restrictions on the scope of the engagement, the auditor should withdraw from the engagement or disclaim an opinion.

.118 When disclaiming an opinion because of a scope limitation, the auditor should state that he or she does not express an opinion on the effectiveness of internal control and, in a separate paragraph or paragraphs, the substantive reasons for the disclaimer. The auditor should not identify the procedures that were performed nor include the statements describing the characteristics of an examination of internal control (paragraph .107[d–h]); to do so might overshadow the disclaimer.

.119 When the auditor plans to disclaim an opinion and the limited procedures performed by the auditor caused the auditor to conclude that one or more material weaknesses exist, the auditor's report also should include

- the definition of a material weakness.
- a description of any material weaknesses identified in the entity's internal control. This description should address the requirements in paragraph .112 and should provide the users of the report with specific information about the nature of any material weakness and its actual and potential effect on the presentation of the entity's financial statements issued during the existence of the weakness. The auditor also should apply the requirements in paragraph .114.

.120 The auditor may issue a report disclaiming an opinion on internal control as soon as the auditor concludes that a scope limitation will prevent the auditor from obtaining the reasonable assurance necessary to express an opinion.[33] The auditor is not required to perform any additional work prior to issuing a disclaimer when the auditor concludes that he or she will not be able to obtain sufficient appropriate evidence to express an opinion.

.121 If the auditor concludes that he or she cannot express an opinion because there has been a limitation on the scope of the examination, the auditor should communicate, in writing, to management and those charged with governance that the examination of internal control cannot be satisfactorily completed.

Opinion Based, in Part, on the Report of a Component Auditor

.122 When an entity is composed of one or more components (for example, subsidiaries, divisions, or branches), and another auditor has examined the internal control of one or more of the components, the auditor should determine whether it is appropriate to serve as the auditor of the group's internal control and use the work and reports of the component auditor as a basis, in part, for the auditor's opinion. The auditor considering whether to serve as the auditor of the group's internal control may have performed all but a relatively minor portion of the work, or the component auditor may have performed significant parts of the examination. In the latter case, the auditor should decide whether the auditor's own involvement is sufficient to enable the auditor to serve as the auditor of the group's internal control and to report on internal control as such. In deciding this question, the auditor should consider, among other things, the materiality of the portion of internal control the auditor has examined in comparison with the portion examined by the component auditor, the extent of the auditor's knowledge of overall internal control, and the importance of

---

[33] In this case, in following paragraph .110 regarding dating the report, the report date is the date that the auditor has obtained sufficient appropriate evidence to support the representations in the report.

the components examined by the auditor in relation to the group as a whole. [Revised, December 2012, to reflect conforming changes necessary due to the issuance of SAS Nos. 122–126.]

.123 If the auditor decides that it is appropriate to serve as the auditor of the group's internal control, the auditor should then decide whether to make reference in his or her report on the group's internal control to the examination of internal control performed by the component auditor. If the auditor decides to assume responsibility for the work of the component auditor insofar as that work relates to the expression of an opinion on the group's internal control taken as a whole, no reference should be made to the component auditor's work or report. On the other hand, if the auditor decides not to assume responsibility, the auditor's report should make reference to the examination of the component auditor and should clearly indicate the division of responsibility between the auditor and the component auditor in expressing an opinion on the group's internal control. Regardless of the auditor's decision, the auditor remains responsible for the performance of his or her own work and report. [Revised, December 2012, to reflect conforming changes necessary due to the issuance of SAS Nos. 122–126.]

.124 The decision about whether to make reference to a component auditor in the report on the examination of internal control might differ from the corresponding decision as it relates to the audit of the financial statements. For example, the audit report on the financial statements may make reference to the audit of a significant equity investment performed by a component auditor[34] but the report on internal control might not make a similar reference because management's assertion ordinarily would not extend to controls at the equity method investee.[35] [Revised, December 2012, to reflect conforming changes necessary due to the issuance of SAS Nos. 122–126.]

.125 When the auditor of the group's internal control decides to make reference to the report of the component auditor as a basis, in part, for the auditor's opinion on the group's internal control, the auditor should refer to the report of the component auditor when describing the scope of the examination and when expressing the opinion. Whether the component auditor's opinion is expressed on management's assertion or on internal control does not affect the determination of whether the opinion of the auditor of the group's internal control is expressed on management's assertion or on internal control. [Revised, December 2012, to reflect conforming changes necessary due to the issuance of SAS Nos. 122–126.]

Management's Report Contains Additional Information

.126 Management's report accompanying the auditor's report may contain information in addition to the elements described in paragraph .95 that are subject to the auditor's evaluation.[36] If management's report could reasonably

---

[34] AU-C section 600, *Special Considerations—Audits of Group Financial Statements (Including the Work of Component Auditors*, addresses special considerations that apply to group audits, in particular those that involve component auditors. [Footnote added, December 2012, to reflect conforming changes necessary due to the issuance of SAS Nos. 122–126.]

[35] See paragraph .140 for further discussion of the evaluation of the controls for an equity method investment. [Footnote renumbered, December 2012, to reflect conforming changes necessary due to the issuance of SAS Nos. 122–126.]

[36] An entity may publish various documents that contain information in addition to management's report and the auditor's report on internal control. Paragraphs .91–.94 of section 101 provide guidance to the auditor in these circumstances. If management makes the types of disclosures

(continued)

be viewed by users of the report as including such additional information, the auditor should disclaim an opinion on the information.

.127 The auditor may use the following sample language as the last paragraph of the auditor's report to disclaim an opinion on such additional information:

> We do not express an opinion or any other form of assurance on [*describe additional information, such as management's cost-benefit statement*].

.128 If the auditor believes that management's additional information contains a material misstatement of fact, he or she should apply the guidance in paragraphs .92–.94 of section 101 and take appropriate action. If the auditor concludes that a material misstatement of fact remains, the auditor should notify management and those charged with governance, in writing, of the auditor's views concerning the information. AU-C section 250, *Consideration of Laws and Regulations in an Audit of Financial Statements*, also may require the auditor to take additional action. [Revised, December 2012, to reflect conforming changes necessary due to the issuance of SAS Nos. 122–126.]

Subsequent Events

.129 Changes in internal control or other factors that might significantly affect internal control might occur subsequent to the date as of which internal control is being examined but before the date of the auditor's report. The auditor should inquire of management whether there were any such changes or factors and obtain written representations from management relating to such matters, as described in paragraph .97.

.130 To obtain additional information about changes in internal control or other factors that might significantly affect the effectiveness of the entity's internal control, the auditor should inquire about and examine, for this subsequent period, the following:

- Relevant internal audit (or similar functions, such as loan review in a financial institution) reports issued during the subsequent period
- Independent auditor reports (if other than the auditor's) of deficiencies
- Regulatory agency reports on the entity's internal control
- Information about the effectiveness of the entity's internal control obtained through other engagements

.131 The auditor might inquire about and examine other documents for the subsequent period. AU-C section 560, *Subsequent Events and Subsequently Discovered Facts*, establishes requirements and provides guidance on subsequent events for a financial statement audit that also may be helpful to the auditor performing an examination of internal control. [Revised, December 2012, to reflect conforming changes necessary due to the issuance of SAS Nos. 122–126.]

.132 If, subsequent to the date as of which internal control is being examined but before the date of the auditor's report, the auditor obtains knowledge

---

(footnote continued)

described in paragraph .126 outside its report and includes them elsewhere within a document that includes the auditor's report, the auditor would not need to disclaim an opinion on such information. However, in that situation, the auditor's responsibilities are the same as those described in paragraph .128, if the auditor believes that the additional information contains a material misstatement of fact. [Footnote renumbered, December 2012, to reflect conforming changes necessary due to the issuance of SAS Nos. 122–126.]

about a material weakness that existed as of the date specified in management's assertion, the auditor should report directly on internal control and issue an adverse opinion, as required by paragraph .111. The auditor should also follow paragraph .116 if management's assertion states that internal control is effective. If the auditor is unable to determine the effect of the matter on the effectiveness of the entity's internal control as of the date specified in management's assertion, the auditor should disclaim an opinion. As described in paragraph .126, the auditor should disclaim an opinion on management's disclosures about corrective actions taken by the entity, if any.

.133 The auditor may obtain knowledge about conditions that did not exist at the date specified in management's assertion but arose subsequent to that date and before the release of the auditor's report. If a subsequent event of this type has a material effect on the entity's internal control, the auditor should include in his or her report an explanatory paragraph describing the event and its effects or directing the reader's attention to the event and its effects as disclosed in management's report.

.134 The auditor has no responsibility to keep informed of events subsequent to the date of his or her report; however, after the release of the report on internal control, the auditor may become aware of conditions that existed at the report date that might have affected the auditor's opinion had he or she been aware of them. The evaluation of such subsequent information is similar to the evaluation of facts discovered subsequent to the date of the report on an audit of financial statements, as described in AU-C section 560. [Revised, December 2012, to reflect conforming changes necessary due to the issuance of SAS Nos. 122–126.]

Special Topics

Entities With Multiple Locations

.135 In determining the locations or business units at which to perform tests of controls, the auditor should assess the risk of material misstatement to the financial statements associated with the location or business unit and correlate the amount of attention devoted to the location or business unit with the degree of risk. The auditor may eliminate from further consideration locations or business units that, individually or when aggregated with others, do not present a reasonable possibility of material misstatement to the entity's consolidated financial statements.

.136 In assessing and responding to risk, the auditor should test controls over specific risks that present a reasonable possibility of material misstatement to the entity's consolidated financial statements. In lower risk locations or business units, the auditor first might evaluate whether testing entity-level controls, including controls in place to provide assurance that appropriate controls exist throughout the organization, provides the auditor with sufficient appropriate evidence.

.137 In determining the locations or business units at which to perform tests of controls, the auditor may take into account work performed by others on behalf of management. For example, if the internal auditors' planned procedures include relevant audit work at various locations, the auditor may coordinate work with the internal auditors and reduce the number of locations or business units at which the auditor would otherwise need to perform examination procedures.

.138 In applying the requirement in paragraph .81 regarding special considerations for subsequent years' examinations, the auditor should vary the nature, timing, and extent of testing of controls at locations or business units from year to year.

Special Situations

.139 The scope of the examination should include entities that are acquired on or before the date of management's assertion and operations that are accounted for as discontinued operations on the date of management's assertion that are reported in accordance with the applicable financial reporting framework in the entity's financial statements.

.140 For equity method investments, the scope of the examination should include controls over the reporting in accordance with the applicable financial reporting framework, in the entity's financial statements, of the entity's portion of the investees' income or loss, the investment balance, adjustments to the income or loss and investment balance, and related disclosures. The examination ordinarily would not extend to controls at the equity method investee.

.141 In situations in which a regulator allows management to limit its assertion by excluding certain entities, the auditor may limit the examination in the same manner. In these situations, the auditor's opinion would not be affected by a scope limitation. However, the auditor should include, either in an additional explanatory paragraph or as part of the scope paragraph in his or her report, a disclosure similar to management's regarding the exclusion of an entity from the scope of both management's assertion and the auditor's examination of internal control. Additionally, the auditor should evaluate the reasonableness of management's conclusion that the situation meets the criteria of the regulator's allowed exclusion and the appropriateness of any required disclosure related to such a limitation. If the auditor believes that management's disclosure about the limitation requires modification, the auditor should communicate the matter to the appropriate level of management. If, in the auditor's judgment, management does not respond appropriately to the auditor's communication within a reasonable period of time, the auditor should inform those charged with governance of the matter as soon as practicable. If management and those charged with governance do not respond appropriately, the auditor should modify his or her report on the examination of internal control to include an explanatory paragraph describing the reasons why the auditor believes management's disclosure requires modification.

Use of Service Organizations

.142 AU-C section 402 [37] addresses an auditor's responsibility for obtaining sufficient appropriate audit evidence in an audit of the financial statements of an entity that uses one or more service organizations (a user entity). Services provided by a service organization are relevant to the audit of a user entity's financial statements when those services and the controls over them affect the user entity's information system. The auditor may apply the relevant concepts described in AU-C section 402 to the examination of internal control. [Revised,

---

[37] AU-C section 402, *Audit Considerations Relating to an Entity Using a Service Organization*, contains the requirements and application guidance for auditors of the financial statements of entities that use a service organization (user auditors). [Footnote added, August 2011, to reflect conforming changes necessary due to the issuance of SSAE No. 16. Footnote renumbered and revised, December 2012, to reflect conforming changes necessary due to the issuance of SAS Nos. 122–126.]

December 2012, to reflect conforming changes necessary due to the issuance of SAS Nos. 122–126.]

.143 Paragraph .03 of AU-C section 402 identifies the situations in which a service organization's services and controls over them are part of a user entity's information system. If the service organization's services are part of the user entity's information system, as described therein, then they are part of the user entity's internal control. When the service organization's services are part of the user entity's internal control, the auditor should consider the activities of the service organization when determining the evidence required to support his or her opinion. [Revised, December 2012, to reflect conforming changes necessary due to the issuance of SAS Nos. 122–126.]

.144 The auditor should perform the procedures in paragraphs .09–.19 of AU-C section 402 with respect to the activities performed by the service organization. These procedures include

a. obtaining an understanding of the how the user entity uses the services of the service organization in its operations,

b. evaluating the design and implementation of relevant controls at the user entity that relate to the services provided by the service organization), and

c. obtaining evidence that controls at the service organization that are relevant to the auditor's opinion on internal control are operating effectively.

[Revised, December 2012, to reflect conforming changes necessary due to the issuance of SAS Nos. 122–126.]

.145 Evidence that the controls that are relevant to the auditor's opinion on internal control are operating effectively may be obtained by following the procedures described in paragraphs .16–.17 of AU-C section 402. These procedures include one or more of the following:

a. Obtaining and reading a service auditor's report on management's description of a service organization's system and the suitability of the design and operating effectiveness of controls, which includes a description of the service auditor's tests of controls and results (a type 2 report),[38] if available

b. Performing appropriate tests of controls at the service organization

c. Using another auditor to perform tests of controls at the service organization on behalf of the auditor

[Revised, August 2011, to reflect conforming changes necessary due to the issuance of SSAE No. 16. Revised, December 2012, to reflect conforming changes necessary due to the issuance of SAS Nos. 122–126.]

.146 If the auditor plans to use a type 2 report as audit evidence that controls are operating effectively, the auditor should determine whether the type

---

[38] A report on management's description of a service organization's system and the suitability of the design of controls (a type 1 report) does not include a description of the service auditor's tests of controls and results of those tests or the service auditor's opinion on the operating effectiveness of controls and therefore does not provide evidence of the operating effectiveness of controls. Type 1 and type 2 reports are defined in paragraph .07 of section 801, *Reporting on Controls at a Service Organization*. [Footnote renumbered and revised, August 2011, to reflect conforming changes necessary due to the issuance of SSAE No. 16. Footnote renumbered, December 2012, to reflect conforming changes necessary due to the issuance of SAS Nos. 122–126.]

2 report provides sufficient appropriate audit evidence about the effectiveness of the controls to support his or her opinion on internal control by evaluating[39]

- the time period covered by the tests of controls and its relation to the as-of date of management's assertion.
- the scope of the services auditor's work and the services and processes covered, the controls tested, and the tests that were performed and the way in which tested controls relate to the entity's controls.
- the results of those tests of controls and the service auditor's opinion on the operating effectiveness of the controls.

[Revised, August 2011, to reflect conforming changes necessary due to the issuance of SSAE No. 16. Revised, December 2012, to reflect conforming changes necessary due to the issuance of SAS Nos. 122–126.]

.147 If the service auditor's type 2 report contains a statement indicating that the control objectives stated in the description can be achieved only if complementary user entity controls are suitably designed and operating effectively, along with the controls at the service organization, the auditor should determine whether the entity has designed and implemented such controls and, if so, should test their operating effectiveness. [Revised, August 2011, to reflect conforming changes necessary due to the issuance of SSAE No. 16. Revised, December 2012, to reflect conforming changes necessary due to the issuance of SAS Nos. 122–126.]

.148 In determining whether the type 2 service auditor's report provides sufficient appropriate evidence to support the auditor's opinion on internal control, the auditor should be satisfied regarding the following:

- The service auditor's professional competence and independence from the service organization. Appropriate sources of information concerning the service auditor's professional competence and independence are discussed in paragraphs .A21–.A22 of AU-C section 402.
- The adequacy of the standards under which the type 2 report was issued.

[Revised, August 2011, to reflect conforming changes necessary due to the issuance of SSAE No. 16. Revised, December 2012, to reflect conforming changes necessary due to the issuance of SAS Nos. 122–126.]

.149 When a significant period of time has elapsed between the time period covered by the tests of controls in the service auditor's report and the date specified in management's assertion, additional procedures should be performed. The auditor should inquire of management to determine whether management has identified any changes in the service organization's controls subsequent to the period covered by the service auditor's report (such as changes communicated to management from the service organization, changes in personnel at the service organization with whom management interacts, changes in reports or other data received from the service organization, changes in contracts or service level agreements with the service organization, or errors identified in the service organization's processing). If management has identified such changes, the auditor should evaluate the effect of such changes on the effectiveness of the

[39] These factors are similar to factors the auditor would consider in determining whether the report provides sufficient appropriate evidence to support the auditor's assessed level of control risk in an audit of the financial statements, as described in paragraph .A32 of AU-C section 402. [Footnote renumbered, August 2011, to reflect conforming changes necessary due to the issuance of SSAE No. 16. Footnote renumbered and revised, December 2012, to reflect conforming changes necessary due to the issuance of SAS Nos. 122–126.]

entity's internal control. The auditor also should evaluate whether the results of other procedures he or she performed indicate that there have been changes in the controls at the service organization.

.150 As risk increases, the need for the auditor to obtain additional evidence increases. Accordingly, the auditor should determine whether to obtain additional evidence about the operating effectiveness of controls at the service organization based on the procedures performed by management or the auditor and the results of those procedures and on an evaluation of the following risk factors:

- The elapsed time between the time period covered by the tests of controls in the service auditor's report and the date specified in management's assertion
- The significance of the activities of the service organization
- Whether there are errors that have been identified in the service organization's processing
- The nature and significance of any changes in the service organization's controls identified by management or the auditor

.151 If the auditor concludes that additional evidence about the operating effectiveness of controls at the service organization is required, the auditor's additional procedures might include

- evaluating procedures performed by management and the results of those procedures.
- contacting the service organization, through the user entity, to obtain specific information.
- requesting that a service auditor be engaged to perform procedures that will supply the necessary information.
- visiting the service organization and performing such procedures.

.152 The auditor should not refer to the service auditor's report when expressing an opinion on internal control.

Benchmarking of Automated Controls

.153 Entirely automated application controls are generally less susceptible to breakdowns due to human failure. This feature may allow the auditor to use a benchmarking strategy.

.154 If general controls over program changes, access to programs, and computer operations are effective and continue to be tested, and if the auditor verifies that the automated application control has not changed since the auditor established a baseline (that is, last tested the application control), the auditor may conclude that the automated application control continues to be effective without repeating the prior year's specific tests of the operation of the automated application control. The nature and extent of the evidence that the auditor should obtain to verify that the control has not changed may vary depending on the circumstances, including the strength of the entity's program change controls.

.155 The consistent and effective functioning of the automated application controls may be dependent upon the related files, tables, data, and parameters. For example, an automated application for calculating interest income might be dependent on the continued integrity of a rate table used by the automated calculation.

.156 To determine whether to use a benchmarking strategy, the auditor should assess the following risk factors. As these factors indicate lower risk, the control being evaluated might be well-suited for benchmarking. As these factors indicate increased risk, the control being evaluated is less suited for benchmarking. These factors are

- the extent to which the application control can be matched to a defined program within an application.
- the extent to which the application is stable (that is, there are few changes from period to period).
- the availability and reliability of a report of the compilation dates of the programs placed in production. (This information may be used as evidence that controls within the program have not changed.)

.157 Benchmarking automated application controls can be especially effective for entities using purchased software when the possibility of program changes is remote (for example, when the vendor does not allow access or modification to the source code).

.158 After a period of time, the length of which depends upon the circumstances, the baseline of the operation of an automated application control should be reestablished. To determine when to reestablish a baseline, the auditor should evaluate the following factors:

- The effectiveness of the IT control environment, including controls over application and system software acquisition and maintenance, access controls, and computer operations.
- The auditor's understanding of the nature of changes, if any, on the specific programs that contain the controls.
- The nature and timing of other related tests.
- The consequences of errors associated with the application control that was benchmarked.
- Whether the control is sensitive to other business factors that may have changed. For example, an automated control may have been designed with the assumption that only positive amounts will exist in a file. Such a control would no longer be effective if negative amounts (credits) begin to be posted to the account.

Integration With the Financial Statement Audit

Tests of Controls in an Examination of Internal Control

.159 The objective of the tests of controls in an examination of internal control is to obtain evidence about the effectiveness of controls to support the auditor's opinion on the entity's internal control. The auditor's opinion relates to the effectiveness of the entity's internal control as of a point in time and taken as a whole.

.160 To express an opinion on internal control as of a point in time, the auditor should obtain evidence that internal control has operated effectively for a sufficient period of time, which may be less than the entire period (ordinarily one year) covered by the entity's financial statements. To express an opinion on internal control taken as a whole, the auditor should obtain evidence about the effectiveness of selected controls over all relevant assertions. This entails testing the design and operating effectiveness of controls ordinarily not tested when expressing an opinion only on the financial statements.

.161 When concluding on the effectiveness of internal control for purposes of expressing an opinion on internal control, the auditor should incorporate the results of any additional tests of controls performed to achieve the objective related to expressing an opinion on the financial statements, as discussed in the following section.

Tests of Controls in an Audit of Financial Statements

.162 To express an opinion on the financial statements, the auditor ordinarily performs tests of controls and substantive procedures. Tests of controls are performed when the auditor's risk assessment includes an expectation of the operating effectiveness of controls or when substantive procedures alone do not provide sufficient appropriate audit evidence at the relevant assertion level.[40] Tests of controls are designed to obtain sufficient appropriate audit evidence that the controls are operating effectively throughout the period of reliance.[41] However, the auditor is not required to test controls for all relevant assertions and, for a variety of reasons, the auditor may choose not to do so.

.163 When concluding on the effectiveness of controls for the purpose of the financial statement audit, the auditor also should evaluate the results of any additional tests of controls performed by the auditor to achieve the objective related to expressing an opinion on the entity's internal control, as discussed in paragraph .160. Consideration of these results may cause the auditor to alter the nature, timing, and extent of substantive procedures and to plan and perform further tests of controls, particularly in response to identified deficiencies.

Effect of Tests of Controls on Substantive Procedures

.164 If, during the examination of internal control, the auditor identifies a deficiency, he or she should determine the effect of the deficiency, if any, on the nature, timing, and extent of substantive procedures to be performed to reduce audit risk in the audit of the financial statements to an appropriately low level.

.165 Regardless of the assessed risk of material misstatement in connection with the audit of the financial statements, the auditor should perform substantive procedures for all relevant assertions related to each material class of transactions, account balance, and disclosure.[42] Performing procedures to express an opinion on internal control does not diminish this requirement. [Footnote renumbered, August 2011, to reflect conforming changes necessary due to the issuance of SSAE No. 16.]

Effect of Substantive Procedures on Conclusions About the Operating Effectiveness of Controls

.166 In an examination of internal control, the auditor should evaluate the effect of the findings of the substantive procedures performed in the audit of

---

[40] See paragraph .18 of AU-C section 330, *Performing Audit Procedures in Response to Assessed Risks and Evaluating the Audit Evidence Obtained*. [Footnote renumbered, August 2011, to reflect conforming changes necessary due to the issuance of SSAE No. 16. Footnote renumbered and revised, December 2012, to reflect conforming changes necessary due to the issuance of SAS Nos. 122–126.]

[41] See paragraph .11 of AU-C section 330. [Footnote renumbered, August 2011, to reflect conforming changes necessary due to the issuance of SSAE No. 16. Footnote renumbered and revised, December 2012, to reflect conforming changes necessary due to the issuance of SAS Nos. 122–126. Footnote revised, July 2013, to reflect conforming changes necessary due to the issuance of SAS Nos. 122–126.]

[42] See paragraphs .18 and .A45 of AU-C section 330. [Footnote renumbered, August 2011, to reflect conforming changes necessary due to the issuance of SSAE No. 16. Footnote renumbered and revised, December 2012, to reflect conforming changes necessary due to the issuance of SAS Nos. 122–126.]

financial statements on the effectiveness of internal control. This evaluation should include, at a minimum

- the risk assessments in connection with the selection and application of substantive procedures, especially those related to fraud.
- findings with respect to illegal acts and related party transactions.
- indications of management bias in making accounting estimates and in selecting accounting principles.
- misstatements detected by substantive procedures. The extent of such misstatements might alter the auditor's judgment about the effectiveness of controls.

.167 To obtain evidence about whether a selected control is effective, the control should be tested directly; the operating effectiveness of a control cannot be inferred from the absence of misstatements detected by substantive procedures. The absence of misstatements detected by substantive procedures, however, may affect the auditor's risk assessments in determining the testing necessary to conclude on the operating effectiveness of a control.

Effective Date

.168 This section is effective for integrated audits for periods ending on or after December 15, 2008. Earlier implementation is permitted.

.169

Exhibit A—Illustrative Reports

1. The following illustrate the report elements described in this section. These illustrative reports refer to an examination; however, the auditor may refer to the examination of internal control as an audit.[1]

2. Report modifications are discussed beginning at paragraph .115 of this section.

Example 1: Unqualified Opinion on Internal Control

3. The following is an illustrative report expressing an unqualified opinion directly on internal control.

Independent Auditor's Report

[*Introductory paragraph*]

We have examined W Company's internal control over financial reporting as of December 31, 20XX, based on [*identify criteria*].[2] W Company's management is responsible for maintaining effective internal control over financial reporting, and for its assertion about the effectiveness of internal control over financial reporting, included in the accompanying [*title of management's report*]. Our responsibility is to express an opinion on W Company's internal control over financial reporting based on our examination.

[*Scope paragraph*]

We conducted our examination in accordance with attestation standards established by the American Institute of Certified Public Accountants. Those standards require that we plan and perform the examination to obtain reasonable assurance about whether effective internal control over financial reporting was maintained in all material respects. Our examination included obtaining an understanding of internal control over financial reporting, assessing the risk that a material weakness exists, and testing and evaluating the design and operating effectiveness of internal control based on the assessed risk. Our examination also included performing such other procedures as we considered necessary in the circumstances. We believe that our examination provides a reasonable basis for our opinion.

[*Definition paragraph*]

An entity's internal control over financial reporting is a process effected by those charged with governance, management, and other personnel, designed to provide reasonable assurance regarding the preparation of reliable financial statements in accordance with [*applicable financial reporting framework, such as accounting principles generally accepted in the United States of America*]. An entity's internal control over financial reporting includes those policies and procedures that (1) pertain to the maintenance of records that, in reasonable detail, accurately and fairly reflect the transactions and dispositions of the assets of the entity; (2) provide reasonable assurance that transactions are recorded as

---

[1] Because the examination of internal control is integrated with the audit of the financial statements and an examination provides the same level of assurance as an audit, the auditor may refer to the examination of internal control as an audit in his or her report or other communications.

[2] For example, the following may be used to identify the criteria: "criteria established in *Internal Control—Integrated Framework* issued by the Committee of Sponsoring Organizations of the Treadway Commission (COSO)."

necessary to permit preparation of financial statements in accordance with [*applicable financial reporting framework, such as accounting principles generally accepted in the United States of America*], and that receipts and expenditures of the entity are being made only in accordance with authorizations of management and those charged with governance; and (3) provide reasonable assurance regarding prevention, or timely detection and correction of unauthorized acquisition, use, or disposition of the entity's assets that could have a material effect on the financial statements.

[*Inherent limitations paragraph*]

Because of its inherent limitations, internal control over financial reporting may not prevent, or detect and correct misstatements. Also, projections of any evaluation of effectiveness to future periods are subject to the risk that controls may become inadequate because of changes in conditions, or that the degree of compliance with the policies or procedures may deteriorate.

[*Opinion paragraph*]

In our opinion, W Company maintained, in all material respects, effective internal control over financial reporting as of December 31, 20XX, based on [*identify criteria*].

[*Audit of financial statements paragraph*]

We also have audited, in accordance with auditing standards generally accepted in the United States of America, the [*identify financial statements*] of W Company and our report dated [*date of report, which should be the same as the date of the report on the examination of internal control*] expressed [*include nature of opinion*].

[*Signature*]

[*Date*]

Example 2: Unqualified Opinion on Management's Assertion

4. The following is an illustrative report expressing an unqualified opinion on management's assertion.

Independent Auditor's Report

[*Introductory paragraph*]

We have examined management's assertion, included in the accompanying [*title of management report*], that W Company maintained effective internal control over financial reporting as of December 31, 20XX based on [*identify criteria*].[3] W Company's management is responsible for maintaining effective internal control over financial reporting, and for its assertion about the effectiveness of internal control over financial reporting, included in the accompanying [*title of management's report*]. Our responsibility is to express an opinion on management's assertion based on our examination.

[*Scope paragraph*]

We conducted our examination in accordance with attestation standards established by the American Institute of Certified Public Accountants. Those standards require that we plan and perform the examination to obtain reasonable

[3] See footnote 2 of this exhibit.

assurance about whether effective internal control over financial reporting was maintained in all material respects. Our examination included obtaining an understanding of internal control over financial reporting, assessing the risk that a material weakness exists, and testing and evaluating the design and operating effectiveness of internal control based on the assessed risk. Our examination also included performing such other procedures as we considered necessary in the circumstances. We believe that our examination provides a reasonable basis for our opinion.

[*Definition paragraph*]

An entity's internal control over financial reporting is a process effected by those charged with governance, management, and other personnel, designed to provide reasonable assurance regarding the preparation of reliable financial statements in accordance with [*applicable financial reporting framework, such as accounting principles generally accepted in the United States of America*]. An entity's internal control over financial reporting includes those policies and procedures that (1) pertain to the maintenance of records that, in reasonable detail, accurately and fairly reflect the transactions and dispositions of the assets of the entity; (2) provide reasonable assurance that transactions are recorded as necessary to permit preparation of financial statements in accordance with [*applicable financial reporting framework, such as accounting principles generally accepted in the United States of America*], and that receipts and expenditures of the entity are being made only in accordance with authorizations of management and those charged with governance; and (3) provide reasonable assurance regarding prevention, or timely detection and correction of unauthorized acquisition, use, or disposition of the entity's assets that could have a material effect on the financial statements.

[*Inherent limitations paragraph*]

Because of its inherent limitations, internal control over financial reporting may not prevent, or detect and correct misstatements. Also, projections of any evaluation of effectiveness to future periods are subject to the risk that controls may become inadequate because of changes in conditions, or that the degree of compliance with the policies or procedures may deteriorate.

[*Opinion paragraph*]

In our opinion, management's assertion that W Company maintained effective internal control over financial reporting as of December 31, 20XX is fairly stated, in all material respects, based on [*identify criteria*].

[*Audit of financial statements paragraph*]

We also have audited, in accordance with auditing standards generally accepted in the United States of America, the [*identify financial statements*] of W Company and our report dated [*date of report, which should be the same as the date of the report on the examination of internal control*] expressed [*include nature of opinion*].

[*Signature*]

[*Date*]

Example 3: Adverse Opinion on Internal Control

5. The following is an illustrative report expressing an adverse opinion on internal control. In this example, the opinion on the financial statements is not affected by the adverse opinion on internal control.

Independent Auditor's Report

[Introductory paragraph]

We have examined W Company's internal control over financial reporting as of December 31, 20XX, based on [*identify criteria*].[4] W Company's management is responsible for maintaining effective internal control over financial reporting, and for its assertion about the effectiveness of internal control over financial reporting, included in the accompanying [*title of management's report*]. Our responsibility is to express an opinion on W Company's internal control over financial reporting based on our examination.

[Scope paragraph]

We conducted our examination in accordance with attestation standards established by the American Institute of Certified Public Accountants. Those standards require that we plan and perform the examination to obtain reasonable assurance about whether effective internal control over financial reporting was maintained in all material respects. Our examination included obtaining an understanding of internal control over financial reporting, assessing the risk that a material weakness exists, and testing and evaluating the design and operating effectiveness of internal control based on the assessed risk. Our examination also included performing such other procedures as we considered necessary in the circumstances. We believe that our examination provides a reasonable basis for our opinion.

[Definition paragraph]

An entity's internal control over financial reporting is a process effected by those charged with governance, management, and other personnel, designed to provide reasonable assurance regarding the preparation of reliable financial statements in accordance with [*applicable financial reporting framework, such as accounting principles generally accepted in the United States of America*]. An entity's internal control over financial reporting includes those policies and procedures that (1) pertain to the maintenance of records that, in reasonable detail, accurately and fairly reflect the transactions and dispositions of the assets of the entity; (2) provide reasonable assurance that transactions are recorded as necessary to permit preparation of financial statements in accordance with [*applicable financial reporting framework, such as accounting principles generally accepted in the United States of America*], and that receipts and expenditures of the entity are being made only in accordance with authorizations of management and those charged with governance; and (3) provide reasonable assurance regarding prevention, or timely detection and correction of unauthorized acquisition, use, or disposition of the entity's assets that could have a material effect on the financial statements.

[Inherent limitations paragraph]

Because of its inherent limitations, internal control over financial reporting may not prevent, or detect and correct misstatements. Also, projections of any evaluation of effectiveness to future periods are subject to the risk that controls may become inadequate because of changes in conditions, or that the degree of compliance with the policies or procedures may deteriorate.

[Explanatory paragraph]

A material weakness is a deficiency, or a combination of deficiencies, in internal control over financial reporting, such that there is a reasonable possibility

---

[4] See footnote 2 of this exhibit.

that a material misstatement of the entity's financial statements will not be prevented, or detected and corrected on a timely basis. The following material weakness has been identified and included in the accompanying [*title of management's report*].

[*Identify the material weakness described in management's report.*][5]

[*Opinion paragraph*]

In our opinion, because of the effect of the material weakness described above on the achievement of the objectives of the control criteria, W Company has not maintained effective internal control over financial reporting as of December 31, 20XX, based on [*identify criteria*].

[*Audit of financial statements paragraph*]

We also have audited, in accordance with auditing standards generally accepted in the United States of America, the [*identify financial statements*] of W Company. We considered the material weakness identified above in determining the nature, timing, and extent of audit tests applied in our audit of the 20XX financial statements, and this report does not affect our report dated [*date of report, which should be the same as the date of the report on the examination of internal control*], which expressed [*include nature of opinion*].

[*Signature*]

[*Date*]

Example 4: Disclaimer of Opinion on Internal Control

6. The following is an illustrative report expressing a disclaimer of opinion on internal control. In this example, the auditor is applying paragraph .119 of this section because a material weakness was identified during the limited procedures performed by the auditor.

<u>Independent Auditor's Report</u>

[*Introductory paragraph*]

We were engaged to examine W Company's internal control over financial reporting as of December 31, 20XX, based on [*identify criteria*].[6] W Company's management is responsible for maintaining effective internal control over financial reporting, and for its assertion about the effectiveness of internal control over financial reporting, included in the accompanying [*title of management's report*].

[*Paragraph that describes the substantive reasons for the scope limitation*] Accordingly, we were unable to perform auditing procedures necessary to form an opinion on W Company's internal control over financial reporting as of December 31, 20XX.

[*Definition paragraph*]

An entity's internal control over financial reporting is a process effected by those charged with governance, management, and other personnel, designed

---

[5] See paragraphs .111–.114 of this section for specific reporting requirements. The auditor's report need only refer to the material weaknesses described in management's report and need not include a description of each material weakness, provided each material weakness is included and fairly presented in all material respects in management's report.

[6] See footnote 2 of this exhibit.

to provide reasonable assurance regarding the preparation of reliable financial statements in accordance with [*applicable financial reporting framework, such as accounting principles generally accepted in the United States of America*]. An entity's internal control over financial reporting includes those policies and procedures that (1) pertain to the maintenance of records that, in reasonable detail, accurately and fairly reflect the transactions and dispositions of the assets of the entity; (2) provide reasonable assurance that transactions are recorded as necessary to permit preparation of financial statements in accordance with [*applicable financial reporting framework, such as accounting principles generally accepted in the United States of America*], and that receipts and expenditures of the entity are being made only in accordance with authorizations of management and those charged with governance; and (3) provide reasonable assurance regarding prevention, or timely detection and correction of unauthorized acquisition, use, or disposition of the entity's assets that could have a material effect on the financial statements.

[*Inherent limitations paragraph*]

Because of its inherent limitations, internal control over financial reporting may not prevent, or detect and correct misstatements. Also, projections of any evaluation of effectiveness to future periods are subject to the risk that controls may become inadequate because of changes in conditions, or that the degree of compliance with the policies or procedures may deteriorate.

[*Explanatory paragraph*]

A material weakness is a deficiency, or a combination of deficiencies, in internal control over financial reporting, such that there is a reasonable possibility that a material misstatement of the entity's financial statements will not be prevented, or detected and corrected on a timely basis. If one or more material weaknesses exist, an entity's internal control over financial reporting cannot be considered effective. The following material weakness has been identified and included in the accompanying [*title of management's report*].

[*Identify the material weakness described in management's report and include a description of the material weakness, including its nature and its actual and potential effect on the presentation of the entity's financial statements issued during the existence of the material weakness.*]

[*Opinion paragraph*]

Because of the limitation on the scope of our audit described in the second paragraph, the scope of our work was not sufficient to enable us to express, and we do not express, an opinion on the effectiveness W Company's internal control over financial reporting.

[*Audit of financial statements paragraph*]

We have audited, in accordance with auditing standards generally accepted in the United States of America, the [*identify financial statements*] of W Company and our report dated [*date of report*] expressed [*include nature of opinion*]. We considered the material weakness identified above in determining the nature, timing, and extent of audit tests applied in our audit of the 20XX financial statements, and this report does not affect such report on the financial statements.

[*Signature*]

[*Date*]

Example 5: Unqualified Opinion on Internal Control Based, in Part, on the Report of Another Auditor

7. The following is an illustrative report expressing an unqualified opinion on internal control when the auditor decides to refer to the report of another auditor as the basis, in part, for the auditor's own report.

Independent Auditor's Report

[*Introductory paragraph*]

We have examined W Company's internal control over financial reporting as of December 31, 20XX, based on [*identify criteria*].[7] W Company's management is responsible for maintaining effective internal control over financial reporting, and for its assertion about the effectiveness of internal control over financial reporting, included in the accompanying [*title of management's report*]. Our responsibility is to express an opinion on W Company's internal control over financial reporting based on our examination. We did not examine the effectiveness of internal control over financial reporting of B Company, a wholly owned subsidiary, whose financial statements reflect total assets and revenues constituting 20 percent and 30 percent, respectively, of the related consolidated financial statement amounts as of and for the year ended December 31, 20XX. The effectiveness of B Company's internal control over financial reporting was examined by other auditors whose report has been furnished to us, and our opinion, insofar as it relates to the effectiveness of B Company's internal control over financial reporting, is based solely on the report of the other auditors.

[*Scope paragraph*]

We conducted our examination in accordance with attestation standards established by the American Institute of Certified Public Accountants. Those standards require that we plan and perform the examination to obtain reasonable assurance about whether effective internal control over financial reporting was maintained in all material respects. Our examination included obtaining an understanding of internal control over financial reporting, assessing the risk that a material weakness exists, and testing and evaluating the design and operating effectiveness of internal control based on the assessed risk. Our examination also included performing such other procedures as we considered necessary in the circumstances. We believe that our examination and the report of the other auditors provide a reasonable basis for our opinion.

[*Definition paragraph*]

An entity's internal control over financial reporting is a process effected by those charged with governance, management, and other personnel, designed to provide reasonable assurance regarding the preparation of reliable financial statements in accordance with [*applicable financial reporting framework, such as accounting principles generally accepted in the United States of America*]. An entity's internal control over financial reporting includes those policies and procedures that (1) pertain to the maintenance of records that, in reasonable detail, accurately and fairly reflect the transactions and dispositions of the assets of the entity; (2) provide reasonable assurance that transactions are recorded as necessary to permit preparation of financial statements in accordance with [*applicable financial reporting framework, such as accounting principles generally accepted in the United States of America*], and that receipts and expenditures of the entity are being made only in accordance with authorizations of management and those charged with governance; and (3) provide reasonable assurance

[7] See footnote 2 of this exhibit.

regarding prevention, or timely detection and correction of unauthorized acquisition, use, or disposition of the entity's assets that could have a material effect on the financial statements.

[*Inherent limitations paragraph*]

Because of its inherent limitations, internal control over financial reporting may not prevent, or detect and correct misstatements. Also, projections of any evaluation of effectiveness to future periods are subject to the risk that controls may become inadequate because of changes in conditions, or that the degree of compliance with the policies or procedures may deteriorate.

[*Opinion paragraph*]

In our opinion, based on our examination and the report of the other auditors, W Company maintained, in all material respects, effective internal control over financial reporting as of December 31, 20XX, based on [*identify criteria*].[8]

[*Audit of financial statements paragraph*]

We also have audited, in accordance with auditing standards generally accepted in the United States of America, the [*identify financial statements*] of W Company and our report dated [*date of report, which should be the same as the date of the report on the examination of internal control*] expressed [*include nature of opinion*].

[*Signature*]

[*Date*]

Example 6: Combined Report Expressing an Unqualified Opinion on Internal Control and an Unmodified Opinion on the Financial Statements

8. The following is an illustrative combined report expressing an unqualified opinion directly on internal control and an unmodified opinion on the financial statements. This report refers to the examination of internal control as an audit.[9]

Independent Auditor's Report

[*Appropriate Addressee*]

We have audited the accompanying financial statements of W Company, which comprise the balance sheet as of December 31, 20XX, and the related statements of income, changes in stockholder's equity, and cash flows for the year then ended, and the related notes to the financial statements. We also have audited W Company's internal control over financial reporting as of December 31, 20XX, based on [*identify criteria*].[10]

Management's Responsibility for the Financial Statements and Internal Control Over Financial Reporting

Management is responsible for the preparation and fair presentation of these financial statements in accordance with accounting principles generally accepted in the United States of America; this includes the design, implementation, and maintenance of effective internal control over financial reporting relevant to the preparation and fair presentation of these financial statements that are

[8] As discussed in paragraph .125 of this section, whether the other auditor's opinion is expressed on management's assertion or on internal control does not affect the determination of whether the principal auditor's opinion is expressed on management's assertion or on internal control.

[9] See footnote 1 of this exhibit.

[10] See footnote 2 of this exhibit.

free from material misstatement, whether due to error of fraud. Management is also responsible for its assertion about the effectiveness of internal control over financial reporting, included in the accompanying [*title of management's report*].

Auditor's Responsibility

Our responsibility is to express an opinion on these financial statements and an opinion on W Company's internal control over financial reporting based on our audits. We conducted our audit of the financial statements in accordance with auditing standards generally accepted in the United States of America and our audit of internal control over financial reporting in accordance with attestation standards established by the American Institute of Certified Public Accountants. Those standards require that we plan and perform the audits to obtain reasonable assurance about whether the financial statements are free from material misstatement and whether effective internal control over financial reporting was maintained in all material respects.

An audit of financial statements involves performing procedures to obtain audit evidence about the amounts and disclosures in the financial statements. The procedures selected depend on the auditor's judgment, including the assessment of the risks of material misstatement of the financial statements, whether due to fraud or error. In making those risk assessments, the auditor considers internal control relevant to the entity's preparation and fair presentation of the financial statements in order to design audit procedures that are appropriate in the circumstances. An audit of financial statements also includes evaluating the appropriateness of accounting policies used and the reasonableness of significant accounting estimates made by management, as well as evaluating the overall presentation of the financial statements. An audit of internal control over financial reporting involves obtaining an understanding of internal control over financial reporting, assessing the risk that a material weakness exists, testing and evaluating the design and operating effectiveness of internal control over financial reporting based on the assessed risk, and performing such other procedures as we considered necessary in the circumstances.

We believe that the audit evidence we obtained is sufficient and appropriate to provide a basis for our audit opinions.

Definitions and Inherent Limitations of Internal Control Over Financial Reporting

An entity's internal control over financial reporting is a process effected by those charged with governance, management, and other personnel, designed to provide reasonable assurance regarding the preparation of reliable financial statements in accordance with [*applicable financial reporting framework, such as accounting principles generally accepted in the United States of America*]. An entity's internal control over financial reporting includes those policies and procedures that (1) pertain to the maintenance of records that, in reasonable detail, accurately and fairly reflect the transactions and dispositions of the assets of the entity; (2) provide reasonable assurance that transactions are recorded as necessary to permit preparation of financial statements in accordance with [*applicable financial reporting framework, such as accounting principles generally accepted in the United States of America*], and that receipts and expenditures of the entity are being made only in accordance with authorizations of management and those charged with governance; and (3) provide reasonable assurance regarding prevention, or timely detection and correction of unauthorized acquisition, use, or disposition of the entity's assets that could have a material effect on the financial statements.

Because of its inherent limitations, internal control over financial reporting may not prevent, or detect and correct misstatements. Also, projections of any evaluation of effectiveness to future periods are subject to the risk that controls may become inadequate because of changes in conditions, or that the degree of compliance with the policies or procedures may deteriorate.

Opinions

In our opinion, the financial statements referred to above present fairly, in all material respects, the financial position of W Company as of December 31, 20XX, and the results of its operations and its cash flows for the year then ended in accordance with accounting principles generally accepted in the United States of America. Also in our opinion, W Company maintained, in all material respects, effective internal control over financial reporting as of December 31, 20XX, based on [*identify criteria*].

[*Auditor's signature*]

[*Auditor's city and state*]

[*Date of the auditor's report*]

[Revised, December 2012 and July 2013, to reflect conforming changes necessary due to the issuance of SAS Nos. 122–126.]

.170

Exhibit B—Illustrative Communication of Significant Deficiencies and Material Weaknesses

1. The following is an illustrative written communication of significant deficiencies and material weaknesses.

> In connection with our audit of W Company's (the "Company") financial statements as of December 31, 20XX and for the year then ended, and our audit of the Company's internal control over financial reporting as of December 31, 20XX ("integrated audit"), the standards established by the American Institute of Certified Public Accountants require that we advise you of the following internal control matters identified during our integrated audit.
>
> Our responsibility is to plan and perform our integrated audit to obtain reasonable assurance about whether the financial statements are free of material misstatement, whether caused by error or fraud, and whether effective internal control over financial reporting was maintained in all material respects (that is, whether material weaknesses exist as of the date specified in management's assertion). The integrated audit is not designed to detect deficiencies that, individually or in combination, are less severe than a material weakness. However, we are responsible for communicating to management and those charged with governance significant deficiencies and material weaknesses identified during the integrated audit. We are also responsible for communicating to management deficiencies that are of a lesser magnitude than a significant deficiency, unless previously communicated, and inform those charged with governance when such a communication was made.
>
> A deficiency in internal control over financial reporting exists when the design or operation of a control does not allow management or employees, in the normal course of performing their assigned functions, to prevent, or detect and correct misstatements on a timely basis. [*A material weakness is a deficiency, or a combination of deficiencies, in internal control over financial reporting, such that there is a reasonable possibility that a material misstatement of the Company's financial statements will not be prevented, or detected and corrected on a timely basis. We believe the following deficiencies constitute material weaknesses:*]
>
> [*Describe the material weaknesses that were identified during the integrated audit. The auditor may separately identify those material weaknesses that exist as of the date of management's assertion by referring to the auditor's report.*]
>
> [*A significant deficiency is a deficiency, or a combination of deficiencies, in internal control over financial reporting that is less severe than a material weakness, yet important enough to merit attention by those charged with governance. We consider the following deficiencies to be significant deficiencies:*]
>
> [*Describe the significant deficiencies that were identified during the integrated audit.*]
>
> This communication is intended solely for the information and use of management, [*identify the body or individuals charged with governance*], others within the organization, and [*identify any specified governmental authorities*] and is not intended to be and should not be used by anyone other than these specified parties.

.171

Exhibit C—Reporting Under Section 112 of the Federal Deposit Insurance Corporation Improvement Act (FDICIA)

1. In Financial Institution Letter (FIL) 86-94, *Additional Guidance Concerning Annual Audits, Audit Committees and Reporting Requirements*, issued December 23, 1994, the Federal Deposit Insurance Corporation (FDIC) provided guidance on the meaning of the term *financial reporting* for purposes of compliance by insured depository institutions (IDIs) with Section 112 of the Federal Deposit Insurance Corporation Improvement Act (FDICIA) (Section 36 of the Federal Deposit Insurance Act, 12.U.S.C. 1831m), and its implementing regulation, 12 CFR Part 363. The FDIC indicated that financial reporting, at a minimum, includes financial statements prepared in accordance with generally accepted accounting principles (GAAP) and the schedules equivalent to the basic financial statements that are included in the IDI's appropriate regulatory report (for example, Schedules RC, RI, and RI-A in the Consolidated Reports of Condition and Income [Call Report]). Accordingly, to comply with FDICIA and Part 363, management of the IDI (or a parent holding company)[1] and the auditor should identify and test controls over the preparation of GAAP-based financial statements as well as the schedules equivalent to the basic financial statements that are included in the IDI's (or its holding company's) appropriate regulatory report. Further, both management and the auditor should include in their report on the IDI's (or its holding company's) internal control a specific description indicating that the scope of internal control included controls over the preparation of the IDI's (or its holding company's) GAAP-based financial statements as well as the schedules equivalent to the basic financial statements that are included in the IDI's (or its holding company's) appropriate regulatory report.

2. In accordance with paragraph .107 of this section, the auditor's report should include a definition of internal control (the auditor should use the same description of the entity's internal control as management uses in its report). The following is an illustrative definition paragraph that may be used when an IDI that is a bank (which is not subject to Section 404 of the Sarbanes-Oxley Act of 2002) elects to report on controls for FDICIA purposes at the bank holding company level:

> An entity's internal control over financial reporting is a process effected by those charged with governance, management, and other personnel, designed to provide reasonable assurance regarding the preparation of reliable financial statements in accordance with accounting principles generally accepted in the United States of America. Because management's assessment and our examination were conducted to meet the reporting requirements of Section 112 of the Federal Deposit Insurance Corporation Improvement Act (FDICIA), our examination of [*Holding Company's*] internal control over financial reporting included controls over the preparation of financial statements in accordance with accounting principles generally accepted in the United States of America and with the instructions to the Consolidated Financial Statements for Bank

[1] See Financial Institution Letter (FIL) 86-94 for further discussion of reporting at the holding company level for Federal Deposit Insurance Corporation Improvement Act purposes and the application of holding company reporting as it relates to controls over the preparation of "regulatory reports."

Holding Companies (Form FR Y-9C).[2] An entity's internal control over financial reporting includes those policies and procedures that (1) pertain to the maintenance of records that, in reasonable detail, accurately and fairly reflect the transactions and dispositions of the assets of the entity; (2) provide reasonable assurance that transactions are recorded as necessary to permit preparation of financial statements in accordance with accounting principles generally accepted in the United States of America, and that receipts and expenditures of the entity are being made only in accordance with authorizations of management and those charged with governance; and (3) provide reasonable assurance regarding prevention, or timely detection and correction of unauthorized acquisition, use, or disposition of the entity's assets that could have a material effect on the financial statements.

[2] This sentence would be modified if the insured depository institution (IDI) reports at the institution level rather than at the bank holding company level to refer to the Federal Financial Institutions Examination Council Instructions for Consolidated Reports of Condition and Income or the Office of Thrift Supervision Instructions for Thrift Financial Reports instead of to the Form FR Y-9C. This sentence would also be modified if the IDI reports at a holding company level and employs another approach to reporting on controls over the preparation of regulatory reports as permitted by FIL 86-94.

.172

Exhibit D—Illustrative Management Report

1. The following is an illustrative management report containing the reporting elements described in paragraph .95 of this section:

Management's Report on Internal Control Over Financial Reporting

W Company's internal control over financial reporting is a process effected by those charged with governance, management, and other personnel, designed to provide reasonable assurance regarding the preparation of reliable financial statements in accordance with [*applicable financial reporting framework, such as accounting principles generally accepted in the United States of America*]. An entity's internal control over financial reporting includes those policies and procedures that (1) pertain to the maintenance of records that, in reasonable detail, accurately and fairly reflect the transactions and dispositions of the assets of the entity; (2) provide reasonable assurance that transactions are recorded as necessary to permit preparation of financial statements in accordance with [*applicable financial reporting framework, such as accounting principles generally accepted in the United States of America*], and that receipts and expenditures of the entity are being made only in accordance with authorizations of management and those charged with governance; and (3) provide reasonable assurance regarding prevention, or timely detection and correction of unauthorized acquisition, use, or disposition of the entity's assets that could have a material effect on the financial statements.

Management is responsible for establishing and maintaining effective internal control over financial reporting. Management assessed the effectiveness of W Company's internal control over financial reporting as of December 31, 20XX, based on the framework set forth by the Committee of Sponsoring Organizations of the Treadway Commission in *Internal Control—Integrated Framework*. Based on that assessment, management concluded that, as of December 31, 20XX, W Company's internal control over financial reporting is effective based on the criteria established in *Internal Control—Integrated Framework*.

W Company

Report signers, if applicable

Date

AT Section 9501

An Examination of an Entity's Internal Control Over Financial Reporting That Is Integrated With an Audit of Its Financial Statements: Attest Engagements Interpretations of Section 501

Notice of Pending Withdrawal of AT Section 501, *An Examination of an Entity's Internal Control Over Financial Reporting That Is Integrated With an Audit of Its Financial Statements*

In October 2015, the Auditing Standards Board (ASB) issued SAS No. 130, *An Audit of Internal Control Over Financial Reporting That Is Integrated With an Audit of Financial Statements* (sec. 940), which withdraws AT section 501. SAS No. 130 is effective for integrated audits for periods ending on or after December 15, 2016, at which time the content of this section will be removed. The ASB concluded that, because engagements performed under AT section 501 are required to be integrated with an audit of financial statements, it would be appropriate to move the content of this section from the attestation standards into generally accepted auditing standards.

1. Reporting Under Section 112 of the Federal Deposit Insurance Corporation Improvement Act

.01 *Question*—For purposes of compliance by insured depository institutions (IDIs) with Section 112 of the Federal Deposit Insurance Corporation Improvement Act (FDICIA) (Section 36, Independent Annual Audits of Insured Depository Institutions, of the Federal Deposit Insurance Act [*Banks and Banking, U.S. Code* Title 12, Section 1831m]) and its implementing regulation, Title 12 U.S. *Code of Federal Regulations* (CFR) Part 363, an IDI that is a subsidiary of a holding company may use the consolidated holding company's financial statements to satisfy the audited financial statements requirement of 12 CFR 363, provided certain criteria are met.[1] For some IDIs, however, an examination of internal control over financial reporting is required at the IDI level. Paragraph .18 of section 501, *An Examination of an Entity's Internal Control Over Financial Reporting That Is Integrated With an Audit of Its Financial Statements*, requires that an examination of internal control over financial reporting (internal control) be integrated with an audit of financial statements. For IDIs that require an examination of internal control at the IDI level, can the auditor

[1] Refer to Section 36 of the Federal Deposit Insurance Act (FDI Act), Section 363.1: Scope and Definitions, for the requirements pertaining to compliance by subsidiaries of holding companies.

meet the integrated audit requirement when the IDI does not prepare financial statements for external distribution? If so, how can the auditor report on the effectiveness of the IDI's internal control over financial reporting?

.02 *Interpretation*—To comply with the integrated audit requirement in section 501, when the IDI uses the consolidated holding company's financial statements to satisfy the audited financial statements requirement of 12 CFR 363, the auditor would be required to perform procedures necessary to obtain sufficient appropriate audit evidence to enable the auditor to express an opinion on the IDI's financial statements and on its internal control over financial reporting. When the IDI does not prepare financial statements for external distribution, "financial statements" for this purpose may consist of the IDI's financial information in a reporting package or equivalent schedules and analyses that include the IDI information necessary for the preparation of the holding company's consolidated financial statements, including disclosures. The measurement of materiality is determined based on the IDI's financial information rather than the consolidated holding company's financial statements.[2] If the auditor is unable to apply the procedures necessary to obtain sufficient appropriate audit evidence with respect to the IDI's financial information, the auditor is required by paragraph .117 of section 501 to withdraw from the engagement or disclaim an opinion on the effectiveness of the IDI's internal control over financial reporting.

.03 As indicated in exhibit C, "Reporting Under Section 112 of the Federal Deposit Insurance Corporation Improvement Act (FDICIA)," of section 501, the FDIC indicated that financial reporting, at a minimum, includes financial statements prepared in accordance with generally accepted accounting principles (GAAP) and the schedules equivalent to the basic financial statements that are included in the IDI's appropriate regulatory report (for example, Schedules RC, RI, and RI-A in the Consolidated Reports of Condition and Income [call report]). When the IDI does not prepare financial statements for external distribution, the auditor is, nevertheless, required by paragraph .41 of section 501 to evaluate the IDI's period-end financial reporting process. This process includes, among other things, the IDI's procedures for preparing financial information for purposes of the consolidated holding company's financial statements, which are prepared in accordance with GAAP, and the schedules equivalent to the basic financial statements that are included in the IDI's appropriate regulatory report.

.04 The period-end financial reporting process may occur either at the IDI or the holding company, or both. The organizational structure, including where the controls relevant to the IDI's financial information operate, may affect how the auditor evaluates this process. For example,

a. when the period-end financial reporting process occurs at the holding company and the IDI comprises substantially all of the consolidated total assets, there may be no distinguishable difference between the IDI's and its holding company's process for purposes of the integrated audit. This is because the auditor's risk assessment, including the determination of significant accounts and disclosures and relevant assertions, the selection of controls to test, and the determination of the evidence necessary to conclude on the effectiveness of a given control, would likely

---

[2] See paragraph .10 of AU-C section 320, *Materiality in Planning and Performing an Audit*. [Footnote revised, December 2012, to reflect conforming changes necessary due to the issuance of SAS Nos. 122–126.]

be the same for the IDI and the holding company.[3] In this circumstance, the period-end financial reporting process of the holding company would be, in effect, the period-end financial reporting process of the IDI and, therefore, would be included in the scope of the integrated audit of the IDI.

b. when the period-end financial reporting process occurs at the holding company and the IDI does not comprise substantially all of the consolidated total assets, the IDI's financial reporting process may be sufficient for the auditor to meet the requirement in paragraph .41 of section 501, if the necessary GAAP information is prepared by the IDI or the holding company, and the process can be evaluated by the auditor. The auditor may determine that the IDI's preparation of the IDI's appropriate regulatory report, together with other financial information at the IDI level that is incorporated into the consolidated holding company's financial statements, is sufficient for this purpose. In this circumstance, both the period-end financial reporting process of the holding company, as it relates to the financial information of the IDI, and the period-end financial reporting process of the IDI, with respect to the preparation of the schedules equivalent to the basic financial statements that are included in the IDI's appropriate regulatory report, would be included in the scope of the integrated audit of the IDI.

.05 The illustrative reports in exhibit A, "Illustrative Reports," of section 501 may be used to report on the effectiveness of the IDI's internal control over financial reporting. Because 12 CFR 363 does not require the auditor to issue a separate auditor's report on the IDI's financial statements, the requirement in paragraph .109 of section 501 to add a paragraph to the internal control report that references the financial statement audit will not apply when the auditor does not issue a separate auditor's report on the IDI's financial statements. In accordance with paragraph .107 of section 501, the auditor's report on internal control is required to include a definition of *internal control* that uses the same description of internal control as management uses in its report. The following is an illustrative definition paragraph that may be used when an IDI that is not subject to Section 404 of the Sarbanes-Oxley Act of 2002 elects to report on controls for FDICIA purposes at the IDI level, and the IDI uses the consolidated holding company's financial statements to satisfy the audited financial statements requirement of 12 CFR 363:

> An entity's internal control over financial reporting is a process effected by those charged with governance, management, and other personnel, designed to provide reasonable assurance regarding the preparation of reliable financial statements in accordance with generally accepted accounting principles. Because management's assessment and our examination were conducted to meet the reporting requirements of Section 112 of the Federal Deposit Insurance Corporation Improvement Act (FDICIA), our examination of [*IDI's*] internal control over financial reporting included controls over the preparation of financial information for purposes of [*consolidated holding company's*] financial statements in accordance with accounting principles generally accepted in the United States of America and controls over the preparation of schedules equivalent to basic financial statements in accordance with the Federal Financial Institutions Examination Council Instructions for Consolidated Reports of Condition and Income (call report instructions). An entity's internal control over financial reporting includes those policies and procedures that (1) pertain to the maintenance of records that, in reasonable detail, accurately and fairly

[3] See paragraph .23 of section 501, *An Examination of an Entity's Internal Control Over Financial Reporting That Is Integrated With an Audit of Its Financial Statements*.

reflect the transactions and dispositions of the assets of the entity; (2) provide reasonable assurance that transactions are recorded as necessary to permit preparation of financial statements in accordance with generally accepted accounting principles, and that receipts and expenditures of the entity are being made only in accordance with authorizations of management and those charged with governance; and (3) provide reasonable assurance regarding prevention, or timely detection and correction of unauthorized acquisition, use, or disposition of the entity's assets that could have a material effect on the financial statements.

.06 Management may evaluate and report on the effectiveness of the IDI's internal control based on the Committee of Sponsoring Organizations of the Treadway Commission's (COSO) report, *Internal Control—Integrated Framework*. Because COSO establishes control objectives relating to the preparation of reliable "published" financial statements, the COSO criteria, as modified for purposes of reporting under Section 112 of FDICIA, is appropriate only for the IDI and its regulatory agencies. Accordingly, the report is required to be restricted as to use.[4] An example of such a restriction is as follows:

> This report is intended solely for the information and use of management, [*identify the body or individuals charged with governance*], others within the organization, the Federal Deposit Insurance Corporation and [*other federal bank regulatory agency*] and is not intended to be and should not be used by anyone other than these specified parties.

.07 Likewise, the auditor's report and management's assertion refer to the modified COSO criteria. For example, the following may be used to identify the criteria: "criteria established in *Internal Control—Integrated Framework* issued by the Committee of Sponsoring Organizations of the Treadway Commission (COSO) as modified for the express purpose of meeting the regulatory requirements of Section 112 of the Federal Deposit Insurance Corporation Improvement Act (FDICIA)."

[Issue Date: September 2010.]

---

[4] Paragraph .78 of section 101, *Attest Engagements*, requires the report to be restricted as to use "when the criteria used to evaluate the subject matter are determined by the practitioner to be appropriate only for a limited number of parties who either participated in their establishment or can be presumed to have an adequate understanding of the criteria." Although reports on internal control issued in accordance with this interpretation are required to be restricted as to use, Section 36 of the FDI Act and Title 12 U.S. *Code of Federal Regulations* Part 363 require that these reports be available for public inspection.

AT Section 601

Compliance Attestation

Source: SSAE No. 10.

Effective when the subject matter or assertion is as of or for a period ending on or after June 1, 2001. Earlier application is permitted.

Introduction and Applicability

.01 This section provides guidance for engagements related to either (*a*) an entity's compliance with requirements of specified laws, regulations, rules, contracts, or grants or (*b*) the effectiveness of an entity's internal control over compliance with specified requirements.[1] Compliance requirements may be either financial or nonfinancial in nature. An attest engagement conducted in accordance with this section should comply with the general, fieldwork, and reporting standards established in section 50, *SSAE Hierarchy*, and the specific standards set forth in this section. [Revised, November 2006, to reflect conforming changes necessary due to the issuance of SSAE No. 14.]

.02 This section does not—

a. Affect the auditor's responsibility in an audit of financial statements performed in accordance with generally accepted auditing standards (GAAS).

b. Apply to situations in which an auditor reports on specified compliance requirements based solely on an audit of financial statements, as addressed in AU-C section 806, *Reporting on Compliance With Aspects of Contractual Agreements or Regulatory Requirements in Connection With Audited Financial Statements*.

c. Apply to engagements for which the objective is to report in accordance with AU-C section 935, *Compliance Audits*, unless the terms of the engagement specify an attest report under this section.

d. Apply to engagements covered by AU-C section 920, *Letters for Underwriters and Certain Other Requesting Parties*.

e. Apply to the report that encompasses internal control over compliance for a broker or dealer in securities as required by rule 17a-5 of the Securities Exchange Act of 1934 (the 1934 Act).[2]

[Revised, December 2010, to reflect conforming changes necessary due to the issuance of SAS No. 117. Revised, December 2012, to reflect conforming changes necessary due to the issuance of SAS Nos. 122–126.]

---

[1] Throughout this section—

a. An entity's compliance with requirements of specified laws, regulations, rules, contracts, or grants is referred to as *compliance with specified requirements*.

b. An entity's internal control over compliance with specified requirements is referred to as its *internal control over compliance*. The internal control addressed in this section may include parts of but is not the same as internal control over financial reporting.

[2] An example of this report is contained in AICPA Audit and Accounting Guide *Brokers and Dealers in Securities*.

.03 A report issued in accordance with the provisions of this section does not provide a legal determination of an entity's compliance with specified requirements. However, such a report may be useful to legal counsel or others in making such determinations.

Scope of Services

.04 The practitioner may be engaged to perform agreed-upon procedures to assist users in evaluating the following subject matter (or assertions related thereto)—

a. The entity's compliance with specified requirements

b. The effectiveness of the entity's internal control over compliance[3]

c. Both the entity's compliance with specified requirements and the effectiveness of the entity's internal control over compliance

The practitioner also may be engaged to examine the entity's compliance with specified requirements or a written assertion thereon.

.05 An important consideration in determining the type of engagement to be performed is expectations by users of the practitioner's report. Since the users decide the procedures to be performed in an agreed-upon procedures engagement, it often will be in the best interests of the practitioner and users (including the client) to have an agreed-upon procedures engagement rather than an examination engagement. When deciding whether to accept an examination engagement, the practitioner should consider the risks discussed in paragraphs .31–.35.

.06 A practitioner may be engaged to examine the effectiveness of the entity's internal control over compliance or an assertion thereon. However, in accordance with section 50, the practitioner cannot accept an engagement unless he or she has reason to believe that the subject matter is capable of reasonably consistent evaluation against criteria that are suitable and available to users.[4] If a practitioner determines that such criteria do exist for internal

[3] An entity's internal control over compliance is the process by which management obtains reasonable assurance of compliance with specified requirements. Although the comprehensive internal control may include a wide variety of objectives and related policies and procedures, only some of these may be relevant to an entity's compliance with specified requirements. (See footnote 1*b*.) The components of internal control over compliance vary based on the nature of the compliance requirements. For example, internal control over compliance with a capital requirement would generally include accounting procedures, whereas internal control over compliance with a requirement to practice nondiscriminatory hiring may not include accounting procedures.

[4] Criteria issued by regulatory agencies and other groups composed of experts that follow due-process procedures, including exposure of the proposed criteria for public comment, ordinarily should be considered suitable criteria for this purpose. For example, the Committee of Sponsoring Organizations (COSO) of the Treadway Commission's Report, *Internal Control—Integrated Framework*, provides suitable criteria against which management may evaluate and report on the effectiveness of the entity's internal control. However, more detailed criteria relative to specific compliance requirements may have to be developed and an appropriate threshold for measuring the severity of control deficiencies needs to be developed in order to apply the concepts of the COSO report to internal control over compliance.

Criteria established by a regulatory agency that does not follow such due-process procedures also may be considered suitable criteria for use by the regulatory agency. The practitioner should determine whether such criteria are suitable for general use reporting by evaluating them against the attributes in paragraph .24 of section 101. If the practitioner determines that such criteria are suitable for general use reporting, those criteria should also be available to users as discussed in paragraph .33 of section 101.

If the practitioner concludes that the criteria are appropriate only for a limited number of parties or are available only to specified parties, the practitioner's report shall state that the use of the report is restricted to those parties specified in the report. (See paragraphs .30, .34, and .78–.83 of section 101.)

control over compliance, he or she should perform the engagement in accordance with section 101, *Attest Engagements*. Additionally, section 501, *An Examination of an Entity's Internal Control Over Financial Reporting That Is Integrated With an Audit of Its Financial Statements*, may be helpful to a practitioner in such an engagement. [Revised, November 2006, to reflect conforming changes necessary due to the issuance of SSAE No. 14.]

.07 A practitioner should not accept an engagement to perform a review, as defined in paragraph .55 of section 101, of an entity's compliance with specified requirements or about the effectiveness of an entity's internal control over compliance or an assertion thereon.

.08 The practitioner may be engaged to provide other types of services in connection with the entity's compliance with specified requirements or the entity's internal control over compliance. For example, management may engage the practitioner to provide recommendations on how to improve the entity's compliance or related internal control. A practitioner engaged to provide such nonattest services should refer to the guidance in CS section 100, *Consulting Services: Definitions and Standards*.

Conditions for Engagement Performance

.09 A practitioner may perform an agreed-upon procedures engagement related to an entity's compliance with specified requirements or the effectiveness of internal control over compliance if the following conditions are met.

a. The responsible party accepts responsibility for the entity's compliance with specified requirements and the effectiveness of the entity's internal control over compliance.

b. The responsible party evaluates the entity's compliance with specified requirements or the effectiveness of the entity's internal control over compliance.

See also section 201, *Agreed-Upon Procedures Engagements*.

.10 A practitioner may perform an examination engagement related to an entity's compliance with specified requirements if the following conditions are met.

a. The responsible party accepts responsibility for the entity's compliance with specified requirements and the effectiveness of the entity's internal control over compliance.

b. The responsible party evaluates the entity's compliance with specified requirements.

c. Sufficient evidential matter exists or could be developed to support management's evaluation.

.11 As part of engagement performance, the practitioner should obtain from the responsible party a written assertion about compliance with specified requirements or internal control over compliance. The responsible party may present its written assertion in either of the following:

a. A separate report that will accompany the practitioner's report

b. A representation letter to the practitioner

.12 The responsible party's written assertion about compliance with specified requirements or internal control over compliance may take many forms. Throughout this section, for example, the phrase "responsible party's assertion that W Company complied with [*specify compliance requirement*] as of [*date*]," illustrates such an assertion. Other phrases may also be used. However, a practitioner should not accept an assertion that is so subjective (for example, "very effective" internal control over compliance) that people having competence in and using the same or similar criteria would not ordinarily be able to arrive at similar conclusions.

.13 Regardless of whether the practitioner's client is the responsible party, the responsible party's refusal to furnish a written assertion as part of an examination engagement should cause the practitioner to withdraw from the engagement. However, an exception is provided if an examination of an entity's compliance with specified requirements is required by law or regulation. In that instance, the practitioner should disclaim an opinion on compliance unless he or she obtains evidential matter that warrants expressing an adverse opinion. If the practitioner expresses an adverse opinion and the responsible party does not provide an assertion, the practitioner's report should be restricted as to use. (See paragraphs .78–.81 of section 101.) If, as part of an agreed-upon procedures engagement, the practitioner's client is the responsible party, a refusal by that party to provide an assertion requires the practitioner to withdraw from the engagement. However, withdrawal is not required if the engagement is required by law or regulation. If, in an agreed-upon procedures engagement, the practitioner's client is not the responsible party, the practitioner is not required to withdraw but should consider the effects of the responsible party's refusal on the engagement and his or her report.

.14 Additionally, at the beginning of the engagement, the practitioner may want to consider discussing with the client and the responsible party the need for the responsible party to provide the practitioner with a written representation letter at the conclusion of the examination engagement or an agreed-upon procedures engagement in which the client is the responsible party. In that letter, the responsible party will be asked to provide, among other possible items, an acknowledgment of their responsibility for establishing and maintaining effective internal control over compliance and their assertion stating their evaluation of the entity's compliance with specified requirements. The responsible party's refusal to furnish these representations (see paragraphs .68–.70) will constitute a limitation on the scope of the engagement.

Responsible Party

.15 The responsible party is responsible for ensuring that the entity complies with the requirements applicable to its activities. That responsibility encompasses the following.

a. Identify applicable compliance requirements.

b. Establish and maintain internal control to provide reasonable assurance that the entity complies with those requirements.

c. Evaluate and monitor the entity's compliance.

d. Specify reports that satisfy legal, regulatory, or contractual requirements.

The responsible party's evaluation may include documentation such as accounting or statistical data, entity policy manuals, accounting manuals, narrative memoranda, procedural write-ups, flowcharts, completed questionnaires, or internal auditors' reports. The form and extent of documentation will vary depending on the nature of the compliance requirements and the size and complexity of the entity. The responsible party may engage the practitioner to gather information to assist it in evaluating the entity's compliance. Regardless of the procedures performed by the practitioner, the responsible party must accept responsibility for its assertion and must not base such assertion solely on the practitioner's procedures.

Agreed-Upon Procedures Engagement

.16 The objective of the practitioner's agreed-upon procedures is to present specific findings to assist users in evaluating an entity's compliance with specified requirements or the effectiveness of an entity's internal control over compliance based on procedures agreed upon by the users of the report. A practitioner engaged to perform agreed-upon procedures on an entity's compliance with specified requirements or about the effectiveness of an entity's internal control over compliance should follow the guidance set forth herein and in section 201.

.17 The practitioner's procedures generally may be as limited or as extensive as the specified users desire, as long as the specified users (*a*) agree upon the procedures performed or to be performed and (*b*) take responsibility for the sufficiency of the agreed-upon procedures for their purposes. (See paragraph .15 of section 201.)

.18 To satisfy the requirements that the practitioner and the specified users agree upon the procedures performed or to be performed and that the specified users take responsibility for the sufficiency of the agreed-upon procedures for their purposes, ordinarily the practitioner should communicate directly with and obtain affirmative acknowledgment from each of the specified users. For example, this may be accomplished by meeting with the specified users or by distributing a draft of the anticipated report or a copy of an engagement letter to the specified users and obtaining their agreement. If the practitioner is not able to communicate directly with all of the specified users, the practitioner may satisfy these requirements by applying any one or more of the following or similar procedures.

- Compare the procedures to be applied to written requirements of the specified users.
- Discuss the procedures to be applied with appropriate representatives of the specified users involved.
- Review relevant contracts with or correspondence from the specified users.

The practitioner should not report on an engagement when specified users do not agree upon the procedures performed or to be performed and do not take responsibility for the sufficiency of the procedures for their purposes. See paragraph .36 of section 201 for guidance on satisfying these requirements when the practitioner is requested to add other parties as specified parties after the date of completion of the agreed-upon procedures.

.19 In an engagement to perform agreed-upon procedures on an entity's compliance with specified requirements or about the effectiveness of an entity's internal control over compliance, the practitioner is required to perform only the procedures that have been agreed to by users.[5] However, prior to performing such procedures, the practitioner should obtain an understanding of the specified compliance requirements, as discussed in paragraph .20. (See section 201.)

.20 To obtain an understanding of the specified compliance requirements, a practitioner should consider the following:

a. Laws, regulations, rules, contracts, and grants that pertain to the specified compliance requirements, including published requirements

b. Knowledge about the specified compliance requirements obtained through prior engagements and regulatory reports

c. Knowledge about the specified compliance requirements obtained through discussions with appropriate individuals within the entity (for example, the chief financial officer, internal auditors, legal counsel, compliance officer, or grant or contract administrators)

d. Knowledge about the specified compliance requirements obtained through discussions with appropriate individuals outside the entity (for example, a regulator or a third-party specialist)

.21 When circumstances impose restrictions on the scope of an agreed-upon procedures engagement, the practitioner should attempt to obtain agreement from the users for modification of the agreed-upon procedures. When such agreement cannot be obtained (for example, when the agreed-upon procedures are published by a regulatory agency that will not modify the procedures), the practitioner should describe such restrictions in his or her report or withdraw from the engagement.

.22 The practitioner has no obligation to perform procedures beyond the agreed-upon procedures. However, if noncompliance comes to the practitioner's attention by other means, such information ordinarily should be included in his or her report.

.23 The practitioner may become aware of noncompliance that occurs subsequent to the period addressed by the practitioner's report but before the date of the practitioner's report. The practitioner should consider including information regarding such noncompliance in his or her report. However, the practitioner has no responsibility to perform procedures to detect such noncompliance other than obtaining the responsible party's representation about noncompliance in the subsequent period, as described in paragraph .68.

.24 The practitioner's report on agreed-upon procedures on an entity's compliance with specified requirements (or the effectiveness of an entity's internal control over compliance) should be in the form of procedures and findings. The practitioner's report should contain the following elements:

a. A title that includes the word *independent*

b. Identification of the specified parties

c. Identification of the subject matter of the engagement (or management's assertion thereon), including the period or point in time addressed and a reference to the character of the engagement[6]

---

[5] AU-C section 610, *The Auditor's Consideration of the Internal Audit Function in an Audit of Financial Statements*, does not apply to agreed-upon procedures engagements. [Footnote revised, December 2012, to reflect conforming changes necessary due to the issuance of SAS Nos. 122–126.]

[6] Generally, management's assertion about compliance with specified requirements will address a *period* of time, whereas an assertion about internal control over compliance will address a *point* in time.

d. An identification of the responsible party

e. A statement that the subject matter is the responsibility of the responsible party

f. A statement that the procedures, which were agreed to by the specified parties identified in the report, were performed to assist the specified parties in evaluating the entity's compliance with specified requirements or the effectiveness of its internal control over compliance

g. A statement that the agreed-upon procedures engagement was conducted in accordance with attestation standards established by the American Institute of Certified Public Accountants

h. A statement that the sufficiency of the procedures is solely the responsibility of the specified parties and a disclaimer of responsibility for the sufficiency of those procedures

i. A list of the procedures performed (or reference thereto) and related findings (The practitioner should not provide negative assurance. See paragraph .24 of section 201.)

j. Where applicable, a description of any agreed-upon materiality limits (See paragraph .25 of section 201.)

k. A statement that the practitioner was not engaged to and did not conduct an examination of the entity's compliance with specified requirements (or the effectiveness of an entity's internal control over compliance), a disclaimer of opinion thereon, and a statement that if the practitioner had performed additional procedures, other matters might have come to his or her attention that would have been reported

l. A statement restricting the use of the report to the specified parties

m. Where applicable, reservations or restrictions concerning procedures or findings as discussed in paragraphs .33, .35, and .39–.40 of section 201

n. Where applicable, a description of the nature of the assistance provided by the specialist as discussed in paragraphs .19–.21 of section 201

o. The manual or printed signature of the practitioner's firm

p. The date of the report

.25 The following is an illustration of an agreed-upon procedures report on an entity's compliance with specified requirements in which the procedures and findings are enumerated rather than referenced.

<u>Independent Accountant's Report on Applying Agreed-Upon Procedures</u>

We have performed the procedures enumerated below, which were agreed to by [*list specified parties*], solely to assist the specified parties in evaluating [*name of entity*]'s compliance with [*list specified requirements*] during the [*period*] ended [*date*].[7] Management is responsible for [*name of entity*]'s compliance with those requirements. This agreed-upon procedures engagement

[7] If the agreed-upon procedures have been published by a third-party user (for example, a regulator in regulatory policies or a lender in a debt agreement), this sentence might begin, "We have performed the procedures included in [*title of publication or other document*] and enumerated below, which were agreed to by [*list specified parties*], solely to assist the specified parties in evaluating ...."

was conducted in accordance with attestation standards established by the American Institute of Certified Public Accountants. The sufficiency of these procedures is solely the responsibility of those parties specified in this report. Consequently, we make no representation regarding the sufficiency of the procedures described below either for the purpose for which this report has been requested or for any other purpose.

[*Include paragraphs to enumerate procedures and findings.*]

We were not engaged to and did not conduct an examination, the objective of which would be the expression of an opinion on compliance. Accordingly, we do not express such an opinion. Had we performed additional procedures, other matters might have come to our attention that would have been reported to you.

This report is intended solely for the information and use of [*list or refer to specified parties*] and is not intended to be and should not be used by anyone other than these specified parties.

[*Signature*]

[*Date*]

.26 Evaluating compliance with certain requirements may require interpretation of the laws, regulations, rules, contracts, or grants that establish those requirements. In such situations, the practitioner should consider whether he or she is provided with the suitable criteria required to evaluate an assertion under the third general attestation standard. If these interpretations are significant, the practitioner may include a paragraph stating the description and the source of interpretations made by the entity's management. An example of such a paragraph, which should precede the procedures and findings paragraph(s), follows.

We have been informed that, under [*name of entity*]'s interpretation of [*identify the compliance requirement*], [*explain the nature and source of the relevant interpretation*].

.27 The following is an illustration of an agreed-upon procedures report on the effectiveness of an entity's internal control over compliance in which the procedures and findings are enumerated rather than referenced.

Independent Accountant's Report on Applying Agreed-Upon Procedures

We have performed the procedures enumerated below, which were agreed to by [*list specified parties*], solely to assist the specified parties in evaluating the effectiveness of [*name of entity*]'s internal control over compliance with [*list specified requirements*] as of [*date*].[8] Management is responsible for [*name of entity*]'s internal control over compliance with those requirements. This agreed-upon procedures engagement was conducted in accordance with attestation standards established by the American Institute of Certified Public Accountants. The sufficiency of these procedures is solely the responsibility of those parties specified in this report. Consequently, we make no representation regarding the sufficiency of the procedures described below either for the purpose for which this report has been requested or for any other purpose.

---

[8] If the agreed-upon procedures have been published by a third-party user (for example, a regulator in regulatory policies or a lender in a debt agreement), this sentence might begin, "We have performed the procedures included in [*title of publication or other document*] and enumerated below, which were agreed to by [*list specified parties*], solely to assist the specified parties in evaluating the effectiveness of [*name of entity*]'s internal control over compliance ...."

[*Include paragraphs to enumerate procedures and findings.*]

We were not engaged to and did not conduct an examination, the objective of which would be the expression of an opinion on the effectiveness of internal control over compliance. Accordingly, we do not express such an opinion. Had we performed additional procedures, other matters might have come to our attention that would have been reported to you.

This report is intended solely for the information and use of [*list or refer to specified parties*] and is not intended to be and should not be used by anyone other than these specified parties.

[*Signature*]

[*Date*]

.28 In some agreed-upon procedures engagements, procedures may relate to both compliance with specified requirements and the effectiveness of internal control over compliance. In these engagements, the practitioner may issue one report that addresses both. For example, the first sentence of the introductory paragraph would state the following.

We have performed the procedures enumerated below, which were agreed to by [*list users of report*], solely to assist the users in evaluating [*name of entity*]'s compliance with [*list specified requirements*] during the [*period*] ended [*date*] and the effectiveness of [*name of entity*]'s internal control over compliance with the aforementioned compliance requirements as of [*date*].

.29 The date of completion of the agreed-upon procedures should be used as the date of the practitioner's report.

Examination Engagement

.30 The objective of the practitioner's examination procedures applied to an entity's compliance with specified requirements is to express an opinion on an entity's compliance (or assertion related thereto), based on the specified criteria. To express such an opinion, the practitioner accumulates sufficient evidence about the entity's compliance with specified requirements, thereby restricting attestation risk to an appropriately low level.

Attestation Risk

.31 In an engagement to examine compliance with specified requirements, the practitioner seeks to obtain reasonable assurance that the entity complied, in all material respects, based on the specified criteria. This includes designing the examination to detect both intentional and unintentional material noncompliance. Absolute assurance is not attainable because of factors such as the need for judgment, the use of sampling, and the inherent limitations of internal control over compliance and because much of the evidence available to the practitioner is persuasive rather than conclusive in nature. Also, procedures that are effective for detecting noncompliance that is unintentional may be ineffective for detecting noncompliance that is intentional and concealed through collusion between personnel of the entity and a third party or among management or employees of the entity. Therefore, the subsequent discovery that material noncompliance exists does not, in and of itself, evidence inadequate planning, performance, or judgment on the part of the practitioner.

.32 Attestation risk is the risk that the practitioner may unknowingly fail to modify appropriately his or her opinion. It is composed of inherent risk, control risk, and detection risk. For purposes of a compliance examination, these components are defined as follows:

a. *Inherent risk*—The risk that material noncompliance with specified requirements could occur, assuming there are no related controls

b. *Control risk*—The risk that material noncompliance that could occur will not be prevented or detected on a timely basis by the entity's controls

c. *Detection risk*—The risk that the practitioner's procedures will lead him or her to conclude that material noncompliance does not exist when, in fact, such noncompliance does exist

Inherent Risk

.33 In assessing inherent risk, the practitioner should consider factors affecting risk similar to those an auditor would consider when planning an audit of financial statements. Such factors are discussed in paragraph .A75 of AU-C section 240, *Consideration of Fraud in a Financial Statement Audit*. In addition, the practitioner should consider factors relevant to compliance engagements, such as the following:

- The complexity of the specified compliance requirements
- The length of time the entity has been subject to the specified compliance requirements
- Prior experience with the entity's compliance
- The potential impact of noncompliance

[Revised, January 2004, to reflect conforming changes necessary due to the issuance of SAS No. 99. Revised, December 2012, to reflect conforming changes necessary due to the issuance of SAS Nos. 122–126.]

Control Risk

.34 The practitioner should assess control risk as discussed in paragraphs .45–.46. Assessing control risk contributes to the practitioner's evaluation of the risk that material noncompliance exists. The process of assessing control risk (together with assessing inherent risk) provides evidential matter about the risk that such noncompliance may exist. The practitioner uses this evidential matter as part of the reasonable basis for his or her opinion.

Detection Risk

.35 In determining an acceptable level of detection risk, the practitioner assesses inherent risk and control risk and considers the extent to which he or she seeks to restrict attestation risk. As assessed inherent risk or control risk decreases, the acceptable level of detection risk increases. Accordingly, the practitioner may alter the nature, timing, and extent of compliance tests performed based on the assessments of inherent risk and control risk.

Materiality

.36 In an examination of an entity's compliance with specified requirements, the practitioner's consideration of materiality differs from that of an audit of financial statements in accordance with GAAS. In an examination of an entity's compliance with specified requirements, the practitioner's consideration of materiality is affected by (*a*) the nature of the compliance requirements, which may or may not be quantifiable in monetary terms, (*b*) the nature and frequency of noncompliance identified with appropriate consideration of sampling risk, and (*c*) qualitative considerations, including the needs and expectations of the report's users.

.37 In a number of situations, the terms of the engagement may provide for a supplemental report of all or certain noncompliance discovered. Such terms should not change the practitioner's judgments about materiality in planning and performing the engagement or in forming an opinion on an entity's compliance with specified requirements or on the responsible party's assertion about such compliance.

Performing an Examination Engagement

.38 The practitioner should exercise (*a*) due care in planning, performing, and evaluating the results of his or her examination procedures and (*b*) the proper degree of professional skepticism to achieve reasonable assurance that material noncompliance will be detected.

.39 In an examination of the entity's compliance with specified requirements, the practitioner should—

a. Obtain an understanding of the specified compliance requirements. (See paragraph .40.)

b. Plan the engagement. (See paragraphs .41–.44.)

c. Consider relevant portions of the entity's internal control over compliance. (See paragraphs .45–.47.)

d. Obtain sufficient evidence including testing compliance with specified requirements. (See paragraphs .48–.49.)

e. Consider subsequent events. (See paragraphs .50–.52.)

f. Form an opinion about whether the entity complied, in all material respects, with specified requirements (or whether the responsible party's assertion about such compliance is fairly stated in all material respects), based on the specified criteria. (See paragraph .53.)

Obtaining an Understanding of the Specified Compliance Requirements

.40 A practitioner should obtain an understanding of the specified compliance requirements. To obtain such an understanding, a practitioner should consider the following:

a. Laws, regulations, rules, contracts, and grants that pertain to the specified compliance requirements, including published requirements

b. Knowledge about the specified compliance requirements obtained through prior engagements and regulatory reports

c. Knowledge about the specified compliance requirements obtained through discussions with appropriate individuals within the entity (for example, the chief financial officer, internal auditors, legal counsel, compliance officer, or grant or contract administrators)

d. Knowledge about the specified compliance requirements obtained through discussions with appropriate individuals outside the entity (for example, a regulator or third-party specialist)

Planning the Engagement

General Considerations

.41 Planning an engagement to examine an entity's compliance with specified requirements involves developing an overall strategy for the expected conduct and scope of the engagement. The practitioner should consider the planning matters discussed in paragraphs .42–.47 of section 101.

Multiple Components

.42 In an engagement to examine an entity's compliance with specified requirements when the entity has operations in several components (for example, locations, branches, subsidiaries, or programs), the practitioner may determine that it is not necessary to test compliance with requirements at every component. In making such a determination and in selecting the components to be tested, the practitioner should consider factors such as the following:

a. The degree to which the specified compliance requirements apply at the component level

b. Judgments about materiality

c. The degree of centralization of records

d. The effectiveness of the control environment, particularly management's direct control over the exercise of authority delegated to others and its ability to supervise activities at various locations effectively

e. The nature and extent of operations conducted at the various components

f. The similarity of operations over compliance for different components

Using the Work of a Specialist

.43 In some compliance engagements, the nature of the specified compliance requirements may require specialized skill or knowledge in a particular field other than accounting or auditing. In such cases, the practitioner may use the work of a specialist and should follow the relevant performance and reporting guidance in AU-C section 620, *Using the Work of an Auditor's Specialist*. [Revised, December 2012, to reflect conforming changes necessary due to the issuance of SAS Nos. 122–126.]

Internal Audit Function

.44 Another factor the practitioner should consider when planning the engagement is whether the entity has an internal audit function and the extent to which internal auditors are involved in monitoring compliance with the specified requirements. A practitioner should consider the guidance in AU-C section 610, *The Auditor's Consideration of the Internal Audit Function in an Audit of Financial Statements*, when addressing the competence and objectivity of internal auditors, the nature, timing, and extent of work to be performed, and other related matters. [Revised, December 2012, to reflect conforming changes necessary due to the issuance of SAS Nos. 122–126.]

Consideration of Internal Control Over Compliance

.45 The practitioner should obtain an understanding of relevant portions of internal control over compliance sufficient to plan the engagement and to assess control risk for compliance with specified requirements. In planning the examination, such knowledge should be used to identify types of potential noncompliance, to consider factors that affect the risk of material noncompliance, and to design appropriate tests of compliance.

.46 A practitioner generally obtains an understanding of the design of specific controls by performing the following:

a. Inquiries of appropriate management, supervisory, and staff personnel

b. Inspection of the entity's documents

c. Observation of the entity's activities and operations

The nature and extent of procedures a practitioner performs vary from entity to entity and are influenced by factors such as the following:

- The newness and complexity of the specified requirements
- The practitioner's knowledge of internal control over compliance obtained in previous professional engagements
- The nature of the specified compliance requirements
- An understanding of the industry in which the entity operates
- Judgments about materiality

When seeking to assess control risk below the maximum, the practitioner should perform tests of controls to obtain evidence to support the assessed level of control risk.

.47 During the course of an examination engagement, the practitioner may become aware of significant deficiencies or material weaknesses in the design or operation of internal control over compliance that could adversely affect the entity's ability to comply with specified requirements. A practitioner's responsibility to communicate these deficiencies in an examination of an entity's compliance with specified requirements is similar to the auditor's responsibility described in AU-C section 265, *Communicating Internal Control Related Matters Identified in an Audit*. If, in a multiple-party arrangement, the practitioner's client is not the responsible party, the practitioner has no responsibility to communicate significant deficiencies or material weaknesses to the responsible party. For example, if the practitioner is engaged by his or her client to examine the compliance of another entity, the practitioner has no obligation to communicate any significant deficiencies or material weaknesses that he or she becomes aware of to the other entity. However, the practitioner is not precluded from making such a communication. [Revised, May 2006, to reflect conforming changes necessary due to the issuance of SAS No. 112. Revised, January 2010, to reflect conforming changes necessary due to the issuance of SAS No. 115. Revised, December 2012, to reflect conforming changes necessary due to the issuance of SAS Nos. 122–126.]

Obtaining Sufficient Evidence

.48 The practitioner should apply procedures to provide reasonable assurance of detecting material noncompliance. Determining these procedures and evaluating the sufficiency of the evidence obtained are matters of professional judgment. When exercising such judgment, practitioners should consider the guidance contained in paragraphs .51–.54 of section 101 and AU-C section 530, *Audit Sampling*. [Revised, December 2012, to reflect conforming changes necessary due to the issuance of SAS Nos. 122–126.]

.49 For engagements involving compliance with regulatory requirements, the practitioner's procedures should include reviewing reports of significant examinations and related communications between regulatory agencies and the entity and, when appropriate, making inquiries of the regulatory agencies, including inquiries about examinations in progress.

Consideration of Subsequent Events

.50 The practitioner's consideration of subsequent events in an examination of an entity's compliance with specified requirements is similar to the auditor's consideration of subsequent events in a financial statement audit, as outlined in AU-C section 560, *Subsequent Events and Subsequently Discovered Facts*. The practitioner should consider information about such events that comes to his or her attention after the end of the period addressed by the practitioner's report and prior to the issuance of his or her report. [Revised, December 2012, to reflect conforming changes necessary due to the issuance of SAS Nos. 122–126.]

.51 Two types of subsequent events require consideration by the responsible party and evaluation by the practitioner. The first consists of events that provide additional information about the entity's compliance during the period addressed by the practitioner's report and may affect the practitioner's report. For the period from the end of the reporting period (or point in time) to the date of the practitioner's report, the practitioner should perform procedures to identify such events that provide additional information about compliance during the reporting period. Such procedures should include but may not be limited to inquiring about and considering the following information:

- Relevant internal auditors' reports issued during the subsequent period
- Other practitioners' reports identifying noncompliance, issued during the subsequent period
- Regulatory agencies' reports on the entity's noncompliance, issued during the subsequent period
- Information about the entity's noncompliance, obtained through other professional engagements for that entity

.52 The second type consists of noncompliance that occurs subsequent to the period being reported on but before the date of the practitioner's report. The practitioner has no responsibility to detect such noncompliance. However, should the practitioner become aware of such noncompliance, it may be of such a nature and significance that disclosure of it is required to keep users from being misled. In such cases, the practitioner should include in his or her report an explanatory paragraph describing the nature of the noncompliance.

Forming an Opinion

.53 In evaluating whether the entity has complied in all material respects (or whether the responsible party's assertion about such compliance is stated fairly in all material respects), the practitioner should consider (*a*) the nature and frequency of the noncompliance identified and (*b*) whether such noncompliance is material relative to the nature of the compliance requirements, as discussed in paragraph .36.

Reporting

.54 The practitioner may examine and report directly on an entity's compliance (see paragraphs .55–56) or he or she may examine and report on the responsible party's written assertion (see paragraphs .57–.58 and .61), except as described in paragraph .64.

.55 The practitioner's examination report on compliance, which is ordinarily addressed to the entity, should include the following:

a. A title that includes the word *independent*

b. Identification of the specified compliance requirements, including the period covered, and of the responsible party[9]

c. A statement that compliance with the specified requirements is the responsibility of the entity's management

d. A statement that the practitioner's responsibility is to express an opinion on the entity's compliance with those requirements based on his or her examination

e. A statement that the examination was conducted in accordance with attestation standards established by the American Institute of Certified Public Accountants and, accordingly, included examining, on a test basis, evidence about the entity's compliance with those requirements and performing such other procedures as the practitioner considered necessary in the circumstances

f. A statement that the practitioner believes the examination provides a reasonable basis for his or her opinion

g. A statement that the examination does not provide a legal determination on the entity's compliance

h. The practitioner's opinion on whether the entity complied, in all material respects, with specified requirements based on the specified criteria[10] (See paragraph .64 for reporting on material noncompliance.)

i. A statement restricting the use of the report to the specified parties (see the fourth reporting standard)[11] under the following circumstances (See also paragraph .13.):

- When the criteria used to evaluate compliance are determined by the practitioner to be appropriate only for a limited number of parties who either participated in their establishment or can be presumed to have an adequate understanding of the criteria.
- When the criteria used to evaluate compliance are available only to the specified parties

j. The manual or printed signature of the practitioner's firm

k. The date of the examination report

.56 The following is the form of report a practitioner should use when he or she is expressing an opinion on an entity's compliance with specified requirements during a period of time.

---

9 A practitioner also may be engaged to report on an entity's compliance with specified requirements as of point in time. In this case, the illustrative reports in this section should be adapted as appropriate.

10 Frequently, criteria will be contained in the compliance requirements, in which case it is not necessary to repeat the criteria in the practitioner's report; however, if the criteria are not included in the compliance requirement, the practitioner's report should identify the criteria. For example, if a compliance requirement is to "maintain $25,000 in capital," it would not be necessary to identify the $25,000 in the report; however, if the requirement is to "maintain adequate capital," the practitioner should identify the criteria used to define *adequate*.

11 In certain situations, however, criteria that have been specified by management and other report users may be suitable for general use.

Independent Accountant's Report

[Introductory paragraph]

We have examined [*name of entity*]'s compliance with [*list specified compliance requirements*] during the [*period*] ended [*date*]. Management is responsible for [*name of entity*]'s compliance with those requirements. Our responsibility is to express an opinion on [*name of entity*]'s compliance based on our examination.

[Scope paragraph]

Our examination was conducted in accordance with attestation standards established by the American Institute of Certified Public Accountants and, accordingly, included examining, on a test basis, evidence about [*name of entity*]'s compliance with those requirements and performing such other procedures as we considered necessary in the circumstances. We believe that our examination provides a reasonable basis for our opinion. Our examination does not provide a legal determination on [*name of entity*]'s compliance with specified requirements.

[Opinion paragraph]

In our opinion, [*name of entity*] complied, in all material respects, with the aforementioned requirements for the year ended December 31, 20XX.[12]

[*Signature*]

[*Date*]

.57 The practitioner's examination report on an entity's assertion about compliance with specified requirements, which is ordinarily addressed to the entity, should include the following:

a. A title that includes the word *independent*

b. Identification of the responsible party's assertion about the entity's compliance with specified requirements, including the period covered by the responsible party's assertion, and of the responsible party (When the responsible party's assertion does not accompany the practitioner's report, the first paragraph of the report should also contain a statement of the responsible party's assertion.)[13]

c. A statement that compliance with the requirements is the responsibility of the entity's management

d. A statement that the practitioner's responsibility is to express an opinion on the responsible party's assertion on the entity's compliance with those requirements based on his or her examination

e. A statement that the examination was conducted in accordance with attestation standards established by the American Institute of Certified Public Accountants and, accordingly, included examining, on a test basis, evidence about the entity's compliance with those requirements and performing such other procedures as the practitioner considered necessary in the circumstances

---

[12] If it is necessary to identify criteria (see footnote 10), the criteria should be identified in the opinion paragraph (for example, "... in all material respects, based on the criteria set forth in Attachment 1").

[13] A practitioner also may be engaged to report on the responsible party's assertion about an entity's compliance with specified requirements as of a point in time. In this case, the illustrative reports in this section should be adapted as appropriate.

f. A statement that the practitioner believes the examination provides a reasonable basis for his or her opinion

g. A statement that the examination does not provide a legal determination on the entity's compliance

h. The practitioner's opinion on whether the responsible party's assertion about compliance with specified requirements is fairly stated in all material respects based on the specified criteria[14] (See paragraph .64 for reporting on material noncompliance.)

i. A statement restricting the use of the report to the specified parties (see the fourth reporting standard)[15, 16] under the following circumstances:

- When the criteria used to evaluate compliance are determined by the practitioner to be appropriate only for a limited number of parties who either participated in their establishment or can be presumed to have an adequate understanding of the criteria
- When the criteria used to evaluate compliance are available only to the specified parties

j. The manual or printed signature of the practitioner's firm

k. The date of the examination report

.58 The following is the form of report that a practitioner should use when expressing an opinion on management's assertion about compliance with specified requirements.

Independent Accountant's Report

[*Introductory paragraph*]

We have examined management's assertion, included in the accompanying [*title of management report*], that [*name of entity*] complied with [*list specified compliance requirements*] during the [*period*] ended [*date*].[17, 18] Management is responsible for [*name of entity*]'s compliance with those requirements. Our responsibility is to express an opinion on management's assertion about [*name of entity*]'s compliance based on our examination.

[*Standard scope paragraph*]

[*Opinion paragraph*]

---

[14] Frequently, criteria will be contained in the compliance requirements, in which case it is not necessary to repeat the criteria in the practitioner's report; however, if the criteria are not included in the compliance requirement, the practitioner's report should identify the criteria. For example, if a compliance requirement is to "maintain $25,000 in capital," it would not be necessary to identify the $25,000 in the report; however, if the requirement is to "maintain adequate capital," the practitioner should identify the criteria used to define *adequate*.

[15] Although a practitioner's report may be appropriate for general use, the practitioner is not precluded from restricting the use of the report.

[16] In certain situations, however, criteria that have been specified by management and other report users may be suitable for general use.

[17] The practitioner should identify the management report examined by reference to the report title used by management in its report. Further, he or she should use the same description of compliance requirements as management uses in its report.

[18] If management's assertion is stated in the practitioner's report and does not accompany the practitioner's report, the phrase "included in the accompanying [*title of management report*]" would be omitted.

In our opinion, management's assertion that [*name of entity*] complied with the aforementioned requirements during the [*period*] ended [*date*] is fairly stated, in all material respects.[19]

[*Signature*]

[*Date*]

.59 Evaluating compliance with certain requirements may require interpretation of the laws, regulations, rules, contracts, or grants that establish those requirements. In such situations, the practitioner should consider whether he or she is provided with the suitable criteria required to evaluate compliance under the third general attestation standard. If these interpretations are significant, the practitioner may include a paragraph stating the description and the source of interpretations made by the entity's management. The following is an example of such a paragraph, which should directly follow the scope paragraph:

We have been informed that, under [*name of entity*]'s interpretation of [*identify the compliance requirement*], [*explain the source and nature of the relevant interpretation*].

.60 The date of completion of the examination procedures should be used as the date of the practitioner's report.

.61 Nothing precludes the practitioner from examining an assertion but opining directly on compliance.

.62 Paragraphs .78–.83 of section 101 provide guidance on restricting the use of an attest report. Nothing in this section precludes the practitioner from restricting the use of the report. For example, if the practitioner is asked by a client to examine another entity's compliance with certain regulations, he or she may want to restrict the use of the report to the client since the practitioner has no control over how the report may be used by the other entity.

Report Modifications

.63 The practitioner should modify the standard report described in paragraphs .55 and .57, if any of the following conditions exist.

- There is material noncompliance with specified requirements (paragraphs .64–.67).
- There is a restriction on the scope of the engagement.[20]
- The practitioner decides to refer to the report of another practitioner as the basis, in part, for the practitioner's report.[21]

Material Noncompliance

.64 When an examination of an entity's compliance with specified requirements discloses noncompliance with the applicable requirements that the practitioner believes have a material effect on the entity's compliance, the practitioner should modify the report and, to most effectively communicate with the reader of the report, should state his or her opinion on the entity's specified compliance requirements, not on the responsible party's assertion.

---

[19] If it is necessary to identify criteria (see footnote 10), the criteria should be identified in the opinion paragraph (for example, "...in all material respects, based on the criteria set forth in Attachment 1").

[20] The practitioner should refer to paragraphs .73–.74 of section 101 for guidance on scope restrictions.

[21] The practitioner should refer to paragraphs .122–.125 of section 501 for guidance on an opinion based in part on the report of another practitioner and adapt such guidance to the standard reports in this section.

.65 The following is the form of report, modified with explanatory language, that a practitioner should use when he or she has concluded that a qualified opinion is appropriate under the circumstances. It has been assumed that the practitioner has determined that the specified compliance requirements are both suitable for general use and available to users as discussed in paragraphs .23–.33 of section 101, and, therefore, that a restricted use paragraph is not required.

Independent Accountant's Report

[*Introductory paragraph*]

We have examined [*name of entity*]'s compliance with [*list specified compliance requirements*] for the [*period*] ended [*date*]. Management is responsible for compliance with those requirements. Our responsibility is to express an opinion on [*name of entity*]'s compliance based on our examination.

[*Standard scope paragraph*]

[*Explanatory paragraph*]

Our examination disclosed the following material noncompliance with [*type of compliance requirement*] applicable to [*name of entity*] during the [*period*] ended [*date*]. [*Describe noncompliance.*]

[*Opinion paragraph*]

In our opinion, except for the material noncompliance described in the third paragraph, [*name of entity*] complied, in all material respects, with the aforementioned requirements for the [*period*] ended [*date*].

[*Signature*]

[*Date*]

.66 The following is the form of report, modified with explanatory language, that a practitioner should use when he or she concludes that an adverse opinion is appropriate in the circumstances. The practitioner has determined that the specified compliance requirements are both suitable for general use and available to users as discussed in paragraphs .23–.33 of section 101.

Independent Accountant's Report

[*Introductory paragraph*]

We have examined [*name of entity*]'s compliance with [*list specified compliance requirements*] for the [*period*] ended [*date*]. Management is responsible for compliance with those requirements. Our responsibility is to express an opinion on [*name of entity*]'s compliance based on our examination.

[*Standard scope paragraph*]

[*Explanatory paragraph*]

Our examination disclosed the following material noncompliance with [*type of compliance requirement*] applicable to [*name of entity*] during the [*period*] ended [*date*]. [*Describe noncompliance.*]

[*Opinion paragraph*]

In our opinion, because of the effect of the noncompliance described in the third paragraph, [*name of entity*] has not complied with the aforementioned requirements for the [*period*] ended [*date*].

[*Signature*]

[*Date*]

.67 If the practitioner's report on his or her examination of the entity's compliance with specified requirements is included in a document that also includes his or her audit report on the entity's financial statements, the following sentence should be included in the paragraph of an examination report that describes material noncompliance.

> These conditions were considered in determining the nature, timing, and extent of audit tests applied in our audit of the 20XX financial statements, and this report does not affect our report dated [*date of report*] on those financial statements.

The practitioner also may include the preceding sentence when the two reports are not included within the same document.

Representation Letter

.68 In an examination engagement or an agreed-upon procedures engagement, the practitioner should obtain written representations from the responsible party—[22]

a. Acknowledging the responsible party's responsibility for complying with the specified requirements.

b. Acknowledging the responsible party's responsibility for establishing and maintaining effective internal control over compliance.

c. Stating that the responsible party has performed an evaluation of (1) the entity's compliance with specified requirements or (2) the entity's controls for ensuring compliance and detecting noncompliance with requirements, as applicable.

d. Stating the responsible party's assertion about the entity's compliance with the specified requirements or about the effectiveness of internal control over compliance, as applicable, based on the stated or established criteria.

e. Stating that the responsible party has disclosed to the practitioner all known noncompliance.

f. State that the responsible party has made available all documentation related to compliance with the specified requirements.

g. Stating the responsible party's interpretation of any compliance requirements that have varying interpretations.

h. State that the responsible party has disclosed any communications from regulatory agencies, internal auditors, and other practitioners concerning possible noncompliance with the specified requirements, including communications received between the end of the period addressed in the written assertion and the date of the practitioner's report.

i. Stating that the responsible party has disclosed any known noncompliance occurring subsequent to the period for which, or date as of which, the responsible party selects to make its assertion.

---

[22] Paragraph .21 of AU-C section 580, *Written Representations*, states that the written representations should be in the form of a representation letter addressed to the auditor. [Footnote revised, December 2012, to reflect conforming changes necessary due to the issuance of SAS Nos. 122–126.]

.69 The responsible party's refusal to furnish all appropriate written representations in an examination engagement constitutes a limitation on the scope of the engagement sufficient to preclude an unqualified opinion and is ordinarily sufficient to cause the practitioner to disclaim an opinion or withdraw from the engagement. However, based on the nature of the representations not obtained or the circumstances of the refusal, the practitioner may conclude in an examination engagement that a qualified opinion is appropriate. When the practitioner is performing agreed-upon procedures and the practitioner's client is the responsible party, the responsible party's refusal to furnish all appropriate written representations constitutes a limitation on the scope of the engagement sufficient to cause the practitioner to withdraw. When the practitioner's client is not the responsible party, the practitioner is not required to withdraw but should consider the effects of the responsible party's refusal on his or her report. Further, the practitioner should consider the effects of the responsible party's refusal on his or her ability to rely on other representations of the responsible party.

.70 When the practitioner's client is not the responsible party, the practitioner may also want to obtain written representations from the client. For example, when a practitioner's client has entered into a contract with a third party (responsible party) and the practitioner is engaged to examine the responsible party's compliance with that contract, the practitioner may want to obtain written representations from his or her client as to their knowledge of any noncompliance.

Other Information in a Client-Prepared Document Containing Management's Assertion About the Entity's Compliance With Specified Requirements or the Effectiveness of the Internal Control Over Compliance

.71 An entity may publish various documents that contain information (referred to as *other information*) in addition to the practitioner's attest report on either (*a*) the entity's compliance with specified requirements or (*b*) the effectiveness of the entity's internal control over compliance or written assertion thereon. Paragraphs .91–.94 of section 101 provide guidance to the practitioner if the other information is contained in either of the following:

a. Annual reports to holders of securities or beneficial interests, annual reports of organizations for charitable or philanthropic purposes distributed to the public, and annual reports filed with regulatory authorities under the 1934 Act

b. Other documents to which the practitioner, at the client's request, devotes attention

Effective Date

.72 This section is effective when the subject matter or assertion is as of or for a period ending on or after June 1, 2001. Early application is permitted.

AT Section 701

Management's Discussion and Analysis

Source: SSAE No. 10.

Effective when management's discussion and analysis is for a period ending on or after June 1, 2001. Earlier application is permitted.

General

.01 This section sets forth attestation standards and provides guidance to a practitioner concerning the performance of an attest engagement[1] with respect to management's discussion and analysis (MD&A) prepared pursuant to the rules and regulations adopted by the Securities and Exchange Commission (SEC), which are presented in annual reports to shareholders and in other documents.[2]

Applicability

.02 This section is applicable to the following levels of service when a practitioner is engaged by (*a*) a public[3] entity that prepares MD&A in accordance with the rules and regulations adopted by the SEC (see paragraph .04) or (*b*) a nonpublic entity that prepares an MD&A presentation and whose management provides a written assertion that the presentation has been prepared using the rules and regulations adopted by the SEC:[4]

- An examination of an MD&A presentation
- A review of an MD&A presentation for an annual period, an interim period, or a combined annual and interim period[5]

---

[1] Paragraph .01 of section 101, *Attest Engagements*, defines an attest engagement as one in which a practitioner "is engaged to issue or does issue an examination, a review, or an agreed-upon procedures report on subject matter, or an assertion about the subject matter (hereafter referred to as the *assertion*), that is the responsibility of another party."

[2] Because this section provides guidance specific to attest engagements concerning MD&A presentations, a practitioner should not perform a compliance attestation engagement under section 601, *Compliance Attestation*, with respect to an MD&A presentation.

[3] For purposes of this section, a public entity is any entity (*a*) whose securities trade in a public market either on a stock exchange (domestic or foreign) or in the over-the-counter (OTC) market, including securities quoted only locally or regionally, (*b*) that makes a filing with a regulatory agency in preparation for the sale of any class of its securities in a public market, or (*c*) a subsidiary, corporate joint venture, or other entity controlled by an entity covered by (*a*) or (*b*).

[4] Such assertion may be made by any of the following:
(*a*) Including a statement in the body of the MD&A presentation that it has been prepared using the rules and regulations adopted by the SEC.
(*b*) Providing a separate written assertion to accompany the MD&A presentation.
(*c*) Providing a written assertion in a representation letter to the practitioner.

[5] As discussed in paragraph .85*k*, a review report is not intended to be filed with the SEC as a report under the Securities Act of 1933 (the 1993 Act) or the Securities Exchange Act of 1934 (the 1934 Act) and, accordingly, the review report should contain a statement of restrictions on the use of the report to specified parties if the entity is (*a*) a public entity or (*b*) a nonpublic entity that is making or has made an offering of securities and it appears that the securities may subsequently be registered or subject to a filing with the SEC or other regulatory agency.

A practitioner[6] engaged to examine or review MD&A and report thereon should comply with the general, fieldwork, and reporting standards established in section 50, *SSAE Hierarchy*, and the specific standards set forth in this section. A practitioner engaged to perform agreed-upon procedures on MD&A should follow the guidance set forth in section 201, Agreed-Upon Procedures Engagements.[7] [Revised, November 2006, to reflect conforming changes necessary due to the issuance of SSAE No. 14.]

.03 This section does not—

a. Change the auditor's responsibility in an audit of financial statements performed in accordance with generally accepted auditing standards (GAAS).

b. Apply to situations in which the practitioner is requested to provide management with recommendations to improve the MD&A rather than to provide assurance. A practitioner engaged to provide such nonattest services should refer to CS section 100, *Consulting Services: Definitions and Standards*.

c. Apply to situations in which the practitioner is engaged to provide attest services with respect to an MD&A presentation that is prepared based on criteria other than the rules and regulations adopted by the SEC. A practitioner engaged to perform an examination or a review based upon such criteria should refer to the guidance in section 101, or to section 201 if engaged to perform an agreed-upon procedures engagement.[8]

.04 The requirements for MD&A have changed periodically since the first requirement was adopted by the SEC in 1974. As of the date of issuance of this SSAE, the rules and regulations for MD&A adopted by the SEC are found in Item 303 of Regulation S-K, as interpreted by Financial Reporting Release (FRR) No. 36, *Management's Discussion and Analysis of Financial Condition and Results of Operations; Certain Investment Company Disclosures* (Chapter 5 of the "Codification of Financial Reporting Policies"); Item 303 of Regulation S-B for small business issuers; and Item 9 of Form 20-F for Foreign Private Issuers.[9] Item 303 of Regulation S-K, as interpreted by FRR No. 36, Item 303 of Regulation S-B for small business issuers, and Item 9 of Form 20-F for Foreign Private Issuers, provide the relevant rules and regulations adopted by the SEC

---

[6] In this section, the terms *practitioner* or *accountant* generally refer to a person engaged to perform an attest service on MD&A. The term *accountant* may also refer to a person engaged to review financial statements. The term *auditor* refers to a person engaged to audit financial statements. As this section includes certain requirements for the practitioner to have audited or performed a review of financial statements in accordance with AU-C section 930, *Interim Financial Information*, the terms *auditor, practitioner*, or *accountant* may refer, in this section, to the same person. [Footnote revised, December 2012, to reflect conforming changes necessary due to the issuance of SAS Nos. 122–126.]

[7] Practitioners should follow guidance in AU-C section 920, *Letters for Underwriters and Certain Other Requesting Parties*, when requested to perform agreed-upon procedures on MD&A and report thereon in a letter for an underwriter. [Footnote revised, December 2012, to reflect conforming changes necessary due to the issuance of SAS Nos. 122–126.]

[8] The guidance in this section may be helpful when performing an engagement to provide attest services with respect to an MD&A presentation that is based on criteria other than the rules and regulations adopted by the SEC. Such other criteria would have to be suitable and available as discussed in paragraphs .23–.33 of section 101.

[9] The SEC staff from time to time issues guidance related to the SEC's adopted requirements; for example, Staff Accounting Bulletins (SABs), Staff Legal Bulletins, and speeches. Although such guidance may provide additional information with respect to the adopted requirements for MD&A, the practitioner should not be expected to attest to assertions on compliance with such guidance. The practitioner may find it helpful to also familiarize himself or herself with material contained on the SEC's website www.sec.gov that provides further information with respect to the SEC's views concerning MD&A disclosures.

that meet the definition of suitable criteria in paragraphs .23–.32 of section 101. The practitioner should consider whether the SEC has adopted additional rules and regulations with respect to MD&A subsequent to the issuance of this section.

Conditions for Engagement Performance

Examination

.05 The practitioner's objective in an engagement to examine MD&A is to express an opinion on the MD&A presentation taken as a whole by reporting whether—

a. The presentation includes, in all material respects, the required elements of the rules and regulations adopted by the SEC.[10]

b. The historical financial amounts have been accurately derived, in all material respects, from the entity's financial statements.[11]

c. The underlying information, determinations, estimates, and assumptions of the entity provide a reasonable basis for the disclosures contained therein.[12]

.06 A practitioner may accept an engagement to examine MD&A of a public or nonpublic entity, provided the practitioner audits, in accordance with GAAS,[13] the financial statements for at least the latest period to which the MD&A presentation relates and the financial statements for the other periods covered by the MD&A presentation have been audited by the practitioner or a predecessor auditor. A base knowledge of the entity and its operations gained through an audit of the historical financial statements and knowledge about the industry and the environment is necessary to provide the practitioner with sufficient knowledge to properly evaluate the results of the procedures performed in connection with the examination.

.07 If a predecessor auditor has audited the financial statements for a prior period covered by the MD&A presentation, the practitioner (the successor auditor) should also consider whether, under the particular circumstances, he or she can acquire sufficient knowledge of the business and of the entity's accounting and financial reporting practices for such period so that he or she would be able to—

a. Identify types of potential material misstatements in MD&A and consider the likelihood of their occurrence.

---

[10] The required elements as of the date of issuance of this SSAE include a discussion of the entity's financial condition, changes in financial condition, and results of operations, including a discussion of liquidity and capital resources.

[11] Whether historical financial amounts are accurately derived from the financial statements includes both amounts that are derived from the face of the financial statements (which includes the notes to the financial statements) and financial statement schedules and those that are derived from underlying records supporting elements, accounts, or items included in the financial statements.

[12] Whether the underlying information, determinations, estimates, and assumptions of the entity provide a reasonable basis for the disclosures contained therein requires consideration of management's interpretation of the disclosure criteria for MD&A, management's determinations as to the relevancy of information to be included, and estimates and assumptions made by management that affect reported information.

[13] Restrictions on the scope of the audit of the financial statements will not necessarily preclude the practitioner from accepting an engagement to examine MD&A. Note that the SEC will generally not accept an auditor's report that is modified for a scope limitation. The practitioner should consider the nature and magnitude of the scope limitation and the form of the auditor's report in assessing whether an examination of MD&A could be performed.

b. Perform the procedures that will provide the practitioner with a basis for expressing an opinion as to whether the MD&A presentation includes, in all material respects, the required elements of the rules and regulations adopted by the SEC.

c. Perform the procedures that will provide the practitioner with a basis for expressing an opinion on the MD&A presentation with respect to whether the historical financial amounts have been accurately derived, in all material respects, from the entity's financial statements for such period.

d. Perform the procedures that will provide the practitioner with a basis for expressing an opinion as to whether the underlying information, determinations, estimates, and assumptions of the entity provide a reasonable basis for the disclosures contained therein.

Refer to paragraphs .99–.101 for guidance regarding the review of the predecessor auditor's working papers.

Review

.08 The objective of a review of MD&A is to report whether any information came to the practitioner's attention to cause him or her to believe that—

a. The MD&A presentation does not include, in all material respects, the required elements of the rules and regulations adopted by the SEC.

b. The historical financial amounts included therein have not been accurately derived, in all material respects, from the entity's financial statements.

c. The underlying information, determinations, estimates, and assumptions of the entity do not provide a reasonable basis for the disclosures contained therein.

A review consists principally of applying analytical procedures and making inquiries of persons responsible for financial, accounting, and operational matters. A review ordinarily does not contemplate (*a*) tests of accounting records through inspection, observation, or confirmation, (*b*) obtaining corroborating evidential matter in response to inquiries, or (*c*) the application of certain other procedures ordinarily performed during an examination of MD&A. A review may bring to the practitioner's attention significant matters affecting the MD&A, but it does not provide assurance that the practitioner will become aware of all significant matters that would be disclosed in an examination.

.09 A practitioner may accept an engagement to review the MD&A presentation of a public entity for an annual period provided the practitioner has audited, in accordance with GAAS, the financial statements for at least the latest annual period to which the MD&A presentation relates and the financial statements for the other periods covered by the MD&A presentation have been audited by the practitioner or a predecessor auditor.[14] A base knowledge of the entity and its operations gained through an audit of the historical financial

[14] As discussed in paragraph .85*k*, a review report is not intended to be filed with the SEC as a report under the 1933 Act or the 1934 Act and, accordingly, the review report should contain a statement of restrictions on the use of the report to specified parties if the entity is (*a*) a public entity or (*b*) a nonpublic entity that is making or has made an offering of securities and it appears that the securities may subsequently be registered or subject to a filing with the SEC or other regulatory agency.

statements and knowledge about the industry and the environment is necessary to provide the practitioner with sufficient knowledge to properly evaluate the results of the procedures performed in connection with the review.

.10 If a predecessor auditor has audited the financial statements for a prior period covered by the MD&A presentation, the practitioner should also consider whether, under the particular circumstances, he or she can acquire sufficient knowledge of the business and of the entity's accounting and financial reporting practices for such period so he or she would be able to—

a. Identify types of potential material misstatements in the MD&A and consider the likelihood of their occurrence.

b. Perform the procedures that will provide the practitioner with a basis for reporting whether any information has come to the practitioner's attention to cause him or her to believe any of the following.

   (1) The MD&A presentation does not include, in all material respects, the required elements of the rules and regulations adopted by the SEC.

   (2) The historical financial amounts included therein have not been accurately derived, in all material respects, from the entity's financial statements for such period.

   (3) The underlying information, determinations, estimates, and assumptions of the entity do not provide a reasonable basis for the disclosures contained therein.

.11 A practitioner may accept an engagement to review the MD&A presentation of a public entity for an interim period provided that both of the following conditions are met.

a. The practitioner performs either (*1*) a review of the historical financial statements for the related comparative interim periods and issues a review report thereon in accordance with AU-C section 930, *Interim Financial Information*, or (*2*) an audit of the interim financial statements.

b. The MD&A presentation for the most recent fiscal year has been or will be examined or reviewed by either the practitioner or a predecessor auditor.

[Revised, December 2012, to reflect conforming changes necessary due to the issuance of SAS Nos. 122–126.]

.12 If a predecessor auditor examined or reviewed the MD&A presentation of a public entity for the most recent fiscal year, the practitioner should not accept an engagement to review the MD&A presentation for an interim period unless he or she can acquire sufficient knowledge of the business and of the entity's accounting and financial reporting practices for the interim period to perform the procedures described in paragraph .10.

.13 If a nonpublic entity chooses to prepare MD&A, the practitioner should not accept an engagement to perform a review of such MD&A for an annual period under this section unless both of the following conditions are met.

a. The annual financial statements for the periods covered by the MD&A presentation have been or will be audited and the practitioner has audited or will audit the most recent year (refer to paragraph .07 if the financial statements for prior years were audited by a predecessor auditor).

b. Management will provide a written assertion that the presentation has been prepared using the rules and regulations adopted by the SEC as the criteria. (See paragraph .02.)

.14 A practitioner may accept an engagement to review the MD&A presentation of a nonpublic entity for an interim period provided that all of the following conditions are met.

a. The practitioner performs one of the following:

(1) A review of the historical financial statements for the related interim periods under the Statements on Standards for Accounting and Review Services (SSARSs) and issues a review report thereon

(2) A review of the condensed interim financial information for the related interim periods under AU-C section 930 and issues a review report thereon, and such interim financial information is accompanied by complete annual financial statements for the most recent fiscal year that have been audited

(3) An audit of the interim financial statements

b. The MD&A presentation for the most recent fiscal year has been or will be examined or reviewed.

c. Management will provide a written assertion stating that the presentation has been prepared using the rules and regulations adopted by the SEC as the criteria. (See paragraph .02.)

[Revised, December 2012, to reflect conforming changes necessary due to the issuance of SAS Nos. 122–126.]

Engagement Acceptance Considerations

.15 In determining whether to accept an engagement, the practitioner should consider whether management (and others engaged by management to assist them, such as legal counsel) has the appropriate knowledge of the rules and regulations adopted by the SEC to prepare MD&A.

Responsibilities of Management

.16 Management is responsible for the preparation of the entity's MD&A pursuant to the rules and regulations adopted by the SEC. The preparation of MD&A in conformity with the rules and regulations adopted by the SEC requires management to interpret the criteria, accurately derive the historical amounts from the entity's books and records, make determinations as to the relevancy of information to be included, and make estimates and assumptions that affect reported information.

.17 An entity should not name the practitioner in a client-prepared document as having examined or reviewed MD&A unless the MD&A presentation and related practitioner's report and the related financial statements and auditor's (or accountant's review) report are included in the document (or, in the case of a public entity, incorporated by reference to such information filed with a regulatory agency). If such a statement is made in a document that does not include (or incorporate by reference) such information, the practitioner should request that neither his or her name nor reference to the practitioner be made with respect to the MD&A information, or that such document be revised to include the required presentations and reports. If the client does not comply, the practitioner should advise the client that he or she does not consent to either the use of his or her name or the reference to the practitioner, and he or she should consider what other actions might be appropriate.[15]

Obtaining an Understanding of the SEC Rules and Regulations and Management's Methodology for the Preparation of MD&A

.18 The practitioner should obtain an understanding of the rules and regulations adopted by the SEC for MD&A. (Refer to paragraph .04.)

.19 The practitioner should inquire of management regarding the method of preparing MD&A, including matters such as the sources of the information, how the information is gathered, how management evaluates the types of factors having a material effect on financial condition (including liquidity and capital resources), results of operations, and cash flows, and whether there have been any changes in the procedures from the prior year.

Timing of Procedures

.20 Proper planning by the practitioner contributes to the effectiveness of the attest procedures in an examination or a review of MD&A. Performing some of the work in conjunction with the audit of the historical financial statements or the review of interim financial statements may permit the work to be carried out in a more efficient manner and to be completed at an earlier date. When performing an examination or a review of MD&A, the practitioner may consider the results of tests of controls, analytical procedures,[16] and substantive tests performed in a financial statement audit or analytical procedures and inquiries made in a review of financial statements or interim financial information.

Materiality

.21 The practitioner should consider the concept of materiality in planning and performing the engagement. The objective of an examination or a review is to report on the MD&A presentation taken as a whole and not on the individual amounts and disclosures contained therein. In the context of an MD&A presentation, the concept of materiality encompasses both material omissions (for example, the omission of trends, events, and uncertainties that are currently known to management that are reasonably likely to have material effects on the entity's financial condition, results of operations, liquidity, or capital resources) and material misstatements in MD&A, both of which are referred to herein as a misstatement. Assessing the significance of a misstatement of some items in MD&A may be more dependent upon qualitative than

---

[15] In considering what other actions, if any, may be appropriate in these circumstances, the practitioner may wish to consult his or her legal counsel.

[16] AU-C section 520, *Analytical Procedures*, defines analytical procedures as "evaluations of financial information through analysis of plausible relationships among both financial and nonfinancial data. Analytical procedures also encompass such investigation, as is necessary, of identified fluctuations or relationships that are inconsistent with other relevant information or that differ from expected values by a significant amount." In applying analytical procedures to MD&A, the practitioner develops expectations of matters that would be discussed in MD&A by identifying and using plausible relationships that are reasonably expected to exist based on the practitioner's understanding of the client and of the industry in which the client operates, and the knowledge of relationships among the various financial elements gained through the audit of financial statements or review of interim financial information. Refer to AU-C section 520 for further discussion of analytical procedures. [Footnote revised, December 2012, to reflect conforming changes necessary due to the issuance of SAS Nos. 122–126.]

quantitative considerations. Qualitative aspects of materiality relate to the relevance and reliability of the information presented (for example, qualitative aspects of materiality are considered in assessing whether the underlying information, determinations, estimates, and assumptions of the entity provide a reasonable basis for the disclosures in the MD&A). Furthermore, quantitative information is often more meaningful when accompanied by qualitative disclosures. For example, quantitative information about market risk-sensitive instruments is more meaningful when accompanied by qualitative information about an entity's market risk exposures and how those exposures are managed. Materiality is also a concept that is judged in light of the expected range of reasonableness of the information; therefore, users should not expect prospective information (information about events that have not yet occurred) to be as precise as historical information.

.22 In expressing an opinion, or providing the limited assurance of a review engagement, on the presentation, the practitioner should consider the omission or misstatement of an individual assertion (see paragraph .34) to be material if the magnitude of the omission or misstatement—individually or when aggregated with other omissions or misstatements—is such that a reasonable person using the MD&A presentation would be influenced by the inclusion or correction of the individual assertion. The relative rather than absolute size of an omission or misstatement may determine whether it is material in a given situation.

Inclusion of Pro Forma Financial Information

.23 Management may include pro forma financial information with respect to a business combination or other transactions in MD&A. The practitioner should consider the guidance in paragraph .10 of section 401, *Reporting on Pro Forma Financial Information*, when performing procedures with respect to such information, even if management indicates in MD&A that certain information has been derived from unaudited financial statements. For example, in an examination of MD&A, the practitioner's procedures would ordinarily include obtaining an understanding of the underlying transaction or event, discussing with management their assumptions, obtaining sufficient evidence in support of the adjustments, and other procedures for the purpose of expressing an opinion on the MD&A presentation taken as a whole and not for expressing an opinion on (or providing the limited assurance of a review of) the pro forma financial information included therein under section 401.

Inclusion of External Information

.24 An entity may also include in its MD&A information external to the entity, such as the rating of its debt by certain rating agencies or comparisons with statistics from a trade association. Such external information should also be subjected to the practitioner's examination or review procedures. For example, in an examination, the practitioner might compare information concerning the statistics of a trade organization to a published source; however, the practitioner would not be expected to test the underlying support for the trade association's calculation of such statistics.

Inclusion of Forward-Looking Information

.25 An entity may include certain forward-looking disclosures in the MD&A presentation, including cautionary language concerning the achievability of the matters disclosed. Although any forward-looking disclosures that are included in the MD&A presentation should be subjected to the practitioner's examination or review, such information is subjected to testing only for the purpose of expressing an opinion that the underlying information, determinations, estimates, and assumptions provide a reasonable basis for the disclosures contained therein or providing the limited assurance of a review on the MD&A presentation taken as a whole. The practitioner may consider the guidance in section 301, *Financial Forecasts and Projections*, when performing procedures with respect to forward-looking information. The practitioner may also consider whether meaningful cautionary language has been included with the forward-looking information.

.26 Section 27A of the Securities Act of 1933 (the 1933 Act) and Section 21E of the Securities Exchange Act of 1934 (the 1934 Act) provide a safe harbor from liability in private litigation with respect to forward-looking statements that include or make reference to meaningful cautionary language. However, such sections also include exclusions from safe harbor protection in certain situations. Whether an entity's forward-looking statements and the practitioner's report thereon qualify for safe harbor protection is a legal matter.

Inclusion of Voluntary Information

.27 An entity may voluntarily include other information in the MD&A presentation that is not required by the rules and regulations adopted by the SEC for MD&A. When the entity includes in MD&A additional information required by other rules and regulations of the SEC (for example, Item 305 of Regulation S-K, *Quantitative and Qualitative Disclosures About Market Risk*), the practitioner should also consider such other rules and regulations in subjecting such information to his or her examination or review procedures.[17]

Examination Engagement

.28 To express an opinion about whether (*a*) the presentation includes, in all material respects, the required elements of the rules and regulations adopted by the SEC, (*b*) the historical financial amounts have been accurately derived, in all material respects, from the entity's financial statements, and (*c*) the underlying information, determinations, estimates, and assumptions of the entity provide a reasonable basis for the disclosures contained therein, the practitioner seeks to obtain reasonable assurance by accumulating sufficient evidence in support of the disclosures and assumptions, thereby restricting attestation risk to an appropriately low level.

Attestation Risk

.29 In an engagement to examine MD&A, the practitioner plans and performs the examination to obtain reasonable assurance of detecting both intentional and unintentional misstatements that are material to the MD&A presentation taken as a whole. Absolute assurance is not attainable because of factors such as the need for judgment regarding the areas to be tested and the nature, timing, and extent of tests to be performed; the concept of selective testing of the data; and the inherent limitations of the controls applicable to the preparation of MD&A. The practitioner exercises professional judgment in

[17] To the extent that the voluntary information includes forward-looking information, refer to paragraphs .25–.26.

assessing the significant determinations made by management as to the relevancy of information to be included, and the estimates and assumptions that affect reported information. As a result of these factors, in the great majority of cases, the practitioner has to rely on evidence that is persuasive rather than convincing. Also, procedures may be ineffective for detecting an intentional misstatement that is concealed through collusion among client personnel and third parties or among management or employees of the client. Therefore, the subsequent discovery that a material misstatement exists in the MD&A does not, in and of itself, evidence (*a*) failure to obtain reasonable assurance; (*b*) inadequate planning, performance, or judgment on the part of the practitioner; (*c*) the absence of due professional care; or (*d*) a failure to comply with this section.

.30 Factors to be considered by the practitioner in planning an examination of MD&A include (*a*) the anticipated level of attestation risk related to assertions embodied in the MD&A presentation, (*b*) preliminary judgments about materiality for attest purposes, (*c*) the items within the MD&A presentation that are likely to require revision or adjustment, and (*d*) conditions that may require extension or modification of attest procedures. For purposes of an engagement to examine MD&A, the components of attestation risk are defined as follows.

a. *Inherent risk* is the susceptibility of an assertion within MD&A to a material misstatement, assuming that there are no related controls. (See paragraphs .34–.38.)

b. *Control risk* is the risk that a material misstatement that could occur in an assertion within MD&A will not be prevented or detected on a timely basis by the entity's controls; some control risk will always exist because of the inherent limitations of any internal control.

c. *Detection risk* is the risk that the practitioner will not detect a material misstatement that exists in an assertion within MD&A.

Inherent Risk

.31 The level of inherent risk varies with the nature of the assertion. For example, the inherent risk concerning financial information included in the MD&A presentation may be low, whereas the inherent risk concerning the completeness of the disclosure of the entity's risks or liquidity may be high.

Control Risk

.32 The practitioner should assess control risk as discussed in paragraphs .53–.57. Assessing control risk contributes to the practitioner's evaluation of the risk that material misstatement in the MD&A exists. In the process of assessing control risk (together with assessing inherent risk), the practitioner may obtain evidential matter about the risk that such misstatement may exist. The practitioner uses this evidential matter as part of the reasonable basis for his or her opinion on the MD&A presentation taken as a whole.

Detection Risk

.33 In determining an acceptable level of detection risk, the practitioner assesses inherent risk and control risk, and considers the extent to which he or she seeks to restrict attestation risk. As assessed inherent risk or control risk decreases, the acceptable level of detection risk increases. Accordingly, the practitioner may alter the nature, timing, and extent of tests performed based on the assessments of inherent risk and control risk.

Nature of Assertions

.34 Assertions are representations by management that are embodied in the MD&A presentation. They can be either explicit or implicit and can be classified according to the following broad categories:

a. Occurrence

b. Consistency with the financial statements

c. Completeness

d. Presentation and disclosure

.35 Assertions about occurrence address whether reported transactions or events have occurred during a given period. Assertions about consistency with the financial statements address whether—

a. Reported transactions, events, and explanations are consistent with the financial statements.

b. Historical financial amounts have been accurately derived from the financial statements and related records.

c. Nonfinancial data have been accurately derived from related records.

.36 Assertions about completeness address whether descriptions of transactions and events necessary to obtain an understanding of the entity's financial condition (including liquidity and capital resources), changes in financial condition, results of operations, and material commitments for capital resources are included in MD&A; and whether known events, transactions, conditions, trends, demands, commitments, or uncertainties that will result in or are reasonably likely to result in material changes to these items are appropriately described in the MD&A presentation.

.37 For example, if management asserts that the reason for an increase in revenues is a price increase in the current year, they are explicitly asserting that both an increase in revenues and a price increase have occurred in the current year, and implicitly asserting that any historical financial amounts included are consistent with the financial statements for such period. They are also implicitly asserting that the explanation for the increase in revenues is complete; that there are no other significant reasons for the increase in revenues.

.38 Assertions about presentation and disclosure address whether information included in the MD&A presentation is properly classified, described, and disclosed. For example, management asserts that any forward-looking information included in MD&A is properly classified as being based on management's present assessment and includes an appropriate description of the expected results. To further disclose the nature of such information, management may also include a statement that actual results in the future may differ materially from management's present assessment. (See paragraphs .25–.26.)

.39 The auditor of the underlying financial statements is responsible for designing and performing audit procedures to obtain sufficient appropriate audit evidence to be able to draw reasonable conclusions on which to base the auditor's opinion, as discussed in AU-C section 500, *Audit Evidence*. Although procedures designed to achieve the practitioner's objective of forming an opinion on the MD&A presentation taken as a whole may test certain assertions embodied in the underlying financial statements, the practitioner is not expected to test the underlying financial statement assertions in an examination of MD&A. For example, the practitioner is not expected to test the completeness of revenues or the existence of inventory when testing the assertions in MD&A concerning an increase in revenues or an increase in inventory levels; assurance related to completeness of revenues or for existence of inventory would be obtained as part of the audit. The practitioner is, however, responsible for testing the completeness of the explanation for the increase in revenues or the increase in inventory levels. [Revised, December 2012, to reflect conforming changes necessary due to the issuance of SAS Nos. 122–126.]

Performing an Examination Engagement

.40 The practitioner should exercise (*a*) due professional care in planning, performing, and evaluating the results of his or her examination procedures and (*b*) the proper degree of professional skepticism to obtain reasonable assurance that material misstatements will be detected.

.41 In an examination of MD&A, the practitioner should perform the following.

a. Obtain an understanding of the rules and regulations adopted by the SEC for MD&A and management's method of preparing MD&A. (See paragraphs .18–.19.)

b. Plan the engagement. (See paragraphs .42–.48.)

c. Consider relevant portions of the entity's internal control applicable to the preparation of MD&A. (See paragraphs .49–.58.)

d. Obtain sufficient evidence, including testing completeness. (See paragraphs .59–.64.)

e. Consider the effect of events subsequent to the balance-sheet date. (See paragraphs .65–.66.)

f. Obtain written representations from management concerning its responsibility for MD&A, completeness of minutes, events subsequent to the balance-sheet date, and other matters about which the practitioner believes written representations are appropriate. (See paragraphs .110–.112.)

g. Form an opinion about whether the MD&A presentation includes, in all material respects, the required elements of the rules and regulations adopted by the SEC, whether the historical financial amounts included therein have been accurately derived, in all material respects, from the entity's financial statements, and whether the underlying information, determinations, estimates, and assumptions of the entity provide a reasonable basis for the disclosures contained in the MD&A. (See paragraph .67.)

Planning the Engagement

General Considerations

.42 Planning an engagement to examine MD&A involves developing an overall strategy for the expected scope and performance of the engagement. When developing an overall strategy for the engagement, the practitioner should consider factors such as the following:

- Matters affecting the industry in which the entity operates, such as financial reporting practices, economic conditions, laws and regulations, and technological changes
- Knowledge of the entity's internal control applicable to the preparation of MD&A obtained during the audit of the financial statements and the extent of recent changes, if any
- Matters relating to the entity's business, including its organization, operating characteristics, capital structure, and distribution methods
- The types of relevant information that management reports to external analysts (for example, press releases and presentations to lenders and rating agencies, if any, concerning past and future performance)
- How the entity analyzes actual performance compared to budgets and the types of information provided in documents submitted to the board of directors for purposes of the entity's day-to-day operations and long-range planning
- The extent of management's knowledge of and experience with the rules and regulations adopted by the SEC for MD&A
- If the entity is a nonpublic entity, the intended use of the MD&A presentation
- Preliminary judgments about (*a*) materiality, (*b*) inherent risk at the individual assertion level, and (*c*) factors (for example, matters identified during the audit or review of the historical financial statements) relating to significant deficiencies in internal control applicable to the preparation of MD&A (See paragraph .58.)
- The fraud risk factors or other conditions identified during the audit of the most recent annual financial statements and the practitioner's response to such risk factors
- The type and extent of evidential matter supporting management's assertions and disclosures in the MD&A presentation
- The nature of complex or subjective matters potentially material to the MD&A presentation that may require special skill or knowledge and whether such matters may require using the work of a specialist to obtain sufficient evidential matter (See paragraph .47.)
- The presence of an internal audit function (See paragraph .48.)

.43 In planning an engagement when MD&A has not previously been examined, the practitioner should consider the degree to which the entity has information available for such prior periods and the continuity of the entity's personnel and their ability to respond to inquiries with respect to such periods. In addition, the practitioner should obtain an understanding of the entity's internal control in prior years applicable to the preparation of MD&A.

Consideration of Audit Results

.44 The practitioner should also consider the results of the audits of the financial statements for the periods covered by the MD&A presentation on the examination engagement, such as matters relating to the following:

- The availability and condition of the entity's records
- The nature and magnitude of audit adjustments

- Misstatements[18] that were not corrected in the financial statements that may affect MD&A disclosures (for example, misclassifications between financial statement line items)

[Revised, December 2012, to reflect conforming changes necessary due to the issuance of SAS Nos. 122–126.]

.45 The practitioner should also consider the possible impact on the scope of the examination engagement of any modification or contemplated modification of the auditor's report, including matters addressed in explanatory language. For example, if the auditor has modified the auditor's report to include a going-concern uncertainty explanatory paragraph, the practitioner would consider such a matter in assessing attestation risk.

Multiple Components

.46 In an engagement to examine MD&A, if the entity has operations in several components (for example, locations, branches, subsidiaries, or programs), the practitioner examining the group's MD&A should determine the components to which procedures should be applied. In making such a determination and in selecting the components to be tested, the practitioner examining the group's MD&A should consider factors such as the following:

- The relative importance of each component to the applicable disclosure in the group's MD&A
- The degree of centralization of records
- The effectiveness of controls, particularly those that affect group management's direct control over the exercise of authority delegated to others and its ability to supervise activities at various locations effectively
- The nature and extent of operations conducted at the various components
- The similarity of operations and internal control for different components

The practitioner examining the group's MD&A should consider whether the audit base of the components is consistent with the components that are disclosed in MD&A Accordingly, it may be desirable for the practitioner examining the group's MD&A to coordinate the audit work with the components that will be disclosed. [Revised, December 2012, to reflect conforming changes necessary due to the issuance of SAS Nos. 122–126.]

Using the Work of a Specialist

.47 In some engagements to examine MD&A, the nature of complex or subjective matters potentially material to the MD&A presentation may require specialized skill or knowledge in a particular field other than accounting or auditing. For example, the entity may include information concerning plant production capacity, which would ordinarily be determined by an engineer. In such cases, the practitioner may use the work of a specialist and should consider the relevant guidance in AU-C section 620, *Using the Work of an Auditor's Specialist*. An auditor's specialist may be either an auditor's internal specialist (for example, a partner of the auditor's firm) or an external specialist. [Revised,

[18] Refer to paragraphs .05–.06 and .11–.13 of AU-C section 320, *Materiality in Planning and Performing an Audit*, and paragraph .10 of AU-C section 450, *Evaluation of Misstatements Identified During the Audit*. [Footnote revised, December 2012, to reflect conforming changes necessary due to the issuance of SAS Nos. 122–126.]

December 2012, to reflect conforming changes necessary due to the issuance of SAS Nos. 122–126.]

Internal Audit Function

.48 Another factor the practitioner should consider when planning the engagement is whether the entity has an internal audit function and the extent to which internal auditors are involved in directly testing the MD&A presentation, in monitoring the entity's internal control applicable to the preparation of MD&A, or in testing the underlying records supporting disclosures in the MD&A. A practitioner should consider the guidance in AU-C section 610, *The Auditor's Consideration of the Internal Audit Function in an Audit of Financial Statements*, when addressing the competence and objectivity of internal auditors; the nature, timing, and extent of work to be performed; and other related matters. [Revised, December 2012, to reflect conforming changes necessary due to the issuance of SAS Nos. 122–126.]

Consideration of Internal Control Applicable to the Preparation of MD&A

.49 The practitioner should obtain an understanding of the entity's internal control applicable to the preparation of MD&A sufficient to plan the engagement and to assess control risk. Generally, controls that are relevant to an examination pertain to the entity's objective of preparing MD&A in conformity with the rules and regulations adopted by the SEC, and may include controls within the control environment, risk assessment, information and communication, control activities, and monitoring components.

.50 The controls relating to operations and compliance objectives may be relevant to an examination if they pertain to data the practitioner evaluates or uses in applying examination procedures. For example, controls over the gathering of information, which are different from financial statement controls, and controls relating to nonfinancial data that are included in the MD&A presentation, may be relevant to an examination engagement.

.51 In planning the examination, knowledge of such controls should be used to identify types of potential misstatement (including types of potential material omissions), to consider factors that affect the risk of material misstatement and to design appropriate tests.

.52 A practitioner generally obtains an understanding of the design of the entity's internal control applicable to the preparation of MD&A by making inquiries of appropriate management, supervisory, and staff personnel; by inspection of the entity's documents; and by observation of the entity's relevant activities, including controls over matters discussed, nonfinancial data included, and management evaluation of the reasonableness of information included. The nature and extent of procedures a practitioner performs vary from entity to entity and are influenced by factors such as the entity's complexity, the length of time that the entity has prepared MD&A pursuant to the rules and regulations adopted by the SEC, the practitioner's knowledge of the entity's controls obtained in audits and previous professional engagements, and judgments about materiality.

.53 After obtaining an understanding of the entity's internal control applicable to the preparation of MD&A, the practitioner assesses control risk for the assertions embodied in the MD&A presentation. (Refer to paragraphs .34–.39.) The practitioner may assess control risk at the maximum level (the greatest probability that a material misstatement that could occur in an assertion will not be prevented or detected on a timely basis by an entity's controls) because the practitioner believes controls are unlikely to pertain to an assertion, are unlikely to be effective, or because evaluating their effectiveness would be inefficient. Alternatively, the practitioner may obtain evidential matter about the effectiveness of both the design and operation of a control that supports a lower assessed level of control risk. Such evidential matter may be obtained from tests of controls planned and performed concurrently with obtaining the understanding of the internal control or from procedures performed to obtain the understanding that were not specifically planned as tests of controls.

.54 After obtaining the understanding and assessing control risk, the practitioner may desire to seek a further reduction in the assessed level of control risk for certain assertions. In such cases, the practitioner considers whether evidential matter sufficient to support a further reduction is likely to be available and whether performing additional tests of controls to obtain such evidential matter would be efficient.

.55 When seeking to assess control risk below the maximum for controls over financial and nonfinancial data, the practitioner should perform tests of controls to obtain evidence to support the assessed level of control risk. For example, the practitioner may perform tests of controls directed toward the effectiveness of the design or operation of internal control over the accumulation of the number of units sold for a manufacturing company, average interest rates earned and paid for a financial institution, or average net sales per square foot for a retail entity.

.56 The practitioner uses the knowledge provided by the understanding of internal control applicable to the preparation of MD&A and the assessed level of control risk in determining the nature, timing, and extent of substantive tests for the MD&A assertions.

.57 The practitioner should document the understanding of the internal control components obtained to plan the examination and the assessment of control risk. The form and extent of this documentation is influenced by the size and complexity of the entity, as well as the nature of the entity's controls applicable to the preparation of MD&A.

.58 During the course of an engagement to examine MD&A, the practitioner may become aware of control deficiencies in the design or operation of controls applicable to the preparation of MD&A that could adversely affect the entity's ability to prepare MD&A in accordance with the rules and regulations adopted by the SEC. The practitioner should consider the implications of such control deficiencies on his or her ability to rely on management's explanations and on comparisons to summary accounting records. A practitioner's responsibility to communicate these control deficiencies in an examination of MD&A is similar to the auditor's responsibility described in AU-C section 265, *Communicating Internal Control Related Matters Identified in an Audit*, and AU-C section 260, *The Auditor's Communication With Those Charged With Governance*. [Revised, March 2006, to reflect conforming changes necessary due to the issuance of SAS No. 112. Revised, January 2010, to reflect conforming changes necessary due to the issuance of SAS No. 115. Revised, December 2012, to reflect conforming changes necessary due to the issuance of SAS Nos. 122–126.]

Obtaining Sufficient Evidence

.59 The practitioner should apply procedures to obtain reasonable assurance of detecting material misstatements. In an audit of historical financial statements, the practitioner will have applied audit procedures to some of the information included in the MD&A. However, because the objective of those audit procedures is to have a reasonable basis for expressing an opinion on the financial statements taken as a whole rather than on the MD&A, certain additional examination procedures should be performed as discussed in paragraphs .60–.64. Determining these procedures and evaluating the sufficiency of the evidence obtained are matters of professional judgment.

.60 The practitioner ordinarily should apply the following procedures.

a. Read the MD&A and compare the content for consistency with the audited financial statements; compare financial amounts to the audited financial statements or related accounting records and analyses; recompute the increases, decreases, and percentages disclosed.

b. Compare nonfinancial amounts to the audited financial statements, if applicable, or to other records. (Refer to paragraphs .62–.64.)

c. Consider whether the explanations in MD&A are consistent with the information obtained during the audit; investigate further those explanations that cannot be substantiated by information in the audit working papers through inquiry (including inquiry of officers and other executives having responsibility for operational areas) and inspection of client records.

d. Examine internally generated documents (for example, variance analyses, sales analyses, wage cost analyses, sales or service pricing sheets, and business plans or programs) and externally generated documents (for example, correspondence, contracts, or loan agreements) in support of the existence, occurrence, or expected occurrence of events, transactions, conditions, trends, demands, commitments, and uncertainties disclosed in the MD&A.

e. Obtain available prospective financial information (for example, budgets; sales forecasts; forecasts of labor, overhead, and materials costs; capital expenditure requests; and financial forecasts and projections) and compare such information to forward-looking MD&A disclosures. Inquire of management as to the procedures used to prepare the prospective financial information. Evaluate whether the underlying information, determinations, estimates, and assumptions of the entity provide a reasonable basis for the MD&A disclosures of events, transactions, conditions, trends, demands, commitments, or uncertainties.[19]

f. Consider obtaining available prospective financial information relating to prior periods and comparing actual results with forecasted and projected amounts.

g. Make inquiries of officers and other executives having responsibility for operational areas (such as sales, marketing, and production) and financial and accounting matters, as to their plans and expectations for the future that could affect the entity's liquidity and capital resources.

h. Consider obtaining external information concerning industry trends, inflation, and changing prices and comparing the related MD&A disclosures to such information.

i. Compare the information in MD&A with the rules and regulations adopted by the SEC and consider whether the presentation includes the required elements of such rules and regulations.

---

[19] Refer to paragraph .26 for a discussion concerning the safe harbor rules for forward-looking statements.

j. Read the minutes of meetings to date of the board of directors and other significant committees to identify matters that may affect MD&A; consider whether such matters are appropriately addressed in MD&A.

k. Inquire of officers as to the entity's prior experience with the SEC and the extent of comments received upon review of documents by the SEC; read correspondence between the entity and the SEC with respect to such review, if any.

l. Obtain public communications (for example, press releases and quarterly reports) and the related supporting documentation dealing with historical and future results; consider whether MD&A is consistent with such communications.

m. Consider obtaining other types of publicly available information (for example, analyst reports and news articles); compare the MD&A presentation with such information.

Testing Completeness

.61 The practitioner should design procedures to test the presentation for completeness, including tests of the completeness of explanations that relate to historical disclosures as discussed in paragraphs .36–.37. The practitioner should also consider whether the MD&A discloses matters that could significantly impact future financial condition and results of operations of the entity by considering information that he or she obtained through the following:

a. Audit of the financial statements

b. Inquiries of the entity's officers and other executives directed to current events, conditions, economic changes, commitments and uncertainties, within both the entity and its industry

c. Other information obtained through procedures such as those listed in paragraphs .60 and .65–.66

As discussed in paragraph .31, the inherent risk concerning the completeness of disclosures may be high; if it is, the practitioner may extend the procedures (for example, by making additional inquiries of management or by examining additional internally generated documents).

Nonfinancial Data

.62 Management may include nonfinancial data (such as units produced; the number of units sold, locations, or customers; plant utilization; or square footage) in the MD&A. The practitioner should consider whether the definitions used by management for such nonfinancial data are reasonable for the particular disclosure in the MD&A and whether there are suitable criteria (for example, industry standards with respect to square footage for retail operations), as discussed in paragraphs .23–.32 of section 101.

.63 In some situations, the nonfinancial data or the controls over the nonfinancial data may have been tested by the practitioner in conjunction with the financial statement audit; however, the practitioner's consideration of the nature of the procedures to apply to nonfinancial data in an examination of MD&A is based on the concept of materiality with respect to the MD&A presentation. The practitioner should consider whether industry standards exist for the nonfinancial data or whether there are different methods of measurement that may be used, and, if such methods could result in significantly different results, whether the method of measurement selected by management is reasonable and consistent between periods covered by the MD&A presentation. For example, the number of customers reported by management could vary depending on whether management defines a customer as a subsidiary or "ship to" location of a company rather than the company itself.

.64 In testing nonfinancial data included in the MD&A, the practitioner may seek to assess control risk below the maximum for controls over such nonfinancial data, as discussed in paragraph .55. The practitioner weighs the increase in effort of the examination associated with the additional tests of controls that is necessary to obtain evidential matter against the resulting decrease in examination effort associated with the reduced substantive tests. For those nonfinancial assertions for which the practitioner performs additional tests of controls, the practitioner determines the assessed level of control risk that the results of those tests will support. This assessed level of control risk is used in determining the appropriate detection risk to accept for those nonfinancial assertions and, accordingly, in determining the nature, timing, and extent of substantive tests for such assertions.

Consideration of the Effect of Events Subsequent to the Balance-Sheet Date

.65 As there is an expectation by the SEC that MD&A considers events through a date at or near the filing date,[20] the practitioner should consider information about events[21] that comes to his or her attention after the end of the period addressed by MD&A and prior to the issuance of his or her report that may have a material effect on the entity's financial condition (including liquidity and capital resources), changes in financial condition, results of operations, and material commitments for capital resources. Events or matters that should be disclosed in MD&A include those that—[22]

- Are reasonably expected to have a material favorable or unfavorable impact on net sales or revenues or income from continuing operations.
- Are reasonably likely to result in the entity's liquidity increasing or decreasing in any material way.
- Will have a material effect on the entity's capital resources.
- Would cause reported financial information not to be necessarily indicative of future operating results or of future financial condition.

The practitioner should consider whether events identified during the examination of the MD&A presentation or the audit of the related financial statements require adjustment to or disclosure in the MD&A presentation. When MD&A will be included or incorporated by reference in a 1933 Act document that is filed with the SEC, the practitioner's procedures should extend up to the filing

---

[20] A registration statement under the 1933 Act speaks as of its effective date.

[21] Such events are only referred to as *subsequent events* in relation to an MD&A presentation if they occur after the MD&A presentation has been issued. The annual MD&A presentation ordinarily would not be updated for subsequent events if an MD&A presentation for a subsequent interim period has been issued or the event has been reported through a filing on Form 8-K.

[22] The practitioner should refer to the rules and regulations adopted by the SEC for other examples of events that should be disclosed.

date or as close to it as is reasonable and practicable in the circumstances.[23] If a public entity's MD&A presentation is to be included only in a filing under the 1934 Act (for example, Forms 10-K or 10-KSB), the practitioner's responsibility to consider subsequent events does not extend beyond the date of the report on MD&A. Paragraphs .94–.98 provide guidance when the practitioner is engaged subsequent to the filing of the MD&A presentation.

.66 In an examination of MD&A, the practitioner's fieldwork ordinarily extends beyond the date of the auditor's report on the related financial statements.[24] Accordingly, the practitioner generally should—

a. Read available minutes of meetings of stockholders, the board of directors, and other appropriate committees; as to meetings for which minutes are not available, inquire about matters dealt with at such meetings.

b. Read the latest available interim financial statements for periods subsequent to the date of the auditor's report, compare them with the financial statements for the periods covered by the MD&A, and inquire of and discuss with officers and other executives having responsibility for operational, financial, and accounting matters (limited where appropriate to major locations) matters such as the following:

- Whether interim financial statements have been prepared on the same basis as the audited financial statements
- Whether there were any significant changes in the entity's operations, liquidity, or capital resources in the subsequent period
- The current status of items in the financial statements for which the MD&A has been prepared that were accounted for on the basis of tentative, preliminary, or inconclusive data
- Whether any unusual adjustments were made during the period from the balance-sheet date to the date of inquiry

c. Make inquiries of members of senior management as to the current status of matters concerning litigation, claims, and assessments identified during the audit of the financial statements and of any new matters or unfavorable developments. Consider obtaining updated legal letters from legal counsel.[25]

d. Consider whether there have been any changes in economic conditions or in the industry that could have a significant effect on the entity.

---

[23] Additionally, if the practitioner's report on MD&A is included or incorporated by reference in a 1933 Act document, the practitioner should extend his or her procedures with respect to subsequent events from the date of his or her report on MD&A up to the effective date or as close thereto as is reasonable and practicable in the circumstances.

[24] Undertaking an engagement to examine MD&A does not extend the auditor's responsibility to update the subsequent events review procedures for the financial statements beyond the date of the auditor's report. However, see AU-C section 560, *Events and Subsequently Discovered Facts*. Also, see AU-C section 925, *Filings With the U.S. Securities and Exchange Commission Under the Securities Act of 1933*, as to an auditor's responsibility when his or her report is included in a registration statement filed under the 1933 Act. [Footnote revised, December 2012, to reflect conforming changes necessary due to the issuance of SAS Nos. 122–126.]

[25] See paragraphs .16–.24 of AU-C section 501, *Audit Evidence—Specific Considerations for Selected Items*, for guidance concerning obtaining legal letters. [Footnote revised, December 2012, to reflect conforming changes necessary due to the issuance of SAS Nos. 122–126.]

e. Obtain written representations from appropriate officials as to whether any events occurred subsequent to the latest balance-sheet date that would require disclosure in the MD&A. (See paragraphs .110–.112.)

f. Make such additional inquiries or perform such other procedures as considered necessary and appropriate to address questions that arise in carrying out the foregoing procedures, inquiries, and discussions.

Forming an Opinion

.67 The practitioner should consider the concept of materiality discussed in paragraphs .21–.22, and the impact of any modification of the auditor's report on the historical financial statements in forming an opinion on the examination of MD&A, including the practitioner's ability to evaluate the results of inquiries and other procedures.

Reporting

.68 In order for the practitioner to issue a report on an examination of MD&A, the financial statements for the periods covered by the MD&A presentation and the related auditor's report(s) should accompany the MD&A presentation (or, with respect to a public entity, be incorporated in the document containing the MD&A by reference to information filed with a regulatory agency). In addition, if the entity is a nonpublic entity, one of the following conditions should be met.

a. A statement should be included in the body of the MD&A presentation that it has been prepared using the rules and regulations adopted by the SEC.

b. A separate written assertion should accompany the MD&A presentation or such assertion should be included in a representation letter obtained from the entity.

.69 The practitioner's report on an examination of MD&A should include the following:

a. A title that includes the word *independent*

b. An identification of the MD&A presentation, including the period covered

c. A statement that management is responsible for the preparation of the MD&A pursuant to the rules and regulations adopted by the SEC, and a statement that the practitioner's responsibility is to express an opinion on the presentation based on his or her examination

d. A reference to the auditor's report on the related financial statements, and if the report was other than a standard report, the substantive reasons therefor

e. A statement that the examination was conducted in accordance with attestation standards established by the AICPA and a description of the scope of an examination of MD&A

f. A statement that the practitioner believes the examination provides a reasonable basis for his or her opinion

g. A paragraph stating that—

(1) The preparation of MD&A requires management to interpret the criteria, make determinations as to the relevancy of information to be included, and make estimates and assumptions that affect reported information

(2) Actual results in the future may differ materially from management's present assessment of information regarding the estimated future impact of transactions and events that have occurred or are expected to occur, expected sources of liquidity and capital resources, operating trends, commitments, and uncertainties

h. If the entity is a nonpublic entity, a statement that, although the entity is not subject to the rules and regulations of the SEC, the MD&A presentation is intended to be a presentation in accordance with the rules and regulations adopted by the SEC

i. The practitioner's opinion on whether—

(1) The presentation includes, in all material respects, the required elements of the rules and regulations adopted by the SEC

(2) The historical financial amounts have been accurately derived, in all material respects, from the entity's financial statements

(3) The underlying information, determinations, estimates, and assumptions of the entity provide a reasonable basis for the disclosures contained therein

j. The manual or printed signature of the practitioner's firm

k. The date of the examination report

Appendix A [paragraph .114], "Examination Reports," includes a standard examination report. (See Example 1.)

Dating

.70 The practitioner's report on the examination of MD&A should be dated as of the completion of the practitioner's examination procedures. That date should not precede the date of the auditor's report on the latest historical financial statements covered by the MD&A.

Report Modifications

.71 The practitioner should modify the standard report described in paragraph .69, if any of the following conditions exist.

- The presentation excludes a material required element under the rules and regulations adopted by the SEC. (See paragraph .72.)
- The historical financial amounts have not been accurately derived, in all material respects, from the entity's financial statements. (See paragraph .72.)
- The underlying information, determinations, estimates, and assumptions used by management do not provide the entity with a reasonable basis for the disclosure in the MD&A. (See paragraph .72.)
- There is a restriction on the scope of the engagement. (See paragraph .73.)

- The practitioner decides to refer to the report of another practitioner as the basis in part for his or her report. (See paragraph .74.)
- The practitioner is engaged to examine the MD&A presentation after it has been filed with the SEC or other regulatory agency. (See paragraphs .94–.98.)

.72 The practitioner should express a qualified or an adverse opinion if (*a*) the MD&A presentation excludes a material required element, (*b*) historical financial amounts have not been accurately derived in all material respects, or (*c*) the underlying information, determinations, estimates, and assumptions of the entity do not provide a reasonable basis for the disclosures; for example, if there is a lack of consistency between management's method of measuring nonfinancial data between periods covered by the MD&A presentation. The basis for such opinion should be stated in the practitioner's report. Appendix A [paragraph .114] includes several examples of such modifications. (See Example 2.) Also refer to paragraph .107 for required communications with the audit committee.

.73 If the practitioner is unable to perform the procedures he or she considers necessary in the circumstances, the practitioner should modify the report or withdraw from the engagement. If the practitioner modifies the report, he or she should describe the limitation on the scope of the examination in an explanatory paragraph and qualify his or her opinion, or disclaim an opinion. However, limitations on the ability of the practitioner to perform necessary procedures could also arise because of the lack of adequate support for a significant representation in the MD&A. That circumstance may result in a conclusion that the unsupported representation constitutes a material misstatement of fact and, accordingly, the practitioner may qualify his or her opinion or express an adverse opinion, as described in paragraph .72.

Reference to Report of Another Practitioner

.74 If another practitioner examined the MD&A presentation of a component (refer to paragraph .46), the practitioner examining the group's MD&A may decide to make reference to such report of the component practitioner as a basis for his or her opinion on the group's consolidated MD&A presentation. The practitioner examining the group's MD&A should disclose this fact in the introductory paragraph of the report and should refer to the report of the component practitioner in expressing an opinion on the group's consolidated MD&A presentation. These references indicate (1) that the practitioner examining the group's MD&A is not taking responsibility for the work of the component practitioner, and (2) the source of the examination evidence with respect to those components for which reference to the examination of component practitioners is made. Appendix A [paragraph .114] provides an example of a report for such a situation. (See example 3.) Refer to paragraph .105 for guidance when the other practitioner does not issue a report. [Revised, December 2012, to reflect conforming changes necessary due to the issuance of SAS Nos. 122–126.]

Emphasis of a Matter

.75 In a number of circumstances, the practitioner may wish to emphasize a matter regarding the MD&A presentation. For example, he or she may wish to emphasize that the entity has included information beyond the required elements of the rules and regulations adopted by the SEC. Such explanatory comments should be presented in a separate paragraph of the practitioner's report.

Review Engagement

.76 The objective of a review engagement, including a review of MD&A for an interim period, is to accumulate sufficient evidence to provide the practitioner with a basis for reporting whether any information came to the practitioner's attention to cause him or her to believe that (*a*) the MD&A presentation does not include, in all material respects, the required elements of the rules and regulations adopted by the SEC, (*b*) the historical financial amounts included therein have not been accurately derived, in all material respects, from the entity's financial statements, or (*c*) the underlying information, determinations, estimates, and assumptions of the entity do not provide a reasonable basis for the disclosures contained therein. MD&A for an interim period may be a freestanding presentation or it may be combined with the MD&A presentation for the most recent fiscal year. Procedures for conducting a review of MD&A generally are limited to inquiries and analytical procedures, rather than also including search and verification procedures, concerning factors that have a material effect on financial condition, including liquidity and capital resources, results of operations, and cash flows. In a review engagement, the practitioner should—

a. Obtain an understanding of the rules and regulations adopted by the SEC for MD&A and management's method of preparing MD&A. (See paragraphs .18–.19.)

b. Plan the engagement. (See paragraph .77.)

c. Consider relevant portions of the entity's internal control applicable to the preparation of the MD&A. (See paragraph .78.)

d. Apply analytical procedures and make inquiries of management and others. (See paragraphs .79–.80.)

e. Consider the effect of events subsequent to the balance-sheet date. The practitioner's consideration of such events in a review of MD&A is similar to the practitioner's consideration in an examination. (See paragraphs .65–.66.)

f. Obtain written representations from management concerning its responsibility for MD&A, completeness of minutes, events subsequent to the balance-sheet date, and other matters about which the practitioner believes written representations are appropriate. (See paragraph .110.)

g. Form a conclusion as to whether any information came to the practitioner's attention that causes him or her to believe any of the following.

   (1) The MD&A presentation does not include, in all material respects, the required elements of the rules and regulations adopted by the SEC.

   (2) The historical financial amounts included therein have not been accurately derived, in all material respects, from the entity's financial statements.

   (3) The underlying information, determinations, estimates, and assumptions of the entity do not provide a reasonable basis for the disclosures contained therein.

Planning the Engagement

.77 Planning an engagement to review MD&A involves developing an overall strategy for the analytical procedures and inquiries to be performed. When developing an overall strategy for the review engagement, the practitioner should consider factors such as the following:

- Matters affecting the industry in which the entity operates, such as financial reporting practices, economic conditions, laws and regulations, and technological changes
- Matters relating to the entity's business, including its organization, operating characteristics, capital structure, and distribution methods
- The types of relevant information that management reports to external analysts (for example, press releases or presentations to lenders and rating agencies concerning past and future performance)
- The extent of management's knowledge of and experience with the rules and regulations adopted by the SEC for MD&A
- If the entity is a nonpublic entity, the intended use of the MD&A presentation
- Matters identified during the audit or review of the historical financial statements relating to MD&A reporting, including knowledge of the entity's internal control applicable to the preparation of MD&A and the extent of recent changes, if any
- Matters identified during prior engagements to examine or review MD&A
- Preliminary judgments about materiality
- The nature of complex or subjective matters potentially material to the MD&A that may require special skill or knowledge
- The presence of an internal audit function and the extent to which internal auditors are involved in directly testing the MD&A presentation or underlying records

Consideration of Internal Control Applicable to the Preparation of MD&A

.78 To perform a review of MD&A, the practitioner needs to have sufficient knowledge of the entity's internal control applicable to the preparation of MD&A to—

- Identify types of potential misstatements in MD&A, including types of material omissions, and consider the likelihood of their occurrence.
- Select the inquiries and analytical procedures that will provide a basis for reporting whether any information causes the practitioner to believe the following.
  - — The MD&A presentation does not include, in all material respects, the required elements of the rules and regulations adopted by the SEC, or the historical financial amounts included therein have not been accurately derived, in all material respects, from the entity's financial statements.
  - — The underlying information, determinations, estimates, and assumptions of the entity do not provide a reasonable basis for the disclosures contained therein.

Application of Analytical Procedures and Inquiries

.79 The practitioner ordinarily would not obtain corroborating evidential matter of management's responses to the practitioner's inquiries in performing a review of MD&A. The practitioner should, however, consider the consistency of management's responses in light of the results of other inquiries and the application of analytical procedures. The practitioner ordinarily should apply the following analytical procedures and inquiries.

a. Read the MD&A presentation and compare the content for consistency with the audited financial statements (or reviewed interim financial information if MD&A includes interim information); compare financial amounts to the audited or reviewed financial statements or related accounting records and analyses; recompute the increases, decreases, and percentages disclosed.

b. Compare nonfinancial amounts to the audited (or reviewed) financial statements, if applicable, or to other records. (Refer to paragraph .80.)

c. Consider whether the explanations in MD&A are consistent with the information obtained during the audit or the review of interim financial information; make further inquiries of officers and other executives having responsibility for operational areas as necessary.

d. Obtain available prospective financial information (for example, budgets; sales forecasts; forecasts of labor, overhead, and materials costs; capital expenditure requests; and financial forecasts and projections) and compare such information to forward-looking MD&A disclosures. Inquire of management as to the procedures used to prepare the prospective financial information. Consider whether information came to the practitioner's attention that causes him or her to believe that the underlying information, determinations, estimates, and assumptions of the entity do not provide a reasonable basis for the disclosures of trends, demands, commitments, events, or uncertainties.[26]

e. Make inquiries of officers and other executives having responsibility for operational areas (such as sales, marketing, and production) and financial and accounting matters, as to any plans and expectations for the future that could affect the entity's liquidity and capital resources.

f. Compare the information in MD&A with the rules and regulations adopted by the SEC and consider whether the presentation includes the required elements of such rules and regulations.

g. Read the minutes of meetings to date of the board of directors and other significant committees to identify actions that may affect MD&A; consider whether such matters are appropriately addressed in the MD&A presentation.

h. Inquire of officers as to the entity's prior experience with the SEC and the extent of comments received upon review of documents by the SEC; read correspondence between the entity and the SEC with respect to such review, if any.

i. Inquire of management regarding the nature of public communications (for example, press releases and quarterly reports) dealing with historical and future results and consider whether the MD&A presentation is consistent with such communications.

---

[26] Refer to paragraph .26 for a discussion concerning the safe harbor rules for forward-looking statements.

.80 If nonfinancial data are included in the MD&A presentation, the practitioner should inquire as to the nature of the records from which such information was derived and observe the existence of such records, but need not perform other tests of such records beyond analytical procedures and inquiries of individuals responsible for maintaining them. The practitioner should consider whether such nonfinancial data are relevant to users of the MD&A presentation and whether such data are clearly defined in the MD&A presentation. The practitioner should make inquiries regarding whether the definition of the nonfinancial data was consistently applied during the periods reported.

.81 However, if the practitioner becomes aware that the presentation may be incomplete or contain inaccuracies, or is otherwise unsatisfactory, the practitioner should perform the additional procedures he or she deems necessary to achieve the limited assurance contemplated by a review engagement.

Reporting

.82 In order for the practitioner to issue a report on a review of MD&A for an annual period, the financial statements for the periods covered by the MD&A presentation and the related auditor's report(s) should accompany the MD&A presentation (or with respect to a public entity be incorporated in the document containing the MD&A by reference to information filed with a regulatory agency).

.83 If the MD&A presentation relates to an interim period and the entity is a public entity, the financial statements for the interim periods covered by the MD&A presentation and the related accountant's review report(s) should accompany the MD&A presentation, or be incorporated in the document containing the MD&A by reference to information filed with a regulatory agency. The comparative financial statements for the most recent annual period and the related MD&A should accompany the MD&A presentation for the interim period, or be incorporated by reference to information filed with a regulatory agency. Generally, the requirement for inclusion of the annual financial statements and related MD&A is satisfied by a public entity that has met its reporting responsibility for filing its annual financial statements and MD&A in its annual report on Form 10-K.

.84 If the MD&A presentation relates to an interim period and the entity is a nonpublic entity, the following documents should accompany the interim MD&A presentation in order for the practitioner to issue a review report:

a. The MD&A presentation for the most recent fiscal year and related accountant's examination or review report(s)

b. The financial statements for the periods covered by the respective MD&A presentations (most recent fiscal year and interim periods and the related auditor's report(s) and accountant's review report(s))

In addition, one of the following conditions should be met.

- A statement should be included in the body of the MD&A presentation that it has been prepared using the rules and regulations adopted by the SEC.
- A separate written assertion should accompany the MD&A presentation or such assertion should be included in a representation letter obtained from the entity.

.85 The practitioner's report on a review of MD&A should include the following:

a. A title that includes the word *independent*

b. An identification of the MD&A presentation, including the period covered

c. A statement that management is responsible for the preparation of the MD&A pursuant to the rules and regulations adopted by the SEC

d. A reference to the auditor's report on the related financial statements, and, if the report was other than a standard report, the substantive reasons therefor

e. A statement that the review was conducted in accordance with attestation standards established by the AICPA

f. A description of the procedures for a review of MD&A

g. A statement that a review of MD&A is substantially less in scope than an examination, the objective of which is an expression of opinion regarding the MD&A presentation, and accordingly, no such opinion is expressed

h. A paragraph stating that—

(1) The preparation of MD&A requires management to interpret the criteria, make determinations as to the relevancy of information to be included, and make estimates and assumptions that affect reported information

(2) Actual results in the future may differ materially from management's present assessment of information regarding the estimated future impact of transactions and events that have occurred or are expected to occur, expected sources of liquidity and capital resources, operating trends, commitments, and uncertainties

i. If the entity is a nonpublic entity, a statement that although the entity is not subject to the rules and regulations of the SEC, the MD&A presentation is intended to be a presentation in accordance with the rules and regulations adopted by the SEC

j. A statement about whether any information came to the practitioner's attention that caused him or her to believe that—

(1) The MD&A presentation does not include, in all material respects, the required elements of the rules and regulations adopted by the SEC

(2) The historical financial amounts included therein have not been accurately derived, in all material respects, from the entity's financial statements

(3) The underlying information, determinations, estimates, and assumptions of the entity do not provide a reasonable basis for the disclosures contained therein

k. If the entity is a public entity as defined in paragraph .02, or a nonpublic entity that is making or has made an offering of securities and it appears that the securities may subsequently be registered or subject to a filing with the SEC or other regulatory agency (for example, certain offerings of securities under Rule 144A of the 1933 Act that purport to conform to Regulation S-K), a statement of restrictions on the use of the report to specified parties, because it is not intended to be filed with the SEC as a report under the 1933 Act or the 1934 Act.

l. The manual or printed signature of the practitioner's firm

m. The date of the review report

Appendix B [paragraph .115], "Review Reports," provides examples of a standard review report for an annual and interim period.

Dating

.86 The practitioner's report on the review of MD&A should be dated as of the completion of the practitioner's review procedures. That date should not precede the date of the accountant's report on the latest historical financial statements covered by the MD&A.

Report Modifications

.87 The practitioner should modify the standard review report described in paragraph .86 if any of the following conditions exist.

- The presentation excludes a material required element of the rules and regulations adopted by the SEC. (See paragraph .89.)
- The historical financial amounts have not been accurately derived, in all material respects, from the entity's financial statements. (See paragraph .89.)
- The underlying information, determinations, estimates, and assumptions used by management do not provide the entity with a reasonable basis for the disclosures in the MD&A. (See paragraph .89.)
- The practitioner decides to refer to the report of another practitioner as the basis, in part, for his or her report. (See paragraph .90.)
- The practitioner is engaged to review the MD&A presentation after it has been filed with the SEC or other regulatory agency. (See paragraphs .94–.98.)

.88 When the practitioner is unable to perform the inquiry and analytical procedures he or she considers necessary to achieve the limited assurance provided by a review, or the client does not provide the practitioner with a representation letter, the review will be incomplete. A review that is incomplete is not an adequate basis for issuing a review report. If the practitioner is unable to complete a review because of a scope limitation, the practitioner should consider the implications of that limitation with respect to possible misstatements of the MD&A presentation. In those circumstances, the practitioner should also refer to paragraphs .107–.109 for guidance concerning communications with the audit committee.

.89 If the practitioner becomes aware that the MD&A is materially misstated, the practitioner should modify the review report to describe the nature of the misstatement. Appendix B [paragraph .115] contains an example of such a modification of the accountant's report. (See Example 3.)

.90 If another practitioner reviewed or examined the MD&A for a material component, the practitioner may decide to make reference to such report of the other practitioner in reporting on the consolidated MD&A presentation. Such reference indicates a division of responsibility for performance of the review.

Emphasis of a Matter

.91 In some circumstances, the practitioner may wish to emphasize a matter regarding the MD&A presentation. For example, he or she may wish to emphasize that the entity has included information beyond the required elements of the rules and regulations adopted by the SEC. Such explanatory comments should be presented in a separate paragraph of the practitioner's report.

Combined Examination and Review Report on MD&A

.92 A practitioner may be engaged both to examine an MD&A presentation as of the most recent fiscal year-end and to review a separate MD&A presentation for a subsequent interim period. If the examination and review are completed at the same time, a combined report may be issued. Appendix C [paragraph .116], "Combined Reports," contains an example of a combined report on an examination of an annual MD&A presentation and the review of a separate MD&A presentation for an interim period. (See Example 1.)

.93 If an entity prepares a combined MD&A presentation for annual and interim periods in which there is a discussion of liquidity and capital resources only as of the most recent interim period but not as of the most recent annual period, the practitioner is limited to performing the highest level of service that is provided with respect to the historical financial statements for any of the periods covered by the MD&A presentation. For example, if the annual financial statements have been audited and the interim financial statements have been reviewed, the practitioner may be engaged to perform a review of the combined MD&A presentation. Appendix C [paragraph .116] contains an example of a review report on a combined MD&A presentation for annual and interim periods. (See Example 2.)

When Practitioner Is Engaged Subsequent to the Filing of MD&A

.94 Management's responsibility for updating an MD&A presentation for events occurring subsequent to the issuance of MD&A depends on whether the entity is a public or nonpublic entity. A public entity is required to report significant subsequent events in a Form 8-K or Form 10-Q, or in a registration statement; therefore, a public company would ordinarily not modify its MD&A presentation once it is filed with the SEC (or other regulatory agency).

.95 Therefore, if the practitioner is engaged to examine (or review) an MD&A presentation of a public entity that has already been filed with the SEC (or other regulatory agency), the practitioner should consider whether material subsequent events are appropriately disclosed in a Form 8-K or 10-Q, or a registration statement that includes or incorporates by reference such MD&A presentation. Refer to paragraphs .65–.66 for guidance concerning consideration of events up to the filing date when the practitioner's report on MD&A will be included (or incorporated by reference) in a 1933 Act document filed with the SEC that will require a consent.

.96 If subsequent events of a public entity are appropriately disclosed in a Form 8-K or 10-Q, or in a registration statement, or if there have been no material subsequent events, the practitioner should add the following paragraph to his or her examination or review report following the opinion or concluding paragraph, respectively.

> The accompanying Management's Discussion and Analysis does not consider events that have occurred subsequent to Month XX, 20X6, the date as of which it was filed with the Securities and Exchange Commission.

.97 If there has been a material subsequent event that has not been disclosed in a manner described in paragraph .95 and if the practitioner determines that it is appropriate to issue a report even though the MD&A presentation has not been updated for such material subsequent event (for example, because the filing of the Form 10-Q that will disclose such events has not yet occurred), the practitioner should express a qualified or an adverse opinion (or appropriately modify the review report) on the MD&A presentation. As discussed in paragraph .107, if such material subsequent event is not appropriately disclosed, the practitioner should evaluate (*a*) whether to resign from the engagement related to the MD&A presentation and (*b*) whether to remain as the entity's auditor or stand for re-election to audit the entity's financial statements.

.98 Because a nonpublic entity is not subject to the filing requirements of the SEC, an MD&A presentation of a nonpublic entity should be updated for material subsequent events through the date of the practitioner's report.

When a Predecessor Auditor Has Audited Prior Period Financial Statements

.99 If a predecessor auditor has audited the financial statements for a prior period covered by the MD&A, the need by the practitioner reporting on the MD&A for an understanding of the business and the entity's accounting and financial reporting practices for such prior period, as discussed in paragraph .07, is not diminished and the practitioner should apply the appropriate procedures. In applying the appropriate procedures, the practitioner may consider reviewing the predecessor auditor's working papers with respect to audits of financial statements and examinations or reviews of MD&A presentations for such prior periods.

.100 Information that may be obtained from the audit or attest working papers of the predecessor auditor will not provide a sufficient basis in itself for the practitioner to express an opinion with respect to the MD&A disclosures for such prior periods. If the practitioner has audited the current year, the results of such audit may be considered in planning and performing the examination of MD&A and may provide evidential matter that is useful in performing the examination, including with respect to matters disclosed for prior periods. For example, an increase in salaries expense may be the result of an acquisition in the last half of the prior year. Auditing procedures applied to payroll expense in the current year that validate the increase as a result of the acquisition may provide evidential matter with respect to the increase in salaries expense in the prior year attributed to the acquisition.

.101 In addition to the procedures described in paragraphs .49–.66, the practitioner will need to make inquiries of the predecessor auditor and management as to audit adjustments proposed by the predecessor auditor that were not recorded in the financial statements.

Communications Between Predecessor and Successor Auditors

.102 If the practitioner is appointed as the successor auditor, he or she follows the guidance AU-C section 210, *Terms of Engagement*, in considering whether or not to accept the engagement. If, at the time of the appointment as auditor, the practitioner is also being engaged to examine or review MD&A, the practitioner should also make specific inquiries of the predecessor auditor regarding MD&A. [Revised, December 2012, to reflect conforming changes necessary due to the issuance of SAS Nos. 122–126.]

.103 The practitioner's examination may be facilitated by (*a*) making specific inquiries of the predecessor regarding matters that the successor believes may affect the conduct of the examination (or review), such as areas that required an inordinate amount of time or problems that arose from the condition of the records, and (*b*) if the predecessor previously examined or reviewed MD&A, reviewing the predecessor's working papers for the predecessor's examination or review engagement.

.104 If, subsequent to his or her engagement to audit the financial statements, the practitioner is requested to examine MD&A, the practitioner should request the client to authorize the predecessor auditor to allow a review of the predecessor's audit working papers related to the financial statement periods included in the MD&A presentation. Although the practitioner may previously have had access to the predecessor auditor's working papers in connection with the successor's audit of the financial statements, ordinarily the predecessor auditor should permit the practitioner to review those audit working papers relating to matters that are disclosed or that would likely be disclosed in MD&A.

Another Auditor Audits a Significant Part of the Financial Statements

.105 When one or more component auditors audits a significant part of a group's financial statements, the practitioner[27] may request that the component auditor perform procedures with respect to the MD&A or the practitioner may perform the procedures directly with respect to such component(s).[28] Unless the component auditor issues an examination or review report on a separate MD&A presentation of such component(s) (see paragraph .74), the practitioner examining the group's MD&A should not make reference to the work of the component practitioner on MD&A in his or her report on MD&A[29] Accordingly, if the practitioner examining the group's MD&A has requested such component auditor to perform procedures, the practitioner examining the group's MD&A should perform those procedures that he or she considers necessary to take responsibility for the work of the other auditor. Such procedures may include one or more of the following:

a. Visiting the component auditor and discussing the procedures followed and the results thereof.

---

[27] The practitioner serving as auditor of the group's financial statements is presumed to have an audit base for purposes of examining or reviewing the consolidated MD&A presentation. [Footnote revised, December 2012, to reflect conforming changes necessary due to the issuance of SAS Nos. 122–126.]

[28] The practitioner should consider whether he or she has sufficient industry expertise with respect to a subsidiary audited by a component auditor to take sole responsibility for the group's consolidated MD&A presentation. [Footnote revised, December 2012, to reflect conforming changes necessary due to the issuance of SAS Nos. 122–126.]

[29] This does not preclude the practitioner from referring to the component auditor's report on the financial statements in his or her report on the group's MD&A. [Footnote revised, December 2012, to reflect conforming changes necessary due to the issuance of SAS Nos. 122–126.]

b. Reviewing the working papers of the component auditor with respect to the component.

c. Participating in discussions with the component's management regarding matters that may affect the preparation of the component's MD&A.

d. Making supplemental tests with respect to such component.

The determination of the extent of the procedures to be applied by the practitioner examining the group's MD&A rests with that practitioner alone in the exercise of his or her professional judgment and in no way constitutes a reflection on the adequacy of the component auditor's work. Because the practitioner examining the group's MD&A in this case assumes responsibility for his or her opinion on the MD&A presentation without making reference to the procedures performed by the other auditor, the judgment of the practitioner examining the group's MD&A should govern as to the extent of procedures to be undertaken. [Revised, December 2012, to reflect conforming changes necessary due to the issuance of SAS Nos. 122–126.]

Responsibility for Other Information in Documents Containing MD&A

.106 A client may publish annual reports containing MD&A and other documents to which the practitioner, at the client's request, devotes attention. See paragraphs .91–.94 of section 101 for pertinent guidance in these circumstances. See Appendix D of this section [paragraph .117], "Comparison of Activities Performed Under SAS No. 8, *Other Information in Documents Containing Audited Financial Statements*, Versus a Review or an Examination Attest Engagement." The guidance in AU-C section 925, *Filings With the U.S. Securities and Exchange Commission Under the Securities Act of 1933*, is pertinent when the practitioner's report on MD&A is included in a registration statement, proxy statement, or periodic report filed under the federal securities statutes. [Revised, December 2012, to reflect conforming changes necessary due to the issuance of SAS Nos. 122–126.]

Communications With the Audit Committee

.107 If the practitioner concludes that the MD&A presentation contains material inconsistencies with other information included in the document containing the MD&A presentation or with the historical financial statements,[30] material omissions, or material misstatements of fact, and management refuses to take corrective action, the practitioner should inform the audit committee or others with equivalent authority and responsibility. If the MD&A is not revised, the practitioner should evaluate (*a*) whether to resign from the engagement related to the MD&A, and (*b*) whether to remain as the entity's auditor or stand for re-election to audit the entity's financial statements. The practitioner may wish to consult with his or her attorney when making these evaluations.

.108 If the practitioner is engaged after the MD&A presentation has been filed with the SEC (or other regulatory agency), and becomes aware that such MD&A presentation on file with the SEC (or other regulatory agency) has not been revised for a matter for which the practitioner has or would qualify his or her opinion, the practitioner should discuss such matter with the audit committee and request that the MD&A presentation be revised. If the audit

[30] See AU-C section 720, *Information in Documents Containing Audited Financial Statements*, for guidance on the impact of material inconsistencies or material misstatements of fact on the auditor's report on the related historical financial statements. [Footnote revised, December 2012, to reflect conforming changes necessary due to the issuance of SAS Nos. 122–126.]

committee fails to take appropriate action, the practitioner should consider whether to resign as the independent auditor of the company. The practitioner may consider paragraphs .21–.23 and .27 of AU-C section 250, *Consideration of Laws and Regulations in an Audit of Financial Statements*, concerning communication with the audit committee and other considerations. [Revised, December 2012, to reflect conforming changes necessary due to the issuance of SAS Nos. 122–126.]

.109 If, as a result of performing an examination or a review of MD&A, the practitioner has determined that there is evidence that fraud may exist, that matter should be brought to the attention of an appropriate level of management. This is generally appropriate even if the matter might be considered clearly inconsequential. If the matter relates to the audited financial statements, the practitioner should consider the guidance in AU-C section 240, *Consideration of Fraud in a Financial Statement Audit*, concerning communication responsibilities, and the effect on the auditor's report on the financial statements. [Revised, December 2012, to reflect conforming changes necessary due to the issuance of SAS Nos. 122–126.]

Obtaining Written Representations

.110 In an examination or a review engagement, the practitioner should obtain written representations from management.[31] The specific written representations obtained by the practitioner will depend on the circumstances of the engagement and the nature of the MD&A presentation. Specific representations should relate to the following matters:

a. Management's acknowledgment of its responsibility for the preparation of MD&A and management's assertion that the MD&A presentation has been prepared in accordance with the rules and regulations adopted by the SEC for MD&A[32]

b. A statement that the historical financial amounts included in MD&A have been accurately derived from the entity's financial statements

c. Management's belief that the underlying information, determinations, estimates, and assumptions of the entity provide a reasonable basis for the disclosures contained in the MD&A

d. A statement that management has made available all significant documentation related to compliance with SEC rules and regulations for MD&A

e. Completeness and availability of all minutes of meetings of stockholders, directors, and committees of directors

f. For a public entity, whether any communications from the SEC were received concerning noncompliance with or deficiencies in MD&A reporting practices

---

[31] Paragraph .21 of AU-C section 580, *Written Representations*, requires that written representations be in the form of a representation letter addressed to the auditor. Paragraph .09*b* of AU-C section 925 requires the auditor to obtain updated written representations from management at or shortly before the effective date of the registration statement, about (*a*) whether any information has come to management's attention that would cause management to believe that any of the previous representations should be modified, and (*b*) whether any events have occurred subsequent to the date of the financial statements that would require adjustment to, or disclosure in, those financial statements. (See paragraph .65.) [Footnote revised, December 2012, to reflect conforming changes necessary due to the issuance of SAS Nos. 122–126.]

[32] Management should specify the SEC rules (for example, Item 303 of Regulation S-K, Item 303 of Regulation S-B, or Item 9 of Form 20-F). For nonpublic entities, the practitioner also obtains a written assertion that the presentation has been prepared using the rules and regulations adopted by the SEC. (See paragraph .02.)

g. Whether any events occurred subsequent to the latest balance-sheet date that would require disclosure in the MD&A

h. If forward-looking information is included, a statement that—

- The forward-looking information is based on management's best estimate of expected events and operations, and is consistent with budgets, forecasts, or operating plans prepared for such periods
- The accounting principles expected to be used for the forward-looking information are consistent with the principles used in preparing the historical financial statements
- Management has provided the latest version of such budgets, forecasts, or operating plans, and has informed the practitioner of any anticipated changes or modifications to such information that could affect the disclosures contained in the MD&A presentation

i. If voluntary information is included that is subject to the rules and regulations adopted by the SEC (for example, information required by Item 305, *Quantitative and Qualitative Disclosures About Market Risk*), a statement that such voluntary information has been prepared in accordance with the related rules and regulations adopted by the SEC for such information

j. If pro forma information is included, a statement that—

- Management is responsible for the assumptions used in determining the pro forma adjustments
- Management believes that the assumptions provide a reasonable basis for presenting all the significant effects directly attributable to the transaction or event, that the related pro forma adjustments give appropriate effect to those assumptions, and that the pro forma column reflects the proper application of those adjustments to the historical financial statements
- Management believes that the significant effects directly attributable to the transaction or event are appropriately disclosed in the pro forma financial information

.111 In an examination, management's refusal to furnish written representations constitutes a limitation on the scope of the engagement sufficient to preclude an unqualified opinion and is ordinarily sufficient to cause a practitioner to disclaim an opinion or withdraw from the examination engagement. However, based on the nature of the representations not obtained or the circumstances of the refusal, the practitioner may conclude that a qualified opinion is appropriate in an examination engagement. In a review engagement, management's refusal to furnish written representations constitutes a limitation of the scope of the engagement sufficient to require withdrawal from the review engagement. Further, the practitioner should consider the effects of the refusal on his or her ability to rely on other management representations.

.112 If the practitioner is precluded from performing procedures he or she considers necessary in the circumstances with respect to a matter that is material to the MD&A presentation, even though management has given representations concerning the matter, there is a limitation on the scope of the engagement, and the practitioner should qualify his or her opinion or disclaim an opinion in an examination engagement, or withdraw from a review engagement.

Effective Date

.113 This section is effective when management's discussion and analysis is for a period ending on or after June 1, 2001. Early application is permitted.

.114

Appendix A

Examination Reports

Example 1: Standard Examination Report

1. The following is an illustration of a standard examination report.

Independent Accountant's Report

[*Introductory paragraph*]

We have examined XYZ Company's Management's Discussion and Analysis taken as a whole, included [*incorporated by reference*] in the Company's [*insert description of registration statement or document*]. Management is responsible for the preparation of the Company's Management's Discussion and Analysis pursuant to the rules and regulations adopted by the Securities and Exchange Commission. Our responsibility is to express an opinion on the presentation based on our examination. We have audited, in accordance with auditing standards generally accepted in the United States of America, the financial statements of XYZ Company, which comprise the balance sheets as of December 31, 20X5 and 20X4, and the related statements of income, changes in stockholder's equity, and cash flows for each of the years in the three-year period ended December 31, 20X5, and the related notes to the financial statements. In our report dated [*Month*] XX, 20X6, we expressed an unmodified opinion on those financial statements.[33]

[*Scope paragraph*]

Our examination of Management's Discussion and Analysis was conducted in accordance with attestation standards established by the American Institute of Certified Public Accountants and, accordingly, included examining, on a test basis, evidence supporting the historical amounts and disclosures in the presentation. An examination also includes assessing the significant determinations made by management as to the relevancy of information to be included and the estimates and assumptions that affect reported information. We believe that our examination provides a reasonable basis for our opinion.

---

[33] If prior financial statements were audited by other auditors, this sentence would be replaced by the following:

> We have audited, in accordance with auditing standards generally accepted in the United States of America, the financial statements of XYZ Company, which comprise the balance sheet as of December 31, 20X5, and the related statement of income, changes in stockholder's equity, and cash flows for the year then ended, and the related notes to the financial statements. In our report dated [*Month*] XX, 20X6, we expressed an unmodified opinion on those financial statements. The financial statements of XYZ Company; which comprise the balance sheet as of December 31, 20X4, and the related statement of income, changes in stockholder's equity, and cash flows for each of the years in the two-year period then ended, and the notes to the financial statements; were audited by other auditors, whose report dated [*Month*] XX, 20X5, expressed an unmodified opinion on those financial statements.

If the practitioner's opinion on the financial statements is based on the report of component auditors, this sentence would be replaced by the following:

> We have audited, in accordance with auditing standards generally accepted in the United States of America, the financial statements of XYZ Company which comprise the balance sheets as of December 31, 20X5 and 20X4, and the related statements of income, changes in stockholders' equity, and cash flows for each of the years in the three-year period ended December 31, 20X5, and the notes to the financial statements. In our report dated [*Month*] XX, 20X6, we expressed an unmodified opinion on those financial statements based on our audits and the report of component auditors.

Refer to Example 3 if the practitioner's opinion on MD&A is based on the report of another practitioner on a component of the entity. [Footnote revised, December 2012, to reflect conforming changes necessary due to the issuance of SAS Nos. 122–126.]

[*Explanatory paragraph*][34]

The preparation of Management's Discussion and Analysis requires management to interpret the criteria, make determinations as to the relevancy of information to be included, and make estimates and assumptions that affect reported information. Management's Discussion and Analysis includes information regarding the estimated future impact of transactions and events that have occurred or are expected to occur, expected sources of liquidity and capital resources, operating trends, commitments, and uncertainties. Actual results in the future may differ materially from management's present assessment of this information because events and circumstances frequently do not occur as expected.

[*Opinion paragraph*]

In our opinion, the Company's presentation of Management's Discussion and Analysis includes, in all material respects, the required elements of the rules and regulations adopted by the Securities and Exchange Commission; the historical financial amounts included therein have been accurately derived, in all material respects, from the Company's financial statements; and the underlying information, determinations, estimates, and assumptions of the Company provide a reasonable basis for the disclosures contained therein.

[*Signature*]

[*Date*]

Example 2: Modifications to Examination Report for a Qualified Opinion

2. An example of a modification of an examination report for a qualified opinion due to a material omission described in paragraph .72 follows.

[*Additional explanatory paragraph preceding the opinion paragraph*]

Based on information furnished to us by management, we believe that the Company has excluded a discussion of the significant capital outlay required for its plans to expand into the telecommunications industry and the possible effects on the Company's financial condition, liquidity, and capital resources.

[*Opinion paragraph*]

In our opinion, except for the omission of the matter described in the preceding paragraph, the Company's presentation of Management's Discussion and Analysis includes, in all material respects, the required elements of the rules and regulations adopted by the Securities and Exchange Commission; the historical financial amounts included therein have been accurately derived, in all material respects, from the Company's financial statements; and the underlying information, determinations, estimates, and assumptions of the Company provide a reasonable basis for the disclosures contained therein.

3. An example of a modification of an examination report for a qualified opinion when overly subjective assertions are included in MD&A follows.

[*Additional explanatory paragraph preceding the opinion paragraph*]

Based on information furnished to us by management, we believe that the underlying information, determinations, estimates, and assumptions used by

---

[34] The following sentence should be added to the beginning of the explanatory paragraph if the entity is a nonpublic entity, as discussed in paragraph .69*h*:

Although XYZ Company is not subject to the rules and regulations of the Securities and Exchange Commission, the accompanying Management's Discussion and Analysis is intended to be a presentation in accordance with the rules and regulations adopted by the Securities and Exchange Commission.

management do not provide the Company with a reasonable basis for the disclosure concerning [*describe*] in the Company's Management's Discussion and Analysis.

[*Opinion paragraph*]

In our opinion, except for the disclosure regarding [*describe*] discussed in the preceding paragraph, the Company's presentation of Management's Discussion and Analysis includes, in all material respects, the required elements of the rules and regulations adopted by the Securities and Exchange Commission; the historical financial amounts included therein have been accurately derived, in all material respects, from the Company's financial statements; and the underlying information, determinations, estimates, and assumptions of the Company provide a reasonable basis for the disclosures contained therein.

Example 3: Examination Report With Reference to the Report of Another Practitioner

4. The following is an illustration of an examination report indicating a division of responsibility with another practitioner, who has examined a separate MD&A presentation of a wholly-owned subsidiary, when the practitioner reporting is serving as the auditor of the related group's consolidated financial statements.

Independent Accountant's Report

[*Introductory paragraphs*]

We have examined XYZ Company's Management's Discussion and Analysis taken as a whole, included [*incorporated by reference*] in the Company's [*insert description of registration statement or document*]. Management is responsible for the preparation of the Company's Management's Discussion and Analysis pursuant to the rules and regulations adopted by the Securities and Exchange Commission. Our responsibility is to express an opinion on the presentation based on our examination. We did not examine Management's Discussion and Analysis of ABC Corporation, a wholly-owned subsidiary, included in ABC Corporation's [*insert description of registration statement or document*]. Such Management's Discussion and Analysis was examined by other accountants, whose report has been furnished to us, and our opinion, insofar as it relates to information included for ABC Corporation, is based solely on the report of the other accountants.

We have audited, in accordance with auditing standards generally accepted in the United States of America, the consolidated financial statements of XYZ Company, which comprise the consolidated balance sheets as of December 31, 20X5 and 20X4, and the related consolidated statements of income, changes in stockholders' equity, and cash flows, for each of the years in the three-year period ended December 31, 20X5. In our report dated [*Month*] XX, 20X6, we expressed an unmodified opinion on those financial statements based on our audits and the report of other auditors.

[*Scope paragraph*]

Our examination of Management's Discussion and Analysis was conducted in accordance with attestation standards established by the American Institute of Certified Public Accountants and, accordingly, included examining, on a test basis, evidence supporting the historical amounts and disclosures in the presentation. An examination also includes assessing the significant determinations made by management as to the relevancy of information to be included and the estimates and assumptions that affect reported information. We believe that our examination and the report of other accountants provide a reasonable basis for our opinion.

[*Explanatory paragraph*][35]

The preparation of Management's Discussion and Analysis requires management to interpret the criteria, make determinations as to the relevancy of information to be included, and make estimates and assumptions that affect reported information. Management's Discussion and Analysis includes information regarding the estimated future impact of transactions and events that have occurred or are expected to occur, expected sources of liquidity and capital resources, operating trends, commitments, and uncertainties. Actual results in the future may differ materially from management's present assessment of this information because events and circumstances frequently do not occur as expected.

[*Opinion paragraph*]

In our opinion, based on our examination and the report of other accountants, the Company's presentation of Management's Discussion and Analysis included [*incorporated by reference*] in the Company's [*insert description of registration statement or document*] includes, in all material respects, the required elements of the rules and regulations adopted by the Securities and Exchange Commission; the historical financial amounts included therein have been accurately derived, in all material respects, from the Company's financial statements; and the underlying information, determinations, estimates, and assumptions of the Company provide a reasonable basis for the disclosures contained therein.

[*Signature*]

[*Date*]

[Revised, December 2012, to reflect conforming changes necessary due to the issuance of SAS Nos. 122–126.]

---

[35] The following sentence should be added to the beginning of the explanatory paragraph if the entity is a nonpublic entity, as discussed in paragraph .69*h*.

> Although XYZ Company is not subject to the rules and regulations of the Securities and Exchange Commission, the accompanying Management's Discussion and Analysis is intended to be a presentation in accordance with the rules and regulations adopted by the Securities and Exchange Commission.

.115

Appendix B

Review Reports

Example 1: Standard Review Report on an Annual MD&A Presentation

1. The following is an illustration of a standard review report on an annual MD&A presentation.

Independent Accountant's Report

[Introductory paragraph]

We have reviewed XYZ Company's Management's Discussion and Analysis taken as a whole, included *[incorporated by reference]* in the Company's *[insert description of registration statement or document]*. Management is responsible for the preparation of the Company's Management's Discussion and Analysis pursuant to the rules and regulations adopted by the Securities and Exchange Commission. We have audited, in accordance with auditing standards generally accepted in the United States of America, the financial statements of XYZ Company, which comprise the balance sheets as of December 31, 20X5 and 20X4, and the related statements of income, changes in stockholders' equity, and cash flows for each of the years in the three-year period ended December 31, 20X5. In our report dated *[Month]* XX, 20X6, we expressed an unqualified opinion on those financial statements.

[Scope paragraph]

We conducted our review of Management's Discussion and Analysis in accordance with attestation standards established by the American Institute of Certified Public Accountants. A review of Management's Discussion and Analysis consists principally of applying analytical procedures and making inquiries of persons responsible for financial, accounting, and operational matters. It is substantially less in scope than an examination, the objective of which is the expression of an opinion on the presentation. Accordingly, we do not express such an opinion.

[Explanatory paragraph][36]

The preparation of Management's Discussion and Analysis requires management to interpret the criteria, make determinations as to the relevancy of information to be included, and make estimates and assumptions that affect reported information. Management's Discussion and Analysis includes information regarding the estimated future impact of transactions and events that have occurred or are expected to occur, expected sources of liquidity and capital resources, operating trends, commitments, and uncertainties. Actual results in the future may differ materially from management's present assessment of this information because events and circumstances frequently do not occur as expected.

[Concluding paragraph]

---

[36] The following sentence should be added to the beginning of the explanatory paragraph if the entity is a nonpublic entity, as discussed in paragraph .85*i*.

Although XYZ Company is not subject to the rules and regulations of the Securities and Exchange Commission, the accompanying Management's Discussion and Analysis is intended to be a presentation in accordance with the rules and regulations adopted by the Securities and Exchange Commission.

Based on our review, nothing came to our attention that caused us to believe that the Company's presentation of Management's Discussion and Analysis does not include, in all material respects, the required elements of the rules and regulations adopted by the Securities and Exchange Commission, that the historical financial amounts included therein have not been accurately derived, in all material respects, from the Company's financial statements, or that the underlying information, determinations, estimates and assumptions of the Company do not provide a reasonable basis for the disclosures contained therein.

[Restricted use paragraph][37]

This report is intended solely for the information and use of [*list or refer to specified parties*] and is not intended to be and should not be used by anyone other than the specified parties.

[*Signature*]

[*Date*]

Example 2: Standard Review Report on an Interim MD&A Presentation

2. The following is an illustration of a standard review report on an MD&A presentation for an interim period.

<u>Independent Accountant's Report</u>

[Introductory paragraph]

We have reviewed XYZ Company's Management's Discussion and Analysis taken as a whole included in the Company's [*insert description of registration statement or document*]. Management is responsible for the preparation of the Company's Management's Discussion and Analysis pursuant to the rules and regulations adopted by the Securities and Exchange Commission. We have reviewed, in accordance with standards established by the American Institute of Certified Public Accountants, the interim financial information of XYZ Company as of June 30, 20X6 and 20X5, and for the three-month and six-month periods then ended, and have issued our report thereon dated July XX, 20X6.

[Scope paragraph]

We conducted our review of Management's Discussion and Analysis in accordance with attestation standards established by the American Institute of Certified Public Accountants. A review of Management's Discussion and Analysis consists principally of applying analytical procedures and making inquiries of persons responsible for financial, accounting, and operational matters. It is substantially less in scope than an examination, the objective of which is the expression of an opinion on the presentation. Accordingly, we do not express such an opinion.

[Explanatory paragraph][38]

---

[37] This paragraph may be omitted for certain nonpublic entities. (Refer to paragraph .85*k*.)

[38] The following sentence should be added to the beginning of the explanatory paragraph if the entity is a nonpublic entity, as discussed in paragraph .85*i*.

> Although XYZ Company is not subject to the rules and regulations of the Securities and Exchange Commission, the accompanying Management's Discussion and Analysis is intended to be a presentation in accordance with the rules and regulations adopted by the Securities and Exchange Commission.

The preparation of Management's Discussion and Analysis requires management to interpret the criteria, make determinations as to the relevancy of information to be included, and make estimates and assumptions that affect reported information. Management's Discussion and Analysis includes information regarding the estimated future impact of transactions and events that have occurred or are expected to occur, expected sources of liquidity and capital resources, operating trends, commitments, and uncertainties. Actual results in the future may differ materially from management's present assessment of this information because events and circumstances frequently do not occur as expected.

[*Concluding paragraph*]

Based on our review, nothing came to our attention that caused us to believe that the Company's presentation of Management's Discussion and Analysis does not include, in all material respects, the required elements of the rules and regulations adopted by the Securities and Exchange Commission, that the historical financial amounts included therein have not been accurately derived, in all material respects, from the Company's financial statements, or that the underlying information, determinations, estimates, and assumptions of the Company do not provide a reasonable basis for the disclosures contained therein.

[*Restricted use paragraph*][39]

This report is intended solely for the information and use of [*list or refer to specified parties*] and is not intended to be and should not be used by anyone other than the specified parties.

[*Signature*]

[*Date*]

Example 3: Modification to Review Report for a Material Misstatement

3. An example of a modification of the accountant's report when MD&A is materially misstated, as discussed in paragraph .89, follows.

[*Additional explanatory paragraph preceding the concluding paragraph*]

Based on information furnished to us by management, we believe that the Company has excluded a discussion of the significant capital outlay required for its plans to expand into the telecommunications industry and the possible effects on the Company's financial condition, liquidity, and capital resources.

[*Concluding paragraph*]

Based on our review, with the exception of the matter described in the preceding paragraph, nothing came to our attention that caused us to believe that the Company's presentation of Management's Discussion and Analysis does not include, in all material respects, the required elements of the rules and regulations adopted by the Securities and Exchange Commission, that the historical financial amounts included therein have not been accurately derived, in all material respects, from the Company's financial statements, or that the underlying information, determinations, estimates and assumptions of the Company do not provide a reasonable basis for the disclosures contained therein.

[Revised, December 2012, to reflect conforming changes necessary due to the issuance of SAS Nos. 122–126.]

[39] This paragraph may be omitted for certain nonpublic entities. (Refer to paragraph .85*k*.)

.116

Appendix C

Combined Reports

Example 1: Combined Examination and Review Report on MD&A

1. An example of a combined report on an examination of an annual MD&A presentation and the review of MD&A for an interim period discussed in paragraph .92 follows.

Independent Accountant's Report

[*Introductory paragraph*]

We have examined XYZ Company's Management's Discussion and Analysis taken as a whole for the three-year period ended December 31, 20X5, included [*incorporated by reference*] in the Company's [*insert description of registration statement or document*]. Management is responsible for the preparation of the Company's Management's Discussion and Analysis pursuant to the rules and regulations adopted by the Securities and Exchange Commission. Our responsibility is to express an opinion on the annual presentation based on our examination. We have audited, in accordance with auditing standards generally accepted in the United States of America, the financial statements of XYZ Company as of December 31, 20X5 and 20X4, and for each of the years in the three-year period ended December 31, 19X5, and in our report dated [*Month*] XX, 20X6, we expressed an unqualified opinion on those financial statements.

[*Scope paragraph*]

Our examination of Management's Discussion and Analysis was conducted in accordance with attestation standards established by the American Institute of Certified Public Accountants and, accordingly, included examining, on a test basis, evidence supporting the historical amounts and disclosures in the presentation. An examination also includes assessing the significant determinations made by management as to the relevancy of information to be included and the estimates and assumptions that affect reported information. We believe that our examination provides a reasonable basis for our opinion.

[*Explanatory paragraph*][40]

The preparation of Management's Discussion and Analysis requires management to interpret the criteria, make determinations as to the relevancy of information to be included, and make estimates and assumptions that affect reported information. Management's Discussion and Analysis includes information regarding the estimated future impact of transactions and events that have occurred or are expected to occur, expected sources of liquidity and capital resources, operating trends, commitments, and uncertainties. Actual results in

---

[40] The following sentence should be added to the beginning of the explanatory paragraph if the entity is a nonpublic entity, as discussed in paragraph .69*h*.

Although XYZ Company is not subject to the rules and regulations of the Securities and Exchange Commission, the accompanying Management's Discussion and Analysis is intended to be a presentation in accordance with the rules and regulations adopted by the Securities and Exchange Commission.

the future may differ materially from management's present assessment of this information because events and circumstances frequently do not occur as expected.

[*Opinion paragraph*]

In our opinion, the Company's presentation of Management's Discussion and Analysis for the three-year period ended December 31, 20X5, includes, in all material respects, the required elements of the rules and regulations adopted by the Securities and Exchange Commission; the historical financial amounts included therein have been accurately derived, in all material respects, from the Company's financial statements; and the underlying information, determinations, estimates, and assumptions of the Company provide a reasonable basis for the disclosures contained therein.

[*Paragraphs on interims*]

We have also reviewed XYZ Company's Management's Discussion and Analysis taken as a whole for the six-month period ended June 30, 20X6 included [*incorporated by reference*] in the Company's [*insert description of registration statement or document*]. We have reviewed, in accordance with standards established by the American Institute of Certified Public Accountants, the interim financial information of XYZ Company as of June 30, 20X6 and 20X5, and for the six-month periods then ended, and have issued our report thereon dated July XX, 20X6.

We conducted our review of Management's Discussion and Analysis in accordance with attestation standards established by the American Institute of Certified Public Accountants. A review of Management's Discussion and Analysis consists principally of applying analytical procedures and making inquiries of persons responsible for financial, accounting, and operational matters. It is substantially less in scope than an examination, the objective of which is the expression of an opinion on the presentation. Accordingly, we do not express such an opinion.

Based on our review, nothing came to our attention that caused us to believe that the Company's presentation of Management's Discussion and Analysis for the six-month period ended June 30, 20X6, does not include, in all material respects, the required elements of the rules and regulations adopted by the Securities and Exchange Commission, that the historical financial amounts included therein have not been accurately derived, in all material respects, from the Company's unaudited interim financial statements, or that the underlying information, determinations, estimates, and assumptions of the Company do not provide a reasonable basis for the disclosures contained therein.

[*Restricted use paragraph*][41]

This report is intended solely for the information and use of [*list or refer to specified parties*] and is not intended to be and should not be used by anyone other than the specified parties.

[*Signature*]

[*Date*]

Example 2: Review Report on a Combined Annual and Interim MD&A Presentation

2. An example of a review report on a combined MD&A presentation for annual and interim periods follows.

[41] This paragraph may be omitted for certain nonpublic entities. (Refer to paragraph .85*k*.)

Independent Accountant's Report

[*Introductory paragraph*]

We have reviewed XYZ Company's Management's Discussion and Analysis taken as a whole included [*incorporated by reference*] in the Company's [*insert description of registration statement or document*]. Management is responsible for the preparation of the Company's Management's Discussion and Analysis pursuant to the rules and regulations adopted by the Securities and Exchange Commission. We have audited, in accordance with auditing standards generally accepted in the United States of America, the financial statements of XYZ Company as of December 31, 20X5 and 20X4, and for each of the years in the three-year period ended December 31, 20X5, and in our report dated [*Month*] XX, 20X6, we expressed an unqualified opinion on those financial statements. We have reviewed, in accordance with standards established by the American Institute of Certified Public Accountants, the interim financial information of XYZ Company as of June 30, 20X6 and 20X5, and for the six-month periods then ended, and have issued our report thereon dated July XX, 20X6.

[*Scope paragraph*]

We conducted our review of Management's Discussion and Analysis in accordance with attestation standards established by the American Institute of Certified Public Accountants. A review of Management's Discussion and Analysis consists principally of applying analytical procedures and making inquiries of persons responsible for financial, accounting, and operational matters. It is substantially less in scope than an examination, the objective of which is the expression of an opinion on the presentation. Accordingly, we do not express such an opinion.

[*Explanatory paragraph*][42]

The preparation of Management's Discussion and Analysis requires management to interpret the criteria, make determinations as to the relevancy of information to be included, and make estimates and assumptions that affect reported information. Management's Discussion and Analysis includes information regarding the estimated future impact of transactions and events that have occurred or are expected to occur, expected sources of liquidity and capital resources, operating trends, commitments, and uncertainties. Actual results in the future may differ materially from management's present assessment of this information because events and circumstances frequently do not occur as expected.

[*Concluding paragraph*]

Based on our review, nothing came to our attention that caused us to believe that the Company's presentation of Management's Discussion and Analysis does not include, in all material respects, the required elements of the rules and regulations adopted by the Securities and Exchange Commission, that the historical financial amounts included therein have not been accurately derived, in all material respects, from the Company's financial statements, or that the underlying information, determinations, estimates, and assumptions of the Company do not provide a reasonable basis for the disclosures contained therein.

[*Restricted use paragraph*][43]

---

[42] The following sentence should be added to the beginning of the explanatory paragraph if the entity is a nonpublic entity, as discussed in paragraph .69*h*.

Although XYZ Company is not subject to the rules and regulations of the Securities and Exchange Commission, the accompanying Management's Discussion and Analysis is intended to be a presentation in accordance with the rules and regulations adopted by the Securities and Exchange Commission.

[43] This paragraph may be omitted for certain nonpublic entities. (Refer to paragraph .85*k*.)

This report is intended solely for the information and use of [*list or refer to specified parties*] and is not intended to be and should not be used by anyone other than the specified parties.

[*Signature*]

[*Date*]

.117

Appendix D

Comparison of Activities Performed Under SAS No. 118, *Other Information in Documents Containing Audited Financial Statements* [AU-C Section 720], Versus a Review or an Examination Attest Engagement*

Activities	*SAS No. 118 (AU-C Section 720)*	*Review*	*Examination*
Obtain an understanding of SEC rules and regulations and management's methodology for the preparation of Management's Discussion and Analysis (MD&A).	Not applicable (N/A)—Auditor is only required to read the information in the MD&A in order to identify material inconsistencies, if any, with the audited financial statements.	Obtain an understanding of the rules and regulations adopted by the SEC for MD&A. Inquire of management regarding the method of preparing MD&A.	Same as for a review.
Plan the engagement.	N/A	Develop an overall strategy for the analytical procedures and inquiries to be performed to provide negative assurance.	Develop an overall strategy for the expected scope and performance of the engagement to obtain reasonable assurance to express an opinion.
Consider internal control.	N/A	Consider relevant portions of the entity's internal control applicable to the preparation of MD&A to identify the types of potential misstatements and to select the inquiries and analytical procedures; no testing of controls would be performed.	Obtain an understanding of internal control applicable to the preparation of MD&A sufficient to plan the engagement and to assess control risk; controls may be tested by performing inquiries of client personnel, inspection of documents, and observation of relevant activities.

* Refer to AU-C section 720, *Other Information in Documents Containing Audited Financial Statements*. [Footnote revised, December 2012, to reflect conforming changes necessary due to the issuance of SAS Nos. 122–126.]

(continued)

Activities	*SAS No. 118 (AU-C Section 720)*	*Review*	*Examination*
Test assertions.	N/A	Apply the following analytical procedures and make inquiries of management and others; no corroborating evidential matter is obtained: • Read the MD&A and compare the content for consistency with the financial statements; compare financial amounts to the financial statements or related accounting records and analyses; recompute increases, decreases and percentages disclosed. • Compare nonfinancial amounts to the financial statements or other records. • Consider whether MD&A explanations are consistent with information obtained during the audit or review of financial statements; make further inquiries, as necessary. (Note: Such additional inquiries may result in a decision to perform other procedures or detail tests.) • Compare information in MD&A with the rules and regulations adopted by the SEC. • Obtain and read available prospective financial information; inquire of management as to the procedures used to prepare such information; consider whether information came to the practitioner's attention that causes him or her to believe that the underlying information, determinations, estimates, and assumptions do not provide a reasonable basis for the MD&A disclosures.	Apply the following analytical and corroborative procedures to obtain reasonable assurance of detecting material misstatements: • Read the MD&A and compare the content for consistency with the financial statements; compare financial amounts to the financial statements or related accounting records and analyses; recompute increases, decreases and percentages disclosed. • Compare nonfinancial amounts to the financial statements or other records; perform tests on other records based on the concept of materiality. • Consider whether explanations are consistent with the information obtained during the audit of financial statements; investigate further explanations that cannot be substantiated by information in the audit working papers through inquiry and inspection of client records. • Examine internally and externally generated documents in support of the existence, occurrence, or expected occurrence of events, transactions, conditions, trends, demands, commitments, and uncertainties disclosed in MD&A. • Compare information in MD&A with the rules and regulations adopted by the SEC.

Activities	*SAS No. 118 (AU-C Section 720)*	*Review*	*Examination*
Test assertions. *(continued)*		• Obtain public communications and minutes of meetings for comparison with disclosures in MD&A. • Make inquiries of the officers or executives with responsibility for operational areas and financial and accounting matters as to their plans and expectations for the future. • Inquire as to prior experience with the SEC and the extent of comments received; read correspondence. • Consider whether there are any additional matters that should be disclosed in the MD&A based on the results of the preceding procedures and knowledge obtained during the audit or review of the financial statements.	• Obtain and read available prospective financial information; inquire of management as to the procedures used to prepare such information; evaluate whether the underlying information, determinations, estimates, and assumptions provide a reasonable basis for the MD&A disclosures. • Obtain public communications and minutes of meetings; consider obtaining other types of publicly available information for comparison with the disclosures in MD&A. • Make inquiries of the officers or executives with responsibility for operational areas and financial and accounting matters as to their plans and expectations for the future. • Inquire as to prior experience with the SEC and the extent of comments received; read correspondence. • Test completeness by considering the results of the preceding procedures and knowledge obtained during the audit of the financial statements, and whether such matters are appropriately disclosed in the MD&A; extend procedures if the inherent risk relating to completeness of disclosures is high.

(continued)

Activities	*SAS No. 118 (AU-C Section 720)*	*Review*	*Examination*
Consider the effect of events subsequent to the balance-sheet date.	Yes	Yes	Yes
Obtain written representations from management.	Yes	Yes	Yes
Form a conclusion and report.	The auditor has no reporting responsibility with respect to MD&A unless the auditor concludes that there is a material inconsistency in the MD&A that has not been eliminated. In such a situation, the auditor may add an other matter paragraph to the auditor's report on the audited financial statements describing the material inconsistency or withhold the auditor's report. If, while reading the MD&A, the auditor becomes aware of an apparent material misstatement of fact, the auditor should discuss such matter with management and take other actions based on management's response.	Form a conclusion based on the results of the preceding procedures and report in the form of negative assurance.	Form an opinion based on the results of the preceding procedures and report conclusion by expressing an opinion.

[Revised, December 2010, to reflect conforming changes necessary due to the issuance of SAS Nos. 118–120. Revised, December 2012, to reflect conforming changes necessary due to the issuance of SAS Nos. 122–126.]

AT Section 801

Reporting on Controls at a Service Organization

(Supersedes the guidance for service auditors in Statement on Auditing Standards No. 70, Service Organizations, as amended.)

Source: SSAE No. 16.

Effective for service auditors' reports for periods ending on or after June 15, 2011. Earlier implementation is permitted.

Introduction

Scope of This Section

.01 This section addresses examination engagements undertaken by a service auditor to report on controls at organizations that provide services to user entities when those controls are likely to be relevant to user entities' internal control over financial reporting. It complements AU-C section 402, *Audit Considerations Relating to an Entity Using a Service Organization*, in that reports prepared in accordance with this section may provide appropriate evidence under AU-C section 402. (Ref: par. .A1) [Revised, December 2012, to reflect conforming changes necessary due to the issuance of SAS Nos. 122–126.]

.02 The focus of this section is on controls at service organizations likely to be relevant to user entities' internal control over financial reporting. The guidance herein also may be helpful to a practitioner performing an engagement under section 101, *Attest Engagements*, to report on controls at a service organization

a. other than those that are likely to be relevant to user entities' internal control over financial reporting (for example, controls that affect user entities' compliance with specified requirements of laws, regulations, rules, contracts, or grants, or controls that affect user entities' production or quality control). Section 601, *Compliance Attestation*, is applicable if a practitioner is reporting on an entity's own compliance with specified requirements or on its controls over compliance with specified requirements. (Ref: par. .A2–.A3)

b. when management of the service organization is not responsible for the design of the system (for example, when the system has been designed by the user entity or the design is stipulated in a contract between the user entity and the service organization). (Ref: par. .A4)

.03 In addition to performing an examination of a service organization's controls, a service auditor may be engaged to (*a*) examine and report on a user entity's transactions or balances maintained by a service organization, or (*b*) perform and report the results of agreed upon procedures related to the controls of a service organization or to transactions or balances of a user entity maintained by a service organization. However, these engagements are not addressed in this section.

.04 The requirements and application material in this section are based on the premise that management of the service organization (also referred to as management) will provide the service auditor with a written assertion that is included in or attached to management's description of the service organization's system. Paragraph .10 of this section addresses the circumstance in which management refuses to provide such a written assertion. Section 101 indicates that when performing an attestation engagement, a practitioner may report directly on the subject matter or on management's assertion. For engagements conducted under this section, the service auditor is required to report directly on the subject matter.

Effective Date

.05 This section is effective for service auditors' reports for periods ending on or after June 15, 2011. Earlier implementation is permitted.

Objectives

.06 The objectives of the service auditor are to

a. obtain reasonable assurance about whether, in all material respects, based on suitable criteria,

   i. management's description of the service organization's system fairly presents the system that was designed and implemented throughout the specified period (or in the case of a type 1 report, as of a specified date).

   ii. the controls related to the control objectives stated in management's description of the service organization's system were suitably designed throughout the specified period (or in the case of a type 1 report, as of a specified date).

   iii. when included in the scope of the engagement, the controls operated effectively to provide reasonable assurance that the control objectives stated in management's description of the service organization's system were achieved throughout the specified period.

b. report on the matters in 6(a) in accordance with the service auditor's findings.

Definitions

.07 For purposes of this section, the following terms have the meanings attributed in the subsequent text:

Carve-out method. Method of addressing the services provided by a subservice organization whereby management's description of the service organization's system identifies the nature of the services performed by the subservice organization and excludes from the description and from the scope of the service auditor's engagement, the subservice organization's relevant control objectives and related controls. Management's description of the service organization's system and the scope of the service auditor's engagement include controls at the service organization that monitor the effectiveness of controls at the subservice organization, which may include management of the service organization's review of a service auditor's report on controls at the subservice organization.

Complementary user entity controls. Controls that management of the service organization assumes, in the design of the service provided by the service organization, will be implemented by user entities, and which, if necessary to achieve the control objectives stated in management's description of the service organization's system, are identified as such in that description.

Control objectives. The aim or purpose of specified controls at the service organization. Control objectives address the risks that controls are intended to mitigate.

Controls at a service organization. The policies and procedures at a service organization likely to be relevant to user entities' internal control over financial reporting. These policies and procedures are designed, implemented, and documented by the service organization to provide reasonable assurance about the achievement of the control objectives relevant to the services covered by the service auditor's report. (Ref: par. .A5)

Controls at a subservice organization. The policies and procedures at a subservice organization likely to be relevant to internal control over financial reporting of user entities of the service organization. These policies and procedures are designed, implemented, and documented by a subservice organization to provide reasonable assurance about the achievement of control objectives that are relevant to the services covered by the service auditor's report.

Criteria. The standards or benchmarks used to measure and present the subject matter and against which the service auditor evaluates the subject matter. (Ref: par. .A6)

Inclusive method. Method of addressing the services provided by a subservice organization whereby management's description of the service organization's system includes a description of the nature of the services provided by the subservice organization as well as the subservice organization's relevant control objectives and related controls. (Ref: par. .A7–.A9)

Internal audit function. The service organization's internal auditors and others, for example, members of a compliance or risk department, who perform activities similar to those performed by internal auditors. (Ref: par. .A10)

Report on management's description of a service organization's system and the suitability of the design of controls (referred to in this section as a *type 1 report*). A report that comprises the following:

a. Management's description of the service organization's system.

b. A written assertion by management of the service organization about whether, in all material respects, and based on suitable criteria,

   i. management's description of the service organization's system fairly presents the service organization's system that was designed and implemented as of a specified date.

   ii. the controls related to the control objectives stated in management's description of the service organization's system were suitably designed to achieve those control objectives as of the specified date.

c. A service auditor's report that expresses an opinion on the matters in (b)(i)–(b)(ii).

Report on management's description of a service organization's system and the suitability of the design and operating effectiveness of controls (referred to in this section as a *type 2 report*). A report that comprises the following:

a. Management's description of the service organization's system.

b. A written assertion by management of the service organization about whether in all material respects, and based on suitable criteria,

i. management's description of the service organization's system fairly presents the service organization's system that was designed and implemented throughout the specified period.

ii. the controls related to the control objectives stated in management's description of the service organization's system were suitably designed throughout the specified period to achieve those control objectives.

iii. the controls related to the control objectives stated in management's description of the service organization's system operated effectively throughout the specified period to achieve those control objectives.

c. A service auditor's report that

i. expresses an opinion on the matters in (b)(i)–(b)(iii).

ii. includes a description of the tests of controls and the results thereof.

Service auditor. A practitioner who reports on controls at a service organization.

Service organization. An organization or segment of an organization that provides services to user entities, which are likely to be relevant to those user entities' internal control over financial reporting.

Service organization's assertion. A written assertion about the matters referred to in part (b) of the definition of *Report on management's description of a service organization's system and the suitability of the design and operating effectiveness of controls*, for a type 2 report; and, for a type 1 report, the matters referred to in part (b) of the definition of *Report on management's description of a service organization's system and the suitability of the design of controls*.

Service organization's system. The policies and procedures designed, implemented, and documented, by management of the service organization to provide user entities with the services covered by the service auditor's report. Management's description of the service organization's system identifies the services covered, the period to which the description relates (or in the case of a type 1 report, the date to which the description relates), the control objectives specified by management or an outside party, the party specifying the control objectives (if not specified by management), and the related controls. (Ref: par. .A11)

Subservice organization. A service organization used by another service organization to perform some of the services provided to user entities that are likely to be relevant to those user entities' internal control over financial reporting.

Test of controls. A procedure designed to evaluate the operating effectiveness of controls in achieving the control objectives stated in management's description of the service organization's system.

User auditor. An auditor who audits and reports on the financial statements of a user entity.

User entity. An entity that uses a service organization.

Requirements

Management and Those Charged With Governance

.08 When this section requires the service auditor to inquire of, request representations from, communicate with, or otherwise interact with management of the service organization, the service auditor should determine the appropriate person(s) within the service organization's management or governance structure with whom to interact. This should include consideration of which person(s) have the appropriate responsibilities for and knowledge of the matters concerned. (Ref: par. .A12)

Acceptance and Continuance

.09 A service auditor should accept or continue an engagement to report on controls at a service organization only if (Ref: par. .A13)

a. the service auditor has the capabilities and competence to perform the engagement. (Ref: par. .A14–.A15)

b. the service auditor's preliminary knowledge of the engagement circumstances indicates that

i. the criteria to be used will be suitable and available to the intended user entities and their auditors;

ii. the service auditor will have access to sufficient appropriate evidence to the extent necessary; and

iii. the scope of the engagement and management's description of the service organization's system will not be so limited that they are unlikely to be useful to user entities and their auditors.

c. management agrees to the terms of the engagement by acknowledging and accepting its responsibility for the following:

i. Preparing its description of the service organization's system and its assertion, including the completeness, accuracy, and method of presentation of the description and assertion. (Ref: par. .A16)

ii. Having a reasonable basis for its assertion. (Ref: par. .A17)

iii. Selecting the criteria to be used and stating them in the assertion.

iv. Specifying the control objectives, stating them in the description of the service organization's system, and, if the control objectives are specified by law, regulation, or another party (for example, a user group or a professional body), identifying in the description the party specifying the control objectives.

v. Identifying the risks that threaten the achievement of the control objectives stated in the description and designing, implementing, and documenting controls that are suitably designed and operating effectively to provide reasonable assurance that the control objectives stated in the description of the service organization's system will be achieved. (Ref: par. .A18)

vi. Providing the service auditor with

(1) access to all information, such as records and documentation, including service level agreements, of which management is aware that is relevant to the description of the service organization's system and the assertion;

(2) additional information that the service auditor may request from management for the purpose of the examination engagement;

(3) unrestricted access to personnel within the service organization from whom the service auditor determines it is necessary to obtain evidence relevant to the service auditor's engagement; and

(4) written representations at the conclusion of the engagement.

vii. Providing a written assertion that will be included in, or attached to management's description of the service organization's system, and provided to user entities.

.10 If management will not provide the service auditor with a written assertion, the service auditor should not circumvent the requirement to obtain an assertion by performing a service auditor's engagement under section 101. (Ref: par. .A19)

.11 Management's subsequent refusal to provide a written assertion represents a scope limitation and consequently, the service auditor should withdraw from the engagement. If law or regulation does not allow the service auditor to withdraw from the engagement, the service auditor should disclaim an opinion.

Request to Change the Scope of the Engagement

.12 If management requests a change in the scope of the engagement before the completion of the engagement, the service auditor should be satisfied, before agreeing to the change, that a reasonable justification for the change exists. (Ref: par. .A20–.A21)

Assessing the Suitability of the Criteria (Ref: par. .A6 and .A22–.A23)

.13 As required by paragraph .23 of section 101, the service auditor should assess whether management has used suitable criteria

a. in preparing its description of the service organization's system;

b. in evaluating whether controls were suitably designed to achieve the control objectives stated in the description; and

c. in the case of a type 2 report, in evaluating whether controls operated effectively throughout the specified period to achieve the control objectives stated in the description of the service organization's system.

.14 In assessing the suitability of the criteria to evaluate whether management's description of the service organization's system is fairly presented, the service auditor should determine if the criteria include, at a minimum,

a. whether management's description of the service organization's system presents how the service organization's system was designed and implemented, including the following information about the service organization's system, if applicable:

i. The types of services provided including, as appropriate, the classes of transactions processed.

ii. The procedures, within both automated and manual systems, by which services are provided, including, as appropriate, procedures by which transactions are initiated, authorized, recorded, processed, corrected as necessary, and transferred to the reports and other information prepared for user entities.

iii. The related accounting records, whether electronic or manual, and supporting information involved in initiating, authorizing, recording, processing, and reporting transactions; this includes the correction of incorrect information and how information is transferred to the reports and other information prepared for user entities.

iv. How the service organization's system captures and addresses significant events and conditions other than transactions.

v. The process used to prepare reports and other information for user entities.

vi. The specified control objectives and controls designed to achieve those objectives, including as applicable, complementary user entity controls contemplated in the design of the service organization's controls.

vii. Other aspects of the service organization's control environment, risk assessment process, information and communication systems (including the related business processes), control activities, and monitoring controls that are relevant to the services provided. (Ref: par. A17 and .A24)

b. in the case of a type 2 report, whether management's description of the service organization's system includes relevant details of changes to the service organization's system during the period covered by the description. (Ref: par. .A44)

c. whether management's description of the service organization's system does not omit or distort information relevant to the service organization's system, while acknowledging that management's description of the service organization's system is prepared to meet the common needs of a broad range of user entities and their user auditors, and may not, therefore, include every aspect of the service organization's system that each individual user entity and its user auditor may consider important in its own particular environment.

.15 In assessing the suitability of the criteria to evaluate whether the controls are suitably designed, the service auditor should determine if the criteria include, at a minimum, whether

- *a.* the risks that threaten the achievement of the control objectives stated in management's description of the service organization's system have been identified by management.
- *b.* the controls identified in management's description of the service organization's system would, if operating as described, provide reasonable assurance that those risks would not prevent the control objectives stated in the description from being achieved.

.16 In assessing the suitability of the criteria to evaluate whether controls operated effectively to provide reasonable assurance that the control objectives stated in management's description of the service organization's system were achieved, the service auditor should determine if the criteria include, at a minimum, whether the controls were consistently applied as designed throughout the specified period, including whether manual controls were applied by individuals who have the appropriate competence and authority.

Materiality

.17 When planning and performing the engagement, the service auditor should evaluate materiality with respect to the fair presentation of management's description of the service organization's system, the suitability of the design of controls to achieve the related control objectives stated in the description and, in the case of a type 2 report, the operating effectiveness of the controls to achieve the related control objectives stated in the description. (Ref: par. .A25–.A27)

Obtaining an Understanding of the Service Organization's System (Ref: par. .A28–.A30)

.18 The service auditor should obtain an understanding of the service organization's system, including controls that are included in the scope of the engagement.

Obtaining Evidence Regarding Management's Description of the Service Organization's System (Ref: par. .A26 and .A31–.A35)

.19 The service auditor should obtain and read management's description of the service organization's system and should evaluate whether those aspects of the description that are included in the scope of the engagement are presented fairly, including whether

- *a.* the control objectives stated in management's description of the service organization's system are reasonable in the circumstances. (Ref: par. .A34)
- *b.* controls identified in management's description of the service organization's system were implemented. (Ref: par. .A35)
- *c.* complementary user entity controls, if any, are adequately described. (Ref: par. .A32)
- *d.* services performed by a subservice organization, if any, are adequately described, including whether the inclusive method or the carve-out method has been used in relation to them.

.20 The service auditor should determine through inquiries made in combination with other procedures whether the service organization's system has been implemented. Such other procedures should include observation and inspection of records and other documentation of the manner in which the service organization's system operates and controls are applied. (Ref: par. .A35)

Obtaining Evidence Regarding the Design of Controls (Ref: par .A26 and .A36–.A39)

.21 The service auditor should determine which of the controls at the service organization are necessary to achieve the control objectives stated in management's description of the service organization's system and should assess whether those controls were suitably designed to achieve the control objectives by

a. identifying the risks that threaten the achievement of the control objectives stated in management's description of the service organization's system, and (Ref: par. .A36)

b. evaluating the linkage of the controls identified in management's description of the service organization's system with those risks.

Obtaining Evidence Regarding the Operating Effectiveness of Controls (Ref: par. .A26 and .A40–.A45)

Assessing Operating Effectiveness

.22 When performing a type 2 engagement, the service auditor should test those controls that the service auditor has determined are necessary to achieve the control objectives stated in management's description of the service organization's system and should assess their operating effectiveness throughout the period. Evidence obtained in prior engagements about the satisfactory operation of controls in prior periods does not provide a basis for a reduction in testing, even if it is supplemented with evidence obtained during the current period. (Ref: par. .A40–.A44)

.23 When performing a type 2 engagement, the service auditor should inquire about changes in the service organization's controls that were implemented during the period covered by the service auditor's report. If the service auditor believes the changes would be considered significant by user entities and their auditors, the service auditor should determine whether those changes are included in management's description of the service organization's system. If such changes are not included in the description, the service auditor should describe the changes in the service auditor's report and determine the effect on the service auditor's report. If the superseded controls are relevant to the achievement of the control objectives stated in the description, the service auditor should, if possible, test the superseded controls before the change. If the service auditor cannot test superseded controls relevant to the achievement of the control objectives stated in the description, the service auditor should determine the effect on the service auditor's report. (Ref: par. .A42(c) and .A45)

.24 When designing and performing tests of controls, the service auditor should

a. perform other procedures in combination with inquiry to obtain evidence about the following:

i. How the control was applied.

ii. The consistency with which the control was applied.

iii. By whom or by what means the control was applied.

b. determine whether the controls to be tested depend on other controls, and if so, whether it is necessary to obtain evidence supporting the operating effectiveness of those other controls.

c. determine an effective method for selecting the items to be tested to meet the objectives of the procedure.

.25 When determining the extent of tests of controls and whether sampling is appropriate, the service auditor should consider the characteristics of the population of the controls to be tested, including the nature of the controls, the frequency of their application (for example, monthly, daily, many times per day), and the expected rate of deviation. AU-C section 530, *Audit Sampling*, addresses the auditor's use of statistical and nonstatistical sampling when designing and selecting the audit sample, performing tests of controls and tests of details, and evaluating the results from the sample. If the service auditor determines that sampling is appropriate, the service auditor should apply AU-C section 530. [Revised, December 2012, to reflect conforming changes necessary due to the issuance of SAS Nos. 122–126.]

Nature and Cause of Deviations

.26 The service auditor should investigate the nature and cause of any deviations identified, and should determine whether

a. identified deviations are within the expected rate of deviation and are acceptable. If so, the testing that has been performed provides an appropriate basis for concluding that the control operated effectively throughout the specified period.

b. additional testing of the control or of other controls is necessary to reach a conclusion about whether the controls related to the control objectives stated in management's description of the service organization's system operated effectively throughout the specified period.

c. the testing that has been performed provides an appropriate basis for concluding that the control did not operate effectively throughout the specified period.

.27 If, as a result of performing the procedures in paragraph .26, the service auditor becomes aware that any identified deviations have resulted from intentional acts by service organization personnel, the service auditor should assess the risk that management's description of the service organization's system is not fairly presented, the controls are not suitably designed, and in a type 2 engagement, the controls are not operating effectively. (Ref: par. .A31)

Using the Work of the Internal Audit Function

Obtaining an Understanding of the Internal Audit Function (Ref: par. .A46–.A47)

.28 If the service organization has an internal audit function, the service auditor should obtain an understanding of the nature of the responsibilities of the internal audit function and of the activities performed in order to determine whether the internal audit function is likely to be relevant to the engagement.

Planning to Use the Work of the Internal Audit Function

.29 When the service auditor intends to use the work of the internal audit function, the service auditor should determine whether the work of the internal audit function is likely to be adequate for the purposes of the engagement by evaluating the following:

a. The objectivity and technical competence of the members of the internal audit function

b. Whether the work of the internal audit function is likely to be carried out with due professional care

c. Whether it is likely that effective communication will occur between the internal audit function and the service auditor, including consideration of the effect of any constraints or restrictions placed on the internal audit function by the service organization

.30 If the service auditor determines that the work of the internal audit function is likely to be adequate for the purposes of the engagement, in determining the planned effect of the work of the internal audit function on the nature, timing, or extent of the service auditor's procedures, the service auditor should evaluate the following:

a. The nature and scope of specific work performed, or to be performed, by the internal audit function

b. The significance of that work to the service auditor's conclusions

c. The degree of subjectivity involved in the evaluation of the evidence gathered in support of those conclusions

Using the Work of the Internal Audit Function (Ref: par. .A48)

.31 In order for the service auditor to use specific work of the internal audit function, the service auditor should evaluate and perform procedures on that work to determine its adequacy for the service auditor's purposes.

.32 To determine the adequacy of specific work performed by the internal audit function for the service auditor's purposes, the service auditor should evaluate whether

a. the work was performed by members of the internal audit function having adequate technical training and proficiency;

b. the work was properly supervised, reviewed, and documented;

c. sufficient appropriate evidence was obtained to enable the internal audit function to draw reasonable conclusions;

d. conclusions reached are appropriate in the circumstances and any reports prepared by the internal audit function are consistent with the results of the work performed; and

e. exceptions relevant to the engagement or unusual matters disclosed by the internal audit function are properly resolved.

Effect on the Service Auditor's Report

.33 If the work of the internal audit function has been used, the service auditor should not make reference to that work in the service auditor's opinion. Notwithstanding its degree of autonomy and objectivity, the internal audit function is not independent of the service organization. The service auditor has sole responsibility for the opinion expressed in the service auditor's report and, accordingly, that responsibility is not reduced by the service auditor's use of the work of the internal audit function. (Ref: par. .A49)

.34 In the case of a type 2 report, if the work of the internal audit function has been used in performing tests of controls, that part of the service auditor's report that describes the service auditor's tests of controls and results thereof should include a description of the internal auditor's work and of the service auditor's procedures with respect to that work. (Ref: par. .A50)

Direct Assistance

.35 When the service auditor uses members of the service organization's internal audit function to provide direct assistance, the service auditor should adapt and apply the requirements in paragraph .27 of AU-C section 610, *The Auditor's Consideration of the Internal Audit Function in an Audit of Financial Statements*. [Revised, December 2012, to reflect conforming changes necessary due to the issuance of SAS Nos. 122–126.]

Written Representations (Ref: par. .A51–.A55)

.36 The service auditor should request management to provide written representations that

a. reaffirm its assertion included in or attached to the description of the service organization's system;

b. it has provided the service auditor with all relevant information and access agreed to; and[1]

c. it has disclosed to the service auditor any of the following of which it is aware:

i. Instances of noncompliance with laws and regulations or uncorrected errors attributable to the service organization that may affect one or more user entities.

ii. Knowledge of any actual, suspected, or alleged intentional acts by management or the service organization's employees, that could adversely affect the fairness of the presentation of management's description of the service organization's system or the completeness or achievement of the control objectives stated in the description.

iii. Design deficiencies in controls.

iv. Instances when controls have not operated as described.

v. Any events subsequent to the period covered by management's description of the service organization's system up to the date of the service auditor's report that could have a significant effect on management's assertion.

.37 If a service organization uses a subservice organization and management's description of the service organization's system uses the inclusive method, the service auditor also should obtain the written representations identified in paragraph .36 from management of the subservice organization.

.38 The written representations should be in the form of a representation letter addressed to the service auditor and should be as of the same date as the date of the service auditor's report.

.39 If management does not provide one or more of the written representations requested by the service auditor, the service auditor should do the following:

a. Discuss the matter with management

---

[1] See paragraph .09(c)(vi)(1).

b. Evaluate the effect of such refusal on the service auditor's assessment of the integrity of management and evaluate the effect that this may have on the reliability of management's representations and evidence in general

c. Take appropriate actions, which may include disclaiming an opinion or withdrawing from the engagement

If management refuses to provide the representations in paragraphs .36(a)–.36(b) of this section, the service auditor should disclaim an opinion or withdraw from the engagement.

Other Information (Ref: par. .A56–.A57)

.40 The service auditor should read other information, if any, included in a document containing management's description of the service organization's system and the service auditor's report to identify material inconsistencies, if any, with that description. While reading the other information for the purpose of identifying material inconsistencies, the service auditor may become aware of an apparent misstatement of fact in the other information.

.41 If the service auditor becomes aware of a material inconsistency or an apparent misstatement of fact in the other information, the service auditor should discuss the matter with management. If the service auditor concludes that there is a material inconsistency or a misstatement of fact in the other information that management refuses to correct, the service auditor should take further appropriate action.[2]

Subsequent Events

.42 The service auditor should inquire whether management is aware of any events subsequent to the period covered by management's description of the service organization's system up to the date of the service auditor's report that could have a significant effect on management's assertion. If the service auditor becomes aware, through inquiry or otherwise, of such an event, or any other event that is of such a nature and significance that its disclosure is necessary to prevent users of a type 1 or type 2 report from being misled, and information about that event is not disclosed by management in its description, the service auditor should disclose such event in the service auditor's report.

.43 The service auditor has no responsibility to keep informed of events subsequent to the date of the service auditor's report; however, after the release of the service auditor's report, the service auditor may become aware of conditions that existed at the report date that might have affected management's assertion and the service auditor's report had the service auditor been aware of them. The evaluation of such subsequent information is similar to the evaluation of facts discovered subsequent to the date of the report on an audit of financial statements, as described in AU-C section 560, *Subsequent Events and Subsequently Discovered Facts*, and therefore, the service auditor should adapt and apply AU-C section 560. [Revised, December 2012, to reflect conforming changes necessary due to the issuance of SAS Nos. 122–126.]

Documentation (Ref: par. .A58)

.44 The service auditor should prepare documentation that is sufficient to enable an experienced service auditor, having no previous connection with the engagement, to understand the following:

---

[2] See paragraphs .91–.94 of section 101, *Attest Engagements*.

a. The nature, timing, and extent of the procedures performed to comply with this section and with applicable legal and regulatory requirements

b. The results of the procedures performed and the evidence obtained

c. Significant findings or issues arising during the engagement, the conclusions reached thereon, and significant professional judgments made in reaching those conclusions

.45 In documenting the nature, timing, and extent of procedures performed, the service auditor should record the following:

a. Identifying characteristics of the specific items or matters being tested

b. Who performed the work and the date such work was completed

c. Who reviewed the work performed and the date and extent of such review

.46 If the service auditor uses specific work of the internal audit function, the service auditor should document the conclusions reached regarding the evaluation of the adequacy of the work of the internal audit function and the procedures performed by the service auditor on that work.

.47 The service auditor should document discussions of significant findings or issues with management and others, including the nature of the significant findings or issues, when the discussions took place, and with whom.

.48 If the service auditor has identified information that is inconsistent with the service auditor's final conclusion regarding a significant finding or issue, the service auditor should document how the service auditor addressed the inconsistency.

.49 The service auditor should assemble the engagement documentation in an engagement file and complete the administrative process of assembling the final engagement file on a timely basis, no later than 60 days following the service auditor's report release date.

.50 After the assembly of the final engagement file has been completed, the service auditor should not delete or discard documentation before the end of its retention period.

.51 If the service auditor finds it necessary to modify existing engagement documentation or add new documentation after the assembly of the final engagement file has been completed, the service auditor should, regardless of the nature of the modifications or additions, document the following:

a. The specific reasons for making them

b. When and by whom they were made and reviewed

Preparing the Service Auditor's Report

Content of the Service Auditor's Report (Ref: par. .A59)

.52 A service auditor's type 2 report should include the following elements:

a. A title that includes the word *independent*.

b. An addressee.

c. Identification of

i. management's description of the service organization's system and the function performed by the system.

ii. any parts of management's description of the service organization's system that are not covered by the service auditor's report. (Ref: par. .A56)

iii. any information included in a document containing the service auditor's report that is not covered by the service auditor's report. (Ref: par. .A56)

iv. the criteria.

v. any services performed by a subservice organization and whether the carve-out method or the inclusive method was used in relation to them. Depending on which method is used, the following should be included:

(1) If the carve-out method was used, a statement that management's description of the service organization's system excludes the control objectives and related controls at relevant subservice organizations, and that the service auditor's procedures do not extend to the subservice organization.

(2) If the inclusive method was used, a statement that management's description of the service organization's system includes the subservice organization's specified control objectives and related controls, and that the service auditor's procedures included procedures related to the subservice organization.

d. If management's description of the service organization's system refers to the need for complementary user entity controls, a statement that the service auditor has not evaluated the suitability of the design or operating effectiveness of complementary user entity controls, and that the control objectives stated in the description can be achieved only if complementary user entity controls are suitably designed and operating effectively, along with the controls at the service organization.

e. A reference to management's assertion and a statement that management is responsible for (Ref: par. .A60)

i. preparing the description of the service organization's system and the assertion, including the completeness, accuracy, and method of presentation of the description and assertion;

ii. providing the services covered by the description of the service organization's system;

iii. specifying the control objectives unless the control objectives are specified by law, regulation, or another party, and stating them in the description of the service organization's system;

iv. identifying the risks that threaten the achievement of the control objectives;

v. selecting the criteria; and

vi. designing, implementing, and documenting controls that are suitably designed and operating effectively to achieve the related control objectives stated in the description of the service organization's system.

f. A statement that the service auditor's responsibility is to express an opinion on the fairness of the presentation of management's description of the service organization's system and on the suitability of the design and operating effectiveness of the controls to achieve the related control objectives stated in the description, based on the service auditor's examination.

g. A statement that the examination was conducted in accordance with attestation standards established by the American Institute of Certified Public Accountants and that those standards require the service auditor to plan and perform the examination to obtain reasonable assurance about whether management's description of the service organization's system is fairly presented and the controls are suitably designed and operating effectively throughout the specified period to achieve the related control objectives.

h. A statement that an examination of management's description of a service organization's system and the suitability of the design and operating effectiveness of the service organization's controls to achieve the related control objectives stated in the description involves performing procedures to obtain evidence about the fairness of the presentation of the description and the suitability of the design and operating effectiveness of those controls to achieve the related control objectives stated in the description.

i. A statement that the examination included assessing the risks that management's description of the service organization's system is not fairly presented and that the controls were not suitably designed or operating effectively to achieve the related control objectives.

j. A statement that the examination also included testing the operating effectiveness of those controls that the service auditor considers necessary to provide reasonable assurance that the related control objectives stated in management's description of the service organization's system were achieved.

k. A statement that an examination engagement of this type also includes evaluating the overall presentation of management's description of the service organization's system and suitability of the control objectives stated in the description.

l. A statement that the service auditor believes the examination provides a reasonable basis for his or her opinion.

m. A statement about the inherent limitations of controls, including the risk of projecting to future periods any evaluation of the fairness of the presentation of management's description of the service organization's system or conclusions about the suitability of the design or operating effectiveness of controls.

n. The service auditor's opinion on whether, in all material respects, based on the criteria described in management's assertion,

  i. management's description of the service organization's system fairly presents the service organization's system that was designed and implemented throughout the specified period.

  ii. the controls related to the control objectives stated in management's description of the service organization's system were suitably designed to provide reasonable assurance that those control objectives would be achieved if the controls operated effectively throughout the specified period.

iii. the controls the service auditor tested, which were those necessary to provide reasonable assurance that the control objectives stated in management's description of the service organization's system were achieved, operated effectively throughout the specified period.

iv. if the application of complementary user entity controls is necessary to achieve the related control objectives stated in management's description of the service organization's system, a reference to this condition.

o. A reference to a description of the service auditor's tests of controls and the results thereof, that includes

i. identification of the controls that were tested, whether the items tested represent all or a selection of the items in the population, and the nature of the tests in sufficient detail to enable user auditors to determine the effect of such tests on their risk assessments. (Ref: par. .A50)

ii. if deviations have been identified in the operation of controls included in the description, the extent of testing performed by the service auditor that led to the identification of the deviations (including the number of items tested), and the number and nature of the deviations noted (even if, on the basis of tests performed, the service auditor concludes that the related control objective was achieved). (Ref: par. .A65)

p. A statement restricting the use of the service auditor's report to management of the service organization, user entities of the service organization's system during some or all of the period covered by the service auditor's report, and the independent auditors of such user entities. (Ref: par. .A61–.A64)

q. The date of the service auditor's report.

r. The name of the service auditor and the city and state where the service auditor maintains the office that has responsibility for the engagement.

.53 A service auditor's type 1 report should include the following elements:

a. A title that includes the word *independent*.

b. An addressee.

c. Identification of

i. management's description of the service organization's system and the function performed by the system.

ii. any parts of management's description of the service organization's system that are not covered by the service auditor's report. (Ref: par. .A56)

iii. any information included in a document containing the service auditor report that is not covered by the service auditor's report. (Ref: par. .A56)

iv. the criteria.

v. any services performed by a subservice organization and whether the carve-out method or the inclusive method was used in relation to them. Depending on which method is used, the following should be included:

(1) If the carve-out method was used, a statement that management's description of the service organization's system excludes the control objectives and related controls at relevant subservice organizations, and that the service auditor's procedures do not extend to the subservice organization.

(2) If the inclusive method was used, a statement that management's description of the service organization's system includes the subservice organization's specified control objectives and related controls, and that the service auditor's procedures included procedures related to the subservice organization.

d. If management's description of the service organization's system refers to the need for complementary user entity controls, a statement that the service auditor has not evaluated the suitability of the design or operating effectiveness of complementary user entity controls, and that the control objectives stated in the description can be achieved only if complementary user entity controls are suitably designed and operating effectively, along with the controls at the service organization.

e. A reference to management's assertion and a statement that management is responsible for (Ref: par. .A60)

i. preparing the description of the service organization's system and assertion, including the completeness, accuracy, and method of presentation of the description and assertion;

ii. providing the services covered by the description of the service organization's system;

iii. specifying the control objectives, unless the control objectives are specified by law, regulation, or another party, and stating them in the description of the service organization's system;

iv. identifying the risks that threaten the achievement of the control objectives,

v. selecting the criteria; and

vi. designing, implementing, and documenting controls that are suitably designed and operating effectively to achieve the related control objectives stated in the description of the service organization's system.

f. A statement that the service auditor's responsibility is to express an opinion on the fairness of the presentation of management's description of the service organization's system and on the suitability of the design of the controls to achieve the related control objectives stated in the description, based on the service auditor's examination.

g. A statement that the examination was conducted in accordance with attestation standards established by the American Institute of Certified Public Accountants, and that those standards require the service auditor to plan and perform the examination to obtain reasonable assurance about whether management's description of the service organization's system is fairly presented and the controls are suitably designed as of the specified date to achieve the related control objectives.

h. A statement that the service auditor has not performed any procedures regarding the operating effectiveness of controls and, therefore, expresses no opinion thereon.

i A statement that an examination of management's description of a service organization's system and the suitability of the design of the service organization's controls to achieve the related control objectives stated in the description involves performing procedures to obtain evidence about the fairness of the presentation of the description and the suitability of the design of those controls to achieve the related control objectives stated in the description.

j. A statement that the examination included assessing the risks that management's description of the service organization's system is not fairly presented and that the controls were not suitably designed to achieve the related control objectives.

k. A statement that an examination engagement of this type also includes evaluating the overall presentation of management's description of the service organization's system and suitability of the control objectives stated in the description.

l. A statement that the service auditor believes the examination provides a reasonable basis for his or her opinion.

m. A statement about the inherent limitations of controls, including the risk of projecting to future periods any evaluation of the fairness of the presentation of management's description of the service organization's system or conclusions about the suitability of the design of the controls to achieve the related control objectives.

n. The service auditor's opinion on whether, in all material respects, based on the criteria described in management's assertion,

i. management's description of the service organization's system fairly presents the service organization's system that was designed and implemented as of the specified date.

ii. the controls related to the control objectives stated in management's description of the service organization's system were suitably designed to provide reasonable assurance that those control objectives would be achieved if the controls operated effectively as of the specified date.

iii. if the application of complementary user entity controls is necessary to achieve the related control objectives stated in management's description of the service organization's system, a reference to this condition.

o. A statement restricting the use of the service auditor's report to management of the service organization, user entities of the service organization's system as of the end of the period covered by the service auditor's report, and the independent auditors of such user entities. (Ref: par. .A61–.A64)

p. The date of the service auditor's report.

q. The name of the service auditor and the city and state where the service auditor maintains the office that has responsibility for the engagement.

Report Date

.54 The service auditor should date the service auditor's report no earlier than the date on which the service auditor has obtained sufficient appropriate evidence to support the service auditor's opinion.

Modified Opinions (Ref: par. .A66)

.55 The service auditor's opinion should be modified and the service auditor's report should contain a clear description of all the reasons for the modification, if the service auditor concludes that

a. management's description of the service organization's system is not fairly presented, in all material respects;

b. the controls are not suitably designed to provide reasonable assurance that the control objectives stated in management's description of the service organization's system would be achieved if the controls operated as described;

c. in the case of a type 2 report, the controls did not operate effectively throughout the specified period to achieve the related control objectives stated in management's description of the service organization's system; or

d. the service auditor is unable to obtain sufficient appropriate evidence

.56 If the service auditor plans to disclaim an opinion because of the inability to obtain sufficient appropriate evidence, and, based on the limited procedures performed, has concluded that,

a. certain aspects of management's description of the service organization's system are not fairly presented, in all material respects;

b. certain controls were not suitably designed to provide reasonable assurance that the control objectives stated in management's description of the service organization's system would be achieved if the controls operated as described; or

c. in the case of a type 2 report, certain controls did not operate effectively throughout the specified period to achieve the related control objectives stated in management's description of the service organization's system,

the service auditor should identify these findings in his or her report.

.57 If the service auditor plans to disclaim an opinion, the service auditor should not identify the procedures that were performed nor include statements describing the characteristics of a service auditor's engagement in the service auditor's report; to do so might overshadow the disclaimer.

Other Communication Responsibilities

.58 If the service auditor becomes aware of incidents of noncompliance with laws and regulations, fraud, or uncorrected errors attributable to management or other service organization personnel that are not clearly trivial and that may affect one or more user entities, the service auditor should determine the effect of such incidents on management's description of the service organization's system, the achievement of the control objectives, and the service auditor's report.

Additionally, the service auditor should determine whether this information has been communicated appropriately to affected user entities. If the information has not been so communicated, and management of the service organization is unwilling to do so, the service auditor should take appropriate action. (Ref: par. .A67)

Application and Other Explanatory Material

Scope of This Section

.A1 *Internal control* is a process designed to provide reasonable assurance regarding the achievement of objectives related to the reliability of financial reporting, effectiveness and efficiency of operations, and compliance with applicable laws and regulations. Controls related to a service organization's operations and compliance objectives may be relevant to a user entity's internal control over financial reporting. Such controls may pertain to assertions about presentation and disclosure relating to account balances, classes of transactions or disclosures, or may pertain to evidence that the user auditor evaluates or uses in applying auditing procedures. For example, a payroll processing service organization's controls related to the timely remittance of payroll deductions to government authorities may be relevant to a user entity because late remittances could incur interest and penalties that would result in a liability for the user entity. Similarly, a service organization's controls over the acceptability of investment transactions from a regulatory perspective may be considered relevant to a user entity's presentation and disclosure of transactions and account balances in its financial statements. (Ref: par. .01)

.A2 Paragraph .02 of this section refers to other engagements that the practitioner may perform and report on under section 101 to report on controls at a service organization. Paragraph .02 is not, however, intended to

- provide for the alteration of the definitions of *service organization* and *service organization's system* in paragraph .07 to permit reports issued under this section to include in the description of the service organization's system aspects of their services (including relevant control objectives and related controls) not likely to be relevant to user entities' internal control over financial reporting, or
- permit a report to be issued that combines reporting under this section on a service organization's controls that are likely to be relevant to user entities' internal control over financial reporting, with reporting under section 101 on controls that are not likely to be relevant to user entities' internal control over financial reporting. (Ref: par. .02(a))

.A3 When a service auditor conducts an engagement under section 101 to report on controls at a service organization other than those controls likely to be relevant to user entities' internal control over financial reporting, and the service auditor intends to use the guidance in this section in planning and performing that engagement, the service auditor may encounter issues that differ significantly from those associated with engagements to report on a service organization's controls likely to be relevant to user entities' internal control over financial reporting. For example,

- identification of suitable and available criteria, as prescribed in paragraphs .23–.34 of section 101, for evaluating the fairness of presentation of management's description of the service organization's system and the suitability of the design and the operating effectiveness of the controls.
- identification of appropriate control objectives, and the basis for evaluating the reasonableness of the control objectives in the circumstances of the particular engagement.

- identification of the intended users of the report and the manner in which they intend to use the report.
- relevance and appropriateness of the definitions in paragraph .07 of this section, many of which specifically relate to internal control over financial reporting.
- application of references to auditing standards (AU-C sections) that are intended to provide the service auditor with guidance relevant to internal control over financial reporting.
- application of the concept of materiality in the circumstances of the particular engagement.
- developing the language to be used in the practitioner's report, including addressing paragraphs .84–.87 of section 101, which identify the elements to be included in an examination report. (Ref: par. .02(a))

.A4 When management of the service organization is not responsible for the design of the system, it is unlikely that management of the service organization will be in a position to assert that the system is suitably designed. Controls cannot operate effectively unless they are suitably designed. Because of the inextricable link between the suitability of the design of controls and their operating effectiveness, the absence of an assertion with respect to the suitability of design will likely preclude the service auditor from opining on the operating effectiveness of controls. As an alternative, the practitioner may perform tests of controls in either an agreed-upon procedures engagement under section 201, *Agreed Upon Procedures Engagements*, or an examination of the operating effectiveness of the controls under section 101. (Ref: par. .02(b))

Definitions

Controls at a Service Organization (Ref: par. .07)

.A5 The policies and procedures referred to in the definition of *controls at a service organization* in paragraph .07 include aspects of user entities' information systems maintained by the service organization and may also include aspects of one or more of the other components of internal control at a service organization. For example, the definition of *controls at a service organization* may include aspects of the service organization's control environment, monitoring, and control activities when they relate to the services provided. Such definition does not, however, include controls at a service organization that are not related to the achievement of the control objectives stated in management's description of the service organization's system; for example, controls related to the preparation of the service organization's own financial statements.

Criteria (Ref: par. .07 and .14–.16)

.A6 For the purposes of engagements performed in accordance with this section, criteria need to be available to user entities and their auditors to enable them to understand the basis for the service organization's assertion about the fair presentation of management's description of the service organization's system, the suitability of the design of controls that address control objectives stated in the description of the system and, in the case of a type 2 report, the operating effectiveness of such controls. Information about suitable criteria is provided in paragraphs .23–.34 of section 101. Paragraphs .14–.16 of this section discuss the criteria for evaluating the fairness of the presentation of management's description of the service organization's system and the suitability of the design and operating effectiveness of the controls.

Inclusive Method (Ref: par. .07)

.A7 As indicated in the definition of *inclusive method* in paragraph .07, a service organization that uses a subservice organization presents management's description of the service organization's system to include a description of the services provided by the subservice organization as well as the subservice organization's relevant control objectives and related controls. When the inclusive method is used, the requirements of this section also apply to the services provided by the subservice organization, including the requirement to obtain management's acknowledgement and acceptance of responsibility for the matters in paragraph .09(c)(i)–(vii) as they relate to the subservice organization.

.A8 Performing procedures at the subservice organization entails coordination and communication between the service organization, the subservice organization, and the service auditor. The inclusive method generally is feasible if, for example, the service organization and the subservice organization are related, or if the contract between the service organization and the subservice organization provides for issuance of a service auditor's report. If the service auditor is unable to obtain an assertion from the subservice organization regarding management's description of the service organization's system provided, including the relevant control objectives and related controls at the subservice organization, the service auditor is unable to use the inclusive method but may instead use the carve-out method.

.A9 There may be instances when the service organization's controls, such as monitoring controls, permit the service organization to include in its assertion the relevant aspects of the subservice organization's system, including the relevant control objectives and related controls of the subservice organization. In such instances, the service auditor is basing his or her opinion solely on the controls at the service organization, and hence, the inclusive method is not applicable.

Internal Audit Function (Ref: par. .07)

.A10 The "others" referenced in the definition of *internal audit function* may be individuals who perform activities similar to those performed by internal auditors and include service organization personnel (in addition to internal auditors), and third parties working under the direction of management or those charged with governance.

Service Organization's System (Ref: par. .07)

.A11 The policies and procedures referred to in the definition of *service organization's system* refer to the guidelines and activities for providing transaction processing and other services to user entities and include the infrastructure, software, people, and data that support the policies and procedures.

Management and Those Charged With Governance (Ref: par. .08)

.A12 Management and governance structures vary by entity, reflecting influences such as size and ownership characteristics. Such diversity means that it is not possible for this section to specify for all engagements the person(s) with whom the service auditor is to interact regarding particular matters. For example, the service organization may be a segment of an organization and not a separate legal entity. In such cases, identifying the appropriate management personnel or those charged with governance from whom to request written representations may require the exercise of professional judgment.

Acceptance and Continuance

.A13 If one or more of the conditions in paragraph .09 are not met and the service auditor is nevertheless required by law or regulation to accept or continue an engagement to report on controls at a service organization, the service auditor is required, in accordance with the requirements in paragraphs .55–.56, to determine the effect on the service auditor's report of one or more of such conditions not being met. (Ref: par. .09)

Capabilities and Competence to Perform the Engagement (Ref: par. .09a)

.A14 Relevant capabilities and competence to perform the engagement include matters such as the following:

- Knowledge of the relevant industry
- An understanding of information technology and systems
- Experience in evaluating risks as they relate to the suitable design of controls
- Experience in the design and execution of tests of controls and the evaluation of the results

.A15 In performing a service auditor's engagement, the service auditor need not be independent of each user entity. (Ref: par. .09a)

Management's Responsibility for Documenting the Service Organization's System (Ref: par. .09(c)(i))

.A16 Management of the service organization is responsible for documenting the service organization's system. No one particular form of documentation is prescribed and the extent of documentation may vary depending on the size and complexity of the service organization and its monitoring activities.

Reasonable Basis for Management's Assertion (Ref: par. .07, definition of service organization's system; par. .09(c)(ii) and .14(a)(vii))

.A17 Management's monitoring activities may provide evidence of the design and operating effectiveness of controls in support of management's assertion. *Monitoring of controls* is a process to assess the effectiveness of internal control performance over time. It involves assessing the effectiveness of controls on a timely basis, identifying and reporting deficiencies to appropriate individuals within the service organization, and taking necessary corrective actions. Management accomplishes monitoring of controls through ongoing activities, separate evaluations, or a combination of the two. Ongoing monitoring activities are often built into the normal recurring activities of an entity and include regular management and supervisory activities. Internal auditors or personnel performing similar functions may contribute to the monitoring of a service organization's activities. Monitoring activities may also include using information communicated by external parties, such as customer complaints and regulator comments, which may indicate problems or highlight areas in need of improvement. The greater the degree and effectiveness of ongoing monitoring, the less need for separate evaluations. Usually, some combination of ongoing monitoring and separate evaluations will ensure that internal control maintains its effectiveness over time. The service auditor's report on controls is not a substitute for the service organization's own processes to provide a reasonable basis for its assertion.

Identification of Risks (Ref: par. .09(c)(v))

.A18 Control objectives relate to risks that controls seek to mitigate. For example, the risk that a transaction is recorded at the wrong amount or in the wrong period can be expressed as a control objective that transactions are recorded at the correct amount and in the correct period. Management is responsible for identifying the risks that threaten achievement of the control objectives stated in management's description of the service organization's system. Management may have a formal or informal process for identifying relevant risks. A formal process may include estimating the significance of identified risks, assessing the likelihood of their occurrence, and deciding about actions to address them. However, because control objectives relate to risks that controls seek to mitigate, thoughtful identification by management of control objectives when designing, implementing, and documenting the service organization's system may itself comprise an informal process for identifying relevant risks.

Management's Refusal to Provide a Written Assertion

.A19 A recent change in service organization management or the appointment of the service auditor by a party other than management are examples of situations that may cause management to be unwilling to provide the service auditor with a written assertion. However, other members of management may be in a position to, and will agree to, sign the assertion so that the service auditor can meet the requirement of paragraph .09(c)(vii). (Ref: par. .10)

Request to Change the Scope of the Engagement (Ref: par. .12)

.A20 A request to change the scope of the engagement may not have a reasonable justification if, for example, the request is made

- to exclude certain control objectives at the service organization from the scope of the engagement because of the likelihood that the service auditor's opinion would be modified with respect to those control objectives.
- to prevent the disclosure of deviations identified at a subservice organization by requesting a change from the inclusive method to the carve-out method.

.A21 A request to change the scope of the engagement may have a reasonable justification when, for example, the request is made to exclude from the engagement a subservice organization because the service organization cannot arrange for access by the service auditor, and the method used for addressing the services provided by that subservice organization is changed from the inclusive method to the carve-out method.

Assessing the Suitability of the Criteria (Ref: par. .13–.16)

.A22 Section 101 requires a practitioner, among other things, to determine whether the subject matter is capable of evaluation against criteria that are suitable and available to users. As indicated in paragraph .27 of section 101, regardless of who establishes or develops the criteria, management is responsible for selecting the criteria and for determining whether the criteria are appropriate. The subject matter is the underlying condition of interest to intended users of an attestation report. The following table identifies the subject matter and minimum criteria for each of the opinions in type 2 and type 1 reports.

	Subject Matter	*Criteria*	*Comment*
Opinion on the fair presentation of management's description of the service organization's system (type 1 and type 2 reports).	Management's description of the service organization's system that is likely to be relevant to user entities' internal control over financial reporting and is covered by the service auditor's report, and management's assertion about whether the description is fairly presented.	Management's description of the service organization's system is fairly presented if it *a.* presents how the service organization's system was designed and implemented including, as appropriate, the matters identified in paragraph .14(a) and, in the case of a type 2 report, includes relevant details of changes to the service organization's system during the period covered by the description. *b.* does not omit or distort information relevant to the service organization's system, while acknowledging that management's description of the service organization's system is prepared to meet the common needs of a broad range of user entities and may not, therefore, include every aspect of the service organization's system that each individual user entity may consider important in its own particular environment.	The specific wording of the criteria for this opinion may need to be tailored to be consistent with criteria established by, for example, law, regulation, user groups, or a professional body. Criteria for evaluating management's description of the service organization's system are provided in paragraph .14. Paragraphs .19–.20 and .A31–.A33 offer further guidance on determining whether these criteria are met.

(continued)

	Subject Matter	*Criteria*	*Comment*	
Opinion on suitability of design and operating effectiveness (type 2 reports).	The design and operating effectiveness of the controls that are necessary to achieve the control objectives stated in management's description of the service organization's system.	The controls are suitably designed and operating effectively to achieve the control objectives stated in management's description of the service organization's system if *a.* management has identified the risks that threaten the achievement of the control objectives stated in management's description of the service organization's system. *b.* the controls identified in management's description of the service organization's system would, if operating as described, provide reasonable assurance that those risks would not prevent the control objectives stated in the description from being achieved. *c.* the controls were consistently applied as designed throughout the specified period. This includes whether manual controls were applied by individuals who have the appropriate competence and authority.	When the criteria for this opinion are met, controls will have provided reasonable assurance that the related control objectives stated in management's description of the service organization's system were achieved throughout the specified period.	The control objectives stated in management's description of the service organization's system are part of the criteria for these opinions. The control objectives stated in the description will differ from engagement to engagement. If the service auditor concludes that the control objectives stated in the description are not fairly presented, then those control objectives would not be suitable as part of the criteria for forming an opinion on the design and operating effectiveness of the controls.

	Subject Matter	Criteria	Comment
Opinion on suitability of design (type 1 reports).	The suitability of the design of the controls necessary to achieve the control objectives stated in management's description of the service organization's system and relevant to the services covered by the service auditor's report.	The controls are suitably designed to achieve the control objectives stated in management's description of the service organization's system if *a.* management has identified the risks that threaten the achievement of the control objectives stated in its description of the service organization's system. *b.* the controls identified in management's description of the service organization's system would, if operating as described, provide reasonable assurance that those risks would not prevent the control objectives stated in the description from being achieved.	Meeting these criteria does not, of itself, provide any assurance that the control objectives stated in management's description of the service organization's system were achieved because no evidence has been obtained about the operating effectiveness of the controls.

.A23 Paragraph .14(a) identifies a number of elements that are included in management's description of the service organization's system as appropriate. These elements may not be appropriate if the system being described is not a system that processes transactions; for example, if the system relates to general controls over the hosting of an IT application but not the controls embedded in the application itself. (Ref: par. .14)

.A24 The requirement to include in management's description of the service organization's system "other aspects of the service organization's control environment, risk assessment process, information and communication systems (including the related business processes), control activities, and monitoring controls, that are relevant to the services provided" is also applicable to the internal control components of subservice organizations used by the service organization when the inclusive method is used. See AU-C section 315, *Understanding the Entity and Its Environment and Assessing the Risks of Material Misstatement*, for a discussion of these components. (Ref: par. .14(a)(vii)) [Revised, December 2012, to reflect conforming changes necessary due to the issuance of SAS Nos. 122–126.]

Materiality (Ref: par. .17)

.A25 In an engagement to report on controls at a service organization, the concept of materiality relates to the information being reported on, not the financial statements of user entities. The service auditor plans and performs procedures to determine whether management's description of the service organization's system is fairly presented, in all material respects; whether controls at the service organization are suitably designed in all material respects to achieve the control objectives stated in the description; and in the case of a type 2 report, whether controls at the service organization operated effectively throughout the specified period in all material respects to achieve the control objectives stated in the description. The concept of materiality takes into account that the service auditor's report provides information about the service organization's system to meet the common information needs of a broad range of user entities and their auditors who have an understanding of the manner in which the system is being used by a particular user entity for financial reporting.

.A26 Materiality with respect to the fair presentation of management's description of the service organization's system and with respect to the design of controls primarily includes the consideration of qualitative factors; for example, whether

- management's description of the service organization's system includes the significant aspects of the processing of significant transactions.
- management's description of the service organization's system omits or distorts relevant information.
- the controls have the ability, as designed, to provide reasonable assurance that the control objectives stated in management's description of the service organization's system would be achieved.

Materiality with respect to the operating effectiveness of controls includes the consideration of both quantitative and qualitative factors; for example, the tolerable rate and observed rate of deviation (a quantitative matter) and the nature and cause of any observed deviations (a qualitative matter).

.A27 The concept of materiality is not applied when disclosing, in the description of the tests of controls, the results of those tests when deviations have been identified. This is because, in the particular circumstances of a specific user entity or user auditor, a deviation may have significance beyond whether or not, in the opinion of the service auditor, it prevents a control from operating effectively. For example, the control to which the deviation relates may be particularly significant in preventing a certain type of error that may be material in the particular circumstances of a user entity's financial statements.

Obtaining an Understanding of the Service Organization's System (Ref: par. .18)

.A28 Obtaining an understanding of the service organization's system, including related controls, assists the service auditor in the following:

- Identifying the boundaries of the system and how it interfaces with other systems
- Assessing whether management's description of the service organization's system fairly presents the service organization's system that has been designed and implemented
- Determining which controls are necessary to achieve the control objectives stated in management's description of the service organization's system, whether controls were suitably designed to achieve those control objectives, and, in the case of a type 2 report, whether controls were operating effectively throughout the period to achieve those control objectives

.A29 Management's description of the service organization's system includes "aspects of the service organization's control environment, risk assessment process, information and communication systems (including relevant business processes), control activities and monitoring activities that are relevant to the services provided." Although aspects of the service organization's control environment, risk assessment process, and monitoring activities may not be presented in the description in the context of control objectives, they may nevertheless be necessary to achieve the specified control objectives stated in the description. Likewise, deficiencies in these controls may have an effect on the service auditor's assessment of whether the controls, taken as a whole, were suitably designed or operating effectively to achieve the specified control objectives. See AU-C section 315 for a discussion of these components of internal control. [Revised, December 2012, to reflect conforming changes necessary due to the issuance of SAS Nos. 122–126.]

.A30 The service auditor's procedures to obtain the understanding referred to in paragraph .A28 may include the following:

- Inquiring of management and others within the service organization who, in the service auditor's judgment, may have relevant information
- Observing operations and inspecting documents, reports, and printed and electronic records of transaction processing
- Inspecting a selection of agreements between the service organization and user entities to identify their common terms
- Reperforming the application of a control

One or more of the preceding procedures may be accomplished through the performance of a walkthrough.

Obtaining Evidence Regarding Management's Description of the Service Organization's System (Ref: par. .19–.20)

.A31 In a service auditor's examination engagement, the service auditor plans and performs the engagement to obtain reasonable assurance of detecting errors or omissions in management's description of the service organization's system and instances in which control objectives were not achieved. Absolute assurance is not attainable because of factors such as the need for judgment, the use of sampling, and the inherent limitations of controls at the service organization that affect whether the description is fairly presented and the controls are suitably designed and operating effectively to achieve the control objectives, and because much of the evidence available to the service auditor is persuasive rather than conclusive in nature. Also, procedures that are effective for detecting unintentional errors or omissions in the description, and instances in which control objectives were not achieved, may be ineffective for detecting intentional errors or omissions in the description and instances in which the control objectives were not achieved that are concealed through collusion between service organization personnel and a third party or among management or employees of the service organization. Therefore, the subsequent discovery of the existence of material omissions or errors in the description or instances in which control objectives were not achieved does not, in and of itself, evidence inadequate planning, performance, or judgment on the part of the service auditor. (Ref: par. .27)

.A32 Considering the following questions may assist the service auditor in determining whether management's description of the service organization's system is fairly presented, in all material respects:

- Does management's description address the major aspects of the service provided and included in the scope of the engagement that could reasonably be expected to be relevant to the common needs of a broad range of user auditors in planning their audits of user entities' financial statements?

- Is the description prepared at a level of detail that could reasonably be expected to provide a broad range of user auditors with sufficient information to obtain an understanding of internal control in accordance with AU-C section 315? The description need not address every aspect of the service organization's processing or the services provided to user entities and need not be so detailed that it would potentially enable a reader to compromise security or other controls at the service organization.
- Is the description prepared in a manner that does not omit or distort information that might affect the decisions of a broad range of user auditors; for example, does the description contain any significant omissions or inaccuracies regarding processing of which the service auditor is aware?
- Does the description include relevant details of changes to the service organization's system during the period covered by the description when the description covers a period of time?
- Have the controls identified in the description actually been implemented?
- Are complementary user entity controls, if any, adequately described? In most cases, the control objectives stated in the description are worded so that they are capable of being achieved through the effective operation of controls implemented by the service organization alone. In some cases, however, the control objectives stated in the description cannot be achieved by the service organization alone because their achievement requires particular controls to be implemented by user entities. This may be the case when, for example, the control objectives are specified by a regulatory authority. When the description does include complementary user entity controls, the description separately identifies those controls along with the specific control objectives that cannot be achieved by the service organization alone. (Ref: par. .19(c))
- If the inclusive method has been used, does the description separately identify controls at the service organization and controls at the subservice organization? If the carve-out method is used, does the description identify the functions that are performed by the subservice organization? When the carve-out method is used, the description need not describe the detailed processing or controls at the subservice organization.

[Revised, December 2012, to reflect conforming changes necessary due to the issuance of SAS Nos. 122–126.]

.A33 The service auditor's procedures to evaluate the fair presentation of management's description of the service organization's system may include the following:

- Considering the nature of the user entities and how the services provided by the service organization are likely to affect them; for example, the predominant types of user entities, and whether the user entities are regulated by government agencies
- Reading contracts with user entities to gain an understanding of the service organization's contractual obligations

- Observing procedures performed by service organization personnel
- Reviewing the service organization's policy and procedure manuals and other documentation of the system; for example, flowcharts and narratives
- Performing walkthroughs of transactions through the service organization's system

.A34 Paragraph .19(a) requires the service auditor to evaluate whether the control objectives stated in management's description of the service organization's system are reasonable in the circumstances. Considering the following questions may assist the service auditor in this evaluation:

- Have the control objectives stated in the description been specified by the service organization or by outside parties, such as regulatory authorities, a user group, a professional body, or others?
- Do the control objectives stated in the description and specified by the service organization relate to the types of assertions commonly embodied in the broad range of user entities' financial statements to which controls at the service organization could reasonably be expected to relate (for example, assertions about existence and accuracy that are affected by access controls that prevent or detect unauthorized access to the system)? Although the service auditor ordinarily will not be able to determine how controls at a service organization specifically relate to the assertions embodied in individual user entities' financial statements, the service auditor's understanding of the nature of the service organization's system, including controls, and the services being provided is used to identify the types of assertions to which those controls are likely to relate.
- Are the control objectives stated in the description and specified by the service organization complete? Although a complete set of control objectives can provide a broad range of user auditors with a framework to assess the effect of controls at the service organization on assertions commonly embodied in user entities' financial statements, the service auditor ordinarily will not be able to determine how controls at a service organization specifically relate to the assertions embodied in individual user entities' financial statements and cannot, therefore, determine whether control objectives are complete from the viewpoint of individual user entities or user auditors. It is the responsibility of individual user entities or user auditors to assess whether the service organization's description addresses the particular control objectives that are relevant to their needs. If the control objectives are specified by an outside party, including control objectives specified by law or regulation, the outside party is responsible for their completeness and reasonableness. (Ref: par. .19(a))

.A35 The service auditor's procedures to determine whether the system described by the service organization has been implemented may be similar to, and performed in conjunction with, procedures to obtain an understanding of that system. Other procedures that the service auditor may use in combination with inquiry of management and other service organization personnel include observation, inspection of records and other documentation, as well as reperformance of the manner in which transactions are processed through the system and controls are applied. (Ref: par. .19(b) and .20)

Obtaining Evidence Regarding the Design of Controls (Ref: par. .21)

.A36 The risks and control objectives identified in paragraph .21(a) encompass intentional and unintentional acts that threaten the achievement of the control objectives. (Ref: par. .21(a))

.A37 From the viewpoint of a user auditor, a control is suitably designed to achieve the control objectives stated in management's description of the service organization's system if individually or in combination with other controls, it would, when complied with satisfactorily, provide reasonable assurance that material misstatements are prevented, or detected and corrected. A service auditor, however, is not aware of the circumstances at individual user entities that would affect whether or not a misstatement resulting from a control deficiency is material to those user entities. Therefore, from the viewpoint of a service auditor, a control is suitably designed if individually or in combination with other controls, it would, when complied with satisfactorily, provide reasonable assurance that the control objective(s) stated in the description of the service organization's system are achieved.

.A38 A service auditor may consider using flowcharts, questionnaires, or decision tables to facilitate understanding the design of the controls.

.A39 Controls may consist of a number of activities directed at the achievement of various control objectives. Consequently, if the service auditor evaluates certain activities as being ineffective in achieving a particular control objective, the existence of other activities may allow the service auditor to conclude that controls related to the control objective are suitably designed to achieve the control objective.

Obtaining Evidence Regarding the Operating Effectiveness of Controls (Ref: par. .22–.27)

.A40 From the viewpoint of a user auditor, a control is operating effectively if individually or in combination with other controls, it provides reasonable assurance that material misstatements whether due to fraud or error are prevented, or detected and corrected. A service auditor, however, is not aware of the circumstances at individual user entities that would affect whether or not a misstatement resulting from a control deviation is material to those user entities. Therefore, from the viewpoint of a service auditor, a control is operating effectively if individually or in combination with other controls, it provides reasonable assurance that the control objectives stated in management's description of the service organization's system are achieved. Similarly, a service auditor is not in a position to determine whether any observed control deviation would result in a material misstatement from the viewpoint of an individual user entity. (Ref: par. .22)

.A41 Obtaining an understanding of controls sufficient to opine on the suitability of their design is not sufficient evidence regarding their operating effectiveness unless some automation provides for the consistent operation of the controls as they were designed and implemented. For example, obtaining information about the implementation of a manual control at a point in time does not provide evidence about operation of the control at other times. However, because of the inherent consistency of IT processing, performing procedures to determine the design of an automated control and whether it has been implemented may serve as evidence of that control's operating effectiveness, depending on the service auditor's assessment and testing of controls such as those over program changes. (Ref: par. .22)

.A42 A type 2 report that covers a period that is less than six months is unlikely to be useful to user entities and their auditors. If management's description of the service organization's system covers a period that is less than six months, the description may describe the reasons for the shorter period and the service auditor's report may include that information as well. Circumstances that may result in a report covering a period of less than six months include the following:

- The service auditor was engaged close to the date by which the report on controls is to be issued, and controls cannot be tested for operating effectiveness for a six month period.
- The service organization or a particular system or application has been in operation for less than six months.
- Significant changes have been made to the controls, and it is not practicable either to wait six months before issuing a report or to issue a report covering the system both before and after the changes. (Ref: par. .23)

.A43 Evidence about the satisfactory operation of controls in prior periods does not provide evidence of the operating effectiveness of controls during the current period. The service auditor expresses an opinion on the effectiveness of controls throughout each period; therefore, sufficient appropriate evidence about the operating effectiveness of controls throughout the current period is required for the service auditor to express that opinion for the current period. Knowledge of deviations observed in prior engagements may, however, lead the service auditor to increase the extent of testing during the current period. (Ref: par. .22)

.A44 Determining the effect of changes in the service organization's controls that were implemented during the period covered by the service auditor's report involves gathering information about the nature and extent of such changes, how they affect processing at the service organization, and how they might affect assertions in the user entities' financial statements. (Ref: par. .14(b) and .23)

.A45 Certain controls may not leave evidence of their operation that can be tested at a later date and, accordingly, the service auditor may find it appropriate to test the operating effectiveness of such controls at various times throughout the reporting period. (Ref: par. .22)

Using the Work of an Internal Audit Function

Obtaining an Understanding of the Internal Audit Function (Ref: par. .28)

.A46 An internal audit function may be responsible for providing analyses, evaluations, assurances, recommendations, and other information to management and those charged with governance. An internal audit function at a service organization may perform activities related to the service organization's internal control or activities related to the services and systems, including controls that the service organization provides to user entities.

.A47 The scope and objectives of an internal audit function vary widely and depend on the size and structure of the service organization and the requirements of management and those charged with governance. Internal audit function activities may include one or more of the following:

- Monitoring the service organization's internal control or the application processing systems. This may include controls relevant to the services provided to user entities. The internal audit function may be assigned specific responsibility for reviewing controls, monitoring their operation, and recommending improvements thereto.
- Examination of financial and operating information. The internal audit function may be assigned to review the means by which the service organization identifies, measures, classifies, and reports financial and operating information; to make inquiries about specific matters; and to perform other procedures including detailed testing of transactions, balances, and procedures.
- Evaluation of the economy, efficiency, and effectiveness of operating activities including nonfinancial activities of the service organization.
- Evaluation of compliance with laws, regulations, and other external requirements and with management policies, directives, and other internal requirements.

Using the Work of the Internal Audit Function (Ref: par .31–.32)

.A48 The nature, timing, and extent of the service auditor's procedures on specific work of the internal auditors will depend on the service auditor's assessment of the significance of that work to the service auditor's conclusions (for example, the significance of the risks that the controls tend to mitigate), the evaluation of the internal audit function, and the evaluation of the specific work of the internal auditors. Such procedures may include the following:

- Examination of items already examined by the internal auditors
- Examination of other similar items
- Observation of procedures performed by the internal auditors

Effect on the Service Auditor's Report (Ref: par. .33–.34)

.A49 The responsibility to report on management's description of the service organization's system and the suitability of the design and operating effectiveness of controls rests solely with the service auditor and cannot be shared with the internal audit function. Therefore, the judgments about the significance of deviations in the design or operating effectiveness of controls, the sufficiency of tests performed, the evaluation of identified deficiencies, and other matters affecting the service auditor's report are those of the service auditor. In making judgments about the extent of the effect of the work of the internal audit function on the service auditor's procedures, the service auditor may determine, based on risk associated with the controls and the significance of the judgments relating to them, that the service auditor will perform the work relating to some or all of the controls rather than using the work performed by the internal audit function.

.A50 In the case of a type 2 report, when the work of the internal audit function has been used in performing tests of controls, the service auditor's description of that work and of the service auditor's procedures with respect to that work may be presented in a number of ways, for example, (Ref: par. .34 and .52(o)(i))

- by including introductory material to the description of tests of controls indicating that certain work of the internal audit function was used in performing tests of controls.

- attribution of individual tests to internal audit.

Written Representations (Ref: par. .36–.39)

.A51 Written representations reaffirming the service organization's assertion about the effective operation of controls may be based on ongoing monitoring activities, separate evaluations, or a combination of the two. (Ref: par. .A12)

.A52 In certain circumstances, a service auditor may obtain written representations from parties in addition to management of the service organization, such as those charged with governance.

.A53 The written representations required by paragraph .36 are separate from and in addition to the assertion included in or attached to management's description of the service organization's system required by paragraph .09(c)(vii).

.A54 If the service auditor is unable to obtain written representations regarding relevant control objectives and related controls at the subservice organization, management of the service organization would be unable to use the inclusive method but could use the carve-out method.

.A55 In addition to the written representations required by paragraph .36, the service auditor may consider it necessary to request other written representations.

Other Information

.A56 The "other information" referred to in paragraphs .40–.41 may be the following:

- Information provided by the service organization and included in a section of the service auditor's type 1 or type 2 report, or
- Information outside the service auditor's type 1 or type 2 report included in a document that contains the service auditor's report. This other information may be provided by the service organization or by another party. (Ref: par. .40, .52(c)(ii)–(iii), and .53(c)(ii)–(iii))

.A57 If other information included in a document containing management's description of the service organization's system and the service auditor's report contains future-oriented information that cannot be reasonably substantiated, the service auditor may request that the information be removed or revised. (Ref: par. .41)

Documentation

.A58 Paragraph 57 of Statement on Quality Control Standards No. 8, *A Firm's System of Quality Control*, requires the firm to establish policies and procedures that address engagement performance, supervision responsibilities, and review responsibilities. The requirement to document who reviewed the work performed and the extent of the review, in accordance with the firm's policies and procedures addressing review responsibilities, does not imply a need for each specific working paper to include evidence of review. The requirement, however, means documenting what work was reviewed, who reviewed such work, and when it was reviewed. (Ref: par. .44)

Preparing the Service Auditor's Report

Content of the Service Auditor's Report (Ref: par. .52–.53)

.A59 Examples of service auditors' reports are presented in appendixes A–C and illustrative assertions by management of the service organization are presented in exhibit A.

.A60 The service organization's assertion may be presented in management's description of the service organization's system or may be attached to the description. (Ref: par. .52(e) and .53(e))

Use of the Service Auditor's Report (Ref: par. .52(p) and .53(o))

.A61 Paragraph .79 of section 101 requires that the use of a practitioner's report be restricted to specified parties when the criteria used to evaluate or measure the subject matter are available only to specified parties or appropriate only for a limited number of parties who either participated in their establishment or can be presumed to have an adequate understanding of the criteria. The criteria used for engagements to report on controls at a service organization are relevant only for the purpose of providing information about the service organization's system, including controls, to those who have an understanding of how the system is used for financial reporting by user entities and, accordingly, the service auditor's report states that the report and the description of tests of controls are intended only for use by management of the service organization, user entities of the service organization ("during some or all of the period covered by the report" for a type 2 report, and "as of the ending date of the period covered by the report" for a type 1 report), and their user auditors. (The illustrative service auditor's reports in appendix A illustrate language for a paragraph restricting the use of a service auditor's report.)

.A62 Paragraph .79 of section 101 indicates that the need for restriction on the use of a report may result from a number of circumstances, including the potential for the report to be misunderstood when taken out of the context in which it was intended to be used, and the extent to which the procedures performed are known or understood.

.A63 Although a service auditor is not responsible for controlling a service organization's distribution of a service auditor's report, a service auditor may inform the service organization of the following:

- A service auditor's type 1 report is not intended for distribution to parties other than the service organization, user entities of the service organization's system as of the end of the period covered by the service auditor's report, and their user auditors.
- A service auditor's type 2 report is not intended for distribution to parties other than the service organization, user entities of the service organization's system during some or all of the period covered by the service auditor's report, and their user auditors.

.A64 A user entity is also considered a user entity of the service organization's subservice organizations if controls at subservice organizations are relevant to internal control over financial reporting of the user entity. In such case, the user entity is referred to as an indirect or downstream user entity of the subservice organization. Consequently, an indirect or downstream user entity may be included in the group to whom use of the service auditor's report is restricted if controls at the service organization are relevant to internal control over financial reporting of such indirect or downstream user entity.

Description of the Service Auditor's Tests of Controls and the Results Thereof (Ref: par. .52(o)(ii))

.A65 In describing the service auditor's tests of controls for a type 2 report, it assists readers if the service auditor's report includes information about causative factors for identified deviations, to the extent the service auditor has identified such factors.

Modified Opinions (Ref: par. .55–.57)

.A66 Examples of elements of modified service auditor's reports are presented in appendix B.

Other Communication Responsibilities (Ref: par. .58)

.A67 Actions that a service auditor may take when he or she becomes aware of noncompliance with laws and regulations, fraud, or uncorrected errors at the service organization (after giving additional consideration to instances in which the service organization has not appropriately communicated this information to affected user entities, and the service organization is unwilling to do so) include the following:

- Obtaining legal advice about the consequences of different courses of action
- Communicating with those charged with governance of the service organization
- Disclaiming an opinion, modifying the service auditor's opinion, or adding an emphasis paragraph
- Communicating with third parties, for example, a regulator, when required to do so
- Withdrawing from the engagement

.A68

Appendix A: Illustrative Service Auditor's Reports

The following illustrative reports are for guidance only and are not intended to be exhaustive or applicable to all situations.

Example 1: Type 2 Service Auditor's Report

Independent Service Auditor's Report on a Description of a Service Organization's System and the Suitability of the Design and Operating Effectiveness of Controls

To: XYZ Service Organization

Scope

We have examined XYZ Service Organization's description of its [*type or name of*] system for processing user entities' transactions [*or identification of the function performed by the system*] throughout the period [*date*] to [*date*] (description) and the suitability of the design and operating effectiveness of controls to achieve the related control objectives stated in the description.

Service organization's responsibilities

On page XX of the description, XYZ Service Organization has provided an assertion about the fairness of the presentation of the description and suitability of the design and operating effectiveness of the controls to achieve the related control objectives stated in the description. XYZ Service Organization is responsible for preparing the description and for the assertion, including the completeness, accuracy, and method of presentation of the description and the assertion, providing the services covered by the description, specifying the control objectives and stating them in the description, identifying the risks that threaten the achievement of the control objectives, selecting the criteria, and designing, implementing, and documenting controls to achieve the related control objectives stated in the description.

Service auditor's responsibilities

Our responsibility is to express an opinion on the fairness of the presentation of the description and on the suitability of the design and operating effectiveness of the controls to achieve the related control objectives stated in the description, based on our examination. We conducted our examination in accordance with attestation standards established by the American Institute of Certified Public Accountants. Those standards require that we plan and perform our examination to obtain reasonable assurance about whether, in all material respects, the description is fairly presented and the controls were suitably designed and operating effectively to achieve the related control objectives stated in the description throughout the period [*date*] to [*date*].

An examination of a description of a service organization's system and the suitability of the design and operating effectiveness of the service organization's controls to achieve the related control objectives stated in the description involves performing procedures to obtain evidence about the fairness of the presentation of the description and the suitability of the design and operating effectiveness of those controls to achieve the related control objectives stated in the description. Our procedures included assessing the risks that the description is not fairly presented and that the controls were not suitably designed or operating effectively to achieve the related control objectives stated in the description. Our procedures also included testing the operating effectiveness of those controls that we consider necessary to provide reasonable assurance that the related control objectives stated in the description were achieved. An examination engagement of this type also includes evaluating the overall presentation of the description and the suitability of the control objectives stated therein, and the suitability of the criteria specified by the service organization and described at page *[aa]*. We believe that the evidence we obtained is sufficient and appropriate to provide a reasonable basis for our opinion.

Inherent limitations

Because of their nature, controls at a service organization may not prevent, or detect and correct, all errors or omissions in processing or reporting transactions [*or identification of the function performed by the system*]. Also, the projection to the future of any evaluation of the fairness of the presentation of the description, or conclusions about the suitability of the design or operating effectiveness of the controls to achieve the related control objectives is subject to the risk that controls at a service organization may become inadequate or fail.

Opinion

In our opinion, in all material respects, based on the criteria described in XYZ Service Organization's assertion on page [*aa*],

a. the description fairly presents the [*type or name of*] system that was designed and implemented throughout the period [*date*] to [*date*].

b. the controls related to the control objectives stated in the description were suitably designed to provide reasonable assurance that the control objectives would be achieved if the controls operated effectively throughout the period [*date*] to [*date*].

c. the controls tested, which were those necessary to provide reasonable assurance that the control objectives stated in the description were achieved, operated effectively throughout the period [*date*] to [*date*].

Description of tests of controls

The specific controls tested and the nature, timing, and results of those tests are listed on pages [*yy–zz*].

Restricted use

This report, including the description of tests of controls and results thereof on pages [*yy–zz*], is intended solely for the information and use of XYZ Service Organization, user entities of XYZ Service Organization's [*type or name of*] system during some or all of the period [*date*] to [*date*], and the independent auditors of such user entities, who have a sufficient understanding to consider it, along with other information including information about controls implemented by user entities themselves, when assessing the risks of material misstatements of user entities' financial statements. This report is not intended to be and should not be used by anyone other than these specified parties.

[*Service auditor's signature*]

[*Date of the service auditor's report*]

[*Service auditor's city and state*]

Following is a modification of the scope paragraph in a type 2 service auditor's report if the description refers to the need for complementary user entity controls. (New language is shown in boldface italics):

> We have examined XYZ Service Organization's description of its [*type or name of*] system for processing user entities' transactions [*or identification of the function performed by the system*] throughout the period [*date*] to [*date*] (description) and the suitability of the design and operating effectiveness of controls to achieve the related control objectives stated in the description. ***The description indicates that certain control objectives specified in the description can be achieved only if complementary user entity controls contemplated in the design of XYZ Service Organization's controls are suitably designed and operating effectively, along with related controls at the service organization. We have not evaluated the suitability of the design or operating effectiveness of such complementary user entity controls.***

Following is a modification of the applicable subparagraphs of the opinion paragraph of a type 2 service auditor's report if the application of complementary user entity controls is necessary to achieve the related control objectives stated in the description of the service organization's system (New language is shown in boldface italics):

> *b.* The controls related to the control objectives stated in the description were suitably designed to provide reasonable assurance that those control objectives would be achieved if the controls operated effectively throughout the period [*date*] to [*date*] ***and user entities applied the complementary user entity controls contemplated in the design of XYZ Service Organization's controls throughout the period [date] to [date].***
>
> *c.* The controls tested, which ***together with the complementary user entity controls referred to in the scope paragraph of this report, if operating effectively,*** were those necessary to provide reasonable assurance that the control objectives stated in the description were achieved, operated effectively throughout the period [*date*] to [*date*].

Following is a modification of the paragraph that describes the responsibilities of management of the service organization for use in a type 2 service auditor's report when the control objectives have been specified by an outside party. (New language is shown in boldface italics):

> On page XX of the description, XYZ Service Organization has provided an assertion about the fairness of the presentation of the description and suitability of the design and operating effectiveness of the controls to achieve the related control objectives stated in the description. XYZ Service Organization is responsible for preparing the description and for its assertion], including the completeness, accuracy, and method of presentation of the description and assertion, providing the services covered by the description, selecting the criteria, and designing, implementing, and documenting controls to achieve the related control objectives stated in the description. ***The control objectives have been specified by [name of party specifying the control objectives] and are stated on page [aa] of the description.***

Example 2: Type 1 Service Auditor's Report

Independent Service Auditor's Report on a Description of a Service Organization's System and the Suitability of the Design of Controls

To: XYZ Service Organization

Scope

We have examined XYZ Service Organization's description of its [*type or name of*] system for processing user entities' transactions [*or identification of the function performed by the system*] as of [*date*], and the suitability of the design of controls to achieve the related control objectives stated in the description.

Service organization's responsibilities

On page XX of the description, XYZ Service Organization has provided an assertion about the fairness of the presentation of the description and suitability of the design of the controls to achieve the related control objectives stated in the description. XYZ Service Organization is responsible for preparing the description and for its assertion, including the completeness, accuracy, and method of presentation of the description and the assertion, providing the services covered by the description, specifying the control objectives and stating them in the description, identifying the risks that threaten the achievement of the control objectives, selecting the criteria, and designing, implementing, and documenting controls to achieve the related control objectives stated in the description.

Service auditor's responsibilities

Our responsibility is to express an opinion on the fairness of the presentation of the description and on the suitability of the design of the controls to achieve the related control objectives stated in the description, based on our examination. We conducted our examination in accordance with attestation standards established by the American Institute of Certified Public Accountants. Those standards require that we plan and perform our examination to obtain reasonable assurance, in all material respects, about whether the description is fairly presented and the controls were suitably designed to achieve the related control objectives stated in the description as of [*date*].

An examination of a description of a service organization's system and the suitability of the design of the service organization's controls to achieve the related control objectives stated in the description involves performing procedures to obtain evidence about the fairness of the presentation of the description of the system and the suitability of the design of the controls to achieve the related control objectives stated in the description. Our procedures included assessing the risks that the description is not fairly presented and that the controls were not suitably designed to achieve the related control objectives stated in the description. An examination engagement of this type also includes evaluating the overall presentation of the description and the suitability of the control objectives stated therein, and the suitability of the criteria specified by the service organization and described at page *[aa]*.

We did not perform any procedures regarding the operating effectiveness of the controls stated in the description and, accordingly, do not express an opinion thereon.

We believe that the evidence we obtained is sufficient and appropriate to provide a reasonable basis for our opinion.

Inherent limitations

Because of their nature, controls at a service organization may not prevent, or detect and correct, all errors or omissions in processing or reporting transactions [*or identification of the function performed by the system*]. The projection to the future of any evaluation of the fairness of the presentation of the description, or any conclusions about the suitability of the design of the controls to achieve the related control objectives is subject to the risk that controls at a service organization may become ineffective or fail.

Opinion

In our opinion, in all material respects, based on the criteria described in XYZ Service Organization's assertion,

a. the description fairly presents the [*type or name of*] system that was designed and implemented as of [*date*], and

b. the controls related to the control objectives stated in the description were suitably designed to provide reasonable assurance that the control objectives would be achieved if the controls operated effectively as of [*date*].

Restricted use

This report is intended solely for the information and use of XYZ Service Organization, user entities of XYZ Service Organization's [*type or name of*] system as of [*date*], and the independent auditors of such user entities, who have a sufficient understanding to consider it, along with other information including information about controls implemented by user entities themselves, when obtaining an understanding of user entities information and communication systems relevant to financial reporting. This report is not intended to be and should not be used by anyone other than these specified parties.

[*Service auditor's signature*]

[*Date of the service auditor's report*]

[*Service auditor's city and state*]

Following is a modification of the scope paragraph in a type 1 report if the description of the service organization's system refers to the need for complementary user entity controls. (New language is shown in boldface italics)

> We have examined XYZ Service Organization's description of its [type or name of] system (description) made available to user entities of the system for processing their transactions [or identification of the function performed by the system] as of [date], and the suitability of the design of controls to achieve the related control objectives stated in the description. ***The description indicates that certain complementary user entity controls must be suitably designed and implemented at user entities for related controls at the service organization to be considered suitably designed to achieve the related control objectives. We have not evaluated the suitability of the design or operating effectiveness of such complementary user entity controls.***

Following is a modification of the applicable subparagraph in the opinion paragraph of a type 1 report if the application of complementary user entity controls is necessary to achieve the related control objectives stated in management's description of the service organization's system (New language is shown in boldface italics):

> *b.* The controls related to the control objectives stated in the description were suitably designed to provide reasonable assurance that those control objectives would be achieved if the controls operated effectively as of [*date*] ***and user entities applied the complementary user entity controls contemplated in the design of XYZ Service Organization's controls as of [date].***

Following is a modification of the paragraph that describes management of XYZ Service Organization's responsibilities to be used in a type 1 report when the control objectives have been specified by an outside party. (New language is shown in boldface italics):

> On page XX of the description, XYZ Service Organization has provided an assertion about the fairness of the presentation of the description and suitability of the design of the controls to achieve the related control objectives stated in the description. XYZ Service Organization is responsible for preparing the description and assertion, including the completeness, accuracy, and method of presentation of the description and assertion, providing the services covered by the description, selecting the criteria, and designing, implementing, and documenting controls to achieve the related control objectives stated in the description. ***The control objectives have been specified by [name of party specifying the control objectives] and are stated on page [aa] of the description***.

.A69

Appendix B: Illustrative Modified Service Auditor's Reports

The following examples of modified service auditor's reports are for guidance only and are not intended to be exhaustive or applicable to all situations. They are based on the illustrative reports in appendix A.

Example 1: Qualified Opinion for a Type 2 Report—The Description of the Service Organization's System is Not Fairly Presented in All Material Respects

The following is an illustrative paragraph describing the basis for the qualified opinion. The paragraph would be inserted before the modified opinion paragraph. All other report paragraphs are unchanged.

Basis for qualified opinion

The accompanying description states on page [*mn*] that XYZ Service Organization uses operator identification numbers and passwords to prevent unauthorized access to the system. Based on inquiries of staff personnel and observation of activities, we have determined that operator identification numbers and passwords are employed in applications A and B but are not required to access the system in applications C and D.

Opinion

In our opinion, except for the matter described in the preceding paragraph, and based on the criteria described in XYZ Service Organization's assertion on page *[aa]*, in all material respects. . .

Example 2: Qualified Opinion—The Controls are Not Suitably Designed to Provide Reasonable Assurance That the Control Objectives Stated in the Description of the Service Organization's System Would be Achieved if the Controls Operated Effectively

The following is an illustrative paragraph describing the basis for the qualified opinion. The paragraph would be inserted before the modified opinion paragraph. All other report paragraphs are unchanged.

Basis for qualified opinion

As discussed on page [*mn*] of the accompanying description, from time to time, XYZ Service Organization makes changes in application programs to correct deficiencies or to enhance capabilities. The procedures followed in determining whether to make changes, in designing the changes, and in implementing them do not include review and approval by authorized individuals who are independent from those involved in making the changes. There also are no specified requirements to test such changes or provide test results to an authorized reviewer prior to implementing the changes. As a result the controls are not suitably designed to achieve the control objective, "Controls provide reasonable assurance that changes to existing applications are authorized, tested, approved, properly implemented, and documented."

Opinion

In our opinion, except for the matter described in the preceding paragraph, and based on the criteria described in XYZ Service Organization's assertion on page *[aa]*, in all material respects. . .

Example 3: Qualified Opinion for a Type 2 Report—The Controls Did Not Operate Effectively Throughout the Specified Period to Achieve the Control Objectives Stated in the Description of the Service Organization's System

The following is an illustrative paragraph describing the basis for the qualified opinion. The paragraph would be inserted before the modified opinion paragraph. All other report paragraphs are unchanged.

Basis for qualified opinion

XYZ Service Organization states in its description that it has automated controls in place to reconcile loan payments received with the various output reports. However, as noted on page [*mn*] of the description of tests of controls and results thereof, this control was not operating effectively throughout the period [*date*] to [*date*] due to a programming error. This resulted in the nonachievement of the control objective, "Controls provide reasonable assurance that loan payments received are properly recorded" throughout the period January 1, 20X1, to April 30, 20X1. XYZ Service Organization implemented a change to the program performing the calculation as of May 1, 20X1, and our tests indicate that it was operating effectively throughout the period May 1, 20X1, to December 31, 20X1.

Opinion

In our opinion, except for the matter described in the preceding paragraph, and based on the criteria described in XYZ Service Organization's assertion on page [*aa*], in all material respects. . . .

Example 4: Qualified Opinion—The Service Auditor is Unable to Obtain Sufficient Appropriate Evidence

The following is an illustrative paragraph describing the basis for the qualified opinion. The paragraph would be inserted before the modified opinion paragraph. All other report paragraphs are unchanged.

Basis for qualified opinion

XYZ Service Organization states in its description that it has automated controls in place to reconcile loan payments received with the output generated. However, electronic records of the performance of this reconciliation for the period from [*date*] to [*date*] were deleted as a result of a computer processing error and, therefore, we were unable to test the operation of this control for that period. Consequently, we were unable to determine whether the control objective, "Controls provide reasonable assurance that loan payments received are properly recorded" was achieved throughout the period [*date*] to [*date*].

Opinion

In our opinion, except for the matter described in the preceding paragraph, and based on the criteria described in XYZ Service Organization's assertion on page [*aa*], in all material respects. . .

.A70

Appendix C: Illustrative Report Paragraphs for Service Organizations That Use a Subservice Organization

Following are modifications of the illustrative type 2 report in example 1 of appendix A for use in engagements in which the service organization uses a subservice organization. (New language is shown in boldface italics; deleted language is shown by strikethrough.)

Example 1: Carve-Out Method

Scope

We have examined XYZ Service Organization's description of its system for processing user entities' transactions [*or identification of the function performed by the system*] throughout the period [*date*] to [*date*] (description) and the suitability of the design and operating effectiveness of controls to achieve the related control objectives stated in the description.

XYZ Service Organization uses a computer processing service organization for all of its computerized application processing. The description on pages [bb–cc] includes only the controls and related control objectives of XYZ Service Organization and excludes the control objectives and related controls of the computer processing service organization. Our examination did not extend to controls of the computer processing service organization.

All other report paragraphs are unchanged.

Example 2: Inclusive Method

Scope

We have examined XYZ Service Organization's ***and ABC Subservice Organization's*** description of ~~its~~ ***their*** [*type or name of*] system for processing user entities' transactions [*or identification of the function performed by the system*] throughout the period [*date*] to [*date*] (description) and the suitability of the design and operating effectiveness of ***XYZ Service Organization's and ABC Subservice Organization's*** controls to achieve the related control objectives stated in the description. ***ABC Subservice Organization is an independent service organization that provides computer processing services to XYZ Service Organization. XYZ Service Organization's description includes a description of ABC Subservice Organization's* [type or name of] *system used by XYZ Service Organization to process transactions for its user entities, as well as relevant control objectives and controls of ABC Subservice Organization.***

XYZ Service Organization's responsibilities

On page XX of the description, XYZ Service Organization ***and ABC Subservice Organization*** ~~has~~ ***have*** provided ~~an~~ ***their*** assertion***s*** about the fairness of the presentation of the description and suitability of the design and operating effectiveness of the controls to achieve the related control objectives stated in the description. XYZ Service Organization ***and ABC Subservice Organization are*** ~~is~~ responsible for preparing the description and assertion***s***, including the completeness, accuracy, and method of presentation of the description and assertion***s***, providing the services covered by the description, specifying the control objectives and stating them in the description, identifying the risks that threaten the achievement of the control objectives, selecting the criteria, and designing, implementing, and documenting controls to achieve the related control objectives stated in the description.

Inherent limitations

Because of their nature, controls at a service organization ***or subservice organization*** may not prevent, or detect and correct, all errors or omissions in processing or reporting transactions. Also, the projection to the future of any evaluation of the fairness of the presentation of the description or any conclusions about the suitability of the design or operating effectiveness of the controls to achieve the related control objectives is subject to the risk that controls at a service organization ***or subservice organization*** may become ineffective or fail.

Opinion

In our opinion, in all material respects, based on the criteria specified in XYZ Service Organization**'s and ABC Subservice Organization's** assertions on page [*aa*],

a. the description fairly presents ***XYZ Service Organization's*** ~~the~~ [*type or name of*] system ***and ABC Subservice Organization's [type or name of] system used by XYZ Service Organization to process transactions for its user entities [or identification of the function performed by the service organization's system]*** that ***were*** ~~was~~ designed and implemented throughout the period [*date*] to [*date*].

b. the controls related to the control objectives ***of XYZ Service Organization and ABC Subservice Organization*** stated in the description were suitably designed to provide reasonable assurance that the control objectives would be achieved if the controls operated effectively throughout the period [*date*] to [*date*].

c. the controls ***of XYZ Service Organization and ABC Subservice Organization that*** we tested, which were those necessary to provide reasonable assurance that the control objectives stated in the description were achieved, operated effectively throughout the period [*date*] to [*date*].

All other report paragraphs are unchanged.

.A71

Exhibit A: Illustrative Assertions by Management of a Service Organization

The assertion by management of the service organization may be included in management's description of the service organization's system or may be attached to the description. The following illustrative assertions are intended for assertions that are included in the description.

The following illustrative management assertions are for guidance only and are not intended to be exhaustive or applicable to all situations.

Example 1: Assertion by Management of a Service Organization for a Type 2 Report

XYZ Service Organization's Assertion

We have prepared the description of XYZ Service Organization's [*type or name of*] system (description) for user entities of the system during some or all of the period [*date*] to [*date*], and their user auditors who have a sufficient understanding to consider it, along with other information, including information about controls implemented by user entities of the system themselves, when assessing the risks of material misstatements of user entities' financial statements. We confirm, to the best of our knowledge and belief, that

a. the description fairly presents the [*type or name of*] system made available to user entities of the system during some or all of the period [*date*] to [*date*] for processing their transactions [*or identification of the function performed by the system*]. The criteria we used in making this assertion were that the description

i. presents how the system made available to user entities of the system was designed and implemented to process relevant transactions, including

(1) the classes of transactions processed.

(2) the procedures, within both automated and manual systems, by which those transactions are initiated, authorized, recorded, processed, corrected as necessary, and transferred to the reports presented to user entities of the system.

(3) the related accounting records, supporting information, and specific accounts that are used to initiate, authorize, record, process, and report transactions; this includes the correction of incorrect information and how information is transferred to the reports presented to user entities of the system.

(4) how the system captures and addresses significant events and conditions, other than transactions.

(5) the process used to prepare reports or other information provided to user entities' of the system.

(6) specified control objectives and controls designed to achieve those objectives.

(7) other aspects of our control environment, risk assessment process, information and communication systems (including the related business processes), control activities, and monitoring controls that are relevant to processing and reporting transactions of user entities of the system.

ii. does not omit or distort information relevant to the scope of the [*type or name of*] system, while acknowledging that the description is prepared to meet the common needs of a broad range of user entities of the system and the independent auditors of those user entities, and may not, therefore, include every aspect of the [*type or name of*] system that each individual user entity of the system and its auditor may consider important in its own particular environment.

b. the description includes relevant details of changes to the service organization's system during the period covered by the description when the description covers a period of time.

c. the controls related to the control objectives stated in the description were suitably designed and operated effectively throughout the period [*date*] to [*date*] to achieve those control objectives. The criteria we used in making this assertion were that

i. the risks that threaten the achievement of the control objectives stated in the description have been identified by the service organization;

ii. the controls identified in the description would, if operating as described, provide reasonable assurance that those risks would not prevent the control objectives stated in the description from being achieved; and

iii. the controls were consistently applied as designed, including whether manual controls were applied by individuals who have the appropriate competence and authority.

Example 2: Assertion by Management of a Service Organization for a Type 1 Report

XYZ Service Organization's Assertion

We have prepared the description of XYZ Service Organization's [*type or name of*] system (description) for user entities of the system as of [*date*], and their user auditors who have a sufficient understanding to consider it, along with other information including information about controls implemented by user entities themselves, when obtaining an understanding of user entities' information and communication systems relevant to financial reporting. We confirm, to the best of our knowledge and belief, that

a. the description fairly presents the [*type or name of*] system made available to user entities of the system as of [*date*] for processing their transactions [*or identification of the function performed by the system*]. The criteria we used in making this assertion were that the description

i. presents how the system made available to user entities of the system was designed and implemented to process relevant transactions, including

(1) the classes of transactions processed.

(2) the procedures, within both automated and manual systems, by which those transactions are initiated, authorized, recorded, processed, corrected as necessary, and transferred to the reports presented to user entities of the system.

(3) the related accounting records, supporting information, and specific accounts that are used to initiate, authorize, record, process, and report transactions; this includes the correction of incorrect information and how information is transferred to the reports provided to user entities of the system.

(4) how the system captures and addresses significant events and conditions, other than transactions.

(5) the process used to prepare reports or other information provided to user entities of the system.

(6) specified control objectives and controls designed to achieve those objectives.

(7) other aspects of our control environment, risk assessment process, information and communication systems (including the related business processes), control activities, and monitoring controls that are relevant to processing and reporting transactions of user entities of the system.

ii. does not omit or distort information relevant to the scope of the [*type or name of*] system, while acknowledging that the description is prepared to meet the common needs of a broad range of user entities of the system and the independent auditors of those user entities, and may not, therefore, include every aspect of the [*type or name of*] system that each individual user entity of the system and its auditor may consider important in its own particular environment.

b. the controls related to the control objectives stated in the description were suitably designed as of [*date*] to achieve those control objectives. The criteria we used in making this assertion were that

i. the risks that threaten the achievement of the control objectives stated in the description have been identified by the service organization.

ii. the controls identified in the description would, if operating as described, provide reasonable assurance that those risks would not prevent the control objectives stated in the description from being achieved.

.A72

Exhibit B: Comparison of Requirements of Section 801, *Reporting On Controls at a Service Organization*, With Requirements of International Standard on Assurance Engagements 3402, *Assurance Reports on Controls at a Service Organization*

This analysis was prepared by the AICPA Audit and Attest Standards staff to highlight substantive differences between section 801, *Reporting on Controls at a Service Organization*, and International Standard on Assurance Engagements (ISAE) 3402, *Assurance Reports on Controls at a Service Organization*, and to explain the rationale for those differences. This analysis is not authoritative and is prepared for informational purposes only.

1. Intentional Acts by Service Organization Personnel

Paragraph .26 of this section requires the service auditor to investigate the nature and cause of any deviations identified, as does paragraph 28 of ISAE 3402. Paragraph .27 of this section indicates that if the service auditor becomes aware that the deviations resulted from intentional acts by service organization personnel, the service auditor should assess the risk that the description of the service organization's system is not fairly presented and that the controls are not suitably designed or operating effectively. The ISAE does not contain the requirement included in paragraph .27 of this section. The Auditing Standards Board (ASB) believes that information about intentional acts affects the nature, timing, and extent of the service auditor's procedures. Therefore, paragraph .27 provides follow-up action for the service auditor when he or she obtains information about intentional acts as a result of performing the procedures in paragraph .26 of this section.

Paragraph .36(c)(ii) of this section, which is not included in ISAE 3402, also requires the service auditor to request written representations from management that it has disclosed to the service auditor knowledge of any actual, suspected, or alleged intentional acts by management or the service organization's employees, of which it is aware, that could adversely affect the fairness of the presentation of management's description of the service organization's system or the completeness or achievement of the control objectives stated in the description.

2. Anomalies

Paragraph 29 of ISAE 3402 contains a requirement that enables a service auditor to conclude that a deviation identified in tests of controls involving sampling is not representative of the population from which the sample was drawn. This section does not include this requirement because of concerns about use of terms such as, "in the extremely rare circumstances" and "a high degree of certainty." These terms are not used in U.S professional standards and the ASB believes their introduction in this section could have unintended consequences. The ASB also believes that the deletion of this requirement will enhance examination quality because deviations identified by the service auditor in tests of controls involving sampling will be treated in the same manner as any other deviation identified by the practitioner, rather than as an anomaly.

3. Direct Assistance

Paragraph .35 of this section requires the service auditor to adapt and apply the requirements in paragraph .27 of AU-C section 610, *The Auditor's Consideration of the Internal Audit Function in an Audit of Financial Statements*, when the service auditor uses members of the service organization's internal audit function to provide direct assistance. Because AU-C section 610 provides for an auditor to use the work of the internal audit function in a direct assistance capacity, paragraph .35 of this section also provides for this. The International Standards on Auditing and the ISAEs do not provide for use of the internal audit function for direct assistance.

4. Subsequent Events

With respect to events that occur subsequent to the period covered by the description of the service organization's system up to the date of the service auditor's report, paragraph .42 of this section requires the service auditor to disclose in the service auditor's report, if not disclosed by management in its description, any event that is of such a nature and significance that its disclosure is necessary to prevent users of a type 1 or type 2 report from being misled. The ASB believes that information about such events could be important to user entities and their auditors. ISAE 3402 limits the types of subsequent events that would need to be disclosed in the service auditor's report to those that could have a significant effect on the service auditor's report.

Paragraph .43 of this section requires the service auditor to adapt and apply the guidance in AU-C section 560, *Subsequent Events and Subsequently Discovered Facts*, if, after the release of the service auditor's report, the service auditor becomes aware of conditions that existed at the report date that might have affected management's assertion and the service auditor's report had the service auditor been aware of them. The ISAE does not include a similar requirement. The ASB believes that, by analogy, AU-C section 560 provides needed guidance to a service auditor by presenting the various circumstances that could occur during the subsequent events period and the actions a service auditor should take.

5. Statement Restricting Use of the Service Auditor's Report

This section requires the service auditor's report to include a statement restricting the use of the report to management of the service organization, user entities of the service organization's system, and user auditors. The ASB believes that the unambiguous language in the restricted use statement prevents misunderstanding regarding who the report is intended for. Paragraphs .A61–.A62 of this section explain the reasons for restricting the use of the report. ISAE 3402 requires the service auditor's report to include a statement indicating that the report is intended only for user entities and their auditors, However, the ISAE does not require the inclusion of a statement restricting the use of the report to specified parties, although it does not prohibit the inclusion of restricted use language in the report.

6. Documentation Completion

Paragraph 50 of the ISAE requires the service auditor to assemble the documentation in an engagement file and complete the administrative process of assembling the final engagement file on a timely basis after the date of the service auditor's assurance report. Paragraph .49 of this section also requires the service auditor to assemble the engagement documentation in an engagement file and complete the administrative process of assembling the final engagement file on a timely basis, but also indicates that a timely basis is no later than 60 days following the service auditor's report release date. The ASB made this change to parallel the definition of *documentation completion date* in paragraph .06 of AU-C section 230, *Audit Documentation*.

7. Engagement Acceptance and Continuance

Paragraph .09 of this section establishes conditions for the acceptance and continuance of an engagement to report on controls at a service organization. One of the conditions is that management acknowledge and accept responsibility for providing the service auditor with written representations at the conclusion of the engagement. ISAE 3402 does not include this requirement as a condition of engagement acceptance and continuance.

8. Disclaimer of Opinion

If management does not provide the service auditor with certain written representations, paragraph 40 of ISAE 3402 requires the service auditor, after discussing the matter with management, to disclaim an opinion. In the same circumstances, paragraph .39 of this section requires the service auditor to take appropriate action, which may include disclaiming an opinion or withdrawing from the engagement.

Paragraphs .56–.57 of this section contain certain incremental requirements when the service auditor plans to disclaim an opinion.

9. Elements of the Section 801 Report That Are Not Required in the ISAE 3402 Report

Paragraphs .52–.53 of this section contain certain requirements regarding the content of the service auditor's report, which are incremental to those in ISAE 3402. These incremental requirements are included in paragraphs .52(c)(iii); .52(e)(iv); .52(i); and .52(k) for type 2 reports, and in paragraphs .53(c)(iii); .53(e)(iv); .53(j); and .53(k) for type 1 reports.

[Revised, December 2012, to reflect conforming changes necessary due to the issuance of SAS Nos. 122–126.]

AT Appendixes

TABLE OF CONTENTS

AT Appendix A

AICPA Attestation Guides and Statements of Position

AICPA Attestation Guides

Prospective Financial Information

Reporting on Controls at a Service Organization: Relevant to Security, Availability, Processing Integrity, Confidentiality, or Privacy (SOC 2[SM])

Service Organizations: Reporting on Controls at a Service Organization Relevant to User Entities' Internal Control Over Financial Reporting

Statements of Position—Attestation

Guidance to Practitioners in Conducting and Reporting on an Agreed-Upon Procedures Engagement to Assist Management in Evaluating the Effectiveness of Its Corporate Compliance Program	*5/99*
Performing Agreed-Upon Procedures Engagements That Address Internal Control Over Derivative Transactions as Required by the New York State Insurance Law	*6/01*
Performing Agreed-Upon Procedures Engagements That Address Annual Claims Prompt Payment Reports as Required by the New Jersey Administrative Code	*5/02*
Attestation Engagements That Address Specified Compliance Control Objectives and Related Controls at Entities That Provide Services to Investment Companies, Investment Advisers, or Other Service Providers	*10/07*
Reporting Pursuant to the Global Investment Performance Standards	*10/12*
Attest Engagements on Greenhouse Gas Emissions Information	*4/13*
Performing Agreed-Upon Procedures Engagements That Address the Completeness, Mapping, Consistency, or Structure of XBRL-Formatted Information	*9/13*

AT Appendix B

Other Attestation Publications

This listing identifies *other attestation publications* published by the AICPA that have been reviewed by the AICPA Audit and Attest Standards staff and are, therefore, presumed to be appropriate as defined in AT section 50, *SSAE Hierarchy*. Products may be obtained through www.cpa2biz.com.

AICPA Technical Questions and Answers

Q&A section 9500, *Attestation Engagements*

Current AICPA Attestation Risk Alerts

Service Organization Control Reports¨: *Considerations for User and Service Auditors*

AT TOPICAL INDEX

References are to AT section and paragraph numbers.

J

K

L

M

References are to AT section and paragraph numbers.

AT-C Cross-References to SSAEs

TABLE OF CONTENTS

AT-C Cross-References to SSAEs

Part I—Statements on Standards for Attestation Engagements and Sources of Sections in Current Text

Statements on Standards for Attestation Engagements*

No.	*Date Issued*	*Title*	*AT-C Section*
18	April 2016	*Attestation Standards: Clarification and Recodification*[1]	

Sources of Sections in Current Text

AT-C Section	*Contents*	*Source*
100	**Common Concepts**	
105	*Concepts Common to All Attestation Engagements*	SSAE No. 18
200	**Level of Service**	
205	*Examination Engagements*	SSAE No. 18
210	*Review Engagements*	SSAE No. 18
215	*Agreed-Upon Procedures Engagements*	SSAE No. 18
300	**Subject Matter**	
305	*Prospective Financial Information*	SSAE No. 18
310	*Reporting on Pro Forma Financial Information*	SSAE No. 18
315	*Compliance Attestation*	SSAE No. 18
320	*Reporting on an Examination of Controls at a Service Organization Relevant to User Entities' Internal Control Over Financial Reporting*	SSAE No. 18
395	*Designated for AT Section 701,* Management's Discussion and Analysis	SSAE No. 10[2]

* This table lists Statements on Standards for Attestation Engagements (SSAEs) issued subsequent to SSAE No. 18, *Attestation Standards: Clarification and Recodification*, which was issued in April 2016. Refer to part II, "List of Statement on Standards for Attestation Engagements Nos. 1–17," of this section for SSAEs issued prior to SSAE No. 18.

[1] SSAE No. 18 created various sections throughout *U.S. Attestation Standards—AICPA (Clarified)*. See the following section, "Sources of Sections in Current Text," for a full list.

[2] SSAE No. 18 does not supersede chapter 7, "Management's Discussion and Analysis," of SSAE No. 10, *Attestation Standards: Revision and Recodification*, which is currently codified as AT section 701. The Auditing Standards Board (ASB) has not clarified AT section 701 because practitioners rarely perform attest engagements to report on management's discussion and analysis prepared pursuant to the rules and regulations adopted by the SEC. Therefore, the ASB decided that it would retain AT section 701 in its current unclarified format as AT-C section 395 until further notice.

Part II—List of Statement on Standards for Attestation Engagements Nos. 1–17

No.	*Date Issued*	*Title*
1	Mar. 1986	*Attestation Standards*
1	Dec. 1987	*Attest Services Related to MAS Engagements*
1	Oct. 1985	*Financial Forecasts and Projections*
1	Sept. 1988	*Reporting on Pro Forma Financial Information*
2	May 1993	*Reporting on an Entity's Internal Control Over Financial Reporting*
3	Dec. 1993	*Compliance Attestation*
4	Sept. 1995	*Agreed-Upon Procedures Engagements*
5	Nov. 1995	*Amendment to Statement on Standards for Attestation Engagements No. 1,* Attestation Standards
6	Dec. 1995	*Reporting on an Entity's Internal Control Over Financial Reporting: An Amendment to Statement on Standards for Attestation Engagements No. 2*
7	Oct. 1997	*Establishing an Understanding With the Client*
8	Mar. 1998	*Management's Discussion and Analysis*
9	Jan. 1999	*Amendments to Statement on Standards for Attestation Engagements Nos. 1, 2, and 3*
10	Jan. 2001	*Attestation Standards: Revision and Recodification*
11	Jan. 2002	*Attest Documentation*
12	Sept. 2002	*Amendment to Statement on Standards for Attestation Engagements No. 10,* Attestation Standards: Revision and Recodification
13	Dec. 2005	*Defining Professional Requirements in Statements on Standards for Attestation Engagements*
14	Nov. 2006	*SSAE Hierarchy*
15	Sept. 2008	*An Examination of an Entity's Internal Control Over Financial Reporting That Is Integrated With an Audit of Its Financial Statements*
16	April 2010	*Reporting on Controls at a Service Organization*
17	Dec. 2010	*Reporting on Compiled Prospective Financial Statements When the Practitioner's Independence Is Impaired*

AT-C Introduction

TABLE OF CONTENTS

AT-C Introduction

Foreword

Attestation Clarity Project

To address concerns over the clarity, length, and complexity of its standards, the Auditing Standards Board (ASB) established clarity drafting conventions and undertook a project to redraft all the standards it issues in clarity format. The redrafting of Statements on Standards for Attestation Engagements (SSAEs or attestation standards) in SSAE No. 18, *Attestation Standards: Clarification and Recodification*, represents the culmination of that process. This section redrafts all SSAEs, except for the following:

- Chapter 7, "Management's Discussion and Analysis," of SSAE No. 10, *Attestation Standards: Revision and Recodification* (AT sec. 701)

  The ASB decided not to clarify AT section 701 because practitioners rarely perform attestation engagements to report on management's discussion and analysis prepared pursuant to the rules and regulations adopted by the U.S. Securities and Exchange Commission. Therefore, the ASB decided that AT section 701 should be retained in its current unclarified format as section 395 until further notice.
- SSAE No. 15, *An Examination of an Entity's Internal Control Over Financial Reporting That Is Integrated With an Audit of Its Financial Statements*, and related Attestation Interpretation No. 1, "Reporting Under Section 112 of the Federal Deposit Insurance Corporation Improvement Act" (AT sec. 501 and 9501)

  The ASB concluded that because engagements performed under AT section 501 are required to be integrated with an audit of financial statements, the content of AT section 501 should be moved to the Statements on Auditing Standards (SASs). As a result, in October 2015, the ASB issued SAS No. 130, *An Audit of Internal Control Over Financial Reporting That Is Integrated With an Audit of Financial Statements* (AU-C sec. 940). AT section 501 and the related interpretation will be withdrawn when SAS No. 130 becomes effective; the effective date for SAS No. 130 is for integrated audits for periods ending on or after December 15, 2016.

The attestation standards are developed and issued in the form of SSAEs and are codified into sections. This section recodifies the "AT" section numbers designated by SSAE Nos. 10–17 using the identifier "AT-C" to differentiate the sections of the clarified attestation standards ("AT-C sections") from the attestation standards that are superseded by SSAE No. 18 ("AT sections"). The AT sections remain effective through April 2017, by which time substantially all engagements for which the AT sections were still effective are expected to be completed.

The attestation standards have been redrafted in accordance with the clarity drafting conventions, which include the following:

- Establishing objectives for each AT-C section

- Including a definitions section, where relevant, in each AT-C section
- Separating requirements from application and other explanatory material
- Numbering application and other explanatory material paragraphs using an A- prefix and presenting them in a separate section that follows the requirements section
- Using formatting techniques, such as bulleted lists, to enhance readability
- Including, when appropriate, special considerations relevant to audits of smaller, less complex entities within the text of the AT-C section
- Including, when appropriate, special considerations relevant to examination, review, or agreed-upon procedures engagements for governmental entities within the text of the AT-C section

Convergence

It is the ASB's general strategy to converge its standards with those of the International Auditing and Assurance Standards Board. Accordingly, the foundation for section 105, *Concepts Common to All Attestation Engagements*; section 205, *Examination Engagements*; and section 210, *Review Engagements*, is International Standard on Assurance Engagements (ISAE) 3000 (Revised), *Assurance Engagements Other Than Audits or Reviews of Historical Financial Information*. Many of the paragraphs in this section have been converged with the related paragraphs in ISAE 3000 (Revised), with certain changes made to reflect U.S. professional standards. Other content included in this section is derived from the extant SSAEs.

The ASB decided not to adopt certain provisions of ISAE 3000 (Revised), for example, in this section, a practitioner is not permitted to issue an examination or review report if the practitioner has not obtained a written assertion from the responsible party, except when the engaging party is not the responsible party. In the ISAEs, an assertion (or representation about the subject matter against the criteria) is not required in order for the practitioner to report.

Section 215, *Agreed-Upon Procedures Engagements*, is based on a redrafting of extant AT section 201, *Agreed-Upon Procedures Engagements*, in clarified format. ISAE 3000 (Revised) does not address agreed-upon procedures engagements.

Authority of the SSAEs

SSAEs are issued by senior committees of the AICPA designated to issue pronouncements on attestation matters applicable to the preparation and issuance of attestation reports for entities that are nonissuers. The "Compliance With Standards Rule" (ET sec. 1.310.001) of the AICPA Code of Professional Conduct requires an AICPA member performing an attestation engagement for a nonissuer (a practitioner) to comply with standards promulgated by the ASB. A practitioner must comply with an unconditional requirement in all cases in which such requirement is relevant. A practitioner also must comply with a presumptively mandatory requirement in all cases in which such requirement is relevant. However, if, in rare circumstances, a practitioner judges it necessary to depart from a relevant presumptively mandatory requirement, the practitioner must document the justification for the departure and how the alternative procedures performed in the circumstances were sufficient to achieve the intent of that requirement.

Exhibits and interpretations to SSAEs are *interpretive publications*, as defined in section 105. Section 105 requires the practitioner to consider applicable interpretive publications in planning and performing the attestation engagement. Interpretive publications are not attestation standards. Interpretive publications are recommendations on the application of the SSAEs in specific circumstances, including engagements for entities in specialized industries. An interpretive publication is issued under the authority of the relevant senior technical committee after all members of the committee have been provided an opportunity to consider and comment on whether the proposed interpretive publication is consistent with the SSAEs. Attestation interpretations are included in AT-C sections. AICPA Guides and Attestation Statements of Position are listed in AT-C appendix A, "AICPA Guides and Statements of Position."

AUDITING STANDARDS BOARD
Bruce P. Webb, *Chair*
Charles E. Landes, *Vice President—Professional Standards and Services*

AT-C Preface*

Preface to the Attestation Standards

.01 The Statements on Standards for Attestation Engagements (SSAEs or attestation standards) establish requirements and provide application guidance for performing and reporting on examination, review, and agreed-upon procedures engagements (attestation engagements). Examples of subject matter for attestation engagements are a schedule of investment returns, the effectiveness of an entity's controls over the security of a system, or a statement of greenhouse gas emissions.

.02 The attestation standards are issued under the "Compliance With Standards Rule" (ET section 1.310.001) of the AICPA Code of Professional Conduct, which requires an AICPA member who performs an attestation engagement to comply with standards promulgated by bodies designated by AICPA council. AICPA council has granted the Auditing Standards Board authority to promulgate the attestation standards, which are issued through a due process that includes deliberation in meetings open to the public, public exposure of proposed attestation standards, and a formal vote by an authorized standard-setting body.

.03 This preface provides an overview of the attestation standards but does not establish requirements and does not carry any authority. It is intended to be helpful in understanding attestation engagements.

.04 The attestation standards are developed and issued in the form of SSAEs and are codified into sections. The identifier "AT-C" is used to differentiate the sections of the clarified attestation standards issued in April 2016 (AT-C sections) from the sections of the attestation standards they supersede (identified as AT sections).

Structure of the Attestation Standards

.05 The attestation standards apply to three levels of service—examination, review, and agreed-upon procedures—and can be applied to innumerable types of subject matter. The applicability of specific AT-C sections to an engagement depends on both the level of service provided and the subject matter on which the practitioner is engaged to report.

.06 Section 105, *Concepts Common to All Attestation Engagements*, contains concepts that are relevant to any attestation engagement. The level of service sections are section 205, *Examination Engagements*; section 210, *Review Engagements*; and section 215, *Agreed-Upon Procedures Engagements*, which contain additional requirements and application guidance specific to examination, review, or agreed-upon procedures engagements, respectively. Under the attestation standards, the applicable requirements and application guidance for any attestation engagement are contained in at least two sections: section 105 and section 205, 210, or 215, depending on the level of service being provided. In addition, incremental performance and reporting requirements and application guidance unique to specific subject matters, such as prospective financial information or compliance with laws and regulations, are contained in

---

* This section contains an "AT-C" identifier, instead of an "AT" identifier, to avoid confusion with references to existing "AT" sections, which remain effective through April 2017.

the subject-matter sections. The applicable requirements and application guidance for a subject-matter-specific engagement is contained in three sections: section 105; section 205, 210, or 215, as applicable; and the applicable subject-matter section.

Purpose of the Engagement and Premise on Which an Attestation Engagement Is Conducted

.07 The purpose of an attestation engagement is to provide users of information, generally third parties, with an opinion, conclusion, or findings regarding the reliability of subject matter or an assertion about the subject matter, as measured against suitable and available criteria. (An examination engagement results in an opinion; a review engagement results in a conclusion; and an agreed-upon procedures engagement results in findings.) The practitioner's report is intended to enhance the degree of confidence that intended users can place in the subject matter.

Responsibilities

.08 An engagement in accordance with the attestation standards is conducted on the premise that the responsible party is responsible for

- the subject matter (and, if applicable, the preparation and presentation of the subject matter) in accordance with (or based on) the criteria
- its assertion about the subject matter;
- measuring, evaluating, and, when applicable, presenting subject matter that is free from material misstatement, whether due to fraud or error; and
- providing the practitioner with
    - — access to all information of which the responsible party is aware that is relevant to the measurement, evaluation, or disclosure of the subject matter;
    - — access to additional information that the practitioner may request from the responsible party for the purpose of the engagement; and
    - — unrestricted access to persons within the appropriate party(ies) from whom the practitioner determines it is necessary to obtain evidence.

.09 Practitioners are responsible for complying with the relevant performance and reporting requirements established in the attestation standards when they are engaged to issue, or do issue, an examination, review, or agreed-upon procedures report on subject matter or an assertion about subject matter that is the responsibility of another party (the responsible party). Although a practitioner may assist the responsible party in developing or presenting the subject matter, the responsible party remains responsible for the subject matter.

Performance

.10 In all services provided under the attestation standards, practitioners are responsible for

- having the appropriate competence and capabilities to perform the engagement,
- complying with relevant ethical requirements,
- maintaining professional skepticism, and
- exercising professional judgment throughout the planning and performance of the engagement.

.11 To express an opinion in an examination, the practitioner obtains reasonable assurance about whether the subject matter, or an assertion about the subject matter, is free from material misstatement, whether due to fraud or error. To obtain reasonable assurance, which is a high but not absolute level of assurance, the practitioner

- plans the work and properly supervises other members of the engagement team.
- identifies and assesses the risks of material misstatement, whether due to fraud or error, based on an understanding of the subject matter, its measurement or evaluation, the criteria, and other engagement circumstances.
- obtains sufficient appropriate evidence about whether material misstatements exist by designing and implementing appropriate responses to the assessed risks. Examination procedures may involve inspection, observation, analysis, inquiry, reperformance, recalculation, or confirmation with outside parties.

.12 To express a conclusion in a review, the practitioner obtains limited assurance about whether any material modification should be made to the subject matter in order for it be in accordance with (or based on) the criteria or to an assertion about the subject matter in order for it to be fairly stated. In a review, the nature and extent of the procedures are substantially less than in an examination. To obtain limited assurance in a review, the practitioner

- plans the work and properly supervises other members of the engagement team.
- focuses procedures in those areas in which the practitioner believes increased risks of misstatements exist, whether due to fraud or error, based on the practitioner's understanding of the subject matter, its measurement or evaluation, the criteria, and other engagement circumstances.
- obtains review evidence, through the application of inquiry and analytical procedures or other procedures as appropriate, to obtain limited assurance that no material modifications should be made to the subject matter in order for it to be in accordance with (or based on) the criteria.

.13 To report on the application of agreed-upon procedures, the practitioner applies procedures determined by the specified parties who are the intended users of the practitioner's report and who are responsible for the sufficiency of the procedures for their purposes. As a result of the engagement, the practitioner reports on the results of the engagement but does not provide an opinion or conclusion on the subject matter or assertion. In an agreed-upon procedures engagement, the practitioner

- plans the work and properly supervises other members of the engagement team.

- applies the procedures agreed to by the specified parties and reports on their results.

Reporting

.14 Based on evidence obtained, the practitioner expresses an opinion in an examination, expresses a conclusion in a review, or reports findings in an agreed-upon procedures engagement. In the case of an examination, the practitioner's report provides an opinion about whether the subject matter, as measured against the criteria, is in accordance with (or based on) the criteria (or whether the assertion about the subject matter is fairly stated), in all material respects. In a review, the report expresses a conclusion about whether, based on the limited procedures, the practitioner is aware of any material modification that should be made to the subject matter in order for it to be in accordance with (or based on) the criteria or to the assertion in order for it to be fairly stated. In an agreed-upon procedures report, the practitioner describes the specified procedures that were applied to the subject matter and the results of those procedures.

AT-C Glossary

Glossary of Terms[1]

Appropriate party. Reference to this term should be read as the *responsible party* or the *engaging party*, as appropriate. Also see **engaging party** and **responsible party**.

Appropriateness of evidence (in the context of section 205, *Examination Engagements*). The measure of the quality of evidence, that is, its relevancy and reliability in providing support for the practitioner's opinion. Also see **evidence**.

Appropriateness of review evidence (in the context of section 210, *Review Engagements*). The measure of the quality of review evidence, that is, its relevancy and reliability in providing support for the practitioner's conclusion. Also see **review evidence**.

Assertion. Any declaration or set of declarations about whether the subject matter is in accordance with (or based on) the criteria.

Attestation engagement. An examination, review, or agreed-upon procedures engagement performed under the attestation standards related to subject matter or an assertion that is the responsibility of another party. The following are the three types of attestation engagements:

- *Examination engagement.* An attestation engagement in which the practitioner obtains reasonable assurance by obtaining sufficient appropriate evidence about the measurement or evaluation of subject matter against criteria in order to be able to draw reasonable conclusions on which to base the practitioner's opinion about whether the subject matter is in accordance with (or based on) the criteria or the assertion is fairly stated, in all material respects.
- *Review engagement.* An attestation engagement in which the practitioner obtains limited assurance by obtaining sufficient appropriate review evidence about the measurement or evaluation of subject matter against criteria in order to express a conclusion about whether any material modification should be made to the subject matter in order for it be in accordance with (or based on) the criteria or to the assertion in order for it to be fairly stated.
- *Agreed-upon procedures engagement.* An attestation engagement in which a practitioner performs specific procedures on subject matter or an assertion and reports the findings without providing an opinion or a conclusion on it. The parties to the engagement (*specified parties*) agree upon and are responsible for the sufficiency of the procedures for their purposes.

Also see **specified party** and **attestation standards**.

---

[1] This glossary lists terms defined in the "Definitions" sections of the attestation standards as well as certain terms defined or explained in other sections of the attestation standards. Terms defined for purposes of a specific section are denoted as such. Terms may appear in more than one section.

Attestation risk. In an examination or review engagement, the risk that the practitioner expresses an inappropriate opinion or conclusion, as applicable, when the subject matter or assertion is materially misstated.

Attestation standards. The Statements on Standards for Attestation Engagements (SSAEs), which are also known as the *attestation standards*, establish requirements and provide guidance for performing and reporting on examination, review, and agreed-upon procedures engagements (attestation engagements). Examples of subject matter for attestation engagements are a schedule of investment returns, the effectiveness of an entity's controls over the security of a system, or a statement of greenhouse gas emissions. The SSAEs apply only to attestation engagements performed under the SSAEs. They are issued under the "Compliance With Standards Rule" (ET sec. 1.310.001) of the AICPA Code of Professional Conduct, which requires an AICPA member who performs an attestation engagement to comply with standards promulgated by bodies designated by AICPA Council. AICPA Council has granted the Auditing Standards Board authority to promulgate the attestation standards, which are issued through a due process that includes deliberation in meetings open to the public, public exposure of proposed attestation standards, and a formal vote by an authorized standard-setting body. Also see **attestation engagement**.

Carve-out method (in the context of section 320, *Reporting on an Examination of Controls at a Service Organization Relevant to User Entities' Internal Control Over Financial Reporting*). Method of addressing the services provided by a subservice organization, whereby management's description of the service organization's system identifies the nature of the services performed by the subservice organization and excludes from the description and from the scope of the service auditor's engagement the subservice organization's relevant control objectives and related controls.

Complementary subservice organization controls (in the context of section 320). Controls that management of the service organization assumes, in the design of the service organization's system, will be implemented by the subservice organizations and are necessary to achieve the control objectives stated in management's description of the service organization's system.

Complementary user entity controls (in the context of section 320). Controls that management of the service organization assumes, in the design of the service organization's system, will be implemented by user entities and are necessary to achieve the control objectives stated in management's description of the service organization's system.

Compliance with specified requirements (in the context of section 315, *Compliance Attestation*). An entity's compliance with specified laws, regulations, rules, contracts, or grants.

Control objectives (in the context of section 320). The aim or purpose of specified controls at the service organization. Control objectives address the risks that controls are intended to mitigate.

Controls at a service organization (in the context of section 320). The policies and procedures at a service organization likely to be relevant to user entities' internal control over financial reporting. These policies and procedures are designed, implemented, and documented by the service organization to provide reasonable assurance about the achievement of the control objectives relevant to the services covered by the service auditor's report.

In the context of section 320, the policies and procedures include aspects of the information and communications component of user entities' internal control maintained by the service organization and control activities related to the information and communications component and may also include aspects of one or more of the other components of internal control at a service organization. For example, the definition of *controls at a service organization* may include aspects of the service organization's control environment, risk assessment, monitoring activities, and control activities when they relate to the services provided. Such definition does not, however, include controls at a service organization that are not related to the achievement of the control objectives stated in management's description of the service organization's system, for example, controls related to the preparation of the service organization's own financial statements.

Criteria. The benchmarks used to measure or evaluate the subject matter.

Criteria for the preparation of pro forma financial information (in the context of section 310, *Reporting on Pro Forma Financial Information*). The basis disclosed in the pro forma financial information that management used to develop the pro forma financial information, including the assumptions underlying the pro forma financial information. Paragraph .11 of section 310 contains the attributes of suitable criteria for an examination or review of pro forma financial information.

Documentation completion date. The date on which the practitioner has assembled for retention a complete and final set of documentation in the engagement file.

Engagement circumstances. The broad context defining the particular engagement, which includes the terms of the engagement; whether it is an examination, review, or agreed-upon procedures engagement; the characteristics of the subject matter; the criteria; the information needs of the intended users; relevant characteristics of the responsible party and, if different, the engaging party and their environment; and other matters, for example, events, transactions, conditions and practices, and relevant laws and regulations, that may have a significant effect on the engagement.

Engagement documentation. The record of procedures performed, relevant evidence obtained, and, in an examination or review engagement, conclusions reached by the practitioner, or in an agreed-upon procedures engagement, findings of the practitioner. (Terms such as *working papers* or *workpapers* are also sometimes used).

Engagement partner. The partner or other person in the firm who is responsible for the attestation engagement and its performance and for the practitioner's report that is issued on behalf of the firm and who, when required, has the appropriate authority from a professional, legal, or regulatory body. *Engagement partner*, *partner*, and *firm* refer to their governmental equivalents when relevant. Also see **firm** and **practitioner**.

Engagement team. All partners and staff performing the engagement and any individuals engaged by the firm or a network firm who perform attestation procedures on the engagement. This excludes a practitioner's external specialist and engagement quality control reviewer engaged by the firm or a network firm. The term *engagement team* also excludes individuals within the client's internal audit function who provide direct assistance.

Engaging party. The party(ies) that engages the practitioner to perform the attestation engagement. Also see **appropriate party** and **responsible party**.

Entity (in the context of section 305, *Prospective Financial Information*). Any unit, existing or to be formed for which financial statements could be prepared in accordance with generally accepted accounting principles or special purpose frameworks. For example, an entity can be an individual, partnership, corporation, trust, estate, association, or governmental unit.

Evidence. Information used by the practitioner in arriving at the opinion, conclusion, or findings on which the practitioner's report is based. Also see **appropriateness of evidence** and **sufficiency of evidence**.

Financial forecast (in the context of section 305). Prospective financial statements that present, to the best of the responsible party's knowledge and belief, an entity's expected financial position, results of operations, and cash flows. A financial forecast is based on the responsible party's assumptions reflecting conditions it expects to exist and the course of action it expects to take. A financial forecast may be expressed in specific monetary amounts as a single-point estimate of forecasted results or as a range, when the responsible party selects key assumptions to form a range within which it reasonably expects, to the best of its knowledge and belief, the item or items subject to the assumptions to actually fall. If a forecast contains a range, the range is not selected in a biased or misleading manner (for example, a range in which one end is significantly less expected than the other).

Financial projection (in the context of section 305). Prospective financial statements that present, to the best of the responsible party's knowledge and belief, given one or more hypothetical assumptions, an entity's expected financial position, results of operations, and cash flows. A financial projection is sometimes prepared to present one or more hypothetical courses of action for evaluation, as in response to a question such as, "What would happen if...?" A financial projection is based on the responsible party's assumptions reflecting conditions it expects would exist and the course of action it expects would be taken, given one or more hypothetical assumptions. A projection, like a forecast, may contain a range.

Firm. A form of organization permitted by law or regulation whose characteristics conform to resolutions of the Council of the AICPA and that is engaged in the practice of public accounting. Also see **engagement partner** and **practitioner**.

Forecast (in the context of section 305). Used alone, this term means forecasted information, which can be either a full presentation (a financial forecast) or a partial presentation. Also see **financial forecast**.

Fraud. An intentional act involving the use of deception that results in a misstatement in the subject matter or the assertion.

General use. Use of a practitioner's report that is not restricted to specified parties.

General use of prospective financial statements (in the context of section 305). Refers to the use of the statements by persons with whom the responsible party is not negotiating directly, for example, in an offering statement of an entity's debt or equity interests. Also see **limited use of**

prospective financial statements and **prospective financial statements**.

Guide (in the context of section 305). The AICPA Guide *Prospective Financial Information*.

Hypothetical assumption (in the context of section 305). An assumption used in a financial projection or in a partial presentation of projected information to present a condition or course of action that is not necessarily expected to occur but is consistent with the purpose of the projection.

Inclusive method (in the context of section 320). Method of addressing the services provided by a subservice organization whereby management's description of the service organization's system includes a description of the nature of the services provided by the subservice organization as well as the subservice organization's relevant control objectives and related controls.

Internal audit function. A function of an entity that performs assurance and consulting activities designed to evaluate and improve the effectiveness of the entity's governance, risk management, and internal control processes.

Internal control over compliance (in the context of section 315). An entity's internal control over compliance with specified requirements. The internal control addressed in section 315 may include part of, but is not the same as, internal control over financial reporting.

Interpretive publications. Interpretive publications are not attestation standards. Interpretive publications are recommendations on the application of the attestation standards in specific circumstances, including engagements for entities in specialized industries. An interpretive publication is issued under the authority of the relevant senior technical committee after all members of the committee have been provided an opportunity to consider and comment on whether the proposed interpretive publication is consistent with the attestation standards. Examples of interpretive publications are interpretations of the attestation standards, exhibits to the attestation standards, attestation guidance included in AICPA guides and attestation Statements of Position (SOPs). Interpretations of the attestation standards and exhibits are included within the sections of the attestation standards. AICPA guides and attestation SOPs are listed in AT-C appendix A, "AICPA Guides and Statements of Position," of the attestation standards. Also see **other attestation publications**.

Key factors (in the context of section 305). The significant matters on which an entity's future results are expected to depend. Such factors are basic to the entity's operations and, thus, encompass matters that affect, among other things, the entity's sales, production, service, and financing activities. Key factors serve as a foundation for prospective financial information and are the bases for the assumptions.

Limited use of prospective financial statements (in the context of section 305). Refers to the use of prospective financial statements by the responsible party alone or by the responsible party and third parties with whom the responsible party is negotiating directly. Examples include use in negotiations for a bank loan, submission to a regulatory agency, and use solely within the entity. Also see **general use of prospective financial statements** and **prospective financial statements**.

Management's description of a service organization's system and a service auditor's report on that description and on the suitability of

the design of controls (referred to in the context of section 320 as a *type 1 report*). A service auditor's report that comprises the following:

i. Management's description of the service organization's system

ii. A written assertion by management of the service organization about whether, based on the criteria

(1) management's description of the service organization's system fairly presents the service organization's system that was designed and implemented as of a specified date

(2) the controls related to the control objectives stated in management's description of the service organization's system were suitably designed to achieve those control objectives as of the specified date

iii. A service auditor's report that expresses an opinion on the matters in (ii)(1)–(ii)(2)

Management's description of a service organization's system and a service auditor's report on that description and on the suitability of the design and operating effectiveness of controls (referred to in the context of section 320 as a *type 2 report*). A service auditor's report that comprises the following:

i. Management's description of the service organization's system

ii. A written assertion by management of the service organization about whether, based on the criteria

(1) management's description of the service organization's system fairly presents the service organization's system that was designed and implemented throughout the specified period

(2) the controls related to the control objectives stated in management's description of the service organization's system were suitably designed throughout the specified period to achieve those control objectives

(3) the controls related to the control objectives stated in management's description of the service organization's system operated effectively throughout the specified period to achieve those control objectives

iii. A service auditor's report that

(1) expresses an opinion on the matters in (ii)(1)–(ii)(3)

(2) includes a description of the tests of controls and the results thereof

Material noncompliance (in the context of section 315). A failure to follow compliance requirements or a violation of prohibitions included in the specified requirements that results in noncompliance that is quantitatively or qualitatively material, either individually or when aggregated with other noncompliance.

Misstatement. A difference between the measurement or evaluation of the subject matter by the responsible party and the proper measurement or evaluation of the subject matter based on the criteria. Misstatements can be intentional or unintentional, qualitative or quantitative, and include omissions. In certain engagements, a misstatement may be referred to as a *deviation*, *exception*, or *instance of noncompliance*. Also see **risk of material misstatement**.

Modified opinion (in the context of section 205). A qualified opinion, an adverse opinion, or a disclaimer of opinion.

Monitoring of controls (in the context of section 320). A process to assess the effectiveness of internal control performance over time. It involves assessing the effectiveness of controls on a timely basis, identifying and reporting deficiencies to appropriate individuals within the service organization, and taking necessary corrective actions.

Network firm. A firm or other entity that belongs to a network, as defined in ET section 0.400, *Definitions*.

Noncompliance with laws or regulations. Acts of omission or commission by the entity, either intentional or unintentional, that are contrary to the prevailing laws or regulations. Such acts include transactions entered into by, or in the name of, the entity or on its behalf by those charged with governance, management, or employees. *Noncompliance* does not include personal misconduct (unrelated to the subject matter) by those charged with governance, management, or employees of the entity.

Nonparticipant party (in the context of section 215, *Agreed-Upon Procedures Engagements*). An additional specified party the practitioner is requested to add as a user of the report subsequent to the completion of the agreed-upon procedures engagement. Also see **specified party**.

Other attestation publications. Publications other than interpretive publications. These include AICPA attestation publications not defined as interpretive publications; attestation articles in the *Journal of Accountancy* and other professional journals; continuing professional education programs and other instruction materials, textbooks, guidebooks, attestation programs, and checklists; and other attestation publications from state CPA societies, other organizations, and individuals. Other attestation publications have no authoritative status; however, they may help the practitioner understand and apply the attestation standards. The practitioner is not expected to be aware of the full body of other attestation publications. Also see **interpretive publications**.

Other practitioner. An independent practitioner who is not a member of the engagement team who performs work on information that will be used as evidence by the practitioner performing the attestation engagement. An other practitioner may be part of the practitioner's firm, a network firm, or another firm.

Partial presentation (in the context of section 305). A presentation of prospective financial information that excludes one or more of the applicable items required for prospective financial statements as described in chapter 8, "Presentation Guidelines," of the AICPA Guide *Prospective Financial Information*.

Pervasive (in the context of section 205). Describes the effects on the subject matter of misstatements or the possible effects on the subject matter of misstatements, if any, that are undetected due to an inability to obtain sufficient appropriate evidence. Pervasive effects on the subject matter are those that, in the practitioner's professional judgment

a. are not confined to specific aspects of the subject matter;

b. if so confined, represent or could represent a substantial proportion of the subject matter; or

c. in relation to disclosures, are fundamental to the intended users' understanding of the subject matter.

Practitioner. The person or persons conducting the attestation engagement, usually the engagement partner or other members of the engagement team, or, as applicable, the firm. When a section of the attestation standards expressly intends that a requirement or responsibility be fulfilled by the engagement partner, the term *engagement partner*, rather than *practitioner*, is used. *Engagement partner* and *firm* are to be read as referring to their governmental equivalents when relevant. Also see **engagement partner** and **firm**.

Practitioner's specialist. An individual or organization possessing expertise in a field other than accounting or attestation, whose work in that field is used by the practitioner to assist the practitioner in obtaining evidence for the service being provided. A practitioner's specialist may be either a practitioner's internal specialist (who is a partner or staff, including temporary staff, of the practitioner's firm or a network firm) or a practitioner's external specialist. *Partner* and *firm* refer to their governmental equivalents when relevant.

Presentation guidelines (in the context of section 305). The criteria for the presentation and disclosure of prospective financial information.

Presumptively mandatory requirements. The category of professional requirements with which the practitioner must comply in all cases in which such a requirement is relevant, except in rare circumstances discussed in paragraph .20 of section 105, *Concepts Common to All Attestation Engagements*. The attestation standards use the word *should* to indicate a presumptively mandatory requirement. Also see **attestation standards** and **unconditional requirements**.

Pro forma financial information (in the context of section 310). A presentation that shows what the significant effects on historical financial information might have been had a consummated or proposed transaction (or event) occurred at an earlier date.

Professional judgment. The application of relevant training, knowledge, and experience, within the context provided by attestation and ethical standards in making informed decisions about the courses of action that are appropriate in the circumstances of the attestation engagement.

Professional skepticism. An attitude that includes a questioning mind, being alert to conditions that may indicate possible misstatement due to fraud or error, and a critical assessment of evidence.

Projection (in the context of section 305). This term can refer to either a financial projection or a partial presentation of projected information. Also see **financial projection**.

Prospective financial information (in the context of section 305). Any financial information about the future. The information may be presented as complete financial statements or limited to one or more elements, items, or accounts.

Prospective financial statements (in the context of section 305). Either financial forecasts or financial projections, including the summaries of significant assumptions and accounting policies. Although prospective financial statements may cover a period that has partially expired, statements for periods that have completely expired are not considered to be prospective financial statements. Pro forma financial statements and partial presentations are not considered to be prospective financial statements. Also see **general use of prospective financial statements** and **limited use prospective financial statements**.

Reasonable assurance. A high but not absolute level of assurance.

Report release date. The date on which the practitioner grants the engaging party permission to use the practitioner's report.

Responsible party. The party(ies) responsible for the subject matter. If the nature of the subject matter is such that no such party exists, a party who has a reasonable basis for making a written assertion about the subject matter may be deemed to be the responsible party. Also see **appropriate party** and **engaging party**.

Review evidence (in the context of section 210). Information used by the practitioner in obtaining limited assurance on which the practitioner's review report is based. Also see **appropriateness of review evidence** and **sufficiency of review evidence**.

Risk of material misstatement (in the context of section 205). The risk that the subject matter is not in accordance with (or based on) the criteria in all material respects or that the assertion is not fairly stated, in all material respects. Also see **misstatement**.

Service auditor (in the context of section 320). A practitioner who reports on controls at a service organization.

Service organization (in the context of section 320). An organization or segment of an organization that provides services to user entities, which are likely to be relevant to those user entities' internal control over financial reporting.

Service organization's assertion (in the context of section 320). A written assertion about the matters referred to in item ii of the definition of *Management's description of a service organization's system and a service auditor's report on that description and on the suitability of the design and operating effectiveness of controls*, for a type 2 report, and, for a type 1 report, the matters referred to in part (*b*) of the definition of *Management's description of a service organization's system and a service auditor's report on that description and on the suitability of the design of controls*.

Service organization's system (in the context of section 320). The policies and procedures designed, implemented, and documented by management of the service organization to provide user entities with the services covered by the service auditor's report. Management's description of the service organization's system identifies the services covered, the period to which the description relates (or in the case of a type 1 report, the date to which the description relates), the control objectives specified by management or an outside party, the party specifying the control objectives (if not specified by management), and the related controls.

In the context of section 320, the policies and procedures refer to the guidelines and activities for providing transaction processing and other services to user entities and include the infrastructure, software, people, and data that support the policies and procedures.

Specified party. The intended user(s) to whom use of the practitioner's written report is limited. Also see **nonparticipant party**.

Statements on Standards for Attestation Engagements (SSAEs). See **attestation standards**.

Subject matter. The phenomenon that is measured or evaluated by applying criteria.

Subservice organization (in the context of section 320). A service organization used by another service organization to perform some of the services provided to user entities that are likely to be relevant to those user entities' internal control over financial reporting.

Sufficiency of evidence (in the context of section 205). The measure of the quantity of evidence. The quantity of the evidence needed is affected by the risks of material misstatement and also by the quality of such evidence. Also see **evidence.**

Sufficiency of review evidence (in the context of section 210). The measure of the quantity of review evidence. The quantity of the review evidence needed is affected by the risks of material misstatement and also by the quality of such evidence. Also see **review evidence.**

Suitable criteria. The benchmarks used to measure or evaluate the subject matter that are established or developed by groups composed of experts that follow due process procedures, including exposure of the proposed criteria for public comment, are ordinarily considered suitable. Criteria promulgated by a body designated by the Council of the AICPA under the AICPA Code of Professional Conduct are, by definition, considered to be suitable. Suitable criteria exhibit all the following characteristics:

- *Relevance*. Criteria are relevant to the subject matter.
- *Objectivity*. Criteria are free from bias.
- *Measurability*. Criteria permit reasonably consistent measurements, qualitative or quantitative, of subject matter.
- *Completeness*. Criteria are complete when subject matter prepared in accordance with them does not omit relevant factors that could reasonably be expected to affect decisions of the intended users made on the basis of that subject matter.

Test of controls (in the context of section 205). A procedure designed to evaluate the operating effectiveness of controls in preventing, or detecting and correcting, material misstatements in the subject matter.

Test of controls (in the context of section 320). A procedure designed to evaluate the operating effectiveness of controls in achieving the control objectives stated in management's description of the service organization's system.

Type 1 report. See **management's description of a service organization's system and a service auditor's report on that description and on the suitability of the design of controls.**

Type 2 report. See **management's description of a service organization's system and a service auditor's report on that description and on the suitability of the design and operating effectiveness of controls.**

Unconditional requirements. The category of professional requirements with which the practitioner must comply in all cases in which such requirement is relevant. The attestation standards use the word *must* to indicate an unconditional requirement. Also see **attestation standards** and **presumptively mandatory requirements.**

User auditor (in the context of section 320). An auditor who audits and reports on the financial statements of a user entity.

User entity (in the context of section 320). An entity that uses a service organization for which controls at the service organization are likely to be relevant to that entity's internal control over financial reporting.

Working papers or **workpapers.** See **engagement documentation**.

AT-C Section 100

COMMON CONCEPTS

The following is a Codification of Statements on Standards for Attestation Engagements (SSAEs) resulting from the Auditing Standards Board's (ASB) project to clarify the SSAEs and related attestation interpretations. SSAEs are issued by senior committees of the AICPA designated to issue pronouncements on attestation matters applicable to the preparation and issuance of attestation reports for entities that are nonissuers. The "Compliance With Standards Rule" (ET sec. 1.310.001) of the AICPA Code of Professional Conduct requires an AICPA member performing an attestation engagement for a nonissuer (a practitioner) to comply with standards promulgated by the ASB. A practitioner must comply with an unconditional requirement in all cases in which such requirement is relevant. A practitioner also must comply with a presumptively mandatory requirement in all cases in which such requirement is relevant; however, if, in rare circumstances, a practitioner judges it necessary to depart from a relevant presumptively mandatory requirement, the practitioner must document the justification for the departure and how the alternative procedures performed in the circumstances were sufficient to achieve the intent of that requirement.

Attestation interpretations are interpretive publications, as defined in section 105, *Concepts Common to All Attestation Engagements*. Section 105 requires the practitioner to consider applicable interpretive publications in planning and performing the attestation engagement. Interpretive publications are not attestation standards. Interpretive publications are recommendations on the application of the SSAEs in specific circumstances, including engagements for entities in specialized industries. An interpretive publication is issued under the authority of the relevant senior technical committee after all members of the committee have been provided an opportunity to consider and comment on whether the proposed interpretive publication is consistent with the SSAEs. Attestation interpretations are included in AT-C sections. AICPA Guides and Attestation Statements of Position are listed in AT-C appendix A, "AICPA Guides and Statements of Position."

TABLE OF CONTENTS

AT-C Section 105*

Concepts Common to All Attestation Engagements

Source: SSAE No. 18.

Effective for practitioners' reports dated on or after May 1, 2017.

Introduction

.01 This section applies to engagements in which a CPA in the practice of public accounting is engaged to issue, or does issue, a practitioner's examination, review, or agreed-upon procedures report on subject matter or an assertion about subject matter (hereinafter referred to as an *assertion*) that is the responsibility of another party. (Ref: par. .A1)

.02 An attestation engagement is predicated on the concept that a party other than the practitioner makes an assertion about whether the subject matter is measured or evaluated in accordance with suitable criteria. Section 205, *Examination Engagements*; section 210, *Review Engagements*; and section 215, *Agreed-Upon Procedures Engagements*, require the practitioner to request such an assertion in writing when performing an examination, review, or agreed-upon procedures engagement.[1] In examination and review engagements, when the engaging party is the responsible party, the responsible party's refusal to provide a written assertion requires the practitioner to withdraw from the engagement when withdrawal is possible under applicable laws and regulations.[2] In examination and review engagements, when the engaging party is not the responsible party and the responsible party refuses to provide a written assertion, the practitioner need not withdraw from the engagement but is required to disclose that refusal in the practitioner's report and restrict the use of the report to the engaging party.[3] In an agreed-upon procedures engagement, the responsible party's refusal to provide a written assertion requires the practitioner to disclose that refusal in the report.[4]

.03 This section is not applicable to professional services for which the AICPA has established other professional standards, for example, services performed in accordance with (Ref: par. .A2–.A3)

a. Statements on Auditing Standards,

b. Statements on Standards for Accounting and Review Services, or

c. Statements on Standards for Tax Services.

.04 An attestation engagement may be part of a larger engagement, for example, a feasibility study or business acquisition study that also includes an

---

* This section contains an "AT-C" identifier, instead of an "AT" identifier, to avoid confusion with references to existing "AT" sections, which remain effective through April 2017.

1 Paragraph .10 of section 205, *Examination Engagements*; paragraph .11 of section 210, *Review Engagements*; and paragraph .15 of section 215, *Agreed-Upon Procedures Engagements*.

2 Paragraph .82 of section 205 and paragraph .59 of section 210.

3 Paragraph .84 of section 205 and paragraph .60 of section 210.

4 Paragraph .36 of section 215.

examination of prospective financial information. In such circumstances, the attestation standards apply only to the attestation portion of the engagement.

Compliance With the Attestation Standards

.05 The "Compliance With Standards Rule" (ET sec. 1.310.001) of the AICPA Code of Professional Conduct requires members who perform professional services to comply with standards promulgated by bodies designated by the Council of the AICPA.

Relationship of Attestation Standards to Quality Control Standards

.06 Quality control systems, policies, and procedures are the responsibility of the firm in conducting its attestation practice. Under QC section 10, *A Firm's System of Quality Control*, the firm has an obligation to establish and maintain a system of quality control to provide it with reasonable assurance that[5] (Ref: par. .A4–.A6)

a. the firm and its personnel comply with professional standards and applicable legal and regulatory requirements and

b. practitioners' reports issued by the firm are appropriate in the circumstances.

.07 Attestation standards relate to the conduct of individual attestation engagements; quality control standards relate to the conduct of a firm's attestation practice as a whole. Thus, attestation standards and quality control standards are related, and the quality control policies and procedures that a firm adopts may affect both the conduct of individual attestation engagements and the conduct of a firm's attestation practice as a whole. However, deficiencies in or instances of noncompliance with a firm's quality control policies and procedures do not, in and of themselves, indicate that a particular engagement was not performed in accordance with the attestation standards.

Effective Date

.08 This section is effective for practitioners' reports dated on or after May 1, 2017.

Objectives

.09 In conducting an attestation engagement, the overall objectives of the practitioner are to

a. apply the requirements relevant to the attestation engagement;

b. report on the subject matter or assertion, and communicate as required by the applicable AT-C section, in accordance with the results of the practitioner's procedures; and

c. implement quality control procedures at the engagement level that provide the practitioner with reasonable assurance that the attestation engagement complies with professional standards and applicable legal and regulatory requirements.

---

[5] Paragraph .12 of QC section 10, *A Firm's System of Quality Control*.

Definitions

.10 For purposes of the attestation standards, the following terms have the meanings attributed as follows:

Assertion. Any declaration or set of declarations about whether the subject matter is in accordance with (or based on) the criteria.

Attestation engagement. An examination, review, or agreed-upon procedures engagement performed under the attestation standards related to subject matter or an assertion that is the responsibility of another party. The following are the three types of attestation engagements:

a. **Examination engagement.** An attestation engagement in which the practitioner obtains reasonable assurance by obtaining sufficient appropriate evidence about the measurement or evaluation of subject matter against criteria in order to be able to draw reasonable conclusions on which to base the practitioner's opinion about whether the subject matter is in accordance with (or based on) the criteria or the assertion is fairly stated, in all material respects. (Ref: par. .A7)

b. **Review engagement.** An attestation engagement in which the practitioner obtains limited assurance by obtaining sufficient appropriate review evidence about the measurement or evaluation of subject matter against criteria in order to express a conclusion about whether any material modification should be made to the subject matter in order for it be in accordance with (or based on) the criteria or to the assertion in order for it to be fairly stated. (Ref: par. .A8)

c. **Agreed-upon procedures engagement.** An attestation engagement in which a practitioner performs specific procedures on subject matter or an assertion and reports the findings without providing an opinion or a conclusion on it. The parties to the engagement (*specified party*), as defined later in this paragraph, agree upon and are responsible for the sufficiency of the procedures for their purposes.

Attestation risk. In an examination or review engagement, the risk that the practitioner expresses an inappropriate opinion or conclusion, as applicable, when the subject matter or assertion is materially misstated. (Ref: par. .A9–.A15)

Criteria. The benchmarks used to measure or evaluate the subject matter. (Ref: par. .A16)

Documentation completion date. The date on which the practitioner has assembled for retention a complete and final set of documentation in the engagement file.

Engagement circumstances. The broad context defining the particular engagement, which includes the terms of the engagement; whether it is an examination, review, or agreed-upon procedures engagement; the characteristics of the subject matter; the criteria; the information needs of the intended users; relevant characteristics of the responsible party and, if different, the engaging party and their environment; and other matters, for example, events, transactions, conditions and practices, and relevant laws and regulations, that may have a significant effect on the engagement.

Engagement documentation. The record of procedures performed, relevant evidence obtained, and, in an examination or review engagement, conclusions reached by the practitioner, or in an agreed-upon procedures engagement, findings of the practitioner. (Terms such as *working papers* or *workpapers* are also sometimes used).

Engagement partner. The partner or other person in the firm who is responsible for the attestation engagement and its performance and for the practitioner's report that is issued on behalf of the firm and who, when required, has the appropriate authority from a professional, legal, or regulatory body. *Engagement partner*, *partner*, and *firm* refer to their governmental equivalents when relevant.

Engagement team. All partners and staff performing the engagement and any individuals engaged by the firm or a network firm who perform attestation procedures on the engagement. This excludes a practitioner's external specialist and engagement quality control reviewer engaged by the firm or a network firm. The term *engagement team* also excludes individuals within the client's internal audit function who provide direct assistance.

Engaging party. The party(ies) that engages the practitioner to perform the attestation engagement. (Ref: par. .A17)

Evidence. Information used by the practitioner in arriving at the opinion, conclusion, or findings on which the practitioner's report is based.

Firm. A form of organization permitted by law or regulation whose characteristics conform to resolutions of the Council of the AICPA and that is engaged in the practice of public accounting.

Fraud. An intentional act involving the use of deception that results in a misstatement in the subject matter or the assertion.

General use. Use of a practitioner's report that is not restricted to specified parties.

Internal audit function. A function of an entity that performs assurance and consulting activities designed to evaluate and improve the effectiveness of the entity's governance, risk management, and internal control processes.

Misstatement. A difference between the measurement or evaluation of the subject matter by the responsible party and the proper measurement or evaluation of the subject matter based on the criteria. Misstatements can be intentional or unintentional, qualitative or quantitative, and include omissions. In certain engagements, a misstatement may be referred to as a *deviation*, *exception*, or *instance of noncompliance*.

Network firm. A firm or other entity that belongs to a network, as defined in ET section 0.400, *Definitions*.

Noncompliance with laws or regulations. Acts of omission or commission by the entity, either intentional or unintentional, that are contrary to the prevailing laws or regulations. Such acts include transactions entered into by, or in the name of, the entity or on its behalf by those charged with governance, management, or employees. *Noncompliance* does not include personal misconduct (unrelated to the subject matter) by those charged with governance, management, or employees of the entity.

Other practitioner. An independent practitioner who is not a member of the engagement team who performs work on information that will be used as evidence by the practitioner performing the attestation engagement. An other practitioner may be part of the practitioner's firm, a network firm, or another firm.

Practitioner. The person or persons conducting the attestation engagement, usually the engagement partner or other members of the engagement team, or, as applicable, the firm. When an AT-C section expressly intends that a requirement or responsibility be fulfilled by the engagement partner, the term *engagement partner*, rather than *practitioner*, is used. *Engagement partner* and *firm* are to be read as referring to their governmental equivalents when relevant.

Practitioner's specialist. An individual or organization possessing expertise in a field other than accounting or attestation, whose work in that field is used by the practitioner to assist the practitioner in obtaining evidence for the service being provided. A practitioner's specialist may be either a practitioner's internal specialist (who is a partner or staff, including temporary staff, of the practitioner's firm or a network firm) or a practitioner's external specialist. *Partner* and *firm* refer to their governmental equivalents when relevant.

Professional judgment. The application of relevant training, knowledge, and experience, within the context provided by attestation and ethical standards in making informed decisions about the courses of action that are appropriate in the circumstances of the attestation engagement.

Professional skepticism. An attitude that includes a questioning mind, being alert to conditions that may indicate possible misstatement due to fraud or error, and a critical assessment of evidence.

Reasonable assurance. A high, but not absolute, level of assurance.

Report release date. The date on which the practitioner grants the engaging party permission to use the practitioner's report.

Responsible party. The party(ies) responsible for the subject matter. If the nature of the subject matter is such that no such party exists, a party who has a reasonable basis for making a written assertion about the subject matter may be deemed to be the responsible party.

Specified party. The intended user(s) to whom use of the written practitioner's report is limited.

Subject matter. The phenomenon that is measured or evaluated by applying criteria.

.11 For the purposes of the attestation standards, references to appropriate party(ies) should be read hereafter as the responsible party or the engaging party, as appropriate. (Ref: par. .A18)

Requirements

Conduct of an Attestation Engagement in Accordance With the Attestation Standards

Complying With AT-C Sections That Are Relevant to the Engagement

.12 When performing an attestation engagement, the practitioner should comply with

- this section;
- sections 205, 210, or 215, as applicable; and
- any subject-matter AT-C section relevant to the engagement when the AT-C section is in effect and the circumstances addressed by the AT-C section exist.

.13 The practitioner should not represent compliance with this or any other AT-C section unless the practitioner has complied with the requirements of this section and all other AT-C sections relevant to the engagement.

.14 Reports issued by a practitioner in connection with services performed under other professional standards should be written to be clearly distinguishable from and not confused with reports issued under the attestation standards. (Ref: par. .A19–.A20)

Text of an AT-C Section

.15 The practitioner should have an understanding of the entire text of each AT-C section that is relevant to the engagement being performed, including its application and other explanatory material, to understand its objectives and apply its requirements properly. (Ref: par. .A21–.A26)

Complying With Relevant Requirements

.16 Subject to paragraph .20, the practitioner should comply with each requirement of the AT-C sections that is relevant to the engagement being performed, including any relevant subject-matter AT-C section, unless, in the circumstances of the engagement,

a. the entire AT-C section is not relevant, or

b. the requirement is not relevant because it is conditional, and the condition does not exist.

.17 When a practitioner undertakes an attestation engagement for the benefit of a government body or agency and agrees to follow specified government standards, guides, procedures, statutes, rules, and regulations, the practitioner should comply with those governmental requirements as well as the applicable AT-C sections. (Ref: par. .A27)

Practitioner's Report Prescribed by Law or Regulation

.18 If the practitioner is required by law or regulation to use a specific layout, form, or wording of the practitioner's report and the prescribed form of report is not acceptable or would cause a practitioner to make a statement that the practitioner has no basis to make, the practitioner should reword the prescribed form of report or attach an appropriately worded separate practitioner's report. (Ref: par. .A28)

Defining Professional Requirements in the Attestation Standards

.19 The attestation standards use the following two categories of professional requirements, identified by specific terms, to describe the degree of responsibility it imposes on practitioners:

- *Unconditional requirements*. The practitioner must comply with an unconditional requirement in all cases in which such requirement is relevant. The attestation standards use the word *must* to indicate an unconditional requirement.
- *Presumptively mandatory requirements*. The practitioner must comply with a presumptively mandatory requirement in all cases in which such a requirement is relevant, except in rare circumstances discussed in paragraph .20. The attestation standards use the word *should* to indicate a presumptively mandatory requirement.

Departure From a Relevant Requirement

.20 In rare circumstances, the practitioner may judge it necessary to depart from a relevant presumptively mandatory requirement. In such circumstances, the practitioner should perform alternative procedures to achieve the intent of that requirement. The need for the practitioner to depart from a relevant, presumptively mandatory requirement is expected to arise only when the requirement is for a specific procedure to be performed and, in the specific circumstances of the engagement, that procedure would be ineffective in achieving the intent of the requirement. (Ref: par. .A29)

Interpretive Publications

.21 The practitioner should consider applicable interpretive publications in planning and performing the attestation engagement. (Ref: par. .A30)

Other Attestation Publications

.22 In applying the attestation guidance included in an other attestation publication, the practitioner should, exercising professional judgment, assess the relevance and appropriateness of such guidance to the circumstances of the attestation engagement. (Ref: par. .A31–.A33)

Acceptance and Continuance

.23 The engagement partner should be satisfied that appropriate procedures regarding the acceptance and continuance of client relationships and attestation engagements have been followed and should determine that conclusions reached in this regard are appropriate.

Preconditions for an Attestation Engagement

.24 The practitioner must be independent when performing an attestation engagement in accordance with the attestation standards unless the practitioner is required by law or regulation to accept the engagement and report on the subject matter or assertion. (Ref: par. .A34)

.25 In order to establish that the preconditions for an attestation engagement are present, the practitioner should determine both of the following:

a. The responsible party is a party other than the practitioner and takes responsibility for the subject matter. (Ref: par. .A35)

b. The engagement exhibits all of the following characteristics:

i. The subject matter is appropriate. (Ref: par. .A36–.A41)

ii. The criteria to be applied in the preparation and evaluation of the subject matter are suitable and will be available to the intended users. (Ref: par. .A43–.A52)

iii. The practitioner expects to be able to obtain the evidence needed to arrive at the practitioner's opinion, conclusion, or findings, including (Ref: par. .A53–.A54)

(1) access to all information of which the responsible party is aware that is relevant to the measurement, evaluation, or disclosure of the subject matter;

(2) access to additional information that the practitioner may request from the responsible party for the purpose of the engagement; and

(3) unrestricted access to persons within the appropriate party(ies) from whom the practitioner determines it necessary to obtain evidence.

iv. The practitioner's opinion, conclusion, or findings, in the form appropriate to the engagement, is to be contained in a written practitioner's report.

.26 If the preconditions in paragraphs .24–.25 are not present, the practitioner should discuss the matter with the engaging party to attempt to resolve the issue.

.27 The practitioner should accept an attestation engagement only when the practitioner

a. has no reason to believe that relevant ethical requirements, including independence, will not be satisfied;

b. is satisfied that those persons who are to perform the engagement collectively have the appropriate competence and capabilities (see also paragraph .32);

c. has determined that the engagement to be performed meets all the preconditions for an attestation engagement (see also paragraphs .24–.25); and

d. has reached a common understanding with the engaging party of the terms of the engagement, including the practitioner's reporting responsibilities.

.28 If it is discovered after the engagement has been accepted that one or more of the preconditions for an attestation engagement is not present, the practitioner should discuss the matter with the appropriate party(ies) and should determine

a. whether the matter can be resolved;

b. whether it is appropriate to continue with the engagement; and

c. if the matter cannot be resolved but it is still appropriate to continue with the engagement, whether, and if so how, to communicate the matter in the practitioner's report.

Acceptance of a Change in the Terms of the Engagement

.29 The practitioner should not agree to a change in the terms of the engagement when no reasonable justification for doing so exists. If a change in the terms of the engagement is made, the practitioner should not disregard evidence that was obtained prior to the change. (Ref: par. .A55–.A56)

.30 If the practitioner concludes, based on the practitioner's professional judgment, that there is reasonable justification to change the terms of the engagement from the original level of service that the practitioner was engaged to perform to a lower level of service, for example, from an examination to a review, and if the practitioner complies with the AT-C sections applicable to the lower level of service, the practitioner should issue an appropriate practitioner's report on the lower level of service. The report should not include reference to (*a*) the original engagement, (*b*) any procedures that may have been performed, or (*c*) scope limitations that resulted in the changed engagement.

Using the Work of an Other Practitioner

.31 When the practitioner expects to use the work of an other practitioner, the practitioner should (Ref: par. .A57–.A58)

a. obtain an understanding of whether the other practitioner understands and will comply with the ethical requirements that are relevant to the engagement and, in particular, is independent.

b. obtain an understanding of the other practitioner's professional competence.

c. communicate clearly with the other practitioner about the scope and timing of the other practitioner's work and findings.

d. if assuming responsibility for the work of the other practitioner, be involved in the work of the other practitioner.

e. evaluate whether the other practitioner's work is adequate for the practitioner's purposes.

f. determine whether to make reference to the other practitioner in the practitioner's report.

Quality Control

Assignment of the Engagement Team and the Practitioner's Specialists

.32 The engagement partner should be satisfied that

a. the engagement team, and any practitioner's external specialists, collectively, have the appropriate competence, including knowledge of the subject matter, and capabilities to (Ref: par. .A59–.A60)

   i. perform the engagement in accordance with professional standards and applicable legal and regulatory requirements and

   ii. enable the issuance of a practitioner's report that is appropriate in the circumstances.

b. to an extent that is sufficient to accept responsibility for the opinion, conclusion, or findings on the subject matter or assertion, the engagement team will be able to be involved in the work of

   i. a practitioner's external specialist when the work of that specialist is to be used and (Ref: par. .A61)

   ii. an other practitioner, when the work of that practitioner is to be used.

c. those involved in the engagement have been informed of their responsibilities, including the objectives of the procedures they are to perform and matters that may affect the nature, timing, and extent of such procedures.

d. engagement team members have been directed to bring to the engagement partner's attention significant questions raised during the engagement so that their significance may be assessed.

Leadership Responsibilities for Quality in Attestation Engagements

.33 The engagement partner should take responsibility for the overall quality on each attestation engagement. This includes responsibility for the following:

a. Appropriate procedures being performed regarding the acceptance and continuance of client relationships and engagements

b. The engagement being planned and performed (including appropriate direction and supervision) to comply with professional standards and applicable legal and regulatory requirements

c. Reviews being performed in accordance with the firm's review policies and procedures and reviewing the engagement documentation on or before the date of the practitioner's report (Ref: par. .A62)

d. Appropriate engagement documentation being maintained to provide evidence of achievement of the practitioner's objectives and that the engagement was performed in accordance with the attestation standards and relevant legal and regulatory requirements

e. Appropriate consultation being undertaken by the engagement team on difficult or contentious matters

Engagement Documentation

.34 The practitioner should prepare engagement documentation on a timely basis. (Ref: par. .A63)

.35 The practitioner should assemble the engagement documentation in an engagement file and complete the administrative process of assembling the final engagement file no later than 60 days following the practitioner's report release date. (Ref: par. .A64)

.36 After the documentation completion date, the practitioner should not delete or discard documentation of any nature before the end of its retention period.

.37 If the practitioner finds it necessary to amend existing engagement documentation or add new engagement documentation after the documentation completion date, the practitioner should, regardless of the nature of the amendments or additions, document

a. the specific reasons for making the amendments or additions and

b. when, and by whom, they were made and reviewed.

.38 Engagement documentation is the property of the practitioner, and some jurisdictions recognize this right of ownership in their statutes. The practitioner should adopt reasonable procedures to retain engagement documentation for a period of time sufficient to meet the needs of the practitioner and to satisfy any applicable legal or regulatory requirements for records retention.

.39 Because engagement documentation often contains confidential information, the practitioner should adopt reasonable procedures to maintain the confidentiality of that information.

.40 The practitioner also should adopt reasonable procedures to prevent unauthorized access to engagement documentation.

.41 If, in rare circumstances, the practitioner judges it necessary to depart from a relevant, presumptively mandatory requirement, the practitioner should document the justification for the departure and how the alternative procedures performed in the circumstances were sufficient to achieve the intent of that requirement. (See paragraph .20.)

Engagement Quality Control Review

.42 For those engagements, if any, for which the firm has determined that an engagement quality control review is required (Ref: par. .A65)

a. the engagement partner should take responsibility for discussing with the engagement quality control reviewer significant findings or issues arising during the engagement, including those identified during the engagement quality control review, and not release the practitioner's report until completion of the engagement quality control review and

b. the engagement quality control reviewer should perform an objective evaluation of the significant judgments made by the engagement team and the conclusions reached in formulating the report. This evaluation should include the following:

  i. Discussion of significant findings or issues with the engagement partner

  ii. Reading the written subject matter or assertion and the proposed report

  iii. Reading selected engagement documentation relating to the significant judgments the engagement team made and the related conclusions it reached

  iv. Evaluation of the conclusions reached in formulating the report and consideration of whether the proposed report is appropriate

Professional Skepticism and Professional Judgment

Professional Skepticism

.43 The practitioner should plan and perform an attestation engagement with professional skepticism. (Ref: par. .A66–.A68)

.44 Unless the practitioner has reason to believe the contrary, the practitioner may accept records and documents as genuine. If conditions identified during the attestation engagement cause the practitioner to believe that a document may not be authentic or that terms in a document have been modified but not disclosed to the practitioner, the practitioner should investigate further.

Professional Judgment

.45 The practitioner should exercise professional judgment in planning and performing an attestation engagement. (Ref: par. .A69–.A74)

Application and Other Explanatory Material

Introduction (Ref: par. .01 and .03)

.A1 The subject matter of an attestation engagement may take many forms, including the following:

a. Historical or prospective performance or condition, for example, historical or prospective financial information, performance measurements, and backlog data

b. Physical characteristics, for example, narrative descriptions or square footage of facilities

c. Historical events, for example, the price of a market basket of goods on a certain date

d. Analyses, for example, break-even analyses

e. Systems and processes, for example, internal control

f. Behavior, for example, corporate governance, compliance with laws and regulations, and human resource practices

The subject matter may be as of a point in time or for a period of time.

.A2 The attestation standards do not apply to litigation services that involve pending or potential legal or regulatory proceedings before a trier of fact when the practitioner has not been engaged to issue, and does not issue, a practitioner's examination, review, or agreed-upon procedures report on subject matter or an assertion that is the responsibility of another party and any of the following circumstances exist:

a. The service comprises being an expert witness.

b. The service comprises being a trier of fact or acting on behalf of one.

c. The practitioner's work under the rules of the proceedings is subject to detailed analysis and challenge by each party to the dispute.

d. The practitioner is engaged by an attorney to do work that will be protected by the attorney's work product or attorney-client privilege, and such work is not intended to be used for other purposes.

.A3 Because performance audits performed pursuant to *Government Auditing Standards* do not require a practitioner's examination, review, or agreed-upon procedures report as described in this section, this section does not apply to performance audits unless the practitioner engaged to conduct a performance audit is also engaged to conduct an AICPA attestation engagement or issues such an examination, review, or agreed-upon procedures report.

Relationship of Attestation Standards to Quality Control Standards (Ref: par. .06)

.A4 The nature and extent of a firm's quality control policies and procedures depend on factors such as its size, the degree of operating autonomy allowed its personnel and its practice offices, the nature of its practice, its organization, and appropriate cost-benefit considerations.

.A5 Within the context of the firm's system of quality control, engagement teams have a responsibility to implement quality control procedures that are applicable to the attestation engagement and provide the firm with relevant information to enable the functioning of that part of the firm's quality control relating to independence.

.A6 Engagement teams are entitled to rely on the firm's system of quality control, unless the engagement partner determines that it is inappropriate to do so based on information provided by the firm or other parties.

Definitions

Examination Engagement (Ref: par. .10)

.A7 The practitioner obtains the same level of assurance in an examination engagement as the practitioner does in a financial statement audit.

Review Engagement (Ref: par. .10)

.A8 The practitioner obtains the same level of assurance in a review engagement as the practitioner does in a review of financial statements.

Attestation Risk (Ref: par. .10)

.A9 Attestation risk does not refer to the practitioner's business risks, such as loss from litigation, adverse publicity, or other events arising in connection with the subject matter or assertion reported on.

.A10 In general, attestation risk can be represented by the following components, although not all of these components will necessarily be present or significant for all engagements:

a. Risks that the practitioner does not directly influence, which consist of

   i. the susceptibility of the subject matter to a material misstatement before consideration of any related controls (inherent risk) and

   ii. the risk that a material misstatement that could occur in the subject matter will not be prevented, or detected and corrected, on a timely basis by the appropriate party(ies)'s internal control (control risk)

b. Risk that the practitioner does directly influence, which consists of the risk that the procedures to be performed by the practitioner will not detect a material misstatement (detection risk)

.A11 The degree to which each of these components of attestation risk is relevant to the engagement is affected by the engagement circumstances, in particular

- the nature of the subject matter or assertion. (For example, the concept of control risk may be more useful when the subject matter or assertion relates to the preparation of information about an entity's performance than when it relates to information about the existence of a physical condition.)
- the type of engagement being performed. (For example, in a review engagement, the practitioner may often decide to obtain evidence by means other than tests of controls, in which case, consideration of control risk may be less relevant than in an examination engagement on the same subject matter or assertion.)

.A12 The consideration of risks is a matter of professional judgment, rather than a matter capable of precise measurement.

.A13 In an examination engagement, the practitioner reduces attestation risk to an acceptably low level in the circumstances of the engagement as the basis for the practitioner's opinion. Reducing attestation risk to zero is not contemplated in an examination engagement and, therefore, reasonable assurance is less than absolute assurance as a result of factors such as the following:

- The use of selective testing
- The inherent limitations of internal control
- The fact that much of the evidence available to the practitioner is persuasive, rather than conclusive
- The use of professional judgment in gathering and evaluating evidence and forming conclusions based on that evidence
- In some cases, the characteristics of the subject matter when evaluated or measured against the criteria

.A14 In a review engagement, attestation risk is greater than it is in an examination engagement. Because the practitioner obtains limited assurance in a review engagement, the types of procedures performed are less extensive than they are in an examination engagement and generally are limited to inquiries and analytical procedures.

.A15 Attestation risk is not applicable to an agreed-upon procedures engagement because in such engagements, the practitioner performs specific procedures (the design of which is the responsibility of the specified parties) on subject matter or an assertion and reports the findings without providing an opinion or conclusion.

Criteria (Ref: par. .10)

.A16 Suitable criteria are required for reasonably consistent measurement or evaluation of subject matter within the context of professional judgment. Without the frame of reference provided by suitable criteria, any conclusion is open to individual interpretation and misunderstanding. The suitability of criteria is context-sensitive, that is, it is determined in the context of the engagement circumstances. Even for the same subject matter, there can be different criteria, which will yield a different measurement or evaluation. For example, one responsible party might select the number of customer complaints resolved to the acknowledged satisfaction of the customer for the subject matter of customer satisfaction; another responsible party might select the number of repeat purchases in the three months following the initial purchase. The suitability of criteria is not affected by the level of assurance, that is, if criteria are unsuitable for an examination engagement, they are also unsuitable for a review engagement and vice versa.

Engaging Party (Ref: par. .10)

.A17 The engaging party, depending on the circumstances, may be management or those charged with governance of the responsible party, a governmental body or agency, the intended users, or another third party.

Appropriate Party(ies) (Ref: par. .11)

.A18 Management and governance structures vary by entity, reflecting influences such as size and ownership characteristics. Such diversity means that it is not possible for the attestation standards to specify for all engagements the person(s) with whom the practitioner is to interact regarding particular matters. For example, an entity may be a segment of an organization and not a separate legal entity. In such cases, identifying the appropriate management personnel or those charged with governance with whom to communicate may require the exercise of professional judgment.

Conduct of an Attestation Engagement in Accordance With the Attestation Standards

Complying With AT-C Sections That Are Relevant to the Engagement (Ref: par. .14)

.A19 A practitioner's report that merely excludes the phrase "was conducted in accordance with attestation standards established by the American Institute of Certified Public Accountants" but is otherwise similar to a practitioner's examination, review, or agreed-upon procedures attestation report is an example of a practitioner's report that is not clearly distinguishable from, and could be confused with, a report issued under the attestation standards.

.A20 Paragraph .14 does not prohibit combining reports issued by a practitioner under the attestation standards with reports issued under other professional standards.

Text of an AT-C Section (Ref: par. .15)

.A21 The AT-C sections contain the objectives of the practitioner and requirements designed to enable the practitioner to meet those objectives. In addition, they contain related guidance in the form of application and other explanatory material, introductory material that provides context relevant to a proper understanding of the section, and definitions.

.A22 Introductory material may include, as needed, such matters as an explanation of the following:

- The purpose and scope of the AT-C section, including how the AT-C section relates to other AT-C sections
- The subject matter of the AT-C section
- The respective responsibilities of the practitioner and others regarding the subject matter of the AT-C section
- The context in which the AT-C section is set

.A23 The application and other explanatory material provides further explanation of the requirements of an AT-C section and guidance for carrying them out. In particular, it may

a. explain more precisely what a requirement means or is intended to cover and

b. include examples of procedures that may be appropriate in the circumstances.

Although such guidance does not, in itself, impose a requirement, it may explain the proper application of the requirements of an AT-C section. The application and other explanatory material may also provide background information on matters addressed in an AT-C section. They do not, however, limit or reduce the responsibility of the practitioner to apply and comply with the requirements in applicable AT-C sections.

.A24 The practitioner is required by paragraph .15 to understand the application and other explanatory material. How the practitioner applies the guidance in the engagement depends on the exercise of professional judgment in the circumstances consistent with the objective of the section. The words *may*, *might*, and *could* are used to describe these actions and procedures.

.A25 An AT-C section may include, in a separate section under the heading "Definition(s)," a description of the meanings attributed to certain terms for purposes of the AT-C section. These are provided to assist in the consistent application and interpretation of the AT-C section and are not intended to override definitions that may be established for other purposes, whether in law, regulation, or otherwise. Unless otherwise indicated, those terms will carry the same meanings in all AT-C sections.

.A26 Appendixes form part of the application and other explanatory material. The purpose and intended use of an appendix are explained in the body of the related AT-C section or within the title and introduction of the appendix itself.

Complying With Relevant Requirements (Ref: par. .17)

.A27 In certain attestation engagements, the practitioner also may be required to comply with other requirements in addition to the attestation standards. The attestation standards do not override law or regulation that governs the attestation engagement. In the event that such law or regulation differs from attestation standards, an attestation engagement conducted only in accordance with law or regulation will not necessarily comply with the attestation standards.

Practitioner's Report Prescribed by Law or Regulation (Ref: par. .18)

.A28 Some report forms can be made acceptable by inserting additional wording to include the elements required by sections 205, 210, and 215.[6] Some report forms required by law or regulation can be made acceptable only by complete revision because the prescribed language of the practitioner's report calls for statements by the practitioner that are not consistent with the practitioner's function or responsibility, for example, a report form that requests the practitioner to "certify" the subject matter.

Departure From a Relevant Requirement (Ref: par. .20)

.A29 Paragraph .41 prescribes documentation requirements when the circumstances described in paragraph .20 occur.

Interpretive Publications (Ref: par. .21)

.A30 *Interpretive publications* are not attestation standards. Interpretive publications are recommendations on the application of the attestation standards in specific circumstances, including engagements for entities in specialized industries. An interpretive publication is issued under the authority of the relevant senior technical committee after all members of the committee have been provided an opportunity to consider and comment on whether the proposed interpretive publication is consistent with the attestation standards. Examples of interpretive publications are interpretations of the attestation standards, exhibits to the AT-C sections, and attestation guidance included in AICPA guides and attestation Statements of Position (SOPs). Interpretations of the AT-C sections and exhibits are included within the AT-C sections. AICPA guides and attestation SOPs are listed in AT-C appendix A, "AICPA Guides and Statements of Position."

---

[6] Paragraphs .63–.66 of section 205, paragraphs .46–.49 of section 210, and paragraph .35 of section 215.

Other Attestation Publications (Ref: par. .22)

.A31 *Other attestation publications* are publications other than interpretive publications. These include AICPA attestation publications not defined as interpretive publications; attestation articles in the *Journal of Accountancy* and other professional journals; continuing professional education programs and other instruction materials, textbooks, guidebooks, attestation programs, and checklists; and other attestation publications from state CPA societies, other organizations, and individuals. Other attestation publications have no authoritative status; however, they may help the practitioner understand and apply the attestation standards. The practitioner is not expected to be aware of the full body of other attestation publications.

.A32 Although the practitioner determines the relevance of these publications in accordance with paragraph .22, the practitioner may presume that other attestation publications published by the AICPA that have been reviewed by the AICPA Audit and Attest Standards staff are appropriate. These other attestation publications are listed in AT-C appendix B, "Other Attestation Publications."

.A33 In determining whether an other attestation publication that has not been reviewed by the AICPA Audit and Attest Standards staff is appropriate to the circumstances of the attestation engagement, the practitioner may wish to consider the degree to which the publication is recognized as being helpful in understanding and applying the attestation standards and the degree to which the issuer or author is recognized as an authority in attestation matters.

Preconditions for an Attestation Engagement (Ref: par. .24-.25b[ii])

.A34 The "Independence Standards for Engagements Performed in Accordance With Statements on Standards for Attestation Engagements" interpretation (ET sec. 1.297) establishes special requirements for independence for services provided under the attestation standards. In addition, the "Conceptual Framework Approach" interpretation (ET sec. 1.210.010) discusses threats to independence not specifically detailed elsewhere, for example, when the practitioner has an interest in the subject matter.

.A35 The responsible party may acknowledge its responsibility for the subject matter or for the written assertion as it relates to the objective of the engagement in a number of ways, for example, in an engagement letter, a representation letter, or the presentation of the subject matter, including the notes thereto, or the written assertion. Examples of other evidence of the responsible party's responsibility for the subject matter include reference to legislation, a regulation, or a contract.

Appropriateness of Subject Matter (Ref: par. .25b[i])

.A36 An element of the appropriateness of subject matter is the existence of a reasonable basis for measuring or evaluating the subject matter. The responsible party in an attestation engagement is responsible for having a reasonable basis for measuring or evaluating the subject matter. What constitutes a reasonable basis will depend on the nature of the subject matter and other engagement circumstances. In some cases, a formal process with extensive internal controls may be needed to provide the responsible party with a reasonable basis for concluding that the measurement or evaluation of the subject matter is free from material misstatement. The fact that the practitioner will report on the subject matter or assertion is not a substitute for the responsible party's own processes to have a reasonable basis for measuring or evaluating the subject matter or assertion.

.A37 An appropriate subject matter

- *a.* is identifiable and capable of consistent measurement or evaluation against the criteria and
- *b.* can be subjected to procedures for obtaining sufficient appropriate evidence to support an opinion, conclusion, or findings, as appropriate.

.A38 If the subject matter is not appropriate for an examination engagement, it also is not appropriate for a review engagement.

.A39 Different subject matters have different characteristics, including the degree to which information about them is qualitative versus quantitative, objective versus subjective, historical versus prospective, and relates to a point in time or covers a period. Such characteristics affect the following:

- *a.* Precision with which the subject matter can be measured or evaluated against criteria
- *b.* The persuasiveness of available evidence

.A40 Identifying such characteristics and considering their effects assists the practitioner when assessing the appropriateness of the subject matter and also in determining the content of the practitioner's report.

.A41 In some cases, the attestation engagement may relate to only one part of a broader subject matter. For example, the practitioner may be engaged to examine one aspect of an entity's contribution to sustainable development, such as the programs run by the entity that have positive environmental outcomes, and may be aware that the practitioner has not been engaged to examine more significant programs with less favorable outcomes. In such cases, in determining whether the engagement exhibits the characteristic of having an appropriate subject matter, it may be appropriate for the practitioner to consider whether information about the aspect that the practitioner is asked to examine is likely to meet the information needs of intended users.

Suitable and Available Criteria (Ref: par. .25b[ii])

.A42 Suitable criteria exhibit all of the following characteristics:

- *Relevance*. Criteria are relevant to the subject matter.
- *Objectivity*. Criteria are free from bias.
- *Measurability*. Criteria permit reasonably consistent measurements, qualitative or quantitative, of subject matter.
- *Completeness*. Criteria are complete when subject matter prepared in accordance with them does not omit relevant factors that could reasonably be expected to affect decisions of the intended users made on the basis of that subject matter.

The relative importance of each characteristic to a particular engagement is a matter of professional judgment.

.A43 Criteria can be developed in a variety of ways, for example, they may be

- embodied in laws or regulations.
- issued by authorized or recognized bodies of experts that follow a transparent due process.

- developed collectively by a group that does not follow a transparent due process.
- published in scholarly journals or books.
- developed for sale on a proprietary basis.
- specifically designed for the purpose of measuring, evaluating, or disclosing the subject matter or assertion in the particular circumstances of the engagement.

How criteria are developed may affect the work that the practitioner carries out to assess their suitability.

.A44 Criteria that are established or developed by groups composed of experts that follow due process procedures, including exposure of the proposed criteria for public comment, are ordinarily considered suitable. Criteria promulgated by a body designated by the Council of the AICPA under the AICPA Code of Professional Conduct are, by definition, considered to be suitable.

.A45 In some cases, laws or regulations prescribe the criteria to be used for the engagement. In the absence of indications to the contrary, such criteria are presumed to be suitable.

.A46 Criteria may be established or developed by the engaging party, the responsible party, industry associations, or other groups that do not follow due process procedures or do not as clearly represent the public interest. The practitioner's determination of whether such criteria are suitable is based on the characteristics described in paragraph .A42.

.A47 Regardless of who establishes or develops the criteria, the responsible party or the engaging party is responsible for selecting the criteria, and the engaging party is responsible for determining that such criteria are appropriate for its purposes.

.A48 Some criteria may be suitable for only a limited number of parties who either participated in their establishment or can be presumed to have an adequate understanding of the criteria. For example, criteria set forth in a lease agreement for override payments may be suitable only for reporting to the parties to the agreement because of the likelihood that such criteria would be misunderstood or misinterpreted by parties other than those who have specifically agreed to the criteria. Such criteria can be agreed upon directly by the parties or through a designated representative.

.A49 Even when established criteria exist for a subject matter, specific users may agree to other criteria for their specific purposes. For example, various frameworks can be used as established criteria for evaluating the effectiveness of internal control. Specific users may, however, develop a more detailed set of criteria that meet their specific information needs.

.A50 If criteria are specifically designed for the purpose of measuring, evaluating, or disclosing the subject matter or assertion in the particular circumstances of the engagement, they are not suitable if they result in subject matter, an assertion, or a practitioner's report that is misleading to the intended users. It is desirable for the intended users or the engaging party to acknowledge that specifically developed criteria are suitable for the intended users' purposes. The absence of such an acknowledgement may affect what is to be done to assess the suitability of the criteria and the information provided about the criteria in the report.

.A51 Criteria need to be available to the intended users to allow them to understand how the subject matter has been measured or evaluated. Criteria are made available to the intended users in one or more of the following ways:

a. Publicly

b. Through inclusion in a clear manner in the presentation of the subject matter

c. Through inclusion in a clear manner in the practitioner's report

d. By general understanding, for example, the criterion for measuring time in hours and minutes

e. Available only to specified parties, for example, terms of a contract or criteria issued by an industry association that are available only to those in the industry

.A52 When criteria are available only to specified parties, sections 205 and 210 require a statement restricting the use of the practitioner's report.[7]

Access to Evidence (Ref: par. .25b[iii])

.A53 The nature of the relationship between the responsible party and, if different, the engaging party, may affect the practitioner's ability to access records, documentation, and other information the practitioner may require as evidence to arrive at the practitioner's opinion, conclusion, or findings. Therefore, the nature of that relationship may be a relevant consideration when determining whether or not to accept the engagement.

.A54 The quantity or quality of available evidence is affected by both of the following:

a. The characteristics of the subject matter, for example, less objective evidence might be expected when the subject matter is future-oriented, rather than historical

b. Other circumstances, such as when evidence that could reasonably be expected to exist is not available, for example, because of the timing of the practitioner's appointment, an entity's document retention policy, inadequate information systems, or a restriction imposed by the responsible party

Acceptance of a Change in the Terms of the Engagement (Ref: par. .29)

.A55 A change in circumstances that affects the requirements of the responsible party or, if different, the engaging party, or a misunderstanding concerning the nature of the engagement originally requested, may be considered reasonable justification for requesting a change in the engagement, for example, from an attestation engagement to a consulting engagement or from an examination engagement to a review engagement. A change may not be considered reasonable if it appears that the change relates to information that is incorrect, incomplete, or otherwise unsatisfactory. An example of such a circumstance is a request to change the engagement from an examination to a review to avoid a modified opinion or a disclaimer of opinion in a situation in which the practitioner is unable to obtain sufficient appropriate evidence regarding the subject matter.

.A56 If the practitioner and the engaging party are unable to agree to a change in the terms of the engagement and the practitioner is not permitted to continue the original engagement, the practitioner may withdraw from the engagement when possible under applicable laws and regulations.

---

[7] Paragraph .64*b* of section 205 and paragraph .47*b* of section 210.

Using the Work of an Other Practitioner (Ref: par. .31)

.A57 The practitioner is responsible for (*a*) the direction, supervision, and performance of the engagement in compliance with professional standards; applicable regulatory and legal requirements; and the firm's policies and procedures and (*b*) determining whether the practitioner's report that is issued is appropriate in the circumstances. The practitioner may, however, use the work of other practitioners to obtain sufficient appropriate evidence to express an opinion, conclusion, or findings on the subject matter or assertion.

.A58 The engagement partner may decide to assume responsibility for the work of the other practitioner or to make reference to the other practitioner in the practitioner's report. Regardless of whether the engagement partner decides to assume responsibility or make reference, the practitioner is required to communicate clearly with the other practitioner and evaluate whether the other practitioner's work is adequate for the purposes of the engagement. The nature, timing, and extent of this involvement are affected by the practitioner's understanding of the other practitioner, such as previous experience with, or knowledge of, the other practitioner and the degree to which the engagement team and the other practitioner are subject to common quality control policies and procedures.

Quality Control

Assignment of the Engagement Team and the Practitioner's Specialists (Ref: par. .32a–b[i])

.A59 The practitioner may obtain knowledge about the specific subject matter to which the procedures are to be applied through formal or continuing education, practical experience, or consultation with others.

.A60 When considering the appropriate competence and capabilities expected of those involved in the engagement, the engagement partner may take into consideration such matters as their

- understanding of, and practical experience with, engagements of a similar nature and complexity through appropriate training and participation.
- understanding of professional standards and applicable legal and regulatory requirements.
- technical expertise, including expertise with relevant IT and specialized areas relevant to the subject matter.
- knowledge of relevant industries in which the entity operates.
- ability to apply professional judgment.
- understanding of the firm's quality control policies and procedures.

.A61 Some of the attestation work may be performed by a multidisciplinary team that includes one or more practitioner's specialists. For example, in an examination engagement, a practitioner's specialist may be needed to assist the practitioner in obtaining an understanding of the subject matter and other engagement circumstances or in assessing or responding to the risk of material misstatement.

Leadership Responsibilities for Quality in Attestation Engagements (Ref: par. .33c)

.A62 Under QC section 10, the firm's review responsibility policies and procedures are determined on the basis that suitably experienced team members review the work of other team members. The engagement partner may delegate part of the review responsibility to other members of the engagement team, in accordance with the firm's system of quality control.

Engagement Documentation (Ref: par. .34-.35)

.A63 Documentation prepared at the time work is performed or shortly thereafter is likely to be more accurate than documentation prepared at a much later time.

.A64 The completion of the assembly of the final engagement file is an administrative process that does not involve the performance of new procedures or the drawing of new conclusions. Changes may, however, be made to the documentation during the final assembly process if they are administrative in nature. Examples of such changes include the following:

- Deleting or discarding superseded documentation
- Sorting, collating, and cross-referencing working papers
- Signing off on completion checklists relating to the file assembly process
- Documenting evidence that the practitioner has obtained, discussed, and agreed with the relevant members of the engagement team before the date of the practitioner's report
- Adding information received after the date of the report, for example, an original confirmation that was previously faxed

Engagement Quality Control Review (Ref: par. .42)

.A65 Other matters that may be considered in an engagement quality control review include the following:

a. The engagement team's evaluation of the firm's independence in relation to the engagement

b. Whether appropriate consultation has taken place on matters involving differences of opinion or other difficult or contentious matters and the conclusions arising from those consultations

c. Whether engagement documentation selected for review reflects the work performed in relation to the significant judgments and supports the conclusions reached

Professional Skepticism and Professional Judgment

Professional Skepticism (Ref: par. .43)

.A66 Professional skepticism includes being alert to matters such as the following:

- Evidence that contradicts other evidence obtained
- Information that brings into question the reliability of documents and responses to inquiries to be used as evidence

- Circumstances that may indicate fraud
- Circumstances that suggest the need for procedures in addition to those required by relevant AT-C sections

.A67 Professional skepticism is necessary to the critical assessment of evidence. This includes questioning contradictory evidence and the reliability of documents and responses to inquiries and other information obtained from the appropriate party. It also includes consideration of the sufficiency and appropriateness of evidence obtained in light of the circumstances.

.A68 The practitioner neither assumes that the appropriate party is dishonest nor assumes unquestioned honesty. The practitioner cannot be expected to disregard past experience of the honesty and integrity of those who provide evidence. Nevertheless, a belief that those who provide evidence are honest and have integrity does not relieve the practitioner of the need to maintain professional skepticism or allow the practitioner to be satisfied with less than sufficient appropriate evidence for the service being provided.

Professional Judgment (Ref: par. .45)

.A69 Professional judgment is essential to the proper conduct of an attestation engagement. This is because interpretation of relevant ethical requirements and relevant AT-C sections and the informed decisions required throughout the engagement cannot be made without the application of relevant knowledge and experience to the facts and circumstances.

.A70 For examination and review engagements, professional judgment is necessary regarding decisions about the following matters:

- Materiality and attestation risk
- The nature, timing, and extent of procedures used to meet the requirements of relevant AT-C sections and gather evidence
- Evaluating whether sufficient appropriate evidence for the service being provided has been obtained and whether more needs to be done to achieve the objectives of this section, section 205, or section 210, and any relevant subject-matter-specific AT-C sections and thereby the overall objectives of the practitioner
- The evaluation of the responsible party's judgments in applying the criteria
- The drawing of conclusions based on the evidence obtained, for example, assessing the reasonableness of the evaluation or measurement of subject matter or an assertion

.A71 The distinguishing feature of professional judgment expected of a practitioner is that such judgment is exercised based on competencies necessary to achieve reasonable judgments developed by the practitioner through relevant training, knowledge, and experience.

.A72 The exercise of professional judgment in any particular case is based on the facts and circumstances that are known by the practitioner. Consultation on difficult or contentious matters during the course of the engagement, both within the engagement team and between the engagement team and others at the appropriate level within or outside the firm, assist the practitioner in making informed and reasonable judgments.

.A73 Professional judgment can be evaluated based on whether the judgment reached reflects a competent application of the attestation standards and measurement or evaluation principles and is appropriate in light of, and consistent with, the facts and circumstances that were known to the practitioner up to the date of the practitioner's report.

.A74 The requirement to exercise professional judgment applies throughout the engagement. Professional judgment also needs to be appropriately documented as required by sections 205 and 210.

AT-C Section 200

LEVEL OF SERVICE

TABLE OF CONTENTS

AT-C Section 205*

Examination Engagements

Source: SSAE No. 18.

Effective for practitioners' examination reports dated on or after May 1, 2017.

Introduction

.01 This section contains performance and reporting requirements and application guidance for all examination engagements. The requirements and guidance in this section supplement the requirements and guidance in section 105, *Concepts Common to All Attestation Engagements*.

Effective Date

.02 This section is effective for practitioners' examination reports dated on or after May 1, 2017.

Objectives

.03 In conducting an examination engagement, the objectives of the practitioner are to

a. obtain reasonable assurance about whether the subject matter as measured or evaluated against the criteria is free from material misstatement;

b. express an opinion in a written report about whether

   i. the subject matter is in accordance with (or based on) the criteria, in all material respects, or

   ii. the responsible party's assertion is fairly stated, in all material respects; and

c. communicate further as required by relevant AT-C sections.

Definitions

.04 For purposes of this section, the following terms have the meanings attributed as follows:

Appropriateness of evidence. The measure of the quality of evidence, that is, its relevancy and reliability in providing support for the practitioner's opinion.

Modified opinion. A qualified opinion, an adverse opinion, or a disclaimer of opinion.

Risk of material misstatement. The risk that the subject matter is not in accordance with (or based on) the criteria in all material

* This section contains an "AT-C" identifier, instead of an "AT" identifier, to avoid confusion with references to existing "AT" sections, which remain effective through April 2017.

respects or that the assertion is not fairly stated, in all material respects.

Sufficiency of evidence. The measure of the quantity of evidence. The quantity of the evidence needed is affected by the risks of material misstatement and also by the quality of such evidence.

Test of controls. A procedure designed to evaluate the operating effectiveness of controls in preventing, or detecting and correcting, material misstatements in the subject matter.

Requirements

Conduct of an Examination Engagement

.05 In performing an examination engagement, the practitioner should comply with this section, section 105, and any subject-matter AT-C section that is relevant to the engagement. A subject-matter AT-C section is relevant to the engagement when it is in effect, and the circumstances addressed by the AT-C section exist. (Ref: par. .A1)

Preconditions for an Examination Engagement

.06 Section 105 indicates that a practitioner must be independent when performing an attestation engagement in accordance with the attestation standards, unless the practitioner is required by law or regulation to accept the engagement and report on the subject matter or assertion.[1] When the practitioner is not independent but is required by law or regulation to accept the engagement and report on the subject matter or assertion, the practitioner should disclaim an opinion and should specifically state that the practitioner is not independent. The practitioner is neither required to provide, nor precluded from providing, the reasons for the lack of independence; however, if the practitioner chooses to provide the reasons for the lack of independence, the practitioner should include all the reasons therefor.

Agreeing on the Terms of the Engagement

.07 The practitioner should agree upon the terms of the engagement with the engaging party. The agreed-upon terms of the engagement should be specified in sufficient detail in an engagement letter or other suitable form of written agreement. (Ref: par. .A2)

.08 The agreed-upon terms of the engagement should include the following:

a. The objective and scope of the engagement

b. The responsibilities of the practitioner (Ref: par. .A3)

c. A statement that the engagement will be conducted in accordance with attestation standards established by the American Institute of Certified Public Accountants

d. The responsibilities of the responsible party and the responsibilities of the engaging party, if different

e. A statement about the inherent limitations of an examination engagement (Ref: par. .A4)

[1] Paragraph .24 of section 105, *Concepts Common to All Attestation Engagements*.

f. Identification of the criteria for the measurement, evaluation, or disclosure of the subject matter

g. An acknowledgement that the engaging party agrees to provide the practitioner with a representation letter at the conclusion of the engagement

.09 Although an engagement may recur, each engagement is considered a separate engagement. The practitioner should assess whether circumstances require revision to the terms of a preceding engagement. If the practitioner concludes that the terms of the preceding engagement need not be revised for the current engagement, the practitioner should remind the engaging party of the terms of the current engagement, and the reminder should be documented.

Requesting a Written Assertion

.10 The practitioner should request from the responsible party a written assertion about the measurement or evaluation of the subject matter against the criteria. When the engaging party is the responsible party and refuses to provide a written assertion, paragraph .82 requires the practitioner to withdraw from the engagement when withdrawal is possible under applicable law or regulation. When the engaging party is not the responsible party, and the responsible party refuses to provide a written assertion, the practitioner need not withdraw from the engagement. In that case, paragraph .84 requires the practitioner to disclose that refusal in the practitioner's report and restrict the use of the report to the engaging party. (Ref: par. .A5–.A8 and .A97)

Planning and Performing the Engagement

.11 The practitioner should establish an overall engagement strategy that sets the scope, timing, and direction of the engagement and guides the development of the engagement plan. (Ref: par. .A9–.A12)

.12 In establishing the overall engagement strategy, the practitioner should

a. identify the characteristics of the engagement that define its scope and ascertain the reporting objectives of the engagement in order to plan the timing of the engagement and the nature of the communications required;

b. consider the factors that, in the practitioner's professional judgment, are significant in directing the engagement team's efforts;

c. consider the results of preliminary engagement activities, such as client acceptance, and, when applicable, whether knowledge gained on other engagements performed by the engagement partner for the entity is relevant; and

d. ascertain the nature, timing, and extent of resources necessary to perform the engagement.

.13 The practitioner should develop a plan that includes a description of the following items:

a. The nature, timing, and extent of planned risk assessment procedures

b. The nature, timing, and extent of planned further procedures (see paragraph .21)

c. Other planned procedures that are required to be carried out so that the engagement complies with the attestation standards

Risk Assessment Procedures

.14 The practitioner should obtain an understanding of the subject matter and other engagement circumstances sufficient to (Ref: par. .A13–.A14)

a. enable the practitioner to identify and assess the risks of material misstatement in the subject matter and

b. provide a basis for designing and performing procedures to respond to the assessed risks and to obtain reasonable assurance to support the practitioner's opinion.

.15 In obtaining an understanding of the subject matter in accordance with paragraph .14, the practitioner should obtain an understanding of internal control over the preparation of the subject matter relevant to the engagement. This includes evaluating the design of those controls relevant to the subject matter and determining whether they have been implemented by performing procedures in addition to inquiry of the personnel responsible for the subject matter.

Materiality in Planning and Performing the Engagement

.16 When establishing the overall engagement strategy, the practitioner should consider materiality for the subject matter. (Ref: par. .A15–.A21)

.17 The practitioner should reconsider materiality for the subject matter if the practitioner becomes aware of information during the engagement that would have caused the practitioner to have initially determined a different materiality.

Identifying Risks of Material Misstatement

.18 The practitioner should identify and assess risks of material misstatement as the basis for designing and performing further procedures whose nature, timing, and extent (Ref: par. .A22–.A23)

a. are responsive to assessed risks of material misstatement and

b. allow the practitioner to obtain reasonable assurance about whether the subject matter is in accordance with (or based on) the criteria, in all material respects.

Responding to Assessed Risks and Obtaining Evidence

.19 To obtain reasonable assurance, the practitioner should obtain sufficient appropriate evidence to reduce attestation risk to an acceptably low level and thereby enable the practitioner to draw reasonable conclusions on which to base the practitioner's opinion.

.20 The practitioner should design and implement overall responses to address the assessed risks of material misstatement for the subject matter or assertion. (Ref: par. .A24–.A25)

Further Procedures

.21 The practitioner should design and perform further procedures whose nature, timing, and extent are based on, and responsive to, the assessed risks of material misstatement.

.22 In designing and performing further procedures in accordance with paragraph .21, the practitioner should

a. consider the reasons for the assessment given to the risk of material misstatement, including
   i. the likelihood of material misstatement due to the particular characteristics of the subject matter and
   ii. whether the practitioner intends to rely on the operating effectiveness of controls in determining the nature, timing, and extent of other procedures, and

b. obtain more persuasive evidence the higher the practitioner's assessment of risk.

.23 When designing and performing procedures, the practitioner should consider the relevance and reliability of the information to be used as evidence. If

a. evidence obtained from one source is inconsistent with that obtained from another,

b. the practitioner has doubts about the reliability of information to be used as evidence, or

c. responses to inquiries of the responsible party or others are inconsistent or otherwise unsatisfactory (for example, vague or implausible),

the practitioner should determine what modifications or additions to procedures are necessary to resolve the matter and should consider the effect of the matter, if any, on other aspects of the engagement.

Tests of Controls

.24 The practitioner should design and perform tests of controls to obtain sufficient appropriate evidence about the operating effectiveness of relevant controls if

a. the practitioner intends to rely on the operating effectiveness of controls in determining the nature, timing, and extent of other procedures;

b procedures other than tests of controls cannot alone provide sufficient appropriate evidence; or

c. the subject matter is internal control.

.25 If the practitioner designed and performed tests of controls to rely on their operating effectiveness and identified deviations in those controls, the practitioner should make specific inquiries and perform other procedures as necessary to understand these matters and their potential consequences. The practitioner also should determine whether

a. the tests of controls that have been performed provide an appropriate basis for reliance on the controls,

b. additional tests of controls are necessary, or

c. the potential risks of misstatement need to be addressed using other procedures.

Procedures Other Than Tests of Controls

.26 Irrespective of the assessed risks of material misstatement, the practitioner should design and perform tests of details or analytical procedures related to the subject matter, except when the subject matter is internal control.

Analytical Procedures Performed in Response to Assessed Risks

.27 When designing and performing analytical procedures in response to assessed risks, the practitioner should (Ref: par. .A26–.A27)

a. determine the suitability of particular analytical procedures for the subject matter, taking into account the assessed risks of material misstatement and any related tests of details;

b. evaluate the reliability of data from which the practitioner's expectation is developed, taking into account the source, comparability, nature, and relevance of information available, and controls over their preparation; and

c. develop an expectation that is sufficiently precise to identify possible material misstatements (taking into account whether analytical procedures are to be performed alone or in combination with tests of details).

.28 If analytical procedures identify fluctuations or relationships that are inconsistent with other relevant information or that differ significantly from expected amounts or ratios, the practitioner should investigate such differences by

a. inquiring of the responsible party and obtaining additional evidence relevant to its responses and

b. performing other procedures as necessary in the circumstances.

Procedures Regarding Estimates

.29 Based on the assessed risks of material misstatement, the practitioner should evaluate whether

a. the responsible party has appropriately applied the requirements of the criteria relevant to any estimated amounts and

b. the methods for making estimates are appropriate and have been applied consistently and whether changes, if any, in reported estimates or in the method for making them from the prior period, if applicable, are appropriate in the circumstances.

.30 When responding to an assessed risk of material misstatement related to an estimate, the practitioner should undertake one or more of the following, taking into account the nature of the estimates:

a. Determine whether events occurring up to the date of the practitioner's report provide evidence regarding the estimate.

b. Test how the responsible party made the estimate and the data on which it is based. In doing so, the practitioner should evaluate whether the

i. method of measurement used is appropriate in the circumstances,

ii. assumptions used by the responsible party are reasonable, and

iii. data on which the estimate is based are sufficiently reliable for the practitioner's purposes.

c. Test the operating effectiveness of the controls over how the responsible party made the estimate, together with other appropriate further procedures.

d. Develop a point estimate or a range to evaluate the responsible party's estimate. For this purpose, if the practitioner

i. uses assumptions or methods that differ from those of the responsible party, the practitioner should obtain an understanding of the responsible party's assumptions or methods sufficient to establish that the practitioner's point estimate or range takes into account relevant variables and to evaluate any significant differences from the responsible party's point estimate.

ii. concludes that it is appropriate to use a range, the practitioner should narrow the range, based on evidence available, until all outcomes within the range are considered reasonable.

Sampling

.31 If sampling is used, the practitioner should, when designing the sample, consider the purpose of the procedure and the characteristics of the population from which the sample will be drawn. Sampling involves (Ref: par. .A28)

a. determining a sample size sufficient to reduce sampling risk to an acceptably low level.

b. selecting items for the sample in such a way that the practitioner can reasonably expect the sample to be representative of the relevant population and likely to provide the practitioner with a reasonable basis for conclusions about the population.

c. treating a selected item to which the practitioner is unable to apply the designed procedures or suitable alternative procedures as a deviation from the prescribed control in the case of tests of controls or a misstatement in the case of tests of details.

d. investigating the nature and cause of deviations or misstatements identified and evaluating their possible effect on the purpose of the procedure and on other areas of the engagement.

e. evaluating the results of the sample, including sampling risk and projecting misstatements found in the sample to the population, and

f. evaluating whether the use of sampling has provided an appropriate basis for conclusions about the population that has been tested.

Fraud, Laws, and Regulations

.32 The practitioner should

a. consider whether risk assessment procedures and other procedures related to understanding the subject matter indicate risk of material misstatement due to fraud or noncompliance with laws or regulations.

b. make inquiries of appropriate parties to determine whether they have knowledge of any actual, suspected, or alleged fraud or noncompliance with laws or regulations affecting the subject matter.

c. evaluate whether there are unusual or unexpected relationships within the subject matter, or between the subject matter and other related information, that indicate risks of material misstatement due to fraud or noncompliance with laws or regulations.

d. evaluate whether other information obtained indicates risk of material misstatement due to fraud or noncompliance with laws or regulations.

.33 The practitioner should respond appropriately to fraud or suspected fraud and noncompliance or suspected noncompliance with laws or regulations affecting the subject matter that is identified during the engagement. (Ref: par. .A29–.A30)

Revision of Risk Assessment

.34 The practitioner's assessment of the risks of material misstatement may change during the course of the engagement as additional evidence is obtained. In circumstances in which the practitioner obtains evidence from performing further procedures, or if new information is obtained, either of which is inconsistent with the evidence on which the practitioner originally based the assessment, the practitioner should revise the assessment and modify the planned procedures accordingly. (Ref: par. .A31–.A32)

Evaluating the Reliability of Information Produced by the Entity

.35 When using information produced by the entity, the practitioner should evaluate whether the information is sufficiently reliable for the practitioner's purposes, including, as necessary, the following: (Ref: par. .A33–.A34)

a. Obtaining evidence about the accuracy and completeness of the information

b. Evaluating whether the information is sufficiently precise and detailed for the practitioner's purposes

Using the Work of a Practitioner's Specialist

.36 When the practitioner expects to use the work of a practitioner's specialist, the practitioner should do the following:

a. Evaluate whether the practitioner's specialist has the necessary competence, capabilities, and objectivity for the practitioner's purposes. In the case of a practitioner's external specialist, the evaluation of objectivity should include inquiry regarding interests and relationships that may create a threat to the objectivity of the practitioner's specialist. (Ref: par. .A38–.A41)

b. Obtain a sufficient understanding of the field of expertise of a practitioner's specialist to enable the practitioner to (Ref: par. .A42)

   i. determine the nature, scope, and objectives of that specialist's work for the practitioner's purposes and

   ii. evaluate the adequacy of that work for the practitioner's purposes.

c. Agree with the practitioner's specialist regarding (Ref: par. .A43)

   i. the nature, scope, and objectives of that practitioner's specialist's work;

   ii. the respective roles and responsibilities of the practitioner and that specialist;

   iii. the nature, timing, and extent of communication between the practitioner and that specialist, including the form of any report or documentation to be provided by that specialist; and

iv. the need for the practitioner's specialist to observe confidentiality requirements.

d. Evaluate the adequacy of the work of the practitioner's specialist for the practitioner's purposes, including

i. the relevance and reasonableness of the findings and conclusions of the practitioner's specialist and their consistency with other evidence;

ii. if the work of the practitioner's specialist involves the use of significant assumptions and methods

(1) obtaining an understanding of those assumptions and methods and

(2) evaluating the relevance and reasonableness of those assumptions and methods in the circumstances, giving consideration to the rationale and support provided by the practitioner's specialist, and in relation to the practitioner's other findings and conclusions;

iii. if the work of the practitioner's specialist involves the use of source data that are significant to the work of the practitioner's specialist, the relevance, completeness, and accuracy of that source data.

.37 If the practitioner determines that the work of the practitioner's specialist is not adequate for the practitioner's purposes, the practitioner should

a. agree with the practitioner's specialist on the nature and extent of further work to be performed by the practitioner's specialist or

b. perform additional procedures appropriate to the circumstances.

.38 The nature, timing, and extent of the procedures a practitioner performs when the practitioner expects to use the work of a practitioner's specialist will vary depending on the circumstances. In determining the nature, timing, and extent of those procedures, the practitioner should consider the following: (See section 105.[2])

a. The significance of that specialist's work in the context of the engagement (See also paragraphs .A35–.A36.)

b. The nature of the matter to which that specialist's work relates

c. The risks of material misstatement in the matter to which that specialist's work relates

d. The practitioner's knowledge of, and experience with, previous work performed by that specialist

e. Whether that specialist is subject to the practitioner's firm's quality control policies and procedures (see also paragraph .A37)

Using the Work of Internal Auditors

.39 When the practitioner expects to use the work of the internal audit function in obtaining evidence or to use internal auditors to provide direct assistance, the practitioner should determine whether the work can be used for purposes of the examination by evaluating (Ref: par. .A44–.A46)

---

[2] Paragraph .32 of section 105.

a. the level of competence of the internal audit function or the individual internal auditors providing direct assistance;

b. the extent to which the internal audit function's organizational status and relevant policies and procedures support the objectivity of the internal audit function or for internal auditors providing direct assistance, the existence of threats to the objectivity of those internal auditors and the related safeguards applied to reduce or eliminate those threats; and

c. when using the work of the internal audit function, the application by the internal audit function of a systematic and disciplined approach, including quality control.

.40 When using the work of the internal audit function, the practitioner should perform sufficient procedures on the body of work of the internal audit function as a whole that the practitioner plans to use to determine its adequacy for the purpose of the examination engagement, including reperforming some of the body of work of the internal audit function that the practitioner intends to use in obtaining evidence.

.41 Prior to using internal auditors to provide direct assistance, the practitioner should obtain written acknowledgment from the responsible party that internal auditors providing direct assistance to the practitioner will be allowed to follow the practitioner's instructions, and that the responsible party will not intervene in the work the internal auditor performs for the practitioner.

.42 When using internal auditors to provide direct assistance to the practitioner, the practitioner should direct, supervise, and review the work of the internal auditors.

.43 Because the practitioner has sole responsibility for the opinion expressed, the practitioner should make all significant judgments in the examination engagement, including when to use the work of the internal audit function in obtaining evidence. To prevent undue use of the internal audit function in obtaining evidence, the external auditor should plan to use less of the work of the function and perform more of the work directly:

a. The more judgment is involved in

  i. planning and performing relevant procedures or

  ii. evaluating the evidence obtained

b. the higher the assessed risk of material misstatement;

c. the less the internal audit function's organizational status and relevant policies and procedures adequately support the objectivity of the internal auditors; and

d. the lower the level of competence of the internal audit function.

.44 Before the conclusion of the engagement, the practitioner should evaluate whether the use of the work of the internal audit function or the use of internal auditors to provide direct assistance results in the practitioner still being sufficiently involved in the examination given the practitioner's sole responsibility for the opinion expressed.

Evaluating the Results of Procedures

.45 The practitioner should accumulate misstatements identified during the engagement other than those that are clearly trivial. (Ref: par. .A47–.A48)

.46 The practitioner should evaluate the sufficiency and appropriateness of the evidence obtained in the context of the engagement and, if necessary, attempt to obtain further evidence. The practitioner should consider all relevant evidence, regardless of whether it appears to corroborate or contradict the measurement or evaluation of the subject matter against the criteria. (Ref: par. .A49–.A53)

.47 If the practitioner is unable to obtain necessary further evidence, the practitioner should consider the implications for the practitioner's opinion in paragraphs .68–.84.

Considering Subsequent Events and Subsequently Discovered Facts

.48 The practitioner should inquire whether the responsible party, and if different, the engaging party, is aware of any events subsequent to the period (or point in time) covered by the examination engagement up to the date of the practitioner's report that could have a significant effect on the subject matter or assertion and should apply other appropriate procedures to obtain evidence regarding such events. If the practitioner becomes aware, through inquiry or otherwise, of such an event, or any other event that is of such a nature and significance that its disclosure is necessary to prevent users of the report from being misled, and information about that event is not adequately disclosed by the responsible party in the subject matter or in its assertion, the practitioner should take appropriate action. (Ref: par. .A54–.A56)

.49 The practitioner has no responsibility to perform any procedures regarding the subject matter or assertion after the date of the practitioner's report. Nevertheless, the practitioner should respond appropriately to facts that become known to the practitioner after the date of the report that, had they been known to the practitioner at that date, may have caused the practitioner to revise the report. (Ref: par. .A57–.A58)

Written Representations

.50 The practitioner should request from the responsible party written representations in the form of a letter addressed to the practitioner. The representations should (Ref: par. .A59–.A62)

a. include the responsible party's assertion about the subject matter based on the criteria. (Ref: par. .A97)

b. state that all relevant matters are reflected in the measurement or evaluation of the subject matter or assertion.

c. state that all known matters contradicting the subject matter or assertion and any communication from regulatory agencies or others affecting the subject matter or assertion have been disclosed to the practitioner, including communications received between the end of the period addressed in the written assertion and the date of the practitioner's report.

d. acknowledge responsibility for

  i. the subject matter and the assertion;

  ii. selecting the criteria, when applicable; and

  iii. determining that such criteria are appropriate for the responsible party's purposes.

e. state that any known events subsequent to the period (or point in time) of the subject matter being reported on that would have a material effect on the subject matter or assertion have been disclosed to the practitioner. (Ref: par. .A61)

f. state that it has provided the practitioner with all relevant information and access.

g. if applicable, state that the responsible party believes the effects of uncorrected misstatements are immaterial, individually and in the aggregate, to the subject matter. (Ref: par. .A62)

h. if applicable, state that significant assumptions used in making any material estimates are reasonable.

i. state that the responsible party has disclosed to the practitioner

   i. all deficiencies in internal control relevant to the engagement of which the responsible party is aware;

   ii. its knowledge of any actual, suspected, or alleged fraud or noncompliance with laws or regulations affecting the subject matter; and

   iii. other matters as the practitioner deems appropriate.

.51 When the engaging party is not the responsible party, and the responsible party refuses to provide the representations in paragraph .50 in writing, the practitioner should make inquiries of the responsible party about, and seek oral responses to, the matters in paragraph .50. (Ref: par. .A63)

.52 When the engaging party is not the responsible party, the practitioner should request written representations from the engaging party, in addition to those requested from the responsible party, in the form of a letter addressed to the practitioner. The representations should

a. acknowledge that the responsible party is responsible for the subject matter and assertion.

b. acknowledge the engaging party's responsibility for selecting the criteria, when applicable.

c. acknowledge the engaging party's responsibility for determining that such criteria are appropriate for its purposes.

d. state that the engaging party is not aware of any material misstatements in the subject matter or assertion.

e. state that the engaging party has disclosed to the practitioner all known events subsequent to the period (or point in time) of the subject matter being reported on that would have a material effect on the subject matter or assertion. (Ref: par. .A61)

f. address other matters as the practitioner deems appropriate.

.53 When written representations are directly related to matters that are material to the subject matter, the practitioner should

a. evaluate their reasonableness and consistency with other evidence obtained, including other representations (oral or written) and

b. consider whether those making the representations can be expected to be well informed on the particular matters.

.54 The date of the written representations should be as of the date of the practitioner's report. The written representations should address the subject matter and periods covered by the practitioner's opinion.

Requested Written Representations Not Provided or Not Reliable

.55 When the engaging party is the responsible party, and one or more of the requested written representations are not provided, or the practitioner concludes that there is sufficient doubt about the competence, integrity, ethical values, or diligence of those providing the written representations, or the practitioner concludes that the written representations are otherwise not reliable, the practitioner should (Ref: par. .A64)

a. discuss the matter with the appropriate party(ies);

b. reevaluate the integrity of those from whom the representations were requested or received and evaluate the effect that this may have on the reliability of representations and evidence in general; and

c. if any of the matters are not resolved to the practitioner's satisfaction, take appropriate action.

.56 When the engaging party is not the responsible party

a. if one or more of the requested representations are not provided in writing by the responsible party, but the practitioner receives satisfactory oral responses to the practitioner's inquiries performed in accordance with paragraph .51 sufficient to enable the practitioner to conclude that the practitioner has sufficient appropriate evidence to form an opinion about the subject matter, the practitioner's report should contain a separate paragraph that restricts the use of the report to the engaging party. (Paragraphs .65–.66 contain requirements for the contents of such a paragraph.) (Ref: par. .A63 and .A65)

b. if one or more of the requested representations are provided neither in writing nor orally from the responsible party in accordance with paragraph .51, a scope limitation exists, and the practitioner should determine the effect on the report, or the practitioner should withdraw from the engagement.(Ref: par. .A66)

Other Information

.57 If prior to or after the release of the practitioner's report on subject matter or an assertion, the practitioner is willing to permit the inclusion of the report in a document that contains the subject matter or assertion and other information, the practitioner should read the other information to identify material inconsistencies, if any, with the subject matter, assertion, or the report. If upon reading the other information, in the practitioner's professional judgment (Ref: par. .A67–.A68)

a. a material inconsistency between that other information and the subject matter, assertion, or the report exists or

b. a material misstatement of fact exists in the other information, the subject matter, assertion, or the report

the practitioner should discuss the matter with the responsible party and take further action as appropriate.

Description of Criteria

.58 The practitioner should evaluate whether the written description of the subject matter or assertion adequately refers to or describes the criteria. (Ref: par. .A69–.A70)

Forming the Opinion

.59 The practitioner should form an opinion about whether the subject matter is in accordance with (or based on) the criteria, in all material respects, or the assertion is fairly stated, in all material respects. In forming that opinion, the practitioner should evaluate

a. the practitioner's conclusion regarding the sufficiency and appropriateness of evidence obtained and (Ref: par. .A71)

b. whether uncorrected misstatements are material, individually or in the aggregate. (Ref: par. .A72)

.60 The practitioner should evaluate, based on the evidence obtained, whether the presentation of the subject matter or assertion is misleading within the context of the engagement. (Ref: par. .A73–.A74)

Preparing the Practitioner's Report

.61 The practitioner's report should be in writing. (Ref: par. .A75–.A76)

.62 A practitioner should report on a written assertion or should report directly on the subject matter. If the practitioner is reporting on the assertion, the assertion should be bound with or accompany the practitioner's report, or the assertion should be clearly stated in the report. (Ref: par. .A77)

Content of the Practitioner's Report

.63 The practitioner's report should include the following, unless the practitioner is disclaiming an opinion, in which case, items .63*f*, and .63*g* should be omitted:

a. A title that includes the word *independent.* (Ref: par. .A78)

b. An appropriate addressee as required by the circumstances of the engagement.

c. An identification or description of the subject matter or assertion being reported on, including the point in time or period of time to which the measurement or evaluation of the subject matter or assertion relates.

d. An identification of the criteria against which the subject matter was measured or evaluated. (Ref: par. .A79)

e. A statement that identifies (Ref: par. .A80–.A81)

   i. the responsible party and its responsibility for the subject matter in accordance with (or based on) the criteria or for its assertion, and

   ii. the practitioner's responsibility to express an opinion on the subject matter or assertion, based on the practitioner's examination.

f. A statement that

   i. the practitioner's examination was conducted in accordance with attestation standards established by the American Institute of Certified Public Accountants.

   ii. those standards require that the practitioner plan and perform the examination to obtain reasonable assurance about whether

(1) the subject matter is in accordance with (or based on) the criteria, in all material respects (or equivalent language regarding the subject matter and criteria, such as the language used in the examples in paragraph .A82) or

(2) the responsible party's assertion is fairly stated, in all material respects.

iii. the practitioner believes the evidence the practitioner obtained is sufficient and appropriate to provide a reasonable basis for the practitioner's opinion.

g. A description of the nature of an examination engagement. (Ref: par. .A83–.A85)

h. A statement that describes significant inherent limitations, if any, associated with the measurement or evaluation of the subject matter against the criteria. (Ref: par. .A86)

i. The practitioner's opinion about whether (Ref: par. .A87–.A90)

i. the subject matter is in accordance with (or based on) the criteria, in all material respects or

ii. the responsible party's assertion is fairly stated, in all material respects.

j. The manual or printed signature of the practitioner's firm.

k. The city and state where the practitioner practices. (Ref: par. .A91)

l. The date of the report. (The report should be dated no earlier than the date on which the practitioner has obtained sufficient appropriate evidence on which to base the practitioner's opinion, including evidence that

i the attestation documentation has been reviewed,

ii. if applicable, the written presentation of the subject matter has been prepared, and

iii. the responsible party has provided a written assertion or, in the circumstances described in paragraph .A66, an oral assertion.)

Restricted Use Paragraph

.64 In the following circumstances, the practitioner's report should include an alert, in a separate paragraph, that restricts the use of the report: (Ref: par. .A94–.A97)

a. The practitioner determines that the criteria used to evaluate the subject matter are appropriate only for a limited number of parties who either participated in their establishment or can be presumed to have an adequate understanding of the criteria.

b. The criteria used to evaluate the subject matter are available only to specified parties.

c. The engaging party is not the responsible party, and the responsible party does not provide the written representations required by paragraph .50, but does provide oral responses to the practitioner's inquiries about the matters in paragraph .50, as provided for in paragraph .51 and .56*a*. In this case, the use of the practitioner's report should be restricted to the engaging party. (Ref: par. .A97)

.65 The alert should

a. state that the practitioner's report is intended solely for the information and use of the specified parties,

b. identify the specified parties for whom use is intended, and (Ref: par. .A98)

c. state that the report is not intended to be, and should not be, used by anyone other than the specified parties. (Ref: par. .A99–.A101)

.66 When the engagement is also performed in accordance with *Government Auditing Standards*, the alert that restricts the use of the practitioner's report should include the following information, rather than the information required by paragraph .65:

a. A description of the purpose of the report

b. A statement that the report is not suitable for any other purpose

Reference to the Practitioner's Specialist

.67 The practitioner should not refer to the work of a practitioner's specialist in the practitioner's report containing an unmodified opinion. (Ref: par. .A102)

Modified Opinions

.68 The practitioner should modify the opinion when either of the following circumstances exist and, in the practitioner's professional judgment, the effect of the matter is or may be material: (Ref: par. .A103–.A104)

a. The practitioner is unable to obtain sufficient appropriate evidence to conclude that the subject matter is in accordance with (or based on) the criteria, in all material respects.

b. The practitioner concludes, based on evidence obtained, that the subject matter is not in accordance with (or based on) the criteria, in all material respects.

.69 When the practitioner modifies the opinion, the practitioner should include a separate paragraph in the practitioner's report that provides a description of the matter(s) giving rise to the modification.

.70 The practitioner should express a qualified opinion when (Ref: par. .A105–.A109)

a. the practitioner, having obtained sufficient appropriate evidence, concludes that misstatements, individually or in the aggregate, are material, but not pervasive to the subject matter or

b. the practitioner is unable to obtain sufficient appropriate evidence on which to base the opinion, but the practitioner concludes that the possible effects on the subject matter of undetected misstatements, if any, could be material, but not pervasive.

.71 When the practitioner expresses a qualified opinion due to a material misstatement of the subject matter, the practitioner should state that, in the practitioner's opinion, except for the effects of the matter(s) giving rise to the modification, the subject matter is presented in accordance with (or based on) the criteria, in all material respects. When the modification arises from an inability to obtain sufficient appropriate evidence, the practitioner should use the corresponding phrase "except for the possible effects of the matter(s) ..." for the modified opinion.

.72 The practitioner should express an adverse opinion when the practitioner, having obtained sufficient appropriate evidence, concludes that misstatements, individually or in the aggregate, are both material and pervasive to the subject matter.

.73 When the practitioner expresses an adverse opinion, the practitioner should state that, in the practitioner's opinion, because of the significance of the matter(s) giving rise to the modification, the subject matter is not presented in accordance with (or based on) the criteria, in all material respects.

.74 The practitioner should disclaim an opinion when the practitioner is unable to obtain sufficient appropriate evidence on which to base the opinion, and the practitioner concludes that the possible effects on the subject matter of undetected misstatements, if any, could be both material and pervasive. (Ref: par. .A110)

.75 When the practitioner disclaims an opinion due to an inability to obtain sufficient appropriate evidence, the practitioner's report should state that

a. because of the significance of the matter(s) giving rise to the modification, the practitioner has not been able to obtain sufficient appropriate evidence to provide a basis for an examination opinion and

b. accordingly, the practitioner does not express an opinion on the subject matter.

Description of the Practitioner's Responsibility When the Practitioner Expresses a Qualified or an Adverse Opinion

.76 When the practitioner expresses a qualified or an adverse opinion, the practitioner should amend the description of the practitioner's responsibility to state that the practitioner believes that the evidence the practitioner has obtained is sufficient and appropriate to provide a basis for the practitioner's modified opinion.

Description of the Practitioner's Responsibility When the Practitioner Disclaims an Opinion

.77 When the practitioner disclaims an opinion due to an inability to obtain sufficient appropriate evidence, the practitioner should amend the practitioner's report to state that the practitioner was engaged to examine the subject matter (or assertion). The practitioner should also amend the description of the practitioner's responsibility and the description of an examination to state only the following:

> Our responsibility is to express an opinion on the subject matter (or assertion) based on conducting the examination in accordance with attestation standards established by the American Institute of Certified Public Accountants. Because of the limitation on the scope of our examination discussed in the preceding paragraph, the scope of our work was not sufficient to enable us to express, and we do not express, an opinion on whether the subject matter is in accordance with (or based on) the criteria, in all material respects.

.78 If the practitioner expresses a modified opinion because of a scope limitation but is also aware of a matter(s) that causes the subject matter to be materially misstated, the practitioner should include in the practitioner's report a clear description of both the scope limitation and the matter(s) that causes the subject matter to be materially misstated.

.79 If the practitioner has concluded that conditions exist that, individually or in combination, result in one or more material misstatements based on the criteria, the practitioner should modify the opinion and express a qualified or adverse opinion directly on the subject matter, not on the assertion, even when the assertion acknowledges the misstatement.

.80 The practitioner's opinion on the subject matter or assertion should be clearly separated from any paragraphs emphasizing matters related to the subject matter or any other reporting responsibilities.

.81 When the opinion is modified, reference to an external specialist is permitted when such reference is relevant to an understanding of the modification to the practitioner's opinion. The practitioner should indicate in the practitioner's report that such reference does not reduce the practitioner's responsibility for that opinion.

Responsible Party Refuses to Provide a Written Assertion

.82 If the engaging party is the responsible party and refuses to provide the practitioner with a written assertion as required by paragraph .10, the practitioner should withdraw from the engagement when withdrawal is possible under applicable law or regulation.

.83 If law or regulation does not allow the practitioner to withdraw from the engagement, the practitioner should disclaim an opinion.

.84 When the engaging party is not the responsible party and the responsible party refuses to provide the practitioner with a written assertion, the practitioner may report on the subject matter but should disclose in the practitioner's report the responsible party's refusal to provide a written assertion and should restrict the use of the practitioner's report to the engaging party. (Ref: par. .A111–.A113)

Communication Responsibilities

.85 The practitioner should communicate to the responsible party known and suspected fraud and noncompliance with laws or regulations, uncorrected misstatements, and, when relevant to the subject matter, internal control deficiencies identified during the engagement. When the engaging party is not the responsible party, the practitioner should also communicate this information to the engaging party. (Ref: par. .A114)

.86 If the practitioner has identified or suspects noncompliance with laws or regulations that are not relevant to the subject matter, the practitioner should determine whether the practitioner has a responsibility to report the identified or suspected noncompliance to parties other than the responsible party and the engaging party (if different). (Ref: par. .A115–.A116)

Documentation

.87 The practitioner should prepare engagement documentation that is sufficient to determine (Ref: par. .A117–.A120)

a. the nature, timing, and extent of the procedures performed to comply with relevant AT-C sections and applicable legal and regulatory requirements, including

i. the identifying characteristics of the specific items or matters tested;

ii. who performed the engagement work and the date such work was completed;

iii. the discussions with the responsible party or others about findings or issues that, in the practitioner's professional judgment, are significant, including the nature of the significant findings or issues discussed, and when and with whom the discussions took place;

iv. when the engaging party is the responsible party and the responsible party will not provide one or more of the requested written representations or the practitioner concludes that there is sufficient doubt about the competence, integrity, ethical values, or diligence of those providing the written representations; or that the written representations are otherwise not reliable, the matters in paragraph .55;

v. when the engaging party is not the responsible party and the responsible party will not provide the written representations regarding the matters in paragraph .50, the oral responses from the responsible party to the practitioner's inquiries regarding the matters in paragraph .50, in accordance with paragraph .51; and

vi. who reviewed the engagement work performed and the date and extent of such review.

b. the results of the procedures performed and the evidence obtained.

.88 If the practitioner identified information that is inconsistent with the practitioner's final conclusion regarding a significant finding or issue, the practitioner should document how the practitioner addressed the inconsistency.

.89 If, in circumstances such as those described in paragraph .49, the practitioner performs new or additional procedures or draws new conclusions after the date of the practitioner's report, the practitioner should document

a. the circumstances encountered;

b. the new or additional procedures performed, evidence obtained, and conclusions reached and their effect on the report; and

c. when and by whom the resulting changes to the documentation were made and reviewed.

Application and Other Explanatory Material

Conduct of an Examination Engagement (Ref: par. .05)

.A1 For example, if a practitioner were examining prospective financial information, section 105, this section, and section 305, *Prospective Financial Information*, would be relevant.

Agreeing on the Terms of the Engagement (Ref: par. .07, .08b, and .08e)

.A2 It is in the interests of both the engaging party and the practitioner to document the agreed-upon terms of the engagement before the commencement of the engagement to help avoid misunderstandings. The form and content of the engagement letter or other suitable form of written agreement will vary with the engagement circumstances.

.A3 A practitioner may further describe the responsibilities of the practitioner by adding the following items to the engagement letter or other suitable form of written agreement:

a. A statement that an examination is designed to obtain reasonable assurance about whether the subject matter as measured or evaluated against the criteria is free from material misstatement

b. A statement that the objective of an examination is the expression of an opinion in a written practitioner's report about whether the subject matter is in accordance with (or based on) the criteria, in all material respects, or whether the responsible party's assertion is fairly stated, in all material respects

.A4 If relevant, a statement about the inherent limitations of an examination engagement may indicate that "because of the inherent limitations of an examination engagement, together with the inherent limitations of internal control, an unavoidable risk exists that some material misstatements may not be detected, even though the examination is properly planned and performed in accordance with the attestation standards."

Requesting a Written Assertion (Ref: par. .10)

.A5 The language of the responsible party's written assertion in paragraph .10 may need to be tailored to reflect the nature of the subject matter and criteria for the engagement. Examples of language that meet the requirements in paragraph .10 include the following:

- The entity maintained effective internal control over the subject matter based on the criteria.
- The subject matter is presented in accordance with (or based on) the criteria.
- The subject matter achieved the objectives, for example, when the objectives are the criteria.
- The subject matter is presented fairly, based on the criteria.

.A6 Situations may arise in which the current responsible party was not present during some or all of the period covered by the practitioner's report. Such persons may contend that they are not in a position to provide a written assertion that covers the entire period because they were not in place during some or all of the period. This fact, however, does not diminish such persons' responsibilities for the subject matter as a whole. Accordingly, the requirement for the practitioner to request a written assertion from the responsible party that covers the entire relevant period(s) still applies.

.A7 Paragraph .50*a* requires the practitioner to request a written representation from the responsible party that is the same as the responsible party's assertion. If the responsible party provides the practitioner with the written representation in paragraph .50*a*, the practitioner need not request a separate written assertion unless a separate written assertion is called for by the engagement circumstances.

.A8 A practitioner may also be engaged to assist the responsible party in measuring or evaluating the subject matter against the criteria in connection with the responsible party providing a written assertion. Regardless of the procedures performed by the practitioner, the responsible party is required to accept responsibility for its assertion and the subject matter and may not base its assertion solely on the practitioner's procedures.[3]

Planning and Performing the Engagement (Ref: par. .11)

.A9 Planning involves the engagement partner and other key members of the engagement team and may involve the practitioner's specialists in developing

- an overall strategy for the scope, timing, and conduct of the engagement and
- an engagement plan, consisting of a detailed approach for the nature, timing, and extent of procedures to be performed.

Adequate planning helps the practitioner to devote appropriate attention to important areas of the engagement, identify potential problems on a timely basis, and properly organize and manage the engagement in order for it to be performed in an effective and efficient manner. Adequate planning also assists the practitioner in properly assigning work to engagement team members and facilitates the direction, supervision, and review of their work. Further, it assists, when applicable, the coordination of work performed by other practitioners and practitioner's specialists. The nature and extent of planning activities will vary with the engagement circumstances, for example, the complexity of the assessment or evaluation of the subject matter and the practitioner's previous experience with it. Examples of relevant matters that may be considered include the following:

- The characteristics of the engagement that define its scope, including the terms of the engagement, the characteristics of the underlying subject matter, and the criteria
- The expected timing and the nature of the communications required
- The results of preliminary engagement activities, such as client acceptance, and, when applicable, whether knowledge gained on other engagements performed by the engagement partner for the appropriate party(ies) is relevant
- The engagement process, including possible sources of evidence, and choices among alternative measurement or evaluation methods
- The practitioner's understanding of the appropriate party(ies) and its (their) environment, including the risks that the subject matter may be materially misstated
- Identification of intended users and their information needs and consideration of materiality and the components of attestation risk
- The risk of fraud relevant to the engagement
- The effect on the engagement of using the internal audit function

.A10 The practitioner may decide to discuss elements of planning with the appropriate party(ies) to facilitate the conduct and management of the engagement (for example, to coordinate some of the planned procedures with the work

---

[3] The "Nonattest Services" subtopic (ET sec. 1.295) of the AICPA Code of Professional Conduct addresses the practitioner's provision of nonattest services for an attest client.

of the responsible party's personnel). Although these discussions often occur, the overall engagement strategy and the engagement plan remain the practitioner's responsibility. When discussing matters included in the overall engagement strategy or engagement plan, care is needed to avoid compromising the effectiveness of the engagement. For example, discussing the nature and timing of detailed procedures with the responsible party may compromise the effectiveness of the engagement by making the procedures too predictable.

.A11 Planning is not a discrete phase but, rather, a cumulative and iterative process throughout the engagement. As a result of unexpected events, changes in conditions, or evidence obtained, the practitioner may need to revise the overall strategy and engagement plan and, thereby, the resulting nature, timing, and extent of planned procedures.

.A12 In smaller or less complex engagements, the entire engagement may be conducted by a very small engagement team, possibly involving the engagement partner (who may be a sole practitioner) working without any other engagement team members. With a smaller team, coordination of, and communication among, team members is easier. In such cases, establishing the overall engagement strategy need not be a complex or time-consuming exercise; it varies according to the size of the entity, complexity of the engagement, and size of the engagement team.

Risk Assessment Procedures (Ref: par. .14)

.A13 Obtaining an understanding of the subject matter and other engagement circumstances provides the practitioner with a frame of reference for exercising professional judgment throughout the engagement, for example, when

- considering the characteristics of the subject matter;
- assessing the suitability of criteria;
- considering the factors that, in the practitioner's professional judgment, are significant in directing the engagement team's efforts, including situations in which special consideration may be necessary (for example, when there is a need for specialized skills or the work of a specialist);
- establishing and evaluating the continued appropriateness of quantitative materiality levels (when appropriate) and considering qualitative materiality factors;
- developing expectations when performing analytical procedures;
- designing and performing procedures;
- evaluating evidence, including the reasonableness of the written representations received by the practitioner.

.A14 In assessing inherent risk, the practitioner may consider factors relevant to examination engagements, such as the following:

- The complexity of the subject matter or assertion
- The length of time during which the entity has had experience with the subject matter or assertion
- Prior experience with the entity's assessment of the subject matter or assertion

Materiality in Planning and Performing the Engagement (Ref: par. .16)

.A15 Materiality is considered in the context of qualitative factors and, when applicable, quantitative factors. The relative importance of qualitative factors and quantitative factors when considering materiality in a particular engagement is a matter for the practitioner's professional judgment.

.A16 Professional judgments about materiality are made in light of surrounding circumstances, but they are not affected by the level of assurance, that is, for the same intended users, materiality for an examination engagement is the same as it is for a review engagement because materiality is based on the information needs of intended users and not the level of assurance.

.A17 In general, misstatements, including omissions, are considered to be material if, individually or in the aggregate, they could reasonably be expected to influence relevant decisions of intended users that are made based on the subject matter. The practitioner's consideration of materiality is a matter of professional judgment and is affected by the practitioner's perception of the common information needs of intended users as a group. In this context, it is reasonable for the practitioner to assume that intended users

a. have a reasonable knowledge of the subject matter and a willingness to study the subject matter with reasonable diligence.

b. understand that the subject matter is measured or evaluated and examined to appropriate levels of materiality and have an understanding of any materiality concepts included in the criteria.

c. understand any inherent uncertainties involved in measuring or evaluating the subject matter.

d. make reasonable decisions on the basis of the subject matter taken as a whole.

Unless the engagement has been designed to meet the particular information needs of specific users, the possible effect of misstatements on specific users, whose information needs may vary widely, is not ordinarily considered.

.A18 Qualitative factors may include the following:

- The interaction between, and relative importance of, various aspects of the subject matter, such as numerous performance indicators
- The wording chosen with respect to subject matter that is expressed in narrative form, for example, the wording chosen does not omit or distort the information
- The characteristics of the presentation adopted for the subject matter when the criteria allow for variations in that presentation
- The nature of a misstatement, for example, the nature of observed deviations in the operation of a control when the responsible party asserts that the control is effective
- Whether a misstatement affects compliance with laws or regulations
- In the case of periodic reporting on a subject matter, whether the effect of an adjustment affects past or current information about the subject matter or is likely to affect future information about the subject matter

- Whether a misstatement is the result of an intentional act or is unintentional
- Whether a misstatement is significant with regard to the practitioner's understanding of known previous communications to users, for example, in relation to the expected outcome of the measurement or evaluation of the subject matter
- Whether a misstatement relates to the relationship between the responsible party, and if different, the engaging party or its relationship with other parties

.A19 Quantitative factors relate to the magnitude of misstatements relative to reported amounts for those aspects of the subject matter, if any, that are

- expressed numerically or
- otherwise related to numerical values, for example, the number of observed deviations in the operation of a control when the examination involves the effectiveness of the control.

.A20 When quantitative factors are applicable, planning the engagement solely to detect individually material misstatements overlooks the fact that the aggregate of individually immaterial misstatements may cause the subject matter to be materially misstated. Applying materiality to elements of the subject matter ordinarily is not a simple mechanical calculation but involves the exercise of professional judgment. It is affected by the practitioner's understanding of the subject matter and the responsible party, updated during the performance of the risk assessment procedures, and consideration of the nature and extent of misstatements identified in previous attestation engagements.

.A21 The criteria may discuss the concept of materiality in the context of the preparation and presentation of the subject matter and thereby provide a frame of reference for the practitioner in considering materiality for the engagement. Although criteria may discuss materiality in different terms, the concept of materiality generally includes the matters discussed in paragraphs .A15–.A20. If the criteria do not include a discussion of the concept of materiality, these paragraphs provide the practitioner with a frame of reference.

Identifying Risks of Material Misstatement (Ref: par. .18)

.A22 Most of the practitioner's work in forming an opinion consists of obtaining and evaluating evidence. Procedures to obtain evidence can include inspection, observation, confirmation, recalculation, reperformance, and analytical procedures, often in some combination, in addition to inquiry.

.A23 In some cases, a subject-matter-specific section may include requirements that affect the nature, timing, and extent of procedures. For example, a subject-matter-specific section may describe the nature or extent of particular procedures to be performed in a particular type of engagement. Even in such cases, determining the exact nature, timing, and extent of procedures is a matter of professional judgment and will vary from one engagement to the next.

Responding to Assessed Risks and Obtaining Evidence (Ref: par. .20)

.A24 Overall responses to address the assessed risks of material misstatement of the subject matter or assertion may include

- emphasizing to the engagement team the need to maintain professional skepticism;
- assigning more experienced staff or those with specialized skills or using specialists;
- providing more supervision;
- incorporating additional elements of unpredictability in the selection of further procedures to be performed; and
- making changes to the nature, timing, or extent of procedures (for example, performing procedures at period-end instead of at an interim date or modifying the nature of procedures to obtain more persuasive evidence).

.A25 The assessment of the risks of material misstatement of the subject matter or assertion is affected by the practitioner's understanding of the control environment. An effective control environment may allow the practitioner to have more confidence in internal control and the reliability of evidence generated internally within the entity and, thus, for example, may allow the practitioner to conduct some procedures at an interim date, rather than at the period-end. Deficiencies in the control environment, however, have the opposite effect, for example, the practitioner may respond to an ineffective control environment by

- conducting more procedures as of the period-end, rather than at an interim date,
- obtaining more extensive evidence from procedures other than tests of controls, and
- increasing the number of locations to be included in the examination scope.

Further Procedures

Analytical Procedures Performed in Response to Assessed Risks (Ref: par. .27)

.A26 An understanding of the purposes of analytical procedures and the limitations of those procedures is important. Accordingly, the identification of the relationships and types of data used, as well as conclusions reached when recorded amounts are compared to expectations, requires professional judgment by the practitioner.

.A27 Analytical procedures involve comparisons of expectations developed by the practitioner to recorded amounts or ratios developed from recorded amounts. The practitioner develops such expectations by identifying and using plausible relationships that are reasonably expected to exist based on the practitioner's understanding of the subject matter; the practices used by the responsible party to measure, recognize, and record the subject matter; and, if applicable, the industry in which the entity operates.

Sampling (Ref: par. .31)

.A28 The AICPA Audit Guide *Audit Sampling* provides guidance that may be useful to a practitioner who has decided to use sampling in performing attestation procedures.

Fraud, Laws, and Regulations (Ref: par. .33)

.A29 In responding to fraud or suspected fraud identified during the engagement, it may be appropriate, unless prohibited by law, regulation, or ethics standards, for the practitioner to, for example,

- discuss the matter with the appropriate party(ies).
- request that the responsible party consult with an appropriately qualified third party, such as the entity's legal counsel or a regulator.
- consider the implications of the matter in relation to other aspects of the engagement, including the practitioner's risk assessment and the reliability of written representations from the responsible party.
- obtain legal advice about the consequences of different courses of action.
- communicate with third parties (for example, a regulator).
- withdraw from the engagement.

.A30 The actions noted in paragraph .A29 also may be appropriate in responding to noncompliance or suspected noncompliance with laws or regulations identified during the engagement. It may be appropriate to describe the matter in a separate paragraph in the practitioner's report, unless the practitioner

a. is precluded by the responsible party from obtaining sufficient appropriate evidence to evaluate whether noncompliance that may be material to the subject matter has, or is likely to have, occurred, in which case, paragraphs .68*a* and .77 apply, or

b. concludes that the noncompliance results in a material misstatement of the subject matter, in which case, paragraph .68*b* applies.

Revision of Risk Assessment (Ref: par. .34)

.A31 Information may come to the practitioner's attention that differs significantly from that on which the determination of planned procedures was based. As the practitioner performs planned procedures, the evidence obtained may cause the practitioner to perform additional procedures. Such procedures may include asking the responsible party to examine the matter identified by the practitioner and to make adjustments to the subject matter if appropriate.

.A32 The practitioner may become aware of a matter(s) that causes the practitioner to believe the subject matter may be materially misstated, for example, when performing analytical procedures the practitioner identifies a fluctuation or relationship that is inconsistent with other relevant information or that differs significantly from expectations.

Evaluating the Reliability of Information Produced by the Entity (Ref: par. .35)

.A33 Reliable information is sufficiently accurate and complete.

.A34 Obtaining evidence about the accuracy and completeness of information produced by the entity may be accomplished concurrently with the actual procedure applied to the information when obtaining such evidence is an integral part of the procedure itself. In other situations, the practitioner may have obtained evidence of the accuracy and completeness of such information by testing controls over the preparation and maintenance of the information. In some situations, however, the practitioner may determine that additional procedures are needed.

Using the Work of a Practitioner's Specialist

Integrating the Work of a Practitioner's Specialist (Ref: par. .38a)

.A35 Examination engagements may be performed on a wide range of subject matters that require specialized skills and knowledge beyond those possessed by the practitioner and for which the work of a practitioner's specialist is used. In some situations, the practitioner's specialist will be consulted to provide advice on an individual matter, but the greater the significance of the work of the practitioner's specialist in the context of the engagement, the more likely it is that the specialist will work as part of a multidisciplinary team comprising subject-matter specialists and other attestation personnel. The more that specialist's work is integrated in nature, timing, and extent with the overall work effort, the more important effective two-way communication is between the practitioner's specialist and other attestation personnel. Effective two-way communication facilitates the proper integration of the specialist's work with the work of others on the engagement.

.A36 When the work of a practitioner's specialist is to be used, it may be appropriate to perform some of the procedures required by paragraph .36 at the engagement acceptance or continuance stage. This is particularly so when the work of the practitioner's specialist is to be used in the early stages of the engagement, for example, during initial planning and risk assessment.

The Practitioner's Firm's Quality Control Policies and Procedures (Ref: par. .38e)

.A37 Engagement teams are entitled to rely on their own firm's system of quality control, unless information provided by the firm or other parties suggests otherwise. The extent of that reliance will vary with the circumstances and may affect the nature, timing, and extent of the practitioner's procedures with respect to matters, such as the following:

- Competence and capabilities, through recruitment and training programs
- The practitioner's evaluation of the objectivity of the practitioner's internal specialist (The practitioner's internal specialists are subject to relevant ethical requirements, including those pertaining to independence.)
- The practitioner's evaluation of the adequacy of the practitioner's internal specialist's work (For example, the firm's training programs may provide the practitioner's internal specialists with an appropriate understanding of the interrelationship of their expertise with the evidence-gathering process. Reliance on such training and other firm processes, such as protocols for scoping the work of the practitioner's internal specialists, may affect the nature, timing, and extent of the practitioner's procedures to evaluate the adequacy of the practitioner's specialist's work.)
- Adherence to regulatory and legal requirements through monitoring processes
- Agreement with the practitioner's specialist

Such reliance does not reduce the practitioner's responsibility to meet the requirements of this section.

The Competence, Capabilities, and Objectivity of a Practitioner's Specialist (Ref: par. .36a)

.A38 Information regarding the competence, capabilities, and objectivity of a practitioner's specialist may come from a variety of sources, such as the following:

- Personal experience with previous work of that specialist
- Discussions with that specialist
- Discussions with other practitioners or others who are familiar with that specialist's work
- Knowledge of that specialist's qualifications, membership of a professional body or industry association, license to practice, or other forms of external recognition
- Published papers or books written by that specialist
- The firm's quality control policies and procedures

.A39 Although a practitioner's specialist does not require the same proficiency as the practitioner in performing all aspects of an examination engagement, a practitioner's specialist whose work is used may need a sufficient understanding of relevant AT-C sections to enable that specialist to relate the work assigned to that specialist to the engagement objective.

.A40 The evaluation of the significance of threats to objectivity and of whether there is a need for safeguards may depend upon the role of the practitioner's specialist and the significance of the specialist's work in the context of the engagement. There may be some circumstances in which safeguards cannot reduce threats to an acceptable level, for example, if in an examination engagement a practitioner's specialist is an individual who has played a significant role in measuring, evaluating, or disclosing the subject matter.

.A41 When evaluating the objectivity of a practitioner's external specialist, it may be relevant to

- inquire of the appropriate party(ies) about any known interests or relationships that the appropriate party(ies) has with the practitioner's external specialist that may affect that specialist's objectivity.
- discuss with that specialist any applicable safeguards, including any professional requirements that apply to that specialist, and evaluate whether the safeguards are adequate to reduce threats to an acceptable level. Interests and relationships that may be relevant to discuss with the practitioner's specialist include
  - — financial interests.
  - — business and personal relationships.
  - — provision of other services by the specialist, including by the organization in the case of an external specialist that is an organization.

In some cases, it may also be appropriate for the practitioner to obtain a written representation from the practitioner's external specialist about any interests or relationships with the appropriate party(ies) of which that specialist is aware.

Obtaining an Understanding of the Field of Expertise of a Practitioner's Specialist (Ref: par. .36b)

.A42 Aspects of a practitioner's specialist's field of expertise relevant to the practitioner's understanding may include the following:

- Whether that specialist's field has areas of specialty within it that are relevant to the engagement
- Whether any professional or other standards and regulatory or legal requirements apply
- What assumptions and methods, including models, when applicable, are used by the practitioner's specialist and whether they are generally accepted within that specialist's field and appropriate in the circumstances of the engagement
- The nature of internal and external data or information the practitioner's specialist uses

Agreement With a Practitioner's Specialist (Ref: par. .36c)

.A43 The matters noted in paragraph .A37 may affect the level of detail and formality of the agreement between the practitioner and the practitioner's specialist, including whether it is appropriate that the agreement be in writing. The agreement between the practitioner and a practitioner's external specialist is often in the form of an engagement letter.

Using the Work of Internal Auditors (Ref: par. .39)

.A44 Activities similar to those performed by an internal audit function may be conducted by functions with other titles within an entity. Some or all of the activities of an internal audit function may also be outsourced to a third-party service provider. Neither the title of the function nor whether it is performed by the entity or a third-party service provider are sole determinants of whether or not the practitioner can use the work of internal auditors. Rather, it is the nature of the activities, the extent to which the internal audit function's organizational status and relevant policies and procedures support the objectivity of the internal auditors, the competence of the internal auditors, and the systematic and disciplined approach of the function that are relevant. References in this section to the work of the internal audit function include relevant activities of other functions or third-party providers that have these characteristics.

.A45 A practitioner planning to use the work of the internal audit function to obtain evidence may find it effective and efficient to discuss the planned use of the work with the internal audit function as a basis for coordinating activities.

.A46 The practitioner has sole responsibility for the opinion expressed, and that responsibility is not reduced by the practitioner's use of the work of internal auditors on the engagement. The objectivity and competence of internal auditors are important in determining whether to use their work and, if so, the nature and extent of the use of their work. However, a high degree of objectivity cannot compensate for a low degree of competence, nor can a high degree of competence compensate for a low degree of objectivity. Additionally, neither a high level of competence nor strong support for the objectivity of the internal auditors compensates for the lack of a systematic and disciplined approach when using the work of the internal audit function.

Evaluating the Results of Procedures (Ref: par. .45–.46)

.A47 Uncorrected misstatements are accumulated during the engagement for the purpose of evaluating whether, individually or in aggregate, they are material when forming the practitioner's opinion. (See also paragraph .59*b*)

.A48 "Clearly trivial" is not another expression for "not material." Matters that are clearly trivial will be of a wholly different (smaller) order of magnitude than materiality and will be matters that are clearly inconsequential, whether taken individually or in the aggregate and whether judged by any criteria of size, nature, or circumstances. When there is any uncertainty about whether one or more items are clearly trivial, the matter is considered not to be clearly trivial.

.A49 Sufficient appropriate evidence is necessary to support the practitioner's opinion and report. It is cumulative in nature and is primarily obtained from procedures performed during the course of the engagement. It may, however, also include information obtained from other sources such as previous engagements (provided the practitioner has determined whether changes have occurred since the previous engagement that may affect its relevance to the current engagement) or a firm's quality control procedures for client acceptance and continuance. Evidence may come from sources inside and outside the appropriate party(ies). Also, information that may be used as evidence may have been prepared by a specialist employed or engaged by the appropriate party(ies). *Evidence* comprises both information that supports and corroborates aspects of the subject matter and any information that contradicts aspects of the subject matter. In addition, in some cases, the absence of information (for example, refusal by the appropriate party(ies) to provide a requested representation) is considered by the practitioner and, therefore, also constitutes evidence.

.A50 The sufficiency and appropriateness of evidence are interrelated. Sufficiency of evidence is the measure of the quantity of evidence. The quantity of the evidence needed is affected by the risks of material misstatement and also by the quality of such evidence.

.A51 *Appropriateness of evidence* is the measure of the quality of evidence, that is, its relevance and reliability in providing support for the practitioner's opinion. The reliability of evidence is influenced by its source and nature and is dependent on the individual circumstances under which it is obtained. Generalizations about the reliability of various kinds of evidence can be made; however, such generalizations are subject to important exceptions. Even when evidence is obtained from sources external to the responsible party, circumstances may exist that could affect its reliability. For example, evidence obtained from an independent external source may not be reliable if the source is not knowledgeable. Recognizing that exceptions may exist, the following generalizations about the reliability of evidence may be useful:

- Evidence is more reliable when it is obtained from independent sources outside the appropriate party(ies).
- Evidence that is generated internally is more reliable when the related controls are effective.
- Evidence obtained directly by the practitioner (for example, observation of the application of a control) is more reliable than evidence obtained indirectly or by inference (for example, inquiry about the application of a control).

- Evidence is more reliable when it exists in documentary form, whether paper, electronic, or other media (for example, a contemporaneously written record of a meeting is ordinarily more reliable than a subsequent oral representation of what was discussed).
- Evidence provided by original documents is more reliable than evidence provided by photocopies, facsimiles, or documents that have been filmed, digitized, or otherwise transformed into electronic form, the reliability of which may depend on the controls over their preparation and maintenance.

.A52 Evidence obtained from different sources or of a different nature ordinarily provides more assurance than evidence from items considered individually. In addition, obtaining evidence from different sources or of a different nature may indicate that an individual item of evidence is not reliable. For example, corroborating information obtained from a source independent of the responsible party may increase the assurance the practitioner obtains from a representation from the responsible party. Conversely, when evidence obtained from one source is inconsistent with that obtained from another, the practitioner determines what additional procedures are necessary to resolve the inconsistency.

.A53 Whether sufficient appropriate evidence has been obtained on which to base the practitioner's opinion is a matter of professional judgment.

Considering Subsequent Events and Subsequently Discovered Facts (Ref: par. .48–.49)

.A54 For certain subject-matter AT-C sections, specific subsequent events requirements and related application guidance have been developed for engagement performance and reporting.

.A55 Procedures that a practitioner may perform to identify subsequent events include inquiring about and considering information

- contained in relevant reports issued during the subsequent period by internal auditors, other practitioners, or regulatory agencies.
- obtained through other professional engagements for that entity.

.A56 If the responsible party refuses to disclose a subsequent event for which disclosure is necessary to prevent users of the practitioner's report from being misled, appropriate actions the practitioner may take include

- disclosing the event in the practitioner's report and modifying the practitioner's opinion.
- withdrawing from the engagement.

.A57 Subsequent to the date of the practitioner's report, the practitioner may become aware of facts that, had they been known to the practitioner at that date, may have caused the practitioner to revise the report. In such circumstances, the practitioner undertakes to determine whether the facts existed at the date of the report and, if so, whether persons who would attach importance to these facts are currently using, or are likely to use, the report and related subject matter or assertion. This may include discussing the matter with the appropriate party(ies) and requesting the appropriate party(ies)'s cooperation in whatever investigation or further action that may be necessary. The specific actions to be taken in a particular case by the appropriate party(ies) and the practitioner may vary with the circumstances. Consideration may be given to, among other things, the time elapsed since the date of the report and whether issuance of a subsequent report is imminent. The practitioner may need to perform additional procedures deemed necessary to determine whether the subject matter or assertion needs revision and whether the previously issued report continues to be appropriate.

.A58 Depending on the circumstances, the practitioner may determine that notification of the situation by the appropriate party(ies) to persons who would attach importance to the facts and who are currently using, or are likely to use, the practitioner's report is necessary. This may be the case, for example, when

a. the report is not to be relied upon because the subject matter or assertion needs revision or the practitioner is unable to determine whether revision is necessary, and

b. issuance of a subsequent report is not imminent.

If the appropriate party(ies) failed to take the necessary steps to prevent reliance on the report, the practitioner's course of action depends upon the practitioner's legal and ethical rights and obligations. Consequently, the practitioner may consider it appropriate to seek legal advice prior to making any disclosure of the situation. Disclosure of the situation directly by the practitioner may include a description of the nature of the matter and its effect on the subject matter or assertion and the report, avoiding comments concerning the conduct or motives of any person.

Written Representations (Ref: par. .50–.51, .52e, and .56a)

.A59 Written confirmation of oral representations reduces the possibility of misunderstandings between the practitioner and the responsible party. The person(s) from whom the practitioner requests written representations is ordinarily a member of senior management or those charged with governance depending on, for example, the management and governance structure of the responsible party(ies), which may vary by entity, reflecting influences such as size and ownership characteristics.

.A60 Representations by the responsible party cannot replace other evidence the practitioner could reasonably expect to be available. Although written representations provide evidence, they do not provide sufficient appropriate evidence on their own about any of the matters with which they deal. Furthermore, the fact that the practitioner has received reliable written representations does not affect the nature or extent of other evidence that the practitioner obtains.

.A61 A discussion of what is considered a material effect on the subject matter or assertion may be included explicitly in the representation letter in qualitative or quantitative terms.

.A62 A summary of uncorrected misstatements ordinarily is included in or attached to the written representation.

.A63 Certain subject-matter AT-C sections do not permit the practitioner to perform the alternative procedures described in paragraphs .51 and .56*a* (making inquiries of the responsible party and restricting the use of the practitioner's report).

Requested Written Representations Not Provided or Not Reliable (Ref: par. .55–.56)

.A64 In the situation discussed in paragraph .55, the refusal to furnish such evidence in the form of written representations constitutes a limitation on the scope of an examination sufficient to preclude an unmodified opinion and may be sufficient to cause the practitioner to withdraw from the engagement.

.A65 Even when the responsible party provides oral responses to the matters in paragraph .50, the practitioner may find it appropriate to consider whether there are significant concerns about the competence, integrity, ethical values, or diligence of those providing the oral responses or whether the oral responses are otherwise not reliable and the potential effect, if any, on the practitioner's report.

.A66 Paragraph .10 provides an exception to the requirement for a written assertion when the engaging party is not the responsible party. Nonetheless, because the assertion is the representation called for by paragraph .50*a*, application of paragraph .56*a* requires the practitioner to obtain an oral assertion when a written assertion is not obtained. Paragraph .56*b* applies when the responsible party provides neither a written nor an oral assertion.

Other Information (Ref: par. .57)

.A67 Further actions that may be appropriate if the practitioner identifies a material inconsistency or becomes aware of a material misstatement of fact include, for example, the following:

- Requesting the appropriate party(ies) to consult with a qualified third party, such as the appropriate party(ies)'s legal counsel
- Obtaining legal advice about the consequences of different courses of action
- If required or permissible, communicating with third parties (for example, a regulator)
- Describing the material inconsistency in the practitioner's report
- Withdrawing from the engagement, when withdrawal is possible under applicable laws and regulations

.A68 Other information does not include information contained on the appropriate party(ies)'s website. Websites are a means of distributing information and are not, themselves, documents for the purposes of paragraph .57.

Description of Criteria (Ref: par. .58)

.A69 The description of the criteria on which the subject matter or assertion is based is particularly important when there are significant differences among various criteria regarding how particular matters may be treated in the subject matter.

.A70 A description of the criteria that states that the subject matter is prepared in accordance with (or based on) particular criteria is appropriate only if the subject matter complies with all relevant requirements of those criteria that are effective.

Forming the Opinion (Ref: par. .59–.60)

.A71 The practitioner's professional judgment regarding what constitutes sufficient appropriate evidence is influenced by such factors as the following:

- The significance of a potential misstatement and the likelihood that it will have a material effect, individually or aggregated with other potential misstatements, on the subject matter or assertion
- The effectiveness of the responsible party's responses to address the known risks
- The experience gained during previous examination or review engagements with respect to similar potential misstatements
- The results of procedures performed, including whether such procedures identified specific misstatements
- The source and reliability of the available information
- The persuasiveness of the evidence
- The practitioner's understanding of the responsible party and its environment

.A72 An examination engagement is a cumulative and iterative process. As the practitioner performs planned procedures, the evidence obtained may cause the practitioner to change the nature, timing, or extent of other planned procedures. Information that differs significantly from the information on which the risk assessments and planned procedures were based may come to the practitioner's attention, for example

- the extent of the misstatements that the practitioner detects is greater than expected. (This may alter the practitioner's professional judgment about the reliability of particular sources of information.)
- the practitioner may become aware of discrepancies in relevant information or conflicting or missing evidence.
- procedures performed toward the end of the engagement may indicate a previously unrecognized risk of material misstatement. In such circumstances, the practitioner may need to reevaluate the planned procedures.

.A73 In making the evaluation required by paragraph .60, the practitioner may consider whether additional disclosures are necessary to describe the subject matter, assertion, or criteria. Additional disclosures may, for example, include

- the measurement or evaluation methods used when the criteria allow for choice among methods;
- significant interpretations made in applying the criteria in the engagement circumstances;
- subsequent events, depending on their nature and significance; and
- whether there have been any changes in the measurement or evaluation methods used.

.A74 Paragraph .60 does not require the practitioner to determine whether the presentation discloses all matters related to the subject matter, assertion, or criteria or all matters intended users may consider in making decisions based on the presentation.

Preparing the Practitioner's Report (Ref: par. .61–.62)

.A75 Oral and other forms of expressing an opinion can be misunderstood without the support of a written practitioner's report. For this reason, the practitioner may not report orally or by use of symbols (such as a web seal) under the attestation standards without also providing a written report that is readily available whenever the oral report is provided or the symbol is used. For example, a symbol could be hyperlinked to a written report on the Internet.

.A76 This section does not require a standardized format for reporting on all examination engagements. Instead, it identifies the basic elements that the practitioner's report is to include. The report is tailored to the specific engagement circumstances. The practitioner may use headings, separate paragraphs, paragraph numbers, typographical devices (for example, the bolding of text), and other mechanisms to enhance the clarity and readability of the report.

.A77 All of the following reporting options are available to a practitioner, except when the circumstances described in paragraph .79 exist:

The practitioner's report may state that the practitioner examined	*and*	*expresses an opinion on*
the subject matter		the subject matter
the responsible party's assertion		the responsible party's assertion
the responsible party's assertion		the subject matter

Content of the Practitioner's Report

Title (Ref: par. .63a)

.A78 A title indicating that the practitioner's report is the report of an independent practitioner (for example, "Independent Practitioner's Report," "Report of Independent Certified Public Accountant," or "Independent Accountant's Report") affirms that the practitioner has met all the relevant ethical requirements regarding independence and, therefore, distinguishes the independent practitioner's report from reports issued by others.

Criteria (Ref: par. .63d)

.A79 The practitioner's report may include the criteria or refer to them if they are included in the subject matter presentation, in the assertion, or are otherwise readily available. It may be relevant in the circumstances to disclose the source of the criteria or the relevant matters discussed in paragraph .A73.

Relevant Responsibilities (Ref: par. .63e)

.A80 Identifying relative responsibilities informs the intended users that the responsible party is responsible for the subject matter, and the practitioner's role is to independently express an opinion about it.

.A81 The practitioner may wish to expand the discussion of the responsible party's responsibility, for example, to indicate that the responsible party is responsible for the preparation and presentation of the subject matter in accordance with (or based on) the criteria, including the design, implementation, and maintenance of internal control to prevent, or detect and correct, misstatement of the subject matter, due to fraud or error.

Statement About the Subject Matter and the Criteria (Ref: par. .63f[ii][1])

.A82 The language in paragraph .63*f*(ii)(1) may need to be tailored to reflect the nature of the subject matter and criteria for the engagement. Examples of language that meet the requirements in paragraph .63*f*(ii)(1) include, "to obtain reasonable assurance about whether

- the entity maintained effective internal control over the subject matter, based on the criteria, in all material respects."
- the subject matter is presented in accordance with (or based on) the criteria, in all material respects."
- the subject matter achieves the objectives, in all material respects." (For example, when the objectives are the criteria.)
- the subject matter is presented fairly, in all material respects, based on the criteria." (The practitioner's professional judgment concerning the fairness of the presentation of the subject matter relates to whether the measurement, recognition, presentation, and disclosure of all material items in the presentation of the subject matter achieve fair presentation.)

Description of the Nature of an Examination Engagement (Ref: par. .63g)

.A83 A description of the nature of an examination engagement may state, for example, that

- an examination involves performing procedures to obtain evidence about the subject matter and that the nature, timing, and extent of the procedures selected depend on the practitioner's judgment, including an assessment of the risks of material misstatement of the subject matter, whether due to fraud or error.
- an examination also involves examining evidence about the subject matter or assertion.
- in making an assessment of the risks of material misstatement, the practitioner considered and obtained an understanding of internal control relevant to the subject matter in order to design procedures that are appropriate in the circumstances, but not for the purpose of expressing an opinion on the effectiveness of internal control. Accordingly, no such opinion is expressed.

.A84 The practitioner may decide to more fully describe the practitioner's responsibility, for example, to

- perform procedures to obtain evidence based on the practitioner's assessment of the risk of material misstatement about whether the subject matter is presented in accordance with (or based on) the criteria.
- obtain an understanding of internal control over the subject matter.

.A85 A practitioner may be requested to provide in a separate section of the practitioner's report a description of the procedures performed and the results thereof in support of the practitioner's opinion. The following factors are relevant when determining whether to include such a description in the report:

- Whether such a description is likely to overshadow the practitioner's overall opinion or cause report users to misunderstand the opinion

- Whether the parties making the request have an appropriate business need or reasonable basis for requesting the information (for example, the specified parties are required to maintain and monitor controls that either encompass or are dependent on controls that are the subject of an examination and, therefore, need information about the tests of controls to enable them to have a basis for concluding that they have met the requirements applicable to them)
- Whether the parties have an understanding of the nature and subject matter of the engagement and experience in using the information in such reports
- Whether the practitioner's procedures performed directly relate to the subject matter of the engagement

The addition of procedures performed and the results thereof in a separate section of an examination report may increase the potential for the report to be misunderstood when taken out of the context of the knowledge of the requesting parties. This potential for an increase in the risk of misunderstanding may lead the practitioner to add a restricted-use paragraph to the practitioner's report.

Inherent Limitations (Ref: par. .63h)

.A86 In some cases, identification of specific inherent limitations is required by an AT-C section. For example, section 305, *Prospective Financial Information*, requires that the practitioner's report include a statement indicating that the prospective results may not be achieved.[4] To implement that requirement, the illustrative practitioner's examination report on a forecast in section 305 states, "There will usually be differences between the forecasted and actual results because events and circumstances frequently do not occur as expected, and those differences may be material."[5] When not explicitly required by an AT-C section, identification in the report of inherent limitations is based on the practitioner's judgment

Opinion (Ref: par. .63i)

.A87 The practitioner's opinion can be worded either in terms of the subject matter and the criteria (for example, "In our opinion, the schedule of investment returns of XYZ Company for the year ended December 31, 20XX, is in accordance with [or based on] the ABC criteria set forth in Note 1, in all material respects."), or in terms of an assertion made by the responsible party (for example, "In our opinion, management's assertion that the accompanying schedule of investment returns of XYZ Company for the year ended December 31, 20XX, is presented in accordance with [or based on] the ABC criteria set forth in Note 1 is fairly stated, in all material respects.").

.A88 The language of the practitioner's opinion in paragraph .63*i*(i) may need to be tailored to reflect the nature of the subject matter and criteria for the engagement. Examples of language that meet the requirements in paragraph .63*i*(i) include the following:

- The entity maintained effective internal control over the subject matter, in all material respects, based on the criteria.
- The subject matter is presented in accordance with (or based on) the criteria, in all material respects.

---

4 Paragraph .32*i* of section 305, *Prospective Financial Information*.

5 Example 1 in paragraph .A43 of section 305.

- The subject matter achieved the objectives, in all material respects (when the objectives are the criteria).
- The subject matter is free from material misstatement based on the criteria.
- The subject matter is presented fairly, in all material respects, based on the criteria. (The practitioner's professional judgment concerning the fairness of the presentation of the subject matter relates to whether the measurement, recognition, presentation, and disclosure of all material items in the presentation of the subject matter achieve fair presentation.)

.A89 A single practitioner's report may cover more than one aspect of a subject matter or an assertion about the subject matter. When that is the case, the report may contain separate opinions or conclusions on each aspect of the subject matter or assertion (for example, examination level related to some aspects or assertions and review level related to others, or an unmodified opinion on some aspects or assertions and a modified opinion on others).

.A90 A practitioner may report on subject matter or an assertion at multiple dates or covering multiple periods during which criteria have changed (for example, a practitioner's report on comparative information). Criteria are clearly described when they identify the criteria for each period and how the criteria have changed from one period to the next. If the criteria for the current date or period have changed from the criteria for a preceding date or period, changes in the criteria may be significant to users of the report. If so, the criteria and the fact that they have changed may be disclosed in the presentation of the subject matter, in the written assertion, or in the report, even if the subject matter for the preceding date or period is not presented.

Location (Ref: par. .63k)

.A91 In the United States, the location of the issuing office is the city and state. In another country, it may be the city and country.

Date (Ref: par. .63l)

.A92 Including the date of the practitioner's report informs the intended users that the practitioner has considered the effect of the events that occurred up to that date on the subject matter and the report.

.A93 Because the practitioner expresses an opinion on the subject matter or assertion and the subject matter or assertion is the responsibility of the responsible party, the practitioner is not in a position to conclude that sufficient appropriate evidence has been obtained until evidence is obtained that all the elements that the subject matter or assertion comprises, including any related notes, when applicable, have been prepared, and the responsible party has accepted responsibility for them.

Restricted-Use Paragraph (Ref: par. .10, .50, .64, and .65b–c)

.A94 A practitioner's report for which the conditions in paragraph .64 do not apply need not include an alert that restricts its use. However, nothing in the attestation standards precludes a practitioner from including such an alert in any practitioner's report or other practitioner's written communication.

.A95 A practitioner's report that is required by paragraph .64 to include an alert that restricts the use of the report may be included in a document that also contains a practitioner's report that is for general use. In such circumstances, the use of the general use report is not affected.

.A96 A practitioner may also issue a single combined practitioner's report that includes (*a*) a practitioner's report that is required by paragraph .64 to include an alert that restricts its use, and (*b*) a report that is for general use. If these two types of reports are clearly differentiated within the combined report, such as through the use of appropriate headings, the alert that restricts the use of the report may be limited to the report required by paragraph .64 to include such an alert. In such circumstances, the use of the general use report is not affected.

.A97 The written representations required by paragraph .50 include an assertion. If the engaging party is not the responsible party and the responsible party provides an oral assertion rather than a written assertion, paragraph .64*c* calls for an alert that restricts the use of the practitioner's report to the engaging party.

.A98 The practitioner may identify the specified parties by naming them, referring to a list of those parties, or identifying the class of parties, for example, "all customers of XYZ Company during some or all of the period January 1, 20XX to December 31, 20XX." The method of identifying the specified parties is determined by the practitioner.

.A99 In some cases, the criteria used to measure or evaluate the subject matter may be designed for a specific purpose. For example, a regulator may require certain entities to use particular criteria designed for regulatory purposes. To avoid misunderstandings, the practitioner alerts users of the practitioner's report to this fact and, therefore, that the report is intended solely for the information and use of the specified parties.

.A100 The alert that restricts the use of the practitioner's report is designed to avoid misunderstandings related to the use of the report, particularly if the report is taken out of the context in which the report is intended to be used. A practitioner may consider informing the responsible party and, if different, the engaging party or other specified parties that the report is not intended for distribution to parties other than those specified in the report. The practitioner may, in connection with establishing the terms of the engagement, reach an understanding with the responsible party or, if different, the engaging party, that the intended use of the report will be restricted and may obtain the responsible party's agreement that the responsible party and specified parties will not distribute such report to parties other than those identified therein. A practitioner is not responsible for controlling, and cannot control, distribution of the report after its release.

.A101 In some cases, a restricted-use practitioner's report filed with regulatory agencies is required by law or regulation to be made available to the public as a matter of public record. Also, a regulatory agency, as part of its oversight responsibility for an entity, may require access to a restricted-use report in which it is not named as a specified party.

Reference to the Practitioner's Specialist (Ref: par. .67)

.A102 The practitioner has sole responsibility for the opinion expressed, and that responsibility is not reduced by the practitioner's use of the work of a practitioner's specialist.

Modified Opinions (Ref: par. .68, .70, and .74)

.A103 The three types of modified opinions are a qualified opinion, an adverse opinion, and a disclaimer of opinion. The decision regarding which type of modified opinion is appropriate depends upon the following:

a. The nature of the matter giving rise to the modification (that is, whether the subject matter of the engagement is in accordance with [or based on] the criteria, in all material respects or, in the case of an inability to obtain sufficient appropriate evidence, may be materially misstated)

b. The practitioner's professional judgment about the pervasiveness of the effects or possible effects of the matter on the subject matter of the engagement

.A104 A practitioner may express an unmodified opinion only when the engagement has been conducted in accordance with the attestation standards. Such standards will not have been complied with if the practitioner has been unable to apply all the procedures that the practitioner considers necessary in the circumstances.

.A105 The term *pervasive* describes the effects on the subject matter of misstatements or the possible effects on the subject matter of misstatements, if any, that are undetected due to an inability to obtain sufficient appropriate evidence. Pervasive effects on the subject matter are those that, in the practitioner's professional judgment

a. are not confined to specific aspects of the subject matter;

b. if so confined, represent or could represent a substantial proportion of the subject matter; or

c. in relation to disclosures, are fundamental to the intended users' understanding of the subject matter.

.A106 The following table illustrates how the practitioner's professional judgment about the nature of the matter giving rise to the modification and the pervasiveness of its effects or possible effects on the subject matter affects the type of practitioner's report to be issued.

Nature of Matter Giving Rise to the Modification	***Practitioner's Professional Judgment About the Pervasiveness of the Effects or Possible Effects on the Subject Matter***	
	Material but Not Pervasive	***Material and Pervasive***
Scope limitation. An inability to obtain sufficient appropriate evidence.	Qualified opinion	Disclaimer of opinion
Subject matter is materially misstated.	Qualified opinion	Adverse opinion

.A107 A scope limitation may arise from the following:

a. Circumstances beyond the control of the appropriate party(ies). For example, documentation that the practitioner considers necessary to inspect may have been accidentally destroyed.

b. Circumstances relating to the nature or timing of the practitioner's work. For example, a physical process that the practitioner considers necessary to observe may have occurred before the practitioner's engagement.

c. Limitations imposed by the responsible party or the engaging party on the practitioner that, for example, may prevent the practitioner from performing a procedure that the practitioner considers necessary in the circumstances. Limitations of this kind may have other implications for the engagement, such as for the practitioner's consideration of risks of material misstatement and engagement acceptance and continuance.

.A108 The inability to obtain written representations from the responsible party ordinarily would result in a scope limitation. However, when the engaging party is not the responsible party, paragraph .51 enables the practitioner to make inquiries of the responsible party and if the responsible party's oral responses enable the practitioner to conclude that the practitioner has sufficient appropriate evidence to form an opinion about the subject matter, paragraph .56*a* indicates this would not cause a scope limitation. Further, paragraph .56*a* requires that the practitioner's report in these circumstances contain an alert paragraph that restricts the use of the report to the engaging party.

.A109 The practitioner's decision to express a qualified opinion, disclaim an opinion, or withdraw from the engagement because of a scope limitation depends on an assessment of the effect of the omitted procedure(s) on the practitioner's ability to express an opinion. This assessment will be affected by the nature and magnitude of the potential effects of the matters in question and by their significance to the subject matter or assertion.

.A110 An inability to perform a specific procedure does not constitute a scope limitation if the practitioner is able to obtain sufficient appropriate evidence by performing alternative procedures.

Responsible Party Refuses to Provide a Written Assertion (Ref: par. .84)

.A111 The following is an example of the disclosure required by paragraph .84:

> Attestation standards established by the American Institute of Certified Public Accountants require that we request a written statement from [*identify the responsible party*] stating that [*identify the subject matter*] that we examined has been accurately measured or evaluated. We requested that [*identify the responsible party*] provide such a written statement but [*identify the responsible party*] refused to do so.

.A112 The practitioner's report discussed in paragraph .84 is appropriate only when the engagement is to report on the subject matter; it is not appropriate for a report on an assertion. When reporting on an assertion, the practitioner is required to obtain a written assertion from the responsible party.

.A113 If the responsible party's failure to provide the practitioner with written representations causes the practitioner to conclude that a scope limitation exists and, thus, qualify or disclaim an opinion, the practitioner need not restrict the use of the practitioner's report but is required by paragraph .69 to describe the matter that gave rise to the modified opinion. Paragraph .A94 notes, however, that the practitioner is not precluded from restricting the use of any report.

Communication Responsibilities (Ref: par. .85–.86)

.A114 Other matters that may be appropriate to communicate to the responsible party or, if different, the engaging party, include bias in the measurement, evaluation, or disclosure of the subject matter. (Ref: par. .85)

.A115 The practitioner's professional duty to maintain the confidentiality of client information may preclude the practitioner from reporting identified or suspected noncompliance with laws or regulations that is not relevant to the subject matter to a party other than the responsible party and, if different, the engaging party. However, the practitioner's legal responsibilities may vary by jurisdiction, and in certain circumstances, the duty of confidentiality may be overridden by statute, the law, or courts of law. In the following circumstances, a duty to notify parties outside the entity may exist:

- In response to a court order
- In compliance with requirements for examinations of entities that receive financial assistance from a government agency

Because potential conflicts with the practitioner's ethical and legal obligations for confidentiality may be complex, the practitioner may consult with legal counsel before discussing noncompliance with parties outside the entity. (Ref: par. .86)

.A116 If the practitioner is performing an examination engagement in accordance with *Government Auditing Standards*, the practitioner may be required to report on compliance with laws, regulations, and provisions of contracts or grant agreements as part of the examination. The practitioner also may be required to communicate instances of noncompliance to appropriate oversight bodies and funding agencies. (Ref: par. .86)

Documentation (Ref: par. .87)

.A117 Documentation includes a record of the practitioner's reasoning on all significant findings or issues that require the exercise of professional judgment and related conclusions. The existence of difficult questions of principle or professional judgment calls for the documentation to include the relevant facts that were known by the practitioner at the time the conclusion was reached.

.A118 It is neither necessary nor practical to document every matter considered, or professional judgment made, during an engagement. Further, it is unnecessary for the practitioner to document separately (as in a checklist, for example) compliance with matters for which compliance is demonstrated by documents included in the engagement file. Similarly, the practitioner need not include in the engagement file superseded drafts of working papers, notes that reflect incomplete or preliminary thinking, previous copies of documents corrected for typographical or other errors, and duplicates of documents.

.A119 In applying professional judgment to assess the extent of documentation to be prepared and retained, the practitioner may consider what is necessary to provide an experienced practitioner, having no previous connection with the engagement, with an understanding of the work performed and the basis of the principal decisions made.

.A120 Documentation ordinarily includes a record of

- issues identified with respect to compliance with relevant ethical requirements and how they were resolved.
- conclusions on compliance with independence requirements that apply to the engagement and any relevant discussions with the firm that support these conclusions.
- conclusions reached regarding the acceptance and continuance of client relationships and attestation engagements.
- the nature and scope of, and conclusions resulting from, consultations undertaken during the course of the engagement.

.A121

Exhibit—Illustrative Practitioner's Examination Reports

The illustrative practitioner's examination reports in this exhibit meet the applicable reporting requirements in paragraphs .61–.84. A practitioner may use alternative language in drafting an examination report, provided that the language meets the applicable requirements in paragraphs .61–.84. The criteria for evaluating the subject matter in examples 1–3 and 5–6 have been determined by the practitioner to be suitable and available to all users of the practitioner's report; therefore, these practitioner's reports may be for general use. The criteria for evaluating the subject matter in example 4 are suitable but available only to specified parties; therefore, use of this practitioner's report is restricted to the specified parties who either participated in the establishment of the criteria or can be presumed to have an adequate understanding of the criteria. (See paragraph .65 for the information to be included in a separate paragraph of the report that contains an alert that restricts the use of the report and paragraph .66 for the content of that paragraph when the engagement is also performed in accordance with *Government Auditing Standards*.)

Example 1: Practitioner's Examination Report on Subject Matter; Unmodified Opinion

The following is an illustrative practitioner's report for an examination engagement in which the practitioner has examined the subject matter and is reporting on the subject matter.

Independent Accountant's Report

[*Appropriate Addressee*]

We have examined [*identify the subject matter, for example, the accompanying schedule of investment returns of XYZ Company for the year ended December 31, 20XX*]. XYZ Company's management is responsible for [*identify the subject matter, for example, presenting the schedule of investment returns*] in accordance with (or based on) [*identify the criteria, for example, the ABC criteria set forth in Note 1*]. Our responsibility is to express an opinion on [*identify the subject matter, for example, the schedule of investment returns*] based on our examination.

Our examination was conducted in accordance with attestation standards established by the American Institute of Certified Public Accountants. Those standards require that we plan and perform the examination to obtain reasonable assurance about whether [*identify the subject matter, for example, the schedule of investment returns*] is in accordance with (or based on) the criteria, in all material respects. An examination involves performing procedures to obtain evidence about [*identify the subject matter, for example, the schedule of investment returns*]. The nature, timing, and extent of the procedures selected depend on our judgment, including an assessment of the risks of material misstatement of [*identify the subject matter, for example, the schedule of investment returns*], whether due to fraud or error. We believe that the evidence we obtained is sufficient and appropriate to provide a reasonable basis for our opinion.

[*Include a description of significant inherent limitations, if any, associated with the measurement or evaluation of the subject matter against the criteria.*]

[Additional paragraph(s) may be added to emphasize certain matters relating to the attestation engagement or the subject matter.]

In our opinion, *[identify the subject matter, for example, the schedule of investment returns of XYZ Company for the year ended December 31, 20XX or the schedule of investment returns referred to above]*, is presented in accordance with (or based on) *[identify the criteria, for example, the ABC criteria set forth in Note 1]*, in all material respects.

[Practitioner's signature]
[Practitioner's city and state]
[Date of practitioner's report]

Example 2: Practitioner's Examination Report on an Assertion; Unmodified Opinion

The following is an illustrative practitioner's report for an examination engagement in which the practitioner has examined the responsible party's assertion and is reporting on that assertion.

Independent Accountant's Report

[Appropriate Addressee]

We have examined management of XYZ Company's assertion that *[identify the assertion, including the subject matter and the criteria, for example, the accompanying schedule of investment returns of XYZ Company for the year ended December 31, 20XX, is presented in accordance with [or based on] the ABC criteria set forth in Note 1]*. XYZ Company's management is responsible for its assertion. Our responsibility is to express an opinion on management's assertion based on our examination.

Our examination was conducted in accordance with attestation standards established by the American Institute of Certified Public Accountants. Those standards require that we plan and perform the examination to obtain reasonable assurance about whether management's assertion is fairly stated, in all material respects. An examination involves performing procedures to obtain evidence about management's assertion. The nature, timing, and extent of the procedures selected depend on our judgment, including an assessment of the risks of material misstatement of management's assertion, whether due to fraud or error. We believe that the evidence we obtained is sufficient and appropriate to provide a reasonable basis for our opinion.

[Include a description of significant inherent limitations, if any, associated with the measurement or evaluation of the subject matter against the criteria.]

[Additional paragraph(s) may be added to emphasize certain matters relating to the attestation engagement or the subject matter.]

In our opinion, management's assertion that *[identify the assertion, including the subject matter and the criteria, for example, the accompanying schedule of investment returns of XYZ Company for the year ended December 31, 20XX, is presented in accordance with [or based on] the ABC criteria set forth in Note 1]* is fairly stated, in all material respects.

[Practitioner's signature]
[Practitioner's city and state]
[Date of practitioner's report]

Example 3: Practitioner's Examination Report in Which the Practitioner Examines Management's Assertion and Reports Directly on the Subject Matter; Unmodified Opinion

The following is an illustrative practitioner's report for an examination engagement in which the practitioner has examined the responsible party's assertion and is reporting directly on the subject matter.

Independent Accountant's Report

[*Appropriate Addressee*]

We have examined management of XYZ Company's assertion that [*identify the assertion, including the subject matter and the criteria, for example, the accompanying schedule of investment returns of XYZ Company for the year ended December 31, 20XX, is presented in accordance with [or based on] the ABC criteria set forth in Note 1*]. XYZ Company's management is responsible for its assertion. Our responsibility is to express an opinion on [*identify the subject matter, for example, the accompanying schedule of investment returns of XYZ Company for the year ended December 31, 20XX*], based on our examination.

Our examination was conducted in accordance with attestation standards established by the American Institute of Certified Public Accountants. Those standards require that we plan and perform the examination to obtain reasonable assurance about whether [*identify the subject matter, for example, the schedule of investment returns*] is presented in accordance with (or based on) the criteria, in all material respects. An examination involves performing procedures to obtain evidence about [*identify the subject matter, for example, the schedule of investment returns*]. The nature, timing, and extent of the procedures selected depend on our judgment, including an assessment of the risks of material misstatement of [*identify the subject matter, for example, the schedule of investment returns*], whether due to fraud or error. We believe that the evidence we obtained is sufficient and appropriate to provide a reasonable basis for our opinion.

[*Include a description of significant inherent limitations, if any, associated with the measurement or evaluation of the subject matter against the criteria.*]

[*Additional paragraph(s) may be added to emphasize certain matters relating to the attestation engagement or the subject matter.*]

In our opinion, [*identify the subject matter, for example, the accompanying schedule of investment returns of XYZ Company for the year ended December 31, 20XX or the schedule of investment returns referred to above*] is presented in accordance with (or based on) [*identify the criteria, for example, the ABC criteria set forth in Note 1*], in all material respects.

[*Practitioner's signature*]
[*Practitioner's city and state*]
[*Date of practitioner's report*]

Example 4: Practitioner's Examination Report on Subject Matter; Unmodified Opinion; Use of the Practitioner's Report Is Restricted to Specified Parties

The following is an illustrative practitioner's report for an examination engagement in which the criteria are suitable, but available only to specified parties; therefore, use of the report is restricted to the specified parties who either participated in the establishment of the criteria or can be presumed to have an adequate understanding of the criteria. The practitioner has examined the subject matter and is reporting on the subject matter.

Independent Accountant's Report

[Appropriate Addressee]

We have examined [*identify the subject matter, for example, the number of widgets sold by XYZ Company to ABC Company (or tons of coal mined by XYZ Company... or gallons of gas sold in the United States by XYZ Company to ABC Company) during the year ended December 31, 20XX,*] to determine whether it has been calculated in accordance with (or based on) [*identify the criteria, for example, the agreement dated (date) between ABC Company and XYZ Company, as further described in Note 1*]. XYZ Company's management is responsible for [*identify the subject matter, for example, calculating the number of widgets sold*]. Our responsibility is to express an opinion on [*identify the subject matter, for example, the number of widgets sold by XYZ Company to ABC Company (or tons of coal mined by XYZ Company... or gallons of gas sold in the United States by XYZ Company to ABC Company) during the year ended December 31, 20XX,*] based on our examination.

Our examination was conducted in accordance with attestation standards established by the American Institute of Certified Public Accountants. Those standards require that we plan and perform the examination to obtain reasonable assurance about whether [*identify the subject matter, for example, the number of widgets sold, tons of coal mined, or gallons of gas sold*] is in accordance with (or based on) the criteria, in all material respects. An examination involves performing procedures to obtain evidence about [*identify the subject matter, for example, the number of widgets sold, tons of coal mined, or gallons of gas sold*]. The nature, timing, and extent of the procedures selected depend on our judgment, including an assessment of the risks of material misstatement of [*identify the subject matter, for example, the number of widgets sold by XYZ Company to ABC Company (or tons of coal mined by XYZ Company, or gallons of gas sold in the United States by XYZ Company to ABC Company*], whether due to fraud or error. We believe that the evidence we obtained is sufficient and appropriate to provide a reasonable basis for our opinion.

[Include a description of significant inherent limitations, if any, associated with the measurement or evaluation of the subject matter against the criteria.]

[Additional paragraph(s) may be added to emphasize certain matters relating to the attestation engagement or the subject matter.]

In our opinion, [*identify the subject matter, for example, the number of widgets sold by XYZ Company to ABC Company (or tons of coal mined by XYZ Company, or gallons of gas sold in the United States by XYZ Company to ABC Company) during the year ended December 31, 20XX,*] has been calculated in accordance with (or based on) [*identify the criteria, for example, the agreement dated (date) between ABC Company and XYZ Company, as further described in Note 1*], in all material respects.

This report is intended solely for the information and use of [*identify the specified parties, for example, ABC Company and XYZ Company*], and is not intended to be and should not be used by anyone other than the specified parties.

[Practitioner's signature]
[Practitioner's city and state]
[Date of practitioner's report]

Example 5: Practitioner's Examination Report on Subject Matter; Qualified Opinion

The following is an illustrative practitioner's report for an examination engagement in which the practitioner expresses a qualified opinion because conditions exist that, individually or in combination, result in one or more material, but not pervasive, misstatements of the subject matter based on (or in certain engagements, deviations from, exceptions to, or instances of noncompliance with) the criteria. The practitioner has examined the subject matter and is reporting on the subject matter. Paragraph .79 states, "If the practitioner has concluded that conditions exist that, individually or in combination, result in one or more material misstatements based on the criteria, the practitioner should modify the opinion and should express a qualified or adverse opinion directly on the subject matter, not on the assertion, even when the assertion acknowledges the misstatement."

Independent Accountant's Report

[*Appropriate Addressee*]

We have examined [*identify the subject matter, for example, the accompanying schedule of investment returns of XYZ Company for the year ended December 31, 20XX*]. XYZ Company's management is responsible for [*identify the subject matter, for example, presenting the schedule of investment returns*] in accordance with (or based on) [*identify the criteria, for example, the ABC criteria set forth in Note 1*]. Our responsibility is to express an opinion on [*identify the subject matter, for example, the schedule of investment returns*] based on our examination.

Our examination was conducted in accordance with attestation standards established by the American Institute of Certified Public Accountants. Those standards require that we plan and perform the examination to obtain reasonable assurance about whether [*identify the subject matter, for example, the schedule of investment returns*] is presented in accordance with (or based on) the criteria, in all material respects. An examination involves performing procedures to obtain evidence about [*identify the subject matter, for example, the schedule of investment returns*]. The nature, timing, and extent of the procedures selected depend on our judgment, including an assessment of the risks of material misstatement of [*identify the subject matter, for example, the schedule of investment returns*], whether due to fraud or error. We believe that the evidence we obtained is sufficient and appropriate to provide a reasonable basis for our opinion.

[*Include a description of significant inherent limitations, if any, associated with the measurement or evaluation of the subject matter against the criteria.*]

[*Additional paragraph(s) may be added to emphasize certain matters relating to the attestation engagement or the subject matter.*]

Our examination disclosed [*describe condition(s) that, individually or in the aggregate, resulted in a material misstatement or deviation from the criteria*].

In our opinion, except for the material misstatement [*or deviation from the criteria*] described in the preceding paragraph, [*identify the subject matter, for example, the accompanying schedule of investment returns of XYZ Company for the year ended December 31, 20XX, or the schedule of investment returns referred to above*], is presented in accordance with (or based on) [*identify the criteria, for example, the ABC criteria set forth in Note 1*], in all material respects.

[*Practitioner's signature*]
[*Practitioner's city and state*]
[*Date of practitioner's report*]

Example 6: Practitioner's Examination Report; Practitioner Engaged to Report on Subject Matter; Disclaimer of Opinion Because of Scope Limitation

The following is an illustrative practitioner's report for an examination engagement in which the practitioner was engaged to report on the subject matter but is disclaiming an opinion because of a scope limitation. (See paragraphs .68–.84 and the related application guidance for reporting guidance when a scope limitation exists.)

Independent Accountant's Report

[*Appropriate Addressee*]

We were engaged to examine [*identify the subject matter, for example, the accompanying schedule of investment returns of XYZ Company for the year ended December 31, 20XX*], in accordance with (or based on) [*identify the criteria, for example, the ABC criteria set forth in Note 1*]. XYZ Company's management is responsible for [*identify the subject matter, for example, presenting the schedule of investment returns*]. Our responsibility is to express an opinion on [*identify the subject matter, for example, the schedule of investment returns*] based on conducting the examination in accordance with attestation standards established by the American Institute of Certified Public Accountants.

[*The first sentence of the practitioner's report has been revised to state, "We were engaged to examine" rather than "We have examined." The standards under which the practitioner conducts an examination have been identified at the end of the second sentence of the report, rather than in a separate sentence in the second paragraph of the report.*

[*The report should omit statements*

- *indicating what those standards require of the practitioner.*
- *indicating that the practitioner believes the evidence obtained is sufficient and appropriate to provide a reasonable basis for the practitioner's opinion.*
- *describing the nature of an examination engagement.*]

[*Include a paragraph to describe scope limitations.*]

Because of the limitation on the scope of our examination discussed in the preceding paragraph, the scope of our work was not sufficient to enable us to express, and we do not express, an opinion on whether [*identify the subject matter, for example, the accompanying schedule of investment returns of XYZ Company for the year ended December 31, 20XX, or the schedule of investment returns referred to above*] is in accordance with (or based on) [*identify the criteria, for example, the ABC criteria set forth in Note 1*], in all material respects.

[*Practitioner's signature*]
[*Practitioner's city and state*]
[*Date of practitioner's report*]

AT-C Section 210*

Review Engagements

Source: SSAE No. 18.

Effective for practitioners' review reports dated on or after May 1, 2017.

Introduction

.01 This section contains performance and reporting requirements and application guidance for all review engagements. The requirements and guidance in this section supplement the requirements and guidance in section 105, *Concepts Common to All Attestation Engagements*.

Effective Date

.02 This section is effective for practitioners' review reports dated on or after May 1, 2017.

Objectives

.03 In conducting a review engagement, the objectives of the practitioner are to

a. obtain limited assurance about whether any material modifications should be made to the subject matter in order for it to be in accordance with (or based on) the criteria;

b. express a conclusion in a written report about whether the practitioner is aware of any material modifications that should be made to

  i. the subject matter in order for it to be in accordance with (or based on) the criteria or

  ii. the responsible party's assertion in order for it to be fairly stated; and

c. communicate further as required by relevant AT-C sections.

Definitions

.04 For purposes of this section, the following terms have the meanings attributed as follows:

Appropriateness of review evidence. The measure of the quality of review evidence, that is, its relevancy and reliability in providing support for the practitioner's conclusion.

Review evidence. Information used by the practitioner in obtaining limited assurance on which the practitioner's review report is based.

---

* This section contains an "AT-C" identifier, instead of an "AT" identifier, to avoid confusion with references to existing "AT" sections, which remain effective through April 2017.

Sufficiency of review evidence. The measure of the quantity of review evidence. The quantity of the review evidence needed is affected by the risks of material misstatement and also by the quality of such evidence.

Requirements

Conduct of a Review Engagement

.05 In performing a review engagement, the practitioner should comply with this section, section 105, and any subject-matter AT-C section that is relevant to the engagement. A subject-matter AT-C section is relevant to the engagement when it is in effect, and the circumstances addressed by the AT-C section exist. (Ref: par. .A1)

.06 The practitioner should consider whether the nature of review procedures would enable the practitioner to obtain sufficient appropriate review evidence to obtain limited assurance. (Ref: par. .A2)

.07 A practitioner should not perform a review of (Ref: par. .A2)

a. prospective financial information,

b. internal control, or

c. compliance with requirements of specified laws, regulations, rules, contracts, or grants.

Agreeing on the Terms of the Engagement

.08 The practitioner should agree upon the terms of the engagement with the engaging party. The agreed-upon terms of the engagement should be specified in sufficient detail in an engagement letter or other suitable form of written agreement. (Ref: par. .A3)

.09 The agreed-upon terms of the engagement should include the following:

a. The objective and scope of the engagement

b. The responsibilities of the practitioner (Ref: par. .A4)

c. A statement that the engagement will be conducted in accordance with attestation standards established by the American Institute of Certified Public Accountants

d. The responsibilities of the responsible party and the responsibilities of the engaging party, if different

e. A statement that a review is substantially less in scope than an examination, the objective of which is to obtain reasonable assurance about whether the subject matter is in accordance with (or based on) the criteria, in all material respects, or the assertion is fairly stated, in all material respects, in order to express an opinion, and that, accordingly, the practitioner will not express such an opinion

f. Identification of the criteria for the measurement, evaluation, or disclosure of the subject matter

g. An acknowledgement that the engaging party agrees to provide the practitioner with a representation letter at the conclusion of the engagement

.10 Although an engagement may recur, each engagement is considered a separate engagement. The practitioner should assess whether circumstances require revision to the terms of a preceding engagement. If the practitioner concludes that the terms of the preceding engagement need not be revised for the current engagement, the practitioner should remind the engaging party of the terms of the current engagement, and the reminder should be documented.

Requesting a Written Assertion

.11 The practitioner should request from the responsible party a written assertion about the measurement or evaluation of the subject matter against the criteria. When the engaging party is the responsible party and refuses to provide a written assertion, paragraph .59 requires the practitioner to withdraw from the engagement, when withdrawal is possible under applicable laws and regulations. When the engaging party is not the responsible party, and the responsible party refuses to provide a written assertion, the practitioner need not withdraw from the engagement. In that case, paragraph .60 requires the practitioner to disclose that refusal in the practitioner's report and restrict the use of the report to the engaging party. (Ref: par. .A5–.A8 and .A76)

Planning and Performing the Engagement

.12 The practitioner should set the scope, timing, and direction of the engagement and determine the nature, timing, and extent of the planned procedures that are required to be carried out in order to achieve the objectives of the engagement. (Ref: par. .A9–.A12)

.13 The practitioner should obtain an understanding of the subject matter and other engagement circumstances sufficient to provide a basis for designing and performing procedures in order to achieve the objectives of the engagement. That understanding should include the practices used to measure, recognize, and record the subject matter. (Ref: par. .A13)

Materiality in Planning and Performing the Engagement

.14 The practitioner should consider materiality when (Ref: par. .A14–.A19)

- planning and performing the review engagement, including when determining the nature, timing, and extent of procedures.
- evaluating whether the practitioner is aware of any material modifications that should be made to the subject matter in order for it to be in accordance with (or based on) the criteria or the assertion in order for it to be fairly stated.

Procedures to Be Performed

.15 To obtain limited assurance, the practitioner should obtain sufficient appropriate review evidence in order to express a conclusion about whether any material modifications should be made to the subject matter in order for it to be in accordance with (or based on) the criteria, or the assertion, in order for it to be fairly stated.

.16 The practitioner should apply professional judgment in determining the specific nature, timing, and extent of review procedures. Based on (Ref: par. .A20–.A23)

a. the practitioner's understanding of

i. the subject matter and the practices used by the responsible party to measure, recognize, and record the subject matter and

ii. the engagement circumstances, and

b. the practitioner's awareness of the risk that the practitioner may unknowingly fail to modify the practitioner's report when the subject matter is materially misstated,

the practitioner should design and perform analytical procedures and make inquiries and perform other procedures, as appropriate, to accumulate review evidence in obtaining limited assurance about whether any material modifications should be made to the subject matter in order for it to be in accordance with (or based on) the criteria, or the assertion, in order for it to be fairly stated.

.17 Analytical procedures may not be possible when the subject matter is qualitative, rather than quantitative. In those circumstances, the practitioner should perform other procedures, in addition to inquiries, that provide equivalent levels of review evidence. (Ref: par. .A24)

.18 The practitioner should place increased focus in those areas in which the practitioner believes there are increased risks that the subject matter may be materially misstated. (Ref: par. .A25–.A26)

Analytical Procedures

.19 When designing and performing analytical procedures, the practitioner should (Ref: par. .A27–.A28)

a. determine the suitability of particular analytical procedures for the subject matter, taking into account the practitioner's awareness of risks;

b. evaluate the reliability of data from which the practitioner's expectation is developed, taking into account the source, comparability, nature, and relevance of information available; and

c. develop an expectation with respect to recorded amounts or ratios.

.20 If analytical procedures identify fluctuations or relationships that are inconsistent with other relevant information or that differ significantly from expected amounts or ratios, the practitioner should (Ref: par. .A29)

a. inquire of the responsible party about such differences and

b. consider the responses to these inquiries to determine whether other procedures are necessary in the circumstances.

Inquiries and Other Review Procedures

.21 The practitioner should inquire of the responsible party about the following: (Ref: par. .A30)

a. Whether the subject matter has been prepared in accordance with (or based on) the criteria

b. The practices used by the responsible party to measure, recognize, and record the subject matter

c. Questions that have arisen in the course of applying the review procedures

d. Communications from regulatory agencies or others, if relevant

.22 The practitioner should consider the reasonableness and consistency of the responsible party's responses in light of the results of other review procedures and the practitioner's knowledge of the subject matter, criteria, and responsible party.

Fraud, Laws, and Regulations

.23 The practitioner should make inquiries of appropriate parties to determine whether they have knowledge of any actual, suspected, or alleged fraud or noncompliance with laws or regulations affecting the subject matter.

.24 The practitioner should respond appropriately to fraud or suspected fraud and noncompliance or suspected noncompliance with laws or regulations affecting the subject matter that is identified during the engagement. (Ref: par. .A31–.A32)

Incorrect, Incomplete, or Otherwise Unsatisfactory Information

.25 During the performance of review procedures, if the practitioner becomes aware that information coming to the practitioner's attention is incorrect, incomplete, or otherwise unsatisfactory, the practitioner should request that the responsible party consider the effect of these matters on the subject matter and communicate the results of its consideration to the practitioner. The practitioner should consider the results communicated to the practitioner by the responsible party and the potential effect, if any, on the practitioner's report.

.26 If the practitioner believes the subject matter may be materially misstated, the practitioner should perform additional procedures sufficient to obtain limited assurance about whether any material modifications should be made to the subject matter in order for it to be in accordance with (or based on) the criteria or the assertion in order for it to be fairly stated.

Using the Work of a Practitioner's Specialist or Internal Auditors

.27 When the practitioner expects to use the work of a practitioner's specialist or internal auditors, the practitioner should apply the requirements in section 205, *Examination Engagements*, and the related application guidance, as appropriate, for a review engagement.[1]

Evaluating the Results of Review Procedures

.28 The practitioner should accumulate misstatements identified during the engagement, other than those that are clearly trivial. (Ref: par. .A33–.A34)

.29 The practitioner should evaluate the sufficiency and appropriateness of the review evidence obtained in the context of the engagement and, if necessary, attempt to obtain further review evidence. The practitioner should consider all relevant review evidence, regardless of whether it appears to corroborate or contradict the measurement or evaluation of the subject matter against the criteria. (Ref: par. .A35–.A37)

.30 If the practitioner concludes that the subject matter is materially misstated or is unable to obtain review evidence sufficient for limited assurance, the practitioner should consider the implications for the practitioner's conclusion in paragraphs .51–.60.

---

[1] Paragraphs .36–.44 of section 205, *Examination Engagements*.

Considering Subsequent Events and Subsequently Discovered Facts

.31 The practitioner should inquire whether the responsible party, and if different, the engaging party, is aware of any events subsequent to the period (or point in time) covered by the review engagement up to the date of the practitioner's report that could have a significant effect on the subject matter or assertion. If the practitioner becomes aware, through inquiry or otherwise, of such an event, or any other event that is of such a nature and significance that its disclosure is necessary to prevent users of the report from being misled, and information about that event is not adequately disclosed by the responsible party in the subject matter or in its assertion, the practitioner should take appropriate action. (Ref: par. .A38–.A40)

.32 The practitioner has no responsibility to perform any procedures regarding the subject matter or assertion after the date of the practitioner's report. Nevertheless, the practitioner should respond appropriately to facts that become known to the practitioner after the date of the report that, had they been known to the practitioner at that date, may have caused the practitioner to revise the report. (Ref: par. .A41–.A42)

Written Representations

.33 The practitioner should request from the responsible party written representations in the form of a letter addressed to the practitioner. The representations should (Ref: par. .A43–.A46)

a. include the responsible party's assertion about the subject matter based on the criteria. (Ref: par. .A76)

b. state that all relevant matters are reflected in the measurement or evaluation of the subject matter or assertion.

c. state that all known matters contradicting the subject matter or assertion and any communication from regulatory agencies or others affecting the subject matter or assertion have been disclosed to the practitioner, including communications received between the end of the period addressed in the written assertion and the date of the practitioner's report.

d. acknowledge responsibility for

i. the subject matter and the assertion;

ii. selecting the criteria, when applicable; and

iii. determining that such criteria are appropriate for the responsible party's purposes.

e. state that any known events subsequent to the period (or point in time) of the subject matter being reported on that would have a material effect on the subject matter or assertion have been disclosed to the practitioner. (Ref: par. .A45)

f. state that it has provided the practitioner with all relevant information and access.

g. if applicable, state that the responsible party believes the effects of uncorrected misstatements are immaterial, individually and in the aggregate, to the subject matter. (Ref: par. .A46)

h. if applicable, state that significant assumptions used in making any material estimates are reasonable.

i. state that the responsible party has disclosed to the practitioner

i. all deficiencies in internal control relevant to the engagement of which the responsible party is aware;

ii. its knowledge of any actual, suspected, or alleged fraud or noncompliance with laws or regulations affecting the subject matter; and

iii. other matters as the practitioner deems appropriate.

.34 When the engaging party is not the responsible party, and the responsible party refuses to provide the representations in paragraph .33 in writing, the practitioner should make inquiries of the responsible party about, and seek oral responses to, the matters in paragraph .33. (Ref: par. .A47)

.35 When the engaging party is not the responsible party, the practitioner should request written representations from the engaging party, in addition to those requested from the responsible party, in the form of a letter addressed to the practitioner. The representations should

a. acknowledge that the responsible party is responsible for the subject matter and assertion.

b. acknowledge the engaging party's responsibility for selecting the criteria, when applicable.

c. acknowledge the engaging party's responsibility for determining that such criteria are appropriate for its purposes.

d. state that the engaging party is not aware of any material misstatements in the subject matter or assertion.

e. state that the engaging party has disclosed to the practitioner all known events subsequent to the period (or point in time) of the subject matter being reported on that would have a material effect on the subject matter or assertion. (Ref: par. .A45)

f. address other matters as the practitioner deems appropriate.

.36 When written representations are directly related to matters that are material to the subject matter, the practitioner should

a. evaluate their reasonableness and consistency with other review evidence obtained, including other representations (oral or written) and

b. consider whether those making the representations can be expected to be well informed on the particular matters.

.37 The date of the written representations should be as of the date of the practitioner's report. The written representations should address the subject matter and periods covered by the practitioner's conclusion.

Requested Written Representations Not Provided or Are Unreliable

.38 When the engaging party is the responsible party, and one or more of the requested written representations are not provided, or the practitioner concludes that there is sufficient doubt about the competence, integrity, ethical values, or diligence of those providing the written representations, or the practitioner concludes that the written representations are otherwise not reliable, the practitioner should

a. discuss the matter with the appropriate party(ies),

b. reevaluate the integrity of those from whom the representations were requested or received and evaluate the effect that this may have on the reliability of representations and review evidence in general, and

c. if any of the matters are not resolved to the practitioner's satisfaction, withdraw from the engagement.

.39 When the engaging party is not the responsible party (Ref: par. .A47–.A49)

a. if one or more of the requested representations are provided in writing by the responsible party, but the practitioner receives satisfactory oral responses to the practitioner's inquiries performed in accordance with paragraph .34 sufficient to enable the practitioner to conclude that the practitioner has sufficient appropriate review evidence to form a conclusion about the subject matter, the practitioner's report should contain a separate paragraph that restricts the use of the practitioner's report to the engaging party. (Paragraphs .48–.49 contain requirements for the contents of such a paragraph.)

b. if one or more of the requested representations are provided neither in writing nor orally from the responsible party in accordance with paragraph .34, a scope limitation exists, and the practitioner should withdraw from the engagement.

Other Information

.40 If prior to or after the release of the practitioner's report on subject matter or an assertion, the practitioner is willing to permit the inclusion of the practitioner's report in a document that contains the subject matter or assertion and other information, the practitioner should read the other information to identify material inconsistencies, if any, with the subject matter, assertion, or the practitioner's report. If on reading the other information, in the practitioner's professional judgment (Ref: par. .A50–.A51)

a. a material inconsistency between that other information and the subject matter, assertion, or the practitioner's report exists, or

b. a material misstatement of fact exists in the other information, the subject matter, assertion, or the practitioner's report

the practitioner should discuss the matter with the responsible party and take further action as appropriate.

Description of Criteria

.41 The practitioner should evaluate whether the written description of the subject matter or assertion adequately refers to or describes the criteria. (Ref: par. .A52–.A53)

Forming the Conclusion

.42 The practitioner should form a conclusion about whether the practitioner is aware of any material modifications that should be made to the subject matter in order for it to be in accordance with (or based on) the criteria or to the responsible party's assertion in order for it to be fairly stated. In forming that conclusion, the practitioner should evaluate

a. the practitioner's conclusion regarding the sufficiency and appropriateness of the review evidence obtained and (Ref: par. .A54) *b.* whether uncorrected misstatements are material, individually or in the aggregate. (Ref: par. .A55)

.43 The practitioner should evaluate, based on the review evidence obtained, whether the presentation of the subject matter or assertion is misleading within the context of the engagement. (Ref: par. .A56–.A57)

Preparing the Practitioner's Report

.44 The practitioner's report should be in writing. (Ref: par. .A58–.A59)

.45 A practitioner should report on a written assertion or should report directly on the subject matter. If the practitioner is reporting on the assertion, the assertion should be bound with or accompany the practitioner's report, or the assertion should be clearly stated in the report. (Ref: par. .A60)

Content of the Practitioner's Report

.46 The practitioner's report should include the following:

a. A title that includes the word *independent*. (Ref: par. .A61)

b. An appropriate addressee as required by the circumstances of the engagement.

c. An identification or description of the subject matter or assertion being reported on, including the point in time or period of time to which the measurement or evaluation of the subject matter or assertion relates.

d. An identification of the criteria against which the subject matter was measured or evaluated. (Ref: par. .A62)

e. A statement that identifies

i. the responsible party and its responsibility for the subject matter in accordance with (or based on) the criteria or for its assertion and (Ref: par. .A63–.A64)

ii. the practitioner's responsibility to express a conclusion on the subject matter or assertion, based on the practitioner's review. (Ref: par. .A63)

f. A statement that

i. the practitioner's review was conducted in accordance with attestation standards established by the American Institute of Certified Public Accountants.

ii. those standards require that the practitioner plan and perform the review to obtain limited assurance about whether any material modifications should be made to

(1) the subject matter in order for it to be in accordance with (or based on) the criteria (or equivalent language regarding the subject matter and criteria, such as the language used in the examples in paragraph .A65) or

(2) the responsible party's assertion in order for it to be fairly stated.

iii. a review is substantially less in scope than an examination, the objective of which is to obtain reasonable assurance about whether the subject matter is in accordance with (or based on) the criteria, in all material respects, or

iii. the responsible party's assertion is fairly stated, in all material respects, in order to express an opinion. Accordingly, the practitioner does not express such an opinion.

iv. the practitioner believes the review provides a reasonable basis for the practitioner's conclusion.

g. A statement that describes significant inherent limitations, if any, associated with the measurement or evaluation of the subject matter against the criteria. (Ref: par. .A66)

h. The practitioner's conclusion about whether, based on the review, the practitioner is aware of any material modifications that should be made to (Ref: par. .A67–.A69)

i. the subject matter in order for it be in accordance with (or based on) the criteria (or equivalent language regarding the subject matter and criteria, such as the language used in the examples in paragraph .A67) or

ii. the responsible party's assertion in order for it to be fairly stated.

i. The manual or printed signature of the practitioner's firm.

j. The city and state where the practitioner practices. (Ref: par. .A70)

k. The date of the report. (The report should be dated no earlier than the date on which the practitioner has obtained sufficient appropriate review evidence on which to base the practitioner's conclusion, including evidence that

i. the attestation documentation has been reviewed,

ii. if applicable, the written presentation of the subject matter has been prepared, and

iii. the responsible party has provided a written assertion or, in the circumstance described in paragraph .A49, an oral assertion.) (Ref: par. .A71–.A72)

Restricted-Use Paragraph

.47 In the following circumstances, the practitioner's report should include an alert, in a separate paragraph, that restricts the use of the report: (Ref: par. .A73–.A76)

a. The practitioner determines that the criteria used to evaluate the subject matter are appropriate only for a limited number of parties who either participated in their establishment or can be presumed to have an adequate understanding of the criteria.

b. The criteria used to evaluate the subject matter are available only to specified parties.

c. The engaging party is not the responsible party, and the responsible party does not provide the written representations required by paragraph .33, but does provide oral responses to the practitioner's inquiries about the matters in paragraph .33, as provided for in paragraphs .34 and .39*a*. In this case, use of the report should be restricted to the engaging party. (Ref: par. .A76)

.48 The alert should

a. state that the practitioner's report is intended solely for the information and use of the specified parties,

b. identify the specified parties for whom use is intended, and (Ref: par. .A77)

c. state that the report is not intended to be, and should not be, used by anyone other than the specified parties. (Ref: par. .A78–.A80)

.49 When the engagement is also performed in accordance with *Government Auditing Standards*, the alert that restricts the use of the practitioner's report should include the following information, rather than the information required by paragraph .48:

a. A description of the purpose of the report

b. A statement that the report is not suitable for any other purpose

Reference to the Practitioner's Specialist

.50 The practitioner should not refer to the work of a practitioner's specialist in the practitioner's report containing an unmodified conclusion. (Ref: par. .A81)

Modified Conclusions

Misstatement of Subject Matter

.51 A practitioner who is engaged to perform a review engagement may become aware that the subject matter is misstated. If the misstatement is not corrected, the practitioner should consider whether qualification of the conclusion in the standard practitioner's report is adequate to disclose the misstatement of the subject matter. (Ref: par. .A82)

.52 When the practitioner qualifies the conclusion, the practitioner should include a separate paragraph in the practitioner's report that provides a description of the matter(s) giving rise to the qualification.

.53 The practitioner should express a qualified conclusion when the effects of a matter are material but not pervasive. A qualified conclusion is expressed as being "except for the effects" of the matter to which the qualification relates. When the effects of a matter are material and also pervasive, the practitioner should withdraw from the engagement, when withdrawal is possible under applicable laws and regulations. (Ref: par. .A83)

.54 If the practitioner has concluded that the material misstatement results in a qualified conclusion, the practitioner should report directly on the subject matter, not on the assertion, even when the assertion acknowledges the misstatement.

.55 If the practitioner believes that qualification of the conclusion in the standard practitioner's report is not adequate to indicate the misstatements in the subject matter, the practitioner should withdraw from the engagement.

.56 The practitioner's conclusion on the subject matter or assertion should be clearly separated from any paragraphs emphasizing matters related to the subject matter or any other reporting responsibilities.

.57 When the conclusion is qualified, reference to an external specialist is permitted when such reference is relevant to an understanding of the qualification to the practitioner's conclusion. The practitioner should indicate in the practitioner's report that such reference does not reduce the practitioner's responsibility for that conclusion.

Scope Limitations

.58 If the practitioner is unable to obtain sufficient appropriate review evidence, a scope limitation exists. When a scope limitation exists, the practitioner should withdraw from the engagement, when withdrawal is possible under applicable laws and regulations. (Ref: par. .A84–.A86)

Responsible Party Refuses to Provide a Written Assertion

.59 If the engaging party is the responsible party and refuses to provide the practitioner with a written assertion as required by paragraph .11, the practitioner should withdraw from the engagement when withdrawal is possible under applicable law or regulation.

.60 When the engaging party is not the responsible party and the responsible party refuses to provide the practitioner with a written assertion, the practitioner may report on the subject matter but should disclose in the practitioner's report the responsible party's refusal to provide a written assertion and should restrict the use of the practitioner's report to the engaging party. (Ref: par. .A87–.A88)

Communication Responsibilities

.61 The practitioner should communicate to the responsible party known and suspected fraud and noncompliance with laws or regulations, as well as uncorrected misstatements. When the engaging party is not the responsible party, the practitioner should also communicate this information to the engaging party. (Ref: par. .A89)

Documentation

.62 The practitioner should prepare engagement documentation that is sufficient to determine (Ref: par. .A90–.A93)

a. the nature, timing, and extent of the procedures performed to comply with relevant AT-C sections and applicable legal and regulatory requirements, including

  i. the identifying characteristics of the specific items or matters tested;

  ii. who performed the engagement work and the date such work was completed;

  iii. the discussions with the responsible party or others about findings or issues that, in the practitioner's professional judgment, are significant, including the nature of the significant findings or issues discussed, and when and with whom the discussions took place;

  iv. when the engaging party is the responsible party and the responsible party will not provide one or more of the requested written representations; the practitioner concludes that there is sufficient doubt about the competence, integrity, ethical values, or diligence of those providing the written representations; or that the written representations are otherwise not reliable, the matters in paragraph .38;

  v. when the engaging party is not the responsible party and the responsible party will not provide the written representations regarding the matters in paragraph .33, the oral responses from the responsible party to the practitioner's inquiries regarding the matters in paragraph .33, in accordance with paragraph .34; and

vi. who reviewed the engagement work performed and the date and extent of such review.

b. the results of the procedures performed and the review evidence obtained.

.63 If the practitioner identified information that is inconsistent with the practitioner's final conclusion regarding a significant finding or issue, the practitioner should document how the practitioner addressed the inconsistency.

.64 If, in circumstances such as those described in paragraph .32, the practitioner performs new or additional procedures or draws new conclusions after the date of the practitioner's report, the practitioner should document

a. the circumstances encountered;

b. the new or additional procedures performed, evidence obtained, and conclusions reached and their effect on the report; and

c. when and by whom the resulting changes to the documentation were made and reviewed.

Application and Other Explanatory Material

Conduct of a Review Engagement (Ref: par. .05–.07)

.A1 For example, if a practitioner was reviewing pro forma financial information, section 105, this section, and section 310, *Reporting on Pro Forma Financial Information*, would be relevant.

.A2 Review procedures generally are limited to inquiries and analytical procedures. In circumstances in which inquiry and analytical procedures are not expected to provide sufficient appropriate review evidence, or when the nature of the subject matter does not lend itself to the application of analytical procedures, the practitioner may perform other procedures that he or she believes can provide the practitioner with a level of assurance equivalent to that which inquiries and analytical procedures would have provided. If the practitioner cannot design other procedures to obtain sufficient appropriate review evidence, a review engagement may not be appropriate.

Agreeing on the Terms of the Engagement (Ref: par. .08 and .09*b*)

.A3 It is in the interests of both the engaging party and the practitioner to document the agreed-upon terms of the engagement before the commencement of the engagement to help avoid misunderstandings. The form and content of the engagement letter or other suitable form of written agreement will vary with the engagement circumstances.

.A4 A practitioner may further describe the responsibilities of the practitioner by adding the following items to the engagement letter or other suitable form of written agreement:

a. A statement that a review is designed to obtain limited assurance about whether any material modifications should be made to the subject matter in order for it to be in accordance with (or based on) the criteria

b. A statement that the objective of a review is the expression of a conclusion in a written practitioner's report about whether the practitioner is aware of any material modifications that should be made to

i. the subject matter in order for it be in accordance with (or based on) the criteria or

ii. the responsible party's assertion in order for it to be fairly stated

Requesting a Written Assertion (Ref: par. .11)

.A5 The language of the responsible party's written assertion in paragraph .11 may need to be tailored to reflect the nature of the subject matter and criteria for the engagement. Examples of language that meet the requirements in paragraph .11 include the following:

- The subject matter is presented in accordance with (or based on) the criteria.
- The subject matter achieved the objectives, for example, when the objectives are the criteria.

.A6 Situations may arise in which the current responsible party was not present during some or all of the period covered by the practitioner's report. Such persons may contend that they are not in a position to provide a written assertion that covers the entire period because they were not in place during some or all of the period. This fact, however, does not diminish such persons' responsibilities for the subject matter as a whole. Accordingly, the requirement for the practitioner to request a written assertion from the responsible party that covers the entire relevant period(s) still applies.

.A7 Paragraph .33*a* requires the practitioner to request a written representation from the responsible party that is the same as the responsible party's assertion. If the responsible party provides the practitioner with the written representation in paragraph .33*a*, the practitioner need not request a separate written assertion, unless a separate written assertion is called for by the engagement circumstances. (Ref: par. .11)

.A8 A practitioner may also be engaged to assist the responsible party in measuring or evaluating the subject matter against the criteria in connection with the responsible party providing a written assertion. Regardless of the procedures performed by the practitioner, the responsible party is required to accept responsibility for its assertion and the subject matter and may not base its assertion solely on the practitioner's procedures.[2]

Planning and Performing the Engagement (Ref: par. .12–.13)

.A9 Planning involves the engagement partner and other key members of the engagement team and may involve the practitioner's specialists. Adequate planning helps the practitioner devote appropriate attention to important areas of the engagement, identify potential problems on a timely basis, and properly organize and manage the engagement in order for it to be performed in an effective and efficient manner. Adequate planning also assists the practitioner in properly assigning work to engagement team members, and facilitates the direction, supervision, and the review of their work. Further, it assists, when applicable, the coordination of work performed by other practitioners and practitioner's specialists. The nature and extent of planning activities will vary with

---

[2] The "Nonattest Services" subtopic (ET sec. 1.295) of the AICPA Code of Professional Conduct addresses the practitioner's provision of nonattest services for an attest client.

the engagement circumstances, for example, the complexity of the assessment or evaluation of the subject matter and the practitioner's previous experience with it. Examples of relevant matters that may be considered include the following:

- The characteristics of the engagement that define its scope, including the terms of the engagement, the characteristics of the underlying subject matter, and the criteria
- The expected timing and nature of the communications required
- The results of preliminary engagement activities, such as client acceptance, and, when applicable, whether knowledge gained on other engagements performed by the engagement partner for the appropriate party(ies) is relevant
- The engagement process, including possible sources of review evidence, and choices among alternative measurement or evaluation methods
- The practitioner's understanding of the appropriate party(ies) and its (their) environment, including the risks that the subject matter may be materially misstated
- Identification of intended users and their information needs and consideration of materiality and the components of attestation risk
- The risk of fraud relevant to the engagement
- The effect on the engagement of using the internal audit function

.A10 The practitioner may decide to discuss elements of planning with the appropriate party(ies) to facilitate the conduct and management of the engagement (for example, to coordinate some of the planned procedures with the work of the responsible party's personnel). Although these discussions often occur, the elements of planning remain the practitioner's responsibility. When discussing planning matters, care is needed to avoid compromising the effectiveness of the engagement. For example, discussing the nature and timing of detailed procedures with the responsible party may compromise the effectiveness of the engagement by making the procedures too predictable.

.A11 Planning is not a discrete phase but, rather, a cumulative and iterative process throughout the engagement. As a result of unexpected events, changes in conditions, or review evidence obtained, the practitioner may need to revise the nature, timing, and extent of planned procedures.

.A12 In smaller or less complex engagements, the entire engagement may be conducted by a very small engagement team, possibly involving the engagement partner (who may be a sole practitioner) working without any other engagement team members. With a smaller team, coordination of, and communication among, team members is easier. In such cases, planning the engagement need not be a complex or time-consuming exercise; it varies according to the size of the entity, the complexity of the engagement, and the size of the engagement team.

.A13 Obtaining an understanding of the subject matter and other engagement circumstances provides the practitioner with a frame of reference for exercising professional judgment throughout the engagement, for example, when

- considering the characteristics of the subject matter;
- assessing the suitability of the criteria;

- considering the factors that, in the practitioner's professional judgment, are significant in directing the engagement team's efforts, including situations in which special consideration may be necessary (for example, when there is a need for specialized skills or the work of a specialist);
- establishing and evaluating the continued appropriateness of quantitative materiality levels (when appropriate) and considering qualitative materiality factors;
- developing expectations when performing analytical procedures;
- designing and performing procedures; and
- evaluating review evidence, including the reasonableness of the written representations received by the practitioner.

In some review engagements, the practitioner may obtain an understanding of internal control over the measurement, evaluation, or disclosure of the subject matter.

Materiality in Planning and Performing the Engagement (Ref: par. .14)

.A14 Materiality is considered in the context of qualitative factors and, when applicable, quantitative factors. The relative importance of qualitative factors and quantitative factors when considering materiality in a particular engagement is a matter for the practitioner's professional judgment.

.A15 Professional judgments about materiality are made in light of surrounding circumstances, but they are not affected by the level of assurance, that is, for the same intended users, materiality for a review engagement is the same as it is for an examination engagement because materiality is based on the information needs of intended users and not the level of assurance.

.A16 In general, misstatements, including omissions, are considered to be material if, individually or in the aggregate, they could reasonably be expected to influence relevant decisions of intended users that are made based on the subject matter. The practitioner's consideration of materiality is a matter of professional judgment and is affected by the practitioner's perception of the common information needs of intended users as a group. In this context, it is reasonable for the practitioner to assume that intended users

a. have a reasonable knowledge of the subject matter and a willingness to study the subject matter with reasonable diligence.

b. understand that the subject matter is measured or evaluated and reviewed to appropriate levels of materiality and have an understanding of any materiality concepts included in the criteria.

c. understand any inherent uncertainties involved in measuring or evaluating the subject matter.

d. make reasonable decisions on the basis of the subject matter taken as a whole.

Unless the engagement has been designed to meet the particular information needs of specific users, the possible effect of misstatements on specific users, whose information needs may vary widely, is not ordinarily considered.

.A17 Qualitative factors may include the following:

- The interaction between, and relative importance of, various aspects of the subject matter, such as numerous performance indicators
- The wording chosen with respect to subject matter that is expressed in narrative form, for example, the wording chosen does not omit or distort the information
- The characteristics of the presentation adopted for the subject matter when the criteria allow for variations in that presentation
- The nature of a misstatement
- Whether a misstatement affects compliance with laws or regulations
- In the case of periodic reporting on a subject matter, the effect of an adjustment that affects past or current information about the subject matter or is likely to affect future information about the subject matter
- Whether a misstatement is the result of an intentional act or is unintentional
- Whether a misstatement is significant with regard to the practitioner's understanding of known previous communications to users, for example, in relation to the expected outcome of the measurement or evaluation of the subject matter
- Whether a misstatement relates to the relationship between the responsible party and, if different, the engaging party or its relationship with other parties

.A18 Quantitative factors relate to the magnitude of misstatements relative to reported amounts for those aspects of the subject matter, if any, that are

- expressed numerically or
- otherwise related to numerical values.

.A19 The criteria may discuss the concept of materiality in the context of the preparation and presentation of the subject matter and thereby provide a frame of reference for the practitioner in considering materiality for the engagement. Although criteria may discuss materiality in different terms, the concept of materiality generally includes the matters discussed in paragraphs .A14–.A18. If the criteria do not include a discussion of the concept of materiality, these paragraphs provide the practitioner with a frame of reference.

Procedures to Be Performed (Ref: par. .16–.18)

.A20 Review evidence obtained through the performance of analytical procedures and inquiry will ordinarily provide the practitioner with a reasonable basis for obtaining limited assurance. However, the practitioner may determine it is appropriate to perform additional procedures if the practitioner determines such procedures to be necessary in order to meet the objectives of this section.

.A21 The degree to which procedures beyond analytical procedures and inquiry may be performed may be influenced by factors specific to the engagement. The practitioner may substitute other procedures that provide equivalent levels of review evidence.

.A22 Information may come to the practitioner's attention that differs significantly from that on which the determination of planned procedures was based. As the practitioner performs planned procedures, the review evidence obtained may cause the practitioner to perform additional procedures. Such procedures may include asking the responsible party to examine the matter identified by the practitioner and to make adjustments to the subject matter, if appropriate.

.A23 In some cases, a subject-matter AT-C section may include requirements that affect the nature, timing, and extent of procedures. For example, a subject-matter AT-C section may describe the nature or extent of particular procedures to be performed in a particular type of engagement. Even in such cases, determining the exact nature, timing, and extent of procedures is a matter of professional judgment and will vary from one engagement to the next.

.A24 Review procedures generally are limited to inquiries and analytical procedures. In circumstances in which inquiry and analytical procedures are not expected to provide sufficient appropriate review evidence, or when the nature of the subject matter does not lend itself to the application of analytical procedures, the practitioner may perform other procedures that he or she believes can provide the practitioner with a level of assurance equivalent to that which inquiries and analytical procedures would have provided. If the practitioner cannot design other procedures to obtain sufficient appropriate review evidence, a review engagement may not be appropriate.

.A25 The results of the practitioner's analytical procedures and inquiries may modify the practitioner's risk awareness.

.A26 The practitioner may become aware of a matter(s) that causes the practitioner to believe that the subject matter may be materially misstated when, for example, performing analytical procedures if the practitioner identifies a fluctuation or relationship that is inconsistent with other relevant information or that differs significantly from expected amounts or ratios. In such cases, the practitioner's investigation of such differences may include inquiring of the responsible party or performing other procedures as appropriate in the circumstances.

Analytical Procedures (Ref: par. .19–.20)

.A27 An understanding of the purposes of analytical procedures and the limitations of those procedures is important. Accordingly, the identification of the relationships and types of data used, as well as conclusions reached when recorded amounts are compared to expectations, requires professional judgment by the practitioner.

.A28 Analytical procedures involve comparisons of expectations developed by the practitioner to recorded amounts or ratios developed from recorded amounts. The practitioner develops such expectations by identifying and using plausible relationships that are reasonably expected to exist based on the practitioner's understanding of the subject matter; the practices used by the responsible party to measure, recognize, and record the subject matter; and, if applicable, the industry in which the entity operates.

.A29 Analytical procedures in a review engagement are not designed to identify misstatements with the level of precision expected in an examination engagement. Further, when significant fluctuations, relationships, or differences are identified, appropriate review evidence in a review engagement may often be obtained by making inquiries of the responsible party and considering responses received in the light of known engagement circumstances without obtaining additional evidence required in the case of an examination engagement.

Inquiries and Other Review Procedures (Ref: par. .21)

.A30 The practitioner is not ordinarily required to corroborate the responsible party's responses with other review evidence.

Fraud, Laws, and Regulations (Ref: par. .24)

.A31 In responding to fraud or suspected fraud identified during the engagement, it may be appropriate, unless prohibited by law, regulation, or ethics standards, for the practitioner to, for example

- discuss the matter with the appropriate party(ies).
- request that the responsible party consult with an appropriately qualified third party, such as the entity's legal counsel or a regulator.
- consider the implications of the matter in relation to other aspects of the engagement, including the practitioner's planning and the reliability of written representations from the responsible party.
- obtain legal advice about the consequences of different courses of action.
- communicate with third parties (for example, a regulator).
- withdraw from the engagement.

.A32 The actions noted in paragraph .A31 also may be appropriate in responding to noncompliance or suspected noncompliance with laws or regulations identified during the engagement. It may also be appropriate to describe the matter in a separate paragraph of the practitioner's report, unless the practitioner

a. is precluded by the responsible party from obtaining sufficient appropriate review evidence to evaluate whether noncompliance that may be material to the subject matter has, or is likely to have, occurred, in which case, paragraph .58 applies or

b. concludes that the noncompliance results in a material misstatement of the subject matter, in which case, paragraphs .51–.57 apply.

Evaluating the Results of Review Procedures (Ref: par. .28–.29)

.A33 Uncorrected misstatements are accumulated during the engagement for the purpose of evaluating whether, individually or in aggregate, they are material when forming the practitioner's conclusion. (See paragraph .42*b*.)

.A34 "Clearly trivial" is not another expression for "not material." Matters that are clearly trivial will be of a wholly different (smaller) order of magnitude than materiality and will be matters that are clearly inconsequential, whether taken individually or in the aggregate and whether judged by any criteria of size, nature, or circumstances. When there is any uncertainty about whether one or more items are clearly trivial, the matter is considered not to be clearly trivial.

.A35 Sufficient appropriate review evidence is necessary to support the practitioner's conclusion and report.

.A36 The sufficiency and appropriateness of review evidence are interrelated. Sufficiency of review evidence is the measure of the quantity of review evidence. The quantity of the review evidence needed is affected by the risks of material misstatement and also by the quality of such review evidence.

.A37 Whether sufficient appropriate review evidence has been obtained on which to base the practitioner's conclusion is a matter of professional judgment.

Considering Subsequent Events and Subsequently Discovered Facts (Ref: par. .31–.32)

.A38 For certain subject-matter AT-C sections, specific subsequent events requirements and related application guidance have been developed for engagement performance and reporting.

.A39 Procedures that a practitioner may perform to identify subsequent events include inquiring about and considering information

- contained in relevant reports issued during the subsequent period by internal auditors, other practitioners, or regulatory agencies
- obtained through other professional engagements for that entity

.A40 If the responsible party refuses to disclose a subsequent event for which disclosure is necessary to prevent users of the practitioner's report from being misled, appropriate actions the practitioner may take include

- disclosing the event in the report and modifying the practitioner's conclusion.
- withdrawing from the engagement.

.A41 Subsequent to the date of the practitioner's report, the practitioner may become aware of facts that, had they been known to the practitioner at that date, may have caused the practitioner to revise the report. In such circumstances, the practitioner undertakes to determine whether the facts existed at the date of the report and, if so, whether persons are currently using or likely to use the report and related subject matter or assertion who would attach importance to these facts. This may include discussing the matter with the appropriate party(ies) and requesting the appropriate party(ies)'s cooperation in whatever investigation or further action that may be necessary. The specific actions to be taken in a particular case by the appropriate party(ies) and the practitioner may vary with the circumstances. Consideration may be given to, among other things, the time elapsed since the date of the report and whether issuance of a subsequent report is imminent. The practitioner may need to perform additional procedures deemed necessary to determine whether the subject matter or assertion needs revision and whether the previously issued report continues to be appropriate.

.A42 Depending on the circumstances, the practitioner may determine that notification of the situation by the appropriate party(ies) to persons who would attach importance to these facts and who are currently using, or are likely to use, the practitioner's report who would attach importance to the facts is necessary. This may be the case, for example, when

a. the report is not to be relied upon because the subject matter or assertion needs revision or the practitioner is unable to determine whether revision is necessary, and

b. issuance of a subsequent report is not imminent.

If the appropriate party(ies) failed to take the necessary steps to prevent reliance on the report, the practitioner's course of action depends upon the practitioner's legal and ethical rights and obligations. Consequently, the practitioner may consider it appropriate to seek legal advice prior to making any disclosure of the situation. Disclosure of the situation directly by the practitioner may include a description of the nature of the matter and of its effect on the subject matter or assertion and the report, avoiding comments concerning the conduct or motives of any person.

Written Representations (Ref: par. .33–.34, .35*e*, and .39*a*)

.A43 Written confirmation of oral representations reduces the possibility of misunderstandings between the practitioner and the responsible party. The person(s) from whom the practitioner requests written representations is ordinarily a member of senior management or those charged with governance depending on, for example, the management and governance structure of the responsible party(ies), which may vary by entity, reflecting influences such as size and ownership characteristics.

.A44 Representations by the responsible party cannot replace other review evidence the practitioner could reasonably expect to be available. Although written representations provide review evidence, they do not provide sufficient appropriate review evidence on their own about any of the matters with which they deal. Furthermore, the fact that the practitioner has received reliable written representations does not affect the nature or extent of other review evidence that the practitioner obtains.

.A45 A discussion of what is considered a material effect on the subject matter or assertion may be included explicitly in the representation letter in qualitative or quantitative terms.

.A46 A summary of uncorrected misstatements ordinarily is included in or attached to the written representation.

.A47 Certain subject-matter AT-C sections do not permit the practitioner to perform the alternative procedures described in paragraphs .34 and .39*a* (making inquiries of the responsible party and restricting the use of the practitioner's report).

Requested Written Representations Not Provided or Not Reliable (Ref: par. .39)

.A48 Even when the responsible party provides oral responses to the matters in paragraph .33, the practitioner may find it appropriate to consider whether there are significant concerns about the competence, integrity, ethical values, or diligence of those providing the oral responses or whether the oral responses are otherwise not reliable and the potential effect, if any, on the practitioner's report.

.A49 Paragraph .11 provides an exception to the requirement for a written assertion when the engaging party is not the responsible party. Nonetheless, because the assertion is the representation called for by paragraph .33*a*, application of paragraph .39*a* requires the practitioner to obtain an oral assertion, when a written assertion is not obtained. Paragraph .39*b* applies when the responsible party provides neither a written nor an oral assertion.

Other Information (Ref: par. .40)

.A50 Further actions that may be appropriate if the practitioner identifies a material inconsistency or becomes aware of a material misstatement of fact include, for example, the following:

- Requesting the appropriate party(ies) to consult with a qualified third party, such as the appropriate party(ies)'s legal counsel
- Obtaining legal advice about the consequences of different courses of action
- If required or permissible, communicating with third parties (for example, a regulator)
- Describing the material inconsistency in the practitioner's report
- Withdrawing from the engagement, when withdrawal is possible under applicable law or regulation

.A51 Other information does not include information contained on the appropriate party(ies)'s website. Websites are a means of distributing information and are not, themselves, documents for the purposes of paragraph .40.

Description of Criteria (Ref: par. .41)

.A52 The description of the criteria on which the subject matter or assertion is based is particularly important when there are significant differences between various criteria regarding how particular matters may be treated in the subject matter.

.A53 A description of the criteria that states that the subject matter is prepared in accordance with (or based on) particular criteria is appropriate only if the subject matter complies with all relevant requirements of those criteria that are effective.

Forming the Conclusion (Ref: par. .42–.43)

.A54 The practitioner's professional judgment regarding what constitutes sufficient appropriate review evidence is influenced by such factors as the following:

- The significance of a potential misstatement and the likelihood that it will have a material effect, individually or aggregated with other potential misstatements, on the subject matter or assertion
- The effectiveness of the responsible party's responses to address the known risks
- The experience gained during previous examination or review engagements with respect to similar potential misstatements
- The results of procedures performed, including whether such procedures identified specific misstatements
- The source and reliability of the available information
- The persuasiveness of the review evidence
- The practitioner's understanding of the responsible party and its environment

.A55 A review engagement is a cumulative and iterative process. As the practitioner performs planned procedures, the review evidence obtained may cause the practitioner to change the nature, timing, or extent of other planned procedures. Information that differs significantly from the information on which the planned procedures were based may come to the practitioner's attention, for example

- the extent of the misstatements that the practitioner detects is greater than expected. (This may alter the practitioner's professional judgment about the reliability of particular sources of information.)

- the practitioner may become aware of discrepancies in relevant information or conflicting or missing review evidence.
- procedures performed toward the end of the engagement may indicate a previously unrecognized risk of material misstatement. In such circumstances, the practitioner may need to reevaluate the planned procedures.

.A56 In making the evaluation required by paragraph .43, the practitioner may consider whether additional disclosures are necessary to describe the subject matter, assertion, or criteria. Additional disclosures may, for example, include

- the measurement or evaluation methods used when the criteria allow for choice among methods;
- significant interpretations made in applying the criteria in the engagement circumstances;
- subsequent events, depending on their nature and significance; and
- whether there have been any changes in the measurement or evaluation methods used.

.A57 Paragraph .43 does not require the practitioner to determine whether the presentation discloses all matters related to the subject matter, assertion, or criteria or all matters users may consider in making decisions based on the presentation.

Preparing the Practitioner's Report (Ref: par. .44–.45)

.A58 Oral and other forms of expressing a conclusion can be misunderstood without the support of a written practitioner's report. For this reason, the practitioner may not report orally or by use of symbols (such as a web seal) under the attestation standards without also providing a written report that is readily available whenever the oral report is provided or the symbol is used. For example, a symbol could be hyperlinked to a written report on the Internet.

.A59 This section does not require a standardized format for reporting on all review engagements. Instead, it identifies the basic elements that the practitioner's report is to include. The report is tailored to the specific engagement circumstances. The practitioner may use headings, separate paragraphs, paragraph numbers, typographical devices (for example, the bolding of text), and other mechanisms to enhance the clarity and readability of the report.

.A60 All of the following reporting options are available to a practitioner, except when the circumstances described in paragraph .54 exist.

The practitioner's report may state that the practitioner examined	*and*	*expresses an opinion on*
the subject matter		the subject matter
the responsible party's assertion		the responsible party's assertion
the responsible party's assertion		the subject matter

Content of the Practitioner's Report

Title (Ref: par. .46a)

.A61 A title indicating that the practitioner's report is the report of an independent practitioner (for example, "Independent Practitioner's Report," "Report of Independent Certified Public Accountant," or "Independent Accountant's Review Report") affirms that the practitioner has met all the relevant ethical requirements regarding independence and, therefore, distinguishes the independent practitioner's report from reports issued by others.

Criteria (Ref: par. .46d)

.A62 The practitioner's report may include the criteria or refer to them if they are included in the subject matter presentation, in the assertion, or are otherwise readily available.

Relative Responsibilities (Ref: par. .46e)

.A63 Identifying relative responsibilities informs the intended users that the responsible party is responsible for the subject matter, and the practitioner's role is to independently express a conclusion about it.

.A64 The practitioner may wish to expand the discussion of the responsible party's responsibility, for example, to indicate that the responsible party is responsible for the preparation and presentation of the subject matter in accordance with (or based on) the criteria, including the design, implementation, and maintenance of internal control to prevent, or detect and correct, misstatement of the subject matter, due to fraud or error.

Statement About the Subject Matter and Criteria (Ref: par. 46f[ii][1])

.A65 The language in paragraph .46*f*(ii)(1) may need to be tailored to reflect the nature of the subject matter and criteria for the engagement. Examples of language that meet the requirements in paragraph .46*f*(ii)(1) include, "to obtain limited assurance about whether any material modifications should be made to the subject matter in order for it to

- be presented in accordance with (or based on) the criteria."
- meet the objectives," for example, when the objectives are the criteria.

Inherent Limitations (Ref: par. .46g)

.A66 In some cases, identification of specific inherent limitations may be required by an AT-C section. To communicate specific inherent limitations, the illustrative practitioner's report on a review of pro forma financial information under section 310, for example, indicates that the objective of pro forma financial information is to show what the significant effects on the historical financial information might have been had the transaction (or event) occurred at an earlier date and that the pro forma condensed financial statements are not necessarily indicative of the results of operations or related effects on financial position that would have been attained had the specified transaction (or event) actually occurred earlier.[3] When not explicitly required by an AT-C section, identification in the report of inherent limitations is based on the practitioner's judgment.

---

[3] Paragraph .18*k* and examples 2 and 3 in paragraph .A24 of section 310, *Reporting on Pro Forma Financial Information*.

Conclusion (Ref: par. .46h)

.A67 The practitioner's conclusion can be worded either in terms of the subject matter and the criteria (for example, "Based on our review, we are not aware of any material modifications that should be made to the XYZ schedule in order for it to be in accordance with [or based on] the ABC criteria.") or in terms of an assertion made by the responsible party (for example, "Based on our review, we are not aware of any material modifications that should be made to management of XYZ Company's assertion in order for it to be fairly stated.").

.A68 A single practitioner's report may cover more than one aspect of a subject matter or an assertion about the subject matter. When that is the case, the report may contain separate opinions or conclusions on each aspect of the subject matter or assertion (for example, examination level related to some aspects or assertions and review level related to others, or an unmodified conclusion on some aspects or assertions and a modified conclusion on others).

.A69 A practitioner may report on subject matter or an assertion at multiple dates or covering multiple periods during which criteria have changed (for example, a practitioner's report on comparative information). Criteria are clearly described when they identify the criteria for each period and how the criteria have changed from one period to the next. If the criteria for the current date or period have changed from the criteria for a preceding date or period, changes in the criteria may be significant to users of the report. If so, the criteria and the fact that they have changed may be disclosed in the presentation of the subject matter, in the written assertion, or in the report, even if the subject matter for the preceding date or period is not presented.

Location (Ref: par. .46j)

.A70 In the United States, the location of the issuing office is the city and state. In another country, it may be the city and country.

Date (Ref: par. .46k)

.A71 Including the date of the practitioner's report informs the intended users that the practitioner has considered the effect on the subject matter and on the report of events that occurred up to that date.

.A72 Because the practitioner expresses a conclusion on the subject matter or assertion and the subject matter or assertion is the responsibility of the responsible party, the practitioner is not in a position to conclude that sufficient appropriate review evidence has been obtained until evidence is obtained that all of the elements that the subject matter or assertion comprises, including any related notes, when applicable, have been prepared, and the responsible party has accepted responsibility for them.

Restricted Use Paragraph (Ref: par. .47 and .48b–c)

.A73 A practitioner's report for which the conditions in paragraph .47 do not apply need not include an alert that restricts its use. However, nothing in the attestation standards precludes a practitioner from including such an alert in any practitioner's report or other practitioner's written communication.

.A74 A practitioner's report that is required by paragraph .47 to include an alert that restricts the use of the report may be included in a document that also contains a practitioner's report that is for general use. In such circumstances, the use of the general use report is not affected.

.A75 A practitioner may also issue a single combined practitioner's report that includes (*a*) a practitioner's report that is required by paragraph .47 to include an alert that restricts its use, and (*b*) a report that is for general use. If these two types of reports are clearly differentiated within the combined report, such as through the use of appropriate headers, the alert that restricts the use of the report may be limited to the report required by paragraph .47 to include such an alert. In such circumstances, the use of the general use report is not affected.

.A76 The representations required by paragraph .33 include an assertion. If the engaging party is not the responsible party and the responsible party provides an oral assertion, rather than a written assertion, paragraph .47*c* calls for an alert that restricts the use of the practitioner's report to the engaging party.

.A77 The practitioner may identify the specified parties by naming them, referring to a list of those parties, or identifying the class of parties, for example, "all customers of XYZ Company during some or all of the period January 1, 20XX to December 31, 20XX." The method of identifying the specified parties is determined by the practitioner.

.A78 In some cases, the criteria used to measure or evaluate the subject matter may be designed for a specific purpose. For example, a regulator may require certain entities to use particular criteria designed for regulatory purposes. To avoid misunderstandings, the practitioner alerts users of the practitioner's report to this fact and, therefore, that the report is intended solely for the information and use of the specified parties.

.A79 The alert that restricts the use of the practitioner's report is designed to avoid misunderstandings related to the use of the report, particularly if the report is taken out of the context in which the report is intended to be used. A practitioner may consider informing the responsible party and, if different, the engaging party or other specified parties that the report is not intended for distribution to parties other than those specified in the report. The practitioner may, in connection with establishing the terms of the engagement, reach an understanding with the responsible party or, if different, the engaging party, that the intended use of the report will be restricted and may obtain the responsible party's agreement that the responsible party and specified parties will not distribute such report to parties other than those identified therein. A practitioner is not responsible for controlling, and cannot control, distribution of the report after its release.

.A80 In some cases, a restricted-use practitioner's report filed with regulatory agencies is required by law or regulation to be made available to the public as a matter of public record. Also, a regulatory agency, as part of its oversight responsibility for an entity, may require access to the restricted-use report in which it is not named as a specified party.

Reference to the Practitioner's Specialist (Ref: par. .50)

.A81 The practitioner has sole responsibility for the conclusion expressed, and that responsibility is not reduced by the practitioner's use of the work of a practitioner's specialist.

Modified Conclusions (Ref: par. .51–.53)

.A82 A practitioner may issue an unmodified conclusion only when the engagement has been conducted in accordance with the attestation standards. Such standards will not have been complied with if the practitioner has been unable to apply all the procedures that the practitioner considers necessary in the circumstances.

.A83 Pervasive effects on the subject matter are those that, in the practitioner's professional judgment

a. are not confined to specific aspects of the subject matter;

b. if so confined, represent or could represent a substantial proportion of the subject matter; or

c. in relation to disclosures, are fundamental to the intended users' understanding of the subject matter.

Scope Limitations (Ref: par. .58)

.A84 The procedures performed in a review engagement are, by definition, limited compared with those performed in an examination engagement. Limitations known to exist prior to accepting a review engagement are a relevant consideration when establishing whether the preconditions for a review engagement are present, in particular, whether the practitioner expects to be able to obtain the evidence needed to arrive at the practitioner's conclusion. (See section 105.)[4] If a further limitation is imposed by the appropriate party(ies) after a review engagement has been accepted, it may be appropriate to withdraw from the engagement, when withdrawal is possible under applicable laws and regulations.

.A85 The inability to obtain written representations from the responsible party ordinarily would result in a scope limitation. However, when the engaging party is not the responsible party, paragraph .34 enables the practitioner to make inquiries of the responsible party, and if the responsible party's oral responses enable the practitioner to conclude that the practitioner has sufficient appropriate review evidence to form a conclusion about the subject matter, paragraph .39*a* indicates that this would not cause a scope limitation. Further, paragraph .39*a* requires that the practitioner's report, in these circumstances, contain an alert paragraph that restricts the use of the report to the engaging party.

.A86 An inability to perform a specific procedure does not constitute a scope limitation if the practitioner is able to obtain sufficient appropriate review evidence by performing alternative procedures.

Responsible Party Refuses to Provide a Written Assertion (Ref: par. .60)

.A87 The following is an example of the disclosure required by paragraph .60:

> Attestation standards established by the American Institute of Certified Public Accountants require that we request a written statement from [*identify the responsible party*] stating that [*identify the subject matter*] that we reviewed has been accurately measured or evaluated. We requested that [*identify the responsible party*] provide such a written statement but [*identify the responsible party*] refused to do so.

.A88 The practitioner's report discussed in paragraph .60 is appropriate only when the engagement is to report on the subject matter; it is not appropriate for a report on an assertion. When reporting on an assertion, the practitioner is required to obtain a written assertion from the responsible party.

---

[4] Paragraph .25*b*(iii) of section 105, *Concepts Common to All Attestation Engagements*.

Communication Responsibilities (Ref: par. .61)

.A89 Other matters that may be appropriate to communicate to the responsible party or, if different, the engaging party, include deficiencies in internal control identified during the engagement, or bias in the measurement, evaluation, or disclosure of the subject matter.

Documentation (Ref: par. .62)

.A90 Documentation includes a record of the practitioner's reasoning on all significant findings or issues that require the exercise of professional judgment and related conclusions. The existence of difficult questions of principle or professional judgment calls for the documentation to include the relevant facts that were known by the practitioner at the time the conclusion was reached.

.A91 It is neither necessary nor practical to document every matter considered, or professional judgment made, during an engagement. Further, it is unnecessary for the practitioner to document separately (as in a checklist, for example) compliance with matters for which compliance is demonstrated by documents included in the engagement file. Similarly, the practitioner need not include in the engagement file superseded drafts of working papers, notes that reflect incomplete or preliminary thinking, previous copies of documents corrected for typographical or other errors, and duplicates of documents.

.A92 In applying professional judgment to assess the extent of documentation to be prepared and retained, the practitioner may consider what is necessary to provide an experienced practitioner, having no previous connection with the engagement, with an understanding of the work performed and the basis of the principal decisions made.

.A93 Documentation ordinarily includes a record of

- issues identified with respect to compliance with relevant ethical requirements and how they were resolved.
- conclusions on compliance with independence requirements that apply to the engagement and any relevant discussions with the firm that support these conclusions.
- conclusions reached regarding the acceptance and continuance of client relationships and attestation engagements.
- the nature and scope of, and conclusions resulting from, consultations undertaken during the course of the engagement.

.A94

Exhibit—Illustrative Practitioner's Review Reports

The illustrative practitioner's review reports in this exhibit meet the applicable reporting requirements in paragraphs .44–.60. A practitioner may use alternative language in drafting a review report, provided that the language meets the applicable requirements in paragraphs .44–.60. The criteria for evaluating the subject matter in examples 1 and 3 have been determined by the practitioner to be suitable and available to all users of the report; therefore, these reports may be for general use. The criteria for evaluating the subject matter in example 2 are suitable but available only to specified parties; therefore, use of this report is restricted to the specified parties who either participated in the establishment of the criteria or can be presumed to have an adequate understanding of the criteria. (See paragraph .48 for the information to be included in a separate paragraph of the report that contains an alert that restricts the use of the report and paragraph .49 for the content of that paragraph when the engagement is also performed in accordance with *Government Auditing Standards*.)

Example 1: Practitioner's Review Report on Subject Matter; Unmodified Conclusion

The following is an illustrative practitioner's review report in which the practitioner has reviewed the subject matter and is reporting on the subject matter.

Independent Accountant's Review Report

[*Appropriate Addressee*]

We have reviewed [*identify the subject matter, for example, the accompanying schedule of investment returns of XYZ Company for the year ended December 31, 20XX*]. XYZ Company's management is responsible for [*identify the subject matter, for example, presenting the schedule of investment returns*] in accordance with (or based on) [*identify the criteria, for example, the ABC criteria set forth in Note 1*]. Our responsibility is to express a conclusion on [*identify the subject matter, for example, the schedule of investment returns*] based on our review.

Our review was conducted in accordance with attestation standards established by the American Institute of Certified Public Accountants. Those standards require that we plan and perform the review to obtain limited assurance about whether any material modifications should be made to [*identify the subject matter, for example, the schedule of investment returns*] in order for it to be in accordance with (or based on) the criteria. A review is substantially less in scope than an examination, the objective of which is to obtain reasonable assurance about whether [*identify the subject matter, for example, the schedule of investment returns*] is in accordance with (or based on) the criteria, in all material respects, in order to express an opinion. Accordingly, we do not express such an opinion. We believe that our review provides a reasonable basis for our conclusion.

[*Include a description of significant inherent limitations, if any, associated with the measurement or evaluation of the subject matter against the criteria.*]

[*Additional paragraph(s) may be added to emphasize certain matters relating to the attestation engagement or the subject matter.*]

Based on our review, we are not aware of any material modifications that should be made to [*identify the subject matter, for example, the accompanying schedule of investment returns of XYZ Company for the year ended December 31, 20XX*], in order for it be in accordance with (or based on) [*identify the criteria, for example, the ABC criteria set forth in Note 1*].

[*Practitioner's signature*]
[*Practitioner's city and state*]
[*Date of practitioner's report*]

Example 2: Practitioner's Review Report on an Assertion; Unmodified Conclusion; Use of the Report Is Restricted to Specified Parties

The following is an illustrative practitioner's report for a review engagement in which the practitioner has reviewed the responsible party's assertion and is reporting on that assertion. Although suitable criteria exist for the subject matter, use of the report is restricted to specified parties because the criteria are available only to the specified parties.

Independent Accountant's Review Report

[*Appropriate Addressee*]

We have reviewed management of XYZ Company's assertion that [*identify the assertion, including the subject matter and the criteria, for example, the accompanying schedule of investment returns of XYZ Company for the year ended December 31, 20XX, is presented in accordance with (or based on) the ABC criteria set forth in Note 1*]. XYZ Company's management is responsible for its assertion. Our responsibility is to express a conclusion on management's assertion based on our review.

Our review was conducted in accordance with attestation standards established by the American Institute of Certified Public Accountants. Those standards require that we plan and perform the review to obtain limited assurance about whether any material modifications should be made to management's assertion in order for it to be fairly stated. A review is substantially less in scope than an examination, the objective of which is to obtain reasonable assurance about whether management's assertion is fairly stated, in all material respects, in order to express an opinion. Accordingly, we do not express such an opinion. We believe that our review provides a reasonable basis for our conclusion.

[*Include a description of significant inherent limitations, if any, associated with the measurement or evaluation of the subject matter against the criteria.*]

[*Additional paragraph(s) may be added to emphasize certain matters relating to the attestation engagement or the subject matter.*]

Based on our review, we are not aware of any material modifications that should be made to management of XYZ Company's assertion in order for it to be fairly stated.

This report is intended solely for the information and use of [*identify the specified parties, for example, ABC Company and XYZ Company*], and is not intended to be, and should not be, used by anyone other than the specified parties.

[*Practitioner's signature*]
[*Practitioner's city and state*]
[*Date of practitioner's report*]

Example 3: Practitioner's Review Report on Subject Matter; Qualified Conclusion

The following is an illustrative practitioner's report for a review engagement in which the practitioner expresses a qualified conclusion because the review identified conditions that, individually or in combination, result in one or more material, but not pervasive, misstatements of the subject matter, based on the criteria. The practitioner has reviewed the subject matter and is also reporting on the subject matter. Paragraph .53 states, "If the practitioner has concluded that the material misstatement results in a qualified conclusion, the practitioner should report directly on the subject matter, not on the assertion, even when the assertion acknowledges the misstatement."

Independent Accountant's Review Report

[*Appropriate Addressee*]

We have reviewed [*identify the subject matter, for example, the accompanying schedule of investment returns of XYZ Company for the year ended December 31, 20XX*]. XYZ Company's management is responsible for [*identify the subject matter, for example, presenting the schedule of investment returns*] based on [*identify the criteria, for example, the ABC criteria set forth in Note 1*]. Our responsibility is to express a conclusion on [*identify the subject matter, for example, the schedule of investment returns*] based on our review.

Our review was conducted in accordance with attestation standards established by the American Institute of Certified Public Accountants. Those standards require that we plan and perform the review to obtain limited assurance about whether any material modifications should be made to [*identify the subject matter, for example, the schedule of investment returns*] in order for it to be in accordance with (or based on) the criteria. A review is substantially less in scope than an examination, the objective of which is to obtain reasonable assurance about whether [*identify the subject matter, for example, the schedule of investment returns*] is in accordance with (or based on) the criteria, in all material respects, in order to express an opinion. Accordingly, we do not express such an opinion. We believe that our review provides a reasonable basis for our conclusion.

[*Include a description of significant inherent limitations, if any, associated with the measurement or evaluation of the subject matter against the criteria.*]

[*Additional paragraph(s) may be added to emphasize certain matters relating to the attestation engagement or the subject matter.*]

Our review identified [*describe condition(s) that, individually or in the aggregate, resulted in a material misstatement, or deviation from, the criteria*].

Based on our review, except for the matter(s) described in the preceding paragraph, we are not aware of any material modifications that should be made to [*identify the subject matter, for example, the accompanying schedule of investment returns of XYZ Company for the year ended December 31, 20XX*], in order for it to be in accordance with (or based on) [*identify the criteria, for example, the ABC criteria set forth in Note 1*].

[*Practitioner's signature*]
[*Practitioner's city and state*]
[*Date of practitioner's report*]

AT-C Section 215*

Agreed-Upon Procedures Engagements

Source: SSAE No. 18

Effective for agreed-upon procedures reports dated on or after May 1, 2017.

Introduction

.01 This section contains performance and reporting requirements and application guidance for all agreed-upon procedures engagements. The requirements and guidance in this section supplement the requirements and guidance in section 105, *Concepts Common to All Attestation Engagements*.

.02 An *agreed-upon procedures engagement* is one in which a practitioner is engaged to issue, or does issue, a practitioner's report of findings based on specific agreed-upon procedures applied to subject matter for use by specified parties. Because the specified parties require that findings be independently derived, the services of a practitioner are obtained to perform procedures and report the practitioner's findings. The specified parties determine the procedures they believe to be appropriate to be applied by the practitioner. Because the needs of specified parties may vary widely, the nature, timing, and extent of the agreed-upon procedures may vary, as well; consequently, the specified parties assume responsibility for the sufficiency of the procedures because they best understand their own needs. In an engagement performed under this section, the practitioner does not perform an examination or a review and does not provide an opinion or conclusion. Instead, the report on agreed-upon procedures is in the form of procedures and findings.

.03 When a practitioner performs services pursuant to an engagement to apply agreed-upon procedures to subject matter as part of or in addition to another form of service, this section applies only to those services described herein; other professional standards would apply to the other services. Other services may include an audit, review, or compilation of a financial statement, another attestation service performed pursuant to the attestation standards, or a nonattestation service. A practitioner's report on applying agreed-upon procedures to subject matter may be combined with a report on such other services, provided the types of services can be clearly distinguished, and the applicable standards for each service are followed. (Ref: par. .A1)

.04 This section does not apply to engagements to issue letters (commonly referred to as *comfort letters*) to underwriters and certain other requesting parties.[1]

Effective Date

.05 This section is effective for agreed-upon procedures reports dated on or after May 1, 2017.

---

* This section contains an "AT-C" identifier, instead of an "AT" identifier, to avoid confusion with references to existing "AT" sections, which remain effective through April 2017.

[1] See AU-C section 920, *Letters for Underwriters and Certain Other Requesting Parties*.

Objectives

.06 In conducting an agreed-upon procedures engagement, the objectives of the practitioner are to

a. apply to the subject matter procedures that are established by specified parties who are responsible for the sufficiency of the procedures for their purposes; (Ref: par. .A2)

b. issue a written practitioner's report that describes the procedures applied and the practitioner's findings; and

c. communicate further as required by relevant AT-C sections.

Definition

.07 For purposes of this section, the following term has the meaning attributed as follows:

Nonparticipant party. An additional specified party the practitioner is requested to add as a user of the practitioner's report subsequent to the completion of the agreed-upon procedures engagement. (The term *specified party* is defined in section 105.[2])

Requirements

Conduct of an Agreed-Upon Procedures Engagement

.08 In performing an agreed-upon procedures engagement, the practitioner should comply with this section, section 105, and any subject-matter section that is relevant to the engagement. A subject-matter AT-C section is relevant to the engagement when it is in effect, and the circumstances addressed by the AT-C section exist. (Ref: par. .A3–.A4)

Preconditions for an Agreed-Upon Procedures Engagement

.09 Section 105 indicates that a practitioner must be independent when performing an attestation engagement in accordance with the attestation standards unless the practitioner is required by law or regulation to accept the engagement and report on the subject matter or assertion.[3] When the practitioner is not independent but is required by law or regulation to accept an agreed-upon procedures engagement and report on the procedures performed and findings obtained, the practitioner's report should specifically state that the practitioner is not independent. The practitioner is neither required to provide, nor precluded from providing, the reasons for the lack of independence; however, if the practitioner chooses to provide the reasons for the lack of independence, the practitioner should include all the reasons therefor.

.10 In order to establish that the preconditions for an agreed-upon procedures engagement are present, the practitioner should determine that the following conditions, in addition to the preconditions identified in section 105, are present:[4] (Ref: par. .A5–.A6)

---

[2] Paragraph .10 of section 105, *Concepts Common to All Attestation Engagements*.

[3] Paragraph .24 of section 105.

[4] Paragraphs .24–.28 of section 105.

a. The specified parties agree on the procedures performed, or to be performed, by the practitioner.

b. The specified parties take responsibility for the sufficiency of the agreed-upon procedures for their purposes. (Ref: par. .A6)

c. The practitioner determines that the procedures can be performed and reported on in accordance with this section.

d. The procedures to be applied to the subject matter are expected to result in reasonably consistent findings using the criteria.

e. When applicable, the practitioner agrees to apply any materiality limits established by the specified parties for reporting purposes.

f. Use of the practitioner's report is to be restricted to the specified parties.

.11 The practitioner should not accept an agreed-upon procedures engagement when the specified parties do not agree upon the procedures performed, or to be performed, or do not take responsibility for the sufficiency of the procedures for their purposes. (See paragraphs .38–.40 for the requirements and related application guidance on satisfying these requirements when the practitioner is requested to add a nonparticipant party.) (Ref: par. .A6)

Agreeing on the Terms of the Engagement

.12 The practitioner should agree upon the terms of the engagement with the engaging party. The agreed-upon terms of the engagement should be specified in sufficient detail in an engagement letter or other suitable form of written agreement. (Ref: par. .A7)

.13 The agreement should be addressed to the engaging party.

.14 The agreed-upon terms of the engagement should include the following:

a. The nature of the engagement

b. Identification of the subject matter or assertion, the responsible party, and the criteria to be used (Ref: par. .A8)

c. Identification of specified parties

d. Acknowledgment by the specified parties of their responsibility for the sufficiency of the procedures (Ref: par. .A6)

e. The responsibilities of the practitioner (Ref: par. .A9–.A10)

f. A statement that the engagement will be conducted in accordance with attestation standards established by the American Institute of Certified Public Accountants

g. Agreement on procedures by enumerating (or referring to) the procedures

h. Disclaimers expected to be included in the practitioner's report

i. Use restrictions

j. Assistance to be provided to the practitioner

k. Involvement of a practitioner's external specialist, if applicable

l. Agreed-upon materiality limits specified by the specified parties, if applicable

Requesting a Written Assertion

.15 The practitioner should request from the responsible party a written assertion about the measurement or evaluation of the subject matter against the criteria. (Ref: par. .A11–.A15)

.16 If the engaging party is not the responsible party, and the practitioner is aware that the responsible party refuses to provide the practitioner with a written assertion, the written agreement required by paragraph .12 should make clear that no such assertion will be provided to the practitioner. (Ref: par. .A15)

Procedures to Be Performed

.17 The procedures agreed upon pursuant to paragraph .14*g* should specify the nature, timing, and extent of the procedures. (Ref: par. .A16–.A20)

.18 In some circumstances, the procedures agreed upon evolve or are modified over the course of the engagement. In such circumstances, the practitioner should amend the engagement letter or other suitable form of written agreement, as applicable, to reflect the modified procedures.

.19 The practitioner should not agree to perform procedures that are open to varying interpretations. Terms of uncertain meaning (such as *general review*, *limited review*, *check*, or *test*) should not be used in describing the procedures unless such terms are defined within the agreed-upon procedures. (Ref: par. .A21)

.20 The practitioner should obtain evidence from applying the agreed-upon procedures to provide a reasonable basis for the finding or findings expressed in the practitioner's report but need not perform additional procedures outside the scope of the engagement to gather additional evidence.

Using the Work of a Practitioner's External Specialist

.21 The practitioner and the specified parties should explicitly agree to the involvement of a practitioner's external specialist if assisting a practitioner in the performance of an agreed-upon procedures engagement. (Ref: par. .A22–.A24)

.22 The practitioner's report should describe the nature of the assistance provided by the practitioner's external specialist.

Using the Work of Internal Auditors or Other Practitioners

.23 The agreed-upon procedures to be enumerated or referred to in the practitioner's report should be performed entirely by the engagement team or other practitioners. (Ref: par. .A25–.A27)

Findings

.24 A practitioner should present the results of applying agreed-upon procedures to specific subject matter in the form of findings.

.25 The practitioner's report should not express an opinion or conclusion about whether the subject matter is in accordance with (or based on) the criteria or whether the assertion is fairly stated, for example, the report should not state, "Nothing came to our attention that caused us to believe that the subject matter is not in accordance with (or based on) the criteria, in all material respects, or that the assertion is not fairly stated, in all material respects."

.26 The practitioner should report all findings from application of the agreed-upon procedures. Any agreed-upon materiality limits should be described in the practitioner's report. (Ref: par. .A28)

.27 The practitioner should avoid vague or ambiguous language in reporting findings. (Ref: par. .A29)

Written Representations

.28 The practitioner should request from the responsible party written representations in the form of a letter addressed to the practitioner. The representations should (Ref: par. .A30)

a. include the responsible party's assertion about the subject matter based on the criteria.

b. state that all known matters contradicting the subject matter or assertion and any communication from regulatory agencies or others affecting the subject matter or assertion have been disclosed to the practitioner, including communications received between the end of the period addressed in the written assertion and the date of the practitioner's report.

c. acknowledge responsibility for

   i. the subject matter and the assertion;

   ii. selecting the criteria, when applicable; and

   iii. determining that such criteria are appropriate for the responsible party's purposes.

d. state that it has provided the practitioner with access to all records relevant to the subject matter and the agreed-upon procedures.

e. state that the responsible party has disclosed to the practitioner other matters as the practitioner deems appropriate.

.29 When the engaging party is not the responsible party, the practitioner should request written representations from the engaging party, in addition to those requested from the responsible party, in the form of a letter addressed to the practitioner. The representations should

a. acknowledge that the responsible party is responsible for the subject matter and assertion.

b. acknowledge the engaging party's responsibility for selecting the criteria, when applicable.

c. acknowledge the engaging party's responsibility for determining that such criteria are appropriate for its purposes.

d. state that the engaging party is not aware of any material misstatements in the subject matter or assertion.

e. state that the engaging party has disclosed to the practitioner all known events subsequent to the period (or point in time) of the subject matter being reported on that would have a material effect on the subject matter or assertion.

f. address other matters as the practitioner deems appropriate.

.30 The date of the written representations should be as of the date of the practitioner's report. The written representations should address the subject matter and periods covered by the practitioner's findings.

Requested Written Representations Not Provided or Not Reliable

.31 When the engaging party is the responsible party, and one or more of the requested written representations are not provided, or the practitioner concludes that there is sufficient doubt about the competence, integrity, ethical values, or diligence of those providing the written representations, or the practitioner concludes that the written representations are otherwise not reliable, the practitioner should

a. discuss the matter with the appropriate party(ies);

b. reevaluate the integrity of those from whom the representations were requested or received and evaluate the effect, if any, on the engagement; and

c. if any of the matters are not resolved to the practitioner's satisfaction, take appropriate action. (Ref: par. .A31)

.32 When the engaging party is not the responsible party

a. if one or more of the requested representations in paragraph .28 are not provided in writing by the responsible party, the practitioner should make inquiries of the responsible party about, and seek oral responses to, the matters in paragraph .28. (Ref: par. .A32)

b. if one or more of the requested representations are not provided in writing or orally from the responsible party, the practitioner should take appropriate action. (Ref: par. .A33)

Preparing the Practitioner's Report

.33 The practitioner's report should be in writing. (Ref: par. .A34)

.34 The practitioner's report should be in the form of procedures and findings.

Content of the Practitioner's Agreed-Upon Procedures Report

.35 The practitioner's agreed-upon procedures report should include the following:

a. A title that includes the word *independent*. (Ref: par. .A35)

b. An appropriate addressee as required by the circumstances of the engagement.

c. An identification of the subject matter or assertion and the nature of an agreed-upon procedures engagement. (Ref: par. .A36)

d. An identification of the specified parties.

e. A statement that the procedures performed were those agreed to by the specified parties identified in the report.

f. A statement that identifies the responsible party and its responsibility for the subject matter or its assertion.

g. A statement that

i. the sufficiency of the procedures is solely the responsibility of the parties specified in the report.

   ii. the practitioner makes no representation regarding the sufficiency of the procedures either for the purpose for which the report has been requested or for any other purpose.

h. A list of the procedures performed (or reference thereto) and related findings. (The practitioner should not provide a conclusion. See paragraph .25.)

i. When applicable, a description of any agreed-upon materiality limits.

j. A statement that

   i. the agreed-upon procedures engagement was conducted in accordance with attestation standards established by the American Institute of Certified Public Accountants.

   ii. the practitioner was not engaged to and did not conduct an examination or review, the objective of which would be the expression of an opinion or conclusion, respectively, on the subject matter.

   iii. the practitioner does not express such an opinion or conclusion.

   iv. had the practitioner performed additional procedures, other matters might have come to the practitioner's attention that would have been reported. (Ref: par. .A37)

k. When applicable, a description of the nature of the assistance provided by a practitioner's external specialist, as discussed in paragraphs .21–.22.

l. When applicable, reservations or restrictions concerning procedures or findings. (Ref: par. .A38)

m. An alert, in a separate paragraph, that restricts the use of the report. The alert should

   i. state that the practitioner's report is intended solely for the information and use of the specified parties,

   ii. identify the specified parties for whom use is intended, and

   iii. state that the report is not intended to be, and should not be, used by anyone other than the specified parties. (Ref: par. .A39 –.A40)

n. When the engagement is also performed in accordance with Government Auditing Standards, the alert that restricts the use of the report should include the following information, rather than the information required by paragraph .35*m*:

   i. A description of the purpose of the report, and

   ii. A statement that the report is not suitable for any other purpose.

o. The manual or printed signature of the practitioner's firm.

p. The city and state where the practitioner practices. (Ref: par. .A41)

q. The date of the report. (The report should be dated no earlier than the date on which the practitioner completed the procedures and determined the findings, including that

   i. the attestation documentation has been reviewed,

   ii. if applicable, the written presentation of the subject matter has been prepared, and

iii. the responsible party has provided a written assertion, unless the responsible party refuses to provide an assertion.)

Responsible Party Refuses to Provide a Written Assertion

.36 When the responsible party refuses to provide the practitioner with a written assertion, the practitioner should disclose in the practitioner's report the responsible party's refusal to provide a written assertion. (Ref: par. .A42–.A43)

Restrictions on the Performance of Procedures

.37 When circumstances impose restrictions on the performance of the agreed-upon procedures, the practitioner should attempt to obtain agreement from the specified parties for modification of the agreed-upon procedures. When such agreement cannot be obtained (for example, when the agreed-upon procedures are published by a regulatory agency that will not modify the procedures), the practitioner should describe any restrictions on the performance of procedures in the practitioner's report or withdraw from the engagement.

Adding Specified Parties (Nonparticipant Parties)

.38 If the practitioner agrees to add a nonparticipant party, the practitioner should obtain affirmative acknowledgment, normally in writing, from the nonparticipant party agreeing to the procedures performed and of its taking responsibility for the sufficiency of the procedures. (Ref: par. .A44)

.39 If the practitioner's report is reissued to acknowledge the nonparticipant party, the date of the report should not be changed. (Ref: par. .A44)

.40 If the practitioner provides written acknowledgment that the nonparticipant party has been added as a specified party, such written acknowledgment ordinarily should state that no procedures have been performed subsequent to the date of the practitioner's report.

Knowledge of Matters Outside Agreed-Upon Procedures

.41 Although the practitioner need not perform procedures beyond the agreed-upon procedures, if in connection with the application, and through the completion of, the agreed-upon procedures engagement, matters come to the practitioner's attention by other means that significantly contradict the subject matter or assertion referred to in the practitioner's report, the practitioner should include this matter in the practitioner's report. (Ref: par. .A45–.A46)

Communication Responsibilities

.42 The practitioner should communicate to the responsible party known and suspected fraud and noncompliance with laws or regulations. When the engaging party is not the responsible party, the practitioner should also communicate this information to the engaging party.

Documentation

.43 The practitioner should prepare engagement documentation that is sufficient to determine (Ref: par. .A47)

a. the specified parties' agreement on the procedures.

b. the nature, timing, and extent of the procedures performed to comply with relevant AT-C sections and applicable legal and regulatory requirements, including

  i. the identifying characteristics of the specific items or matters tested;

  ii. who performed the engagement work and the date such work was completed;

  iii. when the engaging party is the responsible party and the responsible party will not provide one or more of the requested written representations or the practitioner concludes that there is sufficient doubt about the competence, integrity, ethical values, or diligence of those providing the written representations, or that the written representations are otherwise not reliable, the matters in paragraph .31*a–c*;

  iv. when the engaging party is not the responsible party and the responsible party will not provide the written representations regarding the matters in paragraph .28, the oral responses from the responsible party to the practitioner's inquiries regarding the matters in paragraph .28, in accordance with paragraph .32; and (Ref: par. .A32)

  v. who reviewed the engagement work performed and the date and extent of such review.

c. the results of the procedures performed and the evidence obtained.

Application and Other Explanatory Material

Introduction (Ref: par. .03)

.A1 A practitioner may issue a single combined practitioner's report that includes (*a*) a practitioner's report on subject matter or a presentation that requires a restriction on use to specified parties and (*b*) a report on subject matter or a presentation that ordinarily does not require such a restriction. The use of such a single combined report may be restricted to the specified parties. In some instances, a separate restricted use report may be included in a document that also contains a general use report. The inclusion of a separate restricted use report in a document that contains a general use report does not affect the intended use of either report. The restricted use report remains restricted as to use, and the general use report continues to be for general use.

Objectives (Ref: par. .06*a*)

.A2 In an agreed-upon procedures engagement, the practitioner applies procedures to the subject matter of the engagement. Even though the procedures are established by the specified parties, the requirements and guidance related to the subject matter and criteria in section 105 apply.

Conduct of an Agreed-Upon Procedures Engagement (Ref: par. .08, .10, and .14*d*)

.A3 For example, if a practitioner were performing agreed-upon procedures related to an entity's compliance with requirements of specified laws, regulations, rules, contracts, or grants, section 105, this section, and section 315, *Compliance Attestation*, would be relevant.

.A4 Although independence is required for agreed-upon procedures engagements, the "Agreed-Upon Procedures Engagements Performed in Accordance With SSAEs" interpretation (ET sec. 1.297.020) establishes independence requirements unique to such engagements.

.A5 To satisfy the requirements that the specified parties agree upon, the procedures performed or to be performed, and that the specified parties take responsibility for the sufficiency of the agreed-upon procedures for their purposes, the practitioner ordinarily communicates directly with and obtains affirmative acknowledgment from each of the specified parties. For example, this may be accomplished by meeting with the specified parties or by distributing a draft of the anticipated practitioner's report or a copy of an engagement letter to the specified parties and obtaining their agreement. If the practitioner is not able to communicate directly with all the specified parties, the practitioner may satisfy these requirements by applying any one or more of the following or similar procedures:

- Compare the procedures to be applied to written requirements of the specified parties.
- Discuss the procedures to be applied with appropriate representatives of the specified parties involved.
- Review relevant contracts with or correspondence from the specified parties.

.A6 Specified parties are responsible for the sufficiency (nature, timing, and extent) of the agreed-upon procedures because they best understand their own needs. The specified parties assume the risk that such procedures might be insufficient for their purposes. In addition, the specified parties assume the risk that they might misunderstand or otherwise inappropriately use findings properly reported by the practitioner.

Agreeing on the Terms of the Engagement (Ref: par. .12 and .14*b* and *e*)

.A7 It is in the interests of both the engaging party and the practitioner to document the agreed-upon terms of the engagement before the commencement of the engagement to help avoid misunderstandings. The form and content of the engagement letter or other suitable form of written agreement will vary with the engagement circumstances.

.A8 The criteria may be indicated in the procedures as opposed to being described separately.

.A9 The responsibility of the practitioner is to carry out the procedures and report the findings in accordance with the attestation standards. The practitioner assumes the risk that misapplication of the procedures may result in inappropriate findings being reported. Furthermore, the practitioner assumes the risk that appropriate findings may not be reported or may be reported inaccurately. The practitioner's risks can be reduced through adequate planning and supervision and due professional care in performing the procedures, accumulating the findings, and preparing the practitioner's report.

.A10 The practitioner has no responsibility to determine the differences between the agreed-upon procedures to be performed and the procedures that the practitioner would have determined to be necessary had the practitioner been engaged to perform another form of attestation engagement. The procedures that the practitioner agrees to perform pursuant to an agreed-upon procedures engagement may be more or less extensive than the procedures that the practitioner would determine to be necessary had he or she been engaged to perform another form of engagement.

Requesting a Written Assertion (Ref: par. .15–.16)

.A11 Situations may arise in which the current responsible party was not present during some or all of the period covered by the practitioner's report. Such persons may contend that they are not in a position to provide a written assertion that covers the entire period because they were not in place during some or all of the period. This fact, however, does not diminish such persons' responsibilities for the subject matter as a whole. Accordingly, the requirement for the practitioner to request a written assertion from the responsible party that covers the entire relevant period(s) still applies.

.A12 Paragraph .28*a* requires the practitioner to request a written representation from the responsible party that is the same as the responsible party's assertion. If the responsible party provides the practitioner with the written representation in paragraph .28*a*, the practitioner need not request a separate written assertion, unless a separate written assertion is called for by the engagement circumstances.

.A13 In an agreed-upon procedures engagement, the procedures that the practitioner is asked to perform frequently consist of comparing information from one source with information from another source to determine whether they agree. For that reason, the criteria identified in the assertion might be the agreement of one amount with another amount.

.A14 The following are examples of assertions the responsible party might make related to accounts receivable in the engagement that results in the practitioner's report illustrated in example 2 of paragraph .A48:

- General ledger account 250, "Accounts Receivable," as of December 31, 20XX, accurately summarizes the accounts receivable aged trial balance, which accurately summarizes individual customer account balances as of that date.
- The accounts receivable subsidiary ledger as of December 31, 20XX accurately summarizes individual account balances in the aged trial balance of accounts receivable as of that date.
- The aged trial balance of accounts receivable as of December 31, 20XX, accurately ages outstanding invoices in the accounts receivable subledger as of that date.
- The accounts receivable trial balance as of December 31, 20XX, accurately summarizes amounts due from customers at that date.

Alternatively, a single assertion such as the following might be appropriate:

- The accounts receivable aged trial balance as of December 31, 20XX, accurately presents the general ledger balance and the amounts and ages of individual customer balances as of that date.
- Additional assertions would be necessary for the engagement resulting in the report in example 2 of paragraph .A48, for example, an assertion about cash, or in the case of a single assertion, the assertion would need to be modified to address cash.

.A15 Paragraph .36 contains reporting requirements for situations in which the responsible party refuses to provide the practitioner with a written assertion.

Procedures to Be Performed (Ref: par. .17 and .19)

.A16 The procedures that the practitioner and specified parties agree upon may be as limited or as extensive as the specified parties desire. However, mere reading of an assertion or specified information about the subject matter does not constitute a procedure sufficient to permit a practitioner to report on the results of applying agreed-upon procedures.

.A17 Examples of appropriate procedures include the following:

- Execution of a sampling application after agreeing on relevant parameters
- Inspection of specified documents evidencing certain types of transactions or detailed attributes thereof
- Confirmation of specific information with third parties
- Comparison of documents, schedules, or analyses with certain specified attributes
- Performance of specific procedures on work performed by others
- Performance of mathematical computations

.A18 Examples of inappropriate procedures include the following:

- Mere reading of the work performed by others solely to describe their findings
- Evaluating the competency or objectivity of another party
- Obtaining an understanding about a particular subject
- Interpreting documents outside the scope of the practitioner's professional expertise

.A19 If the practitioner is selecting a sample, stating the size of the sample and how the selection was made (after agreement by the specified parties regarding the relevant parameters) contributes to the specificity of the description of procedures performed (for example, 50 items starting at the eighth item and selecting every fifteenth item thereafter or invoices issued from May 1 to July 31, 20XX).

.A20 Examples of other information the practitioner may include are the date the procedure was performed and the sources of information used in performing the procedure.

.A21 To avoid vague or ambiguous language, the procedures to be performed are characterized by the action to be taken at a level of specificity sufficient for a reader to understand the nature and extent of the procedures performed. Examples of acceptable descriptions of actions are the following:

- Inspect
- Confirm
- Compare
- Agree
- Trace

- Inquire
- Recalculate
- Observe
- Mathematically check

Conversely, the following descriptions of actions (unless defined to indicate the nature, timing, and extent of the procedures associated with these actions) generally are not acceptable because they are not sufficiently precise or have an uncertain meaning:

- Note
- Review
- General review
- Limited review
- Evaluate
- Analyze
- Check
- Test
- Interpret
- Verify
- Examine

Using the Work of a Practitioner's External Specialist (Ref: par. .21)

.A22 The practitioner's education and experience enable the practitioner to be knowledgeable about business matters in general, but the practitioner is not expected to have the expertise of a person trained for or qualified to engage in the practice of another profession or occupation. In certain circumstances, it may be appropriate to involve a practitioner's external specialist to assist the practitioner in the performance of one or more procedures. The following are examples of such circumstances:

- An attorney providing assistance concerning the interpretation of legal terminology in laws, regulations, rules, contracts, or grants
- A medical specialist providing assistance in understanding the characteristics of diagnosis codes documented in patient medical records
- An environmental engineer providing assistance in interpreting environmental remedial action regulatory directives that may affect the agreed-upon procedures applied to an environmental liabilities account in a financial statement
- A geologist providing assistance in distinguishing between the physical characteristics of a generic minerals group related to information to which the agreed-upon procedures are applied

.A23 The agreement regarding the involvement of a practitioner's external specialists may be reached when obtaining agreement on the procedures performed, or to be performed, and acknowledgment of responsibility for the sufficiency of the procedures, as discussed in paragraph .10*b*.

.A24 A practitioner may agree to apply procedures to the report or work product of a practitioner's external specialist that does not constitute assistance by the external specialist to the practitioner in an agreed-upon procedures engagement. For example, the practitioner may make reference to information contained in a report of a practitioner's external specialist in describing an agreed-upon procedure. However, it is inappropriate for the practitioner to agree to merely read the external specialist's report solely to describe or repeat the findings or to take responsibility for all or a portion of any procedures performed by a practitioner's external specialist or the external specialist's work product.

Using the Work of Internal Auditors or Other Practitioners (Ref: par. .23)

.A25 Internal auditors or other personnel may prepare schedules and accumulate data or provide other information for the practitioner's use in performing the agreed-upon procedures. Also, internal auditors may perform and report separately on procedures that they have carried out. Such procedures may be similar to those that a practitioner may perform under this section.

.A26 A practitioner may agree to perform procedures on information documented in the working papers of internal auditors. For example, the practitioner may agree to

- repeat all or some of the procedures.
- determine whether the internal auditors' documentation indicates procedures performed and whether the findings documented are presented in a report by the internal auditors.

.A27 It is inappropriate for the practitioner to

- agree to merely read the internal auditors' report solely to describe or repeat their findings.
- take responsibility for all or a portion of any procedures performed by internal auditors by reporting those findings as the practitioner's own.
- report in any manner that implies shared responsibility for the procedures with the internal auditors.

Findings (Ref: par. .26–.27)

.A28 The concept of materiality does not apply to findings to be reported in an agreed-upon procedures engagement unless the definition of materiality is agreed to by the specified parties. An example of language that describes a materiality limit is "For purposes of performing these agreed-upon procedures, no exceptions were reported for differences of $1,000 or less resulting solely from the rounding of amounts disclosed."

.A29 The following table provides examples of appropriate and inappropriate descriptions of findings resulting from the application of certain agreed-upon procedures.

Procedures Agreed Upon	*Appropriate Description of Findings*	*Inappropriate Description of Findings*
Inspect the shipment dates for a sample (agreed-upon) of specified shipping documents and determine whether any such dates were subsequent to [*date*].	No shipment dates shown on the sample of shipping documents were subsequent to [*date*].	Nothing came to my attention as a result of applying that procedure.
Recalculate the number of blocks of streets paved during the year ended [*date*], shown on contractors' certificates of project completion; compare the resultant number to the number in an identified chart of performance statistics as of [*date*].	The number of blocks of streets paved in the chart of performance statistics was Y blocks more than the number calculated from the contractors' certificates of project completion.	The number of blocks of streets paved approximated the number of blocks included in the chart of performance statistics.
Recalculate the rate of return on a specified investment (according to an agreed-upon formula) and determine whether the resultant percentage agrees to the percentage in an identified schedule.	No exceptions were found as a result of applying the procedure.	The resultant percentage approximated the predetermined percentage in the identified schedule.
Inspect the quality standards classification codes in identified performance test documents for products produced during [*specified period*]; compare such codes to those shown in the [*identified*] computer printout for [*specified period*] as of [*date*].	All classification codes inspected in the identified documents were the same as those shown in the computer printout, except for the following: [*List all exceptions.*]	All classification codes appeared to comply with such performance documents.
Trace all outstanding checks appearing on a bank reconciliation as of [*date*] to checks cleared in the bank statement of the subsequent month.	All outstanding checks appearing on the bank reconciliation were traced to the list of cleared checks in the subsequent month's bank statement, except for the following: [*List all exceptions.*]	Nothing came to my attention as a result of applying the procedure.

(continued)

Procedures Agreed Upon	*Appropriate Description of Findings*	*Inappropriate Description of Findings*
Compare the amounts of the invoices included in the "over 90 days" column shown in an identified schedule of aged accounts receivable of a specific customer as of [*date*] to the amount and invoice date shown on the corresponding outstanding invoice. Determine whether the dates on the corresponding outstanding invoices precede the date indicated on the schedule by more than 90 days.	All outstanding invoice amounts agreed with the amounts shown on the schedule in the "over 90 days" column, and the dates shown on such outstanding invoices preceded the date indicated on the schedule by more than 90 days.	The outstanding invoice amounts agreed within approximation of the amounts shown on the schedule in the "over 90 days" column, and nothing came to our attention that the dates shown on such outstanding invoices preceded the date indicated on the schedule by more than 90 days.
Obtain from XYZ Company [*personnel specified by management*], the [*date*] bank reconciliations. Confirm with the bank the cash on deposit as of [*date*]. Compare the balance confirmed by the bank to the amount shown on the bank reconciliations.	Obtained from XYZ Company [*personnel specified by management*], the [*date*] bank reconciliations. Obtained bank confirmations of the cash on deposit as of [*date*]. Compared the balance confirmed by the bank to the amount shown on the bank reconciliations. [*List all exceptions.*]	No exceptions were identified in the confirmations received, and nothing came to our attention as a result of applying the procedures.

Written Representations (Ref: par. .28)

.A30 Written confirmation of oral representations reduces the possibility of misunderstandings between the practitioner and the responsible party. The person(s) from whom the practitioner requests written representations is ordinarily a member of senior management or those charged with governance depending on, for example, the management and governance structure of the responsible party(ies), which may vary by entity, reflecting influences such as size and ownership characteristics.

Requested Written Representations Not Provided or Not Reliable (Ref: par. .31*c*, .32, and .43*b*[iv])

.A31 Appropriate actions the practitioner might consider in the circumstances described in paragraph .31*c* include

- withdrawing from the engagement.
- determining the effect on the practitioner's report.

.A32 Documentation requirements regarding the responsible party's oral responses to the practitioner's inquiries about the matters in paragraph .28 are included in paragraph .43*b*(iv).

.A33 Appropriate action the practitioner might consider in the circumstances described in paragraph .32*b* include

- withdrawing from the engagement.
- determining the effect on the practitioner's report.

Preparing the Practitioner's Report (Ref: par. .33)

.A34 This section does not require a standardized format for reporting on all agreed-upon procedures engagements. Instead, it identifies the basic elements that the report is to include. The report is tailored to the specific engagement circumstances. The practitioner may use headings, separate paragraphs, paragraph numbers, typographical devices (for example, the bolding of text), and other mechanisms to enhance the clarity and readability of the report.

Content of the Practitioner's Agreed-Upon Procedures Report

Title (Ref: par. .35a)

.A35 A title indicating that the practitioner's report is the report of an independent practitioner (for example, "Independent Practitioner's Report," "Report of Independent Certified Public Accountant," or "Independent Accountant's Report") affirms that the practitioner has met all of the relevant ethical requirements regarding independence and, therefore, distinguishes the independent practitioner's report from reports issued by others.

Identification of the Subject Matter or Assertion (Ref: par. .35c)

.A36 A practitioner may be asked to apply agreed-upon procedures to more than one subject matter or assertion. In these engagements, the practitioner may issue one practitioner's report that refers to all subject matter covered or assertions presented. Section 315 contains an example of language that may be used in the introductory paragraph to address such circumstances.[5]

Statement When the Subject Matter Consists of Elements, Accounts, or Items of a Financial Statement (Ref: par. .35j)

.A37 If the subject matter consists of elements, accounts, or items of a financial statement, the practitioner's report might, instead, state that the agreed-upon procedures do not constitute an audit (or a review) of financial statements or any part thereof, the objective of which is the expression of an opinion (or conclusion) on the financial statements or a part thereof.

Reservations or Restrictions Concerning Procedures or Findings (Ref: par. .35l)

.A38 The practitioner also may include explanatory paragraph(s) about matters such as the following:

---

[5] Paragraph .A32 of section 315, *Compliance Attestation*.

- Disclosure of stipulated facts, assumptions, or interpretations (including the source thereof) used in the application of agreed-upon procedures
- Description of the condition of records, controls, or data to which the procedures were applied
- Explanation that the practitioner has no responsibility to update the practitioner's report
- Explanation that the sample may not be representative of the population

Restricted Use (Ref: par. .35m)

.A39 The purpose of the restriction on the use of the practitioner's report on applying agreed-upon procedures is to restrict its use to only those parties that have agreed upon the procedures performed and taken responsibility for the sufficiency of the procedures. Paragraph .38 describes the process for adding parties who were not originally contemplated in the agreed-upon procedures engagement.

.A40 In some cases, a restricted-use practitioner's report filed with regulatory agencies is required by law or regulation to be made available to the public as a matter of public record. Also, a regulatory agency, as part of its oversight responsibility for an entity, may require access to a restricted use report in which they are not named as a specified party.

Location (Ref: par. .35p)

.A41 In the United States, the location of the issuing office is the city and state. In another country, it may be the city and country.

Responsible Party Refuses to Provide a Written Assertion (Ref: par. .36)

.A42 The disclosure in the practitioner's report required by paragraph .36 applies regardless of whether the engaging party is the responsible party.

.A43 The following is an example of the disclosure required by paragraph .36:

> Attestation standards established by the American Institute of Certified Public Accountants require that we request a written statement from [*identify the responsible party*] stating that [*identify the subject matter*] to which we applied procedures has been accurately measured or evaluated. We requested that [*identify the responsible party*] provide such a statement but [*identify the responsible party*] refused to do so.

Adding Specified Parties (Nonparticipant Parties) (Ref: par. .38–.39)

.A44 Subsequent to the completion of the agreed-upon procedures engagement, a practitioner may be requested by the engaging party to consider the addition of another party as a specified party (a nonparticipant party). The practitioner may agree to add a nonparticipant party as a specified party, based on consideration of such factors as the identity of the nonparticipant party and the intended use of the practitioner's report. If the nonparticipant party is added after the practitioner has issued the report, the report may be reissued, or the practitioner may provide other written acknowledgment that the nonparticipant party has been added as a specified party.

Knowledge of Matters Outside Agreed-Upon Procedures (Ref: par. .41)

.A45 For example, if, during the course of applying agreed-upon procedures regarding an entity's internal control, the practitioner becomes aware of a material weakness by means other than performance of the agreed-upon procedures, this matter would be included in the practitioner's report.

.A46 When the practitioner applies agreed-upon procedures to an element, account, or item of a financial statement and has performed (or has been engaged to perform) an audit of the entity's related financial statements, and the auditor's report on such financial statements includes a departure from the standard report, the practitioner may include a reference to the auditor's report and the departure from the standard report in the practitioner's agreed-upon procedures report.

Documentation (Ref: par. .43)

.A47 The practitioner need not include in the engagement file superseded drafts of working papers, notes that reflect incomplete or preliminary thinking, previous copies of documents corrected for typographical or other errors, and duplicates of documents.

.A48

Exhibit—Illustrative Practitioner's Agreed-Upon Procedures Reports

The illustrative practitioner's agreed-upon procedures reports in this exhibit meet the applicable reporting requirements in paragraphs .33–.41. A practitioner may use alternative language in drafting an agreed-upon procedures report, provided that the language meets the applicable requirements in paragraphs .33–.41. Example 1 is an illustrative agreed-upon procedures report related to a Statement of Investment Performance Statistics. Examples 2–3 provide illustrations of reports in which the practitioner has applied agreed-upon procedures to elements, accounts, or items of a financial statement.

Example 1: Practitioner's Agreed-Upon Procedures Report Related to a Statement of Investment Performance Statistics

Independent Accountant's Report on Applying Agreed-Upon Procedures

[*Appropriate Addressee*]

We have performed the procedures enumerated below, which were agreed to by [*identify the specified party(ies), for example, the audit committees and managements of ABC Inc. and XYZ Fund*], on [*identify the subject matter, for example, the accompanying Statement of Investment Performance Statistics of XYZ Fund for the year ended December 31, 20X1*]. XYZ Fund's management is responsible for [*identify the subject matter, for example, the Statement of Investment Performance Statistics for the year ended December 31, 20X1*]. The sufficiency of these procedures is solely the responsibility of the parties specified in this report. Consequently, we make no representation regarding the sufficiency of the procedures enumerated below either for the purpose for which this report has been requested or for any other purpose.

[*Include paragraphs to enumerate procedures and findings.*]

This agreed-upon procedures engagement was conducted in accordance with attestation standards established by the American Institute of Certified Public Accountants. We were not engaged to and did not conduct an examination or review, the objective of which would be the expression of an opinion or conclusion, respectively, on [*identify the subject matter, for example, the accompanying Statement of Investment Performance Statistics of XYZ Fund for the year ended December 31, 20X1*]. Accordingly, we do not express such an opinion or conclusion. Had we performed additional procedures, other matters might have come to our attention that would have been reported to you.

[*Additional paragraph(s) may be added to describe other matters.*]

This report is intended solely for the information and use of [*identify the specified party(ies), for example, the audit committees and managements of ABC Inc. and XYZ Fund*], and is not intended to be, and should not be, used by anyone other than the specified parties.

[*Practitioner's signature*]
[*Practitioner's city and state*]
[*Date of practitioner's report*]

Example 2: Practitioner's Agreed-Upon Procedures Report Related to Cash and Accounts Receivable

Independent Accountant's Report on Applying Agreed-Upon Procedures

[Appropriate Addressee]

We have performed the procedures enumerated below, which were agreed to by *[identify the specified party(ies), for example, the boards of directors and managements of ABC Company and XYZ Company]*, on *[identify the subject matter, for example, the cash and accounts receivable information of XYZ Company as of December 31, 20XX, included in the accompanying information provided to us by management of ABC Company]*. XYZ Company is responsible for *[identify the subject matter, for example, the cash and accounts receivable information of XYZ Company as of December 31, 20XX, included in the accompanying information provided to us by management of ABC Company]*. The sufficiency of these procedures is solely the responsibility of the parties specified in this report. Consequently, we make no representation regarding the sufficiency of the procedures enumerated below either for the purpose for which this report has been requested or for any other purpose.

The procedures and the associated findings are as follows:

Cash

1. For the four bank accounts listed below, we obtained
   a. the December 31, 20XX, bank reconciliations from XYZ Company management and
   b. the December 31, 20XX, general ledger from XYZ Company management.
2. We performed the following procedures:
   a. Obtained a bank confirmation directly from each bank of the cash on deposit as of December 31, 20XX
   b. Compared the balance confirmed by the bank to the amount shown on the respective bank reconciliations.
   c. Mathematically checked the bank reconciliations
   d. Compared the cash balances per book listed in the reconciliations below to the respective general ledger account balances.

Cash December 31, 20XX

Bank	*Cash Balance per Book*
DEF National Bank, general ledger account 123	$5,000
LMN State Bank, general ledger account 124	3,776
RST Trust Company regular account, general ledger account 125	86,912
RST Trust Company payroll account, general ledger account 126	5,000
	$110,688

We found no exceptions as a result of the procedures.

Accounts Receivable

3. We obtained the accounts receivable aged trial balance as of December 31, 20XX, from XYZ Company (attached as exhibit A).We mathematically checked that the individual customer account balance subtotals in the aged trial balance of accounts receivable agreed to the total accounts receivable per the aged trial balance. We compared the total accounts receivable per the accounts receivable aged trial balance to the total accounts receivable per general ledger account 250.

   We found no exceptions as a result of the procedures.

4. We obtained the accounts receivable subsidiary ledger as of December 31, 20XX, from XYZ Company. We compared the individual customer account balance subtotals shown in the accounts receivable aged trial balance (exhibit A) as of December 31, 20XX, to the balances shown in the accounts receivable subsidiary ledger.

   We found no exceptions as a result of the procedures.

5. We selected 50 customer account balances from exhibit A by starting at the eighth item and selecting every fifteenth item thereafter until 50 were selected. The sample size selected represents 9.8 percent of the aggregate amount of the customer account balances. We obtained the corresponding invoices from XYZ Company and traced the aging (according to invoice dates) for the 50 customer account balances shown in exhibit A to the details of outstanding invoices in the accounts receivable subsidiary ledger.

   We found no exceptions as a result of the procedures.

6. We mailed confirmations directly to the customers representing the 150 largest customer account balance subtotals selected from the accounts receivable aged trial balance, and we received responses as indicated below. As agreed, any individual differences in a customer account balance of less than $300 were to be considered minor, and no further procedures were performed.

   Of the 150 customer balances confirmed, we received responses from 140 customers; 10 customers did not reply.

   No exceptions were identified in 120 of the confirmations received. The differences in the remaining 20 confirmation replies were less than $300.

   For the 10 customers that did not reply, we traced the items constituting the outstanding customer account balance to invoices and supporting shipping documents.

   A summary of the confirmation results according to the respective aging categories is as follows.

Accounts Receivable December 31, 20XX

Aging Categories	*Customer Account Balances*	*Confirmations Requested*	*Confirmations Received*
Current	$156,000	$76,000	$65,000
Past due:			
Less than one month	60,000	30,000	19,000
One to three months	36,000	18,000	10,000
Over three months	48,000	48,000	8,000
	$300,000	$172,000	$102,000

This agreed-upon procedures engagement was conducted in accordance with attestation standards established by the American Institute of Certified Public Accountants. We were not engaged to and did not conduct an examination or a review, the objective of which would be the expression of an opinion or conclusion, respectively, on [*identify the subject matter, for example, the cash and accounts receivable information of XYZ Company as of December 31, 20XX, included in the accompanying information provided to us by management of ABC Company*]. Accordingly, we do not express such an opinion or conclusion. Had we performed additional procedures, other matters might have come to our attention that would have been reported to you.

[*Additional paragraph(s) may be added to describe other matters.*]

This report is intended solely for the information and use of [*identify the specified party(ies), for example, the boards of directors and managements of ABC Company and XYZ Company*], and is not intended to be and should not be used by anyone other than the specified parties.

[*Practitioner's signature*]
[*Practitioner's city and state*]
[*Date of practitioner's report*]

Example 3: Practitioner's Agreed-Upon Procedures Report in Connection With Claims of Creditors

Independent Accountant's Report on Applying Agreed-Upon Procedures

[*Appropriate Addressee*]

We have performed the procedures enumerated below, which were agreed to by [*identify the specified party(ies), for example, the Trustee of XYZ Company*], on [*identify the subject matter, for example, the claims of creditors of XYZ Company as of May 31, 20XX, as set forth in the accompanying Schedule A*]. XYZ Company is responsible for maintaining records of [*identify the subject matter, for example, the claims of creditors of XYZ Company as of May 31, 20XX, as set forth in the accompanying Schedule A*]. The sufficiency of these procedures is solely the responsibility of the party specified in this report. Consequently, we make no representation regarding the sufficiency of the procedures enumerated below either for the purpose for which this report has been requested or for any other purpose.

The procedures and associated findings are as follows:

1. Obtained the general ledger and the accounts payable trial balance as of May 31, 20XX, from XYZ Company. Compared the total of the accounts payable trial balance to the total accounts payable balance in general ledger account 450.

   The total of the accounts payable trial balance agreed with the total accounts payable balance in the general ledger account number 450.

2. Obtained the claim form submitted by creditors in support of the amounts claimed from XYZ Company. Compared the creditor name and amounts from the claim form to the respective name and amounts shown in the accounts payable trial balance obtained in procedure 1. For any differences identified, requested XYZ Company to provide supporting detail. Compared such identified differences to the supporting detail provided.

   All differences noted are presented in column 3 of Schedule A. Except for those amounts shown in column 4 of Schedule A, all such differences were agreed to [*describe supporting detail*].

3. Using the claim form obtained in procedure 2, compared the name and amount to invoices, and if applicable, receiving reports, provided by XYZ Company.

   No exceptions were found as a result of this procedure.

This agreed-upon procedures engagement was conducted in accordance with attestation standards established by the American Institute of Certified Public Accountants. We were not engaged to and did not conduct an examination or review, the objective of which would be the expression of an opinion or conclusion, respectively, on [*identify the subject matter, for example, the claims of creditors of XYZ Company as of May 31, 20XX, as set forth in the accompanying Schedule A*]. Accordingly, we do not express such an opinion or conclusion. Had we performed additional procedures, other matters might have come to our attention that would have been reported to you.

[*Additional paragraph(s) may be added to describe other matters.*]

This report is intended solely for the information and use of [*identify the specified party(ies), for example, the Trustee of XYZ Company*], and is not intended to be, and should not be, used by anyone other than the specified party.

[*Practitioner's signature*]
[*Practitioner's city and state*]
[*Date of practitioner's report*]

AT-C Section 300
SUBJECT MATTER

TABLE OF CONTENTS

AT-C Section 305*

Prospective Financial Information

Source: SSAE No. 18.

Effective for practitioners' examination and agreed-upon procedures reports on prospective financial information dated on or after May 1, 2017.

Introduction

.01 This section contains performance and reporting requirements and application guidance for a practitioner examining or performing agreed-upon procedures on prospective financial information.

.02 Prospective financial information can take the form of prospective financial statements or partial presentations.

.03 The AICPA Guide *Prospective Financial Information* (guide) provides comprehensive guidance regarding prospective financial information. Chapter 6, "Preparation Guidelines," chapter 7, "Reasonably Objective Basis," chapter 8, "Presentation Guidelines," and chapter 9, "Illustrative Prospective Financial Statements," of the guide establish the preparation and presentation guidelines for financial forecasts and financial projections. The guide also includes information about the types and uses of prospective financial information and interpretive guidance for applying this section.

.04 In addition to complying with this section, a practitioner is required to comply with section 105, *Concepts Common to All Attestation Engagements*, and either section 205, *Examination Engagements*, for examinations of prospective financial information, or section 215, *Agreed-Upon Procedures Engagements*, for agreed-upon procedures engagements that address prospective financial information. In some cases, this section repeats or refers to requirements found in sections 105, 205, and 215 when describing those requirements in the context of engagements that address prospective financial information. Although not all the requirements in sections 105, 205, and 215 are repeated or referred to in this section, the practitioner is responsible for complying with all the requirements in sections 105 and 205, or 105 and 215, as applicable.

.05 Section 210, *Review Engagements*, prohibits a practitioner from performing a review of prospective financial information.[1]

Effective Date

.06 This section is effective for practitioners' examination and agreed-upon procedures reports on prospective financial information dated on or after May 1, 2017.

---

* This section contains an "AT-C" identifier, instead of an "AT" identifier, to avoid confusion with references to existing "AT" sections, which remain effective through April 2017.

[1] Paragraph .07 of section 210, *Review Engagements*.

Objectives of an Examination Engagement

.07 In conducting an examination of prospective financial information, the objectives of the practitioner are to

a. obtain reasonable assurance about whether, in all material respects,

   i. the prospective financial information is presented in accordance with the guidelines for the presentation of prospective financial information established by the AICPA (AICPA presentation guidelines) (Ref: par. .A1) and

   ii. the assumptions underlying the forecast are suitably supported and provide a reasonable basis for the responsible party's forecast, or the assumptions underlying the projection are suitably supported and provide a reasonable basis for the responsible party's projection, given the hypothetical assumptions. (Ref: par. .A2)

b. express an opinion in a written report on the matters in paragraph .07*a*.

Objectives of an Agreed-Upon Procedures Engagement

.08 In conducting an agreed-upon procedures engagement for which the subject matter is prospective financial information, the objectives of the practitioner are to

a. apply to the prospective financial information procedures that are established by specified parties who are responsible for the sufficiency of the procedures for their purposes and

b. issue a written report that describes the procedures applied and the practitioner's findings.

Definitions

.09 For purposes of this section, the following terms have the meanings attributed as follows:[2]

Entity. Any unit, existing or to be formed, for which financial statements could be prepared in accordance with generally accepted accounting principles or special purpose frameworks. For example, an entity can be an individual, partnership, corporation, trust, estate, association, or governmental unit. (Ref: par. .A3)

Financial forecast. Prospective financial statements that present, to the best of the responsible party's knowledge and belief, an entity's expected financial position, results of operations, and cash flows. A financial forecast is based on the responsible party's assumptions reflecting conditions it expects to exist and the course of action it expects to take. A financial forecast may be expressed in specific monetary amounts as a single-point estimate of forecasted results or as a range, when the responsible party selects key assumptions to form a range within which it reasonably expects, to the best of its knowledge and belief, the item or items subject to the assumptions to actually fall. If a forecast contains

---

[2] All definitions in this section, with the exception of the term *presentation guidelines*, are taken from chapter 3, "Definitions," of the AICPA guide *Prospective Financial Information*.

a range, the range is not selected in a biased or misleading manner (for example, a range in which one end is significantly less expected than the other). (Ref: par. .A4)

Financial projection. Prospective financial statements that present, to the best of the responsible party's knowledge and belief, given one or more hypothetical assumptions, an entity's expected financial position, results of operations, and cash flows. A financial projection is sometimes prepared to present one or more hypothetical courses of action for evaluation, as in response to a question such as, "What would happen if...?" A financial projection is based on the responsible party's assumptions reflecting conditions it expects would exist and the course of action it expects would be taken, given one or more hypothetical assumptions. A projection, like a forecast, may contain a range. (Ref: par. .A5–.A6)

Guide. The AICPA Guide *Prospective Financial Information.*

Hypothetical assumption. An assumption used in a financial projection or in a partial presentation of projected information to present a condition or course of action that is not necessarily expected to occur, but is consistent with the purpose of the projection.

Key factors. The significant matters on which an entity's future results are expected to depend. Such factors are basic to the entity's operations and, thus, encompass matters that affect, among other things, the entity's sales, production, service, and financing activities. Key factors serve as a foundation for prospective financial information and are the bases for the assumptions.

Partial presentation. A presentation of prospective financial information that excludes one or more of the applicable items required for prospective financial statements as described in chapter 8 of the guide. (Ref: par. .A7)

Presentation guidelines. The criteria for the presentation and disclosure of prospective financial information. (Ref: par. .A8)

Prospective financial information. Any financial information about the future. The information may be presented as complete financial statements or limited to one or more elements, items, or accounts.

Prospective financial statements. Either financial forecasts or financial projections, including the summaries of significant assumptions and accounting policies. Although prospective financial statements may cover a period that has partially expired, statements for periods that have completely expired are not considered to be prospective financial statements. Pro forma financial statements and partial presentations are not considered to be prospective financial statements. (Ref: par. .A9–.A10)

Requirements

Preconditions for an Examination Engagement

.10 Because a financial projection is not appropriate for general use, a practitioner should not agree to the use of the practitioner's name in conjunction with a financial projection that the practitioner believes will be distributed to those who will not be negotiating directly with the responsible party. (Ref: par. .A4–.A5 and .A11)

.11 Unless required by law or regulation to do so, a practitioner should not accept an engagement to examine

a. a forecast or projection, unless the responsible party has agreed to disclose the significant assumptions

b. a financial projection, unless the responsible party has agreed to identify in the presentation which of the assumptions are hypothetical and to describe the limitations on the usefulness of the projection.

c. a partial presentation that does not describe the limitations on the usefulness of the presentation.

.12 A practitioner should not examine a forecast or projection that discloses none of the significant assumptions. If after accepting the engagement the practitioner determines that the forecast or projection discloses none of the significant assumptions, the practitioner should withdraw from the engagement, unless required by law or regulation to report on the financial forecast or projection, in which case, the practitioner should express an adverse opinion in the practitioner's report.

.13 If after accepting the engagement, the practitioner determines that the forecast or projection fails to disclose one or more of the significant assumptions, the practitioner should describe the assumption(s) in the practitioner's report and express an adverse opinion.

.14 If after accepting the engagement the practitioner determines that a projection fails to identify which of the assumptions are hypothetical or describe the limitations on the usefulness of the projection, the practitioner should withdraw from the engagement, unless required by law or regulation to report on the projection, in which case, the practitioner should express an adverse opinion in the practitioner's report.

Training and Proficiency

.15 The practitioner should understand the guidelines for the preparation and presentation of prospective financial statements contained in the guide.

.16 The practitioner should possess or obtain a level of knowledge of the industry and the accounting principles and practices of the industry in which the entity operates, or will operate, that will enable the practitioner to examine prospective financial information that is appropriate for an entity operating in that industry.

.17 The practitioner should obtain knowledge of the key factors on which the entity's prospective financial information is based. (Ref: par. .A12)

Requesting a Written Assertion

.18 The practitioner should request from the responsible party a written assertion. If the responsible party refuses to provide a written assertion, the practitioner should withdraw from the engagement when withdrawal is possible under applicable law or regulation. (Ref: par. .A13)

Planning

.19 In accordance with section 205, the practitioner should establish an overall engagement strategy that sets the scope, timing, and direction of the engagement and guides the development of the engagement plan.[3] (Ref: par. .A14)

Examination Procedures

.20 The examination procedures should be based on the practitioner's consideration of the following:

a. The nature and materiality of the information to the prospective financial information taken as a whole

b. The likelihood of material misstatements

c. Knowledge obtained during current and previous engagements

d. The responsible party's competence with respect to prospective financial information

e. The extent to which the prospective financial information is affected by the responsible party's judgment, for example, its judgment in selecting the significant assumptions used to prepare the prospective financial information

f. The support for the responsible party's assumptions

.21 The practitioner should evaluate whether the responsible party has a reasonably objective basis for the forecast and should consider whether sufficiently objective assumptions can be developed for each key factor. (Ref: par. .A15)

.22 The practitioner should perform those procedures the practitioner considers necessary in the circumstances to report on whether the assumptions underlying the forecast are suitably supported and provide a reasonable basis for the forecast, or whether the assumptions underlying the projection are suitably supported and provide a reasonable basis for the projection, given the hypothetical assumptions. (Ref: par. .A16–.A17)

.23 The practitioner should evaluate the support for the significant assumptions individually and in the aggregate. Assumptions are suitably supported if the preponderance of the information supports each significant assumption. In an examination of a projection, the practitioner need not obtain support for the hypothetical assumptions, although the practitioner should evaluate whether they are consistent with the purpose of the presentation. (Ref: par. .A18–.A20)

.24 In an evaluation of whether the assumptions provide a reasonable basis for the forecast, the practitioner should evaluate the assumptions in the aggregate. If certain assumptions do not have a material effect on the presentation, they may not have to be individually evaluated. Nonetheless, the practitioner should evaluate the aggregate effect of individually insignificant assumptions in making the practitioner's overall evaluation.

.25 The practitioner should evaluate the assumptions related to an expired portion of the prospective period. (Ref: par. .A21–.A23)

.26 In evaluating the preparation and presentation of the prospective financial information, the practitioner should perform procedures to obtain reasonable assurance about whether the

a. presentation reflects the identified assumptions,

---

[3] Paragraph .11 of section 205, *Examination Engagements*.

b. computations made to translate the assumptions into prospective amounts are mathematically accurate,

c. assumptions are internally consistent,

d. accounting principles used in the forecast or projection are appropriate, (Ref: par. .A24)

e. prospective financial information is presented in accordance with the AICPA presentation guidelines, and

f. assumptions have been adequately disclosed in accordance with the AICPA presentation guidelines.

.27 The practitioner should conclude whether the prospective financial information, including related disclosures, should be revised because of any of the following: (Ref: par. .A25)

a. Mathematical errors

b. Unreasonable or internally inconsistent assumptions

c. Inappropriate or incomplete presentation

d. Inadequate disclosure

Written Representations in an Examination Engagement

.28 In an examination of a forecast, in addition to the written representations from the responsible party required by section 205, the practitioner should request from the responsible party written representations that[4]

a. the forecast presents the expected financial position, results of operations, and cash flows for the forecast period and that the forecast reflects the responsible party's judgment, based on present circumstances, of the expected conditions and its expected course of action;

b. the assumptions on which the forecast is based are reasonable and suitably supported; and

c. if the forecast contains a range, the item or items subject to the assumptions are reasonably expected to fall within the range and that the range was not selected in a biased or misleading manner.

.29 In an examination of a projection, in addition to the written representations from the responsible party required by section 205, the practitioner should request from the responsible party written representations that[5]

a. identify the hypothetical assumptions;

b. identify which of the hypothetical assumptions, if any, are improbable;

c. describe the limitations of the usefulness of the presentation;

d. the projection presents the expected financial position, results of operations, and cash flows for the projection period given the hypothetical assumptions, and that the projection reflects the responsible party's judgment, based on present circumstances, of expected conditions and its expected course of action given the occurrence of the hypothetical events;

---

[4] Paragraph .50 of section 205.

[5] See footnote 4.

e. the assumptions other than the hypothetical assumptions are reasonable, given the hypothetical assumptions, and are suitably supported; and

f. if the projection contains a range, given the hypothetical assumptions, the item or items subject to the assumption are reasonably expected to actually fall within the range and that the range was not selected in a biased or misleading manner.

.30 In an examination of prospective financial information, the written representation required by section 205 regarding whether the subject matter is in accordance with (or based on) the criteria should indicate that the forecast (or projection) is presented in accordance with (or based on) the guidelines for the presentation of a financial forecast (or financial projection) established by the American Institute of Certified Public Accountants.[6] (Ref: par. .A26)

.31 In an examination of prospective financial information, the practitioner should request from the responsible party the written representations required by section 205 and paragraphs .28 or .29 of this section, as applicable, even if the engaging party is not the responsible party.[7] The alternative to obtaining the required written representations provided for in section 205 is not permitted in an engagement to examine prospective financial information.[8] The responsible party's refusal to furnish the written representations required by section 205 and paragraphs .28 or .29 of this section, as applicable, constitutes a limitation on the scope of the engagement sufficient to preclude an unmodified opinion and may be sufficient to cause the practitioner to withdraw from the examination engagement, when withdrawal is possible under applicable laws and regulations.[9]

Content of the Practitioner's Examination Report

.32 The practitioner's examination report on prospective financial information should include the following, unless the practitioner is disclaiming an opinion, in which case, items .32*f*, and .32*g* should be omitted: (Ref: par. .A27–.A30)

a. A title that includes the word *independent.*

b. An appropriate addressee as required by the circumstances of the engagement.

c. An identification of the prospective financial information being reported on, including the period of time to which the prospective financial information relates.

d. An indication that the criteria against which the prospective financial information was measured or evaluated are the guidelines for the presentation of a forecast (or projection) established by the American Institute of Certified Public Accountants.

e. A statement that identifies

i. the responsible party and its responsibility for preparing and presenting the prospective financial information in accordance with the guidelines for the presentation of a forecast (or projection) established by the American Institute of Certified Public Accountants.

---

6 Paragraph .50*a* of section 205.

7 See footnote 4.

8 Paragraph .51 of section 205.

9 Paragraphs .50, .55, and .A64 of section 205.

ii. the practitioner's responsibility is to express an opinion on the prospective financial information, based on the practitioner's examination.

f. A statement that

i. the practitioner's examination was conducted in accordance with attestation standards established by the American Institute of Certified Public Accountants.

ii. those standards require that the practitioner plan and perform the examination to obtain reasonable assurance about whether the forecast (or projection) is presented in accordance with the guidelines for the presentation of a forecast (or projection) established by the American Institute of Certified Public Accountants, in all material respects.

iii. the practitioner believes the evidence obtained is sufficient and appropriate to provide a reasonable basis for the practitioner's opinion.

g. A description of the nature of an examination engagement.

h. The practitioner's opinion about whether the forecast (or projection) is presented, in all material respects, in accordance with the guidelines for the presentation of a forecast (or projection) established by the American Institute of Certified Public Accountants, and whether the underlying assumptions are suitably supported and provide a reasonable basis for the forecast or a reasonable basis for the projection given the hypothetical assumptions.

i. A statement indicating that the prospective results may not be achieved and describing other significant inherent limitations, if any.

j. A statement that the practitioner has no responsibility to update the report for events and circumstances occurring after the date of the report.

k. The manual or printed signature of the practitioner's firm.

l. The city and state where the practitioner practices.

m. The date of the report. (The report should be dated no earlier than the date on which the practitioner has obtained sufficient appropriate evidence on which to base the practitioner's opinion, including evidence that

i. the attestation documentation has been reviewed,

ii. the prospective financial information has been prepared, and

iii. the responsible party has provided a written assertion.)

.33 When a practitioner examines a projection, the practitioner's opinion regarding the assumptions should be conditioned on the hypothetical assumptions, that is, the practitioner should express an opinion on whether the assumptions provide a reasonable basis for the projection, given the hypothetical assumptions. In addition to the required elements for a practitioner's report on an examination of a forecast, a report on an examination of a projection should include (Ref: par. .A27 and .A31–.A32)

a. an identification of the hypothetical assumptions,

b. a description of the special purpose for which the projection was prepared, and *c.* an alert, in a separate paragraph, that restricts the use of the report. The alert should

i. state that the report is intended solely for the information and use of the specified parties,

ii. identify the specified parties for whom use is intended, and

iii. state that the report is not intended to be, and should not be, used by anyone other than the specified parties.

d. When the engagement is also performed in accordance with *Government Auditing Standards*, the alert that restricts the use of the report should include the following information, rather than the information required by paragraph .33*c*:

i. a description of the purpose of the report, and

ii. a statement that the report is not suitable for any other purpose.

.34 When the prospective financial information contains a range, the practitioner's report should also include a separate paragraph that states that the responsible party has elected to portray the expected results of one or more assumptions as a range. (Ref: par. .A27 and .A33)

Modified Opinions

.35 The following are circumstances that require the practitioner to modify the opinion and the type of modified opinion the practitioner should express in each circumstance: (Ref: par. .A34–.A38)

a. If, in the practitioner's judgment, the prospective financial information materially departs from AICPA presentation guidelines, the practitioner should express a qualified or adverse opinion. (Ref: par. .A35–.A36)

b. If the prospective financial information fails to disclose assumptions that, in the practitioner's professional judgment, are significant, or misapplies the accounting principles, the practitioner should express an adverse opinion. (Ref: par. .A37)

c. If the practitioner believes that one or more significant assumptions are not suitably supported or do not provide a reasonable basis for the forecast, or for the projection given the hypothetical assumptions, the practitioner should express an adverse opinion. (Ref: par. .A37)

d. If the practitioner is unable to obtain sufficient appropriate evidence, the practitioner should disclaim an opinion and describe the scope limitation in the practitioner's report. (Ref: par. .A38)

Partial Presentations

.36 When examining a partial presentation, the practitioner should give appropriate consideration to whether key factors affecting elements, accounts, or items that are interrelated with those in the partial presentation have been considered, including key factors that may not necessarily be obvious to the user of a partial presentation (for example, production capacity relative to a sales forecast), and whether all significant assumptions have been disclosed. (Ref: par. .A39–.A40 and .A29)

.37 Because partial presentations are generally appropriate only for limited use, practitioners' reports on partial presentations of both forecasted and projected financial information should include a description of any limitations on the usefulness of the presentation.

Preconditions for an Agreed-Upon Procedures Engagement

.38 In addition to determining that the preconditions for accepting or continuing an agreed-upon procedures engagement enumerated in section 105 and section 215 are met, the practitioner should not perform an agreed-upon procedures engagement on a forecast or projection unless the prospective financial information includes a summary of significant assumptions.

Content of the Practitioner's Agreed-Upon Procedures Report

.39 The practitioner's report on the application of agreed-upon procedures to a forecast or projection should include the following: (Ref: par. .A41–.A42)

a. A title that includes the word *independent*.

b. An appropriate addressee as required by the circumstances of the engagement.

c. An identification of the prospective financial information and the nature of an agreed-upon procedures engagement.

d. An identification of the specified parties.

e. A statement that the procedures performed were those agreed to by the specified parties identified in the report.

f. A statement that identifies the responsible party and its responsibility for preparing and presenting the forecast (or projection) in accordance with the guidelines for the presentation of a forecast (or projection) established by the American Institute of Certified Public Accountants.

g. A statement that

   i. the sufficiency of the procedures is solely the responsibility of the parties specified in the report.

   ii. the practitioner makes no representation regarding the sufficiency of the procedures either for the purpose for which the report has been requested or for any other purpose.

h. A list of the procedures performed (or reference thereto) and related findings. (The practitioner should not provide a conclusion.)

i. When applicable, a description of any agreed-upon materiality limits.

j. A statement that

   i. the agreed-upon procedures engagement was conducted in accordance with attestation standards established by the American Institute of Certified Public Accountants.

   ii. the practitioner was not engaged to and did not conduct an examination or review, the objective of which would be the expression of an opinion or a conclusion, respectively, on

      (1) whether the presentation of the forecast (or projection) is in accordance with guidelines for the presentation of a forecast (or projection) established by the American Institute of Certified Public Accountants,

(2) whether the underlying assumptions are suitably supported, and

(3) whether the underlying assumptions provide a reasonable basis for the forecast or a reasonable basis for the projection given the hypothetical assumptions.

iii. the practitioner does not express such an opinion or conclusion.

iv. had the practitioner performed additional procedures, other matters might have come to the practitioner's attention that would have been reported.

k. When applicable, a description of the nature of the assistance provided by a practitioner's external specialist.

l. A statement indicating that the prospective results may not be achieved and describing other significant inherent limitations, if any.

m. A statement that the practitioner has no responsibility to update the report for events and circumstances occurring after the date of the report.

n. When applicable, reservations or restrictions concerning procedures or findings.

o. An alert, in a separate paragraph, that restricts the use of the report. The alert should

i. state that the report is intended solely for the information and use of the specified parties,

ii. identify the specified parties for whom use is intended, and

iii. state that the report is not intended to be, and should not be, used by anyone other than the specified parties.

p. When the engagement is also performed in accordance with *Government Auditing Standards*, the alert that restricts the use of the report should include the following information, rather than the information required by paragraph .39*o*.

i. A description of the purpose of the report

ii. A statement indicating that the report is not suitable for any other purpose

q. The manual or printed signature of the practitioner's firm.

r. The city and state where the practitioner practices.

s. The date of the report. (The report should be dated no earlier than the date on which the practitioner completed the procedures and determined the findings, including that

i. the attestation documentation has been reviewed,

ii. the prospective financial information has been prepared, and

iii. the responsible party has provided a written assertion, unless the responsible party refuses to provide an assertion.)

Application and Other Explanatory Material

Objectives of an Examination Engagement (Ref: par. .07*a*)

.A1 The practitioner's objective in an examination of prospective financial information is to obtain sufficient appropriate evidence to reduce attestation risk to a level that is, in the practitioner's professional judgment, acceptably low to express an opinion about whether the prospective financial information is presented in accordance with AICPA presentation guidelines and the assumptions are suitably supported and provide either a reasonable basis for the responsible party's forecast or a reasonable basis for the responsible party's projection, given the hypothetical assumptions. The practitioner's opinion does not address whether the prospective results can be achieved because events and circumstances frequently do not occur as expected, and achievement of the prospective results is dependent on the actions, plans, and assumptions of the responsible party.

.A2 The concept of *suitably supported* is discussed in paragraphs .23 and .A18–.A20.

Definitions

Entity (Ref: par. .09)

.A3 The term *entity* is used elsewhere in the attestation standards. However, the definition of the term *entity* in paragraph .09 is applicable only to this section.

Financial Forecast (Ref: par. .09–.10)

.A4 As indicated in chapter 4, "Types of Prospective Financial Information and Their Uses," of the guide, prospective financial statements are for either general use or limited use. *General use of prospective financial statements* refers to the use of the statements by persons with whom the responsible party is not negotiating directly—for example, in an offering statement of an entity's debt or equity interests. Because recipients of prospective financial statements distributed for general use are unable to ask the responsible party directly about the presentation, the presentation most useful to them is one that portrays, to the best of the responsible party's knowledge and belief, the expected results. Thus, only a financial forecast is appropriate for general use.

Financial Projection (Ref: par. .09–.10)

.A5 *Limited use of prospective financial statements* refers to the use of prospective financial statements by the responsible party alone or by the responsible party and third parties with whom the responsible party is negotiating directly. Examples include use in negotiations for a bank loan, submission to a regulatory agency, and use solely within the entity. Third-party recipients of prospective financial statements intended for limited use can ask questions of the responsible party and negotiate terms directly with it. Any type of prospective financial statements that would be useful in the circumstances would normally be appropriate for limited use. Thus, the presentation may be a financial forecast or a financial projection.

.A6 Generally, as the number or significance of the hypothetical assumptions increases, the less likely that it is appropriate for the responsible party to present a financial projection.

Partial Presentation (Ref: par. .09)

.A7 Chapter 23, "Partial Presentations of Prospective Financial Information," of the guide establishes a limitation on the use of partial presentations. Chapter 23 of the guide states, in part

> ...partial presentations are not ordinarily appropriate for general use. Accordingly, a partial presentation ordinarily should not be distributed to third parties who will not be *negotiating directly* with the responsible party (for example, in an offering document for an entity's debt or equity interests). In this context, negotiating directly is defined as a third-party user's ability to ask questions of, and negotiate the terms or structure of a transaction directly with, the responsible party.

Presentation Guidelines (Ref: par. .09)

.A8 Chapter 8 of the guide contains the guidelines for the presentation and disclosure of prospective financial information.

Prospective Financial Statements (Ref: par. .09)

.A9 Prospective financial statements may take the form of complete financial statements or may be summarized or condensed, as described in chapter 8 of the guide. Presentations that exclude one or more relevant elements described in that section are defined as *partial presentations*. For the purposes of this section, the term *forecast* used alone means forecasted information, which can be either a full presentation (a financial forecast) or a partial presentation. The term *projection* can refer to either a financial projection or a partial presentation of projected information.

.A10 The objective of pro forma financial information is to show what the significant effects on the historical financial statements might have been had a consummated or proposed transaction or event occurred at an earlier date. Although the transaction in question might be prospective, this section does not apply to such presentations because they are essentially historical financial statements and do not purport to be prospective financial statements. See section 310, *Reporting on Pro Forma Financial Information*.

Preconditions for an Examination Engagement (Ref: par. .10)

.A11 Paragraph .10 indicates that it is not appropriate for a practitioner to agree to the use of the practitioner's name in conjunction with a financial projection that the practitioner believes will be distributed to those who will not be negotiating directly with the responsible party. An example of such a situation is the inclusion of a financial projection in an offering statement of an entity's debt or equity interests, unless the projection is used to supplement a financial forecast for the period covered by the forecast (that is, the financial projection would be presented in the same document as the financial forecast and the period covered by the projection would not begin before, or extend beyond, the period covered by the forecast).

Training and Proficiency (Ref: par. .17)

.A12 In obtaining knowledge of the entity's business, accounting policies, and the key factors upon which its future financial results appear to depend, the practitioner may focus on areas such as the following:

- The availability and cost of resources needed to operate, for example, raw materials, labor, short-term and long-term financing, and plant and equipment.

- The nature and condition of markets in which the entity sells its goods or services, including final consumer markets if the entity sells to intermediate markets
- Factors specific to the industry, including competitive conditions, sensitivity to economic conditions, accounting policies, specific regulatory requirements, and technology
- Patterns of past performance for the entity or comparable entities, including trends in revenue and costs, turnover of assets, uses and capacities of physical facilities, and management policies

Requesting a Written Assertion (Ref: par. .18)

.A13 Paragraph .18 applies regardless of whether the responsible party is the engaging party.

Planning (Ref: par. .19)

.A14 Factors that may be considered by the practitioner in planning the examination of prospective financial information include the following:

- The financial reporting framework to be used and the type of presentation
- Preliminary judgments about materiality levels
- Items within the prospective financial information that are subject to risk of material misstatement
- Conditions that may require extension or modification of the practitioner's examination procedures
- Knowledge of the entity's business and its industry
- The responsible party's experience in preparing prospective financial information
- The length of the period covered by the prospective financial information
- The process by which the responsible party develops its prospective financial information

Examination Procedures (Ref: par. .21–.23, .25, .26*d*, and .27)

.A15 Chapter 7 of the guide indicates that a reasonably objective basis for a forecast cannot exist if the premise on which the assumptions are based is too subjective. A forecast has to be based on a realistic premise, which has to be supportable. In contrast, the basic premise for a projection does not have to be supportable, although the hypothetical assumptions should be consistent with the purpose of the presentation. Accordingly, in a projection, the responsible party need not have a reasonably objective basis for the hypothetical assumptions.

.A16 *Forecast.* The practitioner can form an opinion that the assumptions provide a reasonable basis for the financial forecast if the responsible party represents that the presentation reflects, to the best of its knowledge and belief, its estimate of expected financial position, results of operations, and cash flows for the prospective period, and the practitioner concludes that, based on the practitioner's examination, (*a*) the responsible party has explicitly identified all key factors expected to materially affect the operations of the entity during the prospective period and has developed appropriate assumptions with respect to such factors, and (*b*) the assumptions are suitably supported.

.A17 *Projection.* The practitioner can form an opinion that the assumptions provide a reasonable basis for the financial projection given the hypothetical assumptions if the responsible party represents that the presentation reflects, to the best of its knowledge and belief, expected financial position, results of operations, and cash flows for the prospective period given the hypothetical assumptions, and the practitioner concludes, based on the practitioner's examination, that

a. the responsible party has explicitly identified all key factors that would materially affect the operations of the entity during the prospective period if the hypothetical assumptions were to materialize and has developed appropriate assumptions with respect to such factors, and

b. the other assumptions are suitably supported given the hypothetical assumptions. However, as the number and significance of the hypothetical assumptions increase, the practitioner may not be able to be satisfied about the presentation as a whole by obtaining support for the remaining assumptions.

.A18 A preponderance of information exists for an assumption if the weight of available information supports that assumption. Furthermore, because of the judgments involved in developing assumptions, different people may arrive at somewhat different, but equally reasonable, assumptions based on the same information.

.A19 In evaluating support for assumptions other than hypothetical assumptions in a projection, the practitioner can conclude that they are suitably supported if the preponderance of information supports each significant assumption given the hypothetical assumptions.

.A20 Appropriate considerations for forecasts and projections include whether

a. sufficient pertinent sources of information about the assumptions have been considered. Examples of external sources the practitioner might consider are government publications, industry publications, economic forecasts, existing or proposed legislation, and reports of changing technology. Examples of internal sources are budgets, labor agreements, patents, royalty agreements and records, sales backlog records, debt agreements, and actions of the board of directors involving entity plans.

b. the assumptions are consistent with the sources from which they are derived.

c. the assumptions are consistent with each other.

d. the historical financial information and other data used in developing the assumptions are sufficiently reliable for that purpose. Reliability can be assessed by inquiry and analytical or other procedures, some of which may have been completed in past audits or reviews of the historical financial statements.

e. the historical financial information and other data used in developing the assumptions are comparable over the periods specified or whether the effects of any lack of comparability were considered in developing the assumptions.

f. the logical arguments or theory, considered with the data supporting the assumptions, are reasonable.

.A21 The procedures the practitioner performs to evaluate these assumptions depends on

- the significance of the period,
- whether financial statements have been prepared for the expired period, and
- whether the forecast or projection incorporates the historical results.

.A22 The practitioner may obtain evidence regarding the actual results by applying audit or review procedures to the historical results.

.A23 At some point the historical results become such a large portion of the prospective results that the practitioner might consider it inappropriate to examine the prospective financial information.

.A24 Under the AICPA presentation guidelines, the accounting principles used in a financial projection need not be those expected to be used in the historical financial statements for the prospective period if use of a different principle is consistent with the purpose of the presentation.

.A25 The practitioner's consideration of materiality is discussed in section 205.[10] Materiality is a concept that is judged in light of the expected range of reasonableness of the information; therefore, users would not expect prospective financial information (information about events that have not yet occurred) to be as precise as historical information.

Written Representations in an Examination Engagement (Ref: par. .30)

.A26 Section 205 requires the practitioner to request written representations from the responsible party, including a representation that it has disclosed to the practitioner all known matters contradicting the subject matter.[11] Because no one can know the future, "known matters," in the context of prospective financial information, refers to what the responsible party expects. The required disclosure in the written representations relates to assumptions that are not consistent with the responsible party's expectations, or in the case of a projection, not consistent with the responsible party's expectations given the occurrence of the hypothetical assumptions.

Content of the Practitioner's Examination Report (Ref: par. .32–.34, and .36)

.A27 The list of elements in paragraphs .32–.34 constitutes all the required elements for a practitioner's report on an examination of prospective financial information, including the elements required by section 205.[12] Application guidance regarding the elements of an examination report is included in section 205.[13]

.A28 Example 1 in the exhibit, "Illustrative Practitioner's Examination and Agreed-Upon Procedures Reports Related to Prospective Financial

---

[10] Paragraph .16 of section 205.

[11] Paragraph .50c of section 205.

[12] Paragraphs .63–.66 of section 205.

[13] Paragraphs .A78–.A101 of section 205.

Information," to this section provides an illustration of a practitioner's report on an examination of a financial forecast.

.A29 The requirements in paragraph .32 are applicable to practitioners' reports on prospective financial statements and on partial presentations.

.A30 When the practitioner's examination of prospective financial information is part of a larger engagement, for example, a financial feasibility study or business acquisition study, the practitioner may expand the practitioner's report on the examination of the prospective financial information to describe the entire engagement. Chapter 17, "The Practitioner's Examination Report," of the guide addresses reporting when the examination engagement is part of a larger engagement.

.A31 Section 205 notes that the specified parties may be identified by naming them, referring to a list of them, or identifying them as a class.[14]

.A32 Example 2 in the exhibit to this section provides an illustration of a practitioner's examination report on a financial projection.

.A33 The following is an example of a separate paragraph to be added to the practitioner's report when the practitioner examines prospective financial statements, in this case, a forecast that contains a range:

> As described in the summary of significant assumptions, management of XYZ Company has elected to portray forecasted [*describe the financial statement element or elements for which the expected results of one or more assumptions fall within a range, and identify assumptions expected to fall within a range, for example, revenue in the amounts of $X,XXX and $Y,YYY, which is predicated upon occupancy rates of XX percent and YY percent of available apartments*] rather than as a single point estimate. Accordingly, the accompanying forecast presents forecasted financial position, results of operations, and cash flows [*describe one or more assumptions expected to fall within a range, for example, "at such occupancy rates"*]. However, there is no assurance that the actual results will fall within the range of [*describe one or more assumptions expected to fall within a range, for example, occupancy rates*] presented.

Modified Opinions (Ref: par. .35)

.A34 Because of the nature, sensitivity, and interrelationship of prospective financial information, a user of a practitioner's report may find it difficult to interpret a practitioner's opinion that is qualified because of a misapplication of accounting principles, the failure to disclose a significant assumption, the unreasonableness of the underlying assumptions, an assumption that is not suitably supported, or a scope limitation. Using language such as "except for . . ." in the practitioner's opinion about these items may result in misunderstanding by users of the report. For that reason, when a misapplication of accounting principles, a failure to disclose a significant assumption, an unreasonable assumption, an assumption that is not suitably supported, or a limitation on the scope of the practitioner's examination has led the practitioner to conclude that the practitioner cannot express an unmodified opinion, paragraph .35 identifies the type of modified opinion to be expressed.

.A35 A qualified opinion may result from the failure to disclose matters (other than the significant assumptions) required by AICPA presentation guidelines, for example, the failure to disclose significant accounting policies, which is required by chapter 8 of the guide. (As indicated in paragraph

[14] Paragraph .A98 of section 205.

.35*b*, the failure to disclose significant assumptions would result in an adverse opinion.)

.A36 Section 205 indicates that a qualified opinion is expressed as being "except for the effects of the matter to which the qualification relates.[15] Section 205 also requires that the practitioner's opinion be separated from any paragraphs emphasizing matters related to the subject matter or any other reporting responsibilities.[16] Accordingly, the opinion paragraph would refer to a separate paragraph that describes the matter giving rise to the qualification. The following is an illustration of the separate paragraph that describes the matter giving rise to the qualification and the opinion paragraph when a financial forecast contains a departure from AICPA presentation guidelines:

> The forecast does not disclose significant accounting policies. Disclosure of such policies is required by guidelines for the presentation of a forecast established by the American Institute of Certified Public Accountants.
>
> In our opinion, except for the omission of the disclosures related to significant accounting policies as discussed in the preceding paragraph, the accompanying forecast is presented in accordance with the guidelines for the presentation of a forecast established by the American Institute of Certified Public Accountants, and the underlying assumptions are suitably supported and provide a reasonable basis for management's forecast.

.A37 In an adverse opinion, the practitioner's opinion states that the presentation is not in accordance with the AICPA presentation guidelines and, when applicable, also states that in the practitioner's opinion, the assumptions are not suitably supported and do not provide a reasonable basis for the prospective financial statements. The following are illustrative paragraphs for use when the practitioner expresses an adverse opinion because the financial forecast contains a significant assumption that is unreasonable:

> As discussed under the caption "Sales" in the summary of significant forecast assumptions, the forecasted sales include, among other things, revenue from the Company's federal defense contracts continuing at the current level. The Company's present federal defense contracts will expire in March 20XX. No new contracts have been signed, and no negotiations are underway for new federal defense contracts. Furthermore, the federal government has entered into contracts with another company to supply the items being manufactured under the Company's present contracts.
>
> In our opinion, the accompanying forecast is not presented in accordance with the guidelines for the presentation of a forecast established by the American Institute of Certified Public Accountants because management's assumptions, as discussed in the preceding paragraph, are not suitably supported and do not provide a reasonable basis for management's forecast.

.A38 In a disclaimer of opinion, the paragraph of the practitioner's report that describes the matters giving rise to the opinion modification describes the respects in which the examination did not comply with attestation standards applicable to an examination engagement. The practitioner states that because of the respects in which the examination did not comply with such standards, the scope of the examination was not sufficient to enable the practitioner to express, and the practitioner does not express, an opinion on the presentation of or the assumptions underlying the forecast or projection. The following is an illustrative report on an examination of prospective financial statements, in

---

[15] Paragraph .71 of section 205.

[16] Paragraph .80 of section 205.

this case, a financial forecast, for which a significant assumption could not be evaluated.

> We were engaged to examine the accompanying forecast of XYZ Company, which comprises the forecasted balance sheet as of December 31, 20XX, and the related forecasted statements of income, stockholders' equity, and cash flows for the year then ending. XYZ Company's management is responsible for preparing and presenting the forecast in accordance with the guidelines for the presentation of a forecast established by the American Institute of Certified Public Accountants.
>
> As discussed under the caption, "Income From Investee" in the summary of significant forecast assumptions, the forecast includes income from an equity investee constituting 23 percent of forecasted net income, which is management's estimate of the Company's share of the investee's income to be accrued for 20XX. The investee has not prepared a forecast for the year ending December 31, 20XX, and we were, therefore, unable to obtain suitable support for this assumption.
>
> Because, as described in the preceding paragraph, we are unable to evaluate management's assumption regarding income from an equity investee and other assumptions that depend thereon, the scope of our work was not sufficient to express, and we do not express, an opinion with respect to the presentation of or the assumptions underlying the accompanying forecast.
>
> We have no responsibility to update this report for events and circumstances occurring after the date of this report.

Partial Presentations (Ref: par. .36)

.A39 Chapter 23 of the guide addresses partial presentations.

.A40 The practitioner's procedures on a partial presentation may be affected by the nature of the information presented. Many elements of prospective financial statements are interrelated. The nature and extent of the procedures performed in an examination of some partial presentations may need to be similar to the procedures performed in an examination of a full presentation of prospective financial statements. For example, the scope of a practitioner's procedures when the practitioner examines forecasted results of operations (a partial presentation) would likely be similar to that of procedures used for the examination of prospective financial statements because the practitioner would most likely need to consider the interrelationships of all accounts in the examination of results of operations.

Content of the Practitioner's Agreed-Upon Procedures Report (Ref: par. .39)

.A41 The list of elements in paragraph .39 constitutes all the required elements for a practitioner's report on the application of agreed-upon procedures to a forecast or projection, including the elements required by section 215.[17] Application guidance regarding the elements of an agreed-upon procedures report is included in section 215.[18]

.A42 Example 3 in the exhibit to this section provides an illustration of a practitioner's agreed-upon procedures report.

---

[17] Paragraph .35 of section 215, *Agreed-Upon Procedures Engagements*

[18] Paragraphs .A35–.A41 of section 215.

.A43

Exhibit—Illustrative Practitioner's Examination and Agreed-Upon Procedures Reports Related to Prospective Financial Information

Example 1: Practitioner's Examination Report on a Financial Forecast

The following is an illustrative practitioner's report for an examination of a financial forecast that does not contain a range.

Independent Accountant's Report

[*Appropriate Addressee*]

We have examined the accompanying forecast of XYZ Company, which comprises [*identify the statements, for example, the forecasted balance sheet as of December 31, 20XX, and the related forecasted statements of income, stockholders' equity, and cash flows for the year then ending*], based on the guidelines for the presentation of a forecast established by the American Institute of Certified Public Accountants. XYZ Company's management[1] is responsible for preparing and presenting the forecast in accordance with the guidelines for the presentation of a forecast established by the American Institute of Certified Public Accountants.[2] Our responsibility is to express an opinion on the forecast based on our examination.

Our examination was conducted in accordance with attestation standards established by the American Institute of Certified Public Accountants. Those standards require that we plan and perform the examination to obtain reasonable assurance about whether the forecast is presented in accordance with the guidelines for the presentation of a forecast established by the American Institute of Certified Public Accountants, in all material respects. An examination involves performing procedures to obtain evidence about the forecast. The nature, timing, and extent of the procedures selected depend on our judgment, including an assessment of the risks of material misstatement of the forecast, whether due to fraud or error. We believe that the evidence we obtained is sufficient and appropriate to provide a reasonable basis for our opinion.

In our opinion, the accompanying forecast is presented, in all material respects, in accordance with the guidelines for the presentation of a forecast established by the American Institute of Certified Public Accountants, and the underlying assumptions are suitably supported and provide a reasonable basis for management's forecast.

There will usually be differences between the forecasted and actual results because events and circumstances frequently do not occur as expected, and those differences may be material. We have no responsibility to update this report for events and circumstances occurring after the date of this report.

[*Practitioner's signature*]
[*Practitioner's city and state*]
[*Date of practitioner's report*]

---

[1] If the responsible party is other than management, the references to management in this illustrative practitioner's report would be changed to refer to the party who has responsibility for the assumptions.

[2] When the presentation is summarized as illustrated in exhibit 9-2 of the AICPA Guide *Prospective Financial Information*, this sentence might read, "We have examined the accompanying summarized forecast of XYZ Company as of December 31, 20XX, and for the year then ending..."

Example 2: Practitioner's Examination Report on a Financial Projection

The following is an illustrative practitioner's report for an examination of a financial projection that does not contain a range.

Independent Accountant's Report

[*Appropriate Addressee*]

We have examined the accompanying projection of XYZ Company, which comprises [*identify the statements, for example, the projected balance sheet as of December 31, 20XX, and the related projected statements of income, stockholders' equity, and cash flows for the year then ending*] based on the guidelines for the presentation of a projection established by the American Institute of Certified Public Accountants.[3] XYZ Company's management[4] is responsible for preparing and presenting the projection based on [*identify the hypothetical assumption, for example, the granting of the requested loan as described in the summary of significant assumptions*] in accordance with the guidelines for the presentation of a projection established by the American Institute of Certified Public Accountants. The projection was prepared for [*describe the special purpose, for example, the purpose of negotiating a loan to expand XYZ Company's plant*]. Our responsibility is to express an opinion on the projection based on our examination.

Our examination was conducted in accordance with attestation standards established by the American Institute of Certified Public Accountants. Those standards require that we plan and perform the examination to obtain reasonable assurance about whether the projection is presented in accordance with the guidelines for the presentation of a projection established by the American Institute of Certified Public Accountants, in all material respects. An examination involves performing procedures to obtain evidence about the projection. The nature, timing, and extent of the procedures selected depend on our judgment, including an assessment of the risks of material misstatement of the projection, whether due to fraud or error. We believe that the evidence we obtained is sufficient and appropriate to provide a reasonable basis for our opinion.

In our opinion, [*describe the hypothetical assumption(s), for example, assuming the granting of the requested loan for the purpose of expanding XYZ Company's plant as described in the summary of significant assumptions*] the projection referred to above is presented, in all material respects, in accordance with the guidelines for the presentation of a projection established by the American Institute of Certified Public Accountants, and the underlying assumptions are suitably supported and provide a reasonable basis for management's projection given the hypothetical assumption(s).

Even if [*identify the hypothetical assumption, for example, the loan is granted and the plant is expanded,*], there will usually be differences between the projected and actual results because events and circumstances frequently do not occur as expected, and those differences may be material. We have no responsibility to update this report for events and circumstances occurring after the date of this report.

---

[3] When the presentation is summarized as illustrated in exhibit 9-2 of the AICPA Guide *Prospective Financial Information*, this sentence might read, "We have examined the accompanying summarized projection of XYZ Company as of December 31, 20XX, and for the year then ending...."

[4] If the responsible party is other than management, the references to management in this illustrative practitioner's report would be changed to refer to the party who has responsibility for the assumptions.

The accompanying projection and this report are intended solely for the information and use of [*identify specified parties, for example, XYZ Company and DEF National Bank*], and are not intended to be and should not be used by anyone other than these specified parties.

[*Practitioner's signature*]
[*Practitioner's city and state*]
[*Date of practitioner's report*]

Example 3: Practitioner's Agreed-Upon Procedures Report Related to a Financial Forecast

The following is an illustrative practitioner's report for an engagement to apply agreed-upon procedures to a financial forecast.

Independent Accountant's Agreed-Upon Procedures Report

[*Appropriate Addressee*]

We have performed the procedures enumerated below, which were agreed to by [*identify the specified parties, for example, the boards of directors of XYZ Corporation and ABC Company*], on [*identify the statements, for example, the forecasted balance sheet as of December 31, 20XX and the related forecasted statements of income, stockholders' equity, and cash flows of DEF Company, a subsidiary of ABC Company, for the year then ending*]. DEF Company's management[5] is responsible for preparing and presenting the forecast in accordance with the guidelines for the presentation of a forecast established by the American Institute of Certified Public Accountants. The sufficiency of these procedures is solely the responsibility of those parties specified in this report. Consequently, we make no representation regarding the sufficiency of the procedures enumerated below either for the purpose for which this report has been requested or for any other purpose.

[*Include paragraphs to enumerate procedures and findings.*]

This agreed-upon procedures engagement was conducted in accordance with attestation standards established by the American Institute of Certified Public Accountants. We were not engaged to and did not conduct an examination or review, the objective of which would be the expression of an opinion or conclusion, respectively, about whether the forecast is presented in accordance with the guidelines for the presentation of a forecast established by the American Institute of Certified Public Accountants or whether the underlying assumptions are suitably supported or provide a reasonable basis for management's forecast. Accordingly, we do not express such an opinion or conclusion. Had we performed additional procedures, other matters might have come to our attention that would have been reported to you.

There will usually be differences between the forecasted and actual results because events and circumstances frequently do not occur as expected, and those differences may be material. We have no responsibility to update this report for events and circumstances occurring after the date of this report.

This report is intended solely for the information and use of [*identify the specified parties, for example, the boards of directors of ABC Company and XYZ*

[5] If the responsible party is other than management, the references to management in this illustrative report would be changed to refer to the party who has responsibility for the assumptions.

Corporation], and is not intended to be, and should not be, used by anyone other than these specified parties.

[*Practitioner's signature*]
[*Practitioner's city and state*]
[*Date of practitioner's report*]

AT-C Section 310*

Reporting on Pro Forma Financial Information

Source: SSAE No. 18.

Effective for practitioners' examination and review reports on pro forma financial information dated on or after May 1, 2017.

Introduction

.01 This section contains performance and reporting requirements and application guidance for a practitioner examining or reviewing pro forma financial information.

.02 This section does not apply when

- a practitioner is performing agreed-upon procedures related to pro forma financial information. Section 105, *Concepts Common to All Attestation Engagements*, and section 215, *Agreed-Upon Procedures Engagements*, are applicable to such engagements.
- certain requesting parties request a comfort letter or ask a practitioner to perform procedures on pro forma financial information in connection with an offering. AU-C section 920, *Letters for Underwriters and Certain Other Requesting Parties*, is applicable to such engagements.
- pro forma financial information is presented outside the basic financial statements but within the same document, and the practitioner is not engaged to report on the pro forma financial information. AU-C section 720, *Other Information in Documents Containing Audited Financial Statements*, and AU-C section 925, *Filings With the U.S. Securities and Exchange Commission Under the Securities Act of 1933*, may be applicable to such engagements.
- for purposes of a more meaningful presentation, a transaction consummated after the balance sheet date is reflected in the historical financial statements (such as a revision of debt maturities or a revision of earnings per share calculations for a stock split).
- the applicable financial reporting framework requires the presentation of pro forma financial information in the financial statements or the accompanying notes. For example, generally accepted accounting principles require pro forma financial information in FASB *Accounting Standards Codification* (ASC) 805, *Business Combinations*, FASB ASC 250, *Accounting Changes and Error Corrections*, or, in some cases, pro forma financial information relating to subsequent events.

.03 In addition to complying with this section, a practitioner is required to comply with section 105 and either section 205, *Examination Engagements*,

---

* This section contains an "AT-C" identifier, instead of an "AT" identifier, to avoid confusion with references to existing "AT" sections, which remain effective through April 2017.

for examinations of pro forma financial information or section 210, *Review Engagements*, for reviews of pro forma financial information. In some cases, this section repeats or refers to requirements found in sections 105, 205, and 210 when describing those requirements in the context of an examination or review of pro forma financial information. Although not all the requirements in sections 105, 205, and 210 are repeated or referred to in this section, the practitioner is responsible for complying with all the requirements in sections 105, 205, and 210, as applicable.

Effective Date

.04 This section is effective for practitioners' examination and review reports on pro forma financial information dated on or after May 1, 2017.

Objectives of an Examination Engagement

.05 In conducting an examination of pro forma financial information, the objectives of the practitioner are to

a. obtain reasonable assurance about whether, in accordance with (or based on) the criteria

   i. management's assumptions provide a reasonable basis for presenting the significant effects directly attributable to the underlying transaction (or event), (Ref: par. .A1)

   ii. and, in all material respects

      (1) the related pro forma adjustments give appropriate effect to those assumptions, and

      (2) the pro forma amounts reflect the proper application of those adjustments to the historical financial statement amounts.

b. express an opinion in a written report on the matters in paragraph .05*a*.

Objectives of a Review Engagement

.06 In conducting a review of pro forma financial information, the objectives of the practitioner are to

a. obtain limited assurance about whether, in accordance with (or based on) the criteria, any material modifications should be made to

   i. management's assumptions in order for them to provide a reasonable basis for presenting the significant effects directly attributable to the underlying transaction (or event),

   ii. the related pro forma adjustments in order for them to give appropriate effect to those assumptions, or

   iii. the pro forma amounts in order for them to reflect the proper application of those adjustments to the historical financial statement amounts.

b. express a conclusion in a written report on the matters in paragraph .06*a*.

Definitions

.07 For the purposes of this section, the following terms have the meanings attributed as follows: (Ref: par. .A2–.A5)

Criteria for the preparation of pro forma financial information. The basis disclosed in the pro forma financial information that management used to develop the pro forma financial information, including the assumptions underlying the pro forma financial information. Paragraph .11 contains the attributes of suitable criteria for an examination or review of pro forma financial information.

Pro forma financial information. A presentation that shows what the significant effects on historical financial information might have been had a consummated or proposed transaction (or event) occurred at an earlier date.

Requirements

Preconditions for an Examination or Review Engagement

.08 In order to accept an attestation engagement to examine or review pro forma financial information, in addition to the preconditions for an attestation engagement included in sections 105 and 205, the practitioner[1]

a. should determine that the document that contains the pro forma financial information includes historical financial statements of the entity for the most recent year (or for the preceding year if financial statements for the most recent year are not yet available) or that such financial statements are readily available and, if pro forma financial information is presented for an interim period, the document also either includes historical interim financial information for that period (which may be presented in condensed form) or such interim information is readily available. In the case of a business combination, the document includes the relevant historical financial information for the significant constituent parts of the combined entity. (Ref: par. .A6–.A7)

b. should determine that the historical financial statements of the entity (or in the case of a business combination, of each significant constituent part of the combined entity) on which the pro forma financial information is based, in the case of (Ref: par. .A7–.A8)

i. an examination of pro forma financial information, have been audited, or

ii. a review of pro forma financial information, have been audited or reviewed, (Ref: par. .A8)

and the audit report (or the review report, if issued) is included in the document containing the pro forma financial information (or is readily available) to the extent that the historical financial information is included in the document pursuant to paragraph .08*a*.

---

[1] Paragraphs .24–.28 of section 105, *Concepts Common to All Attestation Engagements*, and paragraph .06 of section 205, *Examination Engagements*.

c. will be able to obtain an appropriate level of knowledge of the accounting and financial reporting practices of the entity (or in the case of a business combination, of each significant constituent part of the combined entity) that will enable the practitioner to perform the procedures necessary to report on the pro forma financial information.

.09 The level of service provided by the practitioner on the pro forma financial information should not exceed that provided on the related historical financial statements. An examination can be performed on pro forma financial information only if the related historical financial statements were audited. A review can be performed on pro forma financial information only if the related historical financial statements were audited or reviewed. In the case of a business combination, the level of service provided by the practitioner on the pro forma financial information should not exceed the lowest level of service provided on the underlying historical financial statements of any significant constituent part of the combined entity. (Ref: par. .A9)

Requesting a Written Assertion

.10 The practitioner should request from management a written assertion. If management refuses to provide a written assertion, the practitioner should withdraw from the engagement when withdrawal is possible under applicable law or regulation (Ref: par. .A10)

Assessing the Suitability of the Criteria

.11 As required by section 105, the practitioner should determine whether management has used suitable criteria in preparing and presenting the pro forma financial information.[2] In assessing the suitability of the criteria, the practitioner should determine whether the criteria include, at a minimum, that

a. the financial information be extracted from audited or reviewed historical financial statements;

b. the pro forma adjustments be

   i. directly attributable to the transaction (or event),

   ii. factually supportable (Ref: par. .A11),

   iii. consistent with the entity's applicable financial reporting framework and its accounting policies under that framework; and

c. the pro forma financial information be appropriately presented and include disclosures that enable intended users to understand the information conveyed.

Understanding the Entity's Accounting and Financial Reporting Policies

.12 The practitioner who is reporting on the pro forma financial information should have or obtain an appropriate level of knowledge of the accounting and financial reporting practices of the entity (or, in the case of a business combination, each significant constituent part of the combined entity). (Ref: par. .A12)

[2] Paragraph .25*b*(ii) of section 105.

Examination and Review Procedures

.13 The procedures the practitioner should apply to the assumptions and pro forma adjustments for either an examination or a review engagement are as follows:

a. Obtain an understanding of the underlying transaction (or event). (Ref: par. .A13)

b. Obtain an understanding of the accounting and financial reporting practices of each significant constituent part of the combined entity in a business combination that will enable the practitioner to perform the required procedures. If another practitioner has performed an audit or a review of the most recent annual or interim period for which the pro forma financial information is presented (or the most recent annual or interim period of a significant constituent part of the combined entity), the need, by a practitioner reporting on the pro forma financial information, for an understanding of such entity's accounting and financial reporting practices is not diminished. In such circumstances, the practitioner should consider whether the practitioner can acquire sufficient knowledge of these matters to perform the procedures necessary to report on the pro forma financial information.

c. Discuss with management their assumptions regarding the effects of the transaction (or event).

d. Evaluate whether pro forma adjustments are included for all significant effects directly attributable to the transaction (or event).

e. Obtain sufficient evidence in support of such adjustments. (Ref: par. .A14)

f. Evaluate whether management's assumptions that underlie the pro forma adjustments are presented in a sufficiently clear and comprehensive manner.

g. Evaluate whether the pro forma adjustments are consistent with each other and with the data used to develop them.

h. Evaluate whether computations of pro forma adjustments are mathematically correct and whether the pro forma column reflects the proper application of those adjustments to the historical financial statements.

i. Read the pro forma financial information and evaluate whether

i. the underlying transaction (or event), the pro forma adjustments, the significant assumptions, and the significant uncertainties, if any, about those assumptions have been appropriately described.

ii. the source of the historical financial information on which the pro forma financial information is based has been appropriately identified.

Written Representations in an Examination and Review Engagement

.14 In addition to the written representations from management required by section 205 for an examination engagement or by section 210 for a review engagement, the practitioner should request written representations from management that[3]

a. it is responsible for the assumptions used in determining the pro forma adjustments;

b. the assumptions are factually supportable;

c. the assumptions provide a reasonable basis for presenting the significant effects directly attributable to the underlying transaction (or event); the related pro forma adjustments give appropriate effect to those assumptions; and the pro forma amounts reflect the proper application of those adjustments to the historical financial statement amounts

d. the pro forma adjustments are consistent with the entity's applicable financial reporting framework and its accounting policies under that framework

e. the pro forma financial information is appropriately presented and discloses the significant effects directly attributable to the transaction (or event). (See paragraph .11*c*.)

.15 In an examination or a review engagement, the practitioner should request from management the written representations required by section 205 or section 210, as applicable, and paragraph .14 of this section, even if the engaging party is not management. The alternative to obtaining the required written representations provided for in sections 205 and 210 is not permitted in an engagement to examine or review pro forma financial information.[4] Management's refusal to furnish the written representations required by section 205 and paragraph .14 of this section constitutes a limitation on the scope of the examination engagement sufficient to preclude an unmodified opinion and may be sufficient to cause the practitioner to withdraw from the examination engagement, when withdrawal is possible under applicable laws and regulations.[5] Management's refusal to furnish the written representations required by section 210 and paragraph .14 of this section constitutes a limitation on the scope of the review engagement sufficient to cause the practitioner to withdraw from the review engagement.[6]

Reporting

.16 The practitioner's report on pro forma financial information may be added to the practitioner's report on historical financial information, or it may appear separately. If the reports are combined and the date of completion of the procedures for the examination or review of the pro forma financial information is after the date the practitioner obtained the evidence necessary to issue a report on the audit or review of the historical financial information, the combined report should be dual-dated. (Ref: par. .A15)

Content of the Practitioner's Examination Report

.17 The practitioner's examination report on pro forma financial information should include the following, unless the practitioner is disclaiming an opinion, in which case, items .17*j* and .17*k* should be omitted: (Ref: par. .A16)

---

[3] Paragraph .50 of section 205 and paragraph .33 of section 210, *Review Engagements*.

[4] Paragraph .51 of section 205 and paragraph .34 of section 210.

[5] Paragraphs .50, .55, and .A64 of section 205.

[6] Paragraphs .33–.38c of section 210.

a. A title that includes the word *independent.*

b. An appropriate addressee as required by the circumstances of the engagement.

c. A reference to the pro forma adjustments included in the pro forma financial information.

d. A reference to management's description of the transaction (or event) to which the pro forma adjustments give effect. (The description is included in the pro forma financial information.)

e. An identification or description of the pro forma financial information being reported on, including the point in time or period of time to which the measurement or evaluation of the pro forma financial information relates.

f. An identification of the criteria against which the pro forma financial information was measured or evaluated.

g. A reference to the financial statements from which the historical financial information is derived, a statement that such financial statements were audited, and, if applicable, whether the financial statements were audited by another auditor. (The report on pro forma financial information should refer to any modification in the auditor's report on the historical financial statements. In the case of a business combination, this paragraph applies to each significant constituent part of the combined entity.) (Ref: par. .A17)

h. A statement that the pro forma adjustments are based on management's assumptions.

i. A statement that identifies

  i. management and its responsibility for the pro forma financial information.

  ii. the practitioner's responsibility to express an opinion on the pro forma financial information based on the practitioner's examination.

j. A statement that

  i. the practitioner's examination was conducted in accordance with attestation standards established by the American Institute of Certified Public Accountants.

  ii. those standards require that the practitioner plan and perform the examination to obtain reasonable assurance about whether, in accordance with (or based on) the criteria

    (1) management's assumptions provide a reasonable basis for presenting the significant effects directly attributable to the underlying transaction (or event),

    (2) and, in all material respects,

      (a) the related pro forma adjustments give appropriate effect to those assumptions, and

      (b) the pro forma amounts reflect the proper application of those adjustments to the historical financial statement amounts.

  iii. an examination involves performing procedures to obtain evidence about

(1) management's assumptions, (Ref: par. .A18)

(2) the related pro forma adjustments, and

(3) the pro forma amounts.

iv. the practitioner believes that the evidence the practitioner obtained is sufficient and appropriate to provide a reasonable basis for the practitioner's opinion.

k. A description of the objectives and limitations of pro forma financial information

l. The practitioner's opinion about whether, in accordance with (or based on) the criteria

i. management's assumptions provide a reasonable basis for presenting the significant effects directly attributable to the transaction (or event), (Ref: par. .A19)

ii. and, in all material respects

(1) the related pro forma adjustments give appropriate effect to those assumptions, and

(2) the pro forma amounts reflect the proper application of those adjustments to the historical financial statement amounts.

m. When the circumstances identified in section 205 are applicable, an alert, in a separate paragraph, that restricts the use of the report or describes the purpose of the report, as applicable.[7]

n. The manual or printed signature of the practitioner's firm.

o. The city and state where the practitioner practices.

p. The date of the report. (The report should be dated no earlier than the date on which the practitioner has obtained sufficient appropriate evidence on which to base the practitioner's opinion, including evidence that

i. the attestation documentation has been reviewed,

ii. the pro forma financial information has been prepared, and

iii. management has provided a written assertion.)

Content of the Practitioner's Review Report

.18 The practitioner's review report on pro forma financial information should include the following: (Ref: par. .A20)

a. A title that includes the word *independent.*

b. An appropriate addressee as required by the circumstances of the engagement.

c. A reference to the pro forma adjustments included in the pro forma financial information.

d. A reference to management's description of the transaction (or event) to which the pro forma adjustments give effect. (The description is included in the pro forma financial information.)

[7] Paragraph .64 of section 205.

e. An identification or description of the pro forma financial information being reported on, including the point in time or period of time to which the measurement or evaluation of the pro forma financial information relates.

f. An identification of the criteria against which the pro forma financial information was measured or evaluated.

g. A reference to the financial statements from which the historical financial information is derived and (Ref: par. .A21)

   i. a statement that such financial statements were audited or reviewed, as applicable.

   ii. if the practitioner issued a review report on the historical financial statements, a statement that a review report was issued, and, if applicable, whether the financial statements were reviewed by another accountant. (The report on pro forma financial information should refer to any modification in the accountant's report on the historical financial information. In the case of a business combination, this paragraph applies to each significant constituent part of the combined entity.)

h. A statement that the pro forma adjustments are based on management's assumptions.

i. A statement that identifies

   i. management and its responsibility for the pro forma financial information.

   ii. the practitioner's responsibility to express a conclusion on the pro forma financial information based on the practitioner's review.

j. A statement that

   i. the practitioner's review was conducted in accordance with attestation standards established by the American Institute of Certified Public Accountants.

   ii. those standards require that the practitioner plan and perform the review to obtain limited assurance about whether, in accordance with (or based on) the criteria, any material modifications should be made to

      (1) management's assumptions in order for them to provide a reasonable basis for presenting the significant effects directly attributable to the underlying transaction (or event), (Ref: par. .A22)

      (2) the related pro forma adjustments in order for them to give appropriate effect to those assumptions, or

      (3) the pro forma amounts in order for them to reflect the proper application of those adjustments to the historical financial statement amounts.

   iii. a review is substantially less in scope than an examination, the objective of which is to obtain reasonable assurance about whether, in accordance with (or based on) the criteria, management's assumptions provide a reasonable basis for presenting the significant effects directly attributable to the underlying transaction (or event), and, in all material respects, the related pro forma adjustments give appropriate effect to those assumptions, and the pro forma amounts reflect the proper application of those adjustments to the historical financial statement amounts in order to express an opinion. Accordingly, the practitioner does not express such an opinion.

iv. the practitioner believes that the practitioner's review provides a reasonable basis for the practitioner's conclusion.

k. a description of the objectives and limitations of pro forma financial information.

l. the practitioner's conclusion about whether, in accordance with (or based on) the review and based on the criteria, the practitioner is aware of any material modifications that should be made to

i. management's assumptions in order for them to provide a reasonable basis for presenting the significant effects directly attributable to the underlying transaction (or event), (Ref: par. .A23)

ii. the related pro forma adjustments in order for them to give appropriate effect to those assumptions, or

iii. the pro forma amounts in order for them to reflect the proper application of those adjustments to the historical financial statement amounts.

m. When the circumstances identified in section 210 are applicable, an alert, in a separate paragraph, that restricts the use of the report or describes the purpose of the report, as applicable.[8]

n. The manual or printed signature of the practitioner's firm.

o. The city and state where the practitioner practices.

p. The date of the report. (The report should be dated no earlier than the date on which the practitioner has obtained sufficient appropriate review evidence on which to base the practitioner's conclusion, including evidence that

i. the attestation documentation has been reviewed,

ii. the pro forma financial information has been prepared, and

iii. management has provided a written assertion.)

Application and Other Explanatory Material

Objectives of an Examination Engagement (Ref: par. .05a[i])

.A1 For the purposes of this section, the responsible party is management of the entity for which the practitioner is reporting on pro forma financial information.

Definitions (Ref: par. .07)

Pro Forma Financial Information

.A2 Pro forma financial information is developed by applying pro forma adjustments to historical financial information. Appropriate pro forma

[8] Paragraph .47c of section 210.

adjustments are based on management's assumptions, give effect to all significant effects directly attributable to the transaction (or event), and are stated on a basis consistent with the financial reporting framework of the reporting entity and its accounting policies under that framework.

.A3 Pro forma financial information is commonly used to show the effects of transactions such as the following:

- Business combination
- Change in capitalization
- Disposition of a significant portion of the business
- Change in the form of business organization or status as an autonomous entity
- Proposed sale of securities and the application of the proceeds

.A4 Adequately disclosed pro forma financial information

- is labeled as such to distinguish it from historical financial information.
- describes the transaction (or event) that is reflected in the pro forma financial information, the date on which the transaction (or event) is assumed to occur, the financial reporting framework of the historical financial statements, the source of the historical financial information on which it is based, the significant assumptions used to develop the pro forma adjustments, and any significant uncertainties about those assumptions.
- indicates that the pro forma financial information should be read in conjunction with related historical financial information and that the pro forma financial information is not necessarily indicative of the results (such as financial position and results of operations, as applicable) that would have been attained had the transaction (or event) actually taken place earlier.

.A5 Article 11 of Regulation S-X provides further guidance on the presentation of pro forma financial information included in filings with the SEC.

Preconditions for an Examination or Review Engagement (Ref: par. .08–.09)

.A6 For pro forma financial information included in an SEC Form 8-K, historical financial information previously included in an SEC filing would meet this requirement. Interim historical financial information may be presented as a column in the pro forma financial information.

.A7 Historical financial statements, historical interim financial information, and audit reports are deemed to be *readily available* if they are obtainable by a third-party user without any further action by the entity. (For example, historical interim financial information on an entity's website may be considered readily available, but being available upon request is not considered readily available.)

.A8 For issuers, the review may be as defined in AU section 722, *Interim Financial Information*, of the PCAOB's interim auditing standards. For nonissuers, the review may be an interim or annual review as described in AR-C section 90, *Review of Financial Statements*, or an interim review as discussed in AU-C section 930, *Interim Financial Information*, when the review of interim financial information meets the provisions of that section.[9] Although AU section 722 does not require an accountant to issue a written report on a review of interim financial information, the SEC requires the report to be filed if, in any filing, the entity states that the interim financial information has been reviewed by an independent public accountant.[10]

.A9 If the underlying historical financial statements of the entity (or, in the case of a business combination, of each significant constituent part of the combined entity) have been audited at year-end and reviewed at an interim date, the practitioner may perform an examination or a review of the pro forma financial information at year-end, but is limited to performing a review of the pro forma financial information at the interim date.

Requesting a Written Assertion (Ref: par. .10)

.A10 Paragraph .10 applies regardless of whether the responsible party is the engaging party.

Assessing the Suitability of the Criteria (Ref: par. .11b[ii])

.A11 Management is responsible for having factually supportable pro forma adjustments. The pro forma adjustments are factually supportable if the preponderance of the information supports each significant assumption underlying the adjustments.

Understanding the Entity's Accounting and Financial Reporting Policies (Ref: par. .12)

.A12 Procedures to obtain knowledge of each significant constituent part of the combined entity in a business combination may include communicating with other practitioners who have audited or reviewed the historical financial information on which the pro forma financial information is based. Matters that may be considered include

- accounting principles and financial reporting practices followed;
- transactions between the entities;
- material contingencies; and
- relevant industry, legal and regulatory, and other external factors pertaining to the entity and any acquiree or divestee.

Examination and Review Procedures (Ref: par. .13a and e)

.A13 An understanding of the underlying transaction (or event) may be obtained, for example, by reading relevant contracts and minutes of meetings of the board of directors and by making inquiries of appropriate officials of the entity, and, if considered necessary in the circumstances, of the entity acquired or to be acquired.

.A14 The evidence required to support the level of assurance obtained is a matter of professional judgment. Sections 205 and 210 provide guidance about the evidence to be obtained in examination and review engagements, respectively. Examples of evidence that the practitioner might consider obtaining are

---

[9] Paragraph .04 of AR-C section 90, *Review of Financial Statements*.

[10] Paragraph .03 of AU section 722, *Interim Financial Information*.

purchase, merger or exchange agreements, appraisal reports, debt agreements, employment agreements, actions of the board of directors, and existing or proposed legislation or regulatory actions.

Reporting (Ref: par. .16)

.A15 The following is an example of how the report would be dual dated:

February 15, 20X2, except for the paragraphs regarding pro forma financial information for which the date is March 20, 20X2.

Content of the Practitioner's Examination Report (Ref: par. .17)

.A16 The list of elements in paragraph .17 constitutes all the required elements for a practitioner's examination report on pro forma financial information, including the elements required by section 205.[11] Application guidance regarding the elements of an examination report is included in section 205.[12]

Reference to Financial Statements From Which Historical Financial Information is Derived (Ref: par. .17g)

.A17 If the historical financial information was previously included in an SEC filing, the practitioner's report would be modified to indicate that the historical financial statements are "incorporated by reference."

Statement That Examination Involves Performing Procedures to Obtain Evidence About Management's Assumptions (Ref: par. .17j[iii][1])

.A18 Because a business combination accounted for in a manner similar to a pooling-of-interests combines the historical amounts of the combined entities retroactively, pro forma adjustments for a transaction that is not yet reflected in the historical financial statements or a proposed transaction generally affect only the equity section of the pro forma condensed balance sheet. Such business combinations would not ordinarily involve a choice of assumptions by management. Accordingly, a practitioner's report on a business combination that will be accounted for in a manner similar to a pooling-of-interests need not address management's assumptions unless the pro forma financial information includes adjustments to conform the accounting principles of the combining entities or gives effect to other transactions (for example, a new contractual arrangement or reduction in interest expense attributable to repayment of debt).

Opinion About Management's Assumptions (Ref: par. .17l[i])

.A19 Uncertainty about whether the transaction (or event) will be consummated would not ordinarily require a modification of the practitioner's report.

Content of the Practitioner's Review Report (Ref: par. .18)

.A20 The list of elements in paragraph .18 constitutes all the required elements for a practitioner's report on a review of pro forma financial information, including the elements required by section 210.[13] Application guidance regarding the elements of a review report is included in section 210.[14]

---

[11] Paragraphs .63–.66 of section 205.

[12] Paragraphs .A78–.A101 of section 205.

[13] Paragraphs .46–.49 of section 210.

[14] Paragraphs .A61–.A80 of section 210.

Reference to Financial Statements From Which Historical Financial Information is Derived (Ref: par. .18g)

.A21 If the historical financial information was previously included in an SEC filing, the practitioner's report would be modified to indicate that the historical financial statements are "incorporated by reference."

Statement That the Practitioner Plans and Performs Review to Obtain Limited Assurance About Management's Assumptions (Ref: par. .18j[ii][1])

.A22 Because a business combination accounted for in a manner similar to a pooling-of-interests combines the historical amounts of the combined entities retroactively, pro forma adjustments for a transaction that is not yet reflected in the historical financial statements or a proposed transaction generally affect only the equity section of the pro forma condensed balance sheet. Such business combinations would not ordinarily involve a choice of assumptions by management. Accordingly, a practitioner's report on a business combination that will be accounted for in a manner similar to a pooling-of-interests need not address management's assumptions unless the pro forma financial information includes adjustments to conform the accounting principles of the combining entities or gives effect to other transactions (for example, a new contractual arrangement or reduction in interest expense attributable to a repayment of debt).

Conclusion About Management's Assumptions (Ref: par. .18l[i])

.A23 Uncertainty about whether the transaction (or event) will be consummated would not ordinarily require a modification of the practitioner's report.

.A24

Exhibit—Illustrative Practitioner's Reports for Examinations and Reviews of Pro Forma Financial Information

The illustrative practitioner's examination reports in this exhibit (examples 1, 3, 4, 5, and 6) meet the reporting requirements of section 205, *Examination Engagements*, and of paragraph .17 of this section.[1] A practitioner may use alternative language in drafting an examination report, provided that the language meets the applicable requirements of section 205 and paragraph .17 of this section.[2]

The illustrative practitioner's review reports in this exhibit (examples 2 and 3) meet the applicable reporting requirements of section 210, *Review Engagements*, and of paragraph .18 of this section.[3] A practitioner may use alternative language in drafting a review report, provided that the language meets the applicable requirements of section 210 and paragraph .18 of this section.[4]

The language in these illustrative examination and review reports assume that one column of pro forma financial information is presented without presenting separate columns of historical financial information and pro forma adjustments.

Example 1: Practitioner's Examination Report on Pro Forma Financial Information: Unmodified Opinion

Independent Accountant's Report

[*Appropriate Addressee*]

We have examined the pro forma adjustments giving effect to the underlying transaction (or event) described in Note 1 and the application of those adjustments to the historical amounts in the accompanying pro forma condensed balance sheet of X Company as of December 31, 20X1, and the related pro forma condensed statement of income for the year then ended (pro forma financial information), based on the criteria in Note 1. The historical condensed financial statements are derived from the historical financial statements of X Company, which were audited by us, and of Y Company, which were audited by other accountants, appearing elsewhere herein [*or "and are readily available"*]. The pro forma adjustments are based on management's assumptions described in Note 1. X Company's management is responsible for the pro forma financial information. Our responsibility is to express an opinion on the pro forma financial information based on our examination.

Our examination was conducted in accordance with attestation standards established by the American Institute of Certified Public Accountants. Those standards require that we plan and perform the examination to obtain reasonable assurance about whether, based on the criteria in Note 1, management's assumptions provide a reasonable basis for presenting the significant effects directly attributable to the underlying transaction (or event), and, in all material respects, the related pro forma adjustments give appropriate effect to

---

1 Paragraphs .61–.84 of section 205, *Examination Engagements*.

2 Paragraphs .61–.84 of section 205.

3 Paragraphs .44–.60 of section 210, *Review Engagements*.

4 See footnote 3.

those assumptions, and the pro forma amounts reflect the proper application of those adjustments to the historical financial statement amounts. An examination involves performing procedures to obtain evidence about management's assumptions, the related pro forma adjustments, and the pro forma amounts in the pro forma condensed balance sheet of X Company as of December 31, 20X1, and the related pro forma condensed statement of income for the year then ended. The nature, timing, and extent of the procedures selected depend on our judgment, including an assessment of the risks of material misstatement of the pro forma financial information, whether due to fraud or error. We believe that the evidence we obtained is sufficient and appropriate to provide a reasonable basis for our opinion.

The objective of this pro forma financial information is to show what the significant effects on the historical financial information might have been had the underlying transaction (or event) occurred at an earlier date. However, the pro forma condensed financial statements are not necessarily indicative of the results of operations or related effects on financial position that would have been attained had the above-mentioned transaction (or event) actually occurred at such earlier date.

In our opinion, based on the criteria in Note 1, management's assumptions provide a reasonable basis for presenting the significant effects directly attributable to the above-mentioned transaction (or event) described in Note 1, and, in all material respects, the related pro forma adjustments give appropriate effect to those assumptions, and the pro forma amounts reflect the proper application of those adjustments to the historical financial statement amounts in the pro forma condensed balance sheet of X Company as of December 31, 20X1, and the related pro forma condensed statement of income for the year then ended.

[*Practitioner's signature*]
[*Practitioner's city and state*]
[*Date of practitioner's report*]

Example 2: Practitioner's Review Report on Pro Forma Financial Information: Unmodified Conclusion

Independent Accountant's Report

[*Appropriate Addressee*]

We have reviewed the pro forma adjustments giving effect to the transaction (or event) described in Note 1 and the application of those adjustments to the historical amounts in the accompanying pro forma condensed balance sheet of X Company as of March 31, 20X2, and the related pro forma condensed statement of income for the three months then ended (pro forma financial information), based on the criteria in Note 1. These historical condensed financial statements are derived from the historical unaudited financial statements of X Company, which were reviewed by us, and of Y Company, which were reviewed by other accountants,[5] appearing elsewhere herein [*or "and are readily available"*]. The pro forma adjustments are based on management's assumptions as described

[5] When one set of historical financial statements is audited and the other set is reviewed, wording similar to the following would be appropriate:

The historical condensed financial statements are derived from the historical financial statements of X Company, which were audited by us, and of Y Company, which were reviewed by other accountants, appearing elsewhere herein [*or "and are readily available"*].

in Note 1. X Company's management is responsible for the pro forma financial information. Our responsibility is to express a conclusion based on our review.

Our review was conducted in accordance with attestation standards established by the American Institute of Certified Public Accountants. Those standards require that we plan and perform our review to obtain limited assurance about whether, based on the criteria in Note 1, any material modifications should be made to management's assumptions in order for them to provide a reasonable basis for presenting the significant effects directly attributable to the underlying transaction (or event); the related pro forma adjustments, in order for them to give appropriate effect to those assumptions; or the pro forma amounts, in order for them to reflect the proper application of those adjustments to the historical financial statement amounts. A review is substantially less in scope than an examination, the objective of which is to obtain reasonable assurance about whether, based on the criteria, management's assumptions provide a reasonable basis for presenting the significant effects directly attributable to the underlying transaction (or event), and, in all material respects, the related pro forma adjustments give appropriate effect to those assumptions, and the pro forma amounts reflect the proper application of those adjustments to the historical financial statement amounts, in order to express an opinion. Accordingly, we do not express such an opinion. We believe that our review provides a reasonable basis for our conclusion.

The objective of this pro forma financial information is to show what the significant effects on the historical financial information might have been had the underlying transaction (or event) occurred at an earlier date. However, the pro forma condensed financial statements are not necessarily indicative of the results of operations or related effects on financial position that would have been attained had the above-mentioned transaction (or event) actually occurred at such earlier date.

Based on our review, we are not aware of any material modifications that should be made to management's assumptions in order for them to provide a reasonable basis for presenting the significant effects directly attributable to the above-mentioned transaction (or event) described in Note 1, the related pro forma adjustments in order for them to give appropriate effect to those assumptions, or the pro forma amounts, in order for them to reflect the proper application of those adjustments to the historical financial statement amounts in the pro forma condensed balance sheet of X Company as of March 31, 20X2, and the related pro forma condensed statement of income for the three months then ended, based on the criteria in Note 1.

[*Practitioner's signature*]
[*Practitioner's city and state*]
[*Date of practitioner's report*]

Example 3: Practitioner's Examination Report on Pro Forma Financial Information at Year-End With a Review of Pro Forma Financial Information for a Subsequent Interim Date: Unmodified Opinion and Unmodified Conclusion

Independent Accountant's Report

[*Appropriate Addressee*]

We have examined the pro forma adjustments giving effect to the transaction (or event) described in Note 1 and the application of those adjustments to the historical amounts in the accompanying pro forma condensed balance sheet of X Company as of December 31, 20X1, and the related pro forma condensed statement of income for the year then ended (pro forma financial information) based on the criteria in Note 1. The historical condensed financial statements are derived from the historical financial statements of X Company, which were audited by us, and of Y Company, which were audited by other accountants, appearing elsewhere herein [*or "and are readily available"*]. The pro forma adjustments are based on management's assumptions described in Note 1. X Company's management is responsible for the pro forma financial information. Our responsibility is to express an opinion on the pro forma financial information based on our examination.

Our examination was conducted in accordance with attestation standards established by the American Institute of Certified Public Accountants. Those standards require that we plan and perform the examination to obtain reasonable assurance about whether, based on the criteria in Note 1, management's assumptions provide a reasonable basis for presenting the significant effects directly attributable to the underlying transaction (or event), and, in all material respects, the related pro forma adjustments give appropriate effect to those assumptions, and the pro forma amounts reflect the proper application of those adjustments to the historical financial statement amounts. An examination involves performing procedures to obtain evidence about management's assumptions, the related pro forma adjustments, and the pro forma amounts in the pro forma condensed balance sheet of X Company as of December 31, 20X1, and the related pro forma condensed statement of income for the year then ended. The nature, timing, and extent of the procedures selected depend on our judgment, including an assessment of the risks of material misstatement of the pro forma financial information, whether due to fraud or error. We believe that the evidence we have obtained is sufficient and appropriate to provide a reasonable basis for our opinion.

In addition, we have reviewed the pro forma adjustments and the application of those adjustments to the historical amounts in the accompanying pro forma condensed balance sheet of X Company as of March 31, 20X2, and the related pro forma condensed statement of income for the three months then ended (pro forma financial information), based on the criteria in Note 1. The historical condensed financial statements are derived from the historical financial statements of X Company, which were reviewed by us, and of Y Company, which were reviewed by other accountants,[6] appearing elsewhere herein [*or "and are readily available"*]. The pro forma adjustments are based on management's assumptions as described in Note 1. X Company's management is responsible for the pro forma financial information. Our responsibility is to express a conclusion based on our review.

Our review was conducted in accordance with attestation standards established by the American Institute of Certified Public Accountants. Those standards require that we plan and perform our review to obtain limited assurance about whether, based on the criteria in Note 1, any material modifications should be made to management's assumptions in order for them to provide a reasonable basis for presenting the significant effects directly attributable to the underlying transaction (or event); the related pro forma adjustments, in order for them to give appropriate effect to those assumptions; or the pro forma amounts, in order for them to reflect the proper application of those

---

[6] When one set of historical financial statements is audited and the other set is reviewed, wording similar to the following would be appropriate:

> The historical condensed financial statements are derived from the historical financial statements of X Company, which were audited by us, and of Y Company, which were reviewed by other accountants, appearing elsewhere herein [*or "and are readily available"*].

adjustments to the historical financial statement amounts. A review is substantially less in scope than an examination, the objective of which is to obtain reasonable assurance about whether, based on the criteria, management's assumptions provide a reasonable basis for presenting the significant effects directly attributable to the underlying transaction (or event), and, in all material respects, the related pro forma adjustments give appropriate effect to those assumptions, and the pro forma amounts reflect the proper application of those adjustments to the historical financial statement amounts, in order to express an opinion. Accordingly, we do not express such an opinion on the pro forma adjustments or on the application of such adjustments to the pro forma condensed balance sheet as of March 31, 20X2, and the pro forma condensed statement of income for the three months then ended. We believe that our review provides a reasonable basis for our conclusion.

The objective of this pro forma financial information is to show what the significant effects on the historical financial information might have been had the underlying transactions (or event) occurred at an earlier date. However, the pro forma condensed financial statements are not necessarily indicative of the results of operations or related effects on financial position that would have been attained had the above-mentioned transaction (or event) actually occurred at such earlier date.

In our opinion, based on the criteria in Note 1, management's assumptions provide a reasonable basis for presenting the significant effects directly attributable to the above-mentioned transaction (or event) described in Note 1, and, in all material respects, the related pro forma adjustments give appropriate effect to those assumptions, and the pro forma amounts reflect the proper application of those adjustments to the historical financial statement amounts in the pro forma condensed balance sheet of X Company as of December 31, 20X1, and the related pro forma condensed statement of income for the year then ended.

Based on our review, we are not aware of any material modifications that should be made to management's assumptions in order for them to provide a reasonable basis for presenting the significant effects directly attributable to the above-mentioned transaction (or event) described in Note 1, the related pro forma adjustments in order for them to give appropriate effect to those assumptions, or the pro forma amounts in order for them to reflect the proper application of those adjustments to the historical financial statement amounts in the pro forma condensed balance sheet of X Company as of March 31, 20X2, and the related pro forma condensed statement of income for the three months then ended based on the criteria in Note 1.

[Practitioner's signature]
[Practitioner's city and state]
[Date of practitioner's report]

Example 4: Practitioner's Examination Report: Qualified Opinion Because of a Scope Limitation

Independent Accountant's Report

[Appropriate Addressee]

We have examined the pro forma adjustments giving effect to the transaction (or event) described in Note 1 and the application of those adjustments to the historical amounts in the accompanying pro forma condensed balance sheet of X Company as of December 31, 20X1, and the related pro forma condensed statement of income for the year then ended (pro forma financial information), based on the criteria in Note 1. The historical condensed financial statements are derived from the historical financial statements of X Company, which were audited by us, and of Y Company, which were audited by other accountants, appearing elsewhere herein [*or "and are readily available"*]. The pro forma adjustments are based upon management's assumptions described in Note 1. X Company's management is responsible for the pro forma financial information. Our responsibility is to express an opinion on the pro forma financial information based on our examination.

Except as discussed below, our examination was conducted in accordance with attestation standards established by the American Institute of Certified Public Accountants. Those standards require that we plan and perform the examination to obtain reasonable assurance about whether, based on the criteria in Note 1, management's assumptions provide a reasonable basis for presenting the significant effects directly attributable to the underlying transaction (or event), and, in all material respects, the related pro forma adjustments give appropriate effect to those assumptions, and the pro forma amounts reflect the proper application of those adjustments to the historical financial statement amounts. An examination involves performing procedures to obtain evidence about management's assumptions, the related pro forma adjustments, and the pro forma amounts in the pro forma condensed balance sheet of X Company as of December 31, 20X1, and the related pro forma condensed statement of income for the year then ended. The nature, timing, and extent of the procedures selected depend on our judgment, including an assessment of the risks of material misstatement of the pro forma financial information, whether due to fraud or error. We believe that the evidence we obtained is sufficient and appropriate to provide a reasonable basis for our opinion.

We were unable to perform the examination procedures we considered necessary with respect to the assumptions relating to the proposed loan described in Adjustment E in Note 1.

The objective of this pro forma financial information is to show what the significant effects on the historical financial information might have been had the underlying transaction (or event) occurred at an earlier date. However, the pro forma condensed financial statements are not necessarily indicative of the results of operations or related effects on financial position that would have been attained had the above-mentioned transaction (or event) actually occurred at such earlier date.

In our opinion, based on the criteria in Note 1, except for the effects of such changes, if any, as might have been determined to be necessary had we been able to satisfy ourselves as to the assumptions relating to the proposed loan, management's assumptions provide a reasonable basis for presenting the significant effects directly attributable to the above-mentioned transaction (or event) described in Note 1, and, in all material respects, the related pro forma adjustments give appropriate effect to those assumptions, and the pro forma amounts reflect the proper application of those adjustments to the historical financial statement amounts in the pro forma condensed balance sheet of X Company as of December 31, 20X1, and the related pro forma condensed statement of income for the year then ended.

[*Practitioner's signature*]
[*Practitioner's city and state*]
[*Date of practitioner's report*]

Example 5: Practitioner's Examination Report: Qualified Opinion Because of Reservations About the Propriety of the Assumptions

Independent Accountant's Report

[Appropriate Addressee]

[Same first three paragraphs as examination report in example 1.]

As discussed in Note 1 to the pro forma financial statements, the pro forma adjustments reflect management's assumption that X Division of the acquired company will be sold. The net assets of this division are reflected at their historical carrying amount; generally accepted accounting principles require these net assets to be recorded at fair value less cost to sell.

In our opinion, based on the criteria in Note 1, except for inappropriate valuation of the net assets of X Division, management's assumptions described in Note 1 provide a reasonable basis for presenting the significant effects directly attributable to the above-mentioned transaction (or event) described in Note 1, and, in all material respects, the related pro forma adjustments give appropriate effect to those assumptions, and the pro forma amounts reflect the proper application of those adjustments to the historical financial statement amounts in the pro forma condensed balance sheet of X Company as of December 31, 20X1, and the related pro forma condensed statement of income for the year then ended.

[Practitioner's signature]
[Practitioner's city and state]
[Date of the practitioner's report]

Example 6: Practitioner's Examination Report: Disclaimer of Opinion Because of a Scope Limitation

Independent Accountant's Report

[Appropriate Addressee]

We were engaged to examine the pro forma adjustments giving effect to the transaction (or event) described in Note 1 and the application of those adjustments to the historical amounts in the accompanying pro forma financial condensed balance sheet of X Company as of December 31, 20X1, and the related pro forma condensed statement of income for the year then ended (pro forma financial information), based on the criteria in Note 1. The historical condensed financial statements are derived from the historical financial statements of X Company, which were audited by us, and of Y Company, which were audited by other accountants, appearing elsewhere herein [*or "and are readily available"*]. The pro forma adjustments are based on management's assumptions described in Note 1. X Company's management is responsible for the pro forma financial information.

As discussed in Note 1 to the pro forma financial statements, the pro forma adjustments reflect management's assumptions that the elimination of duplicate facilities would have resulted in a 30 percent reduction in operating costs. Management could not supply us with sufficient evidence to support this assertion.

[The third paragraph in the practitioner's examination report in example 1 is intentionally omitted from the report with a disclaimer of opinion.]

Because we were unable to evaluate management's assumptions regarding the reduction in operating costs and other assumptions related thereto, the scope of our work was not sufficient to enable us to express, and we do not express, an opinion on whether, based on the criteria in Note 1, management's assumptions provide a reasonable basis for presenting the significant effects directly attributable to the above-mentioned transaction (or event) described in Note 1, or on whether, in all material respects, the related pro forma adjustments give appropriate effect to those assumptions, and the pro forma amounts reflect the proper application of those adjustments to the historical financial statement amounts in the pro forma condensed balance sheet of X Company as of December 31, 20X1, and the related pro forma condensed statement of income for the year then ended.

[*Practitioner's signature*]
[*Practitioner's city and state*]
[*Date of practitioner's report*]

AT-C Section 315*

Compliance Attestation

Source: SSAE No. 18.

Effective for practitioners' examination reports on compliance with specified requirements and for practitioners' agreed-upon procedures reports related to compliance or internal control over compliance with specified requirements dated on or after May 1, 2017.

Introduction

.01 This section contains performance and reporting requirements and application guidance for a practitioner (Ref: par. .A1–.A3)

a. examining an entity's compliance with requirements of specified laws, regulations, rules, contracts, or grants (specified requirements) or an assertion about compliance with specified requirements.

b. performing agreed-upon procedures related to an entity's compliance with specified requirements.

c. performing agreed-upon procedures related to an entity's internal control over compliance with specified requirements.

.02 This section does not apply to

a. reviews of compliance with specified requirements or an entity's internal control over compliance or an assertion thereon because section 210, *Review Engagements*, specifically prohibits such engagements.[1]

b. examination engagements in which a practitioner is reporting on an entity's internal control over compliance with specified requirements. (Ref: par. .A4)

c. situations in which an auditor reports on specified requirements based solely on an audit of financial statements, as addressed in AU-C section 806, *Reporting on Compliance With Aspects of Contractual Agreements or Regulatory Requirements in Connection With Audited Financial Statements.*

d. engagements in which a governmental audit requirement requires an auditor to express an opinion on compliance in accordance with AU-C section 935, *Compliance Audits.*

.03 A practitioner's report issued in accordance with the provisions of this section does not provide a legal determination of an entity's compliance with specified requirements. However, such a report may be useful to legal counsel or others in making such determinations.

.04 In addition to complying with this section, a practitioner is required to comply with section 105, *Concepts Common to All Attestation Engagements*, and

---

* This section contains an "AT-C" identifier, instead of an "AT" identifier, to avoid confusion with references to existing "AT" sections, which remain effective through April 2017.

[1] Paragraph .07 of section 210, *Review Engagements.*

either section 205, *Examination Engagements*, for examinations of compliance, or section 215, *Agreed-Upon Procedures Engagements*, for agreed-upon procedures engagements that address compliance. In some cases, this section repeats or refers to requirements found in sections 105, 205, and 215 when describing those requirements in the context of engagements that address compliance. Although not all the requirements in sections 105, 205, and 215 are repeated or referred to in this section, the practitioner is responsible for complying with all the requirements in sections 105 and 205 or 105 and 215, as applicable.

Effective Date

.05 This section is effective for practitioners' examination reports on compliance with specified requirements and for practitioners' agreed-upon procedures reports related to compliance or internal control over compliance with specified requirements dated on or after May 1, 2017.

Objectives of an Examination Engagement

.06 In conducting an examination of an entity's compliance with specified requirements, the objectives of the practitioner are to (Ref: par. .A5)

a. obtain reasonable assurance about whether the entity complied with the specified requirements, in all material respects,

b. express an opinion in a written report about whether

 i. the entity complied with the specified requirements, in all material respects, or

 ii. management's assertion about its compliance with the specified requirements is fairly stated, in all material respects.

Objectives of an Agreed-Upon Procedures Engagement

.07 In conducting an agreed-upon procedures engagement for which the subject matter is compliance or internal control over compliance with specified requirements, the objectives of the practitioner are to

a. apply to an entity's compliance with specified requirements or an entity's internal control over compliance with specified requirements procedures that are established by specified parties who are responsible for the sufficiency of the procedures for their purposes and

b. issue a written report that describes the procedures applied and the practitioner's findings.

Definitions

.08 For the purposes of this section, the following terms have the meanings attributed as follows:

Compliance with specified requirements. An entity's compliance with specified laws, regulations, rules, contracts, or grants.

Internal control over compliance. An entity's internal control over compliance with specified requirements. The internal control addressed in this section may include part of, but is not the same as, internal control over financial reporting. (Ref: par. .A6)

Material noncompliance. A failure to follow compliance requirements or a violation of prohibitions included in the specified requirements that results in noncompliance that is quantitatively or qualitatively material, either individually or when aggregated with other noncompliance. (Ref: par. .A7)

Requirements

Preconditions for Examination Engagements

.09 In order to accept an attestation engagement to examine compliance with specified requirements, in addition to the preconditions for an examination engagement in sections 105 and 205, the practitioner should determine that[2] (Ref: par. .A8–.A9)

a. management accepts responsibility for the entity's compliance with specified requirements and the entity's internal control over compliance.

b. management evaluates the entity's compliance with specified requirements. (Ref: par. .A9)

.10 In performing an examination under this section, the practitioner should request from management a written assertion. If management refuses to provide a written assertion, the practitioner should withdraw from the engagement when withdrawal is possible under applicable law or regulation. (Ref: par. .A10–.A11)

Reasonable Assurance

.11 In an engagement to examine compliance with specified requirements, the practitioner should seek to obtain reasonable assurance that the entity complied with the specified requirements, in all material respects, including designing the examination to detect both intentional and unintentional material noncompliance.

Materiality

.12 As required by section 205, the practitioner should consider materiality when establishing the overall engagement strategy.[3] (Ref: par. .A12–.A13)

Examination Procedures

.13 The practitioner should obtain an understanding of the specified requirements. The practitioner's procedures to obtain that understanding should include the following: (Ref: par. .A14)

a. Consideration of laws, regulations, rules, contracts, and grants that pertain to the specified requirements, including published requirements

b. Consideration of knowledge about the specified requirements obtained through prior engagements and regulatory reports

---

[2] Paragraphs .24–.28 of section 105, *Concepts Common to All Attestation Engagements*, and paragraph .06 of section 205, *Examination Engagements*.

[3] Paragraph .16 of section 205.

c. Discussion with appropriate individuals within the entity (for example, the chief financial officer, internal auditors, legal counsel, compliance officer, or grant or contract administrators)

.14 In an engagement to examine an entity's compliance with specified requirements when the entity has operations in several components (for example, locations, branches, subsidiaries, or programs), the practitioner should determine the nature, timing, and extent of testing to be performed at individual components. In making such a determination and in selecting the components to be tested, the practitioner should evaluate factors such as the following:

a. The degree to which the specified requirements apply at the component level
b. Judgments about materiality
c. The degree of centralization of records
d. The effectiveness of the control environment, particularly management's direct control over the exercise of authority delegated to others and its ability to supervise activities at various locations effectively
e. The nature and extent of operations conducted at the various components
f. The similarity of operations over compliance for different components

.15 The practitioner should obtain an understanding of relevant portions of internal control over compliance sufficient to plan the engagement and to assess control risk for compliance with specified requirements. In planning the examination, such knowledge should be used to identify types of potential noncompliance, to consider factors that affect the risk of material noncompliance, and to design appropriate tests of compliance. (Ref: par. .A15–.A16)

.16 For engagements involving compliance with regulatory requirements, the practitioner's procedures should include reviewing reports of relevant examinations and related communications between regulatory agencies and the entity and, when appropriate, making inquiries of the regulatory agencies, including inquiries about examinations in progress.

Written Representations in an Examination Engagement

.17 In an examination engagement, in addition to the written representations from management required by section 205, the practitioner should request written representations from management that[4] (Ref: par. .A17)

a. acknowledge management's responsibility for establishing and maintaining effective internal control over compliance.
b. state that management has performed an evaluation of the entity's compliance with specified requirements.
c. state management's interpretation of any compliance requirements that have varying interpretations.

.18 In an examination of compliance, the practitioner should request from management the written representations required by section 205 and paragraph .17 of this section, even if the engaging party is not management.[5] The alternative to obtaining the required written representations provided for in

---

[4] Paragraph .50 of section 205.

[5] See footnote 4.

section 205 is not permitted in an engagement to examine compliance.[6] Management's refusal to furnish the written representations required by section 205 and paragraph .17 of this section constitutes a limitation on the scope of the engagement sufficient to preclude an unmodified opinion and may be sufficient to cause the practitioner to withdraw from the examination engagement, when withdrawal is possible under applicable laws and regulations.[7]

Forming the Opinion

.19 In evaluating whether the entity has complied with the specified requirements, in all material respects, (or whether management's assertion about its compliance with the specified requirements is fairly stated, in all material respects), the practitioner should evaluate (*a*) the nature and frequency of the noncompliance identified and (*b*) whether such noncompliance is material relative to the nature of the compliance requirements.

Content of the Practitioner's Examination Report

.20 The practitioner's examination report on compliance should include the following, unless the practitioner is disclaiming an opinion, in which case, items .20*g* and .20*h* should be omitted: (Ref: par. .A18–.A20)

a. A title that includes the word *independent.*

b. An appropriate addressee as required by the circumstances of the engagement.

c. An identification of the compliance matters that are being reported on or the assertion about such matters, including the point in time or period of time to which the measurement or evaluation of compliance relates.

d. An identification of the specified requirements against which compliance was measured or evaluated. (Ref: par. .A21)

e. A statement that identifies

- i. management and its responsibility for compliance with the specified requirements (when reporting on the subject matter) or for its assertion (when reporting on the assertion).
- ii. the practitioner's responsibility to express an opinion on the entity's compliance with the specified requirements or on management's assertion about the entity's compliance with the specified requirements, based on the practitioner's examination.

f. A statement that

- i. the examination was conducted in accordance with attestation standards established by the American Institute of Certified Public Accountants.
- ii. those standards require that the practitioner plan and perform the examination to obtain reasonable assurance about whether
  - (1) the entity complied with the specified requirements, in all material respects, or

---

[6] Paragraph .51 of section 205.

[7] Paragraphs .50, .55, and .A64 of section 205.

(2) management's assertion about compliance with the specified requirements is fairly stated, in all material respects.

iii. the practitioner believes the evidence obtained is sufficient and appropriate to provide a reasonable basis for the practitioner's opinion.

g. A description of the nature of an examination engagement.

h. A statement that describes significant inherent limitations, if any, associated with the measurement or evaluation of the entity's compliance with specified requirements or its assertion thereon.

i. A statement that the examination does not provide a legal determination on the entity's compliance with specified requirements.

j. The practitioner's opinion about whether, in all material respects

i. the entity complied with the specified requirements or

ii. management's assertion about the entity's compliance with specified requirements is fairly stated.

k. When the circumstances identified in section 205 are applicable, an alert in a separate paragraph that restricts the use of the report or describes the purpose of the report, as applicable.[8]

l. The manual or printed signature of the practitioner's firm.

m. The city and state where the practitioner practices.

n. The date of the report. (The report should be dated no earlier than the date on which the practitioner has obtained sufficient appropriate evidence on which to base the practitioner's opinion, including evidence that

i. the attestation documentation has been reviewed, and

ii. management has provided a written assertion.)

.21 Frequently, criteria will be contained in the compliance requirements, in which case, it is not necessary to repeat the criteria in the practitioner's report; however, if the criteria are not included in the compliance requirement, the report should identify the criteria. (Ref: par. .A21–.A23)

Modified Opinions

.22 If the practitioner determines that there is material noncompliance, the practitioner's report should describe the material noncompliance, and the opinion should be modified in accordance with section 205.[9] (Ref: par. .A24–.A28)

Preconditions for an Agreed-Upon Procedures Engagement

.23 In order to accept an attestation engagement to apply agreed-upon procedures related to compliance with specified requirements or internal control over compliance with specified requirements, in addition to the preconditions for an agreed-upon procedures engagement in sections 105 and 215, the practitioner should determine that[10] (Ref: par. .A29–.A30)

---

[8] Paragraph .64*c* of section 205.

[9] Paragraphs .68–.84 of section 205.

[10] Paragraphs .24–.28 of section 105 and paragraphs .09–.11 of section 215, *Agreed-Upon Procedures Engagements*.

a. management accepts responsibility for the entity's compliance with specified requirements and the entity's internal control over compliance.

b. management evaluates the entity's compliance with specified requirements or the entity's internal control over compliance.

.24 The practitioner should obtain an understanding of the specified requirements. The practitioner's procedures to obtain that understanding should include the following:

a. Consideration of laws, regulations, rules, contracts, and grants that pertain to the specified requirements, including published requirements

b. Consideration of knowledge about the specified requirements obtained through prior engagements and regulatory reports

c. Discussion with appropriate individuals within the entity (for example, the chief financial officer, internal auditors, legal counsel, compliance officer, or grant or contract administrators)

Written Representations in an Agreed-Upon Procedures Engagement

.25 In an agreed-upon procedures engagement, in addition to the written representations from management required by section 215, the practitioner should request written representations from management that[11]

a. acknowledge management's responsibility for establishing and maintaining effective internal control over compliance.

b. state that management has performed an evaluation of (i) the entity's compliance with specified requirements or (ii) the entity's controls for establishing and maintaining internal control over compliance and detecting noncompliance with requirements, as applicable.

c. state management's interpretation of any compliance requirements that have varying interpretations.

d. state that management has disclosed any known noncompliance occurring subsequent to the period covered by the practitioner's report.

Content of the Practitioner's Agreed-Upon Procedures Report

.26 The practitioner's agreed-upon procedures report on compliance should include the following: (Ref: par. .A31–.A34)

a. A title that includes the word *independent.*

b. An appropriate addressee as required by the circumstances of the engagement.

c. An indication that the subject matter of the engagement is the entity's compliance during a period or as of a point in time.

d. An identification of the specified requirements against which the entity's compliance was measured or evaluated.

e. An indication that management of the entity is responsible for the entity's compliance with the specified requirements.

---

[11] Paragraph .28 of section 215.

f. An identification of the specified parties.

g. A statement that

i. the sufficiency of the procedures is solely the responsibility of the parties specified in the report.

ii. the practitioner makes no representation regarding the sufficiency of the procedures either for the purpose for which the report has been requested or for any other purpose.

h. A list of the procedures performed (or reference thereto) and related findings. (The practitioner should not provide a conclusion.)

i. When applicable, a description of any agreed-upon materiality limits.

j. A statement that

i. the agreed-upon procedures engagement was conducted in accordance with attestation standards established by the American Institute of Certified Public Accountants.

ii. the practitioner was not engaged to and did not conduct an examination or review, the objective of which would be the expression of an opinion or conclusion, respectively, on compliance with specified requirements (or internal control over compliance with specified requirements).

iii. the practitioner does not express such an opinion or conclusion.

iv. had the practitioner performed additional procedures, other matters might have come to the practitioner's attention that would have been reported.

k. When applicable, a description of the nature of the assistance provided by a practitioner's external specialist.

l. When applicable, reservations or restrictions concerning procedures or findings.

m. An alert, in a separate paragraph, that restricts the use of the report. The alert should

i. state that the report is intended solely for the information and use of the specified parties,

ii. identify the specified parties for whom use is intended, and

iii. state that the report is not intended to be, and should not be, used by anyone other than the specified parties.

n. When the engagement is also performed in accordance with *Government Auditing Standards*, the alert that restricts the use of the report should include the following information, rather than the information required by paragraph .26*m*:

i. A description of the purpose of the report

ii. A statement indicating that the report is not suitable for any other purpose

o. The manual or printed signature of the practitioner's firm.

p. The city and state where the practitioner practices.

q. The date of the report. (The report should be dated no earlier than the date on which the practitioner completed the procedures and determined the findings, including that

i. the attestation documentation has been reviewed, and

ii. management has provided a written assertion, unless management refuses to provide an assertion).

Application and Other Explanatory Material

Introduction (Ref: par. .01 and .02*b*)

.A1 Compliance requirements may be either financial or nonfinancial in nature.

.A2 The criteria for evaluating or measuring compliance with specified requirements ordinarily are included in the specified requirements but may be otherwise identified.

.A3 A practitioner may be engaged to provide other types of services in connection with an entity's compliance with specified requirements or its internal control over compliance with specified requirements. For example, the practitioner may be engaged to provide recommendations on how to improve the entity's compliance or related internal control. Such an engagement is governed by the guidance in CS section 100, *Consulting Services: Definitions and Standards*.

.A4 An engagement to examine internal control oveAU-C section 940r compliance is governed by sections 105 and 205. Additionally, , *An Audit of an Entity's Internal Control Over Financial Reporting That Is Integrated With an Audit of Its Financial Statements*, may be helpful to a practitioner in such an engagement.

Objectives of an Examination Engagement (Ref: par. .06)

.A5 For the purposes of this section, the responsible party is management of the entity for which the practitioner is reporting on compliance.

Definitions

Internal Control Over Compliance

.A6 An entity's internal control over compliance is the process by which management obtains reasonable assurance of compliance with specified requirements. Although management's internal control may include a wide variety of objectives and related policies and procedures, only some of these may be relevant to an entity's compliance with specified requirements. An entity's internal control over compliance may vary based on the nature of the compliance requirements. For example, internal control over compliance with a capital requirement would generally include accounting procedures, whereas internal control over compliance with a requirement to practice nondiscriminatory hiring may not include accounting procedures.

Material Noncompliance

.A7 Government requirements or other requirements may define material noncompliance for the purpose of the engagement.

Preconditions for Examination Engagements (Ref: par. .09–.10)

.A8 Management is responsible for ensuring that the entity complies with the requirements applicable to its activities. That responsibility encompasses the following:

a. Identifying the specified requirements

b. Designing, implementing, and maintaining internal control to provide reasonable assurance that the entity complies with those requirements

c. Evaluating and monitoring the entity's compliance

d. Specifying reports that satisfy legal, regulatory, or contractual requirements

.A9 Management's evaluation may include documentation such as accounting or statistical data, entity policy manuals, accounting manuals, narrative memoranda, procedural write-ups, flowcharts, completed questionnaires, or internal auditors' reports. The form and extent of documentation will vary depending on the nature of the compliance requirements and the size and complexity of the entity.

.A10 Management's written assertion about compliance with specified requirements may take many forms. Throughout this section, for example, the phrase "management's assertion that W Company complied with [*specify compliance requirement*] as of [*date*]," illustrates such an assertion. Other phrases may also be used. A statement that is so subjective (for example, *substantially complied*) that people having competence in and using the same or similar criteria would not ordinarily be able to arrive at similar conclusions is not an appropriate written assertion.

.A11 Paragraph .10 applies regardless of whether the responsible party is the engaging party.

Materiality (Ref: par. .12)

.A12 The terms of an engagement may provide for a supplemental practitioner's report of all or certain noncompliance discovered. Such terms would not affect the practitioner's judgments about materiality in establishing the overall engagement strategy or in forming an opinion on an entity's compliance with specified requirements or on management's assertion about such compliance.

.A13 In an examination of an entity's compliance with specified requirements, the practitioner's consideration of materiality is affected by (*a*) the nature of the compliance requirements, which may or may not be quantifiable in monetary terms, (*b*) the nature and frequency of noncompliance identified with appropriate consideration of sampling risk, and (*c*) qualitative considerations, including the needs and expectations of the users of the practitioner's report.

Examination Procedures (Ref: par. .13 and .15)

.A14 In certain circumstances, the practitioner may determine that it is necessary to discuss the specified requirements with appropriate individuals outside the entity (for example, a regulator or specialist).

.A15 A practitioner generally obtains an understanding of the design of specific controls by performing the following:

a. Inquiries of appropriate management, supervisory, and staff personnel *b.* Inspection of the entity's documents

c. Observation of the entity's activities and operations

.A16 The nature and extent of procedures a practitioner performs vary from entity to entity and are influenced by factors such as the following:

- The newness and complexity of the specified requirements
- The practitioner's knowledge of internal control over compliance obtained in previous professional engagements
- The nature of the specified requirements
- An understanding of the industry in which the entity operates
- Judgments about materiality

Written Representations in an Examination Engagement (Ref: par. .17)

.A17 At the beginning of the engagement, the practitioner may want to consider discussing with management the need for management to provide the practitioner with a written representation letter at the conclusion of the engagement.

Content of the Practitioner's Examination Report (Ref: par. .20–.21)

.A18 The list of elements in paragraph .20 constitutes all the required elements for a practitioner's report on an examination of compliance with specified requirements, including the elements required by section 205.[12] Application guidance regarding the elements of an examination report is included in section 205.[13]

.A19 Examples 1 and 2 in the exhibit to this section provide illustrations of practitioner's examination reports on compliance.

.A20 Paragraph .20*d* represents the criteria for measuring or evaluating compliance with the specified requirements.

.A21 Ordinarily, the criteria are included in the specified requirements. In that case, the identification may say, "We have examined management of XYZ Company's compliance with [*identify the specified requirements*...]."

.A22 If a compliance requirement is to "maintain $25,000 in capital," it would not be necessary to identify the $25,000 in the practitioner's report; however, if the requirement is subjectively worded, for example, to "maintain adequate capital," the criteria used to define *adequate* would be included in the report.

.A23 When evaluating compliance with certain requirements requires interpretation of the laws, regulations, rules, contracts, or grants that establish those requirements, the practitioner evaluates whether the criteria are suitable for evaluating compliance. If these interpretations are significant, the practitioner may include a paragraph describing the interpretations and identifying

---

[12] Paragraphs .63–.66 of section 205.

[13] Paragraphs .A78–.A101 of section 205.

the source of the interpretations made by the entity's management. The following is an example of such a paragraph:

> We have been informed that, under [*name of entity*]'s interpretation of [*identify the compliance requirement*], [*explain the source and nature of the relevant interpretation*].

Modified Opinions (Ref: par. .22)

Qualified Opinion

.A24 The following is an example of

a. a paragraph that would be added to the practitioner's report to describe the matter giving rise to the qualified opinion, and

b. an opinion paragraph of a report containing the qualified opinion:

> Our examination disclosed the following material noncompliance with [*type of compliance requirement*] applicable to [*name of entity*] during the [*period*] ended [*date*]. [*Describe noncompliance.*]
>
> In our opinion, except for the material noncompliance described in the preceding paragraph, [*name of entity*] complied, in all material respects, with the aforementioned requirements for the [*period*] ended [*date*].

Adverse Opinion

.A25 The following is an example of

a. a paragraph that would be added to the practitioner's report to describe the matter(s) giving rise to the adverse opinion, and

b. an opinion paragraph of a report containing an adverse opinion:

> Our examination disclosed the following material noncompliance with [*type of compliance requirement*] applicable to [*name of entity*] during the [*period*] ended [*date*]. [*Describe noncompliance.*]
>
> In our opinion, because of the effect of the noncompliance described in the preceding paragraph, [*name of entity*] has not complied with the aforementioned requirements for the [*period*] ended [*date*].

.A26 If the practitioner's report containing a qualified or adverse opinion on the entity's compliance with specified requirements is included in a document that also includes the practitioner's audit report on the entity's financial statements, the compliance report may indicate that the noncompliance was considered during the audit.

.A27 The following is an example of an additional sentence that may be included in the opinion paragraph of a practitioner's examination report that describes material noncompliance:

> We considered the effect of these conditions on our audit of the 20XX financial statements. This report on XYZ Company's compliance with [*identify the specified requirements*] does not affect our audit report dated [*date of report*] on those financial statements.

.A28 The practitioner also may include the preceding sentence when the two practitioner's reports are not included in the same document.

Preconditions for an Agreed-Upon Procedures Engagement (Ref: par. .23)

.A29 Management is responsible for ensuring that the entity complies with the requirements applicable to its activities. That responsibility encompasses the following:

a. Identifying the specified requirements

b. Establishing and maintaining internal control to provide reasonable assurance that the entity complies with those requirements

c. Evaluating and monitoring the entity's compliance

d. Specifying reports that satisfy legal, regulatory, or contractual requirements

.A30 Management's evaluation may include documentation such as accounting or statistical data, entity policy manuals, accounting manuals, narrative memoranda, procedural write-ups, flowcharts, completed questionnaires, or internal auditors' reports. The form and extent of documentation will vary depending on the nature of the compliance requirements and the size and complexity of the entity.

Content of the Practitioner's Agreed-Upon Procedures Report (Ref: par. .26)

.A31 The list of elements in paragraph .26 of this section constitutes all the required elements for a practitioner's report on the application of agreed-upon procedures related to an entity's compliance with specified requirements, including the elements required by section 215.[14] Application guidance regarding the elements of an agreed-upon procedures report is included in section 215.[15]

.A32 In some agreed-upon procedures engagements, procedures may relate to both compliance with specified requirements and the entity's internal control over compliance. In these engagements, the practitioner may issue one practitioner's report that addresses both. For example, the first sentence of the introductory paragraph may state the following:

> We have performed the procedures enumerated below, related to [*name of entity*]'s compliance with [*identify the specified requirements*] during the [*period*] ended [*date*] and [*name of entity*]'s internal control over compliance with the aforementioned compliance requirements as of [*date*].

.A33 When performing agreed-upon procedures related to an entity's compliance with specified requirements, or an entity's internal control over compliance with certain requirements requires interpretation of the laws, regulations, rules, contracts, or grants that establish those requirements, the practitioner evaluates whether the criteria are suitable for performing such agreed-upon procedures and reporting findings. If these interpretations are significant, the practitioner may include a paragraph describing the interpretations made by management and the source of the interpretations. An example of such a paragraph, which would precede the procedures and findings paragraph(s), follows:

> We have been informed that, under [*name of entity*]'s interpretation of [*identify the compliance requirement*], [*explain the nature and source of the relevant interpretation.*]

---

14 Paragraphs .35–.36 of section 215.

15 Paragraphs .A35–.A43 of section 215.

.A34 Example 3 in the exhibit to this section provides an illustration of a practitioner's agreed-upon procedures report related to compliance with specified requirements. Example 4 in the exhibit to this section provides an illustration of an agreed-upon procedures report related to internal control over compliance with specified requirements.

.A35

Exhibit—Illustrative Practitioner's Examination and Agreed-Upon Procedures Reports Related to Compliance, and Agreed-Upon Procedures Report Related to Internal Control Over Compliance

The illustrative practitioner's examination reports in this exhibit (examples 1 and 2) meet the reporting requirements of section 205, *Examination Engagements*, and of paragraphs .20–.22 of this section.[1] A practitioner may use alternative language in drafting an examination report, provided that the language meets the applicable requirements of section 205 and paragraphs .20–.22 of this section.[2]

The illustrative practitioner's agreed-upon procedures reports in this exhibit (examples 3 and 4) meet the applicable reporting requirements of section 215, *Agreed-Upon Procedures Engagements*, and paragraph .26 of this section.[3] A practitioner may use alternative language in drafting an agreed-upon procedures report, provided that the language meets the applicable requirements of section 215 and paragraph .26 of this section.[4]

Example 1: Practitioner's Examination Report on Compliance; Unmodified Opinion

The following is an illustrative practitioner's examination report for an engagement in which the practitioner is reporting on subject matter (an entity's compliance with specified requirements during a period of time).

Independent Accountant's Report

[*Appropriate addressee*]

We have examined XYZ Company's compliance with [*identify the specified requirements, for example, the requirements listed in Attachment 1*] during the period January 1, 20X1, to December 31, 20X1. Management of XYZ Company is responsible for XYZ Company's compliance with the specified requirements. Our responsibility is to express an opinion on XYZ Company's compliance with the specified requirements based on our examination.

Our examination was conducted in accordance with attestation standards established by the American Institute of Certified Public Accountants. Those standards require that we plan and perform the examination to obtain reasonable assurance about whether XYZ Company complied, in all material respects, with the specified requirements referenced above. An examination involves performing procedures to obtain evidence about whether XYZ Company complied with the specified requirements. The nature, timing, and extent of the procedures selected depend on our judgment, including an assessment of the risks of material noncompliance, whether due to fraud or error. We believe that the evidence we obtained is sufficient and appropriate to provide a reasonable basis for our opinion.

---

1 Paragraphs .61–.84 of section 205.

2 See footnote 1.

3 Paragraphs .33–.41 of section 215.

4 See footnote 3.

Our examination does not provide a legal determination on XYZ Company's compliance with specified requirements.

In our opinion, XYZ Company complied, in all material respects, with [*identify the specified requirements, for example, the requirements listed in Attachment 1*] during the period January 1, 20X1 to December 31, 20X1.

[*Practitioner's signature*]
[*Practitioner's city and state*]
[*Date of practitioner's report*]

Example 2: Practitioner's Examination Report on an Assertion About Compliance; Unmodified Opinion

The following is an illustrative practitioner's examination report for an engagement in which the practitioner is reporting on the management's assertion about compliance with specified requirements and management's assertion accompanies the report.

Independent Accountant's Report

[*Appropriate Addressee*]

We have examined management of XYZ Company's assertion that XYZ Company complied with [*identify the specified requirements, for example, the requirements listed in Attachment 1*] during the period January 1, 20X1 to December 31, 20X1.[5] XYZ Company's management is responsible for its assertion. Our responsibility is to express an opinion on management's assertion about XYZ Company's compliance with the specified requirements based on our examination.

Our examination was conducted in accordance with attestation standards established by the American Institute of Certified Public Accountants. Those standards require that we plan and perform the examination to obtain reasonable assurance about whether management's assertion about compliance with the specified requirements is fairly stated, in all material respects. An examination involves performing procedures to obtain evidence about whether management's assertion is fairly stated, in all material respects. The nature, timing, and extent of the procedures selected depend on our judgment, including an assessment of the risks of material misstatement of management's assertion, whether due to fraud or error. We believe that the evidence we obtained is sufficient and appropriate to provide a reasonable basis for our opinion.

Our examination does not provide a legal determination on XYZ Company's compliance with the specified requirements.

In our opinion, management's assertion that XYZ Company complied with [*identify the specified requirements, for example, the requirements listed in Attachment 1*], is fairly stated, in all material respects.

[*Practitioner's signature*]
[*Practitioner's city and state*]
[*Date of practitioner's report*]

---

[5] If management's assertion accompanies the practitioner's report, the practitioner would refer to management's assertion by using the same title as management used for its assertion. The report also would use the same description of the specified requirements that management used in its assertion. If management's assertion is stated in the report, rather than accompanying the report, the word *accompanying* would be omitted.

Example 3: Practitioner's Agreed-Upon Procedures Report Related to Compliance

The following is an illustrative practitioner's agreed-upon procedures report related to an entity's compliance with specified requirements in which the procedures and findings are enumerated, rather than referenced.

Independent Accountant's Report on Applying Agreed-Upon Procedures

[*Appropriate Addressee*]

We have performed the procedures enumerated below, which were agreed to by [*identify the specified parties, for example, the management and board of directors of XYZ Company*], related to XYZ Company's compliance with [*identify the specified requirements, for example, the requirements listed in Attachment 1*] during the period January 1, 20X1 to December 31, 20X1].[6] XYZ Company's management is responsible for its compliance with those requirements. The sufficiency of these procedures is solely the responsibility of those parties specified in this report. Consequently, we make no representations regarding the sufficiency of the procedures enumerated below either for the purpose for which this report has been requested or for any other purpose.

[*Include paragraphs to enumerate procedures and findings.*]

This agreed-upon procedures engagement was conducted in accordance with attestation standards established by the American Institute of Certified Public Accountants. We were not engaged to and did not conduct an examination or review, the objective of which would be the expression of an opinion or conclusion, respectively, on compliance with specified requirements. Accordingly, we do not express such an opinion or conclusion. Had we performed additional procedures, other matters might have come to our attention that would have been reported to you.

This report is intended solely for the information and use of [*identify the specified parties, for example, the management and board of directors of XYZ Company*] and is not intended to be, and should not be, used by anyone other than the specified parties.

[*Practitioner's signature*]
[*Practitioner's city and state*]
[*Date of practitioner's report*]

Example 4: Practitioner's Agreed-Upon Procedures Report Related to Internal Control Over Compliance

The following is an illustrative practitioner's agreed-upon procedures report related to an entity's internal control over compliance in which the procedures and findings are enumerated rather than referenced.

---

6 If the agreed-upon procedures have been published by a third-party user (for example, a regulator in regulatory policies or a lender in a debt agreement), this sentence might begin as follows: "We have performed the procedures included in [*title of publication or other document*] and enumerated below..."

Independent Accountant's Report on Applying Agreed-Upon Procedures

[*Appropriate Addressee*]

We have performed the procedures enumerated below, which were agreed to by [*identify the specified parties, for example, the management and board of directors of XYZ Company*], related to XYZ Company's internal control over compliance with [*identify the specified requirements for example, the requirements listed in Attachment 1*], as of December 31, 20X1.[7] XYZ Company's management is responsible for its internal control over compliance with those requirements. The sufficiency of these procedures is solely the responsibility of the parties specified in this report. Consequently, we make no representations regarding the sufficiency of the procedures enumerated below either for the purpose for which this report has been requested or for any other purpose.

[*Include paragraphs to enumerate procedures and findings.*]

This agreed-upon procedures engagement was conducted in accordance with attestation standards established by the American Institute of Certified Public Accountants. We were not engaged to and did not conduct an examination or review, the objective of which would be the expression of an opinion or conclusion, respectively, on internal control over compliance with specified requirements. Accordingly, we do not express such an opinion or conclusion. Had we performed additional procedures, other matters might have come to our attention that would have been reported to you.

This report is intended solely for the information and use of [*identify the specified parties, for example, the management and board of directors of XYZ Company*] and is not intended to be, and should not be, used by anyone other than the specified parties.

[*Practitioner's signature*]
[*Practitioner's city and state*]
[*Date of practitioner's report*]

---

7 If the agreed-upon procedures have been published by a third-party user (for example, a regulator in regulatory policies or a lender in a debt agreement), this sentence might begin as follows: "We have performed the procedures included in [*title of publication or other documents*] and enumerated below..."

AT-C Section 320*

Reporting on an Examination of Controls at a Service Organization Relevant to User Entities' Internal Control Over Financial Reporting

Source: SSAE No. 18

Effective for service auditors' reports dated on or after May 1, 2017.

Introduction

.01 This section contains performance and reporting requirements and application guidance for a service auditor examining controls at organizations that provide services to user entities when those controls are likely to be relevant to user entities' internal control over financial reporting. It complements AU-C section 402, *Audit Considerations Relating to an Entity Using a Service Organization*, in that a service auditor's report prepared in accordance with this section may provide appropriate evidence under AU-C section 402. (Ref: par. .A1)

.02 In addition to complying with this section, a practitioner is required to comply with section 105, *Concepts Common to All Attestation Engagements*, and section 205, *Examination Engagements*. In some cases, this section repeats or refers to requirements in sections 105 and 205 when describing those requirements in the context of examinations that address controls at a service organization likely to be relevant to user entities' internal control over financial reporting. Although not all the requirements in sections 105 and 205 are repeated or referred to in this section, the practitioner is responsible for complying with all the requirements in sections 105 and 205. (Ref: par. .A2)

.03 Section 205 indicates that when performing an attestation engagement, a practitioner should report on a written assertion or should report directly on the subject matter.[1] For engagements conducted under this section, the service auditor reports directly on the subject matter.

.04 The focus of this section is on controls at service organizations likely to be relevant to user entities' internal control over financial reporting. The guidance herein also may be helpful to a practitioner performing an engagement under section 205 to report on controls at a service organization

a. other than those that are likely to be relevant to user entities' internal control over financial reporting (for example, controls that affect user entities' compliance with specified requirements of laws, regulations, rules, contracts, or grants or controls that affect user entities' production or quality control). Section 315,

---

* This section contains an "AT-C" identifier, instead of an "AT" identifier, to avoid confusion with references to existing "AT" sections, which remain effective through April 2017.

[1] Paragraph .62 of section 205, *Examination Engagements*.

Compliance Attestation, is applicable if a practitioner is performing agreed-upon procedures related to an entity's internal control over compliance with specified requirements. Section 205 is applicable if a practitioner is examining an entity's controls over compliance with specified requirements. (Ref: par. .A3–.A4)

b. when management of the service organization does not provide an assertion about the suitability of the design of controls because it is not responsible for the design of the controls (for example, when the controls have been designed by the user entity or the design is stipulated in a contract between the user entity and the service organization). (Ref: par. .A5)

.05 In addition to performing an examination of a service organization's controls, a service auditor may be engaged to (*a*) examine and report on a user entity's transactions or balances maintained by a service organization, or (*b*) perform and report under section 215, *Agreed-Upon Procedures Engagements*, the results of agreed-upon procedures related to the controls of a service organization or to transactions or balances of a user entity maintained by a service organization. However, these engagements are not addressed in this section.

Effective Date

.06 This section is effective for service auditors' reports dated on or after May 1, 2017.

Objectives

.07 The objectives of the service auditor are to

a. obtain reasonable assurance about whether, in all material respects, based on the criteria

i. management's description of the service organization's system fairly presents the service organization's system that was designed and implemented throughout the specified period (or in the case of a type 1 report, as of a specified date)

ii. the controls related to the control objectives stated in management's description of the service organization's system were suitably designed to provide reasonable assurance that the control objectives would be achieved if the controls operated effectively throughout the specified period (or in the case of a type 1 report, as of a specified date).

iii. when included in the scope of the engagement, the controls operated effectively to provide reasonable assurance that the control objectives stated in management's description of the service organization's system were achieved throughout the specified period.

b. express an opinion in a written report about the matters in paragraph .07*a*.

Definitions

.08 For the purposes of this section, the following definitions apply:

Carve-out method. Method of addressing the services provided by a subservice organization, whereby management's description of the service organization's system identifies the nature of the services performed by the subservice organization and excludes from the description and from the scope of the service auditor's engagement the subservice organization's relevant control objectives and related controls.

Complementary subservice organization controls. Controls that management of the service organization assumes, in the design of the service organization's system, will be implemented by the subservice organizations and are necessary to achieve the control objectives stated in management's description of the service organization's system.

Complementary user entity controls. Controls that management of the service organization assumes, in the design of the service organization's system, will be implemented by user entities and are necessary to achieve the control objectives stated in management's description of the service organization's system. (Ref: par. .A6)

Control objectives. The aim or purpose of specified controls at the service organization. Control objectives address the risks that controls are intended to mitigate.

Controls at a service organization. The policies and procedures at a service organization likely to be relevant to user entities' internal control over financial reporting. These policies and procedures are designed, implemented, and documented by the service organization to provide reasonable assurance about the achievement of the control objectives relevant to the services covered by the service auditor's report. (Ref: par. .A7)

Inclusive method. Method of addressing the services provided by a subservice organization whereby management's description of the service organization's system includes a description of the nature of the services provided by the subservice organization as well as the subservice organization's relevant control objectives and related controls.

Management's description of a service organization's system and a service auditor's report on that description and on the suitability of the design of controls (referred to in this section as a *type 1 report*). A service auditor's report that comprises the following:

a. Management's description of the service organization's system

b. A written assertion by management of the service organization about whether, based on the criteria

i. management's description of the service organization's system fairly presents the service organization's system that was designed and implemented as of a specified date

ii. the controls related to the control objectives stated in management's description of the service organization's system were suitably designed to achieve those control objectives as of the specified date

c. A report that expresses an opinion on the matters in *b*(i)–(ii)

Management's description of a service organization's system and a service auditor's report on that description and on the suitability of the design and operating effectiveness of controls (referred to in this section as a *type 2 report*). A service auditor's report that comprises the following:

a. Management's description of the service organization's system

b. A written assertion by management of the service organization about whether, based on the criteria

i. management's description of the service organization's system fairly presents the service organization's system that was designed and implemented throughout the specified period

ii. the controls related to the control objectives stated in management's description of the service organization's system were suitably designed throughout the specified period to achieve those control objectives

iii. the controls related to the control objectives stated in management's description of the service organization's system operated effectively throughout the specified period to achieve those control objectives

c. A report that

i. expresses an opinion on the matters in *b*(i)–(iii)

ii. includes a description of the tests of controls and the results thereof

Service auditor. A practitioner who reports on controls at a service organization.

Service organization. An organization or segment of an organization that provides services to user entities, which are likely to be relevant to those user entities' internal control over financial reporting.

Service organization's assertion. A written assertion about the matters referred to in part (b) of the definition of **management's description of a service organization's system and a service auditor's report on that description and on the suitability of the design and operating effectiveness of controls**, for a type 2 report, and, for a type 1 report, the matters referred to in part (b) of the definition of **management's description of a service organization's system and a service auditor's report on that description and on the suitability of the design of controls.**

Service organization's system. The policies and procedures designed, implemented, and documented by management of the service organization to provide user entities with the services covered by the service auditor's report. Management's description of the service organization's system identifies the services covered, the period to which the description relates (or in the case of a type 1 report, the date to which the description relates), the control objectives specified by management or an outside party, the party specifying the control objectives (if not specified by management), and the related controls. (Ref: par. .A8)

Subservice organization. A service organization used by another service organization to perform some of the services provided to user entities that are likely to be relevant to those user entities' internal control over financial reporting. (Ref: par. .A9)

Test of controls. A procedure designed to evaluate the operating effectiveness of controls in achieving the control objectives stated in management's description of the service organization's system.

Type 1 report. See **management's description of a service organization's system and a service auditor's report on that description and on the suitability of the design of controls.**

Type 2 report. See **management's description of a service organization's system and a service auditor's report on that description and on the suitability of the design and operating effectiveness of controls.**

User auditor. An auditor who audits and reports on the financial statements of a user entity.

User entity. An entity that uses a service organization for which controls at the service organization are likely to be relevant to that entity's internal control over financial reporting.

Requirements

Management and Those Charged With Governance

.09 When this section requires the service auditor to inquire of, request representations from, communicate with, or otherwise interact with management of the service organization, the service auditor should determine the appropriate person(s) within the service organization's management or governance structure with whom to interact. This should include consideration of which person(s) has the appropriate responsibilities for and knowledge of the matters concerned. (Ref: par. .A10–.A11)

Preconditions

.10 A service auditor should accept or continue an engagement to report on controls at a service organization pursuant to this section only if the preconditions for an attestation engagement identified in section 105 and the following conditions are met:[2] (Ref: par. .A12–.A13)

a. The service auditor's preliminary knowledge of the engagement circumstances indicates that the scope of the engagement and management's description of the service organization's system will not be so limited that they are unlikely to be useful to user entities and their auditors.

b. Management acknowledges and accepts its responsibility for the following:

  i. Preparing its description of the service organization's system and its assertion, including the completeness, accuracy, and method of presentation of the description and assertion (Ref: par. .A14)

  ii. Having a reasonable basis for its assertion (Ref: par. .A15)

---

[2] Paragraphs .24–.28 of section 105, *Concepts Common to All Attestation Engagements.*

iii. Selecting the criteria to be used and stating them in the assertion

iv. Specifying the control objectives, stating them in the description of the service organization's system, and, if the control objectives are specified by law, regulation, or another party (for example, a user group or a professional body), identifying in the description the party specifying the control objectives (Ref: par. .A16)

v. Identifying the risks that threaten the achievement of the control objectives stated in the description and designing, implementing, and documenting controls that are suitably designed and operating effectively to provide reasonable assurance that the control objectives stated in the description of the service organization's system will be achieved (Ref: par. .A17)

vi. Providing a written assertion that accompanies management's description of the service organization's system, both of which will be provided to user entities (Ref: par. .A18)

.11 When the inclusive method is used, the service auditor should apply the requirements in sections 105, 205, and this section to the services provided by the subservice organization, as applicable, including the requirement to obtain management of the service organization's acknowledgement and acceptance of responsibility for the matters in paragraph .10*b* of this section as they relate to the subservice organization. (Ref: par. .A19–.A20)

Request to Change the Scope of the Engagement

.12 As required by section 105, if management requests a change in the scope of the engagement before the completion of the engagement, the service auditor should not agree to a change in the terms of the engagement when no reasonable justification for doing so exists.[3] (Ref: par. .A21–.A22 and .A57)

Requesting a Written Assertion

.13 The practitioner should request from management of the service organization a written assertion. If management refuses to provide a written assertion, the practitioner should withdraw from the engagement when withdrawal is possible under applicable law or regulation. (Ref: par. .A23)

Assessing the Suitability of the Criteria

.14 As required by section 105, the service auditor should assess whether management has used suitable criteria in[4] (Ref: par. .A25–.A26)

a. preparing its description of the service organization's system,

b. evaluating whether controls were suitably designed to achieve the control objectives stated in the description, and

c. evaluating whether controls operated effectively throughout the specified period to achieve the control objectives stated in the description of the service organization's system, in the case of a type 2 report.

---

[3] Paragraph .29 of section 105.

[4] Paragraph .25*b*(ii) of section 105.

.15 In assessing the suitability of the criteria to evaluate whether management's description of the service organization's system is fairly presented, the service auditor should determine if the criteria include, at a minimum

a. whether management's description of the service organization's system presents how the service organization's system was designed and implemented, including the following information about the service organization's system, if applicable:

   i. The types of services provided, including, as appropriate, the classes of transactions processed.

   ii. The procedures, within both automated and manual systems, by which services are provided, including, as appropriate, procedures by which transactions are initiated, authorized, recorded, processed, corrected as necessary, and transferred to the reports and other information prepared for user entities.

   iii. The information used in the performance of the procedures, including, if applicable, related accounting records, whether electronic or manual, and supporting information involved in initiating, authorizing, recording, processing, and reporting transactions. This includes the correction of incorrect information and how information is transferred to the reports and other information prepared for user entities.

   iv. How the service organization's system captures and addresses significant events and conditions other than transactions.

   v. The process used to prepare reports and other information for user entities.

   vi. Services performed by a subservice organization, if any, including whether the carve- out method or the inclusive method has been used in relation to them. (Ref: par. .A37)

   vii. The specified control objectives and controls designed to achieve those objectives, including, as applicable, complementary user entity controls and complementary subservice organization controls assumed in the design of the service organization's controls.

   viii. Other aspects of the service organization's control environment, risk assessment process, information and communications (including the related business processes), control activities, and monitoring activities that are relevant to the services provided. (Ref: par. .A15 and .A27)

b. in the case of a type 2 report, whether management's description of the service organization's system includes relevant details of changes to the service organization's system during the period covered by the description. (Ref: par. .A50)

c. whether management's description of the service organization's system does not omit or distort information relevant to the service organization's system, while acknowledging that management's description of the service organization's system is prepared to meet the common needs of a broad range of user entities and their user auditors, and may not, therefore, include every aspect of the service organization's system that each individual user entity and its user auditor may consider important in its own particular environment.

.16 In assessing the suitability of the criteria to evaluate whether the controls are suitably designed, the service auditor should determine if the criteria include, at a minimum, whether

a. the risks that threaten the achievement of the control objectives stated in management's description of the service organization's system have been identified by management.

b. the controls identified in management's description of the service organization's system would, if operating effectively, provide reasonable assurance that those risks would not prevent the control objectives stated in the description from being achieved.

.17 In assessing the suitability of the criteria to evaluate whether controls operated effectively to provide reasonable assurance that the control objectives stated in management's description of the service organization's system were achieved, the service auditor should determine if the criteria include, at a minimum, whether the controls were consistently applied as designed throughout the specified period, including whether manual controls were applied by individuals who have the appropriate competence and authority.

.18 Section 205 requires a practitioner to request from the responsible party a written assertion about the measurement or evaluation of the subject matter against the criteria.[5] The practitioner should determine that management's assertion addresses all the criteria management used to evaluate the fairness of the presentation of the description, the suitability of the design of the controls, and in a type 2 engagement, the operating effectiveness of the controls. (Ref: par. .A24)

Materiality

.19 The service auditor's consideration of materiality should include the fair presentation of management's description of the service organization's system, the suitability of the design of controls to achieve the related control objectives stated in the description and, in the case of a type 2 report, the operating effectiveness of the controls to achieve the related control objectives stated in the description. (Ref: par. .A28–.A30)

Obtaining an Understanding of the Service Organization's System and Assessing the Risk of Material Misstatement

.20 The service auditor should obtain an understanding of the service organization's system, including controls that are included in the scope of the engagement. That understanding should include service organization processes used to (Ref: par. .A31–.A33)

a. prepare the description of the service organization's system, including the determination of control objectives,

b. identify controls designed to achieve the control objectives,

c. assess the suitability of the design of the controls, and

d. in a type 2 report, assess the operating effectiveness of controls.

---

[5] Paragraph .10 of section 205.

.21 If the service organization has an internal audit function, part of the service auditor's understanding of the service organization's system should include the following:

a. The nature of the internal audit function's responsibilities and how the internal audit function fits in the service organization's organizational structure

b. The activities performed, or to be performed, by the internal audit function as it relates to the service organization

.22 As required by section 205, the service auditor should identify the risks of material misstatement.[6] (Ref: par. .A34–.A35)

.23 The service auditor should read the reports of the internal audit function and regulatory examinations that relate to the services provided to user entities and the scope of the engagement, if any, to obtain an understanding of the nature and extent of the procedures performed and the related findings. The findings should be taken into consideration as part of the risk assessment and in determining the nature, timing, and extent of the tests.

Responding to Assessed Risks and Further Procedures

.24 As required by paragraphs .25–.39 of this section and section 205, the service auditor should[7]

a. design and implement overall responses to address the assessed risks of material misstatement for the subject matter and

b. design and perform further procedures whose nature, timing, and extent are based on, and responsive to, the assessed risks of material misstatement.

Obtaining Evidence Regarding Management's Description of the Service Organization's System

.25 The service auditor should obtain and read management's description of the service organization's system and should evaluate whether those aspects of the description that are included in the scope of the engagement are presented fairly, in all material respects, based on the criteria in management's assertion, including whether (Ref: par. .A28–.A29 and .A36–.A40)

a. the control objectives stated in management's description of the service organization's system are reasonable in the circumstances;

b. controls identified in management's description of the service organization's system were implemented;

c. complementary user entity controls and complementary subservice organization controls, if any, are adequately described; and

d. services performed by a subservice organization, if any, are adequately described, including whether the carve-out method or the inclusive method has been used in relation to them.

.26 The service auditor should determine through inquiries made in combination with other procedures whether the service organization's system has been implemented. (Ref: par. .A40)

---

[6] Paragraph .18 of section 205.

[7] Paragraphs .20–.21 of section 205.

Obtaining Evidence Regarding the Design of Controls

.27 The service auditor should assess whether the controls that management identified in its description of the service organization's system as the controls that achieve the control objectives were suitably designed to achieve those control objectives by (Ref: par. .A28–.A29, .A36, and .A41–.A45)

a. obtaining an understanding of management's process for identifying and evaluating the risks that threaten the achievement of the control objectives and assessing the completeness and accuracy of management's identification of those risks,

b. evaluating the linkage of the controls identified in management's description of the service organization's system with those risks, including risks arising from each of the described classes of transactions and risks that IT poses to the user entity's internal control over financial reporting, and

c. determining that the controls have been implemented.

Obtaining Evidence Regarding the Operating Effectiveness of Controls

.28 When performing a type 2 engagement, the service auditor should test those controls that management has identified in its description of the service organization's system as the controls that achieve the control objectives and should assess the operating effectiveness of those controls throughout the period. Evidence obtained in prior engagements about the satisfactory operation of controls in prior periods does not provide a basis for a reduction in testing, even if it is supplemented with evidence obtained during the current period. (Ref: par. .A28–.A30, .A36, and .A46–.A51)

.29 When performing a type 2 engagement, the service auditor should obtain an understanding of changes in the service organization's system that were implemented during the period covered by the service auditor's report. If the service auditor believes the changes would be considered significant by user entities and their auditors, the service auditor should determine whether those changes are included in management's description of the service organization's system. If such changes are not included in the description, the service auditor should describe the changes in the report and determine the effect on the report. If superseded controls are relevant to the achievement of the control objectives stated in the description, the service auditor should, if possible, test the superseded controls before the change. If the service auditor cannot test superseded controls relevant to the achievement of the control objectives stated in the description, the service auditor should determine the effect on the report. (Ref: par. .A50–.A51)

Evaluating the Reliability of Information Produced by the Service Organization

.30 When using information produced by the service organization, section 205 requires the service auditor to evaluate whether such information is sufficiently reliable for the service auditor's purposes by obtaining evidence about its accuracy and completeness and evaluating whether the information is sufficiently precise and detailed.[8] (Ref: par. .A52)

---

[8] Paragraph .35 of section 205.

.31 When designing and performing tests of controls, the service auditor should

a. perform other procedures such as inspection, observation, or reperformance in combination with inquiry to obtain evidence about the following:

i. How the control was applied

ii. The consistency with which the control was applied

iii. By whom or by what means the control was applied

b. determine whether the controls to be tested depend on other controls, and if so, whether it is necessary to obtain evidence supporting the operating effectiveness of those other controls.

c. determine an effective method for selecting the items to be tested to meet the objectives of the procedure.

Nature and Cause of Deviations

.32 The service auditor should investigate the nature and cause of any deviations identified and should determine whether

a. identified deviations are within the expected rate of deviation and are acceptable. If so, the testing that has been performed provides an appropriate basis for concluding that the control operated effectively throughout the specified period.

b. additional testing of the control or other controls is necessary to reach a conclusion about whether the controls related to the control objectives stated in management's description of the service organization's system operated effectively throughout the specified period.

c. the testing that has been performed provides an appropriate basis for concluding that the control did not operate effectively throughout the specified period.

.33 If, as a result of performing the procedures in paragraph .32, the service auditor becomes aware that any identified deviations have resulted from fraud by service organization personnel, the service auditor should assess the risk that management's description of the service organization's system is not fairly presented, the controls are not suitably designed and, in a type 2 engagement, the controls are not operating effectively. (Ref: par. .A36)

.34 If the service auditor becomes aware of incidents of noncompliance with laws or regulations, fraud or uncorrected misstatements attributable to management or other service organization personnel that are not clearly trivial and that may affect one or more user entities, the service auditor should determine the effect of such incidents on management's assertion, management's description of the service organization's system, the achievement of the control objectives, and the service auditor's report.

Subsequent Events

.35 In performing subsequent events procedures as required by section 205, if the service auditor becomes aware of an event that is of such a nature and significance that its disclosure is necessary to prevent users of a type 1 or type 2 report from being misled, and information about that event is not disclosed by management in its description, the service auditor should disclose such event in the service auditor's report.[9]

Written Representations

.36 In addition to the written representations from management required by section 205, the service auditor should request written representations indicating that it has disclosed to the service auditor any of the following of which it is aware:[10] (Ref: par. .A53–.A56)

a. Instances of noncompliance with laws and regulations or uncorrected misstatements attributable to the service organization that may affect one or more user entities

b. Knowledge of any actual, suspected, or alleged fraud by management or the service organization's employees that could adversely affect the fairness of the presentation of management's description of the service organization's system or the completeness or achievement of the control objectives stated in the description

.37 If a service organization uses a subservice organization and management's description of the service organization's system uses the inclusive method, the service auditor should also obtain the written representations identified in section 205 and paragraph .36 of this section from management of the subservice organization.[11] (Ref: par. .A53–.A56)

.38 In a type 1 or type 2 engagement, the practitioner should request from the responsible party (in this case, management of the service organization), the written representations required by section 205 and paragraph .36 of this section, even if the engaging party is not the responsible party. The alternative to obtaining the required written representations provided for in section 205 is not permitted in a type 1 or type 2 engagement.[12] The refusal by management of the service organization (or by management of a subservice organization that is being presented using the inclusive method) to furnish the written representations required by section 205 and paragraph .36 of this section constitutes a limitation on the scope of the engagement sufficient to preclude an unmodified opinion and may be sufficient to cause the service auditor to withdraw from the examination engagement when withdrawal is possible under applicable law or regulation.[13] (Ref: par. .A53–.A57)

Other Information

.39 Section 205 contains requirements for situations in which prior to or after the release of the practitioner's report on subject matter or an assertion, the practitioner is willing to permit the inclusion of the report in a document that contains the subject matter or assertion on which the service auditor reported and other information.[14] (Ref: par. .A58)

---

[9] Paragraph .48 and .A56 of section 205.

[10] Paragraph .50 of section 205.

[11] See footnote 10.

[12] Paragraph .51 of section 205.

[13] Paragraphs .50, .55, and .A64 of section 205.

[14] Paragraph .57 of section 205.

Content of the Service Auditor's Report

.40 A service auditor's type 2 report should include the following: (Ref: par. .A59–.A60)

a. A title that includes the word *independent.*

b. An appropriate addressee as required by the circumstances of the engagement.

c. Identification of the following:

  i. Management's description of the service organization's system, the function performed by the system, and the period to which the description relates

  ii. The criteria identified in management's assertion against which the fairness of the presentation of the description and the suitability of the design and operating effectiveness of the controls to achieve the related control objectives stated in the description were evaluated

  iii. Any information included in a document containing the report that is not covered by the report (Ref: par. .A58)

  iv. Any services performed by a subservice organization and whether the carve-out method or the inclusive method was used in relation to them. Depending on which method is used, the following should be included:

    (1) If the carve-out method was used, a statement indicating that (Ref: par. .A61)

      (a) management's description of the service organization's system excludes the control objectives and related controls of the relevant subservice organizations

      (b) certain control objectives specified by the service organization can be achieved only if complementary subservice organization controls assumed in the design of the service organization's controls are suitably designed and operating effectively

      (c) the service auditor's procedures do not extend to such complementary subservice organization controls

    (2) If the inclusive method was used, a statement that management's description of the service organization's system includes the subservice organization's specified control objectives and related controls, and that the service auditor's procedures included procedures related to the subservice organization

d. A statement that the controls and control objectives included in the description are those that management believes are likely to be relevant to user entities' internal control over financial reporting, and the description does not include those aspects of the system that are not likely to be relevant to user entities' internal control over financial reporting.

e. If management's description of the service organization's system refers to the need for complementary user entity controls, a statement that the service auditor has not evaluated the suitability of the design or operating effectiveness of complementary user entity controls, and that the control objectives stated in the description can be achieved only if complementary user entity controls are suitably designed and operating effectively, along with the controls at the service organization.

f. A reference to management's assertion and a statement that management is responsible for

i. preparing the description of the service organization's system and the assertion, including the completeness, accuracy, and method of presentation of the description and assertion.

ii. providing the services covered by the description of the service organization's system.

iii. specifying the control objectives and stating them in the description of the service organization's system.

iv. identifying the risks that threaten the achievement of the control objectives.

v. selecting the criteria.

vi. designing, implementing, and documenting controls that are suitably designed and operating effectively to achieve the related control objectives stated in the description of the service organization's system.

g. A statement that the service auditor is responsible for expressing an opinion on the fairness of the presentation of management's description of the service organization's system and on the suitability of the design and operating effectiveness of the controls to achieve the related control objectives stated in the description based on the service auditor's examination.

h. A statement that

i. the examination was conducted in accordance with attestation standards established by the American Institute of Certified Public Accountants.

ii. those standards require that the service auditor plan and perform the examination to obtain reasonable assurance about whether, in all material respects, based on the criteria in management's assertion, management's description of the service organization's system is fairly presented and the controls are suitably designed and operating effectively throughout the specified period to achieve the related control objectives.

iii. the service auditor believes the evidence obtained is sufficient and appropriate to provide a reasonable basis for the service auditor's opinion.

i. A statement that an examination of management's description of a service organization's system and the suitability of the design and operating effectiveness of the service organization's controls to achieve the related control objectives stated in the description involves

i. performing procedures to obtain evidence about the fairness of the presentation of the description and the suitability of the design and operating effectiveness of the controls to achieve the related control objectives stated in the description based on the criteria in management's assertion.

ii. assessing the risks that management's description of the service organization's system is not fairly presented and that the controls were not suitably designed or operating effectively to achieve the related control objectives.

iii. testing the operating effectiveness of those controls that management considers necessary to provide reasonable assurance that the related control objectives stated in management's description of the service organization's system were achieved.

iv. evaluating the overall presentation of management's description of the service organization's system, suitability of the control objectives stated in the description, and suitability of the criteria specified by the service organization in its assertion.

j. A description of the inherent limitations of controls, including that projecting to the future any evaluation of the fairness of the presentation of management's description of the service organization's system or conclusions about the suitability of the design or operating effectiveness of the controls to achieve the related control objectives is subject to the risk that controls at a service organization may become ineffective.

k. A reference to a description of the service auditor's tests of controls and the results thereof that includes (Ref: par. .A62)

i. an identification of the controls that were tested.

ii. whether the items tested represent all or a selection of the items in the population.

iii. the nature of the tests in sufficient detail to enable user auditors to determine the effect of such tests on their risk assessments.

iv. any identified deviations in the operation of controls included in the description, the extent of testing performed by the service auditor that led to the identification of the deviations (including the number of items tested), and the number and nature of the deviations noted (even if, on the basis of tests performed, the service auditor concludes that the related control objective was achieved). (Ref: par. .A63)

v. if the work of the internal audit function has been used in tests of controls to obtain evidence, a description of the internal auditor's work and of the service auditor's procedures with respect to that work. (Ref: par. .A64–.A66)

l. The service auditor's opinion on whether, in all material respects, based on the criteria described in management's assertion

i. management's description of the service organization's system fairly presents the service organization's system that was designed and implemented throughout the specified period.

ii. the controls related to the control objectives stated in management's description of the service organization's system were suitably designed to provide reasonable assurance that the control objectives would be achieved if the controls operated effectively throughout the specified period.

iii. the controls operated effectively to provide reasonable assurance that the control objectives stated in management's description of the service organization's system were achieved throughout the specified period.

iv. if the application of complementary user entity controls is necessary to achieve the related control objectives stated in management's description of the service organization's system, a statement to that effect.

v. if the application of complementary subservice organization controls is necessary to achieve the related control objectives stated in management's description of the service organization's system, a statement to that effect.

m. An alert, in a separate paragraph, that restricts the use of the report. The alert should (Ref: par. .A67–.A72)

i. state that the report, including the description of tests of controls and results thereof, is intended solely for the information and use of management of the service organization, user entities of the service organization's system during some or all of the period covered by the report, and the auditors who audit and report on such user entities' financial statements or internal control over financial reporting.

ii. state that the report is not intended to be, and should not be, used by anyone other than the specified parties.[15]

n. The manual or printed signature of the service auditor's firm.

o. The city and state where the service auditor practices.

p. The date of the report. (The report should be dated no earlier than the date on which the service auditor has obtained sufficient appropriate evidence on which to base the service auditor's opinion, including evidence that

i. management's description of the service organization system has been prepared,

ii. management has provided a written assertion, and

iii. the attestation documentation has been reviewed.)

.41 A service auditor's type 1 report should include the following: (Ref: par. .A59 and .A72)

a. A title that includes the word *independent*.

b. An appropriate addressee as required by the circumstances of the engagement.

c. Identification of the following:

i. Management's description of the service organization's system, the function performed by the system, and the specified date to which the description relates.

---

[15] Paragraph .65 or .66 of section 205.

ii. The criteria identified in management's assertion against which the fairness of the presentation of the description and the suitability of the design of the controls to achieve the related control objectives stated in the description were evaluated.

iii. Any information included in a document containing the report that is not covered by the report. (Ref: par. .A58)

iv. Any services performed by a subservice organization and whether the carve-out method or the inclusive method was used in relation to them. Depending on which method is used, the following should be included:

(1) If the carve-out method was used, a statement indicating that (Ref: par. .A61)

(a) management's description of the service organization's system excludes the control objectives and related controls of the relevant subservice organizations.

(b) certain control objectives specified by the service organization can be achieved only if complementary subservice organization controls assumed in the design of the service organization's controls are suitably designed and operating effectively.

(c) the service auditor's procedures do not extend to such complementary subservice organization controls.

(2) If the inclusive method was used, a statement that management's description of the service organization's system includes the subservice organization's specified control objectives and related controls, and that the service auditor's procedures included procedures related to the subservice organization.

d. A statement that the controls and control objectives included in the description are those that management believes are likely to be relevant to user entities' internal control over financial reporting, and the description does not include those aspects of the system that are not likely to be relevant to user entities' internal control over financial reporting.

e. If management's description of the service organization's system refers to the need for complementary user entity controls, a statement that the service auditor has not evaluated the suitability of the design or operating effectiveness of complementary user entity controls, and that the control objectives stated in the description can be achieved only if complementary user entity controls are suitably designed and operating effectively, along with the controls at the service organization.

f. A reference to management's assertion and a statement that management is responsible for

i. preparing the description of the service organization's system and the assertion, including the completeness, accuracy, and method of presentation of the description and assertion.

ii. providing the services covered by the description of the service organization's system.

iii. specifying the control objectives and stating them in the description of the service organization's system.

iv. identifying the risks that threaten the achievement of the control objectives.

v. selecting the criteria.

vi. designing, implementing, and documenting controls that are suitably designed and operating effectively to achieve the related control objectives stated in the description of the service organization's system.

g. A statement that the service auditor is responsible for expressing an opinion on the fairness of the presentation of management's description of the service organization's system and on the suitability of the design of the controls to achieve the related control objectives stated in the description, based on the service auditor's examination.

h. A statement that

i. the examination was conducted in accordance with attestation standards established by the American Institute of Certified Public Accountants.

ii. those standards require that the service auditor plan and perform the examination to obtain reasonable assurance about whether, in all material respects, based on the criteria in management's assertion, management's description of the service organization's system is fairly presented, and the controls are suitably designed as of the specified date to achieve the related control objectives.

iii. the service auditor believes the evidence obtained is sufficient and appropriate to provide a reasonable basis for the service auditor's opinion.

i. A statement that an examination of management's description of a service organization's system and the suitability of the design of the service organization's controls to achieve the related control objectives stated in the description involves

i. performing procedures to obtain evidence about the fairness of the presentation of the description and the suitability of the design of the controls to achieve the related control objectives stated in the description, based on the criteria in management's assertion.

ii. assessing the risks that management's description of the service organization's system is not fairly presented and that the controls were not suitably designed to achieve the related control objectives.

iii. evaluating the overall presentation of management's description of the service organization's system, suitability of the control objectives stated in the description, and suitability of the criteria specified by the service organization in its assertion.

j. A description of the inherent limitations of controls, including that projecting to the future any evaluation of the fairness of the presentation of management's description of the service organization's system or conclusions about the suitability of the design of the controls to achieve the related control objectives is subject to the risk that controls at a service organization may become ineffective.

k. A statement the service auditor has not performed any procedures regarding the operating effectiveness of controls and, therefore, expresses no opinion thereon.

l. The service auditor's opinion on whether, in all material respects, based on the criteria described in management's assertion

   i. management's description of the service organization's system fairly presents the service organization's system that was designed and implemented as of the specified date.

   ii. the controls related to the control objectives stated in management's description of the service organization's system were suitably designed to provide reasonable assurance that the control objectives would be achieved if the controls operated effectively as of the specified date.

   iii. if the application of complementary user entity controls is necessary to achieve the related control objectives stated in management's description of the service organization's system, a statement to that effect.

   iv. if the application of complementary subservice organization controls is necessary to achieve the related control objectives stated in management's description of the service organization's system, a statement to that effect.

m. An alert, in a separate paragraph, that restricts the use of the report. The alert should (Ref: par. .A67–.A72)

   i. state that the report is intended solely for the information and use of management of the service organization, user entities of the service organization's system as of the specified date, and the auditors who audit and report on such user entities' financial statements or internal control over financial reporting.

   ii. state that the report is not intended to be, and should not be, used by anyone other than the specified parties.[16]

n. The manual or printed signature of the service auditor's firm.

o. The city and state where the service auditor practices.

p. The date of the report. (The report should be dated no earlier than the date on which the service auditor has obtained sufficient appropriate evidence on which to base the service auditor's opinion, including evidence that

   i. management's description of the service organization system has been prepared,

   ii. management has provided a written assertion, and

   iii. the attestation documentation has been reviewed.)

---

[16] Paragraph .65 or .66 of section 205.

Modified Opinions

.42 The service auditor's opinion should be modified, and the service auditor's report should contain a clear description of all the reasons for the modification, if the service auditor concludes that, based on the criteria in management's assertion (Ref. par. .A73)

a. management's description of the service organization's system is not fairly presented, in all material respects;

b. the controls are not suitably designed to provide reasonable assurance that the control objectives stated in management's description of the service organization's system would be achieved if the controls operated effectively, in all material respects;

c. in the case of a type 2 report, the controls did not operate effectively throughout the specified period to achieve the related control objectives stated in management's description of the service organization's system, in all material respects; or

d. the service auditor is unable to obtain sufficient appropriate evidence.

.43 If the service auditor plans to disclaim an opinion because of the inability to obtain sufficient appropriate evidence, and, based on the limited procedures performed, has concluded that, in all material respects, based on the criteria in management's assertion

a. certain aspects of management's description of the service organization's system are not fairly presented,

b. certain controls were not suitably designed to provide reasonable assurance that the control objectives stated in management's description of the service organization's system would be achieved if the controls operated effectively, or

c. in the case of a type 2 report, certain controls did not operate effectively throughout the specified period to achieve the related control objectives stated in management's description of the service organization's system, then

the service auditor should identify these findings in the service auditor's report.

.44 If the service auditor plans to disclaim an opinion, the service auditor *should not* identify the procedures that were performed nor include statements describing the characteristics of a service auditor's engagement in the service auditor's report—to do so might overshadow the disclaimer.

Other Communication Responsibilities

.45 In addition to the communication responsibilities in section 205, if the service auditor becomes aware of the matters identified in paragraph .34, the service auditor should determine whether this information has been communicated appropriately to affected user entities.[17] If the information has not been so communicated, and management of the service organization refuses to do so, the service auditor should take appropriate action. (Ref: par. .A74)

[17] Paragraphs .85–.86 of section 205.

Application and Other Explanatory Material

Introduction (Ref: par. .01–.02 and .04)

.A1 Controls related to a service organization's operations and compliance objectives may be relevant to a user entity's internal control over financial reporting. Such controls may pertain to assertions about presentation and disclosure relating to account balances, classes of transactions or disclosures, or may pertain to evidence that the user auditor evaluates or uses in applying auditing procedures. For example, a payroll processing service organization's controls related to the timely remittance of payroll deductions to government authorities may be relevant to a user entity because late remittances could incur interest and penalties that would result in a liability to the user entity. Similarly, a service organization's controls over the acceptability of investment transactions from a regulatory perspective may be considered relevant to a user entity's presentation and disclosure of transactions and account balances in its financial statements.

.A2 Section 105 requires the practitioner to consider applicable interpretive publications when planning and performing an attestation engagement.[18] Additional interpretive guidance for a practitioner examining controls at a service organization relevant to user entities' internal control over financial reporting is provided in the AICPA Guide *Service Organizations: Reporting on Controls at a Service Organization Relevant to User Entities' Internal Control Over Financial Reporting*.

.A3 Paragraph .04 of this section refers to other engagements the practitioner may perform and report on under section 205 when reporting on controls at a service organization. Paragraph .04 is not, however, intended to

- alter the definitions of a *service organization* and *service organization's system* in paragraph .08 to permit reports issued under this section to include in the description of the service organization's system aspects of their services (including relevant control objectives and related controls) not likely to be relevant to user entities' internal control over financial reporting, or
- permit a practitioner's report to be issued that combines reporting under this section on a service organization's controls that are likely to be relevant to user entities' internal control over financial reporting, with reporting under section 205 on controls that are not likely to be relevant to user entities' internal control over financial reporting.

.A4 When a service auditor conducts an engagement under section 205 to report on controls at a service organization other than those controls likely to be relevant to user entities' internal control over financial reporting, and the service auditor intends to use the guidance in this section in planning and performing that engagement, the service auditor may encounter matters that differ significantly from those associated with engagements to report on a service organization's controls likely to be relevant to user entities' internal control over financial reporting. The following are examples of such matters:

- Identification of suitable and available criteria, as prescribed in section 105, for evaluating the fairness of presentation of management's description of the service organization's system and the

---

[18] Paragraph .21 of section 105.

suitability of the design and the operating effectiveness of the controls[19]

- Identification of appropriate control objectives, and the basis for evaluating the reasonableness of the control objectives in the circumstances of the particular engagement
- Identification of the intended users of the report and the manner in which they intend to use the report
- Relevance and appropriateness of the definitions in paragraph .08, many of which specifically relate to internal control over financial reporting
- Application of references to auditing standards (AU-C sections) that are intended to provide the service auditor with guidance relevant to internal control over financial reporting
- Application of the concept of materiality in the circumstances of the particular engagement
- Developing the language to be used and identifying the elements to be included in a practitioner's examination report, as discussed in section 205[20]

.A5 In some circumstances, management of the service organization may not be in a position to assert that the controls are suitably designed, for example, because the controls have been designed by management of the user entity. If management is unable to assert that the controls are suitably designed, management would also be precluded from asserting that the controls are operating effectively because of the inextricable link between the suitability of the design of controls and their operating effectiveness. The absence of an assertion with respect to the suitability of design of controls would preclude the service auditor from expressing an opinion on the operating effectiveness of controls. As an alternative, the practitioner may report under section 205 on whether the controls were operating as described or may perform agreed-upon procedures under section 215.

Definitions (Ref: par. .08)

Complementary User Entity Controls

.A6 Complementary user entity controls are specific and relevant to the services provided by the service organization applicable to user entities' internal control over financial reporting.

Controls at a Service Organization

.A7 The policies and procedures referred to in the definition of *controls at a service organization* in paragraph .08 include aspects of the information and communications component of user entities' internal control maintained by the service organization and control activities related to the information and communications component and may also include aspects of one or more of the other components of internal control at a service organization. For example, the definition of *controls at a service organization* may include aspects of the service organization's control environment, risk assessment, monitoring activities, and control activities when they relate to the services provided. Such

---

[19] Paragraph .25*b*(ii) of section 105.

[20] Paragraphs .63–.66 of section 205.

definition does not, however, include controls at a service organization that are not related to the achievement of the control objectives stated in management's description of the service organization's system, for example, controls related to the preparation of the service organization's own financial statements.

Service Organization's System

.A8 The policies and procedures referred to in the definition of *service organization's system* refer to the guidelines and activities for providing transaction processing and other services to user entities and include the infrastructure, software, people, and data that support the policies and procedures.

Subservice Organization

.A9 There may be instances in which a subservice organization uses the services of another service organization to perform services that are likely to be relevant to user entities' internal control over financial reporting. In those circumstances, the service organization that provides services to the subservice organization is also a subservice organization.

Management and Those Charged With Governance (Ref: par. .09)

.A10 For the purposes of this section, the responsible party is management of the service organization.

.A11 Management and governance structures vary by entity, reflecting influences such as size and ownership characteristics. Such diversity means that it is not possible for this section to specify for all engagements the person(s) with whom the service auditor is to interact regarding particular matters. For example, the service organization may be a segment of an organization and not a separate legal entity. In such cases, identifying the appropriate management personnel or those charged with governance from whom to request written representations may require the exercise of professional judgment.

Preconditions

Service Auditor Need Not Be Independent of User Entities (Ref: par. .10)

.A12 In performing a service auditor's engagement, the service auditor need not be independent of each user entity.

Law or Regulation Requires Acceptance or Continuance of Engagement (Ref: par. .10)

.A13 If one or more of the conditions in paragraph .10 of this section or in section 105 are not met and the service auditor is, nevertheless, required by law or regulation to accept or continue an engagement to report on controls at a service organization, the service auditor is required, in accordance with paragraphs .42–.44, to determine the effect on the service auditor's report of one or more of such conditions not being met.[21]

[21] Paragraphs .24–.28 of section 105.

Management's Responsibility for Documenting the Service Organization's System (Ref: par. .10b[i])

.A14 Management of the service organization is responsible for documenting the service organization's system. No one particular form of documentation is prescribed, and the extent of documentation may vary depending on the size and complexity of the service organization and its monitoring activities.

Reasonable Basis for Management's Assertion (Ref: par. .10b[ii] and .15a[viii])

.A15 Management's monitoring activities may provide evidence of the design and operating effectiveness of controls in support of management's assertion. *Monitoring of controls* is a process to assess the effectiveness of internal control performance over time. It involves assessing the effectiveness of controls on a timely basis, identifying and reporting deficiencies to appropriate individuals within the service organization, and taking necessary corrective actions. Management accomplishes monitoring of controls through ongoing activities, separate evaluations, or a combination of the two. Ongoing monitoring activities are often built into the normal recurring activities of an entity and include regular management and supervisory activities. Internal auditors or personnel performing similar functions may contribute to the monitoring of a service organization's activities. Monitoring activities may also include using information communicated by external parties, such as customer complaints, which may indicate problems or highlight areas in need of improvement. The greater the degree and effectiveness of ongoing monitoring, the less need for separate evaluations. Usually, some combination of ongoing monitoring and separate evaluations will ensure that internal control maintains its effectiveness over time. The service auditor's report on controls is not a substitute for the service organization's own processes to provide a reasonable basis for its assertion.

Management's Responsibility for Control Objectives (Ref. par. 10b[iv])

.A16 The control objectives stated in management's description of the service organization's system relate to the types of financial statement assertions commonly embodied in the broad range of user entities' financial statements to which controls at the service organization could reasonably be expected to relate.

Management's Responsibility for Identifying Risks (Ref: par. .10b[v])

.A17 Control objectives relate to risks that controls seek to mitigate. For example, the risk that a transaction is recorded at the wrong amount or in the wrong period can be expressed as a control objective that transactions are recorded at the correct amount and in the correct period. Management is responsible for identifying the risks that threaten achievement of the control objectives stated in management's description of the service organization's system. A service organization's controls may be designed with the assumption that user entities will have implemented complementary user entity controls or that subservice organizations will have implemented complementary subservice organization controls that are necessary to achieve the control objectives. The risks that management identifies also include the risk that such controls were not implemented by user entities or subservice organizations or that those controls were not operating effectively. Management may have a formal or informal process for identifying relevant risks. A formal process may include estimating the significance of identified risks, assessing the likelihood of their occurrence, and deciding about actions to address them. However, because control objectives relate to risks that controls seek to mitigate, thoughtful identification by management of control objectives when designing, implementing, and documenting the service organization's system may itself comprise an informal process for identifying relevant risks.

Providing a Written Assertion (Ref: par. .10b[vi])

.A18 The service organization's assertion may be attached to the description of the service organization's system or may be included in the description if clearly segregated from the description, for example, through the use of headings. Segregating the assertion from the description clarifies that the assertion is not part of the description. (See subparagraph (b) of the definitions of *management's description of a service organization's system and a service auditor's report on that description and on the suitability of the design of controls* and *management's description of a service organization's system and a service auditor's report on that description and on the suitability of the design and operating effectiveness of controls* in paragraph .08.)

Inclusive Method (Ref: par. .11)

.A19 The inclusive method is generally feasible if, for example, the service organization and the subservice organization are related, or if the contract between the service organization and the subservice organization provides for the use of the inclusive method. In such circumstances, the service organization is the engaging party, and the requirements relative to agreeing on the terms of the engagement may not be applicable.

.A20 If the inclusive method is used, matters to be agreed upon or coordinated by the service organization and the subservice organization include

- the scope of the examination and the period to be covered by the service auditor's report.
- acknowledgment from management of the subservice organization that it will provide the service auditor with a written assertion and representation letter. (Both management of the service organization and management of the subservice organization are responsible for providing the service auditor with a written assertion and representation letter.)
- the planned content and format of the inclusive description.
- the representatives of the subservice organization and the service organization who will be responsible for
  - — providing each entity's description.
  - — integrating the descriptions.
- for a type 2 report, the timing of the tests of controls.

Request to Change the Scope of the Engagement (Ref: par. .12)

.A21 A request to change the scope of the engagement may not have a reasonable justification if, for example, the request is made

- to exclude certain control objectives at the service organization from the scope of the engagement because of the likelihood that the service auditor's opinion would be modified with respect to those control objectives.
- to prevent the disclosure of deviations identified at a subservice organization by requesting a change from the inclusive method to the carve-out method.

.A22 A request to change the scope of the engagement may have a reasonable justification when, for example, the request is made because the service organization, a transfer agent, after providing the description of its system to the service auditor, decides that it would like to remove a control objective related to new fund setup because only one fund was set up during the reporting period, and management of the fund had performed its own testing. The service auditor concluded that the removal of the control objective related to new fund setup was reasonable in the circumstances because the objective was not relevant to a broad range of user entities during the examination period.

Requesting a Written Assertion (Ref: par. .13 and .18)

.A23 Paragraph .13 applies regardless of whether the responsible party is the engaging party.

.A24 Exhibit B, "Illustrative Assertions by Management of a Service Organization," contains illustrative management assertions for type 1 and type 2 engagements.

Assessing the Suitability of the Criteria (Ref: par. .14)

.A25 Section 105 requires a practitioner, among other things, to determine whether the subject matter is capable of evaluation against criteria that are suitable and available to users.[22] Section 105 also indicates that one of the attributes of an appropriate subject matter is that it is identifiable and capable of consistent measurement or evaluation against the criteria.[23] As indicated in section 105, the responsible party (in this case, management of the service organization) or the engaging party is responsible for selecting the criteria, and the engaging party is responsible for determining that such criteria are appropriate for its purposes.[24] Section 105 defines the *subject matter* as the phenomenon that is measured or evaluated by applying criteria.[25]

.A26 For the purposes of engagements performed in accordance with this section, criteria need to be available to user entities and their auditors to enable them to understand the basis for the service organization's assertion about the fair presentation of management's description of the service organization's system, the suitability of the design of controls that address control objectives stated in the description of the system and, in the case of a type 2 report, the operating effectiveness of such controls. Information about suitable criteria is provided in section 105.[26] Paragraphs .15–.17 discuss the criteria for evaluating the fairness of the presentation of management's description of the service organization's system and the suitability of the design and operating effectiveness of the controls.

Monitoring the Effectiveness of Controls at Subservice Organizations (Ref: par. .15a[viii])

.A27 Management's description of the service organization's system and the scope of the service auditor's engagement includes controls at the service organization that monitor the effectiveness of controls at the subservice organization, which may include some combination of ongoing monitoring to

---

22 Paragraph .25*b*(ii) of section 105.

23 Paragraph .A37*a* of section 105.

24 Paragraph .A47 of section 105.

25 Definition of *subject matter* in paragraph .10 of section 105.

26 See footnote 22.

determine that potential issues are identified timely and separate evaluations to determine that the effectiveness of internal control is maintained over time. Such monitoring activities may include

- reviewing and reconciling output reports,
- holding periodic discussions with the subservice organization,
- making regular site visits to the subservice organization,
- testing controls at the subservice organization by members of the service organization's internal audit function,
- reviewing type 1 or type 2 reports on the subservice organization's system prepared pursuant to this section or section 205, and
- monitoring external communications, such as customer complaints relevant to the services by the subservice organization.

Materiality (Ref: par. .19, .25, and .27–.28)

.A28 In an engagement to report on controls at a service organization, the concept of materiality relates to the information being reported on, not the financial statements of user entities. The service auditor plans and performs procedures to determine whether, in all material respects, based on the criteria in management's assertion, management's description of the service organization's system is fairly presented; controls at the service organization are suitably designed to achieve the control objectives stated in the description; and, in the case of a type 2 report, controls at the service organization operated effectively throughout the specified period to achieve the control objectives stated in the description. The concept of materiality takes into account that the service auditor's report provides information about the service organization's system to meet the common information needs of a broad range of user entities and their auditors who have an understanding of the manner in which the system is being used by a particular user entity for financial reporting.

.A29 Materiality with respect to the fair presentation of management's description of the service organization's system and with respect to the design of controls primarily includes the consideration of qualitative factors, for example, whether

- management's description of the service organization's system includes the significant aspects of the processing of transactions.
- management's description of the service organization's system omits or distorts relevant information.
- the controls have the ability, as designed, to provide reasonable assurance that the control objectives stated in management's description of the service organization's system would be achieved.

Materiality with respect to the operating effectiveness of controls includes the consideration of both quantitative and qualitative factors, for example, the tolerable rate and observed rate of deviation (a quantitative matter) and the nature and cause of any observed deviations (a qualitative matter).

.A30 The concept of materiality is not applied when disclosing, in the description of the tests of controls, the results of those tests when deviations have been identified. This is because in the particular circumstances of a specific user entity or user auditor, a deviation may have significance beyond whether or not, in the opinion of the service auditor, it prevents a control from operating effectively. For example, the control to which the deviation relates may be particularly significant in preventing a certain type of error that may be material in the particular circumstances of a user entity's financial statements.

Obtaining an Understanding of the Service Organization's System and Assessing the Risk of Material Misstatement (Ref: par. .20 and .22)

.A31 Obtaining an understanding of the service organization's system, including related controls, assists the service auditor in the following:

- Identifying the boundaries of the system and how it interfaces with other systems
- Assessing whether management's description of the service organization's system fairly presents the service organization's system that has been designed and implemented
- Understanding which controls are necessary to achieve the control objectives stated in management's description of the service organization's system, whether controls were suitably designed to achieve those control objectives, and, in the case of a type 2 report, whether controls were operating effectively throughout the specified period to achieve those control objectives.
- When a separate type 1 or type 2 report exists for a subservice organization, whether management has identified controls that are necessary, either at the service organization or at user entities, to address relevant complementary user entity controls identified in the carved-out subservice organization's description of its system.

.A32 Paragraph .15*a*(viii) indicates that the criteria for assessing whether management's description of the service organization's system is fairly presented should include other aspects of the service organization's control environment, risk assessment process, information and communications (including relevant business processes), control activities, and monitoring activities that are relevant to the services provided. Although aspects of the service organization's control environment, risk assessment process, and monitoring activities may not be presented in the description in the context of control objectives, they may, nevertheless, be necessary to achieve the specified control objectives stated in the description. Likewise, deficiencies in these controls may have an effect on the service auditor's assessment of whether the controls, taken as a whole, were suitably designed or operating effectively to achieve the specified control objectives.

.A33 The service auditor's procedures to obtain the understanding may include the following:

- Inquiring of management and others within the service organization who, in the service auditor's judgment, may have relevant information
- Observing operations and inspecting documents, reports, and printed and electronic records of transaction processing
- Inspecting a selection of agreements between the service organization and user entities to identify their common terms
- Reperforming the application of a control

One or more of the preceding procedures may be accomplished through the performance of a walkthrough.

.A34 In a type 1 or type 2 engagement, the risk of material misstatement relates to the risk that, in all material respects, based on the criteria in management's assertion

- *a.* management's description of the service organization's system is not fairly presented;
- *b.* the controls are not suitably designed to provide reasonable assurance that the control objectives stated in management's description of the service organization's system would be achieved if the controls operated effectively; and
- *c.* in the case of a type 2 report, the controls did not operate effectively throughout the specified period to achieve the related control objectives stated in management's description of the service organization's system.

.A35 The risks identified in paragraph .A34 may include those related to new or changed controls, system changes, significant changes in processing volume, new personnel or significant changes in key management or personnel, new types of transactions, new products or technologies, or modifications to the service auditor's opinion in the service auditor's report for the prior year.

Reasonable Assurance (Ref: par. .25, .27–.28, and .33)

.A36 In a service auditor's examination engagement, the service auditor plans and performs the engagement to obtain reasonable assurance of detecting misstatements in management's description of the service organization's system and instances in which control objectives were not achieved. Absolute assurance is not attainable because of factors such as the need for judgment, the use of sampling, and the inherent limitations of controls at the service organization that affect whether the description is fairly presented and the controls are suitably designed and operating effectively to achieve the control objectives, and because much of the evidence available to the service auditor is persuasive, rather than conclusive, in nature. Also, procedures that are effective for detecting unintentional misstatements in the description, and instances in which control objectives were not achieved, may be ineffective for detecting misstatements in the description resulting from fraud and instances in which the control objectives were not achieved that are concealed through collusion between service organization personnel and a third party or among management or employees of the service organization. Therefore, the subsequent discovery of the existence of material misstatements in the description or instances in which control objectives were not achieved does not, in and of itself, evidence inadequate planning, performance, or judgment on the part of the service auditor.

Obtaining Evidence Regarding Management's Description of the Service Organization's System (Ref: par. .15*a*[vi] and .25–.26)

.A37 Considering the following questions may assist the service auditor in determining whether management's description of the service organization's system is fairly presented, in all material respects, based on the criteria in management's assertion:

- Is the description prepared at a level of detail that could reasonably be expected to provide a broad range of user auditors with sufficient information to obtain an understanding of internal control in accordance with AU-C section 402? The description need not address every aspect of the service organization's processing or the services provided to user entities and need not be so detailed that it would potentially enable a reader to compromise security or other controls at the service organization.

- Is the description prepared in a manner that does not omit or distort information that might affect the decisions of a broad range of user auditors, for example, does the description contain any significant omissions or inaccuracies regarding processing of which the service auditor is aware?
- Does the description include relevant details of changes to the service organization's system during the period covered by the description when the description covers a period of time?
- Have the controls identified in the description actually been implemented?
- If the inclusive method has been used, does the description separately identify controls at the service organization and controls at the subservice organization? Does the description include activities at the service organization that monitor the effectiveness of controls at the subservice organization?
- Are complementary user entity controls, if any, adequately described? In most cases, the control objectives stated in the description are worded so that they are capable of being achieved through the effective operation of controls implemented by the service organization alone. In some cases, however, the control objectives stated in the description cannot be achieved by the service organization alone because their achievement requires particular controls to be implemented by user entities. For example, to achieve the specified control objectives, a user entity may need to review the completeness and accuracy of input provided to the service organization before submitting it to the service organization or the completeness and accuracy of reports provided to the user entity subsequent to processing. When the description does include complementary user entity controls, the description separately identifies those controls, along with the specific control objectives that cannot be achieved by the service organization alone.
- If the carve-out method has been used, does the description identify the functions that are performed by the subservice organization? (When the carve-out method has been used, the description does not describe the detailed processing or controls at the subservice organization.) Does the description include activities at the service organization that monitor the effectiveness of controls at the subservice organization as well as complementary subservice organization controls?

.A38 The service auditor's procedures to evaluate the fair presentation of management's description of the service organization's system may include the following:

- Considering the nature of the user entities and how the services provided by the service organization are likely to affect them, for example, the predominant types of user entities, and whether the user entities are regulated by government agencies
- Reading contracts with user entities to gain an understanding of the service organization's contractual obligations
- Observing procedures performed by service organization personnel

- Reviewing the service organization's policy and procedure manuals and other documentation of the system, for example, flowcharts and narratives
- Performing walkthroughs of transactions through the service organization's system

.A39 Paragraph .25*a* requires the service auditor to evaluate whether the control objectives stated in management's description of the service organization's system are reasonable in the circumstances. Considering the following questions may assist the service auditor in this evaluation:

- Do the control objectives stated in the description relate to the types of assertions commonly embodied in the broad range of user entities' financial statements to which controls at the service organization could reasonably be expected to relate (for example, assertions about existence and accuracy that are affected by access controls that prevent or detect unauthorized access to the system)? Although the service auditor ordinarily will not be able to determine how controls at a service organization specifically relate to the assertions embodied in individual user entities' financial statements, the service auditor considers matters, such as the following, when identifying the types of assertions to which the controls are likely to relate:
  - — The types of services provided by the service organization, including the classes of transactions processed
  - — The contents of reports and other information prepared for user entities
  - — The information used in the performance of procedures
  - — The types of significant events other than transactions that occur in providing the services
  - — Services performed by a subservice organization, if any
  - — The responsibility of the service organization to implement controls, including responsibilities established in contracts and agreements with user entities
  - — The risks to a user entity's internal control over financial reporting arising from information technology used or provided by the service organization
- Are the control objectives stated in the description complete? Although a complete set of control objectives can provide a broad range of user auditors with a framework to assess the effect of controls at the service organization on assertions commonly embodied in user entities' financial statements, the service auditor ordinarily will not be able to determine how controls at a service organization specifically relate to the assertions embodied in individual user entities' financial statements and cannot, therefore, determine whether control objectives are complete from the viewpoint of individual user entities or user auditors. It is the responsibility of individual user entities or user auditors to assess whether the service organization's description addresses the particular control objectives that are relevant to their needs. If the control objectives are specified by an outside party, including control objectives specified by law or regulation, the outside party is responsible for their completeness and reasonableness.

.A40 The service auditor's procedures to determine whether the system described by the service organization has been implemented may be similar to, and performed in conjunction with, procedures to obtain an understanding of that system. Other procedures that the service auditor may use in combination with inquiry of management and other service organization personnel include observation, inspection of records and other documentation, and reperformance of the manner in which transactions are processed through the system and controls are applied.

Obtaining Evidence Regarding the Design of Controls (Ref: par. .27)

.A41 The risks and control objectives identified in paragraph .27 encompass fraud and unintentional acts that threaten the achievement of the control objectives.

.A42 From the viewpoint of a user auditor, a control is suitably designed to achieve the control objectives stated in management's description of the service organization's system if individually or in combination with other controls, it would, when complied with satisfactorily, provide reasonable assurance that material misstatements are prevented, or detected and corrected. A service auditor, however, is not aware of the circumstances at individual user entities that would affect whether or not a misstatement is material to those user entities. Therefore, from the viewpoint of a service auditor, a control is suitably designed if individually or in combination with other controls, it would, when complied with satisfactorily, provide reasonable assurance that the control objective(s) stated in the description of the service organization's system are achieved.

.A43 A service auditor may consider using flowcharts, questionnaires, or decision tables to facilitate understanding the design of the controls.

.A44 Controls may consist of a number of activities directed at the achievement of various control objectives. Consequently, if the service auditor evaluates certain activities as being ineffective in achieving a particular control objective, the existence of other activities may allow the service auditor to conclude that controls related to the control objective are suitably designed to achieve the control objective. (Ref: par. .27)

.A45 The service organization may have different controls in place to address each of the risks associated with the control objective; therefore, multiple controls may be needed in order for the service auditor to conclude on the design of controls relating to each of the risks associated with the control objective.

Obtaining Evidence Regarding the Operating Effectiveness of Controls (Ref: par. .15*b* and .28–.29)

.A46 From the viewpoint of a user auditor, a control is operating effectively if individually or in combination with other controls, it provides reasonable assurance that material misstatements are prevented, or detected and corrected. A service auditor, however, is not aware of the circumstances at individual user entities that would affect whether or not a misstatement resulting from a control deviation is material to those user entities. Therefore, from the viewpoint of a service auditor, a control is operating effectively if, individually or in combination with other controls, it provides reasonable assurance that the control objectives stated in management's description of the service organization's system are achieved. Similarly, a service auditor is not in a position to determine whether any observed control deviation would result in a material misstatement from the viewpoint of an individual user entity.

.A47 Obtaining an understanding of controls sufficient to opine on the suitability of their design is not sufficient evidence regarding their operating effectiveness unless some automation provides for the consistent operation of the controls as they were designed and implemented. For example, obtaining information about the implementation of a manual control at a point in time does not provide evidence about operation of the control at other times. However, because of the inherent consistency of IT processing, performing procedures to determine the design of an automated application control and whether it has been implemented may serve as evidence of that control's operating effectiveness, depending on the service auditor's assessment and testing of IT general controls such as those over program changes.

.A48 Evidence about the satisfactory operation of controls in prior periods does not provide evidence of the operating effectiveness of controls during the current period. The service auditor expresses an opinion on the effectiveness of controls throughout each period; therefore, sufficient appropriate evidence about the operating effectiveness of controls throughout the current period is required for the service auditor to express that opinion for the current period. Knowledge of modifications to the service auditor's report or deviations observed in prior engagements may, however, be considered in assessing risk and lead the service auditor to increase the extent of testing during the current period.

.A49 Generally, a type 2 report(s) is most useful to user entities and their auditors when it covers a substantial portion of the period covered by the user entity's financial statements being audited.

.A50 Determining the effect of changes in the service organization's controls that were implemented during the period covered by the service auditor's report involves gathering information about the nature and extent of such changes, how they affect processing at the service organization, and how they might affect assertions in the user entities' financial statements.

.A51 Certain controls may not leave evidence of their operation that can be tested at a later date and, accordingly, the service auditor may find it appropriate to test the operating effectiveness of such controls at various times throughout the reporting period.

Evaluating the Reliability of Information Produced by the Service Organization (Ref: par. .30)

.A52 The following are examples of information produced by a service organization that are commonly used by a service auditor:

- Population lists the service auditor uses to select a sample of items for testing
- Lists of data that have specific characteristics
- Exception reports
- Transaction reconciliations
- Documentation that provides evidence of the operating effectiveness of controls, such as user access lists
- System-generated reports
- Other system-generated data

Written Representations (Ref: par. .12 and .36–.38)

.A53 Written representations reaffirming the service organization's assertion about the effective operation of controls may be based on ongoing monitoring activities, separate evaluations, or a combination of the two.

.A54 In certain circumstances, a service auditor may obtain written representations from parties in addition to management of the service organization, such as those charged with governance.

.A55 The written representations required by paragraph .36 are separate from and in addition to the assertion that accompanies management's description of the service organization's system.

.A56 In addition to the written representations required by paragraph .36, the service auditor may consider it necessary to request other written representations.

.A57 If the service auditor is unable to obtain written representations regarding relevant control objectives and related controls at the subservice organization, management of the service organization may be able to use the carve-out method.

Other Information (Ref: par. .39, .40*c*[iii], and .41*c*[iii])

.A58 The other information referred to in paragraph .39 may include

- information provided by the service organization and included in a separate section of the type 1 or type 2 report, or
- information outside the type 1 or type 2 report included in a document that contains the service auditor's report. This other information may be provided by the service organization or another party.

Content of the Service Auditor's Report (Ref: par. .40 and .41)

.A59 Examples of service auditors' reports are presented in exhibit A of this section, and illustrative assertions by management of the service organization are presented in exhibit B.

.A60 The list of report elements in paragraphs .40 and .41 constitutes all the required report elements for a service auditor's type 2 and type 1 engagement, respectively, including the elements required by section 205.[27] Application guidance regarding the elements of a practitioner's examination report is included in section 205.[28] (Ref: par. .40)

.A61 The following is an example of the information required by paragraphs .40*c*(iv)(1) and .41*c*(iv)(1):

> As indicated in the description, XYZ Service Organization uses a subservice organization for all of its computerized application processing. The description includes only the control objectives and related controls of XYZ Service Organization and excludes the control objectives and related controls of the subservice organization. The description also indicates that certain control objectives specified by XYZ Service Organization can be achieved only if complementary

---

[27] Paragraphs .63–.66 of section 205.

[28] Paragraphs .A78–.A101.

subservice organization controls assumed in the design of XYZ Service Organization's controls are suitably designed and operating effectively, along with related controls at XYZ Service Organization. Our examination did not extend to controls of the subservice organization, and we have not evaluated the suitability of the design or operating effectiveness of such complementary subservice organization controls.

Description of the Service Auditor's Tests of Controls and the Results Thereof (Ref: par. .40k)

.A62 The service auditor may include in the description of tests of controls and results the procedures the service auditor performed to verify the completeness and accuracy of information provided by the service organization.

.A63 In describing the service auditor's tests of controls and results thereof for a type 2 report, it is helpful to readers if the service auditor's report includes information about causative factors for identified deviations, to the extent the service auditor has identified such factors.

.A64 When the work of the internal audit function has been used in performing tests of controls, the service auditor's description of that work and of the service auditor's procedures with respect to that work may be presented in a number of ways, for example

- by including introductory material to the description of tests of controls indicating that certain work of the internal audit function was used in performing tests of controls and describing the service auditor's procedures with regard to that work.
- by attributing individual tests to internal audit and describing the service auditor's procedures with regard to that work.

.A65 The work of the internal audit function referred to in paragraph .40*k*(v) does not include tests of controls performed by internal auditors as a part of direct assistance.

.A66 Other than the description of the work of the internal auditors referred to in paragraph .40*k*(v), the service auditor's report does not make any reference to the use of the work of the internal audit function to obtain evidence or to the use of internal auditors to provide direct assistance.

Use of the Service Auditor's Report (Ref: par. .40m and .41m)

.A67 Section 205 requires that the use of a practitioner's report be restricted to specified parties when the criteria used to evaluate or measure the subject matter are available only to specified parties or appropriate only for a limited number of parties who either participated in their establishment or can be presumed to have an adequate understanding of the criteria.[29] The criteria used for engagements to report on controls at a service organization are relevant only for the purpose of providing information about the service organization's system, including controls, to those who have an understanding of how the system is used for financial reporting by user entities and, accordingly, the service auditor's report states that the report and the description of tests of controls are intended only for use by management of the service organization, user entities of the service organization ("during some or all of the period covered by the service auditor's report" for a type 2 report, and "as of the specified date" for a type 1 report), and their user auditors. (The illustrative reports in

---

[29] Paragraph .64*b* of section 205.

exhibit A of this section illustrate language for a paragraph restricting the use of the report.)

.A68 Section 205 indicates that the need for restriction on the use of a practitioner's report may result from a number of circumstances, including the potential for the report to be misunderstood when taken out of the context in which it was intended to be used, and the extent to which the procedures performed are known or understood.[30]

.A69 Although the alert language in the service auditor's report restricts the use of the report, a service auditor is not responsible for controlling a service organization's distribution of a report. A service auditor may inform the service organization of the following:

- A service auditor's type 1 report is not intended for distribution to parties other than the service organization, user entities of the service organization's system as of the end of the period covered by the report, and their user auditors.
- A service auditor's type 2 report is not intended for distribution to parties other than the service organization, user entities of the service organization's system during some or all of the period covered by the report, and their user auditors.

.A70 A user entity is also considered a user entity of the service organization's subservice organizations if controls at subservice organizations are relevant to internal control over financial reporting of the user entity. In such case, the user entity is referred to as an *indirect* or *downstream* user entity of the subservice organization. Consequently, an indirect or downstream user entity may be included in the group to whom use of the service auditor's report is restricted if controls at the service organization are relevant to internal control over financial reporting of such indirect or downstream user entity.

.A71 In engagements in which the inclusive method is used, the users of a subservice organization's system that are not users of the service organization's system, are not *user entities*, as defined in paragraph .08.

.A72 In engagements in which the inclusive method is used, management of a subservice organization may be identified as a specified party and, if so, would be included in the alert language described in paragraphs .40*m* and .41*m*.

Modified Opinions (Ref: par. .42)

.A73 The AICPA Guide *Service Organizations: Reporting on Controls at a Service Organization Relevant to User Entities' Internal Control Over Financial Reporting* contains examples of elements of modified service auditor's reports.

Other Communication Responsibilities (Ref: par. .45)

.A74 Actions that a service auditor may take when the service auditor becomes aware of noncompliance with laws or regulations, fraud, or uncorrected misstatements at the service organization (after giving additional consideration to instances in which the service organization has not appropriately communicated this information to affected user entities, and the service organization refuses to do so) include the following:

- Obtaining legal advice about the consequences of different courses of action

[30] Paragraph .A100 of section 205.

- Communicating with those charged with governance of the service organization
- Disclaiming an opinion, modifying the service auditor's opinion, or adding an explanatory paragraph
- Communicating with third parties, for example, a regulator, when required to do so
- Withdrawing from the engagement
- Considering the nature of the user entities and how the services provided by the service organization are likely to affect them, for example, the predominant types of user entities, and whether the user entities are regulated by government agencies
- Reading contracts with user entities to gain an understanding of the service organization's contractual obligations
- Observing procedures performed by service organization personnel
- Reviewing the service organization's policy and procedure manuals and other documentation of the system, for example, flowcharts and narratives
- Performing walkthroughs of transactions through the service organization's system

.A75

Exhibit A—Illustrative Service Auditor's Reports

The following illustrative service auditor's reports contain text in ***boldface italics*** that would be added to the report if the situation described in the text is applicable. These illustrative reports are for guidance only and are not intended to be exhaustive or applicable to all situations. The inclusion of headings in the report may be useful but is not required by this section or section 205.[1] The AICPA Guide *Service Organizations: Reporting on Controls at a Service Organization Relevant to User Entities' Internal Control Over Financial Reporting* includes additional illustrative reports, including reports with modified opinions.

Example 1: Type 2 Service Auditor's Report

Independent Service Auditor's Report[2] on XYZ Service Organization's Description of Its [*type or name of*] System and the Suitability of the Design and Operating Effectiveness of Controls

To: XYZ Service Organization

Scope

We have examined XYZ Service Organization's description of its [*type or name of*] system entitled "XYZ Service Organization's Description of Its [*type or name of*] System" for processing user entities' transactions [*or identification of the function performed by the system*] throughout the period [*date*] to [*date*] (description) and the suitability of the design and operating effectiveness of the controls included in the description to achieve the related control objectives stated in the description, based on the criteria identified in "XYZ Service Organization's Assertion" (assertion). The controls and control objectives included in the description are those that management of XYZ Service Organization believes are likely to be relevant to user entities' internal control over financial reporting, and the description does not include those aspects of the [*type or name of*] system that are not likely to be relevant to user entities' internal control over financial reporting.

[A statement such as the following is added to the service auditor's report when information that is not covered by the report is included in the description of the service organization's system.]

The information included in **[section number where the other information is presented],** ***"Other Information Provided by XYZ Service Organization" is presented by management of XYZ Service Organization to provide additional information and is not a part of XYZ Service Organization's description of its*** **[name or type of]** ***system made available to user entities during the period*** **[date]** ***to*** **[date].** ***Information about XYZ Service Organization's*** **[describe the nature of the information, for example, business continuity planning, privacy practices, and so on]** ***has not been subjected to the procedures applied in the examination of the description of the*** **[name or type of]** ***system and of the suitability of the design and operating effectiveness of controls to achieve the related control objectives stated in the description of the*** **[name or type of]** ***system.***

---

[1] Paragraph .A76 of section 205.

[2] May also be "Report of Independent Service Auditors."

[A statement such as the following is added to the service auditor's report when the service organization uses a subservice organization, the carve-out method is used to present the subservice organization, and complementary subservice organization controls are required to meet the control objectives.]

XYZ Service Organization uses a subservice organization to* [identify the function or service provided by the subservice organization]. *The description includes only the control objectives and related controls of XYZ Service Organization and excludes the control objectives and related controls of the subservice organization. The description also indicates that certain control objectives specified by XYZ Service Organization can be achieved only if complementary subservice organization controls assumed in the design of XYZ Service Organization's controls are suitably designed and operating effectively, along with the related controls at XYZ Service Organization. Our examination did not extend to controls of the subservice organization, and we have not evaluated the suitability of the design or operating effectiveness of such complementary subservice organization controls.

[A statement such as the following is added to the service auditor's report when complementary user entity controls are required to meet the control objectives.]

The description indicates that certain control objectives specified in the description can be achieved only if complementary user entity controls assumed in the design of XYZ Service Organization's controls are suitably designed and operating effectively, along with related controls at the service organization. Our examination did not extend to such complementary user entity controls, and we have not evaluated the suitability of the design or operating effectiveness of such complementary user entity controls.

Service Organization's Responsibilities

In [*section number where the assertion is presented*], XYZ Service Organization has provided an assertion about the fairness of the presentation of the description and suitability of the design and operating effectiveness of the controls to achieve the related control objectives stated in the description. XYZ Service Organization is responsible for preparing the description and assertion, including the completeness, accuracy, and method of presentation of the description and assertion, providing the services covered by the description, specifying the control objectives and stating them in the description, identifying the risks that threaten the achievement of the control objectives, selecting the criteria stated in the assertion, and designing, implementing, and documenting controls that are suitably designed and operating effectively to achieve the related control objectives stated in the description.

Service Auditor's Responsibilities

Our responsibility is to express an opinion on the fairness of the presentation of the description and on the suitability of the design and operating effectiveness of the controls to achieve the related control objectives stated in the description, based on our examination.

Our examination was conducted in accordance with attestation standards established by the American Institute of Certified Public Accountants. Those standards require that we plan and perform the examination to obtain reasonable assurance about whether, in all material respects, based on the criteria in management's assertion, the description is fairly presented and the controls were suitably designed and operating effectively to achieve the related control objectives stated in the description throughout the period [*date*] to [*date*]. We believe that the evidence we obtained is sufficient and appropriate to provide a reasonable basis for our opinion.

An examination of a description of a service organization's system and the suitability of the design and operating effectiveness of controls involves

- performing procedures to obtain evidence about the fairness of the presentation of the description and the suitability of the design and operating effectiveness of the controls to achieve the related control objectives stated in the description, based on the criteria in management's assertion.
- assessing the risks that the description is not fairly presented and that the controls were not suitably designed or operating effectively to achieve the related control objectives stated in the description.
- testing the operating effectiveness of those controls that management considers necessary to provide reasonable assurance that the related control objectives stated in the description were achieved.
- evaluating the overall presentation of the description, suitability of the control objectives stated in the description, and suitability of the criteria specified by the service organization in its assertion.

Inherent Limitations

The description is prepared to meet the common needs of a broad range of user entities and their auditors who audit and report on user entities' financial statements and may not, therefore, include every aspect of the system that each individual user entity may consider important in its own particular environment. Because of their nature, controls at a service organization may not prevent, or detect and correct, all misstatements in processing or reporting transactions [*or identification of the function performed by the system*]. Also, the projection to the future of any evaluation of the fairness of the presentation of the description, or conclusions about the suitability of the design or operating effectiveness of the controls to achieve the related control objectives, is subject to the risk that controls at a service organization may become ineffective.

Description of Tests of Controls

The specific controls tested and the nature, timing, and results of those tests are listed in [*section number where the description of tests of controls is presented*].

Opinion

In our opinion, in all material respects, based on the criteria described in XYZ Service Organization's assertion

a. the description fairly presents the [*type or name of*] system that was designed and implemented throughout the period [*date*] to [*date*].

b. the controls related to the control objectives stated in the description were suitably designed to provide reasonable assurance that the control objectives would be achieved if the controls operated effectively throughout the period [*date*] to [*date*] ***and subservice organizations and user entities applied the complementary controls assumed in the design of XYZ Service Organization's controls throughout the period* [date] *to* [date].**

c. the controls operated effectively to provide reasonable assurance that the control objectives stated in the description were achieved throughout the period [*date*] to [*date*] ***if complementary subservice organization and user entity controls assumed in the design of XYZ Service Organization's controls operated effectively throughout the period* [date] *to* [date].**

Restricted Use

This report, including the description of tests of controls and results thereof in [*section number where the description of tests of controls is presented*], is intended solely for the information and use of management of XYZ Service Organization, user entities of XYZ Service Organization's [*type or name of*] system during some or all of the period [*date*] to [*date*], and their auditors who audit and report on such user entities' financial statements or internal control over financial reporting and have a sufficient understanding to consider it, along with other information, including information about controls implemented by user entities themselves, when assessing the risks of material misstatement of user entities' financial statements. This report is not intended to be, and should not be, used by anyone other than the specified parties.

[*Service auditor's signature*]
[*Service auditor's city and state*]
[*Date of the service auditor's report*]

Example 2: Type 1 Service Auditor's Report

Independent Service Auditor's Report[3] on XYZ Service Organization's Description of Its [*type or name of*] System and the Suitability of the Design of Controls

To: XYZ Service Organization

We have examined XYZ Service Organization's description of its [*type or name of*] system entitled, "XYZ Service Organization's Description of Its [*type or name of*] System," for processing user entities' transactions [*or identification of the function performed by the system*] as of [*date*] (description) and the suitability of the design of the controls included in the description to achieve the related control objectives stated in the description, based on the criteria identified in "XYZ Service Organization's Assertion" (assertion). The controls and control objectives included in the description are those that management of XYZ Service Organization believes are likely to be relevant to user entities' internal control over financial reporting, and the description does not include those aspects of the [*type or name of*] system that are not likely to be relevant to user entities' internal control over financial reporting.

[A statement such as the following is added to the service auditor's report when information that is not covered by the report is included in the description of the service organization's system.]

The information included in* [section number where the other information is presented], *"Other Information Provided by XYZ Service Organization," is presented by management of XYZ Service Organization to provide additional information and is not a part of XYZ Service Organization's description of its* [name or type of] *system made available

---

[3] May also be "Report of Independent Service Auditors."

***to user entities as of* [date]. *Information about XYZ Service Organization's* [describe the nature of the information, for example, business continuity planning, privacy practices, and so on] *has not been subjected to the procedures applied in the examination of the description of the* [name or type of] *system and of the suitability of the design of controls to achieve the related control objectives stated in the description of the* [name or type of] *system*.**

[*A statement such as the following is added to the report when the service organization uses a subservice organization, the carve-out method is used to present the subservice organization, and complementary subservice organization controls are required to meet the control objectives.*]

XYZ Service Organization uses a subservice organization to* [identify the function or service provided by the subservice organization]. *The description includes only the control objectives and related controls of XYZ Service Organization and excludes the control objectives and related controls of the subservice organization. The description also indicates that certain control objectives specified by XYZ Service Organization can be achieved only if complementary subservice organization controls assumed in the design of XYZ Service Organization's controls are suitably designed and operating effectively, along with the related controls at XYZ Service Organization. Our examination did not extend to controls of the subservice organization, and we have not evaluated the design or operating effectiveness of such complementary subservice organization controls.

[*A statement such as the following is added to the service auditor's report when complementary user entity controls are required to meet the control objectives.*]

The description indicates that certain control objectives specified in the description can be achieved only if complementary user entity controls assumed in the design of XYZ Service Organization's controls are suitably designed and operating effectively, along with related controls at the service organization. Our examination did not extend to such complementary user entity controls, and we have not evaluated the suitability of the design or operating effectiveness of such complementary user entity controls.

Service Organization's Responsibilities

In [*section number where assertion is presented*], XYZ Service Organization has provided an assertion about the fairness of the presentation of the description and suitability of the design of the controls to achieve the related control objectives stated in the description. XYZ Service Organization is responsible for preparing the description and its assertion, including the completeness, accuracy, and method of presentation of the description and assertion, providing the services covered by the description, specifying the control objectives and stating them in the description, identifying the risks that threaten the achievement of the control objectives, selecting the criteria stated in the assertion, and designing, implementing, and documenting controls that are suitably designed and operating effectively to achieve the related control objectives stated in the description.

Service Auditor's Responsibilities

Our responsibility is to express an opinion on the fairness of the presentation of the description and on the suitability of the design of the controls to achieve the related control objectives stated in the description, based on our examination.

Our examination was conducted in accordance with attestation standards established by the American Institute of Certified Public Accountants. Those standards require that we plan and perform the examination to obtain reasonable assurance about whether, in all material respects, based on the criteria in management's assertion, the description is fairly presented and the controls were suitably designed to achieve the related control objectives stated in the description as of [*date*]. We believe that the evidence we obtained is sufficient and appropriate to provide a reasonable basis for our opinion.

An examination of a description of a service organization's system and the suitability of the design of controls involves

- performing procedures to obtain evidence about the fairness of the presentation of the description and the suitability of the design of the controls to achieve the related control objectives stated in the description, based on the criteria in management's assertion.
- assessing the risks that the description is not fairly presented and that the controls were not suitably designed to achieve the related control objectives stated in the description.
- evaluating the overall presentation of the description, suitability of the control objectives stated in the description, and suitability of the criteria specified by the service organization in its assertion.

Inherent Limitations

The description is prepared to meet the common needs of a broad range of user entities and their auditors who audit and report on user entities' financial statements and may not, therefore, include every aspect of the system that each individual user entity may consider important in its own particular environment. Because of their nature, controls at a service organization may not prevent, or detect and correct, all misstatements in processing or reporting transactions [*or identification of the function performed by the system*]. Also, the projection to the future of any evaluation of the fairness of the presentation of the description, or conclusions about the suitability of the design of the controls to achieve the related control objectives, is subject to the risk that controls at a service organization may become ineffective.

Other Matter

We did not perform any procedures regarding the operating effectiveness of controls stated in the description and, accordingly, do not express an opinion thereon.

Opinion

In our opinion, in all material respects, based on the criteria described in XYZ Service Organization's assertion

a. the description fairly presents the [*type or name of*] system that was designed and implemented as of [*date*].

b. the controls related to the control objectives stated in the description were suitably designed to provide reasonable assurance that the control objectives would be achieved if the controls operated effectively as of [*date*] ***and subservice organizations and user entities applied the complementary controls assumed in the design of XYZ Service Organization's controls as of*** **[date]**.

Restricted Use

This report is intended solely for the information and use of management of XYZ Service Organization, user entities of XYZ Service Organization's [*type or name of*] system as of [*date*], and their auditors who audit and report on such user entities' financial statements or internal control over financial reporting and have a sufficient understanding to consider it, along with other information, including information about controls implemented by user entities themselves, when assessing the risks of material misstatements of user entities' financial statements. This report is not intended to be, and should not be, used by anyone other than the specified parties.

[Service auditor's signature]
[Service auditor's city and state]
[Date of the service auditor's report]

.A76

Exhibit B—Illustrative Assertions by Management of a Service Organization

Paragraph .10*b*(vi) indicates that one of the preconditions for a service auditor to accept or continue an engagement is that management acknowledge and accept responsibility for providing a written assertion that accompanies management's description of the service organization's system. Paragraph .A18 indicates that the service organization has the option of attaching the assertion to the description of the service organization's system or including it in the description and clearly segregating the assertion from the description, for example, through the use of headings. Segregating the assertion from the description clarifies that the assertion is not part of the description.

The following illustrative management assertions contain text in boldface italics that would be added to management's assertion if the situation described in the text is applicable. These illustrative assertions are for guidance only and are not intended to be exhaustive or applicable to all situations.

Example 1: Assertion by Management of a Service Organization for a Type 2 Report

XYZ Service Organization's Assertion

We have prepared the description of XYZ Service Organization's [*type or name of*] system entitled, "XYZ Service Organization's Description of Its [*type or name of*] System," for processing user entities' transactions [*or identification of the function performed by the system*] throughout the period [*date*] to [*date*] (description) for user entities of the system during some or all of the period [*date*] to [*date*], and their auditors who audit and report on such user entities' financial statements or internal control over financial reporting and have a sufficient understanding to consider it, along with other information, ***including information about controls implemented by subservice organizations and user entities of the system themselves,*** when assessing the risks of material misstatement of user entities' financial statements.

[*A statement such as the following is added to the assertion when the service organization uses a subservice organization, the carve-out method is used to present the subservice organization, and complementary subservice organization controls are required to meet the control objectives.*]

XYZ Service Organization uses a subservice organization to **[identify the function or service provided by the subservice organization].** ***The description includes only the control objectives and related controls of XYZ Service Organization and excludes the control objectives and related controls of the subservice organization. The description also indicates that certain control objectives specified in the description can be achieved only if complementary subservice organization controls assumed in the design of our controls are suitably designed and operating effectively, along with the related controls. The description does not extend to controls of the subservice organization.***

[*A statement such as the following is added to the service auditor's report when complementary user entity controls are required to meet the control objectives.*]

The description indicates that certain control objectives specified in the description can be achieved only if complementary user entity controls assumed in the design of XYZ Service Organization's controls are suitably designed and operating effectively, along with related controls at the service organization. The description does not extend to controls of the user entities.

We confirm, to the best of our knowledge and belief, that

a. the description fairly presents the [*type or name of*] system made available to user entities of the system during some or all of the period [*date*] to [*date*] for processing their transactions [*or identification of the function performed by the system*] as it relates to controls that are likely to be relevant to user entities' internal control over financial reporting. The criteria we used in making this assertion were that the description

i. presents how the system made available to user entities of the system was designed and implemented to process relevant user entity transactions, including, if applicable,

(1) the types of services provided, including, as appropriate, the classes of transactions processed.

(2) the procedures, within both automated and manual systems, by which those services are provided, including, as appropriate, procedures by which transactions are initiated, authorized, recorded, processed, corrected as necessary, and transferred to the reports and other information prepared for user entities of the system.

(3) the information used in the performance of the procedures including, if applicable, related accounting records, whether electronic or manual, and supporting information involved in initiating, authorizing, recording, processing, and reporting transactions; this includes the correction of incorrect information and how information is transferred to the reports and other information prepared for user entities.

(4) how the system captures and addresses significant events and conditions other than transactions.

(5) the process used to prepare reports and other information for user entities.

(6) services performed by a subservice organization, if any, including whether the carve-out method or the inclusive method has been used in relation to them.

(7) the specified control objectives and controls designed to achieve those objectives, including, as applicable, complementary user entity controls and complementary subservice organization controls assumed in the design of the service organization's controls.

(8) other aspects of our control environment, risk assessment process, information and communications (including the related business processes),

control activities, and monitoring activities that are relevant to the services provided.

ii. includes relevant details of changes to the service organization's system during the period covered by the description.

iii. does not omit or distort information relevant to the service organization's system, while acknowledging that the description is prepared to meet the common needs of a broad range of user entities of the system and their user auditors, and may not, therefore, include every aspect of the [*type or name of*] system that each individual user entity of the system and its auditor may consider important in its own particular environment.

b. the controls related to the control objectives stated in the description were suitably designed and operating effectively throughout the period [*date*] to [*date*] to achieve those control objectives ***if subservice organizations and user entities applied the complementary controls assumed in the design of XYZ Service Organization's controls throughout the period*** **[date]** ***to*** **[date]**. The criteria we used in making this assertion were that

i. the risks that threaten the achievement of the control objectives stated in the description have been identified by management of the service organization.

ii. the controls identified in the description would, if operating effectively, provide reasonable assurance that those risks would not prevent the control objectives stated in the description from being achieved.

iii. the controls were consistently applied as designed, including whether manual controls were applied by individuals who have the appropriate competence and authority.

Example 2: Assertion by Management of a Service Organization for a Type 1 Report

XYZ Service Organization's Assertion

We have prepared the description of XYZ Service Organization's [*type or name of*] system entitled, "XYZ Service Organization's Description of Its [*type or name of*] System," for processing user entities' transactions [*or identification of the function performed by the system*] as of [*date*] (description) for user entities of the system as of [*date*], and their auditors who audit and report on such user entities' financial statements or internal control over financial reporting and have a sufficient understanding to consider it, along with other information, including information about controls ***implemented by subservice organizations and user entities themselves,*** when obtaining an understanding of user entities' information and communication systems relevant to financial reporting.

[*A statement such as the following is added to the assertion when the service organization uses a subservice organization, the carve-out method is used to present the subservice organization, and complementary subservice organization controls are required to meet the control objectives.*]

XYZ Service Organization uses a subservice organization to **[identify the function or service provided by the subservice organization]**. ***The description includes only the control objectives and related controls of***

XYZ Service Organization and excludes the control objectives and related controls of the subservice organization(s). The description also indicates that certain control objectives specified in the description can be achieved only if complementary subservice organization controls assumed in the design of our controls are suitably designed and operating effectively, along with the related controls. The description does not extend to controls of the subservice organization.

[*A statement such as the following is added to the service auditor's report when complementary user entity controls are required to meet the control objectives.*]

The description indicates that certain control objectives specified in the description can be achieved only if complementary user entity controls assumed in the design of XYZ Service Organization's controls are suitably designed and operating effectively, along with related controls at the service organization. The description does not extend to controls of the user entities.

We confirm, to the best of our knowledge and belief, that

a. the description fairly presents the [*type or name of*] system made available to user entities of the system as of [*date*] for processing their transactions [*or identification of the function performed by the system*] as it relates to controls that are likely to be relevant to user entities' internal control over financial reporting. The criteria we used in making this assertion were that the description

i. presents how the system made available to user entities of the system was designed and implemented to process relevant transactions, including, if applicable

(1) the types of services provided, including, as appropriate, the classes of transactions processed.

(2) the procedures, within both automated and manual systems, by which those services are provided, including, as appropriate, procedures by which transactions are initiated, authorized, recorded, processed, corrected as necessary, and transferred to the reports and other information prepared for user entities of the system.

(3) the information used in the performance of the procedures including, if applicable, related accounting records, whether electronic or manual, and supporting information involved in initiating, authorizing, recording, processing, and reporting transactions; this includes the correction of incorrect information and how information is transferred to the reports and other information prepared for user entities.

(4) how the system captures and addresses significant events and conditions other than transactions.

(5) the process used to prepare reports and other information for user entities.

(6) services performed by a subservice organization, if any, including whether the carve-out method or the inclusive method has been used in relation to them.

(7) the specified control objectives and controls designed to achieve those objectives, including, as applicable, complementary user entity controls and complementary subservice organization controls assumed in the design of the service organization's controls.

(8) other aspects of our control environment, risk assessment process, information and communication systems (including the related business processes), control activities, and monitoring activities that are relevant to the services provided.

ii. does not omit or distort information relevant to the service organization's system, while acknowledging that the description is prepared to meet the common needs of a broad range of user entities of the system and their user auditors, and may not, therefore, include every aspect of the [*type or name of*] system that each individual user entity of the system and its auditor may consider important in its own particular environment.

b. the controls related to the control objectives stated in the description were suitably designed as of [*date*] to achieve those control objectives ***if subservice organizations and user entities applied the complementary controls assumed in the design of XYZ Service Organization's controls as of*** **[date]**. The criteria we used in making this assertion were that

i. the risks that threaten the achievement of the control objectives stated in the description have been identified by management of the service organization.

ii. the controls identified in the description would, if operating effectively, provide reasonable assurance that those risks would not prevent the control objectives stated in the description from being achieved.

AT-C Section 395 *

[Designated for AT Section 701, Management's Discussion and Analysis]

NOTE

SSAE No. 18 does not supersede chapter 7, "Management's Discussion and Analysis," of SSAE No. 10, *Attestation Standards: Revision and Recodification*, which is currently codified as AT section 701.

The Auditing Standards Board (ASB) has not clarified AT section 701 because practitioners rarely perform attest engagements to report on management's discussion and analysis prepared pursuant to the rules and regulations adopted by the U.S. Securities and Exchange Commission. Therefore, the ASB decided that it would retain AT section 701 in its current unclarified format as section 395 until further notice.

AT Section 701—Management's Discussion and Analysis

Source: SSAE No. 10.

Effective when management's discussion and analysis is for a period ending on or after June 1, 2001. Earlier application is permitted.

General

.01 This section sets forth attestation standards and provides guidance to a practitioner concerning the performance of an attest engagement [1] with respect to management's discussion and analysis (MD&A) prepared pursuant to the rules and regulations adopted by the Securities and Exchange Commission (SEC), which are presented in annual reports to shareholders and in other documents. [2]

Applicability

.02 This section is applicable to the following levels of service when a practitioner is engaged by (*a*) a public [3] entity that prepares MD&A in accordance

* This section contains an "AT-C" identifier, instead of an "AT" identifier, to avoid confusion with references to existing "AT" sections, which remain effective through April 2017.

[1] Paragraph .01 of section 101, *Attest Engagements*, defines an attest engagement as one in which a practitioner "is engaged to issue or does issue an examination, a review, or an agreed-upon procedures report on subject matter, or an assertion about the subject matter (hereafter referred to as the *assertion*), that is the responsibility of another party."

[2] Because this section provides guidance specific to attest engagements concerning MD&A presentations, a practitioner should not perform a compliance attestation engagement under section 601, *Compliance Attestation*, with respect to an MD&A presentation.

[3] For purposes of this section, a public entity is any entity (*a*) whose securities trade in a public market either on a stock exchange (domestic or foreign) or in the over-the-counter (OTC) market, including securities quoted only locally or regionally, (*b*) that makes a filing with a regulatory agency in preparation for the sale of any class of its securities in a public market, or (*c*) a subsidiary, corporate joint venture, or other entity controlled by an entity covered by (*a*) or (*b*).

with the rules and regulations adopted by the SEC (see paragraph .04) or (*b*) a nonpublic entity that prepares an MD&A presentation and whose management provides a written assertion that the presentation has been prepared using the rules and regulations adopted by the SEC:[4]

- An examination of an MD&A presentation
- A review of an MD&A presentation for an annual period, an interim period, or a combined annual and interim period[5]

A practitioner[6] engaged to examine or review MD&A and report thereon should comply with the general, fieldwork, and reporting standards established in section 50, *SSAE Hierarchy*, and the specific standards set forth in this section. A practitioner engaged to perform agreed-upon procedures on MD&A should follow the guidance set forth in section 201, Agreed-Upon Procedures Engagements.[7] [Revised, November 2006, to reflect conforming changes necessary due to the issuance of SSAE No. 14.]

.03 This section does not—

a. Change the auditor's responsibility in an audit of financial statements performed in accordance with generally accepted auditing standards (GAAS).

b. Apply to situations in which the practitioner is requested to provide management with recommendations to improve the MD&A rather than to provide assurance. A practitioner engaged to provide such nonattest services should refer to CS section 100, *Consulting Services: Definitions and Standards*.

c. Apply to situations in which the practitioner is engaged to provide attest services with respect to an MD&A presentation that is prepared based on criteria other than the rules and regulations adopted by the SEC. A practitioner engaged to perform an examination or a review based upon such criteria should refer to the guidance in section 101, or to section 201 if engaged to perform an agreed-upon procedures engagement.[8]

---

[4] Such assertion may be made by any of the following:

(*a*) Including a statement in the body of the MD&A presentation that it has been prepared using the rules and regulations adopted by the SEC.

(*b*) Providing a separate written assertion to accompany the MD&A presentation.

(*c*) Providing a written assertion in a representation letter to the practitioner.

[5] As discussed in paragraph .85*k*, a review report is not intended to be filed with the SEC as a report under the Securities Act of 1933 (the 1993 Act) or the Securities Exchange Act of 1934 (the 1934 Act) and, accordingly, the review report should contain a statement of restrictions on the use of the report to specified parties if the entity is (*a*) a public entity or (*b*) a nonpublic entity that is making or has made an offering of securities and it appears that the securities may subsequently be registered or subject to a filing with the SEC or other regulatory agency.

[6] In this section, the terms *practitioner* or *accountant* generally refer to a person engaged to perform an attest service on MD&A. The term *accountant* may also refer to a person engaged to review financial statements. The term *auditor* refers to a person engaged to audit financial statements. As this section includes certain requirements for the practitioner to have audited or performed a review of financial statements in accordance with AU-C section 930, *Interim Financial Information*, the terms *auditor, practitioner*, or *accountant* may refer, in this section, to the same person. [Footnote revised, December 2012, to reflect conforming changes necessary due to the issuance of SAS Nos. 122–126.]

[7] Practitioners should follow guidance in AU-C section 920, *Letters for Underwriters and Certain Other Requesting Parties*, when requested to perform agreed-upon procedures on MD&A and report thereon in a letter for an underwriter. [Footnote revised, December 2012, to reflect conforming changes necessary due to the issuance of SAS Nos. 122–126.]

[8] The guidance in this section may be helpful when performing an engagement to provide attest services with respect to an MD&A presentation that is based on criteria other than the rules and regulations adopted by the SEC. Such other criteria would have to be suitable and available as discussed in paragraphs .23–.33 of section 101.

.04 The requirements for MD&A have changed periodically since the first requirement was adopted by the SEC in 1974. As of the date of issuance of this SSAE, the rules and regulations for MD&A adopted by the SEC are found in Item 303 of Regulation S-K, as interpreted by Financial Reporting Release (FRR) No. 36, *Management's Discussion and Analysis of Financial Condition and Results of Operations; Certain Investment Company Disclosures* (Chapter 5 of the "Codification of Financial Reporting Policies"); Item 303 of Regulation S-B for small business issuers; and Item 9 of Form 20-F for Foreign Private Issuers.[9] Item 303 of Regulation S-K, as interpreted by FRR No. 36, Item 303 of Regulation S-B for small business issuers, and Item 9 of Form 20-F for Foreign Private Issuers, provide the relevant rules and regulations adopted by the SEC that meet the definition of suitable criteria in paragraphs .23–.32 of section 101. The practitioner should consider whether the SEC has adopted additional rules and regulations with respect to MD&A subsequent to the issuance of this section.

Conditions for Engagement Performance

Examination

.05 The practitioner's objective in an engagement to examine MD&A is to express an opinion on the MD&A presentation taken as a whole by reporting whether—

a. The presentation includes, in all material respects, the required elements of the rules and regulations adopted by the SEC.[10]

b. The historical financial amounts have been accurately derived, in all material respects, from the entity's financial statements.[11]

c. The underlying information, determinations, estimates, and assumptions of the entity provide a reasonable basis for the disclosures contained therein.[12]

.06 A practitioner may accept an engagement to examine MD&A of a public or nonpublic entity, provided the practitioner audits, in accordance with GAAS,[13] the financial statements for at least the latest period to which the

---

[9] The SEC staff from time to time issues guidance related to the SEC's adopted requirements; for example, Staff Accounting Bulletins (SABs), Staff Legal Bulletins, and speeches. Although such guidance may provide additional information with respect to the adopted requirements for MD&A, the practitioner should not be expected to attest to assertions on compliance with such guidance. The practitioner may find it helpful to also familiarize himself or herself with material contained on the SEC's website www.sec.gov that provides further information with respect to the SEC's views concerning MD&A disclosures.

[10] The required elements as of the date of issuance of this SSAE include a discussion of the entity's financial condition, changes in financial condition, and results of operations, including a discussion of liquidity and capital resources.

[11] Whether historical financial amounts are accurately derived from the financial statements includes both amounts that are derived from the face of the financial statements (which includes the notes to the financial statements) and financial statement schedules and those that are derived from underlying records supporting elements, accounts, or items included in the financial statements.

[12] Whether the underlying information, determinations, estimates, and assumptions of the entity provide a reasonable basis for the disclosures contained therein requires consideration of management's interpretation of the disclosure criteria for MD&A, management's determinations as to the relevancy of information to be included, and estimates and assumptions made by management that affect reported information.

[13] Restrictions on the scope of the audit of the financial statements will not necessarily preclude the practitioner from accepting an engagement to examine MD&A. Note that the SEC will generally not accept an auditor's report that is modified for a scope limitation. The practitioner should consider the nature and magnitude of the scope limitation and the form of the auditor's report in assessing whether an examination of MD&A could be performed.

MD&A presentation relates and the financial statements for the other periods covered by the MD&A presentation have been audited by the practitioner or a predecessor auditor. A base knowledge of the entity and its operations gained through an audit of the historical financial statements and knowledge about the industry and the environment is necessary to provide the practitioner with sufficient knowledge to properly evaluate the results of the procedures performed in connection with the examination.

.07 If a predecessor auditor has audited the financial statements for a prior period covered by the MD&A presentation, the practitioner (the successor auditor) should also consider whether, under the particular circumstances, he or she can acquire sufficient knowledge of the business and of the entity's accounting and financial reporting practices for such period so that he or she would be able to—

a. Identify types of potential material misstatements in MD&A and consider the likelihood of their occurrence.

b. Perform the procedures that will provide the practitioner with a basis for expressing an opinion as to whether the MD&A presentation includes, in all material respects, the required elements of the rules and regulations adopted by the SEC.

c. Perform the procedures that will provide the practitioner with a basis for expressing an opinion on the MD&A presentation with respect to whether the historical financial amounts have been accurately derived, in all material respects, from the entity's financial statements for such period.

d. Perform the procedures that will provide the practitioner with a basis for expressing an opinion as to whether the underlying information, determinations, estimates, and assumptions of the entity provide a reasonable basis for the disclosures contained therein.

Refer to paragraphs .99–.101 for guidance regarding the review of the predecessor auditor's working papers.

Review

.08 The objective of a review of MD&A is to report whether any information came to the practitioner's attention to cause him or her to believe that—

a. The MD&A presentation does not include, in all material respects, the required elements of the rules and regulations adopted by the SEC.

b. The historical financial amounts included therein have not been accurately derived, in all material respects, from the entity's financial statements.

c. The underlying information, determinations, estimates, and assumptions of the entity do not provide a reasonable basis for the disclosures contained therein.

A review consists principally of applying analytical procedures and making inquiries of persons responsible for financial, accounting, and operational matters. A review ordinarily does not contemplate (*a*) tests of accounting records through inspection, observation, or confirmation, (*b*) obtaining corroborating evidential matter in response to inquiries, or (*c*) the application of certain other procedures ordinarily performed during an examination of MD&A. A review may bring to the practitioner's attention significant matters affecting the

MD&A, but it does not provide assurance that the practitioner will become aware of all significant matters that would be disclosed in an examination.

.09 A practitioner may accept an engagement to review the MD&A presentation of a public entity for an annual period provided the practitioner has audited, in accordance with GAAS, the financial statements for at least the latest annual period to which the MD&A presentation relates and the financial statements for the other periods covered by the MD&A presentation have been audited by the practitioner or a predecessor auditor.[14] A base knowledge of the entity and its operations gained through an audit of the historical financial statements and knowledge about the industry and the environment is necessary to provide the practitioner with sufficient knowledge to properly evaluate the results of the procedures performed in connection with the review.

.10 If a predecessor auditor has audited the financial statements for a prior period covered by the MD&A presentation, the practitioner should also consider whether, under the particular circumstances, he or she can acquire sufficient knowledge of the business and of the entity's accounting and financial reporting practices for such period so he or she would be able to—

a. Identify types of potential material misstatements in the MD&A and consider the likelihood of their occurrence.

b. Perform the procedures that will provide the practitioner with a basis for reporting whether any information has come to the practitioner's attention to cause him or her to believe any of the following.

   (1) The MD&A presentation does not include, in all material respects, the required elements of the rules and regulations adopted by the SEC.

   (2) The historical financial amounts included therein have not been accurately derived, in all material respects, from the entity's financial statements for such period.

   (3) The underlying information, determinations, estimates, and assumptions of the entity do not provide a reasonable basis for the disclosures contained therein.

.11 A practitioner may accept an engagement to review the MD&A presentation of a public entity for an interim period provided that both of the following conditions are met.

a. The practitioner performs either (*1*) a review of the historical financial statements for the related comparative interim periods and issues a review report thereon in accordance with AU-C section 930, *Interim Financial Information*, or (*2*) an audit of the interim financial statements.

b. The MD&A presentation for the most recent fiscal year has been or will be examined or reviewed by either the practitioner or a predecessor auditor.

[Revised, December 2012, to reflect conforming changes necessary due to the issuance of SAS Nos. 122–126.]

---

[14] As discussed in paragraph .85*k*, a review report is not intended to be filed with the SEC as a report under the 1933 Act or the 1934 Act and, accordingly, the review report should contain a statement of restrictions on the use of the report to specified parties if the entity is (*a*) a public entity or (*b*) a nonpublic entity that is making or has made an offering of securities and it appears that the securities may subsequently be registered or subject to a filing with the SEC or other regulatory agency.

.12 If a predecessor auditor examined or reviewed the MD&A presentation of a public entity for the most recent fiscal year, the practitioner should not accept an engagement to review the MD&A presentation for an interim period unless he or she can acquire sufficient knowledge of the business and of the entity's accounting and financial reporting practices for the interim period to perform the procedures described in paragraph .10.

.13 If a nonpublic entity chooses to prepare MD&A, the practitioner should not accept an engagement to perform a review of such MD&A for an annual period under this section unless both of the following conditions are met.

- *a.* The annual financial statements for the periods covered by the MD&A presentation have been or will be audited and the practitioner has audited or will audit the most recent year (refer to paragraph .07 if the financial statements for prior years were audited by a predecessor auditor).
- *b.* Management will provide a written assertion that the presentation has been prepared using the rules and regulations adopted by the SEC as the criteria. (See paragraph .02.)

.14 A practitioner may accept an engagement to review the MD&A presentation of a nonpublic entity for an interim period provided that all of the following conditions are met.

- *a.* The practitioner performs one of the following:
  - (1) A review of the historical financial statements for the related interim periods under the Statements on Standards for Accounting and Review Services (SSARSs) and issues a review report thereon
  - (2) A review of the condensed interim financial information for the related interim periods under AU-C section 930 and issues a review report thereon, and such interim financial information is accompanied by complete annual financial statements for the most recent fiscal year that have been audited
  - (3) An audit of the interim financial statements
- *b.* The MD&A presentation for the most recent fiscal year has been or will be examined or reviewed.
- *c.* Management will provide a written assertion stating that the presentation has been prepared using the rules and regulations adopted by the SEC as the criteria. (See paragraph .02.)

[Revised, December 2012, to reflect conforming changes necessary due to the issuance of SAS Nos. 122–126.]

Engagement Acceptance Considerations

.15 In determining whether to accept an engagement, the practitioner should consider whether management (and others engaged by management to assist them, such as legal counsel) has the appropriate knowledge of the rules and regulations adopted by the SEC to prepare MD&A.

Responsibilities of Management

.16 Management is responsible for the preparation of the entity's MD&A pursuant to the rules and regulations adopted by the SEC. The preparation of MD&A in conformity with the rules and regulations adopted by the SEC requires management to interpret the criteria, accurately derive the historical amounts from the entity's books and records, make determinations as to the relevancy of information to be included, and make estimates and assumptions that affect reported information.

.17 An entity should not name the practitioner in a client-prepared document as having examined or reviewed MD&A unless the MD&A presentation and related practitioner's report and the related financial statements and auditor's (or accountant's review) report are included in the document (or, in the case of a public entity, incorporated by reference to such information filed with a regulatory agency). If such a statement is made in a document that does not include (or incorporate by reference) such information, the practitioner should request that neither his or her name nor reference to the practitioner be made with respect to the MD&A information, or that such document be revised to include the required presentations and reports. If the client does not comply, the practitioner should advise the client that he or she does not consent to either the use of his or her name or the reference to the practitioner, and he or she should consider what other actions might be appropriate.[15]

Obtaining an Understanding of the SEC Rules and Regulations and Management's Methodology for the Preparation of MD&A

.18 The practitioner should obtain an understanding of the rules and regulations adopted by the SEC for MD&A. (Refer to paragraph .04.)

.19 The practitioner should inquire of management regarding the method of preparing MD&A, including matters such as the sources of the information, how the information is gathered, how management evaluates the types of factors having a material effect on financial condition (including liquidity and capital resources), results of operations, and cash flows, and whether there have been any changes in the procedures from the prior year.

Timing of Procedures

.20 Proper planning by the practitioner contributes to the effectiveness of the attest procedures in an examination or a review of MD&A. Performing some of the work in conjunction with the audit of the historical financial statements or the review of interim financial statements may permit the work to be carried out in a more efficient manner and to be completed at an earlier date. When performing an examination or a review of MD&A, the practitioner may consider the results of tests of controls, analytical procedures,[16] and substantive tests performed in a financial statement audit or analytical procedures and inquiries made in a review of financial statements or interim financial information.

---

[15] In considering what other actions, if any, may be appropriate in these circumstances, the practitioner may wish to consult his or her legal counsel.

[16] AU-C section 520, *Analytical Procedures*, defines analytical procedures as "evaluations of financial information through analysis of plausible relationships among both financial and nonfinancial data. Analytical procedures also encompass such investigation, as is necessary, of identified fluctuations or relationships that are inconsistent with other relevant information or that differ from expected values by a significant amount." In applying analytical procedures to MD&A, the practitioner develops expectations of matters that would be discussed in MD&A by identifying and using plausible relationships that are reasonably expected to exist based on the practitioner's understanding of the client and of the industry in which the client operates, and the knowledge of relationships among the various financial elements gained through the audit of financial statements or review of interim financial information. Refer to AU-C section 520 for further discussion of analytical procedures. [Footnote revised, December 2012, to reflect conforming changes necessary due to the issuance of SAS Nos. 122–126.]

Materiality

.21 The practitioner should consider the concept of materiality in planning and performing the engagement. The objective of an examination or a review is to report on the MD&A presentation taken as a whole and not on the individual amounts and disclosures contained therein. In the context of an MD&A presentation, the concept of materiality encompasses both material omissions (for example, the omission of trends, events, and uncertainties that are currently known to management that are reasonably likely to have material effects on the entity's financial condition, results of operations, liquidity, or capital resources) and material misstatements in MD&A, both of which are referred to herein as a misstatement. Assessing the significance of a misstatement of some items in MD&A may be more dependent upon qualitative than quantitative considerations. Qualitative aspects of materiality relate to the relevance and reliability of the information presented (for example, qualitative aspects of materiality are considered in assessing whether the underlying information, determinations, estimates, and assumptions of the entity provide a reasonable basis for the disclosures in the MD&A). Furthermore, quantitative information is often more meaningful when accompanied by qualitative disclosures. For example, quantitative information about market risk-sensitive instruments is more meaningful when accompanied by qualitative information about an entity's market risk exposures and how those exposures are managed. Materiality is also a concept that is judged in light of the expected range of reasonableness of the information; therefore, users should not expect prospective information (information about events that have not yet occurred) to be as precise as historical information.

.22 In expressing an opinion, or providing the limited assurance of a review engagement, on the presentation, the practitioner should consider the omission or misstatement of an individual assertion (see paragraph .34) to be material if the magnitude of the omission or misstatement—individually or when aggregated with other omissions or misstatements—is such that a reasonable person using the MD&A presentation would be influenced by the inclusion or correction of the individual assertion. The relative rather than absolute size of an omission or misstatement may determine whether it is material in a given situation.

Inclusion of Pro Forma Financial Information

.23 Management may include pro forma financial information with respect to a business combination or other transactions in MD&A. The practitioner should consider the guidance in paragraph .10 of section 401, *Reporting on Pro Forma Financial Information*, when performing procedures with respect to such information, even if management indicates in MD&A that certain information has been derived from unaudited financial statements. For example, in an examination of MD&A, the practitioner's procedures would ordinarily include obtaining an understanding of the underlying transaction or event, discussing with management their assumptions, obtaining sufficient evidence in support of the adjustments, and other procedures for the purpose of expressing an opinion on the MD&A presentation taken as a whole and not for expressing an opinion on (or providing the limited assurance of a review of) the pro forma financial information included therein under section 401.

Inclusion of External Information

.24 An entity may also include in its MD&A information external to the entity, such as the rating of its debt by certain rating agencies or comparisons with statistics from a trade association. Such external information should also be subjected to the practitioner's examination or review procedures. For example, in an examination, the practitioner might compare information concerning the statistics of a trade organization to a published source; however, the practitioner would not be expected to test the underlying support for the trade association's calculation of such statistics.

Inclusion of Forward-Looking Information

.25 An entity may include certain forward-looking disclosures in the MD&A presentation, including cautionary language concerning the achievability of the matters disclosed. Although any forward-looking disclosures that are included in the MD&A presentation should be subjected to the practitioner's examination or review, such information is subjected to testing only for the purpose of expressing an opinion that the underlying information, determinations, estimates, and assumptions provide a reasonable basis for the disclosures contained therein or providing the limited assurance of a review on the MD&A presentation taken as a whole. The practitioner may consider the guidance in section 301, *Financial Forecasts and Projections*, when performing procedures with respect to forward-looking information. The practitioner may also consider whether meaningful cautionary language has been included with the forward-looking information.

.26 Section 27A of the Securities Act of 1933 (the 1933 Act) and Section 21E of the Securities Exchange Act of 1934 (the 1934 Act) provide a safe harbor from liability in private litigation with respect to forward-looking statements that include or make reference to meaningful cautionary language. However, such sections also include exclusions from safe harbor protection in certain situations. Whether an entity's forward-looking statements and the practitioner's report thereon qualify for safe harbor protection is a legal matter.

Inclusion of Voluntary Information

.27 An entity may voluntarily include other information in the MD&A presentation that is not required by the rules and regulations adopted by the SEC for MD&A. When the entity includes in MD&A additional information required by other rules and regulations of the SEC (for example, Item 305 of Regulation S-K, *Quantitative and Qualitative Disclosures About Market Risk*), the practitioner should also consider such other rules and regulations in subjecting such information to his or her examination or review procedures. [17]

Examination Engagement

.28 To express an opinion about whether (*a*) the presentation includes, in all material respects, the required elements of the rules and regulations adopted by the SEC, (*b*) the historical financial amounts have been accurately derived, in all material respects, from the entity's financial statements, and (*c*) the underlying information, determinations, estimates, and assumptions of the entity provide a reasonable basis for the disclosures contained therein, the practitioner seeks to obtain reasonable assurance by accumulating sufficient evidence in support of the disclosures and assumptions, thereby restricting attestation risk to an appropriately low level.

---

[17] To the extent that the voluntary information includes forward-looking information, refer to paragraphs .25–.26.

Attestation Risk

.29 In an engagement to examine MD&A, the practitioner plans and performs the examination to obtain reasonable assurance of detecting both intentional and unintentional misstatements that are material to the MD&A presentation taken as a whole. Absolute assurance is not attainable because of factors such as the need for judgment regarding the areas to be tested and the nature, timing, and extent of tests to be performed; the concept of selective testing of the data; and the inherent limitations of the controls applicable to the preparation of MD&A. The practitioner exercises professional judgment in assessing the significant determinations made by management as to the relevancy of information to be included, and the estimates and assumptions that affect reported information. As a result of these factors, in the great majority of cases, the practitioner has to rely on evidence that is persuasive rather than convincing. Also, procedures may be ineffective for detecting an intentional misstatement that is concealed through collusion among client personnel and third parties or among management or employees of the client. Therefore, the subsequent discovery that a material misstatement exists in the MD&A does not, in and of itself, evidence (*a*) failure to obtain reasonable assurance; (*b*) inadequate planning, performance, or judgment on the part of the practitioner; (*c*) the absence of due professional care; or (*d*) a failure to comply with this section.

.30 Factors to be considered by the practitioner in planning an examination of MD&A include (*a*) the anticipated level of attestation risk related to assertions embodied in the MD&A presentation, (*b*) preliminary judgments about materiality for attest purposes, (*c*) the items within the MD&A presentation that are likely to require revision or adjustment, and (*d*) conditions that may require extension or modification of attest procedures. For purposes of an engagement to examine MD&A, the components of attestation risk are defined as follows.

a. *Inherent risk* is the susceptibility of an assertion within MD&A to a material misstatement, assuming that there are no related controls. (See paragraphs .34–.38.)

b. *Control risk* is the risk that a material misstatement that could occur in an assertion within MD&A will not be prevented or detected on a timely basis by the entity's controls; some control risk will always exist because of the inherent limitations of any internal control.

c. *Detection risk* is the risk that the practitioner will not detect a material misstatement that exists in an assertion within MD&A.

Inherent Risk

.31 The level of inherent risk varies with the nature of the assertion. For example, the inherent risk concerning financial information included in the MD&A presentation may be low, whereas the inherent risk concerning the completeness of the disclosure of the entity's risks or liquidity may be high.

Control Risk

.32 The practitioner should assess control risk as discussed in paragraphs .53–.57. Assessing control risk contributes to the practitioner's evaluation of the risk that material misstatement in the MD&A exists. In the process of assessing control risk (together with assessing inherent risk), the practitioner may obtain evidential matter about the risk that such misstatement may exist. The practitioner uses this evidential matter as part of the reasonable basis for his or her opinion on the MD&A presentation taken as a whole.

Detection Risk

.33 In determining an acceptable level of detection risk, the practitioner assesses inherent risk and control risk, and considers the extent to which he or she seeks to restrict attestation risk. As assessed inherent risk or control risk decreases, the acceptable level of detection risk increases. Accordingly, the practitioner may alter the nature, timing, and extent of tests performed based on the assessments of inherent risk and control risk.

Nature of Assertions

.34 Assertions are representations by management that are embodied in the MD&A presentation. They can be either explicit or implicit and can be classified according to the following broad categories:

a. Occurrence

b. Consistency with the financial statements

c. Completeness

d. Presentation and disclosure

.35 Assertions about occurrence address whether reported transactions or events have occurred during a given period. Assertions about consistency with the financial statements address whether—

a. Reported transactions, events, and explanations are consistent with the financial statements.

b. Historical financial amounts have been accurately derived from the financial statements and related records.

c. Nonfinancial data have been accurately derived from related records.

.36 Assertions about completeness address whether descriptions of transactions and events necessary to obtain an understanding of the entity's financial condition (including liquidity and capital resources), changes in financial condition, results of operations, and material commitments for capital resources are included in MD&A; and whether known events, transactions, conditions, trends, demands, commitments, or uncertainties that will result in or are reasonably likely to result in material changes to these items are appropriately described in the MD&A presentation.

.37 For example, if management asserts that the reason for an increase in revenues is a price increase in the current year, they are explicitly asserting that both an increase in revenues and a price increase have occurred in the current year, and implicitly asserting that any historical financial amounts included are consistent with the financial statements for such period. They are also implicitly asserting that the explanation for the increase in revenues is complete; that there are no other significant reasons for the increase in revenues.

.38 Assertions about presentation and disclosure address whether information included in the MD&A presentation is properly classified, described, and disclosed. For example, management asserts that any forward-looking information included in MD&A is properly classified as being based on management's present assessment and includes an appropriate description of the expected results. To further disclose the nature of such information, management may also include a statement that actual results in the future may differ materially from management's present assessment. (See paragraphs .25–.26.)

.39 The auditor of the underlying financial statements is responsible for designing and performing audit procedures to obtain sufficient appropriate audit evidence to be able to draw reasonable conclusions on which to base the auditor's opinion, as discussed in AU-C section 500, *Audit Evidence*. Although procedures designed to achieve the practitioner's objective of forming an opinion on the MD&A presentation taken as a whole may test certain assertions embodied in the underlying financial statements, the practitioner is not expected to test the underlying financial statement assertions in an examination of MD&A. For example, the practitioner is not expected to test the completeness of revenues or the existence of inventory when testing the assertions in MD&A concerning an increase in revenues or an increase in inventory levels; assurance related to completeness of revenues or for existence of inventory would be obtained as part of the audit. The practitioner is, however, responsible for testing the completeness of the explanation for the increase in revenues or the increase in inventory levels. [Revised, December 2012, to reflect conforming changes necessary due to the issuance of SAS Nos. 122–126.]

Performing an Examination Engagement

.40 The practitioner should exercise (*a*) due professional care in planning, performing, and evaluating the results of his or her examination procedures and (*b*) the proper degree of professional skepticism to obtain reasonable assurance that material misstatements will be detected.

.41 In an examination of MD&A, the practitioner should perform the following.

a. Obtain an understanding of the rules and regulations adopted by the SEC for MD&A and management's method of preparing MD&A. (See paragraphs .18–.19.)

b. Plan the engagement. (See paragraphs .42–.48.)

c. Consider relevant portions of the entity's internal control applicable to the preparation of MD&A. (See paragraphs .49–.58.)

d. Obtain sufficient evidence, including testing completeness. (See paragraphs .59–.64.)

e. Consider the effect of events subsequent to the balance-sheet date. (See paragraphs .65–.66.)

f. Obtain written representations from management concerning its responsibility for MD&A, completeness of minutes, events subsequent to the balance-sheet date, and other matters about which the practitioner believes written representations are appropriate. (See paragraphs .110–.112.)

g. Form an opinion about whether the MD&A presentation includes, in all material respects, the required elements of the rules and regulations adopted by the SEC, whether the historical financial amounts included therein have been accurately derived, in all material respects, from the entity's financial statements, and whether the underlying information, determinations, estimates, and assumptions of the entity provide a reasonable basis for the disclosures contained in the MD&A. (See paragraph .67.)

Planning the Engagement

General Considerations

.42 Planning an engagement to examine MD&A involves developing an overall strategy for the expected scope and performance of the engagement.

When developing an overall strategy for the engagement, the practitioner should consider factors such as the following:

- Matters affecting the industry in which the entity operates, such as financial reporting practices, economic conditions, laws and regulations, and technological changes
- Knowledge of the entity's internal control applicable to the preparation of MD&A obtained during the audit of the financial statements and the extent of recent changes, if any
- Matters relating to the entity's business, including its organization, operating characteristics, capital structure, and distribution methods
- The types of relevant information that management reports to external analysts (for example, press releases and presentations to lenders and rating agencies, if any, concerning past and future performance)
- How the entity analyzes actual performance compared to budgets and the types of information provided in documents submitted to the board of directors for purposes of the entity's day-to-day operations and long-range planning
- The extent of management's knowledge of and experience with the rules and regulations adopted by the SEC for MD&A
- If the entity is a nonpublic entity, the intended use of the MD&A presentation
- Preliminary judgments about (*a*) materiality, (*b*) inherent risk at the individual assertion level, and (*c*) factors (for example, matters identified during the audit or review of the historical financial statements) relating to significant deficiencies in internal control applicable to the preparation of MD&A (See paragraph .58.)
- The fraud risk factors or other conditions identified during the audit of the most recent annual financial statements and the practitioner's response to such risk factors
- The type and extent of evidential matter supporting management's assertions and disclosures in the MD&A presentation
- The nature of complex or subjective matters potentially material to the MD&A presentation that may require special skill or knowledge and whether such matters may require using the work of a specialist to obtain sufficient evidential matter (See paragraph .47.)
- The presence of an internal audit function (See paragraph .48.)

.43 In planning an engagement when MD&A has not previously been examined, the practitioner should consider the degree to which the entity has information available for such prior periods and the continuity of the entity's personnel and their ability to respond to inquiries with respect to such periods. In addition, the practitioner should obtain an understanding of the entity's internal control in prior years applicable to the preparation of MD&A.

Consideration of Audit Results

.44 The practitioner should also consider the results of the audits of the financial statements for the periods covered by the MD&A presentation on the examination engagement, such as matters relating to the following:

- The availability and condition of the entity's records
- The nature and magnitude of audit adjustments
- Misstatements[18] that were not corrected in the financial statements that may affect MD&A disclosures (for example, misclassifications between financial statement line items)

[Revised, December 2012, to reflect conforming changes necessary due to the issuance of SAS Nos. 122–126.]

.45 The practitioner should also consider the possible impact on the scope of the examination engagement of any modification or contemplated modification of the auditor's report, including matters addressed in explanatory language. For example, if the auditor has modified the auditor's report to include a going-concern uncertainty explanatory paragraph, the practitioner would consider such a matter in assessing attestation risk.

Multiple Components

.46 In an engagement to examine MD&A, if the entity has operations in several components (for example, locations, branches, subsidiaries, or programs), the practitioner examining the group's MD&A should determine the components to which procedures should be applied. In making such a determination and in selecting the components to be tested, the practitioner examining the group's MD&A should consider factors such as the following:

- The relative importance of each component to the applicable disclosure in the group's MD&A
- The degree of centralization of records
- The effectiveness of controls, particularly those that affect group management's direct control over the exercise of authority delegated to others and its ability to supervise activities at various locations effectively
- The nature and extent of operations conducted at the various components
- The similarity of operations and internal control for different components

The practitioner examining the group's MD&A should consider whether the audit base of the components is consistent with the components that are disclosed in MD&A Accordingly, it may be desirable for the practitioner examining the group's MD&A to coordinate the audit work with the components that will be disclosed. [Revised, December 2012, to reflect conforming changes necessary due to the issuance of SAS Nos. 122–126.]

Using the Work of a Specialist

.47 In some engagements to examine MD&A, the nature of complex or subjective matters potentially material to the MD&A presentation may require specialized skill or knowledge in a particular field other than accounting or auditing. For example, the entity may include information concerning plant production capacity, which would ordinarily be determined by an engineer. In

---

[18] Refer to paragraphs .05–.06 and .11–.13 of AU-C section 320, *Materiality in Planning and Performing an Audit*, and paragraph .10 of AU-C section 450, *Evaluation of Misstatements Identified During the Audit*. [Footnote revised, December 2012, to reflect conforming changes necessary due to the issuance of SAS Nos. 122–126.]

such cases, the practitioner may use the work of a specialist and should consider the relevant guidance in AU-C section 620, *Using the Work of an Auditor's Specialist*. An auditor's specialist may be either an auditor's internal specialist (for example, a partner of the auditor's firm) or an external specialist. [Revised, December 2012, to reflect conforming changes necessary due to the issuance of SAS Nos. 122–126.]

Internal Audit Function

.48 Another factor the practitioner should consider when planning the engagement is whether the entity has an internal audit function and the extent to which internal auditors are involved in directly testing the MD&A presentation, in monitoring the entity's internal control applicable to the preparation of MD&A, or in testing the underlying records supporting disclosures in the MD&A. A practitioner should consider the guidance in AU-C section 610, *The Auditor's Consideration of the Internal Audit Function in an Audit of Financial Statements*, when addressing the competence and objectivity of internal auditors; the nature, timing, and extent of work to be performed; and other related matters. [Revised, December 2012, to reflect conforming changes necessary due to the issuance of SAS Nos. 122–126.]

Consideration of Internal Control Applicable to the Preparation of MD&A

.49 The practitioner should obtain an understanding of the entity's internal control applicable to the preparation of MD&A sufficient to plan the engagement and to assess control risk. Generally, controls that are relevant to an examination pertain to the entity's objective of preparing MD&A in conformity with the rules and regulations adopted by the SEC, and may include controls within the control environment, risk assessment, information and communication, control activities, and monitoring components.

.50 The controls relating to operations and compliance objectives may be relevant to an examination if they pertain to data the practitioner evaluates or uses in applying examination procedures. For example, controls over the gathering of information, which are different from financial statement controls, and controls relating to nonfinancial data that are included in the MD&A presentation, may be relevant to an examination engagement.

.51 In planning the examination, knowledge of such controls should be used to identify types of potential misstatement (including types of potential material omissions), to consider factors that affect the risk of material misstatement and to design appropriate tests.

.52 A practitioner generally obtains an understanding of the design of the entity's internal control applicable to the preparation of MD&A by making inquiries of appropriate management, supervisory, and staff personnel; by inspection of the entity's documents; and by observation of the entity's relevant activities, including controls over matters discussed, nonfinancial data included, and management evaluation of the reasonableness of information included. The nature and extent of procedures a practitioner performs vary from entity to entity and are influenced by factors such as the entity's complexity, the length of time that the entity has prepared MD&A pursuant to the rules and regulations adopted by the SEC, the practitioner's knowledge of the entity's controls obtained in audits and previous professional engagements, and judgments about materiality.

.53 After obtaining an understanding of the entity's internal control applicable to the preparation of MD&A, the practitioner assesses control risk for the assertions embodied in the MD&A presentation. (Refer to paragraphs .34–.39.) The practitioner may assess control risk at the maximum level (the greatest probability that a material misstatement that could occur in an assertion will not be prevented or detected on a timely basis by an entity's controls) because the practitioner believes controls are unlikely to pertain to an assertion, are unlikely to be effective, or because evaluating their effectiveness would be inefficient. Alternatively, the practitioner may obtain evidential matter about the effectiveness of both the design and operation of a control that supports a lower assessed level of control risk. Such evidential matter may be obtained from tests of controls planned and performed concurrently with obtaining the understanding of the internal control or from procedures performed to obtain the understanding that were not specifically planned as tests of controls.

.54 After obtaining the understanding and assessing control risk, the practitioner may desire to seek a further reduction in the assessed level of control risk for certain assertions. In such cases, the practitioner considers whether evidential matter sufficient to support a further reduction is likely to be available and whether performing additional tests of controls to obtain such evidential matter would be efficient.

.55 When seeking to assess control risk below the maximum for controls over financial and nonfinancial data, the practitioner should perform tests of controls to obtain evidence to support the assessed level of control risk. For example, the practitioner may perform tests of controls directed toward the effectiveness of the design or operation of internal control over the accumulation of the number of units sold for a manufacturing company, average interest rates earned and paid for a financial institution, or average net sales per square foot for a retail entity.

.56 The practitioner uses the knowledge provided by the understanding of internal control applicable to the preparation of MD&A and the assessed level of control risk in determining the nature, timing, and extent of substantive tests for the MD&A assertions.

.57 The practitioner should document the understanding of the internal control components obtained to plan the examination and the assessment of control risk. The form and extent of this documentation is influenced by the size and complexity of the entity, as well as the nature of the entity's controls applicable to the preparation of MD&A.

.58 During the course of an engagement to examine MD&A, the practitioner may become aware of control deficiencies in the design or operation of controls applicable to the preparation of MD&A that could adversely affect the entity's ability to prepare MD&A in accordance with the rules and regulations adopted by the SEC. The practitioner should consider the implications of such control deficiencies on his or her ability to rely on management's explanations and on comparisons to summary accounting records. A practitioner's responsibility to communicate these control deficiencies in an examination of MD&A is similar to the auditor's responsibility described in AU-C section 265, *Communicating Internal Control Related Matters Identified in an Audit*, and AU-C section 260, *The Auditor's Communication With Those Charged With Governance*. [Revised, March 2006, to reflect conforming changes necessary due to the issuance of SAS No. 112. Revised, January 2010, to reflect conforming changes necessary due to the issuance of SAS No. 115. Revised, December 2012, to reflect conforming changes necessary due to the issuance of SAS Nos. 122–126.]

Obtaining Sufficient Evidence

.59 The practitioner should apply procedures to obtain reasonable assurance of detecting material misstatements. In an audit of historical financial statements, the practitioner will have applied audit procedures to some of the information included in the MD&A. However, because the objective of those audit procedures is to have a reasonable basis for expressing an opinion on the financial statements taken as a whole rather than on the MD&A, certain additional examination procedures should be performed as discussed in paragraphs .60–.64. Determining these procedures and evaluating the sufficiency of the evidence obtained are matters of professional judgment.

.60 The practitioner ordinarily should apply the following procedures.

a. Read the MD&A and compare the content for consistency with the audited financial statements; compare financial amounts to the audited financial statements or related accounting records and analyses; recompute the increases, decreases, and percentages disclosed.

b. Compare nonfinancial amounts to the audited financial statements, if applicable, or to other records. (Refer to paragraphs .62–.64.)

c. Consider whether the explanations in MD&A are consistent with the information obtained during the audit; investigate further those explanations that cannot be substantiated by information in the audit working papers through inquiry (including inquiry of officers and other executives having responsibility for operational areas) and inspection of client records.

d. Examine internally generated documents (for example, variance analyses, sales analyses, wage cost analyses, sales or service pricing sheets, and business plans or programs) and externally generated documents (for example, correspondence, contracts, or loan agreements) in support of the existence, occurrence, or expected occurrence of events, transactions, conditions, trends, demands, commitments, and uncertainties disclosed in the MD&A.

e. Obtain available prospective financial information (for example, budgets; sales forecasts; forecasts of labor, overhead, and materials costs; capital expenditure requests; and financial forecasts and projections) and compare such information to forward-looking MD&A disclosures. Inquire of management as to the procedures used to prepare the prospective financial information. Evaluate whether the underlying information, determinations, estimates, and assumptions of the entity provide a reasonable basis for the MD&A disclosures of events, transactions, conditions, trends, demands, commitments, or uncertainties.[19]

f. Consider obtaining available prospective financial information relating to prior periods and comparing actual results with forecasted and projected amounts.

g. Make inquiries of officers and other executives having responsibility for operational areas (such as sales, marketing, and production) and financial and accounting matters, as to their plans and

---

[19] Refer to paragraph .26 for a discussion concerning the safe harbor rules for forward-looking statements.

expectations for the future that could affect the entity's liquidity and capital resources.

h. Consider obtaining external information concerning industry trends, inflation, and changing prices and comparing the related MD&A disclosures to such information.

i. Compare the information in MD&A with the rules and regulations adopted by the SEC and consider whether the presentation includes the required elements of such rules and regulations.

j. Read the minutes of meetings to date of the board of directors and other significant committees to identify matters that may affect MD&A; consider whether such matters are appropriately addressed in MD&A.

k. Inquire of officers as to the entity's prior experience with the SEC and the extent of comments received upon review of documents by the SEC; read correspondence between the entity and the SEC with respect to such review, if any.

l. Obtain public communications (for example, press releases and quarterly reports) and the related supporting documentation dealing with historical and future results; consider whether MD&A is consistent with such communications.

m. Consider obtaining other types of publicly available information (for example, analyst reports and news articles); compare the MD&A presentation with such information.

Testing Completeness

.61 The practitioner should design procedures to test the presentation for completeness, including tests of the completeness of explanations that relate to historical disclosures as discussed in paragraphs .36–.37. The practitioner should also consider whether the MD&A discloses matters that could significantly impact future financial condition and results of operations of the entity by considering information that he or she obtained through the following:

a. Audit of the financial statements

b. Inquiries of the entity's officers and other executives directed to current events, conditions, economic changes, commitments and uncertainties, within both the entity and its industry

c. Other information obtained through procedures such as those listed in paragraphs .60 and .65–.66

As discussed in paragraph .31, the inherent risk concerning the completeness of disclosures may be high; if it is, the practitioner may extend the procedures (for example, by making additional inquiries of management or by examining additional internally generated documents).

Nonfinancial Data

.62 Management may include nonfinancial data (such as units produced; the number of units sold, locations, or customers; plant utilization; or square footage) in the MD&A. The practitioner should consider whether the definitions used by management for such nonfinancial data are reasonable for the particular disclosure in the MD&A and whether there are suitable criteria (for example, industry standards with respect to square footage for retail operations), as discussed in paragraphs .23–.32 of section 101.

.63 In some situations, the nonfinancial data or the controls over the nonfinancial data may have been tested by the practitioner in conjunction with the financial statement audit; however, the practitioner's consideration of the nature of the procedures to apply to nonfinancial data in an examination of MD&A is based on the concept of materiality with respect to the MD&A presentation. The practitioner should consider whether industry standards exist for the nonfinancial data or whether there are different methods of measurement that may be used, and, if such methods could result in significantly different results, whether the method of measurement selected by management is reasonable and consistent between periods covered by the MD&A presentation. For example, the number of customers reported by management could vary depending on whether management defines a customer as a subsidiary or "ship to" location of a company rather than the company itself.

.64 In testing nonfinancial data included in the MD&A, the practitioner may seek to assess control risk below the maximum for controls over such nonfinancial data, as discussed in paragraph .55. The practitioner weighs the increase in effort of the examination associated with the additional tests of controls that is necessary to obtain evidential matter against the resulting decrease in examination effort associated with the reduced substantive tests. For those nonfinancial assertions for which the practitioner performs additional tests of controls, the practitioner determines the assessed level of control risk that the results of those tests will support. This assessed level of control risk is used in determining the appropriate detection risk to accept for those nonfinancial assertions and, accordingly, in determining the nature, timing, and extent of substantive tests for such assertions.

Consideration of the Effect of Events Subsequent to the Balance-Sheet Date

.65 As there is an expectation by the SEC that MD&A considers events through a date at or near the filing date,[20] the practitioner should consider information about events[21] that comes to his or her attention after the end of the period addressed by MD&A and prior to the issuance of his or her report that may have a material effect on the entity's financial condition (including liquidity and capital resources), changes in financial condition, results of operations, and material commitments for capital resources. Events or matters that should be disclosed in MD&A include those that—[22]

- Are reasonably expected to have a material favorable or unfavorable impact on net sales or revenues or income from continuing operations.
- Are reasonably likely to result in the entity's liquidity increasing or decreasing in any material way.
- Will have a material effect on the entity's capital resources.
- Would cause reported financial information not to be necessarily indicative of future operating results or of future financial condition.

---

[20] A registration statement under the 1933 Act speaks as of its effective date.

[21] Such events are only referred to as *subsequent events* in relation to an MD&A presentation if they occur after the MD&A presentation has been issued. The annual MD&A presentation ordinarily would not be updated for subsequent events if an MD&A presentation for a subsequent interim period has been issued or the event has been reported through a filing on Form 8-K.

[22] The practitioner should refer to the rules and regulations adopted by the SEC for other examples of events that should be disclosed.

The practitioner should consider whether events identified during the examination of the MD&A presentation or the audit of the related financial statements require adjustment to or disclosure in the MD&A presentation. When MD&A will be included or incorporated by reference in a 1933 Act document that is filed with the SEC, the practitioner's procedures should extend up to the filing date or as close to it as is reasonable and practicable in the circumstances.[23] If a public entity's MD&A presentation is to be included only in a filing under the 1934 Act (for example, Forms 10-K or 10-KSB), the practitioner's responsibility to consider subsequent events does not extend beyond the date of the report on MD&A. Paragraphs .94–.98 provide guidance when the practitioner is engaged subsequent to the filing of the MD&A presentation.

.66 In an examination of MD&A, the practitioner's fieldwork ordinarily extends beyond the date of the auditor's report on the related financial statements.[24] Accordingly, the practitioner generally should—

a. Read available minutes of meetings of stockholders, the board of directors, and other appropriate committees; as to meetings for which minutes are not available, inquire about matters dealt with at such meetings.

b. Read the latest available interim financial statements for periods subsequent to the date of the auditor's report, compare them with the financial statements for the periods covered by the MD&A, and inquire of and discuss with officers and other executives having responsibility for operational, financial, and accounting matters (limited where appropriate to major locations) matters such as the following:

- Whether interim financial statements have been prepared on the same basis as the audited financial statements
- Whether there were any significant changes in the entity's operations, liquidity, or capital resources in the subsequent period
- The current status of items in the financial statements for which the MD&A has been prepared that were accounted for on the basis of tentative, preliminary, or inconclusive data
- Whether any unusual adjustments were made during the period from the balance-sheet date to the date of inquiry

c. Make inquiries of members of senior management as to the current status of matters concerning litigation, claims, and assessments identified during the audit of the financial statements and

---

[23] Additionally, if the practitioner's report on MD&A is included or incorporated by reference in a 1933 Act document, the practitioner should extend his or her procedures with respect to subsequent events from the date of his or her report on MD&A up to the effective date or as close thereto as is reasonable and practicable in the circumstances.

[24] Undertaking an engagement to examine MD&A does not extend the auditor's responsibility to update the subsequent events review procedures for the financial statements beyond the date of the auditor's report. However, see AU-C section 560, *Events and Subsequently Discovered Facts*. Also, see AU-C section 925, *Filings With the U.S. Securities and Exchange Commission Under the Securities Act of 1933*, as to an auditor's responsibility when his or her report is included in a registration statement filed under the 1933 Act. [Footnote revised, December 2012, to reflect conforming changes necessary due to the issuance of SAS Nos. 122–126.]

of any new matters or unfavorable developments. Consider obtaining updated legal letters from legal counsel.[25]

d. Consider whether there have been any changes in economic conditions or in the industry that could have a significant effect on the entity.

e. Obtain written representations from appropriate officials as to whether any events occurred subsequent to the latest balance-sheet date that would require disclosure in the MD&A. (See paragraphs .110–.112.)

f. Make such additional inquiries or perform such other procedures as considered necessary and appropriate to address questions that arise in carrying out the foregoing procedures, inquiries, and discussions.

Forming an Opinion

.67 The practitioner should consider the concept of materiality discussed in paragraphs .21–.22, and the impact of any modification of the auditor's report on the historical financial statements in forming an opinion on the examination of MD&A, including the practitioner's ability to evaluate the results of inquiries and other procedures.

Reporting

.68 In order for the practitioner to issue a report on an examination of MD&A, the financial statements for the periods covered by the MD&A presentation and the related auditor's report(s) should accompany the MD&A presentation (or, with respect to a public entity, be incorporated in the document containing the MD&A by reference to information filed with a regulatory agency). In addition, if the entity is a nonpublic entity, one of the following conditions should be met.

a. A statement should be included in the body of the MD&A presentation that it has been prepared using the rules and regulations adopted by the SEC.

b. A separate written assertion should accompany the MD&A presentation or such assertion should be included in a representation letter obtained from the entity.

.69 The practitioner's report on an examination of MD&A should include the following:

a. A title that includes the word *independent*

b. An identification of the MD&A presentation, including the period covered

c. A statement that management is responsible for the preparation of the MD&A pursuant to the rules and regulations adopted by the SEC, and a statement that the practitioner's responsibility is to express an opinion on the presentation based on his or her examination

---

[25] See paragraphs .16–.24 of AU-C section 501, *Audit Evidence—Specific Considerations for Selected Items*, for guidance concerning obtaining legal letters. [Footnote revised, December 2012, to reflect conforming changes necessary due to the issuance of SAS Nos. 122–126.]

d. A reference to the auditor's report on the related financial statements, and if the report was other than a standard report, the substantive reasons therefor

e. A statement that the examination was conducted in accordance with attestation standards established by the AICPA and a description of the scope of an examination of MD&A

f. A statement that the practitioner believes the examination provides a reasonable basis for his or her opinion

g. A paragraph stating that—

(1) The preparation of MD&A requires management to interpret the criteria, make determinations as to the relevancy of information to be included, and make estimates and assumptions that affect reported information

(2) Actual results in the future may differ materially from management's present assessment of information regarding the estimated future impact of transactions and events that have occurred or are expected to occur, expected sources of liquidity and capital resources, operating trends, commitments, and uncertainties

h. If the entity is a nonpublic entity, a statement that, although the entity is not subject to the rules and regulations of the SEC, the MD&A presentation is intended to be a presentation in accordance with the rules and regulations adopted by the SEC

i. The practitioner's opinion on whether—

(1) The presentation includes, in all material respects, the required elements of the rules and regulations adopted by the SEC

(2) The historical financial amounts have been accurately derived, in all material respects, from the entity's financial statements

(3) The underlying information, determinations, estimates, and assumptions of the entity provide a reasonable basis for the disclosures contained therein

j. The manual or printed signature of the practitioner's firm

k. The date of the examination report

Appendix A [paragraph .114], "Examination Reports," includes a standard examination report. (See Example 1.)

Dating

.70 The practitioner's report on the examination of MD&A should be dated as of the completion of the practitioner's examination procedures. That date should not precede the date of the auditor's report on the latest historical financial statements covered by the MD&A.

Report Modifications

.71 The practitioner should modify the standard report described in paragraph .69, if any of the following conditions exist.

- The presentation excludes a material required element under the rules and regulations adopted by the SEC. (See paragraph .72.)

- The historical financial amounts have not been accurately derived, in all material respects, from the entity's financial statements. (See paragraph .72.)
- The underlying information, determinations, estimates, and assumptions used by management do not provide the entity with a reasonable basis for the disclosure in the MD&A. (See paragraph .72.)
- There is a restriction on the scope of the engagement. (See paragraph .73.)
- The practitioner decides to refer to the report of another practitioner as the basis in part for his or her report. (See paragraph .74.)
- The practitioner is engaged to examine the MD&A presentation after it has been filed with the SEC or other regulatory agency. (See paragraphs .94–.98.)

.72 The practitioner should express a qualified or an adverse opinion if (*a*) the MD&A presentation excludes a material required element, (*b*) historical financial amounts have not been accurately derived in all material respects, or (*c*) the underlying information, determinations, estimates, and assumptions of the entity do not provide a reasonable basis for the disclosures; for example, if there is a lack of consistency between management's method of measuring nonfinancial data between periods covered by the MD&A presentation. The basis for such opinion should be stated in the practitioner's report. Appendix A [paragraph .114] includes several examples of such modifications. (See Example 2.) Also refer to paragraph .107 for required communications with the audit committee.

.73 If the practitioner is unable to perform the procedures he or she considers necessary in the circumstances, the practitioner should modify the report or withdraw from the engagement. If the practitioner modifies the report, he or she should describe the limitation on the scope of the examination in an explanatory paragraph and qualify his or her opinion, or disclaim an opinion. However, limitations on the ability of the practitioner to perform necessary procedures could also arise because of the lack of adequate support for a significant representation in the MD&A. That circumstance may result in a conclusion that the unsupported representation constitutes a material misstatement of fact and, accordingly, the practitioner may qualify his or her opinion or express an adverse opinion, as described in paragraph .72.

Reference to Report of Another Practitioner

.74 If another practitioner examined the MD&A presentation of a component (refer to paragraph .46), the practitioner examining the group's MD&A may decide to make reference to such report of the component practitioner as a basis for his or her opinion on the group's consolidated MD&A presentation. The practitioner examining the group's MD&A should disclose this fact in the introductory paragraph of the report and should refer to the report of the component practitioner in expressing an opinion on the group's consolidated MD&A presentation. These references indicate (1) that the practitioner examining the group's MD&A is not taking responsibility for the work of the component practitioner, and (2) the source of the examination evidence with respect to those components for which reference to the examination of component practitioners is made. Appendix A [paragraph .114] provides an example of a report for such a situation. (See example 3.) Refer to paragraph .105 for guidance when the other practitioner does not issue a report. [Revised, December 2012, to reflect conforming changes necessary due to the issuance of SAS Nos. 122–126.]

Emphasis of a Matter

.75 In a number of circumstances, the practitioner may wish to emphasize a matter regarding the MD&A presentation. For example, he or she may wish to emphasize that the entity has included information beyond the required elements of the rules and regulations adopted by the SEC. Such explanatory comments should be presented in a separate paragraph of the practitioner's report.

Review Engagement

.76 The objective of a review engagement, including a review of MD&A for an interim period, is to accumulate sufficient evidence to provide the practitioner with a basis for reporting whether any information came to the practitioner's attention to cause him or her to believe that (*a*) the MD&A presentation does not include, in all material respects, the required elements of the rules and regulations adopted by the SEC, (*b*) the historical financial amounts included therein have not been accurately derived, in all material respects, from the entity's financial statements, or (*c*) the underlying information, determinations, estimates, and assumptions of the entity do not provide a reasonable basis for the disclosures contained therein. MD&A for an interim period may be a freestanding presentation or it may be combined with the MD&A presentation for the most recent fiscal year. Procedures for conducting a review of MD&A generally are limited to inquiries and analytical procedures, rather than also including search and verification procedures, concerning factors that have a material effect on financial condition, including liquidity and capital resources, results of operations, and cash flows. In a review engagement, the practitioner should—

a. Obtain an understanding of the rules and regulations adopted by the SEC for MD&A and management's method of preparing MD&A. (See paragraphs .18–.19.)

b. Plan the engagement. (See paragraph .77.)

c. Consider relevant portions of the entity's internal control applicable to the preparation of the MD&A. (See paragraph .78.)

d. Apply analytical procedures and make inquiries of management and others. (See paragraphs .79–.80.)

e. Consider the effect of events subsequent to the balance-sheet date. The practitioner's consideration of such events in a review of MD&A is similar to the practitioner's consideration in an examination. (See paragraphs .65–.66.)

f. Obtain written representations from management concerning its responsibility for MD&A, completeness of minutes, events subsequent to the balance-sheet date, and other matters about which the practitioner believes written representations are appropriate. (See paragraph .110.)

g. Form a conclusion as to whether any information came to the practitioner's attention that causes him or her to believe any of the following.

(1) The MD&A presentation does not include, in all material respects, the required elements of the rules and regulations adopted by the SEC.

(2) The historical financial amounts included therein have not been accurately derived, in all material respects, from the entity's financial statements.

(3) The underlying information, determinations, estimates, and assumptions of the entity do not provide a reasonable basis for the disclosures contained therein.

Planning the Engagement

.77 Planning an engagement to review MD&A involves developing an overall strategy for the analytical procedures and inquiries to be performed. When developing an overall strategy for the review engagement, the practitioner should consider factors such as the following:

- Matters affecting the industry in which the entity operates, such as financial reporting practices, economic conditions, laws and regulations, and technological changes
- Matters relating to the entity's business, including its organization, operating characteristics, capital structure, and distribution methods
- The types of relevant information that management reports to external analysts (for example, press releases or presentations to lenders and rating agencies concerning past and future performance)
- The extent of management's knowledge of and experience with the rules and regulations adopted by the SEC for MD&A
- If the entity is a nonpublic entity, the intended use of the MD&A presentation
- Matters identified during the audit or review of the historical financial statements relating to MD&A reporting, including knowledge of the entity's internal control applicable to the preparation of MD&A and the extent of recent changes, if any
- Matters identified during prior engagements to examine or review MD&A
- Preliminary judgments about materiality
- The nature of complex or subjective matters potentially material to the MD&A that may require special skill or knowledge
- The presence of an internal audit function and the extent to which internal auditors are involved in directly testing the MD&A presentation or underlying records

Consideration of Internal Control Applicable to the Preparation of MD&A

.78 To perform a review of MD&A, the practitioner needs to have sufficient knowledge of the entity's internal control applicable to the preparation of MD&A to—

- Identify types of potential misstatements in MD&A, including types of material omissions, and consider the likelihood of their occurrence.

- Select the inquiries and analytical procedures that will provide a basis for reporting whether any information causes the practitioner to believe the following.
  - — The MD&A presentation does not include, in all material respects, the required elements of the rules and regulations adopted by the SEC, or the historical financial amounts included therein have not been accurately derived, in all material respects, from the entity's financial statements.
  - — The underlying information, determinations, estimates, and assumptions of the entity do not provide a reasonable basis for the disclosures contained therein.

Application of Analytical Procedures and Inquiries

.79 The practitioner ordinarily would not obtain corroborating evidential matter of management's responses to the practitioner's inquiries in performing a review of MD&A. The practitioner should, however, consider the consistency of management's responses in light of the results of other inquiries and the application of analytical procedures. The practitioner ordinarily should apply the following analytical procedures and inquiries.

a. Read the MD&A presentation and compare the content for consistency with the audited financial statements (or reviewed interim financial information if MD&A includes interim information); compare financial amounts to the audited or reviewed financial statements or related accounting records and analyses; recompute the increases, decreases, and percentages disclosed.

b. Compare nonfinancial amounts to the audited (or reviewed) financial statements, if applicable, or to other records. (Refer to paragraph .80.)

c. Consider whether the explanations in MD&A are consistent with the information obtained during the audit or the review of interim financial information; make further inquiries of officers and other executives having responsibility for operational areas as necessary.

d. Obtain available prospective financial information (for example, budgets; sales forecasts; forecasts of labor, overhead, and materials costs; capital expenditure requests; and financial forecasts and projections) and compare such information to forward-looking MD&A disclosures. Inquire of management as to the procedures used to prepare the prospective financial information. Consider whether information came to the practitioner's attention that causes him or her to believe that the underlying information, determinations, estimates, and assumptions of the entity do not provide a reasonable basis for the disclosures of trends, demands, commitments, events, or uncertainties.[26]

e. Make inquiries of officers and other executives having responsibility for operational areas (such as sales, marketing, and production) and financial and accounting matters, as to any plans and

[26] Refer to paragraph .26 for a discussion concerning the safe harbor rules for forward-looking statements.

expectations for the future that could affect the entity's liquidity and capital resources.

f. Compare the information in MD&A with the rules and regulations adopted by the SEC and consider whether the presentation includes the required elements of such rules and regulations.

g. Read the minutes of meetings to date of the board of directors and other significant committees to identify actions that may affect MD&A; consider whether such matters are appropriately addressed in the MD&A presentation.

h. Inquire of officers as to the entity's prior experience with the SEC and the extent of comments received upon review of documents by the SEC; read correspondence between the entity and the SEC with respect to such review, if any.

i. Inquire of management regarding the nature of public communications (for example, press releases and quarterly reports) dealing with historical and future results and consider whether the MD&A presentation is consistent with such communications.

.80 If nonfinancial data are included in the MD&A presentation, the practitioner should inquire as to the nature of the records from which such information was derived and observe the existence of such records, but need not perform other tests of such records beyond analytical procedures and inquiries of individuals responsible for maintaining them. The practitioner should consider whether such nonfinancial data are relevant to users of the MD&A presentation and whether such data are clearly defined in the MD&A presentation. The practitioner should make inquiries regarding whether the definition of the nonfinancial data was consistently applied during the periods reported.

.81 However, if the practitioner becomes aware that the presentation may be incomplete or contain inaccuracies, or is otherwise unsatisfactory, the practitioner should perform the additional procedures he or she deems necessary to achieve the limited assurance contemplated by a review engagement.

Reporting

.82 In order for the practitioner to issue a report on a review of MD&A for an annual period, the financial statements for the periods covered by the MD&A presentation and the related auditor's report(s) should accompany the MD&A presentation (or with respect to a public entity be incorporated in the document containing the MD&A by reference to information filed with a regulatory agency).

.83 If the MD&A presentation relates to an interim period and the entity is a public entity, the financial statements for the interim periods covered by the MD&A presentation and the related accountant's review report(s) should accompany the MD&A presentation, or be incorporated in the document containing the MD&A by reference to information filed with a regulatory agency. The comparative financial statements for the most recent annual period and the related MD&A should accompany the MD&A presentation for the interim period, or be incorporated by reference to information filed with a regulatory agency. Generally, the requirement for inclusion of the annual financial statements and related MD&A is satisfied by a public entity that has met its reporting responsibility for filing its annual financial statements and MD&A in its annual report on Form 10-K.

.84 If the MD&A presentation relates to an interim period and the entity is a nonpublic entity, the following documents should accompany the interim MD&A presentation in order for the practitioner to issue a review report:

a. The MD&A presentation for the most recent fiscal year and related accountant's examination or review report(s)

b. The financial statements for the periods covered by the respective MD&A presentations (most recent fiscal year and interim periods and the related auditor's report(s) and accountant's review report(s))

In addition, one of the following conditions should be met.

- A statement should be included in the body of the MD&A presentation that it has been prepared using the rules and regulations adopted by the SEC.

- A separate written assertion should accompany the MD&A presentation or such assertion should be included in a representation letter obtained from the entity.

.85 The practitioner's report on a review of MD&A should include the following:

a. A title that includes the word *independent*

b. An identification of the MD&A presentation, including the period covered

c. A statement that management is responsible for the preparation of the MD&A pursuant to the rules and regulations adopted by the SEC

d. A reference to the auditor's report on the related financial statements, and, if the report was other than a standard report, the substantive reasons therefor

e. A statement that the review was conducted in accordance with attestation standards established by the AICPA

f. A description of the procedures for a review of MD&A

g. A statement that a review of MD&A is substantially less in scope than an examination, the objective of which is an expression of opinion regarding the MD&A presentation, and accordingly, no such opinion is expressed

h. A paragraph stating that—

(1) The preparation of MD&A requires management to interpret the criteria, make determinations as to the relevancy of information to be included, and make estimates and assumptions that affect reported information

(2) Actual results in the future may differ materially from management's present assessment of information regarding the estimated future impact of transactions and events that have occurred or are expected to occur, expected sources of liquidity and capital resources, operating trends, commitments, and uncertainties

i. If the entity is a nonpublic entity, a statement that although the entity is not subject to the rules and regulations of the SEC, the MD&A presentation is intended to be a presentation in accordance with the rules and regulations adopted by the SEC

j. A statement about whether any information came to the practitioner's attention that caused him or her to believe that—

(1) The MD&A presentation does not include, in all material respects, the required elements of the rules and regulations adopted by the SEC

(2) The historical financial amounts included therein have not been accurately derived, in all material respects, from the entity's financial statements

(3) The underlying information, determinations, estimates, and assumptions of the entity do not provide a reasonable basis for the disclosures contained therein

k. If the entity is a public entity as defined in paragraph .02, or a nonpublic entity that is making or has made an offering of securities and it appears that the securities may subsequently be registered or subject to a filing with the SEC or other regulatory agency (for example, certain offerings of securities under Rule 144A of the 1933 Act that purport to conform to Regulation S-K), a statement of restrictions on the use of the report to specified parties, because it is not intended to be filed with the SEC as a report under the 1933 Act or the 1934 Act.

l. The manual or printed signature of the practitioner's firm

m. The date of the review report

Appendix B [paragraph .115], "Review Reports," provides examples of a standard review report for an annual and interim period.

Dating

.86 The practitioner's report on the review of MD&A should be dated as of the completion of the practitioner's review procedures. That date should not precede the date of the accountant's report on the latest historical financial statements covered by the MD&A.

Report Modifications

.87 The practitioner should modify the standard review report described in paragraph .86 if any of the following conditions exist.

- The presentation excludes a material required element of the rules and regulations adopted by the SEC. (See paragraph .89.)
- The historical financial amounts have not been accurately derived, in all material respects, from the entity's financial statements. (See paragraph .89.)
- The underlying information, determinations, estimates, and assumptions used by management do not provide the entity with a reasonable basis for the disclosures in the MD&A. (See paragraph .89.)
- The practitioner decides to refer to the report of another practitioner as the basis, in part, for his or her report. (See paragraph .90.)
- The practitioner is engaged to review the MD&A presentation after it has been filed with the SEC or other regulatory agency. (See paragraphs .94–.98.)

.88 When the practitioner is unable to perform the inquiry and analytical procedures he or she considers necessary to achieve the limited assurance provided by a review, or the client does not provide the practitioner with a representation letter, the review will be incomplete. A review that is incomplete is not an adequate basis for issuing a review report. If the practitioner is unable to complete a review because of a scope limitation, the practitioner should consider the implications of that limitation with respect to possible misstatements of the MD&A presentation. In those circumstances, the practitioner should also refer to paragraphs .107–.109 for guidance concerning communications with the audit committee.

.89 If the practitioner becomes aware that the MD&A is materially misstated, the practitioner should modify the review report to describe the nature of the misstatement. Appendix B [paragraph .115] contains an example of such a modification of the accountant's report. (See Example 3.)

.90 If another practitioner reviewed or examined the MD&A for a material component, the practitioner may decide to make reference to such report of the other practitioner in reporting on the consolidated MD&A presentation. Such reference indicates a division of responsibility for performance of the review.

Emphasis of a Matter

.91 In some circumstances, the practitioner may wish to emphasize a matter regarding the MD&A presentation. For example, he or she may wish to emphasize that the entity has included information beyond the required elements of the rules and regulations adopted by the SEC. Such explanatory comments should be presented in a separate paragraph of the practitioner's report.

Combined Examination and Review Report on MD&A

.92 A practitioner may be engaged both to examine an MD&A presentation as of the most recent fiscal year-end and to review a separate MD&A presentation for a subsequent interim period. If the examination and review are completed at the same time, a combined report may be issued. Appendix C [paragraph .116], "Combined Reports," contains an example of a combined report on an examination of an annual MD&A presentation and the review of a separate MD&A presentation for an interim period. (See Example 1.)

.93 If an entity prepares a combined MD&A presentation for annual and interim periods in which there is a discussion of liquidity and capital resources only as of the most recent interim period but not as of the most recent annual period, the practitioner is limited to performing the highest level of service that is provided with respect to the historical financial statements for any of the periods covered by the MD&A presentation. For example, if the annual financial statements have been audited and the interim financial statements have been reviewed, the practitioner may be engaged to perform a review of the combined MD&A presentation. Appendix C [paragraph .116] contains an example of a review report on a combined MD&A presentation for annual and interim periods. (See Example 2.)

When Practitioner Is Engaged Subsequent to the Filing of MD&A

.94 Management's responsibility for updating an MD&A presentation for events occurring subsequent to the issuance of MD&A depends on whether the entity is a public or nonpublic entity. A public entity is required to report significant subsequent events in a Form 8-K or Form 10-Q, or in a registration statement; therefore, a public company would ordinarily not modify its MD&A presentation once it is filed with the SEC (or other regulatory agency).

.95 Therefore, if the practitioner is engaged to examine (or review) an MD&A presentation of a public entity that has already been filed with the SEC (or other regulatory agency), the practitioner should consider whether material subsequent events are appropriately disclosed in a Form 8-K or 10-Q, or a registration statement that includes or incorporates by reference such MD&A presentation. Refer to paragraphs .65–.66 for guidance concerning consideration of events up to the filing date when the practitioner's report on MD&A will be included (or incorporated by reference) in a 1933 Act document filed with the SEC that will require a consent.

.96 If subsequent events of a public entity are appropriately disclosed in a Form 8-K or 10-Q, or in a registration statement, or if there have been no material subsequent events, the practitioner should add the following paragraph to his or her examination or review report following the opinion or concluding paragraph, respectively.

> The accompanying Management's Discussion and Analysis does not consider events that have occurred subsequent to Month XX, 20X6, the date as of which it was filed with the Securities and Exchange Commission.

.97 If there has been a material subsequent event that has not been disclosed in a manner described in paragraph .95 and if the practitioner determines that it is appropriate to issue a report even though the MD&A presentation has not been updated for such material subsequent event (for example, because the filing of the Form 10-Q that will disclose such events has not yet occurred), the practitioner should express a qualified or an adverse opinion (or appropriately modify the review report) on the MD&A presentation. As discussed in paragraph .107, if such material subsequent event is not appropriately disclosed, the practitioner should evaluate (*a*) whether to resign from the engagement related to the MD&A presentation and (*b*) whether to remain as the entity's auditor or stand for re-election to audit the entity's financial statements.

.98 Because a nonpublic entity is not subject to the filing requirements of the SEC, an MD&A presentation of a nonpublic entity should be updated for material subsequent events through the date of the practitioner's report.

When a Predecessor Auditor Has Audited Prior Period Financial Statements

.99 If a predecessor auditor has audited the financial statements for a prior period covered by the MD&A, the need by the practitioner reporting on the MD&A for an understanding of the business and the entity's accounting and financial reporting practices for such prior period, as discussed in paragraph .07, is not diminished and the practitioner should apply the appropriate procedures. In applying the appropriate procedures, the practitioner may consider reviewing the predecessor auditor's working papers with respect to audits of financial statements and examinations or reviews of MD&A presentations for such prior periods.

.100 Information that may be obtained from the audit or attest working papers of the predecessor auditor will not provide a sufficient basis in itself for the practitioner to express an opinion with respect to the MD&A disclosures for such prior periods. If the practitioner has audited the current year, the results of such audit may be considered in planning and performing the examination of MD&A and may provide evidential matter that is useful in performing the examination, including with respect to matters disclosed for prior periods. For example, an increase in salaries expense may be the result of an acquisition in the last half of the prior year. Auditing procedures applied to payroll expense in the current year that validate the increase as a result of the acquisition may provide evidential matter with respect to the increase in salaries expense in the prior year attributed to the acquisition.

.101 In addition to the procedures described in paragraphs .49–.66, the practitioner will need to make inquiries of the predecessor auditor and management as to audit adjustments proposed by the predecessor auditor that were not recorded in the financial statements.

Communications Between Predecessor and Successor Auditors

.102 If the practitioner is appointed as the successor auditor, he or she follows the guidance AU-C section 210, *Terms of Engagement*, in considering whether or not to accept the engagement. If, at the time of the appointment as auditor, the practitioner is also being engaged to examine or review MD&A, the practitioner should also make specific inquiries of the predecessor auditor regarding MD&A. [Revised, December 2012, to reflect conforming changes necessary due to the issuance of SAS Nos. 122–126.]

.103 The practitioner's examination may be facilitated by (*a*) making specific inquiries of the predecessor regarding matters that the successor believes may affect the conduct of the examination (or review), such as areas that required an inordinate amount of time or problems that arose from the condition of the records, and (*b*) if the predecessor previously examined or reviewed MD&A, reviewing the predecessor's working papers for the predecessor's examination or review engagement.

.104 If, subsequent to his or her engagement to audit the financial statements, the practitioner is requested to examine MD&A, the practitioner should request the client to authorize the predecessor auditor to allow a review of the predecessor's audit working papers related to the financial statement periods included in the MD&A presentation. Although the practitioner may previously have had access to the predecessor auditor's working papers in connection with the successor's audit of the financial statements, ordinarily the predecessor auditor should permit the practitioner to review those audit working papers relating to matters that are disclosed or that would likely be disclosed in MD&A.

Another Auditor Audits a Significant Part of the Financial Statements

.105 When one or more component auditors audits a significant part of a group's financial statements, the practitioner[27] may request that the component auditor perform procedures with respect to the MD&A or the practitioner may perform the procedures directly with respect to such component(s).[28]

[27] The practitioner serving as auditor of the group's financial statements is presumed to have an audit base for purposes of examining or reviewing the consolidated MD&A presentation. [Footnote revised, December 2012, to reflect conforming changes necessary due to the issuance of SAS Nos. 122–126.]

[28] The practitioner should consider whether he or she has sufficient industry expertise with respect to a subsidiary audited by a component auditor to take sole responsibility for the group's consolidated MD&A presentation. [Footnote revised, December 2012, to reflect conforming changes necessary due to the issuance of SAS Nos. 122–126.]

Unless the component auditor issues an examination or review report on a separate MD&A presentation of such component(s) (see paragraph .74), the practitioner examining the group's MD&A should not make reference to the work of the component practitioner on MD&A in his or her report on MD&A [29] Accordingly, if the practitioner examining the group's MD&A has requested such component auditor to perform procedures, the practitioner examining the group's MD&A should perform those procedures that he or she considers necessary to take responsibility for the work of the other auditor. Such procedures may include one or more of the following:

a. Visiting the component auditor and discussing the procedures followed and the results thereof.

b. Reviewing the working papers of the component auditor with respect to the component.

c. Participating in discussions with the component's management regarding matters that may affect the preparation of the component's MD&A.

d. Making supplemental tests with respect to such component.

The determination of the extent of the procedures to be applied by the practitioner examining the group's MD&A rests with that practitioner alone in the exercise of his or her professional judgment and in no way constitutes a reflection on the adequacy of the component auditor's work. Because the practitioner examining the group's MD&A in this case assumes responsibility for his or her opinion on the MD&A presentation without making reference to the procedures performed by the other auditor, the judgment of the practitioner examining the group's MD&A should govern as to the extent of procedures to be undertaken. [Revised, December 2012, to reflect conforming changes necessary due to the issuance of SAS Nos. 122–126.]

Responsibility for Other Information in Documents Containing MD&A

.106 A client may publish annual reports containing MD&A and other documents to which the practitioner, at the client's request, devotes attention. See paragraphs .91–.94 of section 101 for pertinent guidance in these circumstances. See Appendix D of this section [paragraph .117], "Comparison of Activities Performed Under SAS No. 8, *Other Information in Documents Containing Audited Financial Statements*, Versus a Review or an Examination Attest Engagement." The guidance in AU-C section 925, *Filings With the U.S. Securities and Exchange Commission Under the Securities Act of 1933*, is pertinent when the practitioner's report on MD&A is included in a registration statement, proxy statement, or periodic report filed under the federal securities statutes. [Revised, December 2012, to reflect conforming changes necessary due to the issuance of SAS Nos. 122–126.]

Communications With the Audit Committee

.107 If the practitioner concludes that the MD&A presentation contains material inconsistencies with other information included in the document

---

[29] This does not preclude the practitioner from referring to the component auditor's report on the financial statements in his or her report on the group's MD&A. [Footnote revised, December 2012, to reflect conforming changes necessary due to the issuance of SAS Nos. 122–126.]

containing the MD&A presentation or with the historical financial statements,[30] material omissions, or material misstatements of fact, and management refuses to take corrective action, the practitioner should inform the audit committee or others with equivalent authority and responsibility. If the MD&A is not revised, the practitioner should evaluate (*a*) whether to resign from the engagement related to the MD&A, and (*b*) whether to remain as the entity's auditor or stand for re-election to audit the entity's financial statements. The practitioner may wish to consult with his or her attorney when making these evaluations.

.108 If the practitioner is engaged after the MD&A presentation has been filed with the SEC (or other regulatory agency), and becomes aware that such MD&A presentation on file with the SEC (or other regulatory agency) has not been revised for a matter for which the practitioner has or would qualify his or her opinion, the practitioner should discuss such matter with the audit committee and request that the MD&A presentation be revised. If the audit committee fails to take appropriate action, the practitioner should consider whether to resign as the independent auditor of the company. The practitioner may consider paragraphs .21–.23 and .27 of AU-C section 250, *Consideration of Laws and Regulations in an Audit of Financial Statements*, concerning communication with the audit committee and other considerations. [Revised, December 2012, to reflect conforming changes necessary due to the issuance of SAS Nos. 122–126.]

.109 If, as a result of performing an examination or a review of MD&A, the practitioner has determined that there is evidence that fraud may exist, that matter should be brought to the attention of an appropriate level of management. This is generally appropriate even if the matter might be considered clearly inconsequential. If the matter relates to the audited financial statements, the practitioner should consider the guidance in AU-C section 240, *Consideration of Fraud in a Financial Statement Audit*, concerning communication responsibilities, and the effect on the auditor's report on the financial statements. [Revised, December 2012, to reflect conforming changes necessary due to the issuance of SAS Nos. 122–126.]

Obtaining Written Representations

.110 In an examination or a review engagement, the practitioner should obtain written representations from management.[31] The specific written representations obtained by the practitioner will depend on the circumstances of the engagement and the nature of the MD&A presentation. Specific representations should relate to the following matters:

a. Management's acknowledgment of its responsibility for the preparation of MD&A and management's assertion that the

---

[30] See AU-C section 720, *Information in Documents Containing Audited Financial Statements*, for guidance on the impact of material inconsistencies or material misstatements of fact on the auditor's report on the related historical financial statements. [Footnote revised, December 2012, to reflect conforming changes necessary due to the issuance of SAS Nos. 122–126.]

[31] Paragraph .21 of AU-C section 580, *Written Representations*, requires that written representations be in the form of a representation letter addressed to the auditor. Paragraph .09*b* of AU-C section 925 requires the auditor to obtain updated written representations from management at or shortly before the effective date of the registration statement, about (*a*) whether any information has come to management's attention that would cause management to believe that any of the previous representations should be modified, and (*b*) whether any events have occurred subsequent to the date of the financial statements that would require adjustment to, or disclosure in, those financial statements. (See paragraph .65.) [Footnote revised, December 2012, to reflect conforming changes necessary due to the issuance of SAS Nos. 122–126.]

MD&A presentation has been prepared in accordance with the rules and regulations adopted by the SEC for MD&A[32]

b. A statement that the historical financial amounts included in MD&A have been accurately derived from the entity's financial statements

c. Management's belief that the underlying information, determinations, estimates, and assumptions of the entity provide a reasonable basis for the disclosures contained in the MD&A

d. A statement that management has made available all significant documentation related to compliance with SEC rules and regulations for MD&A

e. Completeness and availability of all minutes of meetings of stockholders, directors, and committees of directors

f. For a public entity, whether any communications from the SEC were received concerning noncompliance with or deficiencies in MD&A reporting practices

g. Whether any events occurred subsequent to the latest balance-sheet date that would require disclosure in the MD&A

h. If forward-looking information is included, a statement that—

- The forward-looking information is based on management's best estimate of expected events and operations, and is consistent with budgets, forecasts, or operating plans prepared for such periods
- The accounting principles expected to be used for the forward-looking information are consistent with the principles used in preparing the historical financial statements
- Management has provided the latest version of such budgets, forecasts, or operating plans, and has informed the practitioner of any anticipated changes or modifications to such information that could affect the disclosures contained in the MD&A presentation

i. If voluntary information is included that is subject to the rules and regulations adopted by the SEC (for example, information required by Item 305, *Quantitative and Qualitative Disclosures About Market Risk*), a statement that such voluntary information has been prepared in accordance with the related rules and regulations adopted by the SEC for such information

j. If pro forma information is included, a statement that—

- Management is responsible for the assumptions used in determining the pro forma adjustments
- Management believes that the assumptions provide a reasonable basis for presenting all the significant effects directly attributable to the transaction or event, that the related pro forma adjustments give appropriate effect to those assumptions, and that the pro forma column reflects

---

[32] Management should specify the SEC rules (for example, Item 303 of Regulation S-K, Item 303 of Regulation S-B, or Item 9 of Form 20-F). For nonpublic entities, the practitioner also obtains a written assertion that the presentation has been prepared using the rules and regulations adopted by the SEC. (See paragraph .02.)

the proper application of those adjustments to the historical financial statements

- Management believes that the significant effects directly attributable to the transaction or event are appropriately disclosed in the pro forma financial information

.111 In an examination, management's refusal to furnish written representations constitutes a limitation on the scope of the engagement sufficient to preclude an unqualified opinion and is ordinarily sufficient to cause a practitioner to disclaim an opinion or withdraw from the examination engagement. However, based on the nature of the representations not obtained or the circumstances of the refusal, the practitioner may conclude that a qualified opinion is appropriate in an examination engagement. In a review engagement, management's refusal to furnish written representations constitutes a limitation of the scope of the engagement sufficient to require withdrawal from the review engagement. Further, the practitioner should consider the effects of the refusal on his or her ability to rely on other management representations.

.112 If the practitioner is precluded from performing procedures he or she considers necessary in the circumstances with respect to a matter that is material to the MD&A presentation, even though management has given representations concerning the matter, there is a limitation on the scope of the engagement, and the practitioner should qualify his or her opinion or disclaim an opinion in an examination engagement, or withdraw from a review engagement.

Effective Date

.113 This section is effective when management's discussion and analysis is for a period ending on or after June 1, 2001. Early application is permitted.

.114

Appendix A—Examination Reports

Example 1: Standard Examination Report

1. The following is an illustration of a standard examination report.

Independent Accountant's Report

[*Introductory paragraph*]

We have examined XYZ Company's Management's Discussion and Analysis taken as a whole, included [*incorporated by reference*] in the Company's [*insert description of registration statement or document*]. Management is responsible for the preparation of the Company's Management's Discussion and Analysis pursuant to the rules and regulations adopted by the Securities and Exchange Commission. Our responsibility is to express an opinion on the presentation based on our examination. We have audited, in accordance with auditing standards generally accepted in the United States of America, the financial statements of XYZ Company, which comprise the balance sheets as of December 31, 20X5 and 20X4, and the related statements of income, changes in stockholder's equity, and cash flows for each of the years in the three-year period ended December 31, 20X5, and the related notes to the financial statements. In our report dated [*Month*] XX, 20X6, we expressed an unmodified opinion on those financial statements. [33]

[*Scope paragraph*]

Our examination of Management's Discussion and Analysis was conducted in accordance with attestation standards established by the American Institute of Certified Public Accountants and, accordingly, included examining, on a test basis, evidence supporting the historical amounts and disclosures in the presentation. An examination also includes assessing the significant determinations made by management as to the relevancy of information to be included and the estimates and assumptions that affect reported information. We believe that our examination provides a reasonable basis for our opinion.

---

[33] If prior financial statements were audited by other auditors, this sentence would be replaced by the following.

> We have audited, in accordance with auditing standards generally accepted in the United States of America, the financial statements of XYZ Company, which comprise the balance sheet as of December 31, 20X5, and the related statement of income, changes in stockholder's equity, and cash flows for the year then ended, and the related notes to the financial statements. In our report dated [*Month*] XX, 20X6, we expressed an unmodified opinion on those financial statements. The financial statements of XYZ Company; which comprise the balance sheet as of December 31, 20X4, and the related statement of income, changes in stockholder's equity, and cash flows for each of the years in the two-year period then ended, and the notes to the financial statements; were audited by other auditors, whose report dated [*Month*] XX, 20X5, expressed an unmodified opinion on those financial statements.

If the practitioner's opinion on the financial statements is based on the report of component auditors, this sentence would be replaced by the following:

> We have audited, in accordance with auditing standards generally accepted in the United States of America, the financial statements of XYZ Company which comprise the balance sheets as of December 31, 20X5 and 20X4, and the related statements of income, changes in stockholders' equity, and cash flows for each of the years in the three-year period ended December 31, 20X5, and the notes to the financial statements. In our report dated [*Month*] XX, 20X6, we expressed an unmodified opinion on those financial statements based on our audits and the report of component auditors.

Refer to Example 3 if the practitioner's opinion on MD&A is based on the report of another practitioner on a component of the entity. [Footnote revised, December 2012, to reflect conforming changes necessary due to the issuance of SAS Nos. 122–126.]

[*Explanatory paragraph*][34]

The preparation of Management's Discussion and Analysis requires management to interpret the criteria, make determinations as to the relevancy of information to be included, and make estimates and assumptions that affect reported information. Management's Discussion and Analysis includes information regarding the estimated future impact of transactions and events that have occurred or are expected to occur, expected sources of liquidity and capital resources, operating trends, commitments, and uncertainties. Actual results in the future may differ materially from management's present assessment of this information because events and circumstances frequently do not occur as expected.

[*Opinion paragraph*]

In our opinion, the Company's presentation of Management's Discussion and Analysis includes, in all material respects, the required elements of the rules and regulations adopted by the Securities and Exchange Commission; the historical financial amounts included therein have been accurately derived, in all material respects, from the Company's financial statements; and the underlying information, determinations, estimates, and assumptions of the Company provide a reasonable basis for the disclosures contained therein.

[*Signature*]
[*Date*]

Example 2: Modifications to Examination Report for a Qualified Opinion

2. An example of a modification of an examination report for a qualified opinion due to a material omission described in paragraph .72 follows.

[*Additional explanatory paragraph preceding the opinion paragraph*]

Based on information furnished to us by management, we believe that the Company has excluded a discussion of the significant capital outlay required for its plans to expand into the telecommunications industry and the possible effects on the Company's financial condition, liquidity, and capital resources.

[*Opinion paragraph*]

In our opinion, except for the omission of the matter described in the preceding paragraph, the Company's presentation of Management's Discussion and Analysis includes, in all material respects, the required elements of the rules and regulations adopted by the Securities and Exchange Commission; the historical financial amounts included therein have been accurately derived, in all material respects, from the Company's financial statements; and the underlying information, determinations, estimates, and assumptions of the Company provide a reasonable basis for the disclosures contained therein.

3. An example of a modification of an examination report for a qualified opinion when overly subjective assertions are included in MD&A follows.

---

[34] The following sentence should be added to the beginning of the explanatory paragraph if the entity is a nonpublic entity, as discussed in paragraph .69*h*:

> Although XYZ Company is not subject to the rules and regulations of the Securities and Exchange Commission, the accompanying Management's Discussion and Analysis is intended to be a presentation in accordance with the rules and regulations adopted by the Securities and Exchange Commission.

[*Additional explanatory paragraph preceding the opinion paragraph*]

Based on information furnished to us by management, we believe that the underlying information, determinations, estimates, and assumptions used by management do not provide the Company with a reasonable basis for the disclosure concerning [*describe*] in the Company's Management's Discussion and Analysis.

[*Opinion paragraph*]

In our opinion, except for the disclosure regarding [*describe*] discussed in the preceding paragraph, the Company's presentation of Management's Discussion and Analysis includes, in all material respects, the required elements of the rules and regulations adopted by the Securities and Exchange Commission; the historical financial amounts included therein have been accurately derived, in all material respects, from the Company's financial statements; and the underlying information, determinations, estimates, and assumptions of the Company provide a reasonable basis for the disclosures contained therein.

Example 3: Examination Report With Reference to the Report of Another Practitioner

4. The following is an illustration of an examination report indicating a division of responsibility with another practitioner, who has examined a sepa rate MD&A presentation of a wholly-owned subsidiary, when the practitioner reporting is serving as the auditor of the related group's consolidated financial statements.

Independent Accountant's Report

[*Introductory paragraphs*]

We have examined XYZ Company's Management's Discussion and Analysis taken as a whole, included [*incorporated by reference*] in the Company's [*insert description of registration statement or document*]. Management is responsible for the preparation of the Company's Management's Discussion and Analysis pursuant to the rules and regulations adopted by the Securities and Exchange Commission. Our responsibility is to express an opinion on the presentation based on our examination. We did not examine Management's Discussion and Analysis of ABC Corporation, a wholly-owned subsidiary, included in ABC Corporation's [*insert description of registration statement or document*]. Such Management's Discussion and Analysis was examined by other accountants, whose report has been furnished to us, and our opinion, insofar as it relates to information included for ABC Corporation, is based solely on the report of the other accountants.

We have audited, in accordance with auditing standards generally accepted in the United States of America, the consolidated financial statements of XYZ Company, which comprise the consolidated balance sheets as of December 31, 20X5 and 20X4, and the related consolidated statements of income, changes in stockholders' equity, and cash flows, for each of the years in the three-year period ended December 31, 20X5. In our report dated [*Month*] XX, 20X6, we expressed an unmodified opinion on those financial statements based on our audits and the report of other auditors.

[*Scope paragraph*]

Our examination of Management's Discussion and Analysis was conducted in accordance with attestation standards established by the American Institute of Certified Public Accountants and, accordingly, included examining, on a test basis, evidence supporting the historical amounts and disclosures in the presentation. An examination also includes assessing the significant determinations made by management as to the relevancy of information to be included and the estimates and assumptions that affect reported information. We believe that our examination and the report of other accountants provide a reasonable basis for our opinion.

[*Explanatory paragraph*] [35]

The preparation of Management's Discussion and Analysis requires management to interpret the criteria, make determinations as to the relevancy of information to be included, and make estimates and assumptions that affect reported information. Management's Discussion and Analysis includes information regarding the estimated future impact of transactions and events that have occurred or are expected to occur, expected sources of liquidity and capital resources, operating trends, commitments, and uncertainties. Actual results in the future may differ materially from management's present assessment of this information because events and circumstances frequently do not occur as expected.

[*Opinion paragraph*]

In our opinion, based on our examination and the report of other accountants, the Company's presentation of Management's Discussion and Analysis included [*incorporated by reference*] in the Company's [*insert description of registration statement or document*] includes, in all material respects, the required elements of the rules and regulations adopted by the Securities and Exchange Commission; the historical financial amounts included therein have been accurately derived, in all material respects, from the Company's financial statements; and the underlying information, determinations, estimates, and assumptions of the Company provide a reasonable basis for the disclosures contained therein.

[*Signature*]

[*Date*]

[Revised, December 2012, to reflect conforming changes necessary due to the issuance of SAS Nos. 122–126.]

---

[35] The following sentence should be added to the beginning of the explanatory paragraph if the entity is a nonpublic entity, as discussed in paragraph .69*h*.

Although XYZ Company is not subject to the rules and regulations of the Securities and Exchange Commission, the accompanying Management's Discussion and Analysis is intended to be a presentation in accordance with the rules and regulations adopted by the Securities and Exchange Commission.

.115

Appendix B—Review Reports

Example 1: Standard Review Report on an Annual MD&A Presentation

1. The following is an illustration of a standard review report on an annual MD&A presentation.

Independent Accountant's Report

[*Introductory paragraph*]

We have reviewed XYZ Company's Management's Discussion and Analysis taken as a whole, included [*incorporated by reference*] in the Company's [*insert description of registration statement or document*]. Management is responsible for the preparation of the Company's Management's Discussion and Analysis pursuant to the rules and regulations adopted by the Securities and Exchange Commission. We have audited, in accordance with auditing standards generally accepted in the United States of America, the financial statements of XYZ Company, which comprise the balance sheets as of December 31, 20X5 and 20X4, and the related statements of income, changes in stockholders' equity, and cash flows for each of the years in the three-year period ended December 31, 20X5. In our report dated [*Month*] XX, 20X6, we expressed an unqualified opinion on those financial statements.

[*Scope paragraph*]

We conducted our review of Management's Discussion and Analysis in accordance with attestation standards established by the American Institute of Certified Public Accountants. A review of Management's Discussion and Analysis consists principally of applying analytical procedures and making inquiries of persons responsible for financial, accounting, and operational matters. It is substantially less in scope than an examination, the objective of which is the expression of an opinion on the presentation. Accordingly, we do not express such an opinion.

[*Explanatory paragraph*] [36]

The preparation of Management's Discussion and Analysis requires management to interpret the criteria, make determinations as to the relevancy of information to be included, and make estimates and assumptions that affect reported information. Management's Discussion and Analysis includes information regarding the estimated future impact of transactions and events that have occurred or are expected to occur, expected sources of liquidity and capital resources, operating trends, commitments, and uncertainties. Actual results in the future may differ materially from management's present assessment of this information because events and circumstances frequently do not occur as expected.

[*Concluding paragraph*]

Based on our review, nothing came to our attention that caused us to believe that the Company's presentation of Management's Discussion and Analysis

---

36 The following sentence should be added to the beginning of the explanatory paragraph if the entity is a nonpublic entity, as discussed in paragraph .85*i*.

Although XYZ Company is not subject to the rules and regulations of the Securities and Exchange Commission, the accompanying Management's Discussion and Analysis is intended to be a presentation in accordance with the rules and regulations adopted by the Securities and Exchange Commission.

does not include, in all material respects, the required elements of the rules and regulations adopted by the Securities and Exchange Commission, that the historical financial amounts included therein have not been accurately derived, in all material respects, from the Company's financial statements, or that the underlying information, determinations, estimates and assumptions of the Company do not provide a reasonable basis for the disclosures contained therein.

[*Restricted use paragraph*] [37]

This report is intended solely for the information and use of [*list or refer to specified parties*] and is not intended to be and should not be used by anyone other than the specified parties.

[*Signature*]

[*Date*]

Example 2: Standard Review Report on an Interim MD&A Presentation

2. The following is an illustration of a standard review report on an MD&A presentation for an interim period.

Independent Accountant's Report

[*Introductory paragraph*]

We have reviewed XYZ Company's Management's Discussion and Analysis taken as a whole included in the Company's [*insert description of registration statement or document*]. Management is responsible for the preparation of the Company's Management's Discussion and Analysis pursuant to the rules and regulations adopted by the Securities and Exchange Commission. We have reviewed, in accordance with standards established by the American Institute of Certified Public Accountants, the interim financial information of XYZ Company as of June 30, 20X6 and 20X5, and for the three-month and six-month periods then ended, and have issued our report thereon dated July XX, 20X6.

[*Scope paragraph*]

We conducted our review of Management's Discussion and Analysis in accordance with attestation standards established by the American Institute of Certified Public Accountants. A review of Management's Discussion and Analysis consists principally of applying analytical procedures and making inquiries of persons responsible for financial, accounting, and operational matters. It is substantially less in scope than an examination, the objective of which is the expression of an opinion on the presentation. Accordingly, we do not express such an opinion.

[*Explanatory paragraph*] [38]

The preparation of Management's Discussion and Analysis requires management to interpret the criteria, make determinations as to the relevancy of

---

[37] This paragraph may be omitted for certain nonpublic entities. (Refer to paragraph .85*k*.)

[38] The following sentence should be added to the beginning of the explanatory paragraph if the entity is a nonpublic entity, as discussed in paragraph .85*i*.

> Although XYZ Company is not subject to the rules and regulations of the Securities and Exchange Commission, the accompanying Management's Discussion and Analysis is intended to be a presentation in accordance with the rules and regulations adopted by the Securities and Exchange Commission.

information to be included, and make estimates and assumptions that affect reported information. Management's Discussion and Analysis includes information regarding the estimated future impact of transactions and events that have occurred or are expected to occur, expected sources of liquidity and capital resources, operating trends, commitments, and uncertainties. Actual results in the future may differ materially from management's present assessment of this information because events and circumstances frequently do not occur as expected.

[*Concluding paragraph*]

Based on our review, nothing came to our attention that caused us to believe that the Company's presentation of Management's Discussion and Analysis does not include, in all material respects, the required elements of the rules and regulations adopted by the Securities and Exchange Commission, that the historical financial amounts included therein have not been accurately derived, in all material respects, from the Company's financial statements, or that the underlying information, determinations, estimates, and assumptions of the Company do not provide a reasonable basis for the disclosures contained therein.

[*Restricted use paragraph*] [39]

This report is intended solely for the information and use of [*list or refer to specified parties*] and is not intended to be and should not be used by anyone other than the specified parties.

[*Signature*]

[*Date*]

Example 3: Modification to Review Report for a Material Misstatement

3. An example of a modification of the accountant's report when MD&A is materially misstated, as discussed in paragraph .89, follows.

[*Additional explanatory paragraph preceding the concluding paragraph*]

Based on information furnished to us by management, we believe that the Company has excluded a discussion of the significant capital outlay required for its plans to expand into the telecommunications industry and the possible effects on the Company's financial condition, liquidity, and capital resources.

[*Concluding paragraph*]

Based on our review, with the exception of the matter described in the preceding paragraph, nothing came to our attention that caused us to believe that the Company's presentation of Management's Discussion and Analysis does not include, in all material respects, the required elements of the rules and regulations adopted by the Securities and Exchange Commission, that the historical financial amounts included therein have not been accurately derived, in all material respects, from the Company's financial statements, or that the underlying information, determinations, estimates and assumptions of the Company do not provide a reasonable basis for the disclosures contained therein.

[Revised, December 2012, to reflect conforming changes necessary due to the issuance of SAS Nos. 122–126.]

---

[39] This paragraph may be omitted for certain nonpublic entities. (Refer to paragraph .85*k*.)

.116

Appendix C—Combined Reports

Example 1: Combined Examination and Review Report on MD&A

1. An example of a combined report on an examination of an annual MD&A presentation and the review of MD&A for an interim period discussed in paragraph .92 follows.

Independent Accountant's Report

[*Introductory paragraph*]

We have examined XYZ Company's Management's Discussion and Analysis taken as a whole for the three-year period ended December 31, 20X5, included [*incorporated by reference*] in the Company's [*insert description of registration statement or document*]. Management is responsible for the preparation of the Company's Management's Discussion and Analysis pursuant to the rules and regulations adopted by the Securities and Exchange Commission. Our responsibility is to express an opinion on the annual presentation based on our examination. We have audited, in accordance with auditing standards generally accepted in the United States of America, the financial statements of XYZ Company as of December 31, 20X5 and 20X4, and for each of the years in the three-year period ended December 31, 19X5, and in our report dated [*Month*] XX, 20X6, we expressed an unqualified opinion on those financial statements.

[*Scope paragraph*]

Our examination of Management's Discussion and Analysis was conducted in accordance with attestation standards established by the American Institute of Certified Public Accountants and, accordingly, included examining, on a test basis, evidence supporting the historical amounts and disclosures in the presentation. An examination also includes assessing the significant determinations made by management as to the relevancy of information to be included and the estimates and assumptions that affect reported information. We believe that our examination provides a reasonable basis for our opinion.

[*Explanatory paragraph*] [40]

The preparation of Management's Discussion and Analysis requires management to interpret the criteria, make determinations as to the relevancy of information to be included, and make estimates and assumptions that affect reported information. Management's Discussion and Analysis includes information regarding the estimated future impact of transactions and events that have occurred or are expected to occur, expected sources of liquidity and capital resources, operating trends, commitments, and uncertainties. Actual results in the future may differ materially from management's present assessment of this information because events and circumstances frequently do not occur as expected.

---

[40] The following sentence should be added to the beginning of the explanatory paragraph if the entity is a nonpublic entity, as discussed in paragraph .69*h*.

Although XYZ Company is not subject to the rules and regulations of the Securities and Exchange Commission, the accompanying Management's Discussion and Analysis is intended to be a presentation in accordance with the rules and regulations adopted by the Securities and Exchange Commission.

[Opinion paragraph]

In our opinion, the Company's presentation of Management's Discussion and Analysis for the three-year period ended December 31, 20X5, includes, in all material respects, the required elements of the rules and regulations adopted by the Securities and Exchange Commission; the historical financial amounts included therein have been accurately derived, in all material respects, from the Company's financial statements; and the underlying information, determinations, estimates, and assumptions of the Company provide a reasonable basis for the disclosures contained therein.

[Paragraphs on interims]

We have also reviewed XYZ Company's Management's Discussion and Analysis taken as a whole for the six-month period ended June 30, 20X6 included [*incorporated by reference*] in the Company's [*insert description of registration statement or document*]. We have reviewed, in accordance with standards established by the American Institute of Certified Public Accountants, the interim financial information of XYZ Company as of June 30, 20X6 and 20X5, and for the six-month periods then ended, and have issued our report thereon dated July XX, 20X6.

We conducted our review of Management's Discussion and Analysis in accordance with attestation standards established by the American Institute of Certified Public Accountants. A review of Management's Discussion and Analysis consists principally of applying analytical procedures and making inquiries of persons responsible for financial, accounting, and operational matters. It is substantially less in scope than an examination, the objective of which is the expression of an opinion on the presentation. Accordingly, we do not express such an opinion.

Based on our review, nothing came to our attention that caused us to believe that the Company's presentation of Management's Discussion and Analysis for the six-month period ended June 30, 20X6, does not include, in all material respects, the required elements of the rules and regulations adopted by the Securities and Exchange Commission, that the historical financial amounts included therein have not been accurately derived, in all material respects, from the Company's unaudited interim financial statements, or that the underlying information, determinations, estimates, and assumptions of the Company do not provide a reasonable basis for the disclosures contained therein.

[Restricted use paragraph] [41]

This report is intended solely for the information and use of [*list or refer to specified parties*] and is not intended to be and should not be used by anyone other than the specified parties.

[Signature]

[Date]

Example 2: Review Report on a Combined Annual and Interim MD&A Presentation

2. An example of a review report on a combined MD&A presentation for annual and interim periods follows.

---

[41] This paragraph may be omitted for certain nonpublic entities. (Refer to paragraph .85*k*.)

Independent Accountant's Report

[*Introductory paragraph*]

We have reviewed XYZ Company's Management's Discussion and Analysis taken as a whole included [*incorporated by reference*] in the Company's [*insert description of registration statement or document*]. Management is responsible for the preparation of the Company's Management's Discussion and Analysis pursuant to the rules and regulations adopted by the Securities and Exchange Commission. We have audited, in accordance with auditing standards generally accepted in the United States of America, the financial statements of XYZ Company as of December 31, 20X5 and 20X4, and for each of the years in the three-year period ended December 31, 20X5, and in our report dated [*Month*] XX, 20X6, we expressed an unqualified opinion on those financial statements. We have reviewed, in accordance with standards established by the American Institute of Certified Public Accountants, the interim financial information of XYZ Company as of June 30, 20X6 and 20X5, and for the six-month periods then ended, and have issued our report thereon dated July XX, 20X6.

[*Scope paragraph*]

We conducted our review of Management's Discussion and Analysis in accordance with attestation standards established by the American Institute of Certified Public Accountants. A review of Management's Discussion and Analysis consists principally of applying analytical procedures and making inquiries of persons responsible for financial, accounting, and operational matters. It is substantially less in scope than an examination, the objective of which is the expression of an opinion on the presentation. Accordingly, we do not express such an opinion.

[*Explanatory paragraph*] [42]

The preparation of Management's Discussion and Analysis requires management to interpret the criteria, make determinations as to the relevancy of information to be included, and make estimates and assumptions that affect reported information. Management's Discussion and Analysis includes information regarding the estimated future impact of transactions and events that have occurred or are expected to occur, expected sources of liquidity and capital resources, operating trends, commitments, and uncertainties. Actual results in the future may differ materially from management's present assessment of this information because events and circumstances frequently do not occur as expected.

[*Concluding paragraph*]

Based on our review, nothing came to our attention that caused us to believe that the Company's presentation of Management's Discussion and Analysis does not include, in all material respects, the required elements of the rules and regulations adopted by the Securities and Exchange Commission, that the historical financial amounts included therein have not been accurately derived, in

---

[42] The following sentence should be added to the beginning of the explanatory paragraph if the entity is a nonpublic entity, as discussed in paragraph .69*h*.

> Although XYZ Company is not subject to the rules and regulations of the Securities and Exchange Commission, the accompanying Management's Discussion and Analysis is intended to be a presentation in accordance with the rules and regulations adopted by the Securities and Exchange Commission.

all material respects, from the Company's financial statements, or that the underlying information, determinations, estimates, and assumptions of the Company do not provide a reasonable basis for the disclosures contained therein.

[Restricted use paragraph] [43]

This report is intended solely for the information and use of [*list or refer to specified parties*] and is not intended to be and should not be used by anyone other than the specified parties.

[*Signature*]

[*Date*]

[43] This paragraph may be omitted for certain nonpublic entities. (Refer to paragraph .85*k*.)

.117

Appendix D—Comparison of Activities Performed Under SAS No. 118, *Other Information in Documents Containing Audited Financial Statements* [AU-C Section 720], Versus a Review or an Examination Attest Engagement [*]

Activities	*SAS No. 118 (AU-C Section 720)*	*Review*	*Examination*
Obtain an understanding of SEC rules and regulations and management's methodology for the preparation of Management's Discussion and Analysis (MD&A).	Not applicable (N/A)—Auditor is only required to read the information in the MD&A in order to identify material inconsistencies, if any, with the audited financial statements.	Obtain an understanding of the rules and regulations adopted by the SEC for MD&A.	Same as for a review.
		Inquire of management regarding the method of preparing MD&A.	
Plan the engagement.	N/A	Develop an overall strategy for the analytical procedures and inquiries to be performed to provide negative assurance.	Develop an overall strategy for the expected scope and performance of the engagement to obtain reasonable assurance to express an opinion.
Consider internal control.	N/A	Consider relevant portions of the entity's internal control applicable to the preparation of MD&A to identify the types of potential misstatements and to select the inquiries and analytical procedures; no testing of controls would be performed.	Obtain an understanding of internal control applicable to the preparation of MD&A sufficient to plan the engagement and to assess control risk; controls may be tested by performing inquiries of client personnel, inspection of documents, and observation of relevant activities.

[*] Refer to AU-C section 720, *Other Information in Documents Containing Audited Financial Statements.* [Footnote revised, December 2012, to reflect conforming changes necessary due to the issuance of SAS Nos. 122–126.]

Activities	*SAS No. 118 (AU-C Section 720)*	*Review*	*Examination*
Test assertions.	N/A	Apply the following analytical procedures and make inquiries of management and others; no corroborating evidential matter is obtained:	Apply the following analytical and corroborative procedures to obtain reasonable assurance of detecting material misstatements:
		• Read the MD&A and compare the content for consistency with the financial statements; compare financial amounts to the financial statements or related accounting records and analyses; recompute increases, decreases and percentages disclosed.	• Read the MD&A and compare the content for consistency with the financial statements; compare financial amounts to the financial statements or related accounting records and analyses; recompute increases, decreases and percentages disclosed.
		• Compare nonfinancial amounts to the financial statements or other records.	• Compare nonfinancial amounts to the financial statements or other records; perform tests on other records based on the concept of materiality.
		• Consider whether MD&A explanations are consistent with information obtained during the audit or review of financial statements; make further inquiries, as necessary. (Note: Such additional inquiries may result in a decision to perform other procedures or detail tests.)	• Consider whether explanations are consistent with the information obtained during the audit of financial statements; investigate further explanations that cannot be substantiated by information in the audit working papers through inquiry and inspection of client records.

(continued)

Activities	*SAS No. 118 (AU-C Section 720)*	*Review*	*Examination*
		• Compare information in MD&A with the rules and regulations adopted by the SEC.	• Examine internally and externally generated documents in support of the existence, occurrence, or expected occurrence of events, transactions, conditions, trends, demands, commitments, and uncertainties disclosed in MD&A.
		• Obtain and read available prospective financial information; inquire of management as to the procedures used to prepare such information; consider whether information came to the practitioner's attention that causes him or her to believe that the underlying information, determinations, estimates, and assumptions do not provide a reasonable basis for the MD&A disclosures.	• Compare information in MD&A with the rules and regulations adopted by the SEC.
		• Obtain public communications and minutes of meetings for comparison with disclosures in MD&A.	• Obtain and read available prospective financial information; inquire of management as to the procedures used to prepare such information; evaluate whether the underlying information, determinations, estimates, and assumptions provide a reasonable basis for the MD&A disclosures.
		• Make inquiries of the officers or executives with responsibility for operational areas and financial and accounting matters as to their plans and expectations for the future.	

Activities	*SAS No. 118 (AU-C Section 720)*	*Review*	*Examination*
		• Inquire as to prior experience with the SEC and the extent of comments received; read correspondence.	• Obtain public communications and minutes of meetings; consider obtaining other types of publicly available information for comparison with the disclosures in MD&A.
		• Consider whether there are any additional matters that should be disclosed in the MD&A based on the results of the preceding procedures and knowledge obtained during the audit or review of the financial statements.	• Make inquiries of the officers or executives with responsibility for operational areas and financial and accounting matters as to their plans and expectations for the future.
			• Inquire as to prior experience with the SEC and the extent of comments received; read correspondence.
			• Test completeness by considering the results of the preceding procedures and knowledge obtained during the audit of the financial statements, and whether such matters are appropriately disclosed in the MD&A; extend procedures if the inherent risk relating to completeness of disclosures is high.

(continued)

Activities	*SAS No. 118 (AU-C Section 720)*	*Review*	*Examination*
Consider the effect of events subsequent to the balance-sheet date.	Yes	Yes	Yes
Obtain written representations from management.	Yes	Yes	Yes
Form a conclusion and report.	The auditor has no reporting responsibility with respect to MD&A unless the auditor concludes that there is a material inconsistency in the MD&A that has not been eliminated. In such a situation, the auditor may add an other matter paragraph to the auditor's report on the audited financial statements describing the material inconsistency or withhold the auditor's report. If, while reading the MD&A, the auditor becomes aware of an apparent material misstatement of fact, the auditor should discuss such matter with management and take other actions based on management's response.	Form a conclusion based on the results of the preceding procedures and report in the form of negative assurance.	Form an opinion based on the results of the preceding procedures and report conclusion by expressing an opinion.

[Revised, December 2010, to reflect conforming changes necessary due to the issuance of SAS Nos. 118–120. Revised, December 2012, to reflect conforming changes necessary due to the issuance of SAS Nos. 122–126.]

AT-C Exhibits

TABLE OF CONTENTS

Exhibit

List of AT-C Sections Designated by Statement on Standards for Attestation Engagements No. 18, *Attestation Standards: Clarification and Recodification*, Cross Referenced to List of AT Sections

Part I—AT-C Section to AT Section Cross References

AT-C Sections Designated by SSAE No. 18[1]		*AT Sections Superseded by SSAE No. 18*	
AT-C Section	*Title*	*AT Section*	*Title*
Preface	*Preface to the Attestation Standards*	**Introduction**	*Attestation Standards—Introduction*
100	**Common Concepts**		
105	*Concepts Common to All Attestation Engagements*	20	*Defining Professional Requirements in Statements on Standards for Attestation Engagements*
		50	*SSAE Hierarchy*
		101	*Attest Engagements*
200	**Level of Service**		
205	*Examination Engagements*	101	*Attest Engagements*
210	*Review Engagements*		
215	*Agreed-Upon Procedures Engagements*	201	*Agreed-Upon Procedures Engagements*

(continued)

[1] Statement on Standards for Attestation Engagements (SSAE) No. 18, *Attestation Standards: Clarification and Recodification*, contains "AT-C" section numbers instead of "AT" section numbers to avoid confusion with references to existing "AT" sections, which remain effective through April 2017.

AT-C Sections Designated by SSAE No. 18		AT Sections Superseded by SSAE No. 18	
AT-C Section	*Title*	*AT Section*	*Title*
300	**Subject Matter**		
305 [2]	*Prospective Financial Information*	301	*Financial Forecasts and Projections*
310	*Reporting on Pro Forma Financial Information*	401	*Reporting on Pro Forma Financial Information*
315	*Compliance Attestation*	601	*Compliance Attestation*
320	*Reporting on an Examination of Controls at a Service Organization Relevant to User Entities' Internal Control Over Financial Reporting*	801	*Reporting on Controls at a Service Organization*
395	*Management's Discussion and Analysis*	701 [3]	*Management's Discussion and Analysis*

[2] AT-C section 305, *Prospective Financial Information*, does not address compilations of prospective financial information—a service that is included in AT section 301, *Financial Forecasts and Projections*. Paragraph .01 of AR-C section 80, *Compilation Engagements*, states that AR-C section 80 (which is applicable to compilations of historical financial statements) also may be applied, adapted as necessary in the circumstances, to other historical or prospective financial information. Footnote 1 of AR-C section 80 states that the Accounting and Review Services Committee plans to expose for public comment separate proposed Statements on Standards for Accounting and Review Services that would provide requirements and guidance to accountants with respect to compilation engagements on pro forma or prospective financial information.

[3] The Auditing Standards Board did not clarify AT section 701, *Management's Discussion and Analysis*, because practitioners rarely perform attestation engagements to report on management's discussion and analysis prepared pursuant to the rules and regulations adopted by the SEC. AT section 701 will be retained in its current unclarified format as AT-C section 395, *Management's Discussion and Analysis*, until further notice.

Part II—AT Section to AT-C Section Cross References

AT Sections Superseded by SSAE No. 18		*AT-C Sections Designated by SSAE No. 18*[1]	
AT Section	*Title*	*AT-C Section*	*Title*
20	*Defining Professional Requirements in Statements on Standards for Attestation Engagements*	105	*Concepts Common to All Attestation Engagements*
50	*SSAE Hierarchy*	105	*Concepts Common to All Attestation Engagements*
101	*Attest Engagements*	105	*Concepts Common to All Attestation Engagements*
		205	*Examination Engagements*
		210	*Review Engagements*
201	*Agreed-Upon Procedures Engagements*	215	*Agreed-Upon Procedures Engagements*
301	*Financial Forecasts and Projections*	305[2]	*Prospective Financial Information*
401	*Reporting on Pro Forma Financial Information*	310	*Reporting on Pro Forma Financial Information*
501	*An Examination of an Entity's Internal Control Over Financial Reporting That Is Integrated With an Audit of Its Financial Statements*		Statement on Auditing Standards No. 130, *An Audit of Internal Control Over Financial Reporting That Is Integrated With an Audit of Financial Statements*, withdraws AT section 501[3]

---

[1] Statement on Standards for Attestation Engagements (SSAE) No. 18, *Attestation Standards: Clarification and Recodification*, contains "AT-C" section numbers instead of "AT" section numbers to avoid confusion with references to existing "AT" sections, which remain effective through April 2017.

[2] AT-C section 305, *Prospective Financial Information*, does not address compilations of prospective financial information—a service that is included in AT section 301, *Financial Forecasts and Projections*. Paragraph .01 of AR-C section 80, *Compilation Engagements* , states that AR-C section 80 (which is applicable to compilations of historical financial statements) also may be applied, adapted as necessary in the circumstances, to other historical or prospective financial information. Footnote 1 of AR-C section 80 states that the Accounting and Review Services Committee plans to expose for public comment separate proposed Statements on Standards for Accounting and Review Services that would provide requirements and guidance to accountants with respect to compilation engagements on pro forma or prospective financial information.

[3] The issuance of Statement on Auditing Standards (SAS) No. 130, *An Audit of Internal Control Over Financial Reporting That Is Integrated With an Audit of Financial Statements* (AU-C sec. 940),

(continued)

AT Sections Superseded by SSAE No. 18		AT-C Sections Designated by SSAE No. 18	
AT Section	*Title*	*AT-C Section*	*Title*
601	*Compliance Attestation*	315	*Compliance Attestation*
701[4]	*Management's Discussion and Analysis*	395	*Management's Discussion and Analysis*
801	*Reporting on Controls at a Service Organization*	320	*Reporting on an Examination of Controls at a Service Organization Relevant to User Entities' Internal Control Over Financial Reporting*

(footnote continued)

moves the content of AT section 501, *An Examination of an Entity's Internal Control Over Financial Reporting That Is Integrated With an Audit of Its Financial Statements*, from the SSAEs to the SASs. SAS No. 130 was issued in October 2015 and becomes effective for integrated audits (audits of internal control over financial reporting that are integrated with audits of financial statements) for periods ending on or after December 15, 2016. Upon its effective date, SAS No. 130 withdraws SSAE No. 15, *An Examination of an Entity's Internal Control Over Financial Reporting That Is Integrated With an Audit of Its Financial Statements*, and related Attestation Interpretation No. 1, "Reporting Under Section 112 of the Federal Deposit Insurance Corporation Improvement Act" (AT sec. 501 and 9501).

[4] The Auditing Standards Board did not clarify AT section 701, *Management's Discussion and Analysis*, because practitioners rarely perform attestation engagements to report on management's discussion and analysis prepared pursuant to the rules and regulations adopted by the SEC. AT section 701 will be retained in its current unclarified format as AT-C section 395, *Management's Discussion and Analysis*, until further notice.

AT-C Appendixes

TABLE OF CONTENTS

AT-C Appendix A

AICPA Guides and Statements of Position

AICPA Guides

Prospective Financial Information

Reporting on Controls at a Service Organization: Relevant to Security, Availability, Processing Integrity, Confidentiality, or Privacy (SOC 2®)

Service Organizations: Reporting on Controls at a Service Organization Relevant to User Entities' Internal Control Over Financial Reporting

Statements of Position—Attestation

Guidance to Practitioners in Conducting and Reporting on an Agreed-Upon Procedures Engagement to Assist Management in Evaluating the Effectiveness of Its Corporate Compliance Program	*5/99*
Performing Agreed-Upon Procedures Engagements That Address Internal Control Over Derivative Transactions as Required by the New York State Insurance Law	*6/01*
Performing Agreed-Upon Procedures Engagements That Address Annual Claims Prompt Payment Reports as Required by the New Jersey Administrative Code	*5/02*
Attestation Engagements That Address Specified Compliance Control Objectives and Related Controls at Entities That Provide Services to Investment Companies, Investment Advisers, or Other Service Providers	*10/07*
Reporting Pursuant to the Global Investment Performance Standards	*10/12*
Attest Engagements on Greenhouse Gas Emissions Information	*4/13*
Performing Agreed-Upon Procedures Engagements That Address the Completeness, Mapping, Consistency, or Structure of XBRL-Formatted Information	*9/13*

AT-C Appendix B

Other Attestation Publications

This list identifies *other attestation publications* published by the AICPA that have been reviewed by the AICPA Audit and Attest Standards staff and are, therefore, presumed to be appropriate, as indicated in paragraph .A32 of section 105, *Concepts Common to All Attestation Engagements*. These publications may be obtained at www.AICPAStore.com.

AICPA *Technical Questions and Answers*

Q&A section 9500, *Attestation Engagements*

Current AICPA Alerts

Service Organization Control Reports®: Considerations for User and Service Auditors

AT-C TOPICAL INDEX

References are to AT-C section and paragraph numbers.

References are to AT-C section and paragraph numbers.

W